Introduction to Econometrics

Introduction to **Econometrics**

FOURTH EDITION

Christopher Dougherty
London School of Economics

OXFORD
UNIVERSITY PRESS

OXFORD
UNIVERSITY PRESS

Great Clarendon Street, Oxford OX2 6DP

Oxford University Press is a department of the University of Oxford.
It furthers the University's objective of excellence in research, scholarship,
and education by publishing worldwide in

Oxford New York

Auckland Cape Town Dar es Salaam Hong Kong Karachi
Kuala Lumpur Madrid Melbourne Mexico City Nairobi
New Delhi Shanghai Taipei Toronto

With offices in

Argentina Austria Brazil Chile Czech Republic France Greece
Guatemala Hungary Italy Japan Poland Portugal Singapore
South Korea Switzerland Thailand Turkey Ukraine Vietnam

Oxford is a registered trade mark of Oxford University Press
in the UK and in certain other countries

Published in the United States
by Oxford University Press Inc., New York

Third edition 2007
Second edition 2002
First edition 1992

British Library Cataloguing in Publication Data
Data available

Library of Congress Cataloging in Publication Data
Data available

Typeset by Newgen Imaging Systems (P) Ltd., Chennai, India
Printed in Great Britain
on acid-free paper by
Ashford Colour Press Ltd, Gosport, Hants

ISBN 978–0–19–956708–9

3 5 7 9 10 8 6 4

Preface

Introduction to Econometrics

This is a textbook for a year-long undergraduate course in econometrics. It is intended to fill a need that has been generated by the changing profile of the typical econometrics student. Econometrics courses often used to be optional for economics majors, but now they are becoming compulsory. Several factors are responsible. Perhaps the most important is the recognition that an understanding of empirical research techniques is not just a desirable but an essential part of the basic training of an economist, and that courses limited to applied statistics are inadequate for this purpose. No doubt this has been reinforced by the fact that graduate-level courses in econometrics have become increasingly ambitious, with the consequence that a lack of exposure to econometrics at an undergraduate level is now a handicap in gaining admission to the leading graduate schools. There are also supply-side factors. The wave that has lifted econometrics to prominence in economics teaching comes on the heels of another that did the same for mathematics and statistics. Without this prior improvement in quantitative training, the shift of econometrics to the core of the economics curriculum would not have been possible.

As a consequence of this development, students on econometrics courses are more varied in their capabilities than ever before. No longer are they a self-selected minority of mathematical high-fliers. The typical student now is a regular economics major who has taken basic, but not advanced, courses in calculus and statistics. The democratization of econometrics has created a need for a broader range of textbooks than before, particularly for the wider audience. The mathematical elite has for many years been served by a number of accomplished texts. The wider audience has been less well served. This new edition continues to be chiefly addressed to it.

Objectives of the text

The text is intended to provide a framework for a year's instruction with the depth and breadth of coverage that would enable the student to continue with the subject at the graduate level. It is therefore ambitious in terms of theory and proofs, given the constraints imposed by the nature of its target audience and not making use of linear algebra.

A primary concern has been not to overwhelm the student with information. This is not a reference work. It is hoped that the student will find the text readable and that in the course of a year he or she would comfortably be able to traverse its contents. For the same reason the mathematical demands on the student have been kept to a minimum. For nearly everyone, there is a limit to the rate at which formal mathematical analysis can be digested. If this limit is exceeded, the student spends much mental energy grappling with the technicalities rather than the substance, impeding the development of a unified understanding of the subject.

Although its emphasis is on theory, the text is intended to provide substantial hands-on practical experience in the form of regression exercises using a computer. In particular, the Educational Attainment and Earnings Function data provide opportunities for 60 cross-sectional exercises spread through the first ten chapters of the text. Students start with a simple model and gradually develop it into a more sophisticated one as their knowledge of econometric theory grows. It is hoped that seeing how the specification of their models improves will motivate students and help sustain their interest. The Demand Functions data set, with its 15 time series exercises, is intended to provide a similar experience in the remaining chapters. Further data sets have been provided for specialist applications.

Changes to this edition

The main changes for the new edition are as follows:

1. The initial Review chapter has been extended to include a discussion of the normal distribution and hypothesis testing, bringing forward material that was in Chapter 2, and has a new final section on convergence in distribution and the meaning of asymptotic variance. Even with these additions, it should not be regarded as a substitute for a proper statistics course. As far as the last two sections, it is intended as a straight review that provides an opportunity for students to check that they have a sound understanding of the relevant statistical topics. The last two sections will probably need to be taken more slowly. In a generic statistics course, consistency is defined, but typically the treatment is quite brief. Convergence in distribution is never taught at all, except to explain in general terms the notion of a central limit theorem.
2. Asymptotic variances and simulations are used to illustrate the interplay between asymptotic results and finite-sample distributions throughout the text where such issues arise, starting with the IV estimator in Chapters 7 and 8 and, most especially, with the fitting of the ADL(1,0) model in Chapter 11. As preparation, the regression model assumptions appropriate for time series regressions have been brought forward to Chapter 11 from Chapter 12.

3. The discussions of spurious regressions and unit root tests in Chapter 13 have been greatly extended, simulations being used extensively to investigate not only finite-sample distributions but also the asymptotic distributions themselves. The mathematical demands are such that, at this level, the results must be accepted on trust, but the simulations should inform an appreciation of the issues and demonstrate that the trust is well placed.

The additional material has the overall effect of making the text conceptually a little more demanding than before, although the mathematical requirements are unchanged. In a two-semester sequence, the Review and the first six chapters could be used as an introductory course and the remainder as a second semester for students who are ready to tackle more challenging econometric issues. The aim is to provide a solid intuitive understanding of the material that will serve either as a foundation for further formal study of econometrics or for the self-study of applications.

The simulations have been undertaken using MatLab. I will be happy to email copies of the batch files to anyone interested.

Additional resources

The online resource centre
www.oxfordtextbooks.co.uk/orc/dougherty4e/
offers the following resources for instructors and students:

- PowerPoint® slideshows that offer a graphical treatment of most of the topics in the text. Narrative boxes provide an explanation of the slides.
- Links to data sets and manuals.
- Instructor's manuals for the text and data sets, detailing the exercises and their solutions.
- A student area that provides answers to the starred exercises in the text and offers additional exercises.

It is hoped that the provision of these materials will not only be helpful for the study of econometrics but also make it satisfying and pleasurable.

Christopher Dougherty

Contents

INTRODUCTION 1

Why study econometrics? 1
Aim of this text 2
Mathematics and statistics prerequisites for studying econometrics 2
Additional resources 3
Econometrics software 4

REVIEW: RANDOM VARIABLES, SAMPLING, AND ESTIMATION 5

R.1 **Introduction** 5
R.2 **Discrete random variables and expectations** 6
Discrete random variables 6
Expected values of random variables 8
Expected values of functions of discrete random variables 9
Expected value rules 10
Population variance of a discrete random variable 11
Fixed and random components of a random variable 12
R.3 **Continuous random variables** 14
Probability density 14
R.4 **Population covariance, covariance and variance rules, and correlation** 17
Covariance 17
Independence of random variables 19
Covariance rules 19
Variance rules 21
Correlation 22
R.5 **Samples, the double structure of a variable, and estimators** 23
Sampling 23
Estimators 24
R.6 **Unbiasedness and efficiency** 27
Unbiasedness 27
Efficiency 28
Conflicts between unbiasedness and minimum variance 30

R.7 **Estimators of variance, covariance, and correlation** 33

R.8 **The normal distribution** 34

R.9 **Hypothesis testing** 36
Formulation of a null hypothesis and development of its implications 37
Compatibility, freakiness, and the significance level 38

R.10 **Type II error and the power of a test** 42

R.11 ***t* tests** 47
The reject/fail-to-reject terminology 50

R.12 **Confidence intervals** 51

R.13 **One-sided tests** 56
H_0: $\mu = \mu_0$, H_1: $\mu = \mu_1$ 57
One percent significance test 60
Generalizing from H_0: $\mu = \mu_0$, H_1: $\mu = \mu_1$ to H_0: $\mu = \mu_0$, H_1: $\mu > \mu_0$ 62
H_0: $\mu = \mu_0$, H_1: $\mu < \mu_0$ 63
One-sided t tests 63
Special case: H_0: $\mu = 0$ 63
Anomalous results 64
Justification of the use of a one-sided test 65

R.14 **Probability limits and consistency** 66
Probability limits 67
Consistency 68
Why is consistency of interest? 70
Simulations 72

R.15 **Convergence in distribution and central limit theorems** 74

Key terms 79

Appendix R.1: **Unbiased estimators of the population covariance and variance** 79

Appendix R.2: **Density functions of transformed random variables** 81

1. SIMPLE REGRESSION ANALYSIS 83

1.1 **The simple linear model** 83

1.2 **Least squares regression with one explanatory variable** 85

1.3 **Derivation of the regression coefficients** 88
Least squares regression with one explanatory variable: the general case 90
Two decompositions of the dependent variable 92
Regression model without an intercept 94

1.4 **Interpretation of a regression equation** 95
Changes in the units of measurement 97

1.5 **Two important results relating to OLS regressions** 103
The mean value of the residuals is zero 103

The sample correlation between the observations on *X* and the residuals is zero 103

1.6 **Goodness of fit: R^2** 104

Example of how R^2 is calculated 107

Alternative interpretation of R^2 107

Key terms 108

2. PROPERTIES OF THE REGRESSION COEFFICIENTS AND HYPOTHESIS TESTING 110

2.1 **Types of data and regression model** 110

2.2 **Assumptions for regression models with nonstochastic regressors** 111

2.3 **The random components and unbiasedness of the OLS regression coefficients** 114

The random components of the OLS regression coefficients 114

The unbiasedness of the OLS regression coefficients 118

Normal distribution of the regression coefficients 120

2.4 **A Monte Carlo experiment** 121

2.5 **Precision of the regression coefficients** 125

Variances of the regression coefficients 125

Standard errors of the regression coefficients 129

The Gauss–Markov theorem 132

2.6 **Testing hypotheses relating to the regression coefficients** 134

0.1 percent tests 139

p values 139

One-sided tests 140

Confidence intervals 142

2.7 **The *F* test of goodness of fit** 145

Relationship between the *F* test and the *t* test on the slope coefficient in simple regression analysis 147

Key terms 148

Appendix 2.1 **The Gauss–Markov theorem** 149

3. MULTIPLE REGRESSION ANALYSIS 151

3.1 **Illustration: a model with two explanatory variables** 151

3.2 **Derivation and interpretation of the multiple regression coefficients** 153

The general model 155

Interpretation of the multiple regression coefficients 156

3.3 **Properties of the multiple regression coefficients** 159

Unbiasedness 160

Efficiency 161
Precision of the multiple regression coefficients 161
t tests and confidence intervals 164

3.4 Multicollinearity 165
Multicollinearity in models with more than two explanatory variables 168
Example of multicollinearity 169
What can you do about multicollinearity? 169

3.5 Goodness of fit: R^2 176
F tests 177
Further analysis of variance 180
Relationship between F statistic and t statistic 182
Adjusted' R^2 183

3.6 Prediction 185
Properties of least squares predictors 187

Key terms 190

4. NONLINEAR MODELS AND TRANSFORMATIONS OF VARIABLES 192

4.1 Linearity and nonlinearity 192

4.2 Logarithmic transformations 196
Logarithmic models 196
Semilogarithmic models 200
The disturbance term 202
Comparing linear and logarithmic specifications 205

4.3 Models with quadratic and interactive variables 209
Quadratic variables 209
Higher-order polynomials 211
Interactive explanatory variables 213
Ramsey's RESET test of functional misspecification 216

4.4 Nonlinear regression 218

Key terms 222

5. DUMMY VARIABLES 224

5.1 Illustration of the use of a dummy variable 224
Standard errors and hypothesis testing 227

5.2 Extension to more than two categories and to multiple sets of dummy variables 230
Joint explanatory power of a group of dummy variables 233
Change of reference category 234

The dummy variable trap 235
Multiple sets of dummy variables 237

5.3 Slope dummy variables 240
Joint explanatory power of the intercept and slope dummy variables 243

5.4 The Chow test 245
Relationship between the Chow test and the *F* test of the explanatory power of a set of dummy variables 247

Key terms 249

6. SPECIFICATION OF REGRESSION VARIABLES 250

6.1 Model specification 250

6.2 The effect of omitting a variable that ought to be included 251
The problem of bias 251
Invalidation of the statistical tests 254
R^2 in the presence of omitted variable bias 256

6.3 The effect of including a variable that ought not to be included 260

6.4 Proxy variables 263
Unintentional proxies 266

6.5 Testing a linear restriction 268
F test of a linear restriction 270
The reparameterization of a regression model 270
t test of a linear restriction 273
Multiple restrictions 274
Zero restrictions 275

6.6 Getting the most out of your residuals 278

Key terms 279

7. HETEROSCEDASTICITY 280

7.1 Heteroscedasticity and its implications 280
Possible causes of heteroscedasticity 283

7.2 Detection of heteroscedasticity 285
The Goldfeld–Quandt test 285
The White test 286

7.3 Remedies for heteroscedasticity 288
Nonlinear models 292
White's heteroscedasticity-consistent standard errors 294
How serious are the consequences of heteroscedasticity? 295

Key terms 297

8. STOCHASTIC REGRESSORS AND MEASUREMENT ERRORS 300

8.1 Assumptions for models with stochastic regressors 300
8.2 Finite sample properties of the OLS regression estimators 302
Precision and efficiency 303
8.3 Asymptotic properties of the OLS regression estimators 303
Consistency 304
Asymptotic normality of the regression coefficients 305
8.4 The consequences of measurement errors 306
Measurement errors in the explanatory variable(s) 306
Measurement errors in the dependent variable 309
Imperfect proxy variables 310
8.5 Instrumental variables 316
Asymptotic distribution of the IV estimator 318
Monte Carlo illustration 320
Multiple instruments 325
The Durbin–Wu–Hausman specification test 326
Key terms 329

9. SIMULTANEOUS EQUATIONS ESTIMATION 331

9.1 Simultaneous equations models: structural and reduced form equations 331
9.2 Simultaneous equations bias 333
A Monte Carlo experiment 335
9.3 Instrumental variables estimation 338
Underidentification 341
Overidentification 342
Two-stage least squares 343
The order condition for identification 344
Unobserved heterogeneity 345
Durbin–Wu–Hausman test 346
Key terms 350

10 BINARY CHOICE AND LIMITED DEPENDENT VARIABLE MODELS, AND MAXIMUM LIKELIHOOD ESTIMATION 354

10.1 The linear probability model 354
10.2 Logit analysis 359
Generalization to more than one explanatory variable 361
Goodness of fit and statistical tests 362
10.3 Probit analysis 365
10.4 Censored regressions: tobit analysis 368

10.5 Sample selection bias 374
10.6 An introduction to maximum likelihood estimation 378
Generalization to a sample of n observations 382
Generalization to the case where σ is unknown 383
Application to the simple regression model 385
Goodness of fit and statistical tests 386
Key terms 387
Appendix 10.1 Comparing linear and logarithmic specifications 388

11. MODELS USING TIME SERIES DATA 391

11.1 Assumptions for regressions with time series data 391
11.2 Static models 393
11.3 Models with lagged explanatory variables 398
Estimating long-run effects 400
11.4 Models with a lagged dependent variable 401
The partial adjustment model 404
The error correction model 405
The adaptive expectations model 406
More general autoregressive models 409
11.5 Assumption C.7 and the properties of estimators in autoregressive models 411
Consistency 414
Limiting distributions 415
t tests in an autoregressive model 417
11.6 Simultaneous equations models 419
11.7 Alternative dynamic representations of time series processes 422
Time series analysis 423
Vector autoregressions 425
Key terms 427

12. AUTOCORRELATION 429

12.1 Definition and consequences of autocorrelation 429
Consequences of autocorrelation 431
Autocorrelation with a lagged dependent variable 433
12.2 Detection of autocorrelation 434
The Breusch–Godfrey test 435
The Durbin–Watson test 436
Durbin's h test 438
12.3 Fitting a model subject to AR(1) autocorrelation 440
Issues 441
Inference 442
The common factor test 445

12.4 Apparent autocorrelation 451

12.5 Model specification: specific-to-general versus general-to-specific 457

Comparison of alternative models 458

The general-to-specific approach to model specification 460

Key terms 461

Appendix 12.1: Demonstration that the Durbin–Watson statistic approximates $2 - 2\rho$ in large samples 462

13. INTRODUCTION TO NONSTATIONARY TIME SERIES 463

13.1 Stationarity and nonstationarity 463

Stationary time series 463

Nonstationary time series 469

Deterministic trend 472

Difference-stationarity and trend-stationarity 473

13.2 Spurious regressions 475

Spurious regressions with variables possessing deterministic trends 475

Spurious regressions with variables that are random walks 476

13.3 Graphical techniques for detecting nonstationarity 484

13.4 Tests of nonstationarity 489

Untrended process 491

Trended process 497

Augmented Dickey–Fuller tests 498

Other tests 500

Further complications 502

13.5 Cointegration 504

13.6 Fitting models with nonstationary time series 508

Detrending 509

Differencing 509

Error correction models 510

Key terms 513

14. INTRODUCTION TO PANEL DATA MODELS 514

14.1 Introduction 514

Example of the use of a panel data set to investigate dynamics 515

14.2 Fixed effects regressions 518

Within-groups fixed effects 518

First differences fixed effects 519

Least squares dummy variable fixed effects 520

14.3 **Random effects regressions** 522
Assessing the appropriateness of fixed effects and random effects estimation 525
Random effects or OLS? 526
A note on the random effects and fixed effects terminology 527

Key terms 527

APPENDIX A: Statistical tables 531
APPENDIX B: Data Sets 548
Bibliography 559
Author Index 563
Subject Index 565

Introduction

Why study econometrics?

Econometrics is the term used to describe the application of statistical methods to the quantification and critical assessment of hypothetical relationships using data. The term 'econometrics' suggests that the methods relate only to economic analysis. In fact, applications will be found far more broadly, in virtually all the social sciences and elsewhere. It is true that economics has provided the impetus for much of the development of econometrics, but other disciplines have also made substantial contributions. Indeed, regression analysis, the core technique, appears initially to have been developed in applications to astronomy by Legendre and Gauss in the first few years of the nineteenth century.

It is with the aid of econometrics that we discriminate between competing theories and put numerical clothing on to the successful ones. For economists, econometric analysis may be motivated by a simple desire to improve our understanding of how the economy works, at either the microeconomic or macroeconomic level, but more often it is undertaken with a specific objective in mind. In the private sector, the financial benefits that accrue from a sophisticated understanding of relevant markets and an ability to predict change may be the driving factor. In the public sector, the impetus may come from an awareness that evidence-based policy initiatives are likely to be those that have the greatest impact.

It is now generally recognized that nearly all professional economists, not just those actually working with data, should have a basic understanding of econometrics. There used to be a view that microeconomics and macroeconomics comprised the core training of an economist and that econometrics was an optional extra to be pursued by those with a flair for numbers and an inclination to get their hands dirty with data. In particular, much of early macroeconomic theory was in reality no more than conjecture propounded by (over-)confident theorists who thought that the job of quantifying their theories could safely be left to others with lesser vision and a greater willingness to apply themselves to empirical detail.

That view is long gone. Microeconomic and macroeconomic theories are generally considered to be of little interest if they are not supported by econometric analysis. As a consequence of the recognition of its importance, an introductory course in econometrics now has become an integral component of any serious undergraduate degree in economics and it is a prerequisite for admission to a master's level course in economics or finance.

Even for those who are not actively involved with econometrics, there are two major benefits from its study. One is that it facilitates communication between econometricians and the users of their work. This is especially important in the workshops that are the typical meeting ground for applied econometricians and the policymakers who may be influenced by their work. Would-be policymakers who do not speak the language can expect to be excluded from the discussion. The other benefit is the development of the ability to obtain a perspective on econometric work and to undertake critical evaluation of it. Econometric work is more robust in some contexts than in others. Experience with the practice of econometrics and a knowledge of the potential problems that can arise are essential for developing an instinct for judging how much confidence should be placed on the findings of a particular study.

Aim of this text

With this in mind, the text has three specific objectives:

1. One is to provide you with the practical skills needed to fit models given suitable data, in a relatively straightforward context. This is relatively easy. Generally, such applications will be models fitted with cross-sectional data.
2. The second is to promote the development of an understanding of the statistical properties of these techniques and hence an understanding of why the techniques work satisfactorily in certain contexts and not in others. This is much more demanding.
3. The third, building on the second, is to encourage you to develop a strong intuitive understanding of the material and with it the capacity and confidence to extend it further, either sideways, in applications in a particular field, or vertically, moving on to more advanced study.

Mathematics and statistics prerequisites for studying econometrics

The prerequisite for studying this subject is a solid background in basic college-level mathematics and statistics.

Mathematics: The mathematics requirement is two semesters of college-level calculus, with an emphasis on the differential rather than the integral calculus. This is the official requirement. The real practical requirement is that you should be able to work through a proof involving simple college-level algebra, in comfort and understanding everything as you go. In particular, equations involving Σ notation should not present any difficulty for you. Students who have taken two semesters of calculus in college with reasonable grades should belong to this category.

Linear algebra (matrix algebra) is not used in this text. This is not a serious impediment to acquiring a sound knowledge of econometrics at this level. Although it means that, for the purpose of theoretical analysis, we have to restrict the analysis to models with no more than two explanatory variables, this is not a major constraint. We can still investigate nearly everything that we wish and greater complexity would add very little. If you continue with a higher-level course, you will need to learn how to use linear algebra, but once you have done that, you will find it easy to interpret what we have done here within it. Appendix A, Matrix Algebra, of Greene's *Econometric Analysis* is an excellent resource, giving you just what you need to know for econometrics.

Statistics: You must have a clear understanding of what is meant by the sampling distribution of an estimator and of the principles of statistical inference and hypothesis testing. This is absolutely essential. In my experience, most problems that students have with an introductory econometrics course are not econometric problems at all but problems with statistics, or rather, a lack of understanding of statistics. There are no short cuts. If you do not have this background, you should put your study of econometrics on hold and study statistics first. Otherwise there will be core parts of the econometrics syllabus that you do not begin to understand.

In addition, it would be helpful if you have some knowledge of economics. However, although the examples and exercises relate to economics, most of them are so straightforward that a previous study of economics is not a requirement.

Additional resources

There are two additional major resources that you should check out as soon as you begin to use this text: the slideshows and the study guide. Both are available, at no cost and with no restrictions, on the Oxford University Press website at http://www.oup.com/uk/orc/bin/9780199280964/. Putting 'OUP Dougherty' into Google should bring it up.

Slideshows: The PowerPoint slideshows systematically cover all of the topics treated in the text, typically with greater graphical detail. They are not intended as a substitute for the text, but they should provide substantial support.

Study guide: This provides answers to the starred exercises in the text and additional exercises, also with solutions. It was commissioned by the University of London External Degree as an additional resource for distance-learning students, and the organizers of the External Degree have kindly allowed it to be available to anyone who is interested in using it.

The website also gives unrestricted access to all of the data sets used in the examples and exercises in the text.

Econometrics software

There are at least ten major commercial software packages for econometrics in use around the world and it does not matter which one you use. With little variation, they all have the features and facilities used in econometrics at this level. Many of the tables in this text reproduce output from Stata and EViews, mainly because the format is compact and tidy. Output from other applications looks very similar.

If you do not have access to one of these commercial applications, then download gretl and use that instead. gretl is a powerful, sophisticated econometrics application, easy to use, and free. Go to the OUP website mentioned above, find the link, and follow the instructions. There you will also find a downloadable manual that tells you how to use gretl to do the exercises in this text.

You should not try to use an inferior substitute. In particular, you should not try to use the regression engine built into a spreadsheet application such as Microsoft Excel. Excel and other spreadsheets are invaluable applications, but they are not intended or designed for serious econometrics use. You need a dedicated application and gretl is an excellent one.

The aims of this text have been stated above. There is one further aim, or at least, hope. That is that you will find the study of econometrics intellectually satisfying. By the time that you approach the end of this text, you will find that, although the material in each chapter is new, the same themes and concerns keep reappearing, especially those related to the properties of estimators. When you begin to recognize this, you will be well on your way to becoming a proper econometrician, and not just someone mechanically handling data and performing tests. And, of course, when the time comes for you to fit your own models with your own data, it is hoped that you will find the practice of econometrics enjoyable, too.

Review: Random Variables, Sampling, and Estimation

R.1 Introduction

A course in basic mathematical statistics is a non-negotiable prerequisite for any serious course in econometrics. The reason for this is that econometrics courses have two objectives. One is to show how various quantitative techniques can be used to fit models given suitable data. This is relatively easy. The other is to develop an understanding of the statistical properties of these techniques and hence an understanding of why they work satisfactorily in certain contexts and not in others. This is much more demanding and it does require a good basic knowledge of statistical theory.

This review chapter is not intended to serve as an accelerated substitute for a statistics course. A common problem with statistics courses is that they attempt to cover some of the material too fast. Any abbreviated introduction to the discipline would be even more susceptible to such problems. The present treatment therefore assumes that a first course has already been completed and it is intended to provide an opportunity to revisit the material, with three objectives:

1. To provide an opportunity for revisiting all of the basic elements of statistical theory that are used in the remainder of the text. This is the function of Sections R.2–R.8, which cover:
   - random variables and expectations,
   - variance, covariance, and correlation,
   - sampling and estimators,
   - unbiasedness and efficiency, and
   - the normal distribution.

   Unless your statistics course was taken some time ago, it should be possible to skim through these sections fairly rapidly.
2. To reinforce the understanding of some standard topics that often require a second visit before being fully understood. This is the function of Sections R.9–R.13, which cover
   - hypothesis testing,
   - Type I error, Type II error, and the significance level (size) and power of a test,

- t tests,
- confidence intervals,
- one-sided t tests.

The discussion of the double structure of a sampled random variable and the distinction between its potential sample values and a realization in Section R.5 may also fall into this category.

3. To provide a treatment of some important topics on asymptotics (large-sample theory) that are often neglected in statistics courses:
   - probability limits and consistency,
   - convergence in distribution and central limit theorems.

   These topics are covered in Sections R.14 and R.15.

As far as Section R.13 is concerned, the material should be mostly revision, perhaps with some upgrading of understanding. However, the material on asymptotics in Sections R.14 and R.15 may be largely or wholly new. Despite the fact that asymptotic theory is of great importance in econometrics, it is usually covered inadequately in basic statistics courses. Typically, it is omitted entirely, apart from a brief reference to consistency and 'the' central limit theorem, often with no explanation of why these topics are useful. The reason for this neglect is that basic statistics courses tend to be service courses catering to students from many disciplines with a wide variety of priorities and interests and as a consequence they usually cover some topics that are of little relevance to future students of econometrics and they give insufficient attention to others. Apart from the core theory on sampling, estimation, and inference, the topics that are relevant to business studies or psychology are quite different from those that are relevant to econometrics. For most students of statistics, the topics in Sections R.14 and R.15 are not of great interest. However, for students of econometrics, they are crucial.

R.2 Discrete random variables and expectations

Discrete random variables

A simple notion of probability is adequate for the purposes of this text. We shall begin with discrete random variables. A random variable is any variable whose value cannot be predicted exactly. A **discrete random variable** is one that has a specific set of possible values. An example is the total score when two dice are thrown. An example of a random variable that is not discrete is the temperature in a room. It can take any one of a continuous range of values and is an example of a **continuous random variable**. We shall come to these later in this review.

Continuing with the example of the two dice, suppose that one of them is green and the other red. When they are thrown, there are 36 possible experimental outcomes, since the green one can be any of the numbers from 1 to 6 and the red one likewise. The random variable defined as their sum, which we will denote X, can take only one of 11 values—the numbers from 2 to 12. The relationship between the experimental outcomes and the values of this random variable is illustrated in Figure R.1.

Assuming that the dice are fair, we can use Figure R.1 to work out the probability of the occurrence of each value of X. Since there are 36 different combinations of the dice, each outcome has probability 1/36. {Green = 1, red = 1} is the only combination that gives a total of 2, so the probability of $X = 2$ is 1/36. To obtain $X = 7$, we would need {green = 1, red = 6} or {green = 2, red = 5} or {green = 3, red = 4} or {green = 4, red = 3} or {green = 5, red = 2} or {green = 6, red = 1}. In this case, six of the possible outcomes would do, so the probability of throwing 7 is 6/36. All the probabilities are given in Table R.1. If you add all the probabilities together, you get exactly 1. This is because it is 100 percent certain that the value must be one of the numbers from 2 to 12.

red / *green*	1	2	3	4	5	6
1	2	3	4	5	6	7
2	3	4	5	6	7	8
3	4	5	6	7	8	9
4	5	6	7	8	9	10
5	6	7	8	9	10	11
6	7	8	9	10	11	12

Figure R.1 Outcomes in the example with two dice

Table R.1 Frequencies and probability distribution, example with two dice

Value of X	2	3	4	5	6	7	8	9	10	11	12
Frequency	1	2	3	4	5	6	5	4	3	2	1
Probability	1/36	2/36	3/36	4/36	5/36	6/36	5/36	4/36	3/36	2/36	1/36

The set of all possible values of a random variable is described as the population from which it is drawn. In this case, the population is the set of numbers from 2 to 12.

Expected values of random variables

The expected value (sometimes described as expectation) of a discrete random variable is the weighted average of all its possible values, taking the probability of each outcome as its weight. You calculate it by multiplying each possible value of the random variable by its probability and adding. In mathematical terms, if the random variable is denoted X, its expected value is denoted $E(X)$.

Let us suppose that X can take n particular values $x_1, x_2, \ldots, x_n$ and that the probability of x_i is p_i. Then

$$E(X) = x_1 p_1 + \cdots + x_n p_n = \sum_{i=1}^{n} x_i p_i. \quad \textbf{(R.1)}$$

In the case of the two dice, the values x_1 to x_n were the numbers 2 to 12: $x_1 = 2, x_2 = 3, \ldots, x_{11} = 12$, and $p_1 = 1/36, p_2 = 2/36, \ldots, p_{11} = 1/36$. The easiest and neatest way to calculate an expected value is to use a spreadsheet. The left half of Table R.2 shows the working in abstract. The right half shows the working for the present example. As you can see from the table, the expected value is equal to 7.

Table R.2 Expected value of X, example with two dice

X	p	Xp	X	p	Xp
x_1	p_1	$x_1 p_1$	2	1/36	2/36
x_2	p_2	$x_2 p_2$	3	2/36	6/36
x_3	p_3	$x_3 p_3$	4	3/36	12/36
...	...	...	5	4/36	20/36
...	...	...	6	5/36	30/36
...	...	...	7	6/36	42/36
...	...	...	8	5/36	40/36
...	...	...	9	4/36	36/36
...	...	...	10	3/36	30/36
...	...	...	11	2/36	22/36
x_n	p_n	$x_n p_n$	12	1/36	12/36
Total		$E(X) = \sum_{i=1}^{n} x_i p_i$			252/36 = 7

Before going any further, let us consider an even simpler example of a random variable, the number obtained when you throw just one die. There are six possible outcomes: $x_1 = 1$, $x_2 = 2$, $x_3 = 3$, $x_4 = 4$, $x_5 = 5$, $x_6 = 6$. Each has probability 1/6. Using these data to compute the expected value, you find that it is equal to 3.5. Thus, in this case, the expected value of the random variable is a number you could not obtain at all.

The expected value of a random variable is frequently described as its population mean. In the case of a random variable X, the population mean is often denoted by μ_X, or just μ, if there is no ambiguity.

Expected values of functions of discrete random variables

Let $g(X)$ be any function of X. Then $E\{g(X)\}$. the expected value of $g(X)$, is given by

$$E\{g(X)\} = g(x_1)p_1 + \cdots + g(x_n)p_n = \sum_{i=1}^{n} g(x_i)p_i, \qquad \textbf{(R.2)}$$

where the summation is taken over all possible values of X.

The left half of Table R.3 illustrates the calculation of the expected value of a function of X. Suppose that X can take the n different values x_1 to x_n, with associated probabilities p_1 to p_n. In the first column, you write down all the values that X can take. In the second, you write down the corresponding probabilities. In the third, you

Table R.3 Expected value of $g(X)$, example with two dice

Expected value of g(X)				*Expected value of X²*			
X	p	$g(X)$	$g(X)p$	X	p	X^2	X^2p
x_1	p_1	$g(x_1)$	$g(x_1)p_1$	2	1/36	4	0.11
x_2	p_2	$g(x_2)$	$g(x_2)p_2$	3	2/36	9	0.50
x_3	p_3	$g(x_3)$	$g(x_3)p_3$	4	3/36	16	1.33
...	...	...	...	5	4/36	25	2.78
...	...	...	...	6	5/36	36	5.00
...	...	...	...	7	6/36	49	8.17
...	...	...	...	8	5/36	64	8.89
...	...	...	...	9	4/36	81	9.00
...	...	...	...	10	3/36	100	8.83
...	...	...	...	11	2/36	121	6.72
x_n	p_n	$g(x_n)$	$g(x_n)p_n$	12	1/36	144	4.00
Total			$E\{g(X)\} = \sum_{i=1}^{n} g(x_i)p_i$				54.83

calculate the value of the function for the corresponding value of X. In the fourth, you multiply columns 2 and 3. The answer is given by the total of column 4.

The right half of Table R.3 shows the calculation of the expected value of X^2 for the example with two dice. You might be tempted to think that this is equal to μ_X^2, but this is not correct. $E(X^2)$ is 54.83. The expected value of X was shown in Table R.2 to be equal to 7. Thus it is not true that $E(X^2)$ is equal to μ_X^2, which means that you have to be careful to distinguish between $E(X^2)$ and $[E(X)]^2$ (the latter being $E(X)$ multiplied by $E(X)$: that is, μ_X^2).

Expected value rules

There are three rules that we are going to use over and over again. They are virtually self-evident, and they are equally valid for discrete and continuous random variables.

Expected value rule 1 The expected value of the sum of several variables is equal to the sum of their expected values. For example, if you have three random variables X, Y, and Z,

$$E(X + Y + Z) = E(X) + E(Y) + E(Z). \quad \textbf{(R.3)}$$

Expected value rule 2 If you multiply a random variable by a constant, you multiply its expected value by the same constant. If X is a random variable and b is a constant,

$$E(bX) = bE(X). \quad \textbf{(R.4)}$$

Expected value rule 3 The expected value of a constant is that constant. For example, if b is a constant,

$$E(b) = b. \quad \textbf{(R.5)}$$

The proof of rule 2 is left as an exercise (Exercise R.5). The proof of rule 3 is trivial in that it follows from the definition of a constant. Although the proof of rule 1 is quite easy, we will omit it here.

Putting the three rules together, you can simplify more complicated expressions. For example, suppose you wish to calculate $E(Y)$, where

$$Y = b_1 + b_2X \quad \textbf{(R.6)}$$

and b_1 and b_2 are constants. Then,

$$\begin{aligned} E(Y) &= E(b_1 + b_2X) \\ &= E(b_1) + E(b_2X) \quad \text{using rule 1} \\ &= b_1 + b_2E(X) \quad \text{using rules 2 and 3.} \end{aligned} \quad \textbf{(R.7)}$$

Therefore, instead of calculating $E(Y)$ directly, you could calculate $E(X)$ and obtain $E(Y)$ from equation (R.7).

Population variance of a discrete random variable

In this text there is only one function of X in which we shall take much interest, and that is its population variance, $\text{var}(X)$, a useful measure of the dispersion of its probability distribution. It is defined as the expected value of the square of the difference between X and its mean, that is, of $(X-\mu_X)^2$, where μ_X is the population mean. In equations it is usually denoted σ_X^2, with the subscript being dropped when it is obvious that it is referring to a particular variable:

$$\begin{aligned}\text{var}(X) &= \sigma_X^2 = E\left\{(X-\mu_X)^2\right\} \\ &= (x_1-\mu_X)^2 p_1 + \cdots + (x_n-\mu_X)^2 p_n = \sum_{i=1}^{n}(x_i-\mu_X)^2 p_i. \qquad \textbf{(R.8)}\end{aligned}$$

From σ_X^2 one obtains σ_X, the standard deviation, an equally popular measure of the dispersion of the probability distribution; the standard deviation of a random variable is the square root of its variance.

We will illustrate the calculation of population variance with the example of the two dice. Since $\mu_X = E(X) = 7$, $(X-\mu_X)^2$ is $(X-7)^2$ in this case. The expected value of $(X-7)^2$ is calculated in Table R.4 using Table R.3 as a pattern. An extra column, $(X-\mu_X)$, has been introduced as a step in the calculation of $(X-\mu_X)^2$. By summing the last column in Table R.4, one finds that σ_X^2 is equal to 5.83. Hence, σ_X, the standard deviation, is equal to $\sqrt{5.83}$, which is 2.41.

Table R.4 Population variance of X, example with two dice

X	p	$X-\mu_X$	$(X-\mu_X)^2$	$(X-\mu_X)^2p$
2	1/36	−5	25	0.69
3	2/36	−4	16	0.89
4	3/36	−3	9	0.75
5	4/36	−2	4	0.44
6	5/36	−1	1	0.14
7	6/36	0	0	0.00
8	5/36	1	1	0.14
9	4/36	2	4	0.44
10	3/36	3	9	0.75
11	2/36	4	16	0.89
12	1/36	5	25	0.69
Total				5.83

One particular use of the expected value rules that is quite important is to show that the population variance of a random variable can be written

$$\sigma_X^2 = E(X^2) - \mu_X^2, \tag{R.9}$$

an expression that is sometimes more convenient than the original definition. The proof is a good exercise in the use of the expected value rules. From its definition,

$$\begin{aligned}
\sigma_X^2 &= E\left\{(X-\mu_X)^2\right\} \\
&= E\left(X^2 - 2\mu_X X + \mu_X^2\right) \\
&= E\left(X^2\right) + E\left(-2\mu_X X\right) + E\left(\mu_X^2\right) \\
&= E\left(X^2\right) - 2\mu_X E(X) + \mu_X^2 \\
&= E\left(X^2\right) - 2\mu_X^2 + \mu_X^2 \\
&= E\left(X^2\right) - \mu_X^2 .
\end{aligned} \tag{R.10}$$

Line 3 uses expected value rule 1. Line 4 uses rules 2 and 3 (μ_X is a constant). Line 5 uses the fact that μ_X is just another way of writing $E(X)$.

Fixed and random components of a random variable

Instead of regarding a random variable as a single entity, it is often convenient to break it down into a fixed component and a pure random component, the fixed component always being the population mean. If X is a random variable and μ_X its population mean, one may make the following decomposition:

$$X = \mu_X + u, \tag{R.11}$$

where u is what will be called the pure random component (in the context of regression analysis, it is usually described as the disturbance term).

You could of course look at it the other way and say that the random component, u, is defined to be the difference between X and μ_X:

$$u = X - \mu_X. \tag{R.12}$$

It follows from its definition that the expected value of u is zero. From equation (R.12),

$$E(u) = E(X - \mu_X) = E(X) + E(-\mu_X) = \mu_X - \mu_X = 0. \tag{R.13}$$

Since all the variation in X is due to u, it is not surprising that the population variance of X is equal to the population variance of u. This is easy to prove. By definition,

$$\sigma_X^2 = E\{(X-\mu_X)^2\} = E(u^2) \tag{R.14}$$

and

$$\begin{aligned}\sigma_u^2 &= E\{(u - \text{mean of } u)^2\} \\ &= E\{(u-0)^2\} = E(u^2). \end{aligned} \tag{R.15}$$

Hence, σ^2 can equivalently be defined to be the variance of X or u.

To summarize, if X is a random variable defined by (R.11), where μ_X is a fixed number and u is a random component, with mean zero and population variance σ^2, then X has population mean μ_X and population variance σ^2.

EXERCISES

R.1 A random variable X is defined to be the difference between the higher value and the lower value when two dice are thrown. If they have the same value, X is defined to be zero. Find the probability distribution for X.

R.2* A random variable X is defined to be the larger of the two values when two dice are thrown, or the value if the values are the same. Find the probability distribution for X. [*Note*: Answers to exercises marked with an asterisk are provided in the *Study Guide*.]

R.3 Find the expected value of X in Exercise R.1.

R.4* Find the expected value of X in Exercise R.2.

R.5 If X is a random variable with mean μ_X, and λ is a constant, prove that the expected value of λX is $\lambda\mu_X$.

R.6 Calculate $E(X^2)$ for X defined in Exercise R.1.

R.7* Calculate $E(X^2)$ for X defined in Exercise R.2.

R.8 Let X be the total when two dice are thrown. Calculate the possible values of Y, where Y is given by

$$Y = 2X + 3,$$

and hence calculate $E(Y)$. Show that this is equal to $2E(X) + 3$.

R.9 Calculate the population variance and the standard deviation of X as defined in Exercise R.1, using the definition given by equation (R.8).

R.10* Calculate the population variance and the standard deviation of X as defined in Exercise R.2, using the definition given by equation (R.8).

R.11 Using equation (R.9), find the variance of the random variable X defined in Exercise R.1 and show that the answer is the same as that obtained in Exercise R.9. (*Note*: You have already calculated μ_X in Exercise R.3 and $E(X^2)$ in Exercise R.6.)

R.12* Using equation (R.9), find the variance of the random variable X defined in Exercise R.2 and show that the answer is the same as that obtained in Exercise R.10. (*Note*: You have already calculated μ_X in Exercise R.4 and $E(X^2)$ in Exercise R.7.)

R.3 Continuous random variables

Probability density

Discrete random variables are very easy to handle in that, by definition, they can take only a finite set of values. Each of these values has a 'packet' of probability associated with it, the sum of the probabilities being equal to 1. This is illustrated in Figure R.2 for the example with two dice. X can take values from 2 to 12 and the associated probabilities are as shown. If you know the size of these packets, you can calculate the population mean and variance in a straightforward fashion.

However, the analysis in this text usually deals with continuous random variables, which can take an infinite number of values. The discussion will be illustrated with the example of the temperature in a room. For the sake of argument, we will initially assume that this varies within the limits of 55 to 75°F, and we will suppose that it is equally likely to be anywhere within this range.

Since there are an infinite number of different values that the temperature can take, it is useless trying to divide the probability into little packets and we have to adopt a different approach. Instead, we talk about the probability of the random variable lying within a given interval, and we represent the probability graphically as an area within the interval. For example, in the present case, the probability of X lying in the interval 59–60°F is 0.05 since this range is one-twentieth of the complete range 55–75°F. Figure R.3 shows the rectangle depicting the probability of X lying in this interval. Since its area is 0.05 and its base is 1, its height must be 0.05. The same is true for all the other one-degree intervals in the range that X can take.

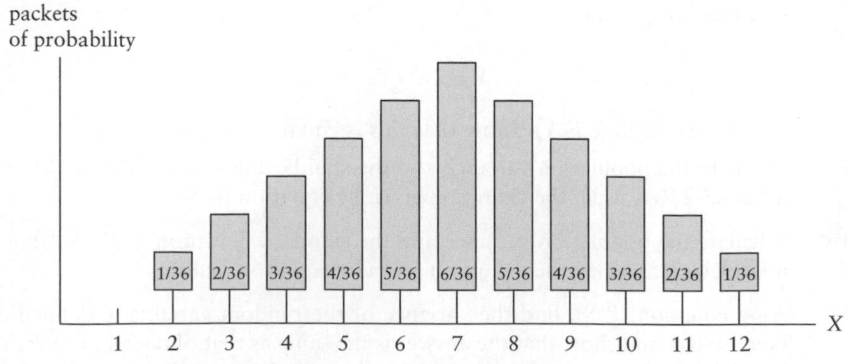

Figure R.2 Discrete probabilities (example with two dice)

Having found the height at all points in the range, we can answer other such questions relating to probabilities. For example, we can determine the probability that the temperature lies between 65 and 70°F. This is given by the area in the interval 65–70°F, represented by the shaded area in Figure R.4. The base of the shaded area is 5, and its height is 0.05, so the area is 0.25. The probability is a quarter, which is obvious anyway in that 65–70°F is a quarter of the whole range.

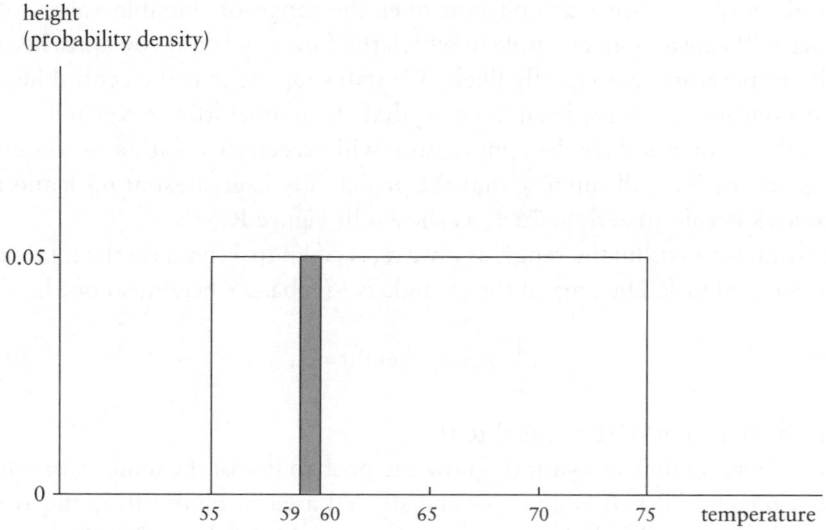

Figure R.3 Probability of the temperature lying in the interval 59–60°F

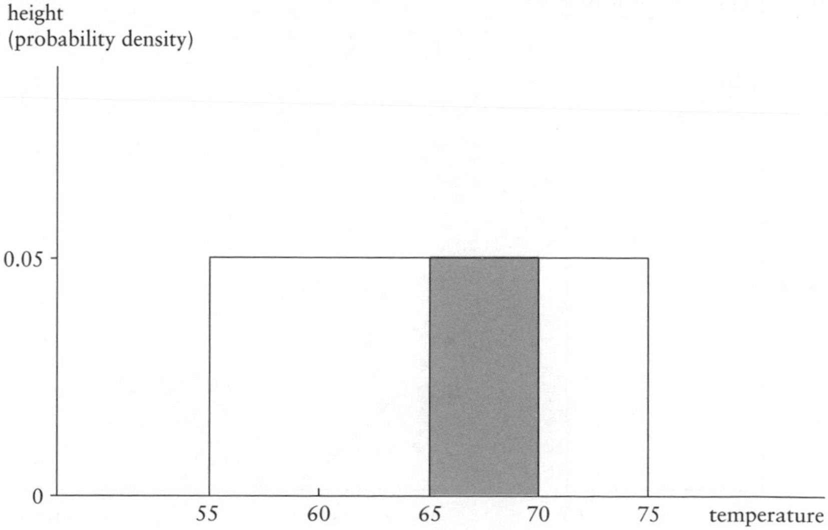

Figure R.4 Probability of the temperature lying in the interval 65–70°F

The height at any point is formally described as the probability density at that point. If the probability density can be written as a function of the random variable, that function is known as the **probability density function**. In this case it is given by $f(X)$, where X is the temperature and

$$f(X) = 0.05 \quad \text{for } 55 \le X \le 75$$
$$f(X) = 0 \quad \text{for } X < 55 \text{ or } X > 75. \tag{R.16}$$

The foregoing example was particularly simple to handle because the probability density function was constant over the range of possible values of X. Next we will consider an example in which the function is not constant, because not all temperatures are equally likely. We will suppose that the central heating and air conditioning have been fixed so that the temperature never falls below 65°F, and that on hot days the temperature will exceed this, with a maximum of 75°F as before. We will suppose that the probability is greatest at 65°F and that it decreases evenly to zero at 75°F, as shown in Figure R.5.

The total area within the range, as always, is equal to 1, because the total probability is equal to 1. The area of the triangle is ½ × base × height, so one has

$$\frac{1}{2} \times 10 \times \text{height} = 1, \tag{R.17}$$

and so the height at 65°F is equal to 0.20.

Suppose again that we want to know the probability of the temperature lying between 65 and 70°F. It is given by the shaded area in Figure R.6, and with a little geometry you should be able to verify that it is equal to 0.75. If you prefer to talk in terms of percentages, this means that there is a 75 percent chance that the temperature will lie between 65 and 70°F, and only a 25 percent chance that it will lie between 70 and 75°F.

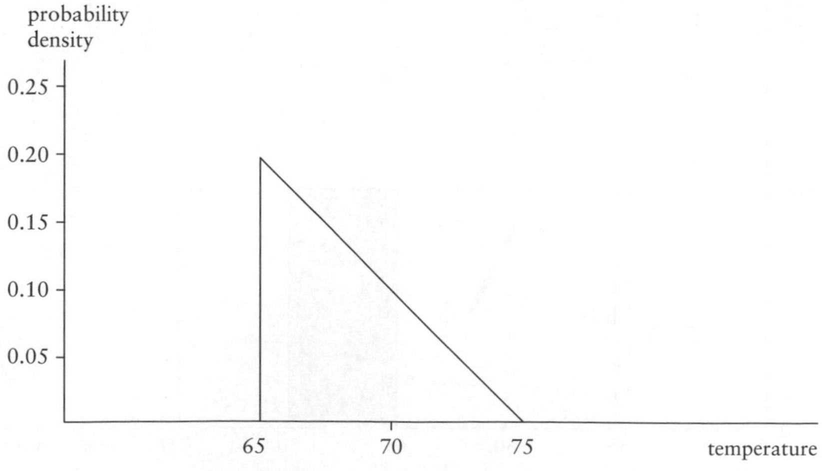

Figure R.5 Triangular density function, 65–75°F

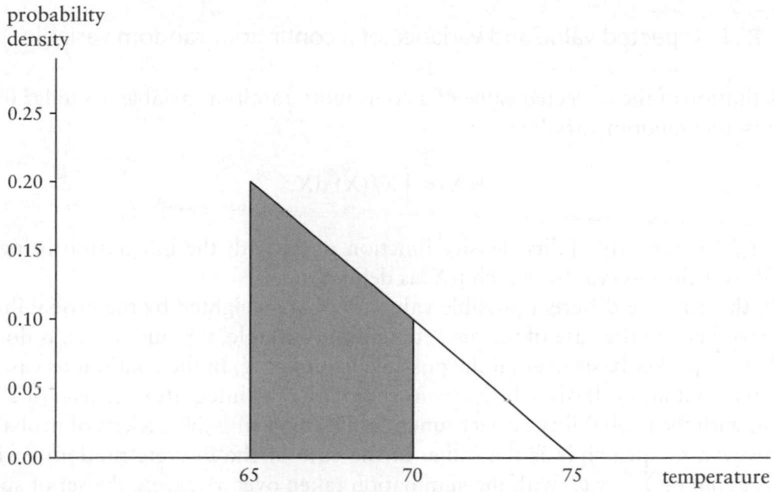

Figure R.6 Probability of the temperature lying in the interval 65–70°F

In this case, the probability density function is given by $f(X)$, where

$$f(X) = 1.5 - 0.02X \quad \text{for } 65 \leq X \leq 75$$

$$f(X) = 0 \quad \text{for } X < 65 \text{ or } X > 75. \qquad \textbf{(R.18)}$$

(You can verify that $f(X)$ gives 0.20 at 65°F and 0 at 75°F.)

If you want to calculate probabilities for more complicated, curved functions, simple geometry will not do. In general, you have to use integral calculus or refer to specialized tables, if they exist. Fortunately, specialized probability tables do exist for all the functions that are going to interest us in practice. Integral calculus is also used in the definitions of the expected value and variance of a continuous random variable. These have much the same meaning for continuous random variables that they have for discrete ones (formal definitions are given in Box R.1), and the expected value rules work in exactly the same way.

R.4 Population covariance, covariance and variance rules, and correlation

Covariance

We come now to some concepts relating to two random variables. The first is covariance. If we have two random variables, X and Y, their population covariance, cov(X, Y), usually written σ_{XY} in equations, is defined to be the expected value of the product of their deviations from their means:

$$\operatorname{cov}(X,Y) = \sigma_{XY} = E\{(X - \mu_X)(Y - \mu_Y)\}, \qquad \textbf{(R.19)}$$

BOX R.1 Expected value and variance of a continuous random variable

The definition of the expected value of a continuous random variable is similar to that for a discrete random variable:

$$E(X) = \int Xf(X)\,dX,$$

where $f(X)$ is the probability density function of X, with the integration being performed over the interval for which $f(X)$ is defined.

In both cases, the different possible values of X are weighted by the probability attached to them. In the case of the discrete random variable, the summation is done on a packet-by-packet basis over all the possible values of X. In the continuous case, it is done on a continuous basis, which means summation by integration instead of Σ summation, with the probability density function $f(X)$ replacing the packets of probability p_i. However, the principle is the same. In the case of the discrete random variable, $E(X)$ is equal to $\sum_{i=1}^{n} x_i p_i$, with the summation taken over $x_1, \ldots, x_n$, the set of specific discrete values that X can take. In the continuous case, it is defined by

$$E(X) = \int Xf(X)\,dX,$$

with the integration taken over the whole range for which $f(X)$ is defined.

Discrete	*Continuous*
$E(X) = \sum_{i=1}^{n} x_i p_i$	$E(X) = \int Xf(X)\,dX$
(Summation over all possible discrete values)	(Integration over the range for which $f(X)$ is defined)

In the section on discrete random variables, it was shown how to calculate the expected value of a function of X, $g(X)$. You make a list of all the different values that $g(X)$ can take, weight each of them by the corresponding probability, and sum. The process is again exactly the same for a continuous random variable, except that it is done on a continuous basis, with integration replacing Σ summation.

$$\text{Discrete} \quad \sum_{i=1}^{n} g(x_i)p_i$$

$$\text{Continuous} \quad E[g(X)] = \int g(X)f(X)\,dX.$$

As in the case of discrete random variables, there is only one function in which we have an interest, the population variance, defined as the expected value of $(X - \mu_X)^2$, where $\mu_X = E(X)$ is the population mean. The variance is the summation of $(X - \mu_X)^2$, weighted by the appropriate probability, over all the possible values of X. In the case of a discrete random variable, this means that you have to evaluate

$$\sigma_X^2 = E\left\{(X-\mu_X)^2\right\} = \sum_{i=1}^{n}(X_i-\mu_X)^2 p_i .$$

The counterpart for the continuous random variable is

$$\sigma_X^2 = E\left\{(X-\mu_X)^2\right\} = \int (X-\mu_X)^2 f(X)dX.$$

As before, when you have evaluated the population variance, you can calculate the standard deviation, σ_X, by taking its square root.

where μ_X and μ_Y are the population means of X and Y, respectively. It is a measure of association, but not as useful as correlation, to be discussed shortly. We are mostly interested in covariance as an ingredient in some of our analysis of the properties of estimators.

Independence of random variables

Two random variables X and Y are said to be **independent** if $E[g(X)h(Y)]$ is equal to $E[g(X)]\,E[h(Y)]$ for any functions $g(X)$ and $h(Y)$. In particular, if X and Y are independent, $E(XY)$ is equal to $E(X)E(Y)$. If X and Y are independent, their population covariance is zero, since then

$$E\{(X-\mu_X)(Y-\mu_Y)\} = E(X-\mu_X)E(Y-\mu_Y) = 0\times 0 \qquad \textbf{(R.20)}$$

by virtue of the fact that $E(X)$ and $E(Y)$ are equal to μ_X and μ_Y, respectively.

Covariance rules

There are some rules that follow in a straightforward way from the definition of covariance, and since they are going to be used frequently in later chapters, it is worthwhile establishing them immediately:

Covariance rule 1 If $Y = V + W$, $\text{cov}(X, Y) = \text{cov}(X, V) + \text{cov}(X, W)$.

Covariance rule 2 If $Y = bZ$, where b is a constant and Z is a variable, $\text{cov}(X, Y) = b\,\text{cov}(X, Z)$.

Covariance rule 3 If $Y = b$, where b is a constant, $\text{cov}(X, Y) = 0$.

Proof of covariance rule 1

Since $Y = V + W$, $\mu_Y = \mu_V + \mu_W$ by virtue of expected value rule 1. Hence,

$$\begin{aligned}\operatorname{cov}(X,Y) &= E\{(X-\mu_X)(Y-\mu_Y)\}\\ &= E\{(X-\mu_X)([V+W]-[\mu_V+\mu_W])\}\\ &= E\{(X-\mu_X)(V-\mu_V)+(X-\mu_X)(W-\mu_W)\}\\ &= \operatorname{cov}(X,V)+\operatorname{cov}(X,W).\end{aligned} \qquad \textbf{(R.21)}$$

Proof of covariance rule 2

If $Y = bZ$, $\mu_Y = b\mu_Z$. Hence,

$$\begin{aligned}\operatorname{cov}(X,Y) &= E\{(X-\mu_X)(Y-\mu_Y)\}\\ &= E\{(X-\mu_X)(bZ-b\mu_Z)\}\\ &= bE\{(X-\mu_X)(Z-\mu_Z)\}\\ &= b\operatorname{cov}(X,Z).\end{aligned} \qquad \textbf{(R.22)}$$

Proof of covariance rule 3

This is trivial. If $Y = b$, $\mu_Y = b$ and

$$\begin{aligned}\operatorname{cov}(X,Y) &= E\{(X-\mu_X)(Y-\mu_Y)\}\\ &= E\{(X-\mu_X)(b-b)\}\\ &= E\{0\}=0.\end{aligned} \qquad \textbf{(R.23)}$$

Further developments

With these basic rules, you can simplify more complicated covariance expressions. For example, if a variable Y is equal to the sum of three variables U, V, and W,

$$\operatorname{cov}(X, Y) = \operatorname{cov}(X, [U + V + W]) = \operatorname{cov}(X, U) + \operatorname{cov}(X, [V + W]), \qquad \textbf{(R.24)}$$

using rule 1 and breaking up Y into two parts, U and $V+W$. Hence,

$$\operatorname{cov}(X, Y) = \operatorname{cov}(X, U) + \operatorname{cov}(X, V) + \operatorname{cov}(X, W), \qquad \textbf{(R.25)}$$

using rule 1 again.

As another example, suppose $Y = b_1 + b_2Z$, where b_1 and b_2 are constants and Z is a variable. Then

$$\begin{aligned}\operatorname{cov}(X, Y) &= \operatorname{cov}(X, [b_1 + b_2Z])\\ &= \operatorname{cov}(X, b_1) + \operatorname{cov}(X, b_2Z) && \text{using rule 1}\\ &= 0 + \operatorname{cov}(X, b_2Z) && \text{using rule 3}\\ &= b_2\operatorname{cov}(X, Z) && \text{using rule 2.}\end{aligned} \qquad \textbf{(R.26)}$$

Variance rules

There are some straightforward rules for variances, the first three of which are counterparts of those for covariance:

Variance rule 1 If $Y = V + W$, $\text{var}(Y) = \text{var}(V) + \text{var}(W) + 2\text{cov}(V, W)$.
Variance rule 2 If $Y = bZ$, where b is a constant, $\text{var}(Y) = b^2\text{var}(Z)$.
Variance rule 3 If $Y = b$, where b is a constant, $\text{var}(Y) = 0$.
Variance rule 4 If $Y = V + b$, where b is a constant, $\text{var}(Y) = \text{var}(V)$.

It is useful to note that the variance of a variable X can be thought of as the covariance of X with itself:

$$\begin{aligned}\text{var}(X) &= E\{(X-\mu_X)^2\} \\ &= E\{(X-\mu_X)(X-\mu_X)\} \\ &= \text{cov}(X,X). \end{aligned} \qquad \textbf{(R.27)}$$

In view of this equivalence, we can make use of the covariance rules to establish the variance rules.

Proof of variance rule 1

If $Y = V + W$,

$$\begin{aligned}\text{var}(Y) &= \text{cov}(Y,Y) = \text{cov}(Y,[V+W]) = \text{cov}(Y,V) + \text{cov}(Y,W) \quad \text{using covariance rule 1} \\ &= \text{cov}([V+W],V) + \text{cov}([V+W],W) \\ &= \text{cov}(V,V) + \text{cov}(W,V) + \text{cov}(V,W) + \text{cov}(W,W) \quad \text{using covariance rule 1 again} \\ &= \text{var}(V) + \text{var}(W) + 2\text{cov}(V,W). \end{aligned} \qquad \textbf{(R.28)}$$

Note that $\text{cov}(W, V)$ and $\text{cov}(V, W)$ are the same. The order of the variables makes no difference in the definition of covariance (R.19).

Proof of variance rule 2

If $Y = bZ$, where b is a constant, using covariance rule 2 twice,

$$\begin{aligned}\text{var}(Y) &= \text{cov}(Y,Y) = \text{cov}(bZ,Y) = b\text{cov}(Z,Y) \\ &= b\text{cov}(Z,bZ) = b^2\text{cov}(Z,Z) = b^2\text{var}(Z). \end{aligned} \qquad \textbf{(R.29)}$$

Proof of variance rule 3

If $Y = b$, where b is a constant, using covariance rule 3,

$$\text{var}(Y) = \text{cov}(b, b) = 0. \qquad \textbf{(R.30)}$$

This is trivial. If Y is a constant, its expected value is the same constant and $(Y - \mu_Y) = 0$. Hence $\text{var}(Y) = 0$.

Proof of variance rule 4

If $Y = V + b$, where V is a variable and b is a constant, using variance rule 1,

$$\begin{aligned}\text{var}(Y) &= \text{var}(V+b) = \text{var}(V) + \text{var}(b) + 2\text{cov}(V, b) \\ &= \text{var}(V). \end{aligned} \quad \textbf{(R.31)}$$

Correlation

As a measure of association between two variables X and Y, $\text{cov}(X, Y)$ is unsatisfactory because it depends on the units of measurement of X and Y. It is the expected value of the product of the deviation of X from its population mean and the deviation of Y from its population mean, $E\{(X - \mu_X)(Y - \mu_Y)\}$. The first deviation is measured in units of X and the second in units of Y. Change the units of measurement and you change the covariance. A better measure of association is the **population correlation coefficient** because it is dimensionless and therefore invariant to changes in the units of measure. It is traditionally denoted ρ, the Greek letter that is the equivalent of 'r', and pronounced 'row', as in 'row a boat'. For variables X and Y it is defined by

$$\rho_{XY} = \frac{\sigma_{XY}}{\sqrt{\sigma_X^2 \sigma_Y^2}}. \quad \textbf{(R.32)}$$

The numerator possesses the units of measurement of both X and Y. The variances of X and Y in the denominator possess the squared units of measurement of those variables. However, once the square root has been taken into account, the units of measurement are the same as those of the numerator, and the expression as a whole is unit free. It is left as an exercise to show that replacing X or Y by a linear function of itself (which is what happens when one changes units) has no effect on the correlation.

If X and Y are independent, ρ_{XY} will be equal to zero because σ_{XY} will be zero. If there is a positive association between them, σ_{XY}, and hence ρ_{XY}, will be positive. If there is an exact positive linear relationship, ρ_{XY} will assume its maximum value of 1. Similarly, if there is a negative relationship, ρ_{XY} will be negative, with a minimum value of –1.

EXERCISES

R.13 Suppose a variable Y is an exact linear function of X:

$$Y = \lambda + \mu X,$$

where λ and μ are constants. Demonstrate that the correlation between X and Y is equal to 1 or –1, according to the sign of μ.

R.14* Suppose a variable Y is an exact linear function of X:

$$Y = \lambda + \mu X,$$

where λ and μ are constants, and suppose that Z is a third variable. Show that $\rho_{XZ} = \rho_{YZ}$.

R.5 Samples, the double structure of a variable, and estimators

So far we have assumed that we have exact information about the random variable under discussion, in particular that we know the probability distribution, in the case of a discrete random variable, or the probability density function, in the case of a continuous variable. With this information, it is possible to derive the population mean and variance and any other population characteristics in which we might be interested.

Now in practice, except for artificially simple random variables such as the numbers on thrown dice, you do not know the exact probability distribution or density function. It follows that you do not know the population mean or variance. However, you would like to obtain an estimate of them or some other population characteristic.

The procedure is always the same. You take a sample of observations and derive an estimate of the population characteristic using some appropriate formula. It is important to be very clear conceptually about what this involves and we will take it one step at a time.

Sampling

We will suppose that we have a random variable X and that we take a sample of n observations with the intention of obtaining information about the distribution of X. We might, for example, wish to estimate its population mean. Before we consider devising estimators, it is useful to make a distinction between the way we think about the sample *before* it has actually been taken and *after* we have taken it.

Once the sample has been generated, the observations are just specific numbers. A statistician would refer to this as a **realization**.

However, before the sample is generated, the potential observations $\{X_1, X_2, \ldots, X_n\}$ themselves may be thought of as a set of random numbers. Let us focus on the first observation, X_1. Before we take the sample, we do not know what the value of X_1 will be. All we know is that it will be generated randomly from the distribution for X. It is itself, therefore, a random variable. Being generated randomly from the distribution for X means that its potential distribution, before the sample is generated, is that of X.

The same is true for all the other observations in the sample, when we are thinking about their potential distribution before the sample is generated.

After the sample has been taken, we have a specific realization and would denote it as $\{x_1, x_2, \ldots, x_n\}$, the lower case indicating that the values are specific numbers.

So we are now thinking about the variable on two levels: the X variable that is the subject of attention, and the X_i components in a potential sample. It is essential to be clear about the **double structure of a variable**. It is the key to understanding the analysis of the properties of estimators based on the sample of observations.

Estimators

An estimator is a general rule, usually just a formula, for estimating an unknown population parameter given the sample of data. It is defined in terms of the $\{X_1, X_2, \ldots, X_n\}$. Once we have obtained a specific sample $\{x_1, x_2, \ldots, x_n\}$ we use it to obtain a specific number that we describe as the estimate. To repeat, the estimator is a formula, whereas the estimate is a number. If we take repeated samples, the estimator will be the same, but the estimate will vary from sample to sample.

An estimator is a special case of a random variable. This is because it is a combination of the $\{X_1, X_2, \ldots, X_n\}$ and, since the $\{X_1, X_2, \ldots, X_n\}$ are random quantities, a combination of them must also be a random variable.

The sample mean $\overline{X}$, the usual estimator of the population mean, provides a simple example since it is just the average of the X_i in the sample:

$$\overline{X} = \frac{1}{n}(X_1 + X_2 + \cdots + X_n) = \frac{1}{n}\sum_{i=1}^{n} X_i. \tag{R.33}$$

The probability density functions of both X and $\overline{X}$ have been drawn in the same diagram in Figure R.7. By way of illustration, X is assumed to have a

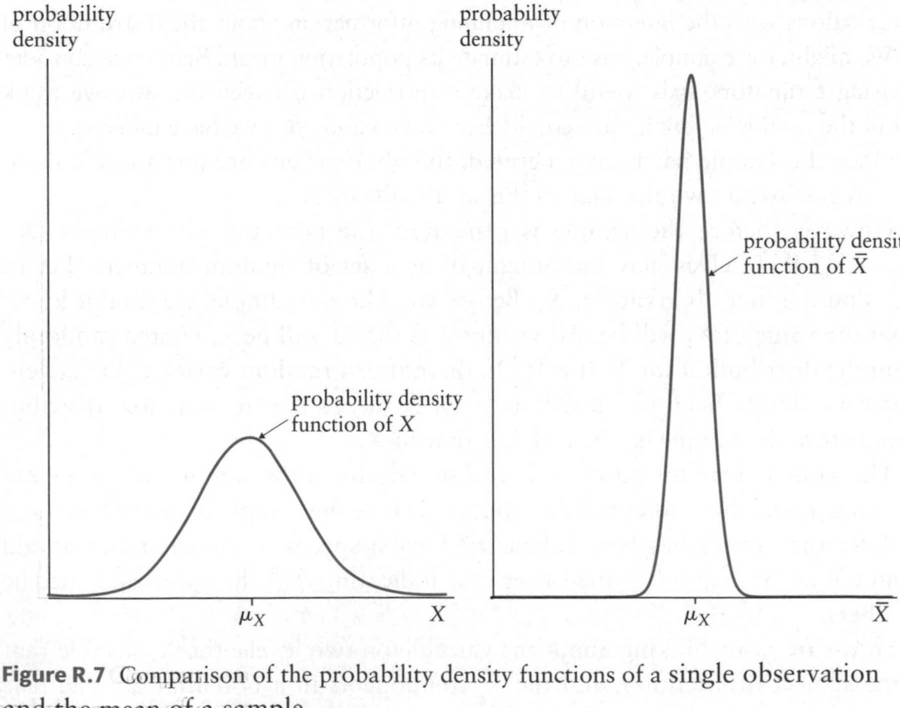

Figure R.7 Comparison of the probability density functions of a single observation and the mean of a sample

normal distribution. You will see that the distributions of both X and $\bar{X}$ are symmetrical about μ_X. The difference between them is that the distribution for $\bar{X}$ is narrower and taller. $\bar{X}$ tends to be closer to μ_X than a single observation on X because it is an average. Some of the X_i in the sample will be greater than the population mean, some will be smaller, and the positive deviations and the negative deviations will to some extent cancel each other out when the average is taken. We will demonstrate that if the distribution of X has variance σ_X^2, the sample mean has variance σ_X^2/n:

$$\begin{aligned}\sigma_{\bar{X}}^2 &= \text{var}\left\{\frac{1}{n}(X_1 + \dots + X_n)\right\} \\ &= \frac{1}{n^2}\text{var}(X_1 + \dots + X_n) \\ &= \frac{1}{n^2}\{\text{var}(X_1) + \dots + \text{var}(X_n)\} \\ &= \frac{1}{n^2}(\sigma_X^2 + \dots + \sigma_X^2) \\ &= \frac{1}{n^2}(n\sigma_X^2) = \frac{\sigma_X^2}{n}.\end{aligned} \quad \textbf{(R.34)}$$

It may be helpful to have some further explanation of equation (R.34). There are some important conceptual issues at stake that are crucial to an understanding of basic statistical theory. We will go through the equation line by line.

The first line simply states what is meant by $\sigma_{\bar{X}}^2$.

The second uses variance rule 2 to take the factor $1/n$ out of the expression. The factor must be squared when it is taken out, as shown in the derivation of the rule in Section R.4.

The third and fourth lines are the ones that sometimes give rise to trouble. The third line uses variance rule 1.

$$\text{var}(X_1 + \dots + X_n) = \text{var}(X_1) + \dots + \text{var}(X_n). \quad \textbf{(R.35)}$$

There are no population covariance terms on the right side of the equation because the observations are assumed to be generated independently. The fourth line reads as

$$\text{var}(X_i) = \sigma_X^2 \quad \text{for all } i. \quad \textbf{(R.36)}$$

What is going on? X has a specific value in observation i, so how can it have a population variance?

The key to this is the double structure. We need to make a distinction between the *potential* distribution of the observations in the sample, as individual random variables, and the sample mean, *before* the sample is generated, and the *actual* realization *after* the sample has been generated.

To illustrate the distinction, we will suppose that X has a normal distribution (the bell-shaped distribution discussed in Section R.8) with population mean 5 and variance 1, and that there are 10 observations in the sample.

The first line of Table R.5 (Sample 1) shows the result of randomly drawing numbers for X_1 to X_{10} from this distribution. The sample mean is 5.04. The numbers that appear in this line are the realization for this sample. The remaining 19 rows are the same as the first, but with different sets of randomly generated numbers.

Next we will focus on the observation X_1. Looking at its values in the 20 samples, we obtain an insight into its *potential* distribution. We see that its average value is 4.95 and its estimated variance (see Section R.7) is 1.11. This is not a surprise, because X_1 has been generated randomly from a normal distribution with population mean 5 and population variance 1. The same is true

Table R.5

sample	X_1	X_2	X_3	X_4	X_5	X_6	X_7	X_8	X_9	X_{10}	$\bar{X}$
1	6.25	4.35	5.30	6.44	4.63	3.13	5.97	5.21	3.88	5.28	5.04
2	3.81	5.19	4.49	5.51	4.41	4.39	5.43	4.75	5.39	5.63	4.90
3	5.65	4.88	6.86	6.42	6.98	4.50	4.92	7.04	5.32	5.77	5.83
4	5.78	4.15	3.99	5.86	6.27	6.32	3.80	4.78	3.67	4.83	4.95
5	2.92	5.48	5.07	4.75	4.73	5.09	5.50	4.46	3.50	4.76	4.63
6	4.82	3.01	5.59	5.02	5.37	4.06	6.04	5.21	6.17	4.59	4.99
7	5.84	4.30	4.69	3.82	5.21	5.74	6.05	7.29	3.77	5.13	5.18
8	5.13	5.02	5.35	4.03	4.90	5.42	4.90	4.21	4.41	5.50	4.89
9	4.13	5.16	5.85	6.11	7.12	5.77	3.91	6.30	3.88	2.81	5.10
10	5.21	4.91	4.01	4.45	5.75	3.20	3.84	3.93	4.08	3.88	4.33
11	7.32	3.96	2.75	5.69	4.60	7.90	3.61	5.88	5.47	3.34	5.05
12	6.52	5.51	5.34	5.47	4.51	5.72	2.78	4.40	4.55	4.80	4.96
13	4.71	5.06	6.22	5.99	4.62	5.00	5.38	3.56	3.90	5.35	4.98
14	4.59	4.54	4.63	4.84	6.38	5.62	4.75	5.86	4.57	4.64	5.04
15	5.13	4.99	7.36	4.60	3.85	5.26	6.13	5.26	5.83	4.83	5.32
16	4.26	4.99	4.49	4.48	4.76	3.77	5.49	5.31	6.66	6.44	5.07
17	4.07	5.55	4.26	5.07	4.96	4.38	5.85	5.51	4.21	5.12	4.90
18	3.83	5.14	5.69	5.24	3.41	4.24	5.00	4.99	5.40	4.09	4.70
19	4.38	5.54	3.70	5.06	5.59	4.00	5.16	4.64	6.25	6.03	5.03
20	4.74	4.45	4.69	5.67	5.51	3.84	5.14	4.89	4.16	4.89	4.80
mean	4.95	4.81	5.02	5.23	5.18	4.87	4.98	5.17	4.75	4.89	4.98
estimated variance	1.11	0.43	1.19	0.64	0.98	1.33	0.89	0.96	0.99	0.77	0.09

for all the other X observations. In each case, their average over the 20 samples is approximately 5, and their variances are approximately 1, and the approximations would have been closer to the population values if we had had more samples. This is what we are referring to when we write

$$\frac{1}{n^2}\left(\sigma_{X_1}^2 + \cdots + \sigma_{X_n}^2\right) = \frac{1}{n^2}\left(\sigma_X^2 + \cdots + \sigma_X^2\right) \qquad \textbf{(R.37)}$$

in equation (R.34). We are saying that the variance of the *potential* distribution of X_1, before a sample is generated, is σ_X^2, because X_1 is drawn randomly from the distribution for X. The same is true for all the other observations.

Of course, we are not interested in the distributions of the individual observations, but in the distribution of the estimator, in this case $\bar{X}$. What we are saying is that the variance of the potential distribution of $\bar{X}$, before the sample is generated, is σ_X^2/n.

R.6 Unbiasedness and efficiency

Much of the analysis in later chapters will be concerned with three properties of estimators: unbiasedness, efficiency, and consistency. The first two, treated in this section, relate to finite sample analysis: analysis where the samples have a finite number of observations. Consistency, a property that relates to analysis when the sample size tends to infinity, is treated in Section R.14.

Unbiasedness

Since estimators are random variables, it follows that only by coincidence will an estimate be exactly equal to the population characteristic. Generally there will be some degree of error, which will be small or large, positive or negative, according to the pure random components of the values of X in the sample.

Although this must be accepted, it is nevertheless desirable that the estimator should not lead us astray by having a tendency either to overestimate or to underestimate the population characteristic. To put it technically, we should like the expected value of the estimator to be equal to the population characteristic. If this is true, the estimator is said to be **unbiased**. If it is not, the estimator is said to be **biased**, and the difference between its expected value and the value of the population characteristic is described as the **bias**.

Let us start with the sample mean. We will show that its expected value is equal to μ_X and that it is therefore an unbiased estimator of the population mean:

$$\begin{aligned} E(\bar{X}) &= E\left\{\frac{1}{n}(X_1 + \cdots + X_n)\right\} = \frac{1}{n}E(X_1 + \cdots + X_n) \\ &= \frac{1}{n}\{E(X_1) + \cdots + E(X_n)\} \\ &= \frac{1}{n}(\mu_X + \cdots + \mu_X) = \frac{1}{n}(n\mu_X) = \mu_X. \end{aligned} \qquad \textbf{(R.38)}$$

Note that when we make the step

$$\frac{1}{n}\{E(X_1)+\cdots+E(X_n)\}=\frac{1}{n}(\mu_X+\cdots+\mu_X), \qquad \textbf{(R.39)}$$

we are referring to the fact that the potential distribution of each X_i, before the sample is actually generated, has population mean μ_X.

We have shown that the sample mean is an unbiased estimator of the population mean μ_X. However, it is not the only unbiased estimator that we could construct. To keep the analysis simple, suppose that we have a sample of just two observations, X_1 and X_2. Any weighted average of the observations X_1 and X_2 will be an unbiased estimator, provided that the weights add up to 1. To see this, suppose we construct a generalized estimator:

$$Z=\lambda_1 X_1+\lambda_2 X_2. \qquad \textbf{(R.40)}$$

The expected value of Z is given by

$$\begin{aligned} E(Z) &= E(\lambda_1 X_1+\lambda_2 X_2)=E(\lambda_1 X_1)+E(\lambda_2 X_2) \\ &= \lambda_1 E(X_1)+\lambda_2 E(X_2)=\lambda_1\mu_X+\lambda_2\mu_X \\ &= (\lambda_1+\lambda_2)\mu_X. \end{aligned} \qquad \textbf{(R.41)}$$

If λ_1 and λ_2 add up to 1, we have $E(Z)=\mu_X$, and Z is an unbiased estimator of μ_X.

Thus, in principle, we have an infinite number of unbiased estimators. How do we choose among them? Why do we always in fact use the sample average, with $\lambda_1=\lambda_2=0.5$? Perhaps you think that it would be unfair to give the observations different weights, or that asymmetry should be avoided on principle. However, we are not concerned with fairness, or with symmetry for its own sake. There is a more compelling reason: efficiency.

Efficiency

Unbiasedness is one desirable feature of an estimator, but it is not the only one. Another important consideration is its reliability. We want the estimator to have as high a probability as possible of giving a close estimate of the population characteristic, which means that we want its probability density function to be as concentrated as possible around the true value. One way of summarizing this is to say that we want its population variance to be as small as possible.

Suppose that we have two estimators of the population mean, that they are calculated using the same information, that they are both unbiased, and that their probability density functions are as shown in Figure R.8. Since the probability density function for estimator B is more highly concentrated than that for estimator A, it is more likely to give an accurate estimate. It is therefore said to be more efficient, to use the technical term.

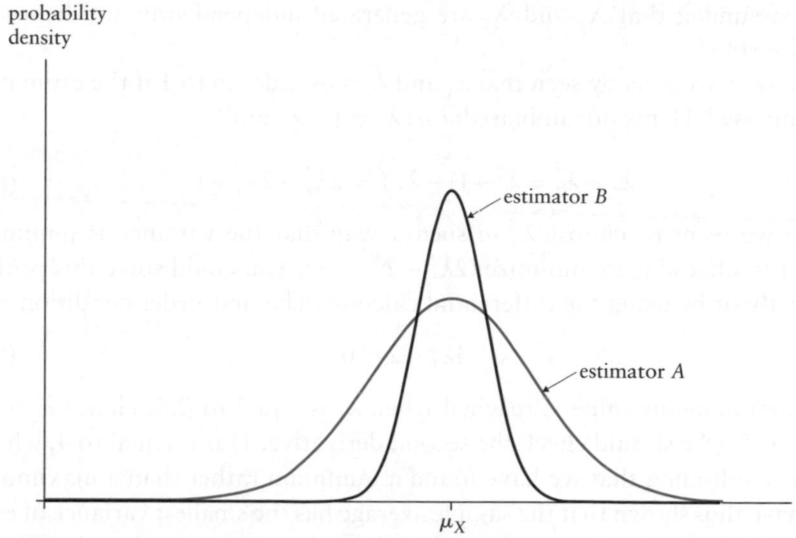

Figure R.8 Efficient and inefficient estimators

Note carefully that the definition says 'more likely'. Even though estimator B is more efficient, that does not mean that it will always give the more accurate estimate. Sometimes it will have a bad day, and estimator A will have a good day, and A will be closer to the true value. But as a matter of probability, B will tend to be more accurate than A.

It is rather like the issue of whether you should fasten your seat belt when driving a vehicle. A large number of surveys in different countries have shown that you are much less likely to be killed or seriously injured in a road accident if you wear a seat belt, but there are always the odd occasions when individuals not wearing belts have miraculously escaped when they might have been killed, had they been strapped in. The surveys do not deny this. They simply conclude that the odds are on the side of belting up. Similarly, the odds are on the side of the efficient estimator.

We have said that we want the variance of an estimator to be as small as possible, and that the efficient estimator is the one with the smallest variance. We shall now investigate the variance of the generalized estimator of the population mean and show that it is minimized when the two observations are given equal weight.

The population variance of the generalized estimator is given by

$$\begin{aligned}\sigma_Z^2 &= \operatorname{var}(\lambda_1 X_1 + \lambda_2 X_2) \\ &= \operatorname{var}(\lambda_1 X_1) + \operatorname{var}(\lambda_2 X_2) + 2\operatorname{cov}(\lambda_1 X_1, \lambda_2 X_2) \\ &= \lambda_1^2 \sigma_{X_1}^2 + \lambda_2^2 \sigma_{X_2}^2 + 2\lambda_1\lambda_2\sigma_{X_1X_2} \\ &= (\lambda_1^2 + \lambda_2^2)\sigma_X^2. \end{aligned} \qquad \textbf{(R.42)}$$

We are assuming that X_1 and X_2 are generated independently and hence that $\sigma_{X_1X_2}$ is zero.

Now, we have already seen that λ_1 and λ_2 must add up to 1 if the estimator is to be unbiased. Hence for unbiasedness, $\lambda_2 = 1 - \lambda_1$ and

$$\lambda_1^2 + \lambda_2^2 = \lambda_1^2 + (1 - \lambda_1)^2 = 2\lambda_1^2 - 2\lambda_1 + 1. \quad \textbf{(R.43)}$$

Since we want to choose λ_1 in such a way that the variance is minimized, we want to choose it to minimize $(2\lambda_1^2 - 2\lambda_1 + 1)$. You could solve this problem graphically or by using the differential calculus. The first-order condition is

$$4\lambda_1 - 2 = 0. \quad \textbf{(R.44)}$$

Thus, the minimum value is reached when λ_1 is equal to 0.5. Hence λ_2 is also equal to 0.5. (We should check the second derivative. This is equal to 4, which is positive, confirming that we have found a minimum rather than a maximum.)

We have thus shown that the sample average has the smallest variance of estimators of this kind. This means that it has the most concentrated probability distribution around the true mean, and hence that (in a probabilistic sense) it is the most accurate. To use the correct terminology, of the set of unbiased estimators, it is the most efficient. Of course, we have shown this only for the case where the sample consists of just two observations, but the conclusions are valid for samples of any size, provided that the observations are independent of one another.

Two final points. First, efficiency is a *comparative* concept. You should use the term only when comparing alternative estimators. You should not use it to summarize changes in the variance of a single estimator. In particular, as we shall see in Section R.14, the variance of an estimator generally decreases as the sample size increases, but it would be wrong to say that the estimator is becoming more efficient. You must reserve the term for comparisons of *different* estimators. Second, you can compare the efficiency of alternative estimators only if they are using the same information: for example, the same set of observations on a number of random variables. If the estimators use different information, one may well have a smaller variance, but it would not be correct to describe it as being more efficient.

Conflicts between unbiasedness and minimum variance

We have seen in this review that it is desirable that an estimator be unbiased and that it have the smallest possible variance. These are two quite different criteria and occasionally they conflict with each other. It sometimes happens that one can construct two estimators of a population characteristic, one of which is unbiased (*A* in Figure R.9), the other being biased but having smaller variance (*B*).

A will be better in the sense that it is unbiased, but *B* is better in the sense that its estimates are always close to the true value. How do you choose between them?

It will depend on the circumstances. If you are not bothered by errors, provided that in the long run they cancel out, you should probably choose *A*. On the other hand, if you can tolerate small errors, but not large ones, you should choose *B*.

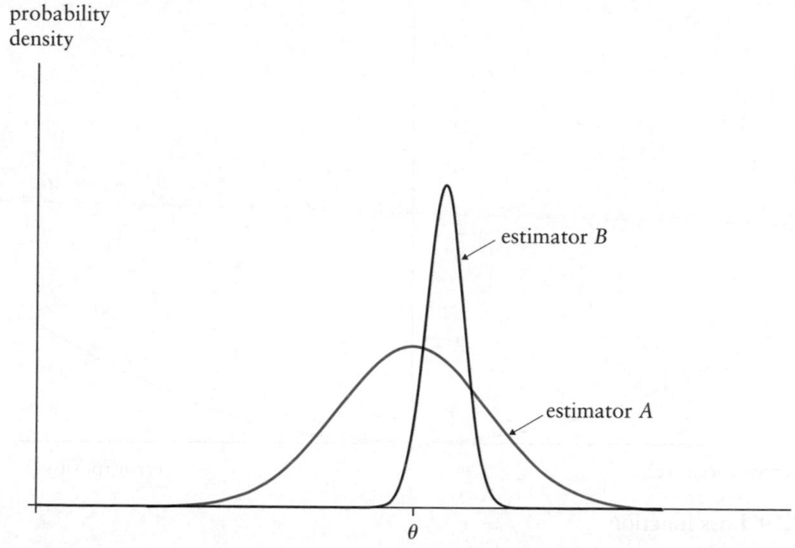

Figure R.9 Which estimator is to be preferred? *A* is unbiased but *B* has smaller variance

Technically speaking, it depends on your loss function, the cost to you of an error as a function of its size. It is usual to choose the estimator that yields the smallest expected loss, which is found by weighting the loss function by the probability density function. (If you are risk averse, you may wish to take the variance of the loss into account as well.)

A common example of a loss function, illustrated by the quadratic curve in Figure R.10, is the square of the error. The expected value of this is known as the mean square error (MSE):

$$\text{MSE of estimator} = E\left\{(Z-\theta)^2\right\}, \quad \textbf{(R.45)}$$

where Z is the estimator and θ is the value of the population characteristic being estimated.

The MSE can be decomposed into the variance of Z plus the square of the bias:

$$\text{MSE of estimator} = \text{variance of estimator} + \text{bias}^2. \quad \textbf{(R.46)}$$

Let the expected value of Z be μ_Z. This will be equal to θ only if Z is an unbiased estimator. In general, there will be a bias, given by $(\mu_Z - \theta)$. The variance of Z is equal to $E\left\{(Z-\mu_Z)^2\right\}$. The MSE of Z can be decomposed as follows:

$$\begin{aligned} E\left\{(Z-\theta)^2\right\} &= E\left\{([Z-\mu_Z]+[\mu_Z-\theta])^2\right\} \\ &= E\left\{(Z-\mu_Z)^2 + 2(Z-\mu_Z)(\mu_Z-\theta) + (\mu_Z-\theta)^2\right\} \\ &= E\left\{(Z-\mu_Z)^2\right\} + 2(\mu_Z-\theta)E(Z-\mu_Z) + E\left\{(\mu_Z-\theta)^2\right\} \quad \textbf{(R.47)} \end{aligned}$$

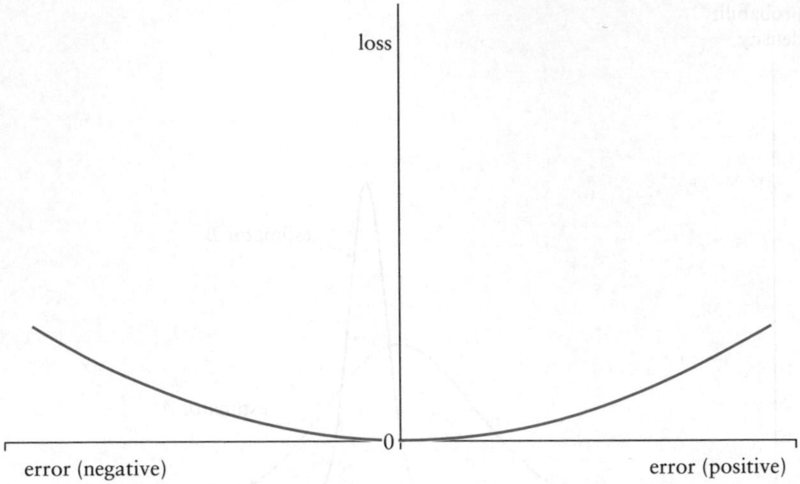

Figure R.10 Loss function

The first term is the population variance of Z. The second term is zero because

$$E(Z-\mu_Z)=E(Z)+E(-\mu_Z)=\mu_Z-\mu_Z=0. \quad \textbf{(R.48)}$$

The expected value of the third term is $(\mu_Z-\theta)^2$, the bias squared, since both μ_z and θ are constants. Hence, we have the decomposition.

In Figure R.9, estimator A has no bias component, but it has a much larger variance component than B and therefore could be inferior by this criterion.

The MSE is often used to generalize the concept of efficiency to cover comparisons of biased as well as unbiased estimators. However, in this text, comparisons of efficiency will mostly be confined to unbiased estimators.

EXERCISES

R.15 For the special case $\sigma^2=1$ and a sample of two observations, calculate the variance of the generalized estimator of the population mean using equation (R.43) with values of λ_1 from 0 to 1 at steps of 0.1, and plot it in a diagram. Is it important that the weights λ_1 and λ_2 should be exactly equal?

R.16* Show that, when you have n observations, the condition that the generalized estimator $(\lambda_1X_1+\dots+\lambda_nX_n)$ should be an unbiased estimator of μ_X is $\lambda_1+\dots+\lambda_n=1$.

R.17 Give examples of applications where you might (1) prefer an estimator of type A, (2) prefer one of type B, in Figure R.9.

R.18 Draw a loss function for getting to an airport later (or earlier) than the official check-in time.

R.19* In general, the variance of the distribution of an estimator decreases when the sample size is increased. Is it correct to describe the estimator as becoming more efficient?

R.20 If you have two estimators of an unknown population parameter, is the one with the smaller variance necessarily more efficient?

R.7 Estimators of variance, covariance, and correlation

The concepts of population variance and covariance were defined in Sections R.2 and R.4. For a random variable X, the population variance σ_X^2 is

$$\text{var}(X) = \sigma_X^2 = E\left\{(X - \mu_X)^2\right\}. \tag{R.49}$$

Given a sample of n observations, the usual estimator of σ_X^2 is the sum of the squared deviations around the sample mean divided by $n - 1$, typically denoted s_X^2:

$$s_X^2 = \frac{1}{n-1}\sum_{i=1}^{n}(X_i - \bar{X})^2. \tag{R.50}$$

Since the population variance is the expected value of the squared deviation of X about its mean, it makes intuitive sense to use the average of the sample squared deviations as an estimator. But why divide by $n - 1$ rather than by n? The reason is that the sample mean is by definition in the middle of the sample, while the unknown population mean is not, except by coincidence. As a consequence, the sum of the squared deviations from the sample mean tends to be slightly smaller than the sum of the squared deviations from the population mean. As a consequence, a simple average of the squared sample deviations is a downwards biased estimator of the population variance. However, the bias can be shown to be a factor of $(n - 1)/n$. Thus, one can allow for the bias by dividing the sum of the squared deviations by $n - 1$ instead of n. A formal proof of the unbiasedness of s_X^2 is given in Appendix R.1.

A similar adjustment has to be made when estimating a population covariance. For two random variables, X and Y, the population covariance σ_{XY} is

$$\text{cov}(X,Y) = \sigma_{XY} = E\{(X - \mu_X)(Y - \mu_Y)\}. \tag{R.51}$$

An unbiased estimator of σ_{XY} is given by the sum of the products of the deviations around the sample means divided by $n - 1$, typically denoted s_{XY}:

$$s_{XY} = \frac{1}{n-1}\sum_{i=1}^{n}(X_i - \bar{X})(Y_i - \bar{Y}). \tag{R.52}$$

Again, for a formal proof of the unbiasedness of s_{XY}, see Appendix R.1.

The population correlation coefficient ρ_{XY} was defined in Section R.4 as

$$\rho_{XY} = \frac{\sigma_{XY}}{\sqrt{\sigma_X^2 \sigma_Y^2}}. \tag{R.53}$$

The sample correlation coefficient, r_{XY} is obtained from this by replacing σ_{XY}, σ_X^2, and σ_Y^2 by their estimators:

$$r_{XY} = \frac{s_{XY}}{\sqrt{s_X^2 s_Y^2}} = \frac{\frac{1}{n-1}\sum (X_i - \bar{X})(Y_i - \bar{Y})}{\sqrt{\frac{1}{n-1}\sum (X_i - \bar{X})^2 \frac{1}{n-1}\sum (Y_i - \bar{Y})^2}}$$

$$= \frac{\sum (X_i - \bar{X})(Y_i - \bar{Y})}{\sqrt{\sum (X_i - \bar{X})^2 \sum (Y_i - \bar{Y})^2}}. \tag{R.54}$$

EXERCISE

R.21* Suppose that you have observations on three variables X, Y, and Z, and suppose that Y is an exact linear function of Z:

$$Y = a + bZ$$

where a and b are constants. Show that $r_{XZ} = r_{XY}$. (This is the counterpart of Exercise R.14.)

R.8 The normal distribution

In the analysis so far, we have discussed the mean and the variance of a distribution of a random variable, but we have not said anything specific about the actual shape of the distribution. It is time to do that. There are only four distributions, all of them continuous, that are going to be of importance to us: the normal distribution, the t distribution, the F distribution, and the chi-squared (χ^2) distribution. We will consider the normal distribution here, the t distribution in Section R.11, the F distribution in Chapter 2, and the chi-squared distribution in Chapter 8.

The **normal distribution** has the graceful, bell-shaped form shown in Figure R.11. The probability density function for a normally distributed random variable X is

$$f(X) = \frac{1}{\alpha\sqrt{2\pi}} e^{-\frac{1}{2}\left(\frac{X-\beta}{\alpha}\right)^2} \tag{R.55}$$

where α and β are parameters. It is in fact an infinite family of distributions since β can be any finite real number and α any finite positive real number. The expression may seem somewhat forbidding at first, but we can make an immediate improvement. It can be shown that the expected value of the distribution, μ,

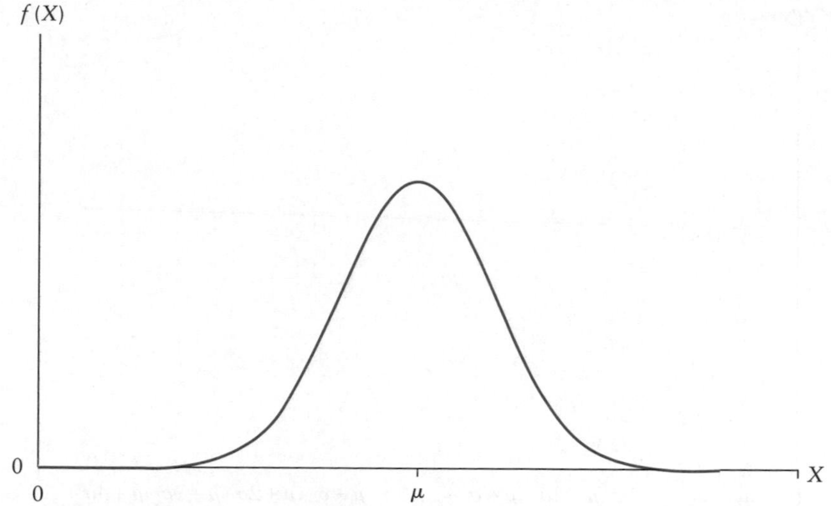

Figure R.11 Normal distribution

is equal to β and its variance, σ^2, is equal to α^2. Thus, it is natural to write the probability density function in the form

$$f(X) = \frac{1}{\sigma\sqrt{2\pi}} e^{-\frac{1}{2}\left(\frac{X-\mu}{\sigma}\right)^2} \quad \textbf{(R.56)}$$

The distribution is symmetric, so it automatically follows that the mean and the mode coincide in the middle of the distribution. Further, its shape is fixed when expressed in terms of standard deviations, so all normal distributions look the same when expressed in terms of μ and σ. This is shown in Figure R.12.

As a matter of mathematical shorthand, if a variable X is normally distributed with mean μ and variance σ^2, this is written

$$X \sim N\left(\mu, \sigma^2\right) \quad \textbf{(R.57)}$$

(the symbol ~ means 'is distributed as'). The first argument in the parentheses refers to the mean and the second to the variance. This, of course, is the general expression. If you had a specific normal distribution, you would replace the arguments with the actual numerical values.

An important special case is the **standardized normal distribution**, where $\mu = 0$ and $\sigma = 1$. This is shown in Figure R.13.

EXERCISE

R.22 A scalar multiple of a normally distributed random variable also has a normal distribution. A random variable X has a normal distribution with mean 5 and variance 10. Sketch the distribution of $Z = X/2$.

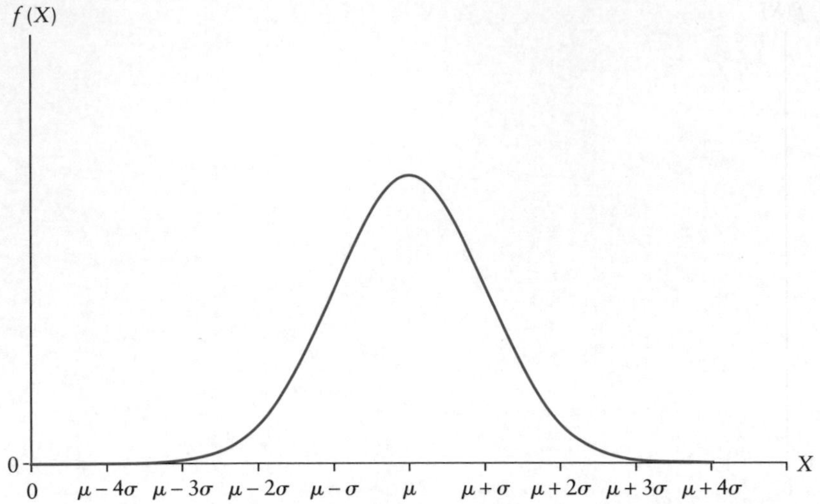

Figure R.12 Structure of the normal distribution in terms of μ and σ

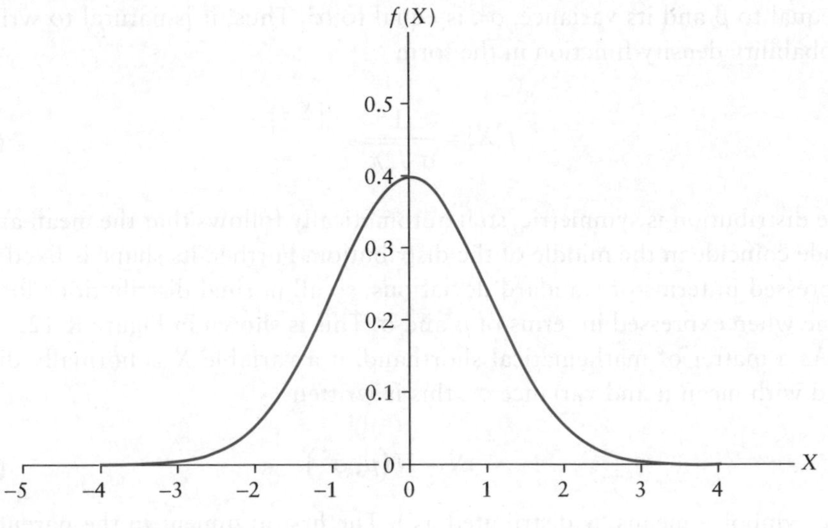

Figure R.13 Standardized normal distribution

R.9 Hypothesis testing

Which comes first, theoretical hypothesizing or empirical research? Perhaps, at the outset, theory might be the starting point, but in practice, theorizing and experimentation rapidly become interactive activities. For this reason, we will approach the topic of hypothesis testing from both directions. On the one hand, we may suppose that the theory has come first and that the purpose of the experiment is to evaluate its plausibility. This will lead to the execution of significance tests. Alternatively, we may perform the experiment first and then consider what theoretical hypotheses would be consistent with the results. This will lead to the construction of confidence intervals.

Formulation of a null hypothesis and development of its implications

Suppose that a random variable X is assumed to have a normal distribution with mean μ and variance σ^2. We will start by assuming that the theory precedes the experiment and that we hypothesize that μ is equal to some specific value μ_0. We then describe

$$H_0: \mu = \mu_0 \qquad \textbf{(R.58)}$$

as our null hypothesis. We also define an alternative hypothesis, denoted H_1, which represents our conclusion if the evidence indicates that H_0 is false. In the present case, H_1 is simply that μ is not equal to μ_0:

$$H_1: \mu \neq \mu_0. \qquad \textbf{(R.59)}$$

Our test strategy consists of generating a sample of n independent observations of X and calculating the sample mean, $\bar{X}$. If the null hypothesis is true, values of $\bar{X}$ obtained in repeated samples will be normally distributed with mean μ_0 and variance σ^2/n. Since the variance of the distribution is σ^2/n, the standard deviation is $\sigma/\sqrt{n}$. The potential distribution of $\bar{X}$, conditional on H_0 being true, is shown in Figure R.14. To draw this figure, we have to know the standard deviation of $\bar{X}$, $\sigma/\sqrt{n}$, which means that we have to know the value of σ. For the time being, to simplify the discussion, we shall assume that we do. In practice, we have to estimate it, so we will eventually need to relax this assumption.

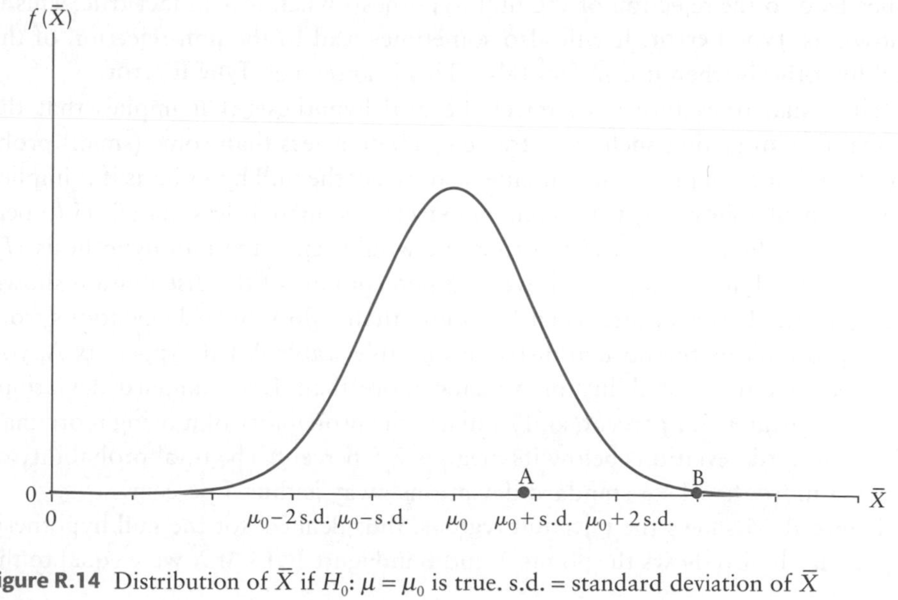

Figure R.14 Distribution of $\bar{X}$ if H_0: $\mu = \mu_0$ is true. s.d. = standard deviation of $\bar{X}$

Compatibility, freakiness, and the significance level

Now we come to the crunch. Suppose that we take an actual sample of observations and calculate $\bar{X}$. Suppose that it lies within one standard deviation of μ_0. The point A in Figure R.14 is an example of such an outcome. It is perfectly compatible with the null hypothesis. We do not anticipate $\bar{X}$ being exactly equal to μ_0, except by freak coincidence, because it has a random component, but we would expect it to be somewhere 'close' to μ_0, in the sense of occurring reasonably frequently if H_0 is true. That is the case with A.

Suppose, on the other hand, that $\bar{X}$ is located at the point B, three standard deviations above μ_0. If the null hypothesis is correct, the probability of being three standard deviations away from the mean, positive or negative, is only 0.0027, which is very low. You could come to either of two conclusions about this problematic result:

1. You could continue to maintain that your null hypothesis H_0: $\mu = \mu_0$ is correct, and that the experiment has given a freak result. You concede that the probability of such a low value of $\bar{X}$ is very small, but nevertheless it does occur 0.27 percent of the time and you reckon that this is one of those times.
2. You could conclude that the hypothesis is contradicted by the sample result. You are not convinced by the explanation in (1) because the probability is so small and you think that a much more likely explanation is that μ is not really equal to μ_0. In other words, you adopt the alternative hypothesis H_1: $\mu \neq \mu_0$ instead.

How do you decide when to choose (1) and when to choose (2)? There is no error-free procedure. The best you can do is to establish some decision rule, but there is no guaranteed way of avoiding mistakes. Any decision rule will sometimes lead to the rejection of the null hypothesis when it is in fact true. This is known as **Type I error**. It will also sometimes lead to the non-rejection of the null hypothesis when it is in fact false. This is known as **Type II error**.

The usual procedure is to reject the null hypothesis if it implies that the probability of getting such an extreme estimate is less than some (small) probability p. For example, we might choose to reject the null hypothesis if it implies that the probability of getting such an extreme estimate is less than 0.05 (5 percent). According to this decision rule, we would reject the null hypothesis H_0: $\mu = \mu_0$ if $\bar{X}$ fell in the upper or lower 2.5 percent tails of the distribution shown in Figure R.14. This occurs when $\bar{X}$ is more than 1.96 standard deviations from μ_0. If you look up the normal distribution table, Table A.1 in Appendix A, you will see that the probability of $\bar{X}$ being more than 1.96 standard deviations above its mean is 2.5 percent, and similarly the probability of it being more than 1.96 standard deviations below its mean is 2.5 percent. The total probability of it being more than 1.96 standard deviations away is thus 5 percent.

Figure R.15 shows the **rejection regions**, thus defined, for the null hypothesis H_0: $\mu = \mu_0$. It also shows the points A and B in Figure R.14. If $\bar{X}$ were equal to the

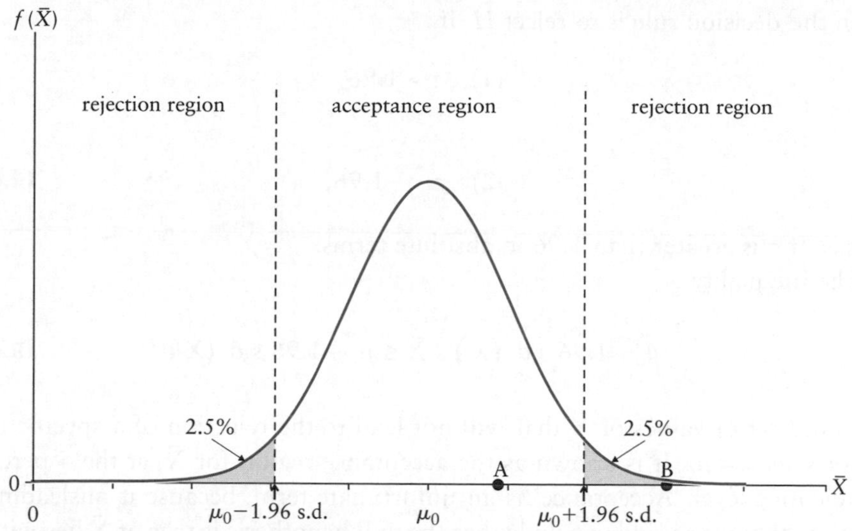

Figure R.15 Rejection regions, conditional on H_0: $\mu = \mu_0$, 5 percent test

value indicated by the point B, H_0 would be rejected. The value indicated by the point A would not lead to rejection. Generalizing, we can see from the figure that we would reject H_0: $\mu = \mu_0$ if

$$(1)\quad \bar{X} > \mu_0 + 1.96 \text{ s.d.}(\bar{X})$$

or

$$(2)\quad \bar{X} < \mu_0 - 1.96 \text{ s.d.}(\bar{X}). \tag{R.60}$$

Rewriting the inequality, we would reject H_0 if

$$(1)\quad \bar{X} - \mu_0 > 1.96 \text{ s.d.}(\bar{X})$$

or

$$(2)\quad \bar{X} - \mu_0 < -1.96 \text{ s.d.}(\bar{X}). \tag{R.61}$$

Dividing through by the standard deviation of $\bar{X}$, we reject H_0 if

$$(1)\quad \frac{\bar{X} - \mu_0}{\text{s.d.}(\bar{X})} > 1.96$$

or

$$(2)\quad \frac{\bar{X} - \mu_0}{\text{s.d.}(\bar{X})} < -1.96\,. \tag{R.62}$$

It is convenient to define a z statistic that is equal to the discrepancy between $\bar{X}$ and μ_0 measured in terms of standard deviations:

$$z = \frac{\bar{X} - \mu_0}{\text{s.d.}(\bar{X})}\,. \tag{R.63}$$

Then the decision rule is to reject H_0 if

$$(1) \quad z > 1.96$$

or

$$(2) \quad z < -1.96, \tag{R.64}$$

that is, if z is greater than 1.96 in absolute terms.

The inequality

$$\mu_0 - 1.96 \text{ s.d.} \left(\bar{X}\right) \leq \bar{X} \leq \mu_0 + 1.96 \text{ s.d.} \left(\bar{X}\right) \tag{R.65}$$

gives the set of values of $\bar{X}$ that will not lead to the rejection of a specific null hypothesis $\mu = \mu_0$. It is known as the acceptance region for $\bar{X}$, at the 5 percent significance level. 'Acceptance' is an unfortunate term, because it misleadingly suggests that we should conclude that the null hypothesis is true, if $\bar{X}$ lies within it. In fact, there will in general be a whole range of null hypotheses not contradicted by the sample result, so it is too strong to talk of 'accepting' H_0. It would be better to talk of the 'fail-to-reject' region, but it is too late to change the terminology now.

The decision procedure described above is not foolproof. Suppose that the null hypothesis H_0: $\mu = \mu_0$ is true. Then there is a 2.5 percent probability that $\bar{X}$ will be so large that it lies in the right rejection region and we decide to reject H_0. Likewise, there is a 2.5 percent probability that it will be so large and negative that it lies in the left rejection region. So there is a 5 percent chance of the occurrence of a Type I error. The significance level of a test is the term used to describe the risk of a Type I error if the null hypothesis is true. Another, equivalent, term is the size of a test.

Of course, we can reduce the risk of making a Type I error by reducing the size of the rejection region. For example, we could change the decision rule to reject the null hypothesis only if it implies that the probability of getting the sample value is less than 0.01 (1 percent). The rejection region now becomes the upper and lower 0.5 percent tails. Looking at the normal distribution table again, you will see that the 0.5 percent tails of a normal distribution start 2.58 standard deviations from the mean, as shown in Figure R.16. Since the probability of making a Type I error, if the null hypothesis is true, is now only 1 percent, the test is said to be a 1 percent significance test.

By definition, the lower is your critical probability, the smaller is the risk of a Type I error. If your significance level is 5 percent, you will reject a true hypothesis 5 percent of the time. If it is 1 percent, you will make a Type I error 1 percent of the time. Thus, the 1 percent significance level is safer in this respect. If you reject the hypothesis at this level, you are almost certainly right to do so. For this reason, the 1 percent significance level is described as *higher* than the 5 percent level.

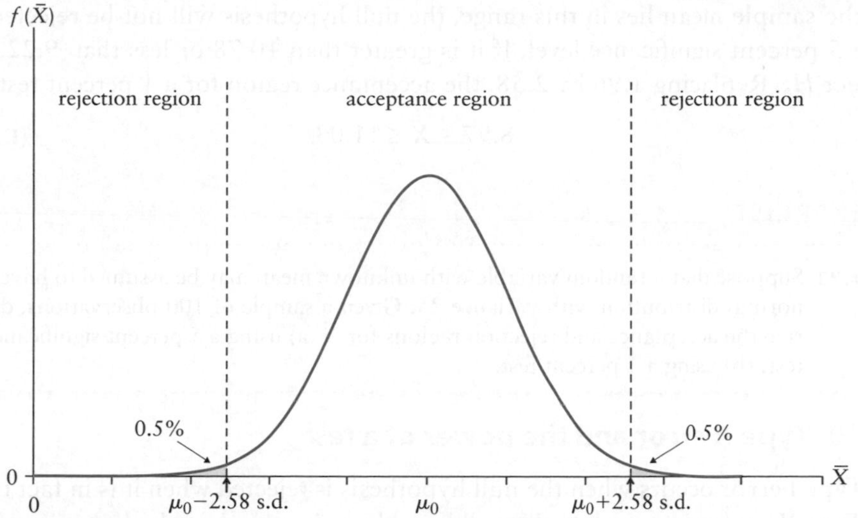

Figure R.16 Rejection regions, conditional on H_0: $\mu = \mu_0$, 1 percent test

Note that the acceptance region for the 5 percent test lies entirely inside the acceptance region for the 1 percent test. This has important implications for the reporting of tests:

1. If you reject the null hypothesis at the 1 percent level, you must also reject it at the 5 percent level. There is no need to mention the 5 percent test. Indeed, you look ignorant if you do.
2. If you do not reject at the 5 percent level, you cannot reject at the 1 percent level. There is no need to mention the 1 percent test, and, again, you look ignorant if you do.
3. You should mention both tests only when you reject at 5 percent but do not reject at 1 percent.

Example

Suppose that a random variable X may be assumed to have a normal distribution with variance 4. It is hypothesized that the unknown mean μ is equal to 10. Given a sample of 25 observations, suppose that we wish to determine the acceptance and rejection regions for $\bar{X}$ under H_0: $\mu = 10$ (a) using a 5 percent significance test, (b) using a 1 percent test.

If the variance of X is 4, its standard deviation is 2 and the standard deviation of $\bar{X}$ is $2/\sqrt{25} = 0.4$. The acceptance region, at the 5 percent significance level, is therefore

$$10 - 1.96 \times 0.4 \leq \bar{X} \leq 10 + 1.96 \times 0.4, \quad \textbf{(R.66)}$$

which is

$$9.22 \leq \bar{X} \leq 10.78. \quad \textbf{(R.67)}$$

If the sample mean lies in this range, the null hypothesis will not be rejected at the 5 percent significance level. If it is greater than 10.78 or less than 9.22, we reject H_0. Replacing 1.96 by 2.58, the acceptance region for a 1 percent test is

$$8.97 \leq \overline{X} \leq 11.03. \tag{R.68}$$

EXERCISE

R.23 Suppose that a random variable with unknown mean may be assumed to have a normal distribution with variance 25. Given a sample of 100 observations, derive the acceptance and rejection regions for $\overline{X}$ (a) using a 5 percent significance test, (b) using a 1 percent test.

R.10 Type II error and the power of a test

A Type I error occurs when the null hypothesis is rejected when it is in fact true. A Type II error occurs when the null hypothesis is not rejected when it is in fact false. We will see that, in general, there is a trade-off between the risk of making a Type I error and the risk of making a Type II error.

BOX R.2 Type I and Type II errors in everyday life

The problem of trying to avoid Type I and Type II errors is pervasive in everyday life. A criminal trial provides a particularly acute example. Taking as the null hypothesis that the defendant is innocent, a Type I error occurs when the jury wrongly decides that the defendant is guilty. A Type II error occurs when the jury wrongly acquits the defendant.

We will consider the case where the null hypothesis, H_0: $\mu = \mu_0$ is false and the actual value of μ is μ_1. This is shown in Figure R.17. If the null hypothesis is tested, it will be rejected only if $\overline{X}$ lies in one of the rejection regions associated with it. To determine the rejection regions, we draw the distribution of $\overline{X}$ conditional on H_0 being true. The distribution is marked with a dashed curve to emphasize that H_0 is not actually true. The rejection regions for a 5 percent test, given this distribution, are marked on the diagram.

If $\overline{X}$ lies in the acceptance region, H_0 will not be rejected, and so a Type II error will occur. What is the probability of this happening? To determine this, we now turn to the actual distribution of $\overline{X}$, given that $\mu = \mu_1$. This is the solid curve on the right. The probability of $\overline{X}$ lying in the acceptance region for H_0 is the area under this curve in the acceptance region. It is the shaded area in Figure R.18. In this particular case, the probability of $\overline{X}$ lying within the acceptance region for H_0, thus causing a Type II error, is 0.15.

The probability of rejecting the null hypothesis, when it is false, is known as the power of a test. By definition, it is equal to 1 minus the probability of making a Type II error. It is therefore 0.85 in this example.

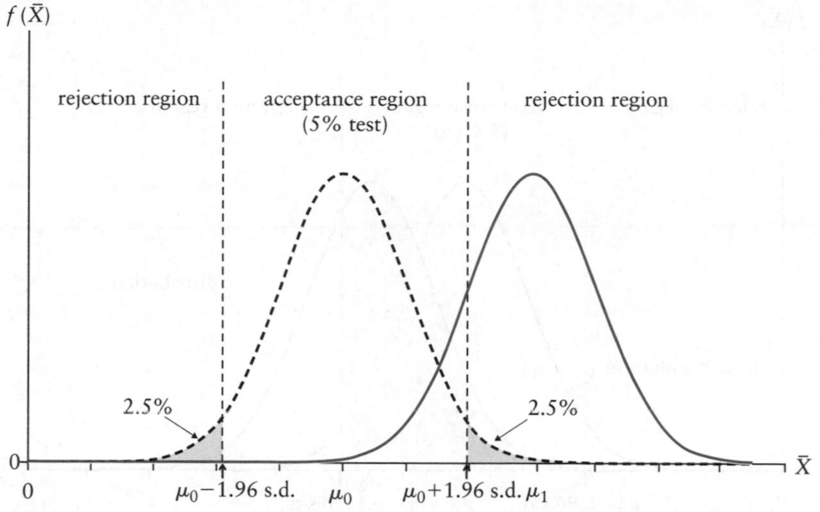

Figure R.17 Acceptance and rejection regions, conditional on H_0: $\mu = \mu_0$, 5 percent test

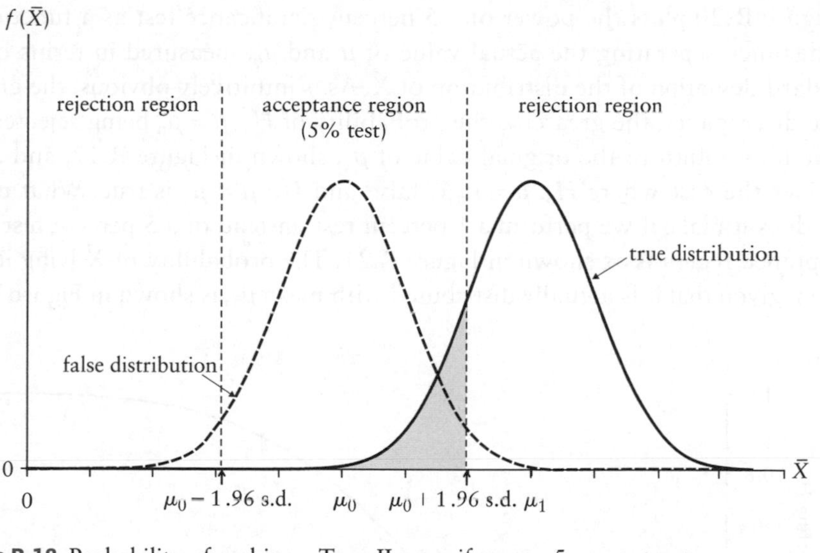

Figure R.18 Probability of making a Type II error if $\mu = \mu_1$, 5 percent test

The power depends on the distance between the value of μ under the false null hypothesis and its actual value. The closer that the actual value is to μ_0, the harder it is to demonstrate that H_0: $\mu = \mu_0$ is false. This is illustrated in Figure R.19. μ_0 is the same as in Figure R.18, and so the acceptance region and rejection regions for the test of H_0: $\mu = \mu_0$ are the same as in Figure R.18. As in Figure R.18, H_0 is false, but now the true value is μ_2, and μ_2 is closer to μ_0. As a consequence, the probability of $\bar{X}$ lying in the acceptance region for H_0 is much greater, 0.68 instead of 0.15, and so the power of the test, 0.32, is much lower.

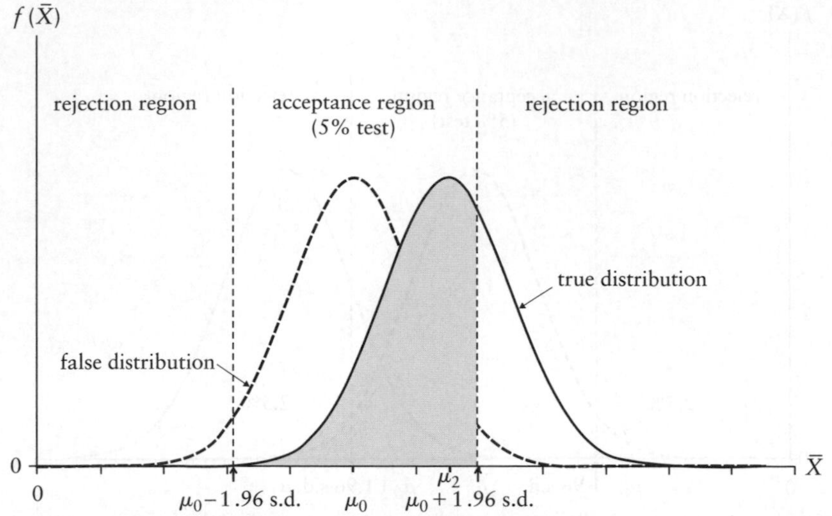

Figure R.19 Probability of making a Type II error if $\mu = \mu_2$, 5 percent test

Figure R.20 plots the power of a 5 percent significance test as a function of the distance separating the actual value of μ and μ_0, measured in terms of the standard deviation of the distribution of $\bar{X}$. As is intuitively obvious, the greater is the discrepancy, the greater is the probability of H_0: $\mu = \mu_0$ being rejected.

We now return to the original value of μ_1, shown in Figure R.17, and again consider the case where H_0: $\mu = \mu_0$ is false and H_1: $\mu = \mu_1$ is true. What difference does it make if we perform a 1 percent test, instead of a 5 percent test? The acceptance region is as shown in Figure R.21. The probability of $\bar{X}$ lying in this region, given that it is actually distributed with mean μ_1, is shown in Figure R.22.

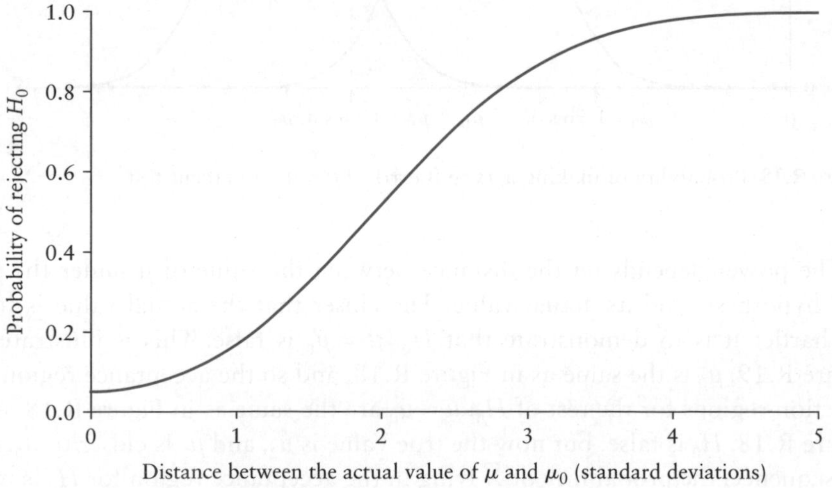

Figure R.20 Power function, 5% significance test

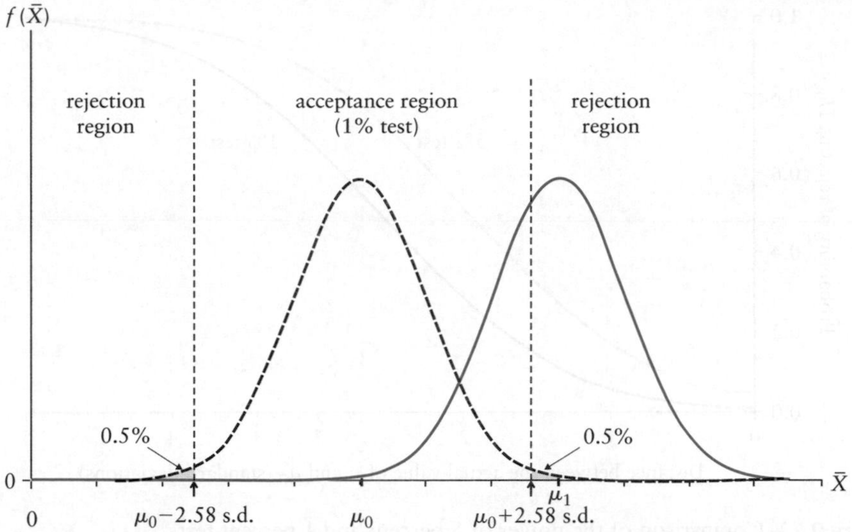

Figure R.21 Acceptance and rejection regions, conditional on H_0: $\mu = \mu_0$, 1 percent test

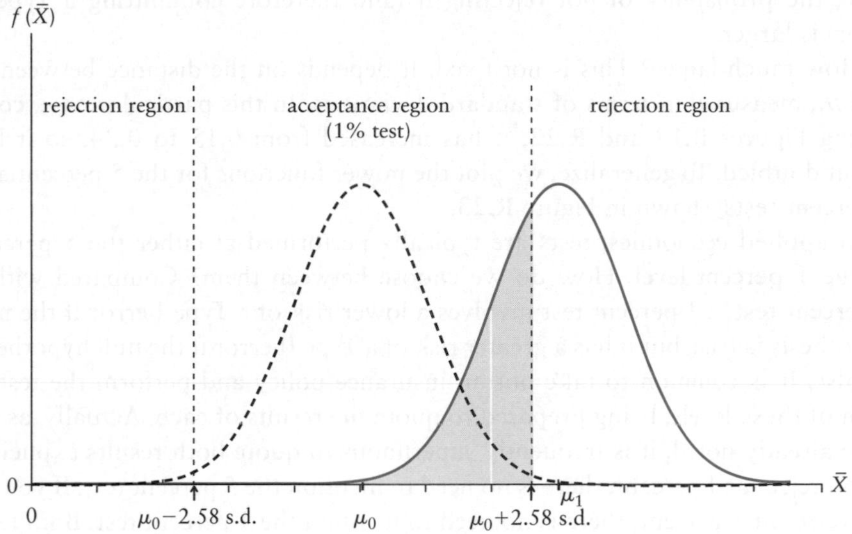

Figure R.22 Probability of making a Type II error if $\mu = \mu_1$, 1 percent test

It is larger than before, 0.34. The vertical white line within it shows the limit of the area in the case of the 5 percent test in Figure R.18.

Thus, we see that there is a trade-off between risk of Type I error and risk of Type II error. If we perform a 1 percent test instead of a 5 percent test, and H_0 is true, the risk of mistakenly rejecting it (and therefore committing a Type

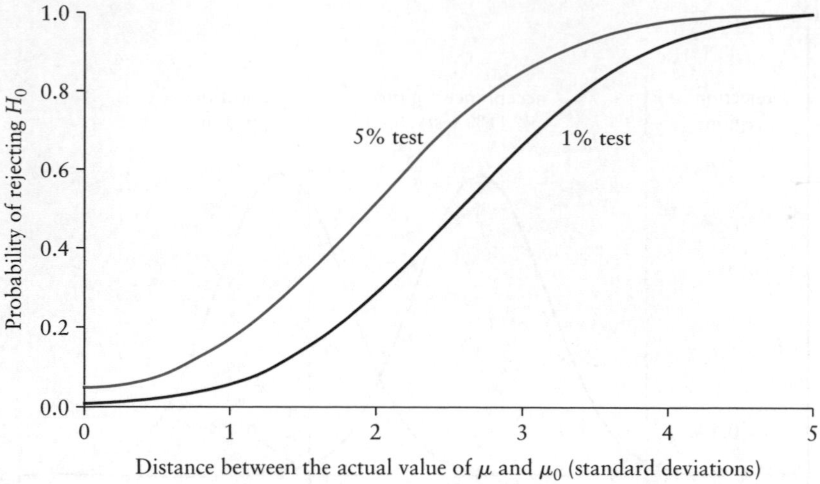

Figure R.23 Comparison of the power of 5 percent and 1 percent tests

I error) is only 1 percent instead of 5 percent. However, if H_0 happens to be false, the probability of not rejecting it (and therefore committing a Type II error) is larger.

How much larger? This is not fixed. It depends on the distance between μ_0 and μ_1, measured in terms of standard deviations. In this particular case, comparing Figures R.18 and R.22, it has increased from 0.15 to 0.34, so it has about doubled. To generalize, we plot the power functions for the 5 percent and 1 percent tests, shown in Figure R.23.

In applied economics, tests are typically performed at either the 5 percent or the 1 percent level. How do we choose between them? Compared with a 5 percent test, a 1 percent test involves a lower risk of a Type I error if the null hypothesis is true, but it has a greater risk of a Type II error if the null hypothesis is false. It is common to take out an insurance policy and perform the test at both of these levels, being prepared to quote the results of each. Actually, as we have already noted, it is frequently superfluous to quote both results explicitly. If you reject at 1 percent, there is no need to mention the 5 percent test. If you do not reject at 5 percent, there is no need to mention the 1 percent test. Both tests should be mentioned only if you reject at 5 percent but not at 1 percent.

EXERCISES

R.24 Give more examples of everyday instances in which decisions involving possible Type I and Type II errors may arise.

R.25 Before beginning a certain course, 36 students are given an aptitude test. The scores and the course results (pass/fail) are given below:

student	*test score*	*course result*	*student*	*test score*	*course result*	*student*	*test score*	*course result*
1	30	fail	13	26	fail	25	9	fail
2	29	pass	14	43	pass	26	36	pass
3	33	fail	15	43	fail	27	61	pass
4	62	pass	16	68	pass	28	79	fail
5	59	fail	17	63	pass	29	57	fail
6	63	pass	18	42	fail	30	46	pass
7	80	pass	19	51	fail	31	70	fail
8	32	fail	20	45	fail	32	31	pass
9	60	pass	21	22	fail	33	68	pass
10	76	pass	22	30	pass	34	62	pass
11	13	fail	23	40	fail	35	56	pass
12	41	pass	24	26	fail	36	36	pass

Do you think that the aptitude test is useful for selecting students for admission to the course, and if so, how would you determine the pass mark? (Discuss the trade-off between Type I and Type II errors associated with the choice of pass mark.)

R.26* Show that, in Figures R.18 and R.22, the probabilities of a Type II error are 0.15 in the case of a 5 percent significance test and 0.34 in the case of a 1 percent test. Note that the distance between μ_0 and μ_1 is three standard deviations. Hence the right-hand 5 percent rejection region begins 1.96 standard deviations to the right of μ_0. This means that it is located 1.04 standard deviations to the left of μ_1. Similarly, for a 1 percent test, the right-hand rejection region starts 2.58 standard deviations to the right of μ_0, which is 0.42 standard deviations to the left of μ_1.

R.27* Explain why the difference in the power of a 5 percent test and a 1 percent test becomes small when the distance between μ_0 and μ_1 becomes large.

R.11 *t* tests

Thus far, we have assumed that the standard deviation of $\bar{X}$ is known, which is most unlikely in practice. It has to be estimated. If the variance of the probability distribution of X is σ^2, the variance of the probability distribution of $\bar{X}$ is

$$\sigma_{\bar{X}}^2 = \frac{\sigma^2}{n} \quad \textbf{(R.69)}$$

for a sample of size n. We estimate this variance as s_X^2/n, where

$$s_X^2 = \frac{1}{n-1}\sum_{i=1}^{n}\left(X_i - \bar{X}\right)^2 . \quad \textbf{(R.70)}$$

Our estimator of the standard deviation of the probability distribution of $\bar{X}$ is therefore

$$\text{s.e.}\left(\bar{X}\right)=\sqrt{\frac{1}{n(n-1)}\sum_{i=1}^{n}\left(X_i-\bar{X}\right)^2}\,. \qquad \textbf{(R.71)}$$

We describe this as the **standard error** of $\bar{X}$, for short. The fact that we have to estimate the standard deviation with the standard error causes two modifications to the test procedure. First, $s_{\bar{X}}$ replaces $\sigma_{\bar{X}}$ in the test statistic. The test statistic

$$z=\frac{\bar{X}-\mu_0}{\sigma_{\bar{X}}} \qquad \textbf{(R.72)}$$

becomes the ***t* statistic**

$$t=\frac{\bar{X}-\mu_0}{\text{s.e.}\left(\bar{X}\right)}. \qquad \textbf{(R.73)}$$

Second, the t statistic has a distribution that is more complex than the normal distribution of the z statistic. Like the z statistic, the t statistic has a random component, $\bar{X}$, in the numerator. It also has a random component in the denominator. $s_{\bar{X}}^2$ provides only an estimate of $\sigma_{\bar{X}}^2$ and, as is obvious from (R.70), it depends on the actual values of the X_i in the sample and so will vary from sample to sample. Hence s.e.$\left(\bar{X}\right)$ will vary from sample to sample. Both the numerator and the denominator of the test statistic contain random elements and as a consequence its distribution is no longer normal, even if X itself has a normal distribution. Its distribution is known as a ***t* distribution**.

There is a further complication. The t distribution is actually a family of distributions varying with what is known as the number of **degrees of freedom** in the sample. This is equal to $n-1$ in the present context. We will not go into the reasons for this, or even describe the t distribution mathematically. Suffice to say that the t distribution is a relative of the normal distribution, its exact shape depending on the number of degrees of freedom in the regression, and that it approximates the normal distribution increasingly closely as the number of degrees of freedom becomes large.

Figure R.24 compares the distributions for 5, 10, and 20 degrees of freedom with that of the normal distribution. It will be seen that differences are noticeable only at the mode and in the tails. The mode of the t distribution is lower than that of the normal distribution and the tails are thicker, the differences being greater, the smaller the number of degrees of freedom. The modal differences are of no consequence. However, the difference in the shape of the tails is important because this is where the rejection regions for tests are defined. If we have decided to perform a two-sided 5 percent significance test, the 2.5 percent tails start 1.96 standard deviations from the mean in the case of a normal distribution. In the case of a t distribution with 10 degrees of freedom, the extra thickness of the tails means that the 2.5 percent tails are reached 2.23 standard

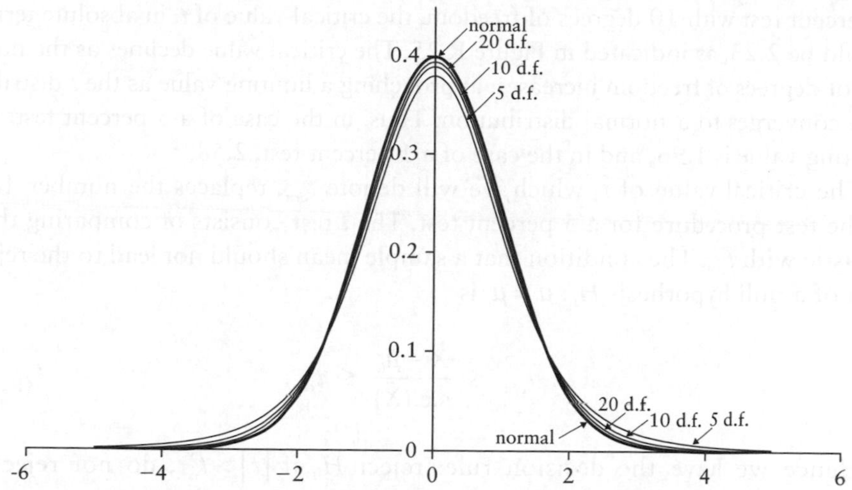

Figure R.24 Normal distribution and t distributions with 5, 10, and 20 degrees of freedom

deviations from the mean. This is shown in Figure R.25. The tail of the normal distribution has lighter shading. That of the t distribution has darker shading. Of course, they overlap.

Table A.2 in Appendix A gives the critical values of t cross-classified by significance level and the number of degrees of freedom. At the top of the table are listed possible significance levels for a test. For the time being, we are performing two-sided tests, so ignore the line for one-sided tests. Thus, the critical values for 5 percent tests are given in the second column and those for 1 percent tests in the fourth. The left-hand vertical column lists degrees of freedom. So, if we were performing a

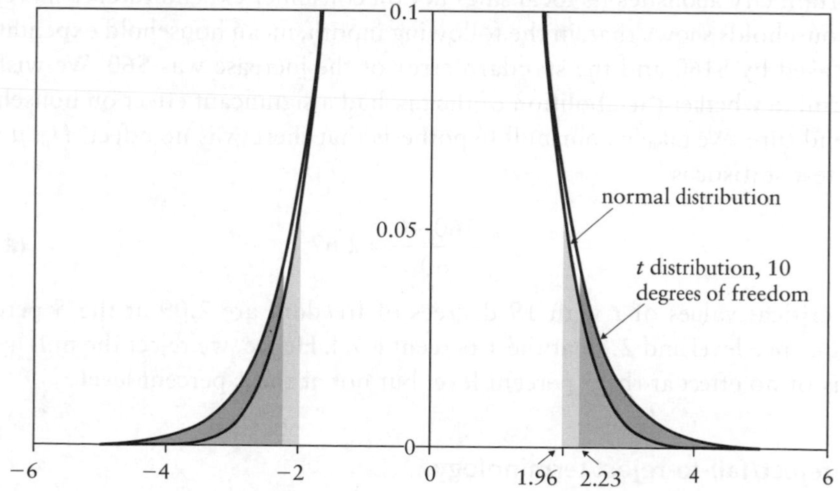

Figure R.25 2.5 percent tails of a normal distribution and a t distribution with 10 degrees of freedom

5 percent test with 10 degrees of freedom, the critical value of t, in absolute terms, would be 2.23, as indicated in Figure R.25. The critical value declines as the number of degrees of freedom increases, approaching a limiting value as the t distribution converges to a normal distribution. Thus, in the case of a 5 percent test, the limiting value is 1.96, and in the case of a 1 percent test, 2.58.

The critical value of t, which we will denote t_{crit}, replaces the number 1.96 in the test procedure for a 5 percent test. The t test consists of comparing the t statistic with t_{crit}. The condition that a sample mean should not lead to the rejection of a null hypothesis H_0: $\mu = \mu_0$ is

$$-t_{crit} \leq \frac{\bar{X} - \mu_0}{\text{s.e.}(\bar{X})} \leq t_{crit}. \qquad \textbf{(R.74)}$$

Hence we have the decision rule: reject H_0 if $|t| > t_{crit}$, do not reject if $|t| \leq t_{crit}$, where

$$|t| = \left| \frac{\bar{X} - \mu_0}{\text{s.e.}(\bar{X})} \right| \qquad \textbf{(R.75)}$$

is the absolute value of t (its numerical value, neglecting the sign). This makes a difference only for relatively small samples, say fewer than 50 observations. If the sample size is larger than 50, the fact that we have to estimate the standard error of $\bar{X}$ makes negligible difference because the t distribution converges on the normal distribution and the critical values of t converge on those for the normal distribution.

Example

A certain city abolishes its local sales tax on consumer expenditure. A survey of 20 households shows that, in the following month, mean household expenditure increased by \$160 and the standard error of the increase was \$60. We wish to determine whether the abolition of the tax had a significant effect on household expenditure. We take as our null hypothesis that there was no effect: H_0: $\mu = 0$. The test statistic is

$$t = \frac{160 - 0}{60} = 2.67. \qquad \textbf{(R.76)}$$

The critical values of t with 19 degrees of freedom are 2.09 at the 5 percent significance level and 2.86 at the 1 percent level. Hence, we reject the null hypothesis of no effect at the 5 percent level but not at the 1 percent level.

The reject/fail-to-reject terminology

In this section, it has been shown that you should reject the null hypothesis if the absolute value of the t statistic is greater than t_{crit}, and that you fail to reject it otherwise. Why 'fail to reject', which is a clumsy expression? Would it not be better just to say that you accept the hypothesis if the absolute value of the t statistic is less than t_{crit}?

The argument against using the term 'accept' is that you might find yourself 'accepting' several mutually exclusive hypotheses at the same time. For instance, in the sales tax example, a null hypothesis H_0: $\mu = 100$ would not be rejected, even at the 5 percent level, because the t statistic

$$t = \frac{200 - 100}{80} = 1.25 \quad \textbf{(R.77)}$$

is lower than 2.09. But the same would be true if the null hypothesis were $\mu = 150$ or $\mu = 250$, with corresponding t statistics 0.63 and –0.63. It is logical to say that you would not reject any of these null hypotheses, but it makes little sense to say that you simultaneously accept all three of them. In the next section you will see that one can define a whole range of hypotheses which would not be rejected by a given experimental result, so it would be incautious to pick out one as being 'accepted'.

EXERCISES

R.28* A researcher is evaluating whether an increase in the minimum hourly wage has had an effect on employment in the manufacturing industry in the following three months. Taking a sample of 25 firms, what should she conclude if

(a) the mean decrease in employment is 9 percent, and the standard error of the mean is 5 percent;
(b) the mean decrease is 12 percent, and the standard error is 5 percent;
(c) the mean decrease is 20 percent, and the standard error is 5 percent;
(d) there is a mean *increase* of 10 percent, and the standard error is 5 percent?

R.29 A drug company asserts that its course of treatment will, on average, reduce a person's cholesterol level by 0.8 mmol/L. A researcher undertakes a trial with a sample of 30 individuals. What should he report if he obtains the following results:

(a) a mean increase of 0.6 units, with standard error 0.2 units;
(b) a mean decrease of 0.4 units, with standard error 0.2 units;
(c) a mean increase of 0.4 units, with standard error 0.2 units?

R.12 Confidence intervals

Thus far, we have been assuming that the hypothesis preceded the empirical investigation. In particular, given a random variable X with unknown population mean μ, we set up a null hypothesis H_0: $\mu = \mu_0$, obtained a sample of n observations, calculated $\bar{X}$, and checked whether it caused H_0 to be rejected or not. A little more systematically, we established the range of sample values of $\bar{X}$ that would not lead to the rejection of H_0. We called this the acceptance region.

In practice, in empirical work, it is much more common to do the opposite. We conduct an experiment and then consider what hypotheses would be compatible with it, in the sense of not being rejected by it at a chosen significance level. For the moment, to be specific, we will adopt the 5 percent significance level. We will generalize from this in due course.

In Figure R.26, we suppose that we have calculated $\bar{X}$ from a sample of observations and we are considering whether a hypothesis $\mu = \mu_0$ would be rejected by it. To determine this, we need to draw the distribution of $\bar{X}$ conditional on H_0 being true, and this is shown. For the moment, we are assuming for simplicity that we know the value of σ and thus $\sigma/\sqrt{n}$, the standard deviation of the distribution. We can see that, in this case, the hypothesis would not be rejected, given the value of $\bar{X}$.

Next we will consider the hypothesis $\mu = \mu_1$. This is shown in Figure R.27, together with the conditional distribution for $\bar{X}$. In this case, $\bar{X}$ lies in the left rejection region of the conditional distribution, so $\bar{X}$ and μ_1 are incompatible and the hypothesis $\mu = \mu_1$ is rejected.

Now we ask ourselves whether we can generalize and establish the entire range of hypotheses that would not be rejected, given the experimental outcome $\bar{X}$, and given our choice of significance level. In particular, we will ask ourselves what is the maximum hypothetical value of μ that would not be rejected, given $\bar{X}$. We will denote it $\mu^{\max}$. The answer is shown graphically in Figure R.28, for the case where we have chosen a 5 percent significance level. The figure shows the probability distribution of $\bar{X}$, conditional on $\mu = \mu^{\max}$ being true. $\bar{X}$ lies just on the edge of the lower rejection region. Any null hypothesis greater than $\mu^{\max}$

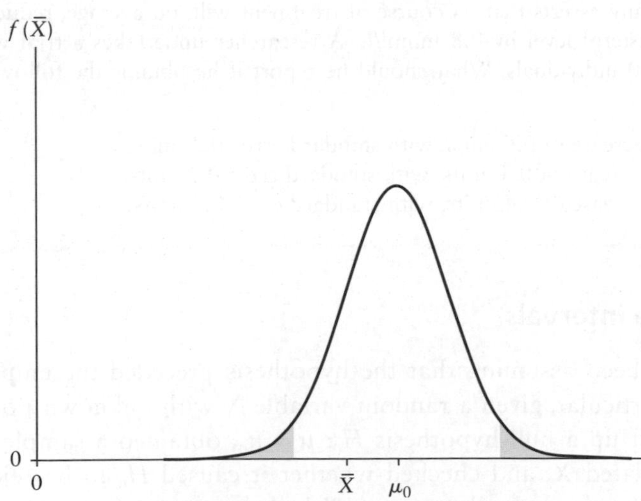

Figure R.26 Distribution of $\bar{X}$ conditional on $\mu = \mu_0$

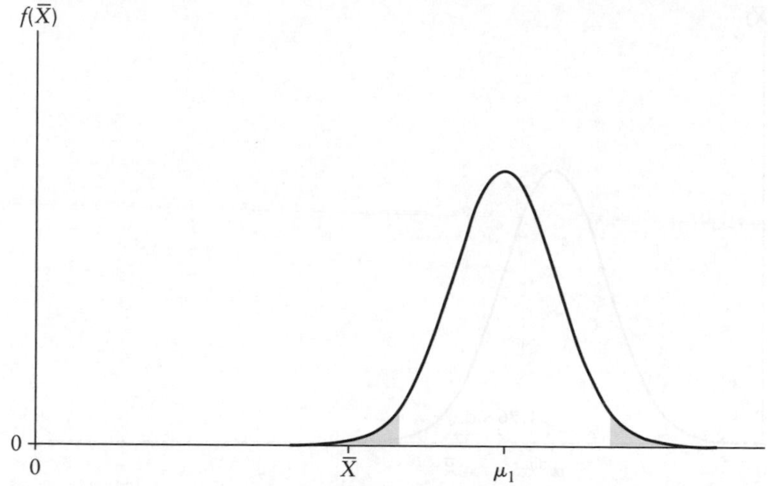

Figure R.27 Distribution of $\overline{X}$ conditional on $\mu = \mu_1$

would be rejected because $\overline{X}$ would lie in the left rejection region for the conditional distribution, as in the case of μ_1 in Figure R.27.

How do we determine $\mu^{\max}$? From the geometry of Figure R.28, we can see that the distance from the middle of the distribution, $\mu^{\max}$, to the limit of the left rejection region is $1.96\sigma_{\overline{X}}$. Hence,

$$\overline{X} = \mu^{\max} - 1.96\sigma_{\overline{X}} \tag{R.78}$$

and so

$$\mu^{\max} = \overline{X} + 1.96\sigma_{\overline{X}}. \tag{R.79}$$

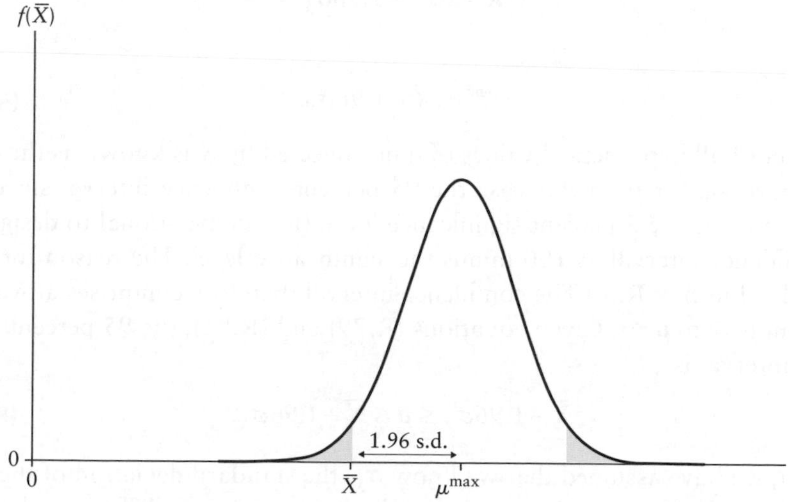

Figure R.28 Distribution of $\overline{X}$ conditional on $\mu = \mu^{\max}$

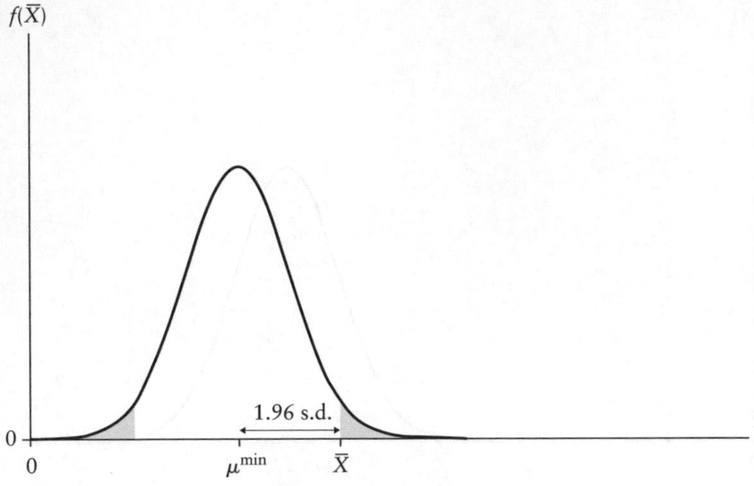

Figure R.29 Distribution of $\overline{X}$ conditional on $\mu = \mu^{\min}$

So far we have been considering hypothetical values of μ that are greater than $\overline{X}$. We should also consider hypothetical values of μ lower than $\overline{X}$. Those that are close enough to $\overline{X}$ will not be rejected by it and those that are too far below it will be rejected. In the same way that we found a limiting value for μ above $\overline{X}$, we can find a limiting value below it. We will call this $\mu^{\min}$. It is the value which, given its conditional distribution for $\overline{X}$, is just not rejected by $\overline{X}$. This is shown in Figure R.29.

To determine $\mu^{\min}$, we note that the distance from the middle of the distribution, $\mu^{\min}$, to the limit of the left rejection region is $1.96\sigma_{\overline{X}}$. Hence,

$$\overline{X} = \mu^{\min} + 1.96\sigma_{\overline{X}} \qquad \textbf{(R.80)}$$

and so

$$\mu^{\min} = \overline{X} - 1.96\sigma_{\overline{X}}. \qquad \textbf{(R.81)}$$

The set of all hypothetical values of μ not rejected by $\overline{X}$ is known as the confidence interval for μ, in this case the 95 percent confidence interval since we have been using the 5 percent significance level. (It is conventional to designate the confidence interval as 100 minus the significance level. The reason for this is explained in Box R.3.) The confidence interval therefore comprises all values of μ from $\mu^{\min}$ to $\mu^{\max}$. Given equations (R.79) and (R.81), the 95 percent confidence interval is

$$\overline{X} - 1.96\sigma_{\overline{X}} \le \mu \le \overline{X} + 1.96\sigma_{\overline{X}}. \qquad \textbf{(R.82)}$$

So far, we have assumed that we know $\sigma_{\overline{X}}$, the standard deviation of the distribution of $\overline{X}$. Of course, in practice we have to estimate it. When we do this, we must replace 1.96, which applies to the normal distribution, with the corresponding critical value of the t distribution. Hence, in practice, the 95 percent confidence interval is computed as

$$\bar{X} - t_{\text{crit, 5\%}} \times \text{s.e.}(\bar{X}) \leq \mu \leq \bar{X} + t_{\text{crit, 5\%}} \times \text{s.e.}(\bar{X}), \quad \textbf{(R.83)}$$

where $t_{\text{crit,5\%}}$ is the critical value of t at the 5 percent level, given the number of degrees of freedom.

We can immediately generalize from this to other significance levels. For example, the 99 percent confidence interval is given by

$$\bar{X} - t_{\text{crit, 1\%}} \times \text{s.e.}(\bar{X}) \leq \mu \leq \bar{X} + t_{\text{crit, 1\%}} \times \text{s.e.}(\bar{X}), \quad \textbf{(R.84)}$$

where $t_{\text{crit,1\%}}$ is the critical value of t at the 1 percent significance level.

BOX R.3 A second interpretation of a confidence interval

When you construct a confidence interval, the numbers you calculate for its upper and lower limits have random components. For example, in inequality (R.83), the lower and upper limits are

$$\bar{X} - t_{\text{crit, 5\%}} \times \text{s.e.}(\bar{X}) \text{ and } \bar{X} + t_{\text{crit, 5\%}} \times \text{s.e.}(\bar{X}).$$

Both $\bar{X}$ and s.e. $(\bar{X})$ are random quantities that depend on the actual values of the X_i in the observations in the sample. One hopes that the confidence interval will include the true value of μ, but sometimes it will be so distorted by the random element that it will fail to do so. This may happen if the sample contains an unusually large number of high or low values of X.

What is the probability that a confidence interval will capture the true value of μ? It can easily be shown, using elementary probability theory, that, in the case of a 95 percent confidence interval, the probability is 95 percent. Similarly, in the case of a 99 percent confidence interval, the probability is 99 percent.

$\bar{X}$ provides a point estimate of μ, but of course the probability of the true value being exactly equal to this estimate is infinitesimal. The confidence interval provides what is known as an *interval estimate* of μ, that is, a range of values that will include the true value with a high, predetermined probability. It is this interpretation that gives the confidence interval its name. The proof is left as an exercise. It is also the reason why, for example, we talk about a 95 percent confidence interval rather than a 5 percent one.

Example

In an example in Section R.11, when a local sales tax was abolished, a survey of 20 households showed that mean household expenditure increased by \$160 and the standard error of the increase was \$60. The 95 percent confidence interval for the effect is

$$160 - 2.09 \times 60 \leq \mu \leq 160 + 2.09 \times 60 \quad \textbf{(R.85)}$$

since the critical value of t with 19 degrees of freedom is 2.09 at the 5 percent significance level. Hence, the interval is

$$35 \leq \mu \leq 285. \tag{R.86}$$

EXERCISES

R.30 Determine the 99 percent confidence interval for the effect of the sales tax in the example.

R.31 Determine the 95 percent confidence interval for the effect of an increase in the minimum wage on employment, given the data in Exercise R.28, for each part of the exercise. How do these confidence intervals relate to the results of the t tests in that exercise?

R.32 Demonstrate that the 95 percent confidence interval defined by equation (R.83) has a 95 percent probability of capturing μ_0 if H_0: $\mu = \mu_0$ is true.

R.13 One-sided tests

In Section R.10 we saw that there is a trade-off between the potential for Type I and Type II errors when performing tests of hypotheses. You can reduce the risk of a Type I error, if the null hypothesis is true, by performing a 1 percent test instead of a 5 percent test. However, if the null hypothesis is false, you thereby increase the risk of making a Type II error. In this section, we will see that we can improve the terms of this trade-off if we are in a position to perform a one-sided test instead of a two-sided test. There will still be a trade-off, but it will be a better one. Holding the risk of making a Type I error constant (if the null hypothesis is true), we will have a smaller risk of making a Type II error (if the null hypothesis is false), if we use a one-sided test instead of a two-sided test.

First, we have to explain what is meant by a one-sided test.

In our discussion of t tests, we started out with our null hypothesis H_0: $\mu = \mu_0$ and tested it to see whether we should reject it or not, given the sample value of $\bar{X}$. Thus far, the alternative hypothesis has been merely the negation of the null hypothesis. However, if we are able to be more specific about the alternative hypothesis, we may be able to improve the testing procedure. We will investigate three cases: first, the very special case where, if $\mu \neq \mu_0$, there is only one possible alternative value, which we will denote μ_1; second, where, if μ is not equal to μ_0, it must be greater than μ_0; and third, where, if μ is not equal to μ_0, it must be less than μ_0.

One-sided tests are used very frequently in hypothesis testing. In the context of regression analysis, they are, or they ought to be, more common than the traditional textbook two-sided tests. It is therefore important that you understand the rationale for their use, and this involves a sequence of small analytical steps. None of this should present any difficulty, but you should avoid the temptation to try to reduce the whole business to the mechanical use of a few formulae.

H_0: $\mu = \mu_0$, H_1: $\mu = \mu_1$

In this case, there are only two possible values of μ, μ_0 and μ_1. For the sake of argument, we will assume for the time being that μ_1 is greater than μ_0.

Suppose that we wish to test H_0 at the 5 percent significance level, and we follow the usual procedure discussed in Section R.9. We locate the limits of the upper and lower 2.5 percent tails under the assumption that H_0 is true, indicated by A and B in Figure R.30, and we reject H_0 if $\overline{X}$ lies to the left of A or to the right of B.

Now, if $\overline{X}$ does lie to the right of B, it is more compatible with H_1 than with H_0; the probability of it lying to the right of B is greater if H_1 is true than if H_0 is true. We should have no hesitation in rejecting H_0. We therefore conclude that H_1 is true.

However, if $\overline{X}$ lies to the left of A, the test procedure will lead us to a perverse conclusion. It tells us to reject H_0, and therefore conclude that H_1 is true, even though the probability of $\overline{X}$ lying to the left of A is smaller (in this case, negligible) if H_1 is true. We have not even drawn the probability density function that far for H_1. If such a value of $\overline{X}$ occurs only once in a million times when H_1 is true, but 2.5 percent of the time when H_0 is true, it is more logical to assume that H_0 is true. Of course, once in a million times you will make a mistake, but the rest of the time you will be right.

Hence we will reject H_0 only if $\overline{X}$ lies in the upper 2.5 percent tail, that is, to the right of B, as in Figure R.31. We are now performing a one-sided test, and we have reduced the probability of making a Type I error to 2.5 percent. Since

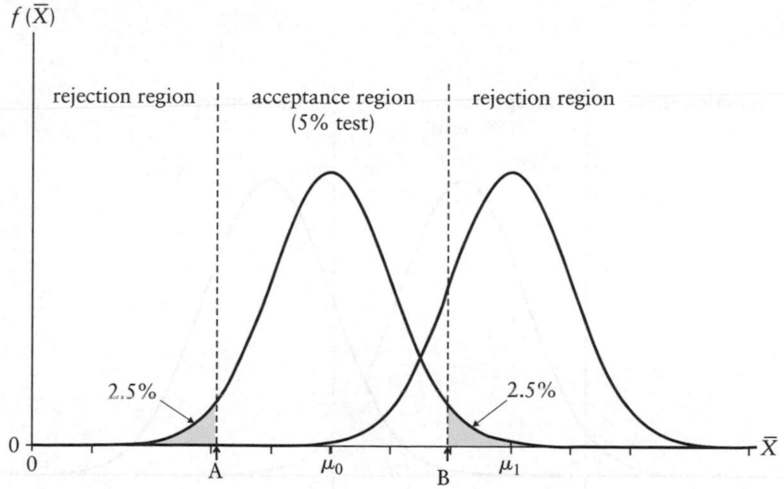

Figure R.30 Distribution of $\overline{X}$ under H_0 and H_1

the significance level is defined to be the probability of making a Type I error, it is now also 2.5 percent.

What difference does this make to the probability of a Type II error? None. A Type II error will occur if the null hypothesis is false (so $\mu = \mu_1$) and $\bar{X}$ lies in the acceptance region for H_0. This is the area under the curve for $\mu = \mu_1$ to the left of the point B. It is shown for the two-sided test in Figure R.32 and for the one-sided test in Figure R.33. Of course, it is the same area. The actual area depends on the distance between μ_0 and μ_1, in terms of standard deviations. In the present example, the probability is 0.15.

The one-sided test is a 2.5 percent significance test because the probability of rejecting H_0: $\mu = \mu_0$, if is true, is 2.5 percent. If we wish to perform a 5 percent

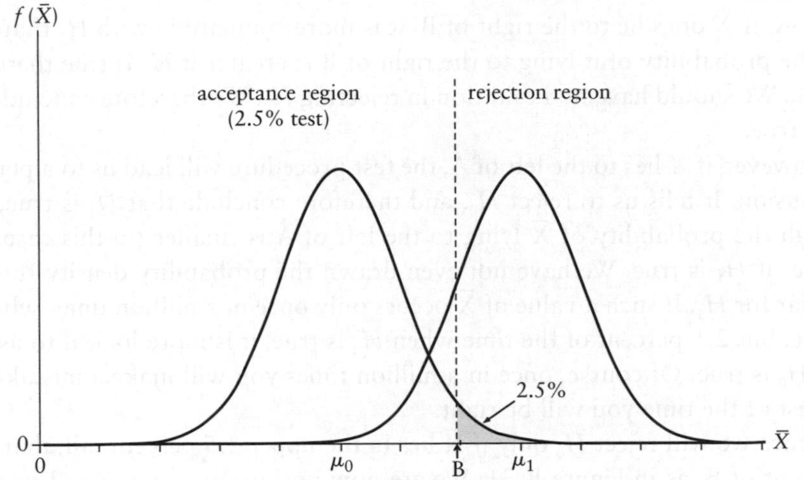

Figure R.31 Rejection region, one-sided test, 2.5% significance level

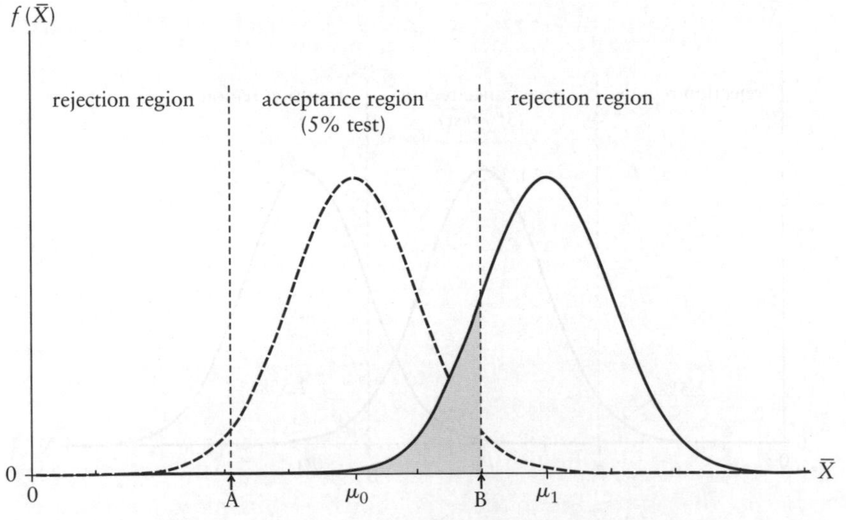

Figure R.32 Probability of Type II error if $\mu = \mu_1$, two-sided test, 5% significance level

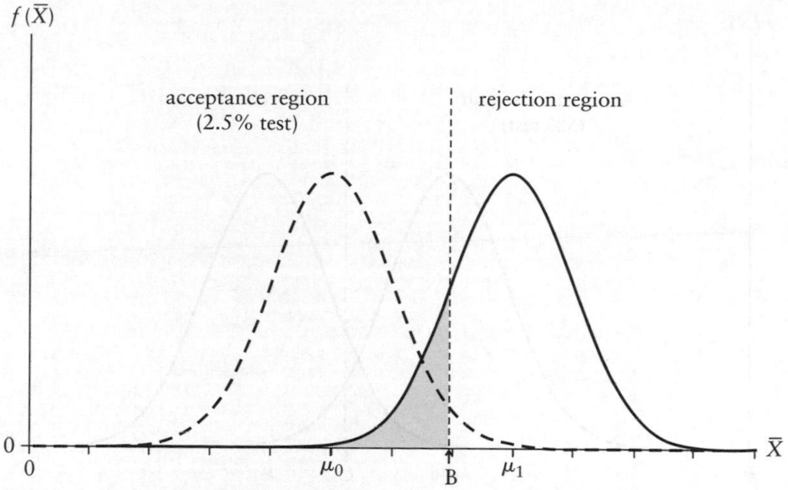

Figure R.33 Probability of Type II error if $\mu = \mu_1$, one-sided test, 2.5% significance level

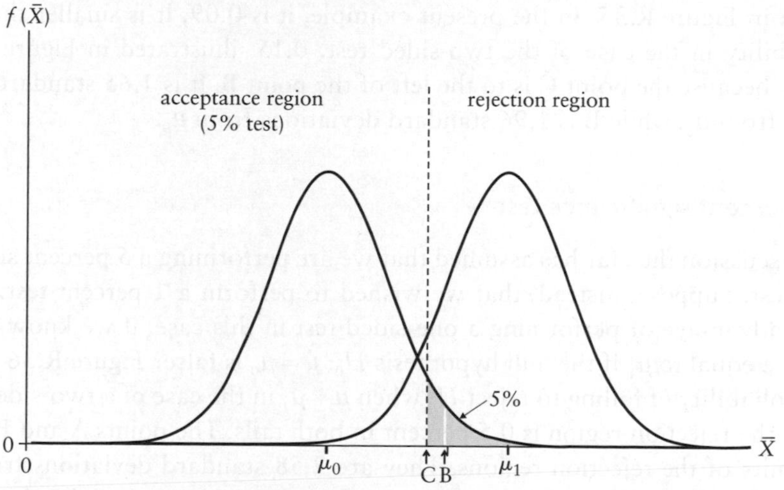

Figure R.34 Rejection region, one-sided test, 5 percent significance level

significance test, we need to increase the right-hand rejection region so that it includes 5 percent of the area under the curve conditional on H_0: $\mu = \mu_0$. This is shown in Figure R.34. The beginning of the rejection region is marked by the point C.

Why should we wish to increase the risk of a Type I error in this way? The answer is that we thereby reduce the probability of a Type II error if H_0 is false.

Suppose that, in fact, $\mu = \mu_1$. We will fail to reject H_0 if $\bar{X}$ lies in the acceptance region for H_0, that is, if it lies to the left of C. The probability of this happening, if $\mu = \mu_1$, is the area under the curve for $\mu = \mu_1$ to the left of the point C. This is

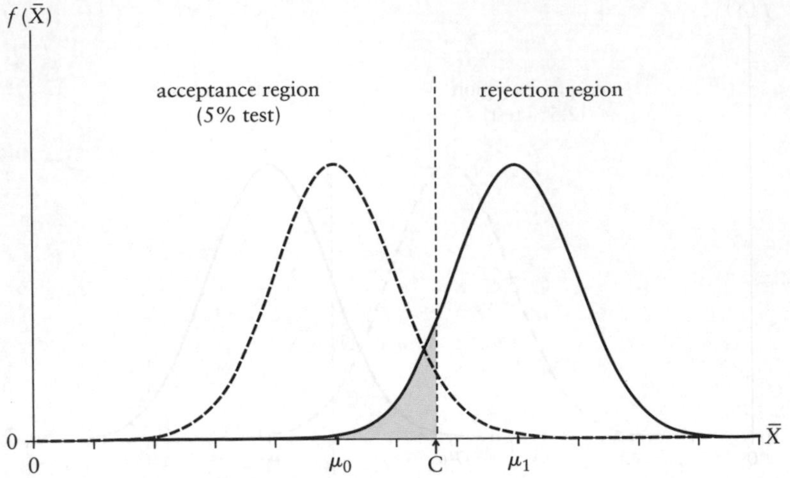

Figure R.35 Probability of Type II error if $\mu = \mu_1$, one-sided test, 5% significance level

shown in Figure R.35. In the present example, it is 0.09. It is smaller than the probability in the case of the two-sided test, 0.15, illustrated in Figure R.33. This is because the point C is to the left of the point B. It is 1.65 standard deviations from μ_0, while B is 1.96 standard deviations from μ_0.

One percent significance test

The discussion thus far has assumed that we are performing a 5 percent significance test. Suppose, instead, that we wished to perform a 1 percent test. What is the advantage of performing a one-sided test in this case, if we know that μ must be equal to μ_1 if the null hypothesis H_0: $\mu = \mu_0$ is false? Figure R.36 shows the probability of failing to reject H_0 when $\mu = \mu_1$ in the case of a two-sided test, where the rejection region is 0.5 percent in both tails. The points A and B mark the limits of the rejection regions. They are 2.58 standard deviations from μ_0. The probability of $\bar{X}$ lying in the acceptance region is the area under the distribution for $\mu = \mu_1$ in the range AB. The probability of a Type II error is 0.34 in the present example.

Figure R.37 shows the probability in the case of a one-sided test. We have eliminated the left tail because, as in the case of the 5 percent test, it is irrational to retain it, and we have increased the right tail to from 0.5 percent to 1 percent. The limit of the right-hand 1 percent tail, marked by the point C, is 2.33 standard deviations from μ_0. The probability of $\bar{X}$ lying in the acceptance region is now the area under the distribution for $\mu = \mu_1$ to the left of C. It is 0.25, in the present example.

Table R.6 summarizes the trade-off between the probabilities of making a Type I error, if H_0 is true, and a Type II error, if H_0 is false, and how the trade-off is altered by performing a one-sided test instead of a two-sided test.

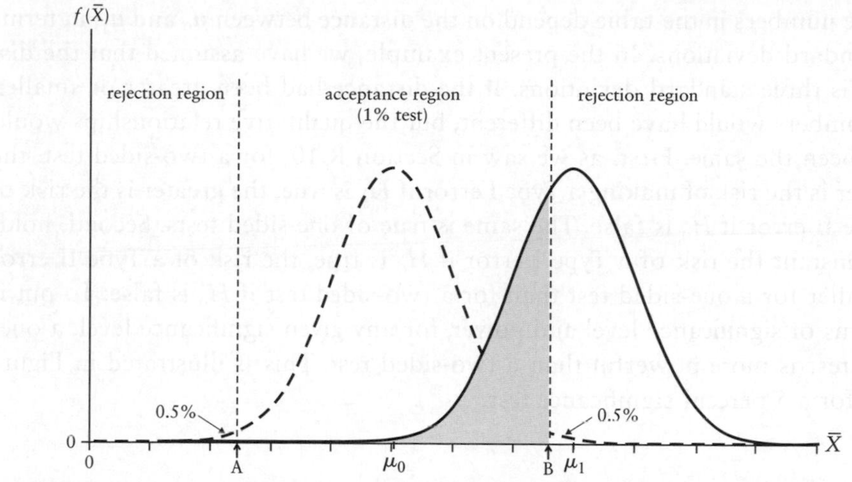

Figure R.36 Probability of Type II error if $\mu = \mu_1$, two-sided test, 1% significance level

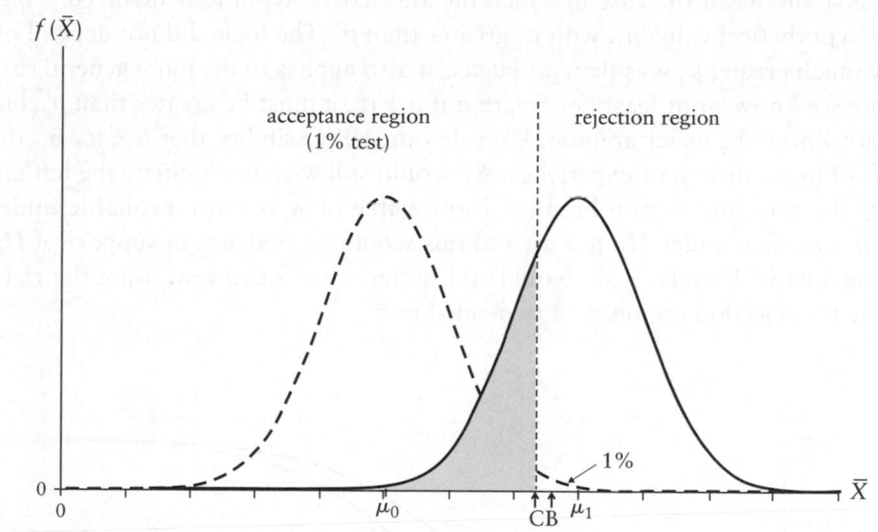

Figure R.37 Probability of Type II error if $\mu = \mu_1$, one-sided test, 1% significance level

Table R.6 Trade-off between Type I and Type II errors, one-sided and two-sided tests

	Probability of Type II error if $\mu = \mu_1$	
	One-sided test	Two-sided test
5 percent significance test	0.09	0.15
2.5 percent significance test	0.15	(not investigated)
1 percent significance test	0.25	0.34

The numbers in the table depend on the distance between μ_0 and μ_1, in terms of standard deviations. In the present example, we have assumed that the distance is three standard deviations. If the distance had been greater or smaller, the numbers would have been different, but the qualitative relationships would have been the same. First, as we saw in Section R.10, for a two-sided test, the smaller is the risk of making a Type I error if H_0 is true, the greater is the risk of a Type II error if H_0 is false. The same is true of one-sided tests. Second, holding constant the risk of a Type I error if H_0 is true, the risk of a Type II error is smaller for a one-sided test than for a two-sided test if H_0 is false. To put it in terms of significance level and power, for any given significance level, a one-sided test is more powerful than a two-sided test. This is illustrated in Figure R.38 for a 5 percent significance test.

Generalizing from H_0: $\mu = \mu_0$, H_1: $\mu = \mu_1$ to H_0: $\mu = \mu_0$, H_1: $\mu > \mu_0$

We have discussed the case in which the alternative hypothesis involved a *specific* hypothetical value μ_1, with μ_1 greater than μ_0. The logic did not depend on how much greater μ_1 was than μ_0. Hence, it also applies to the more general case where we know, or at least believe, that if $\mu \neq \mu_0$, it must be greater than μ_0, but do not know the exact amount. We rule out the possibility that $\mu < \mu_0$ on the basis of logic, theory, or experience. We would still wish to eliminate the left tail from the rejection region because a low value of $\bar{X}$ is more probable under H_0: $\mu = \mu_0$ than under H_1: $\mu > \mu_0$, and this would be evidence in support of H_0, not against it. Therefore, we would still prefer a one-sided test, using the right tail as the rejection region, to a two-sided test.

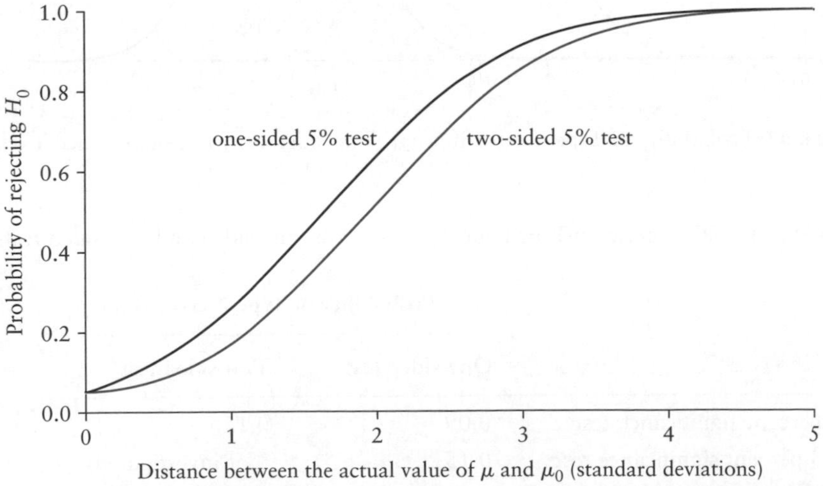

Figure R.38 Comparison of the power of one-sided and two-sided 5 percent tests

Note that, since the true value of μ is not defined specifically under H_1: $\mu > \mu_0$, we now have no way of calculating the probability of a Type II error if H_0 is false. However, we can still be sure that, for any given risk of a Type I error, if H_0 is true, the risk of a Type II error, if H_0 is false, will be lower for a one-sided test than for a two-sided test.

H_0: $\mu = \mu_0$, H_1: $\mu < \mu_0$

Now consider the case where you have two specific alternatives, H_0: $\mu = \mu_0$ and H_1: $\mu = \mu_1$, where μ_1 is less than μ_0. The logic in the first part of this section applies, with the difference that one eliminates the right tail instead of the left tail as a rejection region. If $\bar{X}$ happened to lie in the right tail, this would be even more unlikely under H_1 than under H_0, and so it should not lead to the rejection of H_0. Hence, one should perform a one-sided test, using only the left tail as a rejection region.

Further, as in the previous discussion, the distance between μ_1 and μ_0 makes no difference. It is sufficient that μ_1 should be less than μ_0. Hence, if we are in a position to rule out $\mu > \mu_0$ on the basis of logic, theory, or experience, we should perform a one-sided test in the case of the more general framework H_0: $\mu = \mu_0$, H_1: $\mu < \mu_0$.

One-sided *t* tests

In the discussion so far in this section, we have assumed that we know the standard deviation of $\bar{X}$. Of course, in practice, you have to estimate it, as described in Section R.11. This means that in all of the discussion in this section, we ought to be using *t* distributions rather than normal distributions, and critical values of *t* instead of critical values of the normal distribution if the sample size is relatively small, say fewer than 50 observations.

Special case: H_0: $\mu = 0$

One-sided tests are often particularly useful where the analysis relates to the evaluation of treatment and effect. Suppose that a number of units of observation receive some type of treatment and X_i is a measure of the effect of the treatment for observation *i*. To demonstrate that the treatment did have an effect, we set up the null hypothesis H_0: $\mu = 0$ and see if we can reject it, given the sample average $\bar{X}$. The *t* statistic for testing H_0 is

$$t = \frac{\bar{X} - \mu_0}{\text{s.e.}(\bar{X})} = \frac{\bar{X}}{\text{s.e.}(\bar{X})}. \qquad \textbf{(R.87)}$$

Suppose that we are performing a 5 percent significance test and we have 40 observations. With 39 degrees of freedom, the critical value of *t* is 2.02, using a two-sided test. However, if we can rule out the possibility that the treatment can have a negative effect, we can use a one-sided test, for which the critical value is 1.68. This makes it easier to reject the null hypothesis and demonstrate that the treatment has had a significant effect. Similarly, if we were performing a 1 percent test, the critical values using a two-sided test and a one-sided test are 2.71 and 2.43, respectively. Thus, again, it is easier to reject the null hypothesis with a one-sided test. Consider the following cases for the two-sided test H_0: $\mu = 0$, H_1: $\mu \neq 0$ and the one-sided test H_0: $\mu = 0$, H_1: $\mu > 0$:

(a) $t = 1.20$. One-sided and two-sided tests lead to the same conclusion: H_0 is not rejected at any sensible significance level.
(b) $t = 1.80$. H_0 is not rejected at any sensible significance level using a two-sided test. However, if we use a one-sided test, it is rejected at the 5 percent level and we conclude that the treatment did have an effect, after all.
(c) $t = 2.20$. One-sided and two-sided tests lead to the same conclusion: H_0 is rejected at the 5 percent level (2.02, two-sided, 1.68, one-sided) but not at the 1 percent level (2.71 two-sided, 2.43 one-sided).
(d) $t = 2.60$. H_0 is rejected at the 5 percent level using a two-sided test and at the 1 percent level using a one-sided test.
(e) $t = 3.00$. One-sided and two-sided tests lead to the same conclusion: H_0 is rejected at the 1 percent level (but not at the 0.1 percent level).

In three of the five cases, using a one-sided test leads to the same conclusion. But in cases (b) and (d), there is an advantage in using a one-sided test.

Anomalous results

In this discussion, we have assumed that the treatment cannot have a negative effect. Suppose, however, that in our sample $\bar{X}$ turns out to be negative. What should we then conclude? Let us consider two further cases. Since $\bar{X}$ is negative, the t statistic will be negative.

(f) $t = -0.80$. We should maintain the null hypothesis of no effect. If it is true, the sample $\bar{X}$ will be randomly distributed around zero. In repeated samples, t will be positive half the time, and negative half the time. In this particular case, it is one of the negative times.
(g) $t = -2.40$. If we were performing a two-sided test, this would be significant at the 5 percent level. We would reject H_0 and conclude that the true value was negative. However, on the basis of experience or theory, we have excluded this possibility. We are considering only two possibilities: no effect, under H_0, and a positive effect, under H_1. Under H_0, it would be unusual to obtain a negative estimate with such a large negative t statistic. With 39 degrees of freedom, the probability is about 2 percent. However, the probability of obtaining such an anomalous result would be even lower if the true value of μ were positive. So we should stay with H_0 and conclude that we have a somewhat freakish sample.

This said, it would be reasonable to revisit our assumption that the treatment could not possibly have a negative effect. It might be that we have overlooked something and that we should not be so confident about excluding this possibility. If, in the end, we are sure that the effect cannot be negative, then we would stay with H_0. However, if we decide that, perhaps, we should be performing a two-sided test after all, then we could conclude that we have evidence, significant at the 5 percent level, that the effect is, indeed, negative.

Justification of the use of a one-sided test

The use of a one-sided test has to be justified beforehand on the grounds of logic, theory, common sense, or previous experience. When stating the justification, you should be careful not to exclude the possibility that the null hypothesis is true. For example, suppose that you are testing whether a treatment has an effect. To be specific, suppose that you are evaluating the effect of a training course on the productivity of a sample of workers. You would expect a significant positive effect, given a large enough sample. But your justification should not be that, on the basis of theory and common sense, the effect should be positive. This is too strong, for it eliminates the null hypothesis of no effect, and there is nothing left to test. Instead, you should say that, on the basis of theory and common sense, you would exclude the possibility that the course has a *negative* effect. This then leaves the possibility that the effect is zero and the alternative that it is positive.

Example

We return to the example of the evaluation of the effect on consumer expenditure of the abolition of a local sales tax. The survey of 20 households showed that mean household expenditure increased by \$160 and the standard error of the increase was \$60. The test statistic for H_0: $\mu = 0$ is

$$t = \frac{160 - 0}{60} = 2.67. \qquad \textbf{(R.88)}$$

For a two-sided test, the critical values of t with 19 degrees of freedom are 2.09 at the 5 percent significance level and 2.86 at the 1 percent level, allowing the null hypothesis of no effect to be rejected at the 5 percent level but not at the 1 percent level. However, we should be able to rule out the possibility of the abolition of the sales tax causing a reduction in consumer expenditure, and so we are in a position to perform a one-sided test instead of a two-sided test. For a one-sided test, the critical values of t with 19 degrees of freedom are 1.73 at the 5 percent significance level and 2.54 at the 1 percent level. Hence, with a one-sided test, we establish that the effect was significant at the 1 percent level.

Variation

Suppose that the survey had shown a mean *reduction* of expenditure of \$130, again with standard error \$60. What should we have concluded then? The t statistic for H_0: $\mu = 0$ is -2.17. Hence, if we had unthinkingly performed a two-sided test, we would have come to the strange conclusion that the abolition of the sales tax had a negative effect significant at the 5 percent level. However, if we have decided that we are justified in performing a one-sided test, what should we conclude? One answer would be to say that, although such a large negative estimate is unlikely under H_0, it is even more unlikely under the alternative H_1: $\mu > 0$. So we stay with H_0, and conclude that we have a somewhat freakish sample. At the same time, we should check whether there might be something that we have overlooked that might have given rise to the unexpected result. In the present case, we should definitely check how consumer expenditure is measured. If it is measured excluding the sales tax, then we have an anomalous result. But if it includes the sales tax, then the abolition of the tax could conceivably account for the reduction in measured expenditure. We should re-estimate the effect, excluding the tax.

EXERCISES

R.33* In Exercise R.28, a researcher was evaluating whether an increase in the minimum hourly wage has had an effect on employment in manufacturing industry. Explain whether she might have been justified in performing one-sided tests in cases (a)–(d), and determine whether her conclusions would have been different.

R.34 In Exercise R.29, a researcher was evaluating the assertion of a drug company that its course of treatment will, on average, reduce a person's cholesterol level by 0.8 mmol/L. Explain whether he might have been justified in performing one-sided tests in cases (a)–(c), and determine whether his conclusions would have been different.

R.35 You wish to test H_0: $\mu = 0$. You believe that μ cannot be negative and so the alternative hypothesis is H_1: $\mu > 0$. Accordingly, you decide to perform a one-sided test. However, you are wrong. μ is actually equal to μ_1, and μ_1 is negative. What are the implications for your test results?

R.14 **Probability limits and consistency**

The asymptotic properties of estimators are their limiting properties as the number of observations in a sample becomes very large and approaches infinity. We shall be concerned with the concepts of probability limits and consistency, and the central limit theorem. These topics are usually mentioned in standard statistics texts, but with no great seriousness of purpose, and generally without an explanation of why they are relevant and useful. The reason is that most standard introductory statistics courses cater to a wide variety of students, most of whom will never have any use for these topics. However, for students of econometrics an understanding is essential because the asymptotic properties of estimators lie at the heart of much econometric analysis.

Probability limits

We will start with an abstract definition of a probability limit and then illustrate it with a simple example. A sequence of random quantities Z_n is said to converge in probability to a constant α if

$$\lim_{n\to\infty} P\left(|Z_n - \alpha| > \varepsilon\right) \to 0 \qquad \textbf{(R.89)}$$

for any positive ε, however small. As the sample size becomes large, the probability of Z differing from α by any finite amount, however small, tends to zero. The constant α is described as the probability limit of the sequence, usually abbreviated as plim, and the mathematical statement is simplified to

$$\text{plim } Z = \alpha. \qquad \textbf{(R.90)}$$

We will take as an example the mean of a sample of observations, $\bar{X}$, generated from a random variable X with unknown population mean μ_X and population variance σ_X^2. We will investigate how $\bar{X}$ behaves as the sample size n becomes large. For convenience, we shall assume that X has a normal distribution, but this does not affect the analysis. If X has a normal distribution with mean μ_X, $\bar{X}$ also has a normal distribution with mean μ_X, the difference being that the distribution for $\bar{X}$ has variance σ_X^2/n, as we saw in Section R.5.

As n increases, the variance decreases. This is illustrated in Figure R.39. We are assuming that X has mean 100 and standard deviation 50. If the sample size is 4, the standard deviation of $\bar{X}$, $\sigma_X/\sqrt{n}$, is equal to $50/\sqrt{4} = 25$. If the sample size is 25, the standard deviation is 10. If it is 100, the standard deviation is 5. Figure R.39 shows the corresponding probability density functions. The larger is the sample size, the narrower and taller is the probability density function of $\bar{X}$. As n tends to infinity, the probability density function will collapse to a vertical spike located at μ_X. Formally,

$$\lim_{n\to\infty} P\left(|\bar{X} - \mu_X| > \varepsilon\right) \to 0. \qquad \textbf{(R.91)}$$

The probability of $\bar{X}$ differing from μ_X by any finite amount ε, however small, tends to zero as n becomes large. More simply,

$$\text{plim } \bar{X} = \mu_X. \qquad \textbf{(R.92)}$$

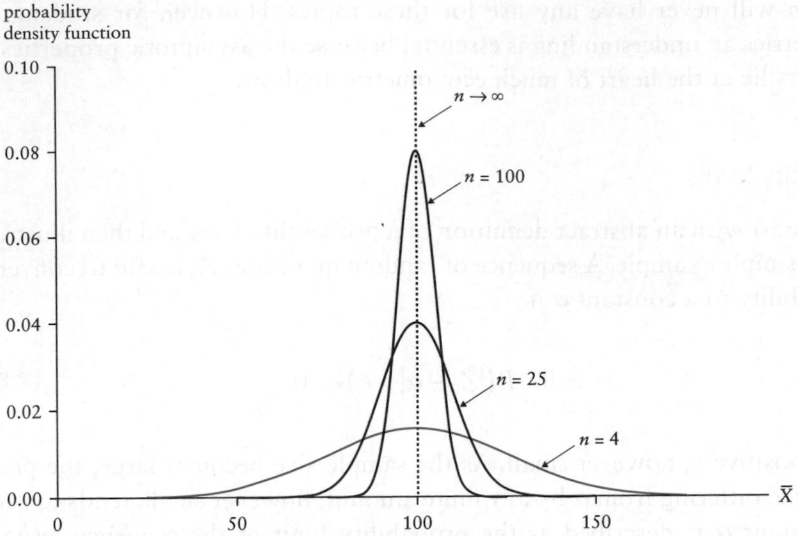

Figure R.39 Effect of increasing the sample size on the distribution of $\overline{X}$

Consistency

An estimator of a population characteristic is said to be consistent if it satisfies two conditions:

1. it possesses a probability limit, and so its distribution collapses to a spike as the sample size becomes large, and
2. the spike is located at the true value of the population characteristic.

The sample mean $\overline{X}$ in our example satisfies both conditions and so it is a consistent estimator of μ_X. Most standard estimators in simple applications satisfy the first condition because their variances are inversely proportional to n and so tend to zero as the sample size becomes large. The only issue then is whether the distribution collapses to a spike at the true value of the population characteristic.

A sufficient condition for consistency is that the estimator should be unbiased and that its variance should tend to zero as n becomes large. It is easy to see why this is a sufficient condition. If the estimator is unbiased for a finite sample, it must stay unbiased as the sample size becomes large. Meanwhile, if the variance of its distribution is inversely proportional to n, its distribution must collapse to a spike. Since the estimator remains unbiased, this spike must be located at the true value. The sample mean is an example of an estimator that satisfies this sufficient condition.

However, the condition is only sufficient, not necessary. It is possible for a biased estimator to be consistent, if the bias vanishes as the sample size becomes large. This is illustrated in principle in Figure R.40. The estimator is biased upwards for finite samples, but nevertheless it is consistent because (1) the bias attenuates as n becomes large, and (2) its distribution collapses to a spike at the true value.

Consider the following estimator of a sample mean

$$Z = \frac{1}{n+1}\sum_{i=1}^{n} X_i. \qquad \textbf{(R.93)}$$

It is biased downwards because

$$E(Z) = \frac{n}{n+1}\mu_X. \qquad \textbf{(R.94)}$$

However, the bias will disappear asymptotically because $n/(n+1)$ will tend to 1. The distribution is said to be asymptotically unbiased because the expectation tends to the true value as the sample size becomes large. The variance of the estimator is given by

$$\operatorname{var}(Z) = \frac{n}{(n+1)^2}\sigma_X^2, \qquad \textbf{(R.95)}$$

which tends to zero as n becomes large. Thus, Z is consistent because its distribution collapses to a spike at the true value.

An estimator is described as inconsistent if its distribution collapses at a point other than the true value. It is also described as inconsistent if its distribution fails to collapse as the sample size becomes large. See Exercise R.37 for a simple example of a non-collapsing distribution. In practice, the distributions of most

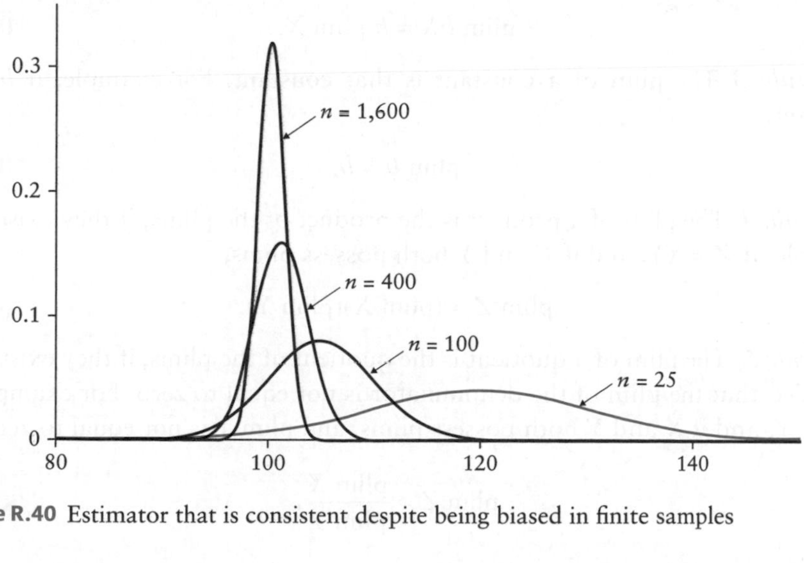

Figure R.40 Estimator that is consistent despite being biased in finite samples

estimators do collapse to a spike and the only issue is whether the spike is at the right value.

Why is consistency of interest?

In practice we deal with finite samples, not infinite ones. So why should we be interested in whether an estimator is consistent? Is this not just an abstract, academic exercise?

One reason for our interest is that estimators of the type shown in Figure R.40 are common in regression analysis, as we shall see later in this text. Sometimes it is impossible to find an estimator that is unbiased for small samples. If you can find one that is at least consistent, that may be better than having no estimator at all, especially if you are able to assess the direction of the bias in finite samples.

A second reason is that often we are unable to say anything at all about the expectation of an estimator. The expected value rules are weak analytical instruments that can be applied only in relatively simple contexts. In particular, the multiplicative rule $E\{g(X)h(Y)\} = E\{g(X)\}\ E\{h(Y)\}$ applies only when X and Y are independent, and in many situations of interest this will not be the case. By contrast, we have a much more powerful set of rules for plims. The first three are the counterparts of those for expectations. The remainder are new.

Plim rule 1 The plim of the sum of several variables is equal to the sum of their plims. For example, if you have three random variables X, Y, and Z, each possessing a plim,

$$\text{plim}\ (X + Y + Z) = \text{plim}\ X + \text{plim}\ Y + \text{plim}\ Z. \quad \textbf{(R.96)}$$

Plim rule 2 If you multiply a random variable possessing a plim by a constant, you multiply its plim by the same constant. If X is a random variable and b is a constant,

$$\text{plim}\ bX = b\ \text{plim}\ X. \quad \textbf{(R.97)}$$

Plim rule 3 The plim of a constant is that constant. For example, if b is a constant,

$$\text{plim}\ b = b. \quad \textbf{(R.98)}$$

Plim rule 4 The plim of a product is the product of the plims, if they exist. For example, if $Z = XY$, and if X and Y both possess plims,

$$\text{plim}\ Z = (\text{plim}\ X)(\text{plim}\ Y). \quad \textbf{(R.99)}$$

Plim rule 5 The plim of a quotient is the quotient of the plims, if they exist, and provided that the plim of the denominator is not equal to zero. For example, if $Z = X/Y$, and if X and Y both possess plims, and plim Y is not equal to zero,

$$\text{plim}\ Z = \frac{\text{plim}\ X}{\text{plim}\ Y}. \quad \textbf{(R.100)}$$

Plim rule 6 The plim of a function of a variable is equal to the function of the plim of the variable, provided that the variable possesses a plim and provided that the function is continuous at that point,

$$\text{plim } f(X) = f(\text{plim } X). \qquad \textbf{(R.101)}$$

To illustrate how the plim rules can lead us to conclusions when the expected value rules do not, consider the following example. Suppose that we hypothesize that a variable Y is a constant multiple of another variable Z:

$$Y = \alpha Z. \qquad \textbf{(R.102)}$$

Z is generated randomly from a fixed distribution with population mean μ_Z and variance σ_Z^2. α is unknown and we wish to estimate it. We have a sample of n observations. Y is measured accurately but Z is measured with random error w with population mean zero and constant variance σ_w^2. Thus, in the sample, we have observations on X, where

$$X = Z + w \qquad \textbf{(R.103)}$$

rather than Z. One estimator of α (not necessarily the best) is $\overline{Y}/\overline{X}$. Given (R.102) and (R.103),

$$\frac{\overline{Y}}{\overline{X}} = \frac{\alpha\overline{Z}}{\overline{Z}+\overline{w}} = \alpha - \alpha\frac{\overline{w}}{\overline{Z}+\overline{w}}. \qquad \textbf{(R.104)}$$

Hence, we have decomposed the estimator into the true value, α, and an error term. To investigate whether the estimator is biased or unbiased, we need to take the expectation of the error term. But we cannot do this. The random quantity $\overline{w}$ appears in both the numerator and the denominator and the expected value rules are too weak to allow us to investigate the expectation analytically. However, we can invoke a law of large numbers that states that, under reasonable assumptions, a sample mean tends to a population mean as the sample size tends to infinity. Hence plim $\overline{w} = 0$ and plim $\overline{Z} = \mu_Z$. Since the plims exist,

$$\text{plim}\left\{\frac{\overline{Y}}{\overline{X}}\right\} = \alpha - \alpha\frac{\text{plim } \overline{w}}{\text{plim } \overline{Z} + \text{plim } \overline{w}} = \alpha - \frac{0}{\mu_Z + 0} = \alpha \qquad \textbf{(R.105)}$$

(provided $\mu_Z \neq 0$). Thus, we are able to show that the estimator is consistent, despite the fact that we cannot say anything about its finite sample properties.

This subsection started out by asking why we are interested in consistency. As a first approximation, the answer is that if we can show that an estimator is consistent, then we may be optimistic about its finite sample properties, whereas if the estimator is inconsistent, in the sense of its distribution collapsing to a spike at the wrong value, we know that for finite samples it will definitely be biased. However, there are reasons for being cautious about preferring consistent estimators to inconsistent ones. First, a consistent estimator may also be biased for finite samples. Second, we are usually also interested in variances. If a consistent estimator has a larger variance than an inconsistent one, the latter might be preferable if judged by the mean square error or a similar criterion that allows a trade-off between bias and variance. How can you resolve these issues? Mathematically they are intractable, otherwise we would not have resorted to large-sample analysis in the first place.

Simulations

The answer is to conduct a **simulation**, directly investigating the distributions of estimators under controlled conditions. We will do this for the example in the previous subsection. We will generate Z as a random variable with a normal distribution with mean 1 and variance 0.25. We will set α equal to 5, so

$$Y = 5Z. \quad \textbf{(R.106)}$$

We will generate the measurement error as a normally distributed random variable with zero mean and unit variance. The value of X in any observation is equal to the value of Z plus this measurement error. Figure R.41 shows the distributions of $\overline{Y}/\overline{X}$ for sample sizes 25, 100, 400, and 1,600, in each case for 10 million samples.

We can see that the standard deviation of the distribution, and hence its variance, diminishes as the sample size increases and it is reasonable to suppose that if the sample size became very large the distribution would collapse to a spike. Further, it is clear that the mean of the distribution is approaching the true value, 5. The actual numbers are given in Table R.7. Although there is some element of bias for a sample of 25 observations, it has mostly disappeared for

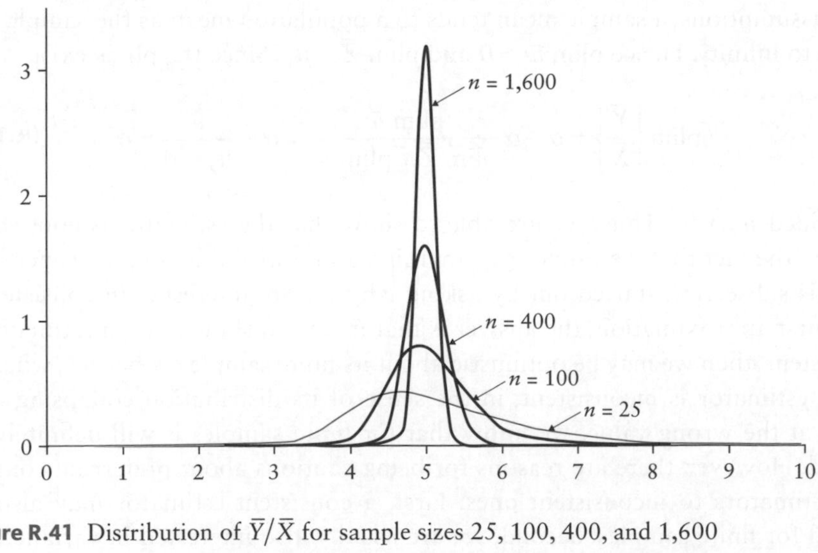

Figure R.41 Distribution of $\overline{Y}/\overline{X}$ for sample sizes 25, 100, 400, and 1,600

Table R.7

Sample size	Mean	Standard deviation
25	5.217	1.181
100	5.052	0.524
400	5.013	0.253
1,600	5.003	0.125

samples of 100 observations and the estimator is virtually unbiased for samples of size 1,600.

Of course, these conclusions are valid only for the particular way in which Z, Y, and X have been generated. However, the conclusions would have been qualitatively the same if we had had a different mean for Z, different standard deviations for Z and the measurement error, or a different value of α. The estimator would have been biased for finite samples, with a skewed distribution, but it would be consistent. We might have found different results for the rate of attenuation of the bias as a function of the sample size. If we were serious about investigating the properties of the estimator, we would perform some further sensitivity analysis. The purpose here was only to show how simulation might in principle shed light where mathematical analysis cannot.

EXERCISES

R.36 A random variable X has unknown population mean μ_X and population variance σ_X^2. A sample of n observations $\{X_1, ..., X_n\}$ is generated. The average of the odd-numbered observations is used to estimate μ_X. Determine whether this estimator is consistent.

R.37* A random variable X has unknown population mean μ_X and population variance σ_X^2. A sample of n observations $\{X_1, ..., X_n\}$ is generated. Show that

$$Z = \frac{1}{2}X_1 + \frac{1}{4}X_2 + \frac{1}{8}X_3 + \cdots + \frac{1}{2^{n-1}}X_{n-1} + \frac{1}{2^{n-1}}X_n$$

is an unbiased estimator of μ_X. Show that the variance of Z does not tend to zero as n tends to infinity and that therefore Z is an inconsistent estimator, despite being unbiased.

R.38 A random variable X has population mean μ and variance σ^2. Given a sample of n independent observations X_i, $i = 1, ..., n$, determine whether the following estimators of μ are consistent (you may assume that $\bar{X}$ is a consistent estimator):

(a) $$\frac{n+2}{n^2+3n+1}\sum_{i=1}^{n} X_i$$

(b) $$\sum_{i=1}^{n} X_i^2 \Big/ \sum_{i=1}^{n} X_i \, .$$

R.15 Convergence in distribution and central limit theorems

If a random variable X has a normal distribution, its sample mean $\bar{X}$ will also have a normal distribution. This fact is useful for the construction of t statistics and confidence intervals if we are employing $\bar{X}$ as an estimator of the population mean. However, what happens if we are *not* able to assume that X is normally distributed?

The standard response is to make use of a central limit theorem. Loosely speaking (we will make a more rigorous statement below), a central limit theorem states that the distribution of $\bar{X}$ will approximate a normal distribution as the sample size becomes large, even if the distribution of X is not normal. There are a number of central limit theorems, differing only in the assumptions that they make in order to obtain this result. Here we shall be content with using the simplest one, the Lindeberg–Levy central limit theorem. It states that, provided that the X_i in the sample are all drawn independently from the same distribution (the distribution of X), and provided that this distribution has finite population mean and variance, the distribution of $\bar{X}$ will converge to a normal distribution. This means that our t statistics and confidence intervals will be approximately valid after all, provided that the sample size is large enough. Of course, we will need to clarify what we mean by 'large enough'.

We will start by looking at two examples. Figure R.42 shows the distribution of $\bar{X}$ for the case where the X has a uniform distribution with range 0 to 1, for 10 million samples. A uniform distribution is one in which all values over the range in question are equally likely. For a sample size of 1, the distribution is the uniform distribution itself, and so it is a horizontal line. The figure also shows the distribution of the sample mean for sample sizes 10, 25, and 100, in each case for 10 million samples. It can be seen that the mean has a distribution very close to a normal distribution even when the sample size is only 10, and for larger sample sizes the approximation is even better.

Figure R.43 shows the corresponding distributions for the case where the underlying distribution is lognormal. A random variable is said to have

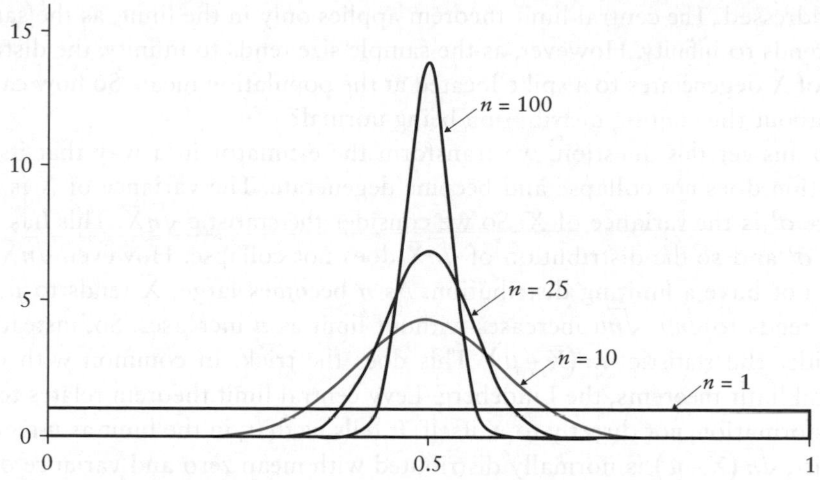

Figure R.42 Distribution of sample mean from a uniform distribution

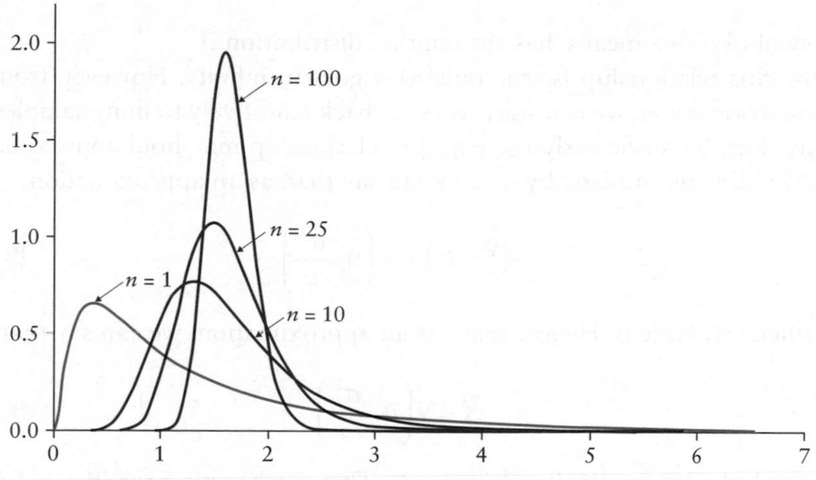

Figure R.43 Distribution of sample mean from a lognormal distribution

a lognormal distribution when its logarithm has a normal distribution. Like the normal distribution, the lognormal distribution is actually a two-parameter family of distributions. The one shown here is based on the standardized normal distribution (log X has a normal distribution with zero mean and unit variance).

As can be seen from the distribution for $n = 1$, the lognormal distribution is highly skewed. Even so, the distribution of $\bar{X}$ is becoming normal-like with sample size 25, and closer still for sample size 100.

In asserting that the distribution of $\bar{X}$ tends to become normal as the sample size increases, we have glossed over an important technical point that needs to be addressed. The central limit theorem applies only in the limit, as the sample size tends to infinity. However, as the sample size tends to infinity, the distribution of $\bar{X}$ degenerates to a spike located at the population mean. So how can we talk about the limiting distribution being normal?

To answer this question, we transform the estimator in a way that its distribution does not collapse and become degenerate. The variance of $\bar{X}$ is σ^2/n, where σ^2 is the variance of X. So we consider the statistic $\sqrt{n}\bar{X}$. This has variance σ^2 and so the distribution of $\sqrt{n}\bar{X}$ does not collapse. However, $\sqrt{n}\bar{X}$ still does not have a limiting distribution. As n becomes large, $\bar{X}$ tends to μ, and $\sqrt{n}\bar{X}$ tends to $\sqrt{n}\mu$. $\sqrt{n}\mu$ increases without limit as n increases. So, instead, we consider the statistic $\sqrt{n}\left(\bar{X}-\mu\right)$. This does the trick. In common with other central limit theorems, the Lindeberg–Levy central limit theorem relates to this transformation, not directly to $\bar{X}$ itself. It tells us that, in the limit as n tends to infinity, $\sqrt{n}\left(\bar{X}-\mu\right)$ is normally distributed with mean zero and variance σ^2. To put this in mathematical notation,

$$\sqrt{n}\left(\bar{X}-\mu\right) \xrightarrow{d} N\left(0,\ \sigma^2\right). \tag{R.107}$$

(The symbol $\xrightarrow{d}$ means 'has the limiting distribution'.)

Now this relationship is true only as n goes to infinity. However, from the limiting distribution, we can start working back tentatively to finite samples. We can say that, for sufficiently large n, the relationship may hold approximately. Then, dividing the statistic by $\sqrt{n}$, we can say that, as an approximation,

$$\left(\bar{X}-\mu\right) \sim N\left(0,\ \frac{\sigma^2}{n}\right) \tag{R.108}$$

for sufficiently large n. Hence, again as an approximation, we can say that

$$\bar{X} \sim N\left(\mu,\ \frac{\sigma^2}{n}\right). \tag{R.109}$$

(The symbol ~ means 'is distributed as'.) This is what we have in mind when we say that $\bar{X}$ is asymptotically distributed as a normal random variable, even though X itself is not.

Of course, this begs the question of what might be considered to be 'sufficiently large' n. To answer this question, the analysis must be supplemented by simulation. Figure R.44 shows the distribution of $\sqrt{n}\left(\bar{X}-\mu\right)$ for the uniform distribution. It is the counterpart of Figure R.42. You can see that the distributions for $n = 10$, 25, and 100 virtually coincide. This is because the distribution is almost perfectly normal for $n = 10$. Figure R.45 shows this more clearly. It compares the distribution for $n = 10$ with the limiting normal distribution (the dashed curve with a slightly higher mode). Thus, in the case of the uniform distribution, a sample size of 10 is sufficiently large.

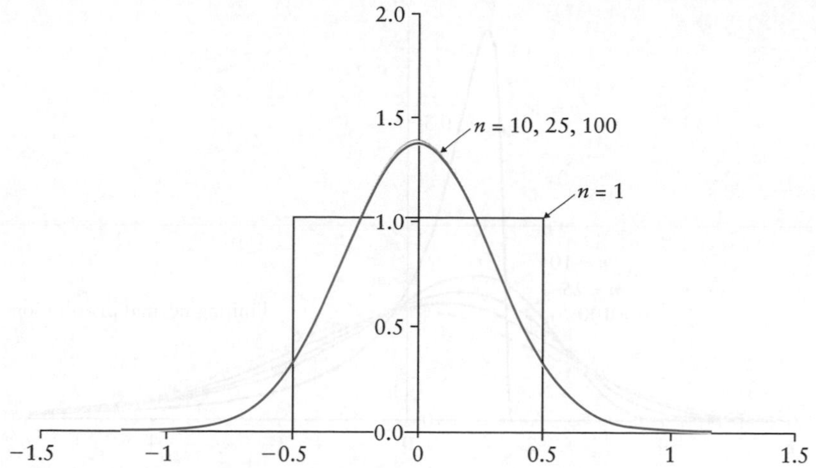

Figure R.44 Distribution of $\sqrt{n}\left(\overline{X}-\mu\right)$ for a uniform distribution

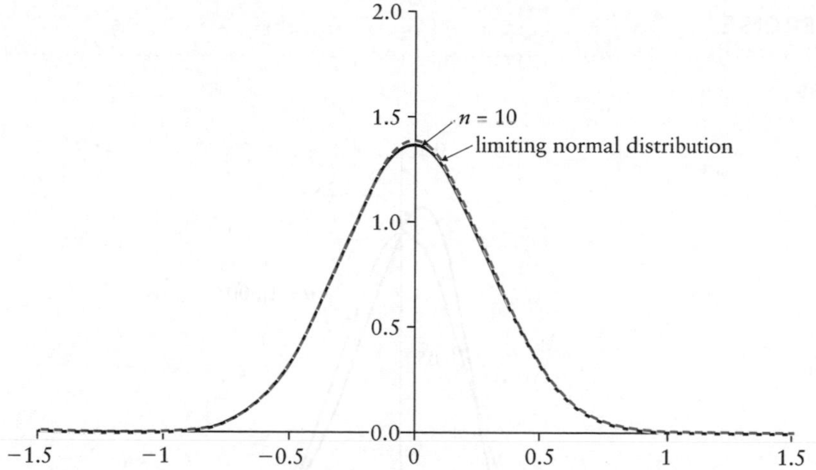

Figure R.45 Distribution of $\sqrt{n}\left(\overline{X}-\mu\right)$ for a uniform distribution, $n = 10$, and limiting normal distribution

Figure R.46 shows the distribution of $\sqrt{n}\left(\overline{X}-\mu\right)$ for the lognormal distribution. Here, we would come to a very different conclusion. In this case, it is evident that a sample size of 100 is not sufficiently large. Even with 100 observations, the distribution of $\sqrt{n}\left(\overline{X}-\mu\right)$ is still clearly different from that of the limiting normal distribution and, as a consequence, the use of conventional test statistics would be likely to lead to misleading results.

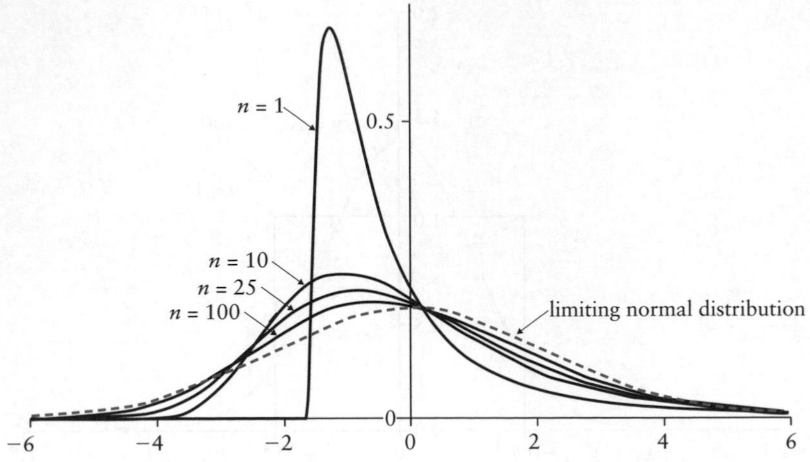

Figure R.46 Distribution of $\sqrt{n}\,(\overline{X}-\mu)$ for a lognormal distribution

EXERCISE

R.39

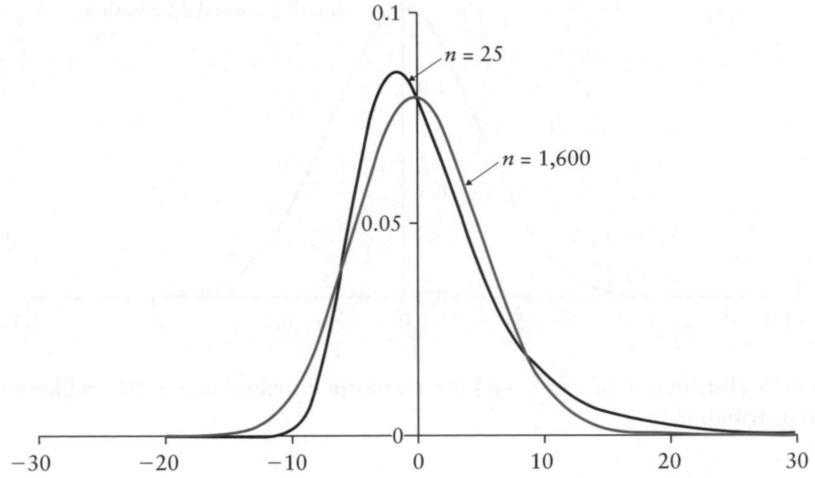

The figure shows the distribution of $\sqrt{n}\left(\frac{\overline{Y}}{\overline{X}}-5\right)$ for the simulation discussed at the end of Section R.14, with $n = 25$ and $n = 1{,}600$. (For clarity, the distributions for $n = 100$ and $n = 400$ have been omitted.) Comment on the relationship between these distributions and the corresponding ones in Figure R.41. Discuss whether one could use $\overline{Y}/\overline{X}$ as a test statistic for hypotheses relating to α.

Key terms

- acceptance region
- alternative hypothesis
- asymptotic properties
- bias, biased
- central limit theorem
- consistent, consistency
- continuous random variable
- degrees of freedom
- discrete random variable
- double structure of a variable
- efficient, efficiency
- estimate
- estimator
- expected value
- inconsistent, inconsistency
- independence
- limiting distribution
- loss function
- mean square error
- normal distribution
- null hypothesis
- one-sided test
- outcome
- plim
- population
- population correlation coefficient
- population covariance
- population mean
- population variance
- power of a test
- probability density function
- probability limit
- realization
- rejection region
- sample correlation coefficient
- significance level of a test
- simulation
- size of a test
- standard error
- standardized normal distribution
- *t* distribution
- *t* statistic
- Type I error
- Type II error
- unbiased

Appendix R.1: Unbiased estimators of the population covariance and variance

We will start with the estimator of the population covariance. The proof of the unbiasedness of the estimator of population variance follows immediately if one treats variances as special cases of covariances.

The estimator of the population covariance of X and Y is

$$s_{XY} = \frac{1}{n-1}\sum_{i=1}^{n}\left(X_i - \bar{X}\right)\left(Y_i - \bar{Y}\right).$$

Rewrite it as

$$s_{XY} = \frac{1}{n-1}\sum_{i=1}^{n}\left(X_i - \mu_X + \mu_X - \bar{X}\right)\left(Y_i - \mu_Y + \mu_Y - \bar{Y}\right).$$

Then

$$s_{XY} = \frac{1}{n-1}\sum_{i=1}^{n}(X_i - \mu_X)(Y_i - \mu_Y) + \frac{1}{n-1}\sum_{i=1}^{n}(X_i - \mu_X)(\mu_Y - \bar{Y})$$
$$+ \frac{1}{n-1}\sum_{i=1}^{n}(\mu_X - \bar{X})(Y_i - \mu_Y) + \frac{1}{n-1}\sum_{i=1}^{n}(\mu_X - \bar{X})(\mu_Y - \bar{Y}).$$

In the second term, $(\mu_Y - \bar{Y})$ is a common factor and can be taken out of the expression. Similarly, in the third term, $(\mu_X - \bar{X})$ is a common factor and can be taken out. The summation in the fourth term consists of n identical products $(\mu_X - \bar{X})(\mu_Y - \bar{Y})$ and is thus equal to $n(\mu_X - \bar{X})(\mu_Y - \bar{Y})$. Hence,

$$s_{XY} = \frac{1}{n-1}\sum_{i=1}^{n}(X_i - \mu_X)(Y_i - \mu_Y) + \frac{1}{n-1}(\mu_Y - \bar{Y})\sum_{i=1}^{n}(X_i - \mu_X)$$
$$+ \frac{1}{n-1}(\mu_X - \bar{X})\sum_{i=1}^{n}(Y_i - \mu_Y) + \frac{n}{n-1}(\mu_X - \bar{X})(\mu_Y - \bar{Y}).$$

Now

$$\sum_{i=1}^{n}(X_i - \mu_X) = \sum_{i=1}^{n}X_i - n\mu_X = n(\bar{X} - \mu_X)$$

and similarly,

$$\sum_{i=1}^{n}(Y_i - \mu_Y) = \sum_{i=1}^{n}Y_i - n\mu_Y = n(\bar{Y} - \mu_Y).$$

Hence,

$$s_{XY} = \frac{1}{n-1}\sum_{i=1}^{n}(X_i - \mu_X)(Y_i - \mu_Y) + \frac{n}{n-1}(\mu_Y - \bar{Y})(\bar{X} - \mu_X)$$
$$+ \frac{n}{n-1}(\mu_X - \bar{X})(\bar{Y} - \mu_Y) + \frac{n}{n-1}(\mu_X - \bar{X})(\mu_Y - \bar{Y})$$
$$= \frac{1}{n-1}\sum_{i=1}^{n}(X_i - \mu_X)(Y_i - \mu_Y) - \frac{n}{n-1}(\bar{X} - \mu_X)(\bar{Y} - \mu_Y)$$
$$- \frac{n}{n-1}(\bar{X} - \mu_X)(\bar{Y} - \mu_Y) + \frac{n}{n-1}(\bar{X} - \mu_X)(\bar{Y} - \mu_Y)$$
$$= \frac{1}{n-1}\sum_{i=1}^{n}(X_i - \mu_X)(Y_i - \mu_Y) - \frac{n}{n-1}(\bar{X} - \mu_X)(\bar{Y} - \mu_Y).$$

Now

$$\left(\bar{X}-\mu_X\right)=\frac{1}{n}\sum_{i=1}^{n}\left(X_i-\mu_X\right) \quad \text{and} \quad \left(\bar{Y}-\mu_Y\right)=\frac{1}{n}\sum_{j=1}^{n}\left(Y_j-\mu_Y\right)$$

Hence,

$$\begin{aligned} s_{XY} &= \frac{1}{n-1}\sum_{i=1}^{n}(X_i-\mu_X)(Y_i-\mu_Y) - \frac{n}{n-1}\frac{1}{n}\sum_{i=1}^{n}(X_i-\mu_X)\frac{1}{n}\sum_{j=1}^{n}(Y_j-\mu_Y) \\ &= \frac{1}{n-1}\sum_{i=1}^{n}(X_i-\mu_X)(Y_i-\mu_Y) - \frac{1}{n(n-1)}\sum_{i=1}^{n}\sum_{j=1}^{n}(X_i-\mu_X)(Y_j-\mu_Y). \end{aligned}$$

By definition, the expected value of any component $\left(X_i-\mu_X\right)\left(Y_j-\mu_Y\right)$ is the population covariance σ_{XY} when j is the same as i. There are n such components in the first term of s_{XY} and n in the second. (There are also $n(n-1)$ components $\left(X_i-\mu_X\right)\left(Y_j-\mu_Y\right)$ in the second term, with j different from i. These have expected value zero.) Hence,

$$E\left(s_{XY}\right)=\frac{1}{n-1}n\sigma_{XY} - \frac{1}{n(n-1)}n\sigma_{XY} = \frac{n-1}{n-1}\sigma_{XY} = \sigma_{XY}$$

and so s_{XY} is an unbiased estimator of the population covariance.

In the special case where Y is the same as X, s_{XY} is s_X^2 and σ_{XY} is σ_X^2. Hence, we have also proved that s_X^2 is an unbiased estimator of the population variance of X.

Appendix R.2: Density functions of transformed random variables

Occasionally, we will need to determine the density functions of transformed random variables. Suppose that we have a random variable Y with density function $f(Y)$. Suppose Z is a transformation of Y:

$$Z=h(Y).$$

What can we say about the density function of Z, $g(Z)$? To keep things simple, we shall assume that $f(Y)$ and $h(Y)$ are both continuous and differentiable and that Z is either an increasing function of Y or a decreasing function. Then, if Y lies in the range $[y_1, y_2]$, Z must lie in the range $[z_1, z_2]$, where $z_1 = h(y_1)$ and $z_2 = h(y_2)$. So the probability of Z lying in the range $[z_1, z_2]$ is equal to the probability of Y lying in the range $[y_1, y_2]$. Mathematically,

$$\int_{z_1}^{z_2} g(Z)\,dZ = \int_{y_1}^{y_2} f(Y)\,dY.$$

Thus, at the margin,

$$g(Z)\,dZ = f(Y)\,dY$$

and so

$$g(Z) = \frac{f(Y)}{dZ/dY}.$$

For example, suppose that $Z = \log(Y)$. Then

$$g(Z) = \frac{f(Y)}{1/Y} = Y f(Y).$$

1. Simple Regression Analysis

This chapter shows how a hypothetical linear relationship between two variables can be quantified using appropriate data. The principle of least squares regression analysis is explained, and expressions for the coefficients are derived.

1.1 The simple linear model

The correlation coefficient may indicate that two variables are associated with one another, but it does not give any idea of the kind of relationship involved. We will now take the investigation a step further in those cases for which we are willing to hypothesize that one variable, usually known as the dependent variable, is determined by other variables, usually known as explanatory variables, independent variables, or regressors. The hypothesized mathematical relationship linking them is known as the regression model. If there is only one regressor, as will be assumed in this chapter and the next, it is described as a simple regression model. If there are two or more regressors, it is described as a multiple regression model.

It must be stated immediately that one would not expect to find an exact relationship between any two economic variables, unless it is true as a matter of definition. In textbook expositions of economic theory, the usual way of dealing with this awkward fact is to write down the relationship as if it were exact and to warn the reader that it is really only an approximation. In statistical analysis, however, one generally acknowledges the fact that the relationship is not exact by explicitly including in it a random factor known as the disturbance term.

We shall start with the simple regression model:

$$Y_i = \beta_1 + \beta_2 X_i + u_i. \tag{1.1}$$

Y_i, the value of the dependent variable in observation i, has two components: (1) the nonrandom component $\beta_1 + \beta_2 X_i$, where β_1 and β_2 are fixed quantities known as the parameters of the equation and X_i is the value of the explanatory variable in observation i, and (2) the disturbance term, u_i.

Figure 1.1 illustrates how these two components combine to determine Y. X_1, X_2, X_3, and X_4 are four hypothetical values of the explanatory variable. If the relationship between Y and X were exact, the corresponding values of Y would

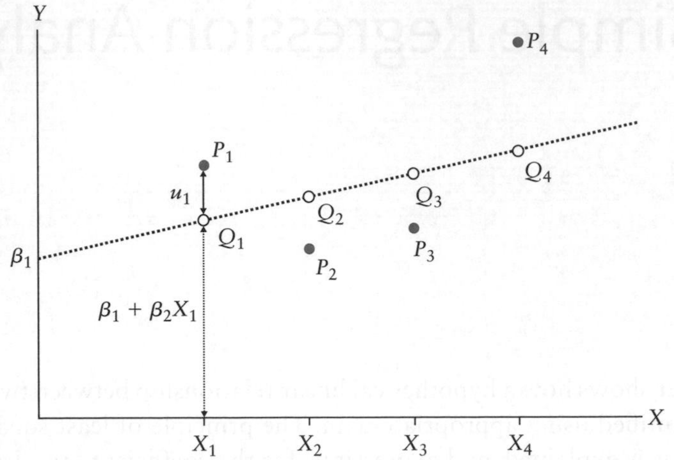

Figure 1.1 True relationship between Y and X

be represented by the points $Q_1 - Q_4$ on the line. The disturbance term causes the actual values of Y to be different. In the diagram, the disturbance term has been assumed to be positive in the first and fourth observations and negative in the other two, with the result that, if one plots the actual values of Y against the values of X, one obtains the points $P_1 - P_4$.

It must be emphasized that in practice the P points are all one can see of Figure 1.1. The actual values of β_1 and β_2, and hence the location of the Q points, are unknown, as are the values of the disturbance term in the observations. The task of regression analysis is to obtain estimates of β_1 and β_2, and hence an estimate of the location of the line, given the P points.

Why does the disturbance term exist? There are several reasons.

1. *Omission of explanatory variables*: The relationship between Y and X is almost certain to be a simplification. In reality, there will be other factors affecting Y that have been left out of equation (1.1), and their influence will cause the points to lie off the line. It often happens that there are variables that you would like to include in the regression equation but cannot because you are unable to measure them. For example, later on in this chapter we will fit an earnings function relating hourly earnings to years of schooling. We know very well that schooling is not the only determinant of earnings and eventually we will improve the model by including other variables, such as years of work experience. However, even the best specified earnings function accounts for at most half of the variation in earnings. Many other factors affect the chances of obtaining a good job, such as the unmeasurable attributes of an individual, and even pure luck in the sense of the individual finding a job that is a good match for his or her attributes. All of these other factors contribute to the disturbance term.

2. *Aggregation of variables*: In many cases, the relationship is an attempt to summarize in aggregate a number of microeconomic relationships. For example, the aggregate consumption function is an attempt to summarize a set of individual expenditure decisions. Since the individual relationships are likely to have different parameters, any attempt to relate aggregate expenditure to aggregate income can only be an approximation. The discrepancy is attributed to the disturbance term.
3. *Model misspecification*: The model may be misspecified in terms of its structure. Just to give one of the many possible examples, if the relationship refers to time series data, the value of Y may depend not on the actual value of X but on the value that had been anticipated in the previous period. If the anticipated and actual values are closely related, there will appear to be a relationship between Y and X, but it will only be an approximation, and again the disturbance term will pick up the discrepancy.
4. *Functional misspecification*: The functional relationship between Y and X may be misspecified mathematically. For example, the true relationship may be nonlinear instead of linear. We will consider the fitting of nonlinear relationships in Chapter 4. Obviously, one should try to avoid this problem by using an appropriate mathematical specification, but even the most sophisticated specification is likely to be only an approximation, and the discrepancy contributes to the disturbance term.
5. *Measurement error*: If the measurement of one or more of the variables in the relationship is subject to error, the observed values will not appear to conform to an exact relationship, and the discrepancy contributes to the disturbance term.

The disturbance term is the collective outcome of all these factors. Obviously, if you were concerned only with measuring the effect of X on Y, it would be much more convenient if the disturbance term did not exist. Were it not for its presence, the P points in Figure 1.1 would coincide with the Q points, you would know that every change in Y from observation to observation was due to a change in X, and you would be able to calculate β_1 and β_2 exactly. However, in fact, part of each change in Y is due to a change in u, and this makes life more difficult. For this reason, u is sometimes described as noise.

1.2 Least squares regression with one explanatory variable

Suppose that you are given the four observations on X and Y represented in Figure 1.1 and you are asked to obtain estimates of the values of β_1 and β_2 in equation (1.1). As a rough approximation, you could do this by plotting the four P points and drawing a line to fit them as best you can. This has been done in Figure 1.2. The intersection of the line with the Y-axis provides an estimate of the intercept β_1, which will be denoted b_1, and the slope provides an estimate of

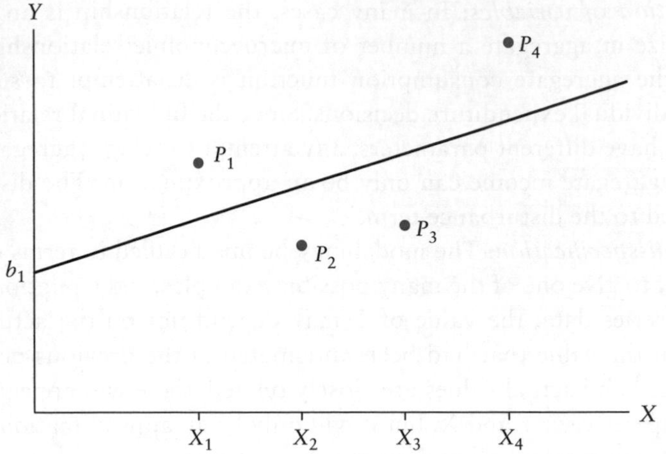

Figure 1.2 Fitted line

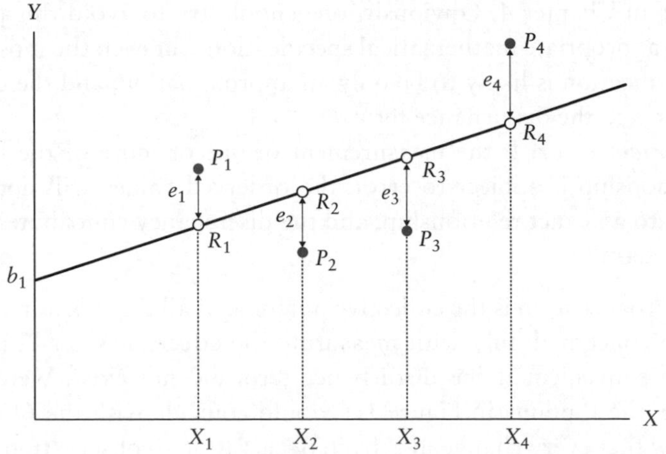

Figure 1.3 Fitted regression line showing residuals

the slope coefficient β_2, which will be denoted b_2. The line, known as the fitted model, will be written

$$\hat{Y}_i = b_1 + b_2 X_i, \tag{1.2}$$

the caret mark over Y indicating that it is the **fitted value** of Y corresponding to X, not the actual value. In Figure 1.3, the fitted points are represented by the points $R_1 - R_4$.

One thing that should be accepted from the beginning is that you can never discover the true values of β_1 and β_2, however much care you take in drawing the line. b_1 and b_2 are only estimates, and they may be good or bad. Once in a while your estimates may be absolutely accurate, but this can only be by coincidence, and even then you will have no way of knowing that you have hit the target exactly.

This remains the case even when you use more sophisticated techniques. Drawing a regression line by eye is all very well, but it leaves a lot to subjective judgment. Furthermore, as will become obvious, it is not even possible when you have a variable Y depending on two or more explanatory variables instead of only one. The question arises, is there a way of calculating good estimates of β_1 and β_2 algebraically?

The first step is to define what is known as a **residual** for each observation. This is the difference between the actual value of Y in any observation and the fitted value given by the regression line: that is, the vertical distance between P_i and R_i in observation i. It will be denoted e_i:

$$e_i = Y_i - \hat{Y}_i. \tag{1.3}$$

The residuals for the four observations are shown in Figure 1.3. Substituting (1.2) into (1.3), we obtain

$$e_i = Y_i - b_1 - b_2 X_i \tag{1.4}$$

and hence the residual in each observation depends on our choice of b_1 and b_2. Obviously, we wish to fit the regression line, that is, choose b_1 and b_2, in such a way as to make the residuals as small as possible. Equally obviously, a line that fits some observations well will fit others badly and vice versa. We need to devise a criterion of fit that takes account of the size of all the residuals simultaneously.

There are a number of possible criteria, some of which work better than others. It is useless minimizing the sum of the residuals, for example. The sum will automatically be equal to zero if you make $b_1 = \overline{Y}$ and $b_2 = 0$, obtaining the horizontal line $Y = \overline{Y}$. The positive residuals will then exactly balance the negative ones but, other than this, the line will not fit the observations.

One way of overcoming the problem is to minimize *RSS*, the **residual sum of squares** (sum of the squares of the residuals). For Figure 1.3,

$$RSS = e_1^2 + e_2^2 + e_3^2 + e_4^2. \tag{1.5}$$

The smaller one can make *RSS*, the better is the fit, according to this criterion. If one could reduce *RSS* to zero, one would have a perfect fit, for this would imply that all the residuals are equal to zero. The line would go through all the points, but of course in general the disturbance term makes this impossible.

There are other quite reasonable solutions, but the **least squares criterion** yields estimates of β_1 and β_2 that are unbiased and the most efficient of their type, provided that certain conditions are satisfied. For this reason, the least squares technique is far and away the most popular in uncomplicated applications of regression analysis. The form used here is usually referred to as **ordinary least squares** and abbreviated OLS. Variants designed to cope with particular problems will be discussed later in the text.

1.3 Derivation of the regression coefficients

We will begin with a very simple example with only three observations, just to show the mechanics working. Y is observed to be equal to 3 when X is equal to 1, 5 when X is equal to 2, and 6 when X is equal to 3, as shown in Figure 1.4.

We shall assume that the true model is

$$Y_i = \beta_1 + \beta_2 X_i + u_i \tag{1.6}$$

and we shall estimate the coefficients b_1 and b_2 of the equation

$$\hat{Y}_i = b_1 + b_2 X_i. \tag{1.7}$$

When X is equal to 1, $\hat{Y}$ is equal to $(b_1 + b_2)$, according to the regression line. When X is equal to 2, $\hat{Y}$ is equal to $(b_1 + 2b_2)$. When X is equal to 3, $\hat{Y}$ is equal to $(b_1 + 3b_2)$. Therefore, we can set up Table 1.1. So the residual for the first observation, e_1, which is given by $(Y_1 - \hat{Y}_1)$, is equal to $(3 - b_1 - b_2)$. Similarly, $e_2 = Y_2 - \hat{Y}_2 = 5 - b_1 - 2b_2$ and $e_3 = Y_3 - \hat{Y}_3 = 6 - b_1 - 3b_2$. Hence,

$$\begin{aligned} RSS &= (3 - b_1 - b_2)^2 + (5 - b_1 - 2b_2)^2 + (6 - b_1 - 3b_2)^2 \\ &= 9 + b_1^2 + b_2^2 - 6b_1 - 6b_2 + 2b_1b_2 \\ &\quad + 25 + b_1^2 + 4b_2^2 - 10b_1 - 20b_2 + 4b_1b_2 \\ &\quad + 36 + b_1^2 + 9b_2^2 - 12b_1 - 36b_2 + 6b_1b_2 \\ &= 70 + 3b_1^2 + 14b_2^2 - 28b_1 - 62b_2 + 12b_1b_2. \end{aligned} \tag{1.8}$$

Now we want to choose b_1 and b_2 to minimize RSS. To do this, we use the calculus and find the values of b_1 and b_2 that satisfy the first-order conditions

$$\frac{\partial RSS}{\partial b_1} = 0 \quad \text{and} \quad \frac{\partial RSS}{\partial b_2} = 0. \tag{1.9}$$

Taking partial differentials,

$$\frac{\partial RSS}{\partial b_1} = 6b_1 + 12b_2 - 28 \tag{1.10}$$

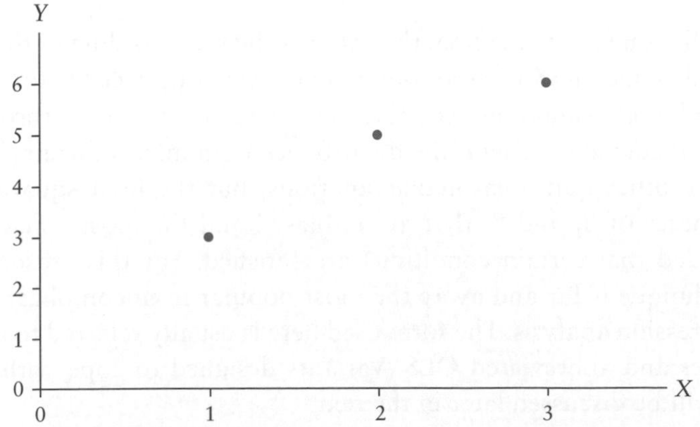

Figure 1.4 Three-observation example

Table 1.1 Three-observation example

X	Y	$\hat{Y}$	e
1	3	$b_1 + b_2$	$3 - b_1 - b_2$
2	5	$b_1 + 2b_2$	$5 - b_1 - 2b_2$
3	6	$b_1 + 3b_2$	$6 - b_1 - 3b_2$

and

$$\frac{\partial RSS}{\partial b_2} = 28b_2 + 12b_1 - 62 \tag{1.11}$$

and so we have

$$3b_1 + 6b_2 - 14 = 0 \tag{1.12}$$

and

$$6b_1 + 14b_2 - 31 = 0. \tag{1.13}$$

Solving these two equations, one obtains $b_1 = 1.67$ and $b_2 = 1.50$. The regression equation is therefore

$$\hat{Y}_i = 1.67 + 1.50X_i. \tag{1.14}$$

The three points and the regression line are shown in Figure 1.5.

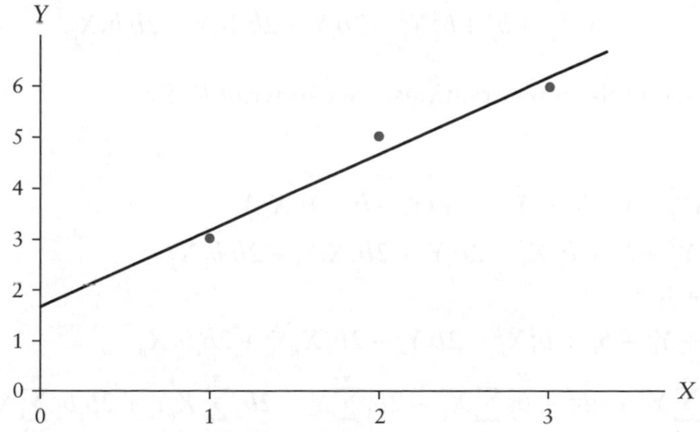

Figure 1.5 Three-observation example with regression line

Least squares regression with one explanatory variable: the general case

We shall now consider the general case where there are n observations on two variables X and Y and, supposing Y to depend on X, we will fit the equation

$$\hat{Y}_i = b_1 + b_2 X_i. \tag{1.15}$$

The fitted value of the dependent variable in observation i, $\hat{Y}_i$, will be $(b_1 + b_2 X_i)$, and the residual e_i will be $(Y_i - b_1 - b_2 X_i)$. We wish to choose b_1 and b_2 so as to minimize the residual sum of the squares, RSS, given by

$$RSS = e_1^2 + \cdots + e_n^2 = \sum_{i=1}^{n} e_i^2. \tag{1.16}$$

We will find that RSS is minimized when

$$b_2 = \frac{\sum_{i=1}^{n}(X_i - \bar{X})(Y_i - \bar{Y})}{\sum_{i=1}^{n}(X_i - \bar{X})^2} \tag{1.17}$$

and

$$b_1 = \bar{Y} - b_2 \bar{X}. \tag{1.18}$$

The derivation of the expressions for b_1 and b_2 will follow the same procedure as the derivation in the preceding example, and you can compare the general version with the example at each step. We will begin by expressing the square of the residual in observation i in terms of b_1, b_2, and the data on X and Y:

$$\begin{aligned} e_i^2 &= (Y_i - \hat{Y}_i)^2 = (Y_i - b_1 - b_2 X_i)^2 \\ &= Y_i^2 + b_1^2 + b_2^2 X_i^2 - 2b_1 Y_i - 2b_2 X_i Y_i + 2b_1 b_2 X_i. \end{aligned} \tag{1.19}$$

Summing over all the n observations, we can write RSS as

$$\begin{aligned} RSS &= (Y_1 - b_1 - b_2 X_1)^2 + \cdots + (Y_n - b_1 - b_2 X_n)^2 \\ &= Y_1^2 + b_1^2 + b_2^2 X_1^2 - 2b_1 Y_1 - 2b_2 X_1 Y_1 + 2b_1 b_2 X_1 \\ &\quad + \cdots \\ &\quad + Y_n^2 + b_1^2 + b_2^2 X_n^2 - 2b_1 Y_n - 2b_2 X_n Y_n + 2b_1 b_2 X_n \\ &= \sum_{i=1}^{n} Y_i^2 + nb_1^2 + b_2^2 \sum_{i=1}^{n} X_i^2 - 2b_1 \sum_{i=1}^{n} Y_i - 2b_2 \sum_{i=1}^{n} X_i Y_i + 2b_1 b_2 \sum_{i=1}^{n} X_i. \end{aligned} \tag{1.20}$$

Note that *RSS* is effectively a quadratic expression in b_1 and b_2, with numerical coefficients determined by the data on X and Y in the sample. We can influence the size of *RSS* only through our choice of b_1 and b_2. The data on X and Y, which determine the locations of the observations in the scatter diagram, are fixed once we have taken the sample. The equation is the generalized version of equation (1.8) in the three-observation example.

The first-order conditions for a minimum, $\partial RSS/\partial b_1 = 0$ and $\partial RSS/\partial b_2 = 0$, yield the following equations:

$$2nb_1 - 2\sum_{i=1}^{n} Y_i + 2b_2 \sum_{i=1}^{n} X_i = 0 \tag{1.21}$$

$$2b_2 \sum_{i=1}^{n} X_i^2 - 2\sum_{i=1}^{n} X_i Y_i + 2b_1 \sum_{i=1}^{n} X_i = 0. \tag{1.22}$$

These equations are known as the normal equations for the regression coefficients and are the generalized versions of (1.12) and (1.13) in the three-observation example. Equation (1.21) allows us to write b_1 in terms of $\overline{Y}$, $\overline{X}$, and the as yet unknown b_2. Noting that $\overline{X} = \frac{1}{n}\sum X_i$ and $\overline{Y} = \frac{1}{n}\sum Y_i$, (1.21) may be rewritten

$$2nb_1 - 2n\overline{Y} + 2b_2 n\overline{X} = 0 \tag{1.23}$$

and hence,

$$b_1 = \overline{Y} - b_2\overline{X}. \tag{1.24}$$

Substituting for b_1 in (1.22), and again noting that $\sum X_i = n\overline{X}$, we obtain

$$2b_2 \sum_{i=1}^{n} X_i^2 - 2\sum_{i=1}^{n} X_i Y_i + 2\left(\overline{Y} - b_2\overline{X}\right)n\overline{X} = 0. \tag{1.25}$$

Separating the terms involving b_2 and not involving b_2 on opposite sides of the equation, we have

$$2b_2\left(\sum_{i=1}^{n} X_i^2 - n\overline{X}^2\right) = 2\sum_{i=1}^{n} X_i Y_i - 2n\overline{X}\overline{Y}. \tag{1.26}$$

Hence,

$$b_2 = \frac{\sum_{i=1}^{n} X_i Y_i - n\overline{X}\overline{Y}}{\sum_{i=1}^{n} X_i^2 - n\overline{X}^2}. \tag{1.27}$$

An alternative form that we shall prefer is

$$b_2 = \frac{\sum_{i=1}^{n}(X_i - \bar{X})(Y_i - \bar{Y})}{\sum_{i=1}^{n}(X_i - \bar{X})^2}. \tag{1.28}$$

To see the equivalence, note that

$$\begin{aligned}\sum_{i=1}^{n}(X_i - \bar{X})(Y_i - \bar{Y}) &= \sum_{i=1}^{n} X_i Y_i - \sum_{i=1}^{n} X_i \bar{Y} - \sum_{i=1}^{n} \bar{X} Y_i + \sum_{i=1}^{n} \bar{X}\bar{Y} \\ &= \sum_{i=1}^{n} X_i Y_i - \bar{Y}\sum_{i=1}^{n} X_i - \bar{X}\sum_{i=1}^{n} Y_i + n\bar{X}\bar{Y} \\ &= \sum_{i=1}^{n} X_i Y_i - \bar{Y}(n\bar{X}) - \bar{X}(n\bar{Y}) + n\bar{X}\bar{Y} \\ &= \sum_{i=1}^{n} X_i Y_i - n\bar{X}\bar{Y}. \end{aligned} \tag{1.29}$$

Similarly,

$$\sum_{i=1}^{n}(X_i - \bar{X})^2 = \sum_{i=1}^{n} X_i^2 - n\bar{X}^2. \tag{1.30}$$

Put X instead of Y in (1.29). Having found b_2 from (1.28), you find b_1 from (1.24). A check of the second-order conditions would confirm that we have minimized RSS.

Example

In the three-observation example, $\bar{Y} = 4.67$, $\bar{X} = 2.00$, $\sum(X_i - \bar{X})(Y_i - \bar{Y}) = 3.00$, and $\sum(X_i - \bar{X})^2 = 2.00$, so

$$b_2 = 3.00/2.00 = 1.50 \tag{1.31}$$

and

$$b_1 = \bar{Y} - b_2\bar{X} = 4.67 - 1.50 \times 2.00 = 1.67, \tag{1.32}$$

which confirms the original calculation.

Two decompositions of the dependent variable

In the preceding analysis we have encountered two ways of decomposing the value of the dependent variable in a regression model. They are going to be used throughout the text, so it is important that they be distinguished conceptually.

The first decomposition relates to the process by which the values of Y are generated:

$$Y_i = \beta_1 + \beta_2 X_i + u_i. \tag{1.33}$$

In observation i, Y_i is generated as the sum of two components, the nonstochastic component, $\beta_1 + \beta_2 X_i$, and the disturbance term u_i. This decomposition is purely theoretical. We will use it in the analysis of the properties of the regression estimators. It is illustrated in Figure 1.6a, where QT is the nonstochastic component of Y and PQ is the disturbance term.

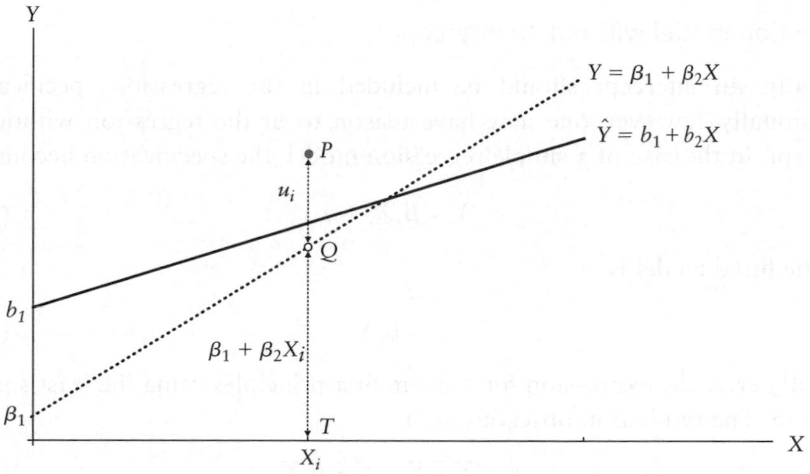

Figure 1.6a Decomposition of Y into nonstochastic component and disturbance term

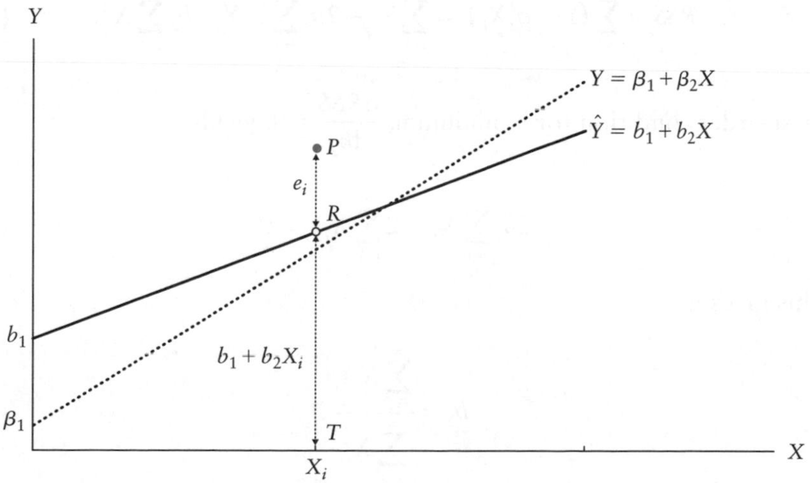

Figure 1.6b Decomposition of Y into fitted value and residual

The other decomposition relates to the regression line:

$$\begin{aligned} Y_i &= \hat{Y}_i + e_i \\ &= b_1 + b_2 X_i + e_i. \end{aligned} \quad \textbf{(1.34)}$$

Once we have chosen the values of b_1 and b_2, each value of Y is split into the fitted value, $\hat{Y}_i$, and the residual, e_i. This decomposition is operational, but it is to some extent arbitrary because it depends on our criterion for determining b_1 and b_2 and it will inevitably be affected by the particular values taken by the disturbance term in the observations in the sample. It is illustrated in Figure 1.6b, where RT is the fitted value and PR is the residual.

Regression model without an intercept

Typically, an intercept should be included in the regression specification. Occasionally, however, one may have reason to fit the regression without an intercept. In the case of a simple regression model, the specification becomes

$$Y_i = \beta_2 X_i + u_i \quad \textbf{(1.35)}$$

and the fitted model is

$$\hat{Y}_i = b_2 X_i. \quad \textbf{(1.36)}$$

We will derive the expression for b_2 from first principles using the least squares criterion. The residual in observation i is

$$e_i = Y_i - \hat{Y}_i = Y_i - b_2 X_i. \quad \textbf{(1.37)}$$

The sum of the squares of the residuals is

$$RSS = \sum_{i=1}^{n} (Y_i - b_2 X_i)^2 = \sum_{i=1}^{n} Y_i^2 - 2b_2 \sum_{i=1}^{n} X_i Y_i + b_2^2 \sum_{i=1}^{n} X_i^2. \quad \textbf{(1.38)}$$

The first-order condition for a minimum, $\frac{dRSS}{db_2} = 0$, yields:

$$2b_2 \sum_{i=1}^{n} X_i^2 - 2\sum_{i=1}^{n} X_i Y_i = 0 \quad \textbf{(1.39)}$$

and this gives us

$$b_2 = \frac{\sum_{i=1}^{n} X_i Y_i}{\sum_{i=1}^{n} X_i^2}. \quad \textbf{(1.40)}$$

The second derivative, $2\sum_{i=1}^{n} X_i^2$, is positive, confirming that we have minimized RSS.

EXERCISES

1.1 Suppose that the fitted line is $\hat{Y} = b_1 + b_2X$, with b_1 and b_2 defined as in equations (1.24) and (1.28). Demonstrate that the fitted line must pass through the point $\{\bar{X}, \bar{Y}\}$ representing the mean of the observations in the sample.

1.2 Using the normal equations (1.21) and (1.22), show that b_1 is defined, but b_2 is not, if $X_i = 0$ for all i. Give an intuitive explanation of this result.

1.3 Demonstrate from first principles that the least squares estimator of β_1 in the primitive model where Y consists simply of a constant plus a disturbance term,

$$Y_i = \beta_1 + u_i$$

is $b_1 = \bar{Y}$. (First define *RSS* and then differentiate.)

1.4 Interpretation of a regression equation

There are two stages in the interpretation of a regression equation. The first is to turn the equation into words so that it can be understood by a noneconometrician. The second is to decide whether this literal interpretation should be taken at face value or whether the relationship should be investigated further.

Both stages are important. We will leave the second until later and concentrate for the time being on the first. It will be illustrated with an earnings function, hourly earnings in 2002, *EARNINGS*, measured in dollars, being regressed on schooling, *S*, measured as highest grade completed, for 540 respondents from the United States National Longitudinal Survey of Youth 1979, the data set that is used for many of the practical illustrations and exercises in this text. See Appendix B for a description of it. This regression uses *EAEF* Data Set 21. The Stata output for the regression is shown in Table 1.2. The scatter diagram and regression line are shown in Figure 1.7.

Table 1.2

```
. reg EARNINGS S

  Source  |       SS          df         MS           Number of obs =    540
--------------------------------------------------    F(1, 538)     = 112.15
   Model  |   19321.5589       1     19321.5589       Prob > F      = 0.0000
Residual  |   92688.6722     538     172.283777       R-squared     = 0.1725
--------------------------------------------------    Adj R-squared = 0.1710
   Total  |   112010.231     539     207.811189       Root MSE      = 13.126

------------------------------------------------------------------------------
EARNINGS  |      Coef.    Std. Err.       t   P>|t|     [95% Conf. Interval]
------------------------------------------------------------------------------
       S  |   2.455321    .2318512    10.59   0.000     1.999876    2.910765
   _cons  |  -13.93347    3.219851    -4.33   0.000    -20.25849   -7.608444
------------------------------------------------------------------------------
```

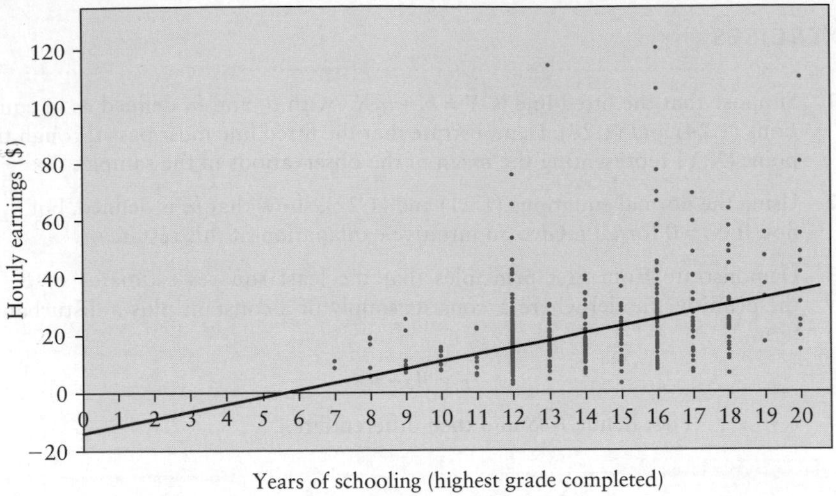

Figure 1.7 A simple earnings function

For the time being, ignore everything except the column headed 'coef.' in the bottom half of the table. This gives the estimates of the coefficient of *S* and the constant, and thus the following fitted equation:

$$\widehat{EARNINGS} = -13.93 + 2.46\ S. \qquad \textbf{(1.41)}$$

Interpreting it literally, the slope coefficient indicates that, as *S* increases by one unit (of *S*), *EARNINGS* increases by 2.46 units (of *EARNINGS*). Since *S* is measured in years, and *EARNINGS* is measured in dollars per hour, the coefficient of *S* implies that hourly earnings increase by $2.46 for every extra year of schooling.

What about the constant term? Strictly speaking, it indicates the predicted level of *EARNINGS* when *S* = 0. Sometimes the constant will have a clear meaning, but sometimes not. If the sample values of the explanatory variable are a long way from zero, extrapolating the regression line back to zero may be dangerous. Even if the regression line gives a good fit for the sample of observations, there is no guarantee that it will continue to do so when extrapolated to the left or to the right.

In this case, a literal interpretation of the constant would lead to the nonsensical conclusion that an individual with no schooling would have hourly earnings of –$13.93. In this data set, no individual had less than seven years of schooling, so it is not surprising that extrapolation to zero leads to trouble.

Box 1.1 gives a general guide to interpreting regression equations when the variables are measured in natural units.

It is important to keep three things in mind when interpreting a regression equation. First, b_1 is only an estimate of β_1 and b_2 is only an estimate of β_2, so the interpretation is really only an estimate. Second, the regression equation refers only to the general tendency for the sample. Any individual case will be further affected by the random factor. Third, the interpretation is conditional on the equation being correctly specified.

BOX 1.1 Interpretation of a linear regression equation

This is a foolproof way of interpreting the coefficients of a linear regression

$$\hat{Y}_i = b_1 + b_2 X_i$$

when Y and X are variables with straightforward natural units (not logarithms or other functions).

The first step is to say that a one-unit increase in X (measured in units of X) will cause a b_2 unit increase in Y (measured in units of Y). The second step is to check to see what the units of X and Y actually are, and to replace the word 'unit' with the actual unit of measurement. The third step is to see whether the result could be expressed in a better way, without altering its substance.

The constant, b_1, gives the predicted value of Y (in units of Y) for X equal to 0. It may or may not have a plausible meaning, depending on the context.

In fact, this is actually a naïve specification of an earnings function. We will reconsider it several times in later chapters. You should be undertaking parallel experiments using one of the other *EAEF* data sets described in Appendix B.

Having fitted a regression, it is natural to ask whether we have any means of telling how accurate our estimates are. This very important issue will be discussed in the next chapter.

Changes in the units of measurement

Suppose that the units of measurement of Y or X are changed. How will this affect the regression results? Intuitively, we would anticipate that nothing of substance will be changed, and this is correct. We will demonstrate this for the estimates of the regression coefficients in this section, and we will trace the implications for the rest of the regression output in due course. We begin by supposing that the true model is

$$Y_i = \beta_1 + \beta_2 X_i + u_i \qquad \textbf{(1.42)}$$

and that the fitted model is

$$\hat{Y}_i = b_1 + b_2 X_i. \qquad \textbf{(1.43)}$$

We now suppose that the units of measurement of Y are changed, with the new measure, Y^*, being related to the old one by

$$Y_i^* = \lambda_1 + \lambda_2 Y_i. \qquad \textbf{(1.44)}$$

Typically, a change of measurement involves a simple multiplicative scaling, such as when we convert pounds into grams. However, one occasionally encounters a full linear transformation. Conversion of temperatures from degrees Celsius to degrees Fahrenheit is an example. Regressing Y^* on X, we have

$$b_2^* = \frac{\sum_{i=1}^{n}(X_i - \bar{X})(Y_i^* - \bar{Y}^*)}{\sum_{i=1}^{n}(X_i - \bar{X})^2} = \frac{\sum_{i=1}^{n}(X_i - \bar{X})([\lambda_1 + \lambda_2 Y_i] - [\lambda_1 + \lambda_2 \bar{Y}])}{\sum_{i=1}^{n}(X_i - \bar{X})^2}$$

$$= \frac{\sum_{i=1}^{n}(X_i - \bar{X})(\lambda_2 Y_i - \lambda_2 \bar{Y})}{\sum_{i=1}^{n}(X_i - \bar{X})^2} = \lambda_2 b_2. \qquad \textbf{(1.45)}$$

The change of measurement has caused the slope coefficient to be multiplied by λ_2. This is logical. A unit change in Y is the same as a change of λ_2 units in Y^*. According to the regression equation, a unit change in X leads to a change of b_2 units in Y, so it should lead to a change of $\lambda_2 b_2$ units in Y^*. The effect on the intercept will be left as an exercise. The effect of a change in the units of measurement of X will also be left as an exercise.

Demeaning

Often the intercept in a regression equation has no sensible interpretation because $X = 0$ is distant from the data range. The earnings function illustrated in Figure 1.7 is an example, with the intercept actually being negative. Sometimes it is useful to deal with the problem by defining X^* as the deviation of X about its sample mean

$$X_i^* = X_i - \bar{X} \qquad \textbf{(1.46)}$$

Table 1.3

```
. sum S

Variable    |Obs  Mean          Std. Dev.  Min          Max
-----------------------------------------------------------------------
       S    |540  13.67222      2.438476   7            20
-----------------------------------------------------------------------

. gen SDEV = S - 13.67
. reg EARNINGS SDEV

   Source   |         SS            df            MS      Number of obs =    540
------------------------------------------------------    F(1, 538)     = 112.15
    Model   |   19321.5587           1    19321.5587      Prob > F      = 0.0000
 Residual   |   92688.6723         538    172.283778      R-squared     = 0.1725
------------------------------------------------------    Adj R-squared = 0.1710
    Total   |   112010.231         539    207.811189      Root MSE      = 13.126

-----------------------------------------------------------------------------------
 EARNINGS   |       Coef.    Std. Err.       t   P>|t|     [95% Conf.   Interval]
-----------------------------------------------------------------------------------
     SDEV   |    2.455321     .2318512   10.59   0.000      1.999876    2.910765
    _cons   |    19.63077     5648401    34.75   0.000       18.5212    20.74033
-----------------------------------------------------------------------------------
```

and regressing Y on X^*. The slope coefficient will not be affected, but the intercept will now be the fitted value of Y at the sample mean of X. Since this is, by construction, in the middle of the sample, it may be more useful for analytical purposes.

Table 1.3 shows the revised output from Table 1.2 when the schooling variable is demeaned. The sum (summarize) command yielded descriptive statistics for S and the gen (generate) command generated the demeaned variable $SDEV$. These are Stata commands but similar commands will be found in all regression applications.

Mean years of schooling was 13.67, that is nearly two years of college. For an individual at the mean, the intercept predicts hourly earnings of $19.63.

EXERCISES

Note: Some of the exercises in this and later chapters require you to fit regressions using one of the *EAEF* data sets. See Appendix B for details.

1.4 The table shows the average annual percentage rates of growth of employment, e, and real GDP, g, for 25 OECD countries for the period 1988–97. The regression output shows the result of regressing e on g. Provide an interpretation of the coefficients.

Average annual percentage rates of growth of employment and real GDP, 1988–97

	Employment	*GDP*		*Employment*	*GDP*
Australia	1.68	3.04	Korea	2.57	7.73
Austria	0.65	2.55	Luxembourg	3.02	5.64
Belgium	0.34	2.16	Netherlands	1.88	2.86
Canada	1.17	2.03	New Zealand	0.91	2.01
Denmark	0.02	2.02	Norway	0.36	2.98
Finland	–1.06	1.78	Portugal	0.33	2.79
France	0.28	2.08	Spain	0.89	2.60
Germany	0.08	2.71	Sweden	–0.94	1.17
Greece	0.87	2.08	Switzerland	0.79	1.15
Iceland	–0.13	1.54	Turkey	2.02	4.18
Ireland	2.16	6.40	United Kingdom	0.66	1.97
Italy	–0.30	1.68	United States	1.53	2.46
Japan	1.06	2.81			

```
. reg e g

 Source   |      SS         df        MS           Number of obs =      25
----------+-----------------------------------     F(1, 23)      =   33.10
 Model    |  14.5753023      1    14.5753023       Prob > F      =  0.0000
Residual  |  10.1266731     23   .440290135        R-squared     =  0.5900
----------+-----------------------------------     Adj R-squared =  0.5722
 Total    |  24.7019754     24    1.02924898       Root MSE      =  .66354
--------------------------------------------------------------------------
       e  |     Coef.   Std. Err.      t  P>|t|     [95% Conf. Interval]
--------------------------------------------------------------------------
       g  |   .489737   .0851184    5.75  0.000     .3136561    .6658179
   _cons  | -.5458912   .2740387   -1.99  0.058    -1.112784    .0210011
--------------------------------------------------------------------------
```

1.5 In Exercise 1.4, $\bar{e} = 0.83$, $\bar{g} = 2.82$, $\sum(e_i - \bar{e})(g_i - \bar{g}) = 29.76$, and $\sum(g_i - \bar{g})^2 = 60.77$. Calculate the regression coefficients and check that they are the same as in the regression output.

1.6 Does educational attainment depend on intellectual ability? In the United States, as in most countries, there is a positive correlation between educational attainment and cognitive ability. *S* (highest grade completed by 2002) is the number of years of schooling of the respondent. *ASVABC* is a composite measure of numerical and verbal ability with mean 50 and standard deviation 10 (both approximately; for further details of the measure, see Appendix B). Perform a regression of *S* on *ASVABC* and interpret the regression results.

1.7 Do earnings depend on education? Using your *EAEF* data set, fit an earnings function parallel to that in Table 1.2, regressing *EARNINGS* on *S*, and give an interpretation of the coefficients.

1.8* The output shows the result of regressing the weight of the respondent in 1985, measured in pounds, on his or her height, measured in inches, using *EAEF* Data Set 21. Provide an interpretation of the coefficients.

```
. reg WEIGHT85 HEIGHT

  Source  |      SS        df        MS            Number of obs =     540
----------+-----------------------------------     F(1, 538)     =  355.97
   Model  |  261111.383     1    261111.383        Prob > F      =  0.0000
Residual  |  394632.365   538    733.517407        R-squared     =  0.3982
----------+-----------------------------------     Adj R-squared =  0.3971
   Total  |  655743.748   539    1216.59322        Root MSE      =  27.084

--------------------------------------------------------------------------
WEIGHT85  |     Coef.    Std. Err.      t  P>|t|    [95% Conf. Interval]
--------------------------------------------------------------------------
  HEIGHT  |   5.192973   .275238    18.87  0.000      4.6523    5.733646
   _cons  |  -194.6815   18.6629   -10.43  0.000   -231.3426   -158.0204
--------------------------------------------------------------------------
```

1.9 The output shows the result of regressing the number of children in the family on the years of schooling of the mother, using *EAEF* Data Set 21. Provide an interpretation of the coefficients. (The data set contains data on siblings, the number of brothers and sisters of the respondent. Therefore the total number of children in the family is the number of siblings plus one.)

```
. g CHILDREN = SIBLINGS + 1
. reg CHILDREN SM

  Source  |       SS         df        MS            Number of obs =     540
----------+-------------------------------          F(1, 538)     =   63.60
   Model  |  272.69684        1   272.69684          Prob > F      =  0.0000
Residual  |  2306.7402      538  4.28762118          R-squared     =  0.1057
----------+-------------------------------          Adj R-squared =  0.1041
   Total  | 2579.43704      539  4.78559747          Root MSE      =  2.0707
-----------------------------------------------------------------------------
CHILDREN  |     Coef.   Std. Err.      t   P>|t|      [95% Conf. Interval]
----------+------------------------------------------------------------------
      SM  | -.2525473   .0316673   -7.98   0.000     -.314754    -.1903406
   _cons  |  7.198478   .3773667   19.08   0.000     6.457186     7.939771
-----------------------------------------------------------------------------
```

1.10* A researcher has international cross-sectional data on aggregate wages, W, aggregate profits, P, and aggregate income, Y, for a sample of n countries. By definition,

$$Y_i = W_i + P_i.$$

The regressions

$$\hat{W}_i = a_1 + a_2 Y_i$$

$$\hat{P}_i = b_1 + b_2 Y_i$$

are fitted using OLS regression analysis. Show that the regression coefficients will automatically satisfy the following equations:

$$a_2 + b_2 = 1$$

$$a_1 + b_1 = 0.$$

Explain intuitively why this should be so.

1.11 Demonstrate that, if the units of Y are changed so that $Y_i^* = \lambda_1 + \lambda_2 Y_i$, the new intercept b_1^* will be given by $b_1^* = \lambda_1 + \lambda_2 b_1$, where b_1 is the intercept in a regression of Y on X.

1.12* Suppose that the units of measurement of X are changed so that the new measure, X^*, is related to the original one by $X_i^* = \mu_1 + \mu_2 X_i$. Show that the new estimate of the slope coefficient is b_2/μ_2, where b_2 is the slope coefficient in the original regression.

1.13* Demonstrate that if X is demeaned but Y is left in its original units, the intercept in a regression of Y on demeaned X will be equal to $\overline{Y}$.

1.14* The regression output shows the result of regressing weight on height using the same sample as in Exercise 1.8, but with weight and height measured in kilos and centimetres: *WMETRIC*=0.454**WEIGHT85* and *HMETRIC*=2.54**HEIGHT*.

Confirm that the estimates of the intercept and slope coefficient are as should be expected from the change in units of measurement.

```
. gen HMETRIC = 2.54*HEIGHT
. gen WMETRIC = WEIGHT85*0.454
. reg WMETRIC HMETRIC
  Source |       SS       df       MS              Number of obs =     540
---------+------------------------------           F(1, 538)     =  355.97
   Model |  53819.2324     1   53819.2324          Prob > F      =  0.0000
Residual |   81340.044   538   151.189673          R-squared     =  0.3982
---------+------------------------------           Adj R-squared =  0.3971
   Total |  135159.276   539   250.759325          Root MSE      =  12.296
------------------------------------------------------------------------------
 WMETRIC |      Coef.   Std. Err.       t   P>|t|      [95% Conf. Interval]
---------+--------------------------------------------------------------------
 HMETRIC |   .9281928    .0491961    18.87  0.000      .8315528    1.024833
   _cons |  -88.38539    8.472958   -10.43  0.000     -105.0295   -71.74125
------------------------------------------------------------------------------
```

1.15* Consider the regression model

$$Y_i = \beta_1 + \beta_2 X_i + u_i.$$

It implies

$$\overline{Y} = \beta_1 + \beta_2 \overline{X} + \overline{u}$$

and hence that

$$Y_i^* = \beta_2 X_i^* + v_i,$$

where $Y_i^* = Y_i - \overline{Y}$, $X_i^* = X_i - \overline{X}$, and $v_i = u_i - \overline{u}$.

Demonstrate that a regression of Y^* on X^* using (1.40) will yield the same estimate of the slope coefficient as a regression of Y on X. (*Note:* (1.40) should be used instead of (1.28) because there is no intercept in this model.)

Evaluate the outcome if the slope coefficient were estimated using (1.28), despite the fact that there is no intercept in the model.

Determine the estimate of the intercept if Y^* were regressed on X^* with an intercept included in the regression specification.

1.16 Two individuals fit earnings functions relating *EARNINGS* to *S* using *EAEF* Data Set 21. The first individual does it correctly and obtains the result found in Table 1.2:

$$\widehat{EARNINGS} = -13.93 + 2.46\,S.$$

The second individual makes a mistake and regresses *S* on *EARNINGS*, obtaining the following result:

$$\hat{S} = 12.29 + 0.070 EARNINGS.$$

From this result the second individual derives

$$\widehat{EARNINGS} = -175.57 + 14.29S.$$

Explain why this equation is different from that fitted by the first individual.

1.5 Two important results relating to OLS regressions

It is convenient at this point to establish two important results relating to OLS regressions. Both of them are purely mechanical. They are valid only if the model includes an intercept (as is usually the case). They hold automatically, irrespective of whether the model is well or poorly specified. Both generalize to the multiple regression case where we have more than one explanatory variable. We will use them and their corollaries immediately in the next section, where we consider goodness of fit. As usual, the true model is assumed to be $Y_i = \beta_1 + \beta_2 X_i + u_i$ and the fitted model to be $\hat{Y}_i = b_1 + b_2 X_i$.

The mean value of the residuals is zero

To demonstrate this, we start with the definition of the residual e_i in observation i:

$$e_i = Y_i - \hat{Y}_i = Y_i - b_1 - b_2 X_i. \tag{1.47}$$

Summing over all the observations in the sample,

$$\sum_{i=1}^{n} e_i = \sum_{i=1}^{n} Y_i - nb_1 - b_2 \sum_{i=1}^{n} X_i. \tag{1.48}$$

Dividing by n,

$$\begin{aligned} \bar{e} &= \bar{Y} - b_1 - b_2\bar{X} \\ &= \bar{Y} - (\bar{Y} - b_2\bar{X}) - b_2\bar{X} = 0. \end{aligned} \tag{1.49}$$

As a corollary, we can immediately demonstrate that the mean of the fitted values of Y is equal to the mean of the actual values of Y. We start again with the definition of the residual,

$$e_i = Y_i - \hat{Y}_i. \tag{1.50}$$

Summing over all the observations in the sample and dividing by n, we have

$$\bar{e} = \bar{Y} - \bar{\hat{Y}}. \tag{1.51}$$

But $\bar{e} = 0$, so $\bar{\hat{Y}} = \bar{Y}$.

The sample correlation between the observations on *X* and the residuals is zero

Intuitively, we would expect this to be the case since the residuals are, by definition, the part of Y not explained by X in the model. We will first demonstrate that $\sum X_i e_i = 0$.

$$\sum_{i=1}^{n} X_i e_i = \sum_{i=1}^{n} X_i \left(Y_i - b_1 - b_2 X_i\right) = \sum_{i=1}^{n} X_i Y_i - b_1 \sum_{i=1}^{n} X_i - b_2 \sum_{i=1}^{n} X_i^2 = 0. \quad \textbf{(1.52)}$$

The final step uses the normal equation (1.22). The numerator of the sample correlation coefficient for X and e can be decomposed as follows, using the fact that $\bar{e} = 0$:

$$\begin{aligned} \frac{1}{n}\sum_{i=1}^{n}\left(X_i - \bar{X}\right)\left(e_i - \bar{e}\right) &= \frac{1}{n}\sum_{i=1}^{n}\left(X_i - \bar{X}\right)e_i \\ &= \frac{1}{n}\sum_{i=1}^{n} X_i e_i - \frac{1}{n}\sum_{i=1}^{n} \bar{X} e_i \\ &= 0 - \bar{X}\frac{1}{n}\sum_{i=1}^{n} e_i = 0. \end{aligned} \quad \textbf{(1.53)}$$

Hence, the correlation coefficient is zero, assuming that it is defined. (This requires that the denominator is nonzero. which in turn requires that the sample variances of X and e are both nonzero.)

As a corollary of (1.52), we have $\sum \hat{Y}_i e_i = 0$:

$$\sum_{i=1}^{n} \hat{Y}_i e_i = \sum_{i=1}^{n} \left(b_1 + b_2 X_i\right) e_i = b_1 \sum_{i=1}^{n} e_i + b_2 \sum_{i=1}^{n} X_i e_i = 0, \quad \textbf{(1.54)}$$

since $\sum e_i = n\bar{e} = 0$. Hence, we may demonstrate that the sample correlation between the fitted values of Y and the residuals is zero. This is left as an exercise.

EXERCISE

1.17* Demonstrate that the fitted values of the dependent variable are uncorrelated with the residuals in a simple regression model. (This result generalizes to the multiple regression case.)

1.6 Goodness of fit: R^2

The aim of regression analysis is to explain the behavior of the dependent variable Y. In any given sample, Y is relatively low in some observations and relatively high in others. We want to know why. The variations in Y in any sample can be summarized by $\sum \left(Y_i - \bar{Y}\right)^2$, the sum of the squared deviations about its sample mean. We should like to be able to account for the size of this statistic.

We have seen that we can split the value of Y_i in each observation into two components, $\hat{Y}_i$ and e_i, after running a regression:

$$Y_i = \hat{Y}_i + e_i. \tag{1.55}$$

We can use this to decompose $\sum \left(Y_i - \overline{Y}\right)^2$:

$$\sum_{i=1}^{n}\left(Y_i - \overline{Y}\right)^2 = \sum_{i=1}^{n}\left(\left[\hat{Y}_i + e_i\right] - \left[\overline{\hat{Y}} + \overline{e}\right]\right)^2 = \sum_{i=1}^{n}\left(\left[\hat{Y}_i - \overline{Y}\right] + e_i\right)^2. \tag{1.56}$$

In the second step, we have used the results $\overline{e} = 0$ and $\overline{\hat{Y}} = \overline{Y}$ from Section 1.5. Hence,

$$\begin{aligned}\sum_{i=1}^{n}\left(Y_i - \overline{Y}\right)^2 &= \sum_{i=1}^{n}\left(\hat{Y}_i - \overline{Y}\right)^2 + \sum_{i=1}^{n} e_i^2 + 2\sum_{i=1}^{n}\left(\left[\hat{Y}_i - \overline{Y}\right]e_i\right) \\ &= \sum_{i=1}^{n}\left(\hat{Y}_i - \overline{Y}\right)^2 + \sum_{i=1}^{n} e_i^2 + 2\sum_{i=1}^{n} \hat{Y}_i e_i - 2\overline{Y}\sum_{i=1}^{n} e_i.\end{aligned} \tag{1.57}$$

Now $\sum \hat{Y}_i e_i = 0$, as demonstrated in Section 1.5, and $\sum e_i = n\overline{e} = 0$. Hence,

$$\sum_{i=1}^{n}\left(Y_i - \overline{Y}\right)^2 = \sum_{i=1}^{n}\left(\hat{Y}_i - \overline{Y}\right)^2 + \sum_{i=1}^{n} e_i^2. \tag{1.58}$$

Thus, we have the decomposition

$$TSS = ESS + RSS, \tag{1.59}$$

where *TSS*, the total sum of squares, is given by the left side of the equation and *ESS*, the 'explained' sum of squares, and *RSS*, the residual ('unexplained') sum of squares, are the two terms on the right side. (*Note:* The words *explained* and *unexplained* have been put in *quotation marks* because the explanation may in fact be false. *Y* might really depend on some other variable *Z*, and *X* might be acting as a proxy for *Z* (more about this later). It would be safer to use the expression *apparently explained* instead of *explained*.)

In view of (1.58), $\sum \left(\hat{Y}_i - \overline{Y}\right)^2 / \sum \left(Y_i - \overline{Y}\right)^2$ is the proportion of the total sum of squares explained by the regression line. This proportion is known as the coefficient of determination or, more usually, R^2:

$$R^2 = \frac{\sum_{i=1}^{n}\left(\hat{Y}_i - \overline{Y}\right)^2}{\sum_{i=1}^{n}\left(Y_i - \overline{Y}\right)^2}. \tag{1.60}$$

Table 1.4

```
. reg EARNINGS S

  Source    |       SS           df           MS              Number of obs =     540
------------+------------------------------------------       F(1, 538)     =  112.15
   Model    |   19321.5589        1       19321.5589          Prob > F      =  0.0000
Residual    |   92688.6722      538     172.28377773          R-squared     =  0.1725
------------+------------------------------------------       Adj R-squared =  0.1710
   Total    |   112010.231      539       207.811189          Root MSE      =  13.126

----------------------------------------------------------------------------------------
EARNINGS    |      Coef.    Std. Err.       t       P>|t|      [95% Conf. Interval]
------------+---------------------------------------------------------------------------
       S    |   2.455321     .2318512     10.59     0.000       1.999876     2.910765
   _cons    |  -13.93347     3.219851     -4.33     0.000      -20.25849    -7.608444
----------------------------------------------------------------------------------------
```

Regression output always includes R^2 and may also present the underlying analysis of variance. Table 1.4 reproduces the Stata earnings function output in Table 1.2. The column heading 'SS' stands for sums of squares. *ESS*, here described as the 'model' sum of squares, is 19,322. *TSS* is 112,010. Dividing *ESS* by *TSS*, we have $R^2 = 19{,}322/112{,}010 = 0.1725$, as stated in the top right quarter of the output. The low R^2 is partly attributable to the fact that important variables, such as work experience, are missing from the model. It is also partly attributable to the fact that unobservable characteristics are important in determining earnings, R^2 seldom being much above 0.5 even in a well-specified model.

The maximum value of R^2 is 1. This occurs when the regression line fits the observations exactly, so that $\hat{Y}_i = Y_i$ in all observations and all the residuals are zero. Then $\sum\left(\hat{Y}_i - \bar{Y}\right)^2 = \sum\left(Y_i - \bar{Y}\right)^2$, $\sum e_i^2 = 0$, and one has a perfect fit. If there is no apparent relationship between the values of Y and X in the sample, R^2 will be close to zero.

Other things being equal, one would like R^2 to be as high as possible. In particular, we would like the coefficients b_1 and b_2 to be chosen in such a way as to maximize R^2. Does this conflict with our criterion that b_1 and b_2 should be chosen to minimize the sum of the squares of the residuals? No, they are easily shown to be equivalent criteria. In view of (1.58), we can rewrite R^2 as

$$R^2 = 1 - \frac{\sum_{i=1}^{n} e_i^2}{\sum_{i=1}^{n}\left(Y_i - \bar{Y}\right)^2} \qquad \textbf{(1.61)}$$

and so the values of b_1 and b_2 that minimize the residual sum of squares automatically maximize R^2.

Note that the results in Section 1.5 depend on the model including an intercept. If there is no intercept, the decomposition (1.58) is invalid and the two definitions of R^2 in equations (1.60) and (1.61) are no longer equivalent. Any definition of R^2 in this case may be misleading and should be treated with caution.

Table 1.5 Analysis of variance in the three-observation example

Observation	X	Y	$\hat{Y}$	e	$Y-\bar{Y}$	$\hat{Y}-\bar{\hat{Y}}$	$(Y-\bar{Y})^2$	$(\hat{Y}-\bar{\hat{Y}})^2$	e^2
1	1	3	3.1667	−0.1667	−1.6667	−1.5	2.7778	2.25	0.0278
2	2	5	4.6667	0.3333	0.3333	0.0	0.1111	0.00	0.1111
3	3	6	6.1667	−0.1667	1.3333	1.5	1.7778	2.25	0.0278
Total	6	14	14				4.6667	4.50	0.1667
Mean	2	4.6667	4.6667						

Example of how R^2 is calculated

R^2 is always calculated by the computer as part of the regression output, so this example is for illustration only. We shall use the primitive three-observation example described in Section 1.3, where the regression line

$$\hat{Y}_i = 1.6667 + 1.5000X_i \tag{1.62}$$

was fitted to the observations on X and Y in Table 1.5. The table also shows $\hat{Y}_i$ and e_i for each observation. $\sum\left(Y_i - \bar{Y}\right)^2 = 4.6667$, $\sum\left(\hat{Y}_i - \bar{Y}\right)^2 = 4.5000$, and $\sum e_i^2 = 0.1667$. From these figures, we can calculate R^2 using either (1.60) or (1.61):

$$R^2 = \frac{\sum_{i=1}^{n}\left(\hat{Y}_i - \bar{Y}\right)^2}{\sum_{i=1}^{n}\left(Y_i - \bar{Y}\right)^2} = \frac{4.5000}{4.6667} = 0.96 \tag{1.63}$$

$$R^2 = 1 - \frac{\sum_{i=1}^{n} e_i^2}{\sum_{i=1}^{n}\left(Y_i - \bar{Y}\right)^2} = 1 - \frac{0.1667}{4.6667} = 0.96. \tag{1.64}$$

Alternative interpretation of R^2

It should be intuitively obvious that, the better is the fit achieved by the regression equation, the higher should be the correlation coefficient for the actual and predicted values of Y. We will show that R^2 is in fact equal to the square of this correlation coefficient, which we will denote $r_{Y,\hat{Y}}$:

$$r_{Y,\hat{Y}} = \frac{\sum_{i=1}^{n}\left(Y_i - \bar{Y}\right)\left(\hat{Y}_i - \bar{Y}\right)}{\sqrt{\sum_{i=1}^{n}\left(Y_i - \bar{Y}\right)^2 \sum_{i=1}^{n}\left(\hat{Y}_i - \bar{Y}\right)^2}}. \tag{1.65}$$

Now

$$\begin{aligned}
\sum_{i=1}^{n}\left(Y_i-\bar{Y}\right)\left(\hat{Y}_i-\bar{Y}\right) &= \sum_{i=1}^{n}\left(\left[\hat{Y}_i+e_i\right]-\left[\bar{Y}+\bar{e}\right]\right)\left(\hat{Y}_i-\bar{Y}\right)\\
&= \sum_{i=1}^{n}\left(\left[\hat{Y}_i-\bar{Y}\right]+e_i\right)\left(\hat{Y}_i-\bar{Y}\right)\\
&= \sum_{i=1}^{n}\left(\hat{Y}_i-\bar{Y}\right)^2+\sum_{i=1}^{n}e_i\hat{Y}_i-\bar{Y}\sum_{i=1}^{n}e_i\\
&= \sum_{i=1}^{n}\left(\hat{Y}_i-\bar{Y}\right)^2. \qquad \textbf{(1.66)}
\end{aligned}$$

In the second line we have used $\bar{e}=0$ and in the fourth we have used $\sum \hat{Y}_i e_i = 0$, as demonstrated in Section 1.5. In the fourth line we have also used $\sum e_i = n\bar{e} = 0$. Hence,

$$r_{Y,\hat{Y}} = \frac{\sum_{i=1}^{n}\left(\hat{Y}_i-\bar{Y}\right)^2}{\sqrt{\sum_{i=1}^{n}\left(Y_i-\bar{Y}\right)^2\sum_{i=1}^{n}\left(\hat{Y}_i-\bar{Y}\right)^2}} = \sqrt{\frac{\sum_{i=1}^{n}\left(\hat{Y}_i-\bar{Y}\right)^2}{\sum_{i=1}^{n}\left(Y_i-\bar{Y}\right)^2}} = \sqrt{R^2}. \qquad \textbf{(1.67)}$$

Key terms

- coefficient of determination
- dependent variable
- disturbance term
- explained sum of squares (*ESS*)
- explanatory variable
- fitted model
- fitted value
- independent variable
- least squares criterion
- multiple regression model
- ordinary least squares (OLS)
- parameter
- R^2
- regression model
- regressor
- residual
- residual sum of squares (*RSS*)
- simple regression model
- total sum of squares (*TSS*)

EXERCISES

1.18 Using the data in Table 1.5, calculate the correlation between Y and $\hat{Y}$ and verify that its square is equal to the value of R^2.

1.19 What was the value of R^2 in the educational attainment regression fitted by you in Exercise 1.6? Comment on it.

1.20 What was the value of R^2 in the earnings function fitted by you in Exercise 1.7? Comment on it.

1.21 Demonstrate that, in a regression with an intercept, a regression of Y^* on X must have the same R^2 as a regression of Y on X, where $Y^* = \lambda_1 + \lambda_2 Y$.

1.22* Demonstrate that, in a regression with an intercept, a regression of Y on X^* must have the same R^2 as a regression of Y on X, where $X^* = \mu_1 + \mu_2 X$.

1.23 In a regression with an intercept, show that R^2 is zero if the estimated slope coefficient is zero.

1.24* The output shows the result of regressing weight in 2002 on height, using *EAEF* Data Set 21. In 2002 the respondents were aged 37–44. Explain why R^2 is lower than in the regression reported in Exercise 1.8.

```
. reg WEIGHT02 HEIGHT

  Source  |       SS        df        MS           Number of obs =     540
----------+------------------------------         F(1, 538)     =  216.95
   Model  |  311260.383      1   311260.383        Prob > F      =  0.0000
Residual  |  771880.527    538   1434.72217        R-squared     =  0.2874
----------+------------------------------         Adj R-squared =  0.2860
   Total  |  1083140.91    539   2009.53787        Root MSE      =  37.878

------------------------------------------------------------------------------
WEIGHT02  |      Coef.   Std. Err.      t   P>|t|      [95% Conf. Interval]
----------+-------------------------------------------------------------------
  HEIGHT  |   5.669766   .3849347   14.73   0.000      4.913606    6.425925
   _cons  |  -199.6832   26.10105   -7.65   0.000     -250.9556   -148.4107
------------------------------------------------------------------------------
```

1.25 In Exercise 1.16 both researchers obtained values of R^2 equal to 0.17 in their regressions. Was this a coincidence?

2. Properties of the Regression Coefficients and Hypothesis Testing

With the aid of regression analysis, we can obtain estimates of the parameters of a relationship. However, they are only *estimates*. The next question to ask is, how reliable are they? What are their properties? We will investigate these questions in this chapter. Both the way that we ask these questions, and their answers, depend upon the assumptions that we are making relating to the regression model, and these in turn depend upon the nature of the data that we are using.

2.1 Types of data and regression model

We shall be applying our regression techniques to three kinds of data: cross-sectional, time series, and panel. **Cross-sectional data** consist of observations relating to units of observation at one moment in time. The units of observation may be individuals, households, enterprises, countries, or any set of elements that are sufficiently similar in nature to allow one reasonably to use them to explore hypothetical relationships. **Time series data** consist of repeated observations through time on the same entities, usually with fixed intervals between the observations. Examples within a macroeconomic context would be quarterly data on gross domestic product, consumption, the money supply, and interest rates. **Panel data**, which can be thought of as combining the features of cross-sectional data and time series data, consist of repeated observations on the same elements through time. An example is the US National Longitudinal Survey of Youth used to illustrate the interpretation of a regression in Section 1.4. This consists of observations on the same individuals from 1979 to the present, interviews having been conducted annually until 1994 and every two years since then.

Following the treatment in Davidson (2000), we will consider three types of regression model:

Model A (for regressions using cross-sectional data): the regressors (explanatory variables) are **nonstochastic**. This means that their values in the observations in a sample do not have **stochastic** (random) components. See Box 2.1 for a brief further discussion.

BOX 2.1 Nonstochastic regressors

For the first part of this text, until Chapter 8, we will assume that the regressors (explanatory variables) in the model do not have stochastic components. This is to simplify the analysis. In fact, it is not easy to think of truly nonstochastic variables, other than time, so the following example is a little artificial. Suppose that we are relating earnings to schooling, S, in terms of highest grade completed. Suppose that we know from the national census that 1 percent of the population have $S = 8$, 3 percent have $S = 9$, 5 percent have $S = 10$, 7 percent have $S = 11$, 43 percent have $S = 12$ (graduation from high school), and so on. Suppose that we have decided to undertake a survey with sample size 1,000 and we want the sample to match the population as closely as possible. We might then select what is known as a stratified random sample, designed so that it includes 10 individuals with $S = 8$, 30 individuals with $S = 9$, and so on. The values of S in the sample would then be predetermined and therefore nonstochastic. In large surveys drawn in such a way as to be representative of the population as a whole, such as the National Longitudinal Survey of Youth, schooling and other demographic variables probably approximate this condition quite well. In Chapter 8 we will acknowledge the restrictiveness of this assumption and replace it with the assumption that the values of the regressors are drawn from defined populations.

Model B (also for regressions using cross-sectional data): the values of the regressors are drawn randomly and independently from defined populations.

Model C (for regressions using time series data): the values of the regressors may exhibit persistence over time. The meaning of 'persistent over time' will be explained when we come to time series regressions in Chapters 11–13.

Regressions with panel data will be treated as an extension of Model B.

The first part of this text will be confined to regressions using cross-sectional data, that is, Models A and B. The reason for this is that regressions with time series data potentially involve complex technical issues that are best avoided initially.

We will start with Model A. We will do this purely for analytical convenience. It enables us to conduct the discussion of regression analysis within the relatively straightforward framework of what is known as the Classical Linear Regression Model. We will replace it in Chapter 8 by the weaker and more realistic assumption, appropriate for regressions with cross-sectional data, that the variables are randomly drawn from defined populations.

2.2 Assumptions for regression models with nonstochastic regressors

To examine the properties of the regression model we need to make some assumptions. In particular, for Model A, we will make the following six assumptions.

A.1 The model is linear in parameters and correctly specified.

$$Y = \beta_1 + \beta_2 X + u. \tag{2.1}$$

'Linear in parameters' means that each term on the right side includes a β as a simple factor and there is no built-in relationship among the βs. An example of a model that is not linear in parameters is

$$Y = \beta_1 X^{\beta_2} + u. \tag{2.2}$$

We will defer a discussion of issues relating to linearity and nonlinearity to Chapter 4.

A.2 There is some variation in the regressor in the sample.

Obviously, if X is constant in the sample, it cannot account for any of the variation in Y. If we tried to regress Y on X, when X is constant, we would find that we would not be able to compute the regression coefficients. X_i would be equal to $\bar{X}$ for all i and hence both the numerator and the denominator of

$$b_2 = \frac{\sum_{i=1}^{n}(X_i - \bar{X})(Y_i - \bar{Y})}{\sum_{i=1}^{n}(X_i - \bar{X})^2} \tag{2.3}$$

would be equal to zero. Since we would not be able to compute b_2, we would not be able to obtain b_1 either, except in the special (and unusual) case where $\bar{X}$ is zero.

A.3 The disturbance term has zero expectation.

$$E(u_i) = 0 \quad \text{for all } i. \tag{2.4}$$

We assume that the expected value of the disturbance term in any observation should be zero. Sometimes the disturbance term will be positive, sometimes negative, but it should not have a systematic tendency in either direction.

Actually, if an intercept is included in the regression equation, it is usually reasonable to assume that this condition is satisfied automatically since the role of the intercept is to pick up any systematic but constant tendency in Y not accounted for by the explanatory variables included in the regression equation. To put this mathematically, suppose that our regression model is

$$Y_i = \beta_1 + \beta_2 X_i + u_i \tag{2.5}$$

and

$$E(u_i) = \mu_u, \tag{2.6}$$

where $\mu_u \neq 0$. Define

$$v_i = u_i - \mu_u. \tag{2.7}$$

Then, using (2.7) to substitute for u_i in (2.5), one has

$$\begin{aligned} Y_i &= \beta_1 + \beta_2 X_i + v_i + \mu_u \\ &= \beta_1' + \beta_2 X_i + v_i, \end{aligned} \tag{2.8}$$

where $\beta_1' = \beta_1 + \mu_u$. The disturbance term in the respecified model now satisfies the condition because

$$E(v_i) = E(u_i - \mu_u) = E(u_i) - E(\mu_u) = \mu_u - \mu_u = 0. \tag{2.9}$$

The price that we pay is that the interpretation of the intercept has changed. It has absorbed the nonzero component of the disturbance term in addition to whatever had previously been responsible for it. Usually this does not matter because we are seldom interested in the intercept in a regression model.

A.4 The disturbance term is homoscedastic.

We assume that the disturbance term is homoscedastic, meaning that its value in each observation is drawn from a distribution with constant population variance. Here we are thinking about the *potential* distribution of the disturbance term *before* the sample is actually generated. Once we have generated the sample, the disturbance term will turn out to be greater in some observations, and smaller in others, but there should not be any reason for it to be more erratic in some observations than in others. Denoting the potential variance of the disturbance term $\sigma_{u_i}^2$ in observation i, the assumption is

$$\sigma_{u_i}^2 = \sigma_u^2 \quad \text{for all } i. \tag{2.10}$$

Since $E(u_i) = \mu_u = 0$ by virtue of Assumption A.3, the population variance of u_i, $E\{(u_i - \mu_u)^2\}$, is equal to $E(u_i^2)$, so the condition may also be written

$$E(u_i^2) = \sigma_u^2 \quad \text{for all } i. \tag{2.11}$$

Of course, σ_u^2 is unknown. One of the tasks of regression analysis is to estimate the variance of the disturbance term.

If Assumption A.4 is not satisfied, the OLS regression coefficients will be inefficient, and it should be possible to obtain more reliable results by using a modification of the regression technique. This will be discussed in Chapter 7.

A.5 The values of the disturbance term have independent distributions.

$$u_i \text{ is distributed independently of } u_j \quad \text{for all } j \neq i. \tag{2.12}$$

We assume that the disturbance term is not subject to autocorrelation, meaning that there should be no systematic association between its values in any two observations. For example, just because the disturbance term is large and positive in one observation, there should be no tendency for it to be large and positive in the next (or large and negative, for that matter, or small and positive, or small and negative). The values of the disturbance term should be absolutely independent of one another.

The assumption implies that $\sigma_{u_i u_j}$, the population covariance between u_i and u_j, is zero, because

$$\begin{aligned}\sigma_{u_i u_j} &= E\{(u_i - \mu_u)(u_j - \mu_u)\} = E(u_i u_j) \\ &= E(u_i)E(u_j) = 0.\end{aligned} \tag{2.13}$$

(Note that $E(u_i u_j)$ can be decomposed as $E(u_i)E(u_j)$ if u_i and u_j are generated independently—see the Review chapter.)

If this assumption is not satisfied, OLS will again give inefficient estimates. Chapter 12 discusses the problems that arise and ways of treating them. Violations of this assumption are rare with cross-sectional data.

With these assumptions, we will show in this chapter that the OLS estimators of the coefficients are BLUE: best (most efficient) linear (function of the observations on Y) unbiased estimators and that the sum of the squares of the residuals divided by the number of degrees of freedom provides an unbiased estimator of σ_u^2.

A.6 The disturbance term has a normal distribution.

We usually assume that the disturbance term has a normal distribution. If u is normally distributed, so will be the regression coefficients, and this will be useful to us later in the chapter when we perform t tests and F tests of hypotheses and construct confidence intervals for β_1 and β_2 using the regression results.

The justification for the assumption depends on the Lindeberg–Feller central limit theorem. In essence, this states that, if a random variable is the composite result of the effects of a large number of other random variables, it will have an approximately normal distribution even if its components do not, provided that none of them is dominant. The disturbance term u is composed of a number of factors not appearing explicitly in the regression equation and so, even if we know nothing about the distributions of these factors (or even their identity), we are usually entitled to assume that the disturbance term is normally distributed. (The Lindeberg–Levy central limit theorem discussed in the Review chapter required all the random components to be drawn from the same distribution; the Lindeberg–Feller theorem is less restrictive.)

2.3 The random components and unbiasedness of the OLS regression coefficients

The random components of the OLS regression coefficients

A least squares regression coefficient is a special form of random variable whose properties depend on those of the disturbance term in the equation. This will be demonstrated first theoretically in this section and again in the next by means of a controlled experiment.

Throughout the discussion we shall continue to work with the simple regression model where Y depends on a nonstochastic variable X according to the relationship

$$Y_i = \beta_1 + \beta_2 X_i + u_i \tag{2.14}$$

and we are fitting the regression equation

$$\hat{Y}_i = b_1 + b_2 X_i \tag{2.15}$$

given a sample of n observations.

First, note that Y_i has two components. It has a nonrandom component ($\beta_1 + \beta_2 X_i$), which owes nothing to the laws of chance (β_1 and β_2 may be unknown, but nevertheless they are fixed constants), and it has the random component u_i.

This implies that, when we calculate b_2 according to the formula

$$b_2 = \frac{\sum_{i=1}^{n}(X_i - \bar{X})(Y_i - \bar{Y})}{\sum_{i=1}^{n}(X_i - \bar{X})^2}, \tag{2.16}$$

b_2 also has a random component. $\sum(X_i - \bar{X})(Y_i - \bar{Y})$ depends on the values of Y, and the values of Y depend on the values of u. If the values of the disturbance term had been different in the n observations, we would have obtained different values of Y, hence of $\sum(X_i - \bar{X})(Y_i - \bar{Y})$, and hence of b_2.

We can in theory decompose b_2 into its nonrandom and random components. In view of (2.14),

$$\begin{aligned}\sum_{i=1}^{n}(X_i - \bar{X})(Y_i - \bar{Y}) &= \sum_{i=1}^{n}(X_i - \bar{X})\left([\beta_1 + \beta_2 X_i + u_i] - [\beta_1 + \beta_2 \bar{X} + \bar{u}]\right) \\ &= \sum_{i=1}^{n}(X_i - \bar{X})\left(\beta_2[X_i - \bar{X}] + [u_i - \bar{u}]\right) \\ &= \beta_2 \sum_{i=1}^{n}(X_i - \bar{X})^2 + \sum_{i=1}^{n}(X_i - \bar{X})(u_i - \bar{u}).\end{aligned} \tag{2.17}$$

Hence,

$$\begin{aligned}b_2 &= \frac{\sum_{i=1}^{n}(X_i - \bar{X})(Y_i - \bar{Y})}{\sum_{i=1}^{n}(X_i - \bar{X})^2} = \frac{\beta_2 \sum_{i=1}^{n}(X_i - \bar{X})^2 + \sum_{i=1}^{n}(X_i - \bar{X})(u_i - \bar{u})}{\sum_{i=1}^{n}(X_i - \bar{X})^2} \\ &= \beta_2 + \frac{\sum_{i=1}^{n}(X_i - \bar{X})(u_i - \bar{u})}{\sum_{i=1}^{n}(X_i - \bar{X})^2}.\end{aligned} \tag{2.18}$$

Thus, we have shown that the regression coefficient b_2 obtained from any sample consists of (1) a fixed component, equal to the true value, β_2, and (2) a random component dependent on the values of the disturbance term in the sample. The random component is responsible for the variations of b_2 around its fixed component β_2. If we wish, we can express this decomposition more tidily:

$$\begin{aligned}\sum_{i=1}^{n}\left(X_i-\bar{X}\right)\left(u_i-\bar{u}\right) &= \sum_{i=1}^{n}\left(X_i-\bar{X}\right)u_i-\bar{u}\sum_{i=1}^{n}\left(X_i-\bar{X}\right)\\ &= \sum_{i=1}^{n}\left(X_i-\bar{X}\right)u_i-\bar{u}\left(\sum_{i=1}^{n}X_i-n\bar{X}\right)\\ &= \sum_{i=1}^{n}\left(X_i-\bar{X}\right)u_i \end{aligned} \tag{2.19}$$

since $\sum_{i=1}^{n}X_i=n\bar{X}$. Hence,

$$b_2=\beta_2+\frac{\sum_{i=1}^{n}\left(X_i-\bar{X}\right)u_i}{\sum_{i=1}^{n}\left(X_i-\bar{X}\right)^2}=\beta_2+\sum_{i=1}^{n}\left\{\frac{\left(X_i-\bar{X}\right)}{\sum_{i=1}^{n}\left(X_i-\bar{X}\right)^2}\right\}u_i=\beta_2+\sum_{i=1}^{n}a_iu_i, \tag{2.20}$$

where

$$a_i=\frac{\left(X_i-\bar{X}\right)}{\sum_{i=1}^{n}\left(X_i-\bar{X}\right)^2}. \tag{2.21}$$

Thus, we have shown that b_2 is equal to the true value, β_2, plus a linear combination of the values of the disturbance term in all the observations in the sample. There is a slight awkwardness in the definition of a_i and it is as well to deal with it before mathematicians start getting excited. The numerator $\left(X_i-\bar{X}\right)$ changes as i changes and is different for each observation. However, the denominator is the sum of the squared deviations for the whole sample and is not dependent on i. So we are using i in two different senses in the definition. To avoid any ambiguity, we will use a different index for the summation and write the denominator $\sum\left(X_j-\bar{X}\right)^2$. It still means the same thing. We could avoid the problem entirely by writing the denominator as $\left(X_1-\bar{X}\right)^2+\cdots+\left(X_n-\bar{X}\right)^2$, but this would be clumsy.

We will note for future reference three properties of the a_i coefficients:

$$\sum_{i=1}^{n}a_i=0,\quad \sum_{i=1}^{n}a_i^2=\frac{1}{\sum_{j=1}^{n}\left(X_j-\bar{X}\right)^2},\quad \text{and}\quad \sum_{i=1}^{n}a_iX_i=1. \tag{2.22}$$

Proofs are supplied in Box 2.2.

BOX 2.2 Proofs of three properties of the a_i coefficients

Proof that $\sum_{i=1}^{n} a_i = 0$:

$$\sum_{i=1}^{n} a_i = \sum_{i=1}^{n}\left(\frac{X_i - \bar{X}}{\sum_{j=1}^{n}(X_j - \bar{X})^2}\right) = \frac{1}{\sum_{j=1}^{n}(X_j - \bar{X})^2}\sum_{i=1}^{n}(X_i - \bar{X}) = 0$$

since

$$\sum_{i=1}^{n}(X_i - \bar{X}) = \sum_{i=1}^{n} X_i - n\bar{X} = n\bar{X} - n\bar{X} = 0$$

using $\bar{X} = \frac{1}{n}\sum X_i$.

Proof that $\sum_{i=1}^{n} a_i^2 = \frac{1}{\sum_{i=1}^{n}(X_i - \bar{X})^2}$:

$$\sum_{i=1}^{n} a_i^2 = \sum_{i=1}^{n}\left(\frac{X_i - \bar{X}}{\sum_{j=1}^{n}(X_j - \bar{X})^2}\right)^2 = \frac{1}{\left(\sum_{j=1}^{n}(X_j - \bar{X})^2\right)^2}\sum_{i=1}^{n}(X_i - \bar{X})^2 = \frac{1}{\sum_{i=1}^{n}(X_i - \bar{X})^2}.$$

Proof that $\sum_{i=1}^{n} a_i X_i = 1$:

First note that

$$\sum_{i=1}^{n}(X_i - \bar{X})^2 = \sum_{i=1}^{n}(X_i - \bar{X})(X_i - \bar{X}) = \sum_{i=1}^{n}(X_i - \bar{X})X_i - \sum_{i=1}^{n}(X_i - \bar{X})\bar{X}$$
$$= \sum_{i=1}^{n}(X_i - \bar{X})X_i - \bar{X}\sum_{i=1}^{n}(X_i - \bar{X}) = \sum_{i=1}^{n}(X_i - \bar{X})X_i$$

since $\sum (X_i - \bar{X}) = 0$ (see above). Then, using the above equation in reverse,

$$\sum_{i=1}^{n} a_i X_i = \sum_{i=1}^{n}\frac{(X_i - \bar{X})X_i}{\sum_{j=1}^{n}(X_j - \bar{X})^2} = \frac{1}{\sum_{j=1}^{n}(X_j - \bar{X})^2}\sum_{i=1}^{n}(X_i - \bar{X})X_i = \frac{\sum_{i=1}^{n}(X_i - \bar{X})^2}{\sum_{j=1}^{n}(X_j - \bar{X})^2} = 1.$$

In a similar manner, one may also show that b_1 has a fixed component equal to the true value, β_1, plus a random component that is a linear combination of the values of the disturbance term:

$$b_1 = \beta_1 + \sum_{i=1}^{n} c_i u_i, \tag{2.23}$$

where $c_i = 1/n - a_i \bar{X}$ and a_i is defined in equation (2.21). The proof is left as an exercise.

Note that you are not able to make these decompositions in practice because you do not know the true values of β_1 and β_2 or the actual values of u in the sample. We are interested in the decompositions because they enable us to analyze the theoretical properties of b_1 and b_2, given the regression model assumptions.

The unbiasedness of the OLS regression coefficients

From (2.20) it follows that b_2 is an unbiased estimator of β_2:

$$E(b_2) = E(\beta_2) + E\left\{\sum_{i=1}^{n} a_i u_i\right\} = \beta_2 + \sum_{i=1}^{n} E(a_i u_i) = \beta_2 + \sum_{i=1}^{n} a_i E(u_i) = \beta_2 \tag{2.24}$$

since $E(u_i) = 0$ for all i by Assumption A.3. The a_i coefficients are nonstochastic given the assumption that the values of X are nonstochastic. Hence, $E(a_i u_i) = a_i E(u_i)$. Unless the random factor in the n observations happens to cancel out exactly, which can happen only by coincidence, b_2 will be different from β_2 for any given sample, but in view of (2.24) there will be no systematic tendency for it to be either higher or lower.

Similarly, b_1 is an unbiased estimator of β_1:

$$E(b_1) = E(\beta_1) + E\left(\sum_{i=1}^{n} c_i u_i\right) = \beta_1 + \sum_{i=1}^{n} c_i E(u_i) = \beta_1. \tag{2.25}$$

OLS estimators of the parameters are not the only unbiased estimators. We will give an example of another. We continue to assume that the true relationship between Y and X is given by $Y_i = \beta_1 + \beta_2 X_i + u_i$. Someone who had never heard of regression analysis, on seeing a scatter diagram of a sample of observations, might be tempted to obtain an estimate of the slope merely by joining the first and the last observations, and by dividing the increase in the height by the horizontal distance between them, as in Figure 2.1. The estimator b_2 would then be given by

$$b_2 = \frac{Y_n - Y_1}{X_n - X_1}. \tag{2.26}$$

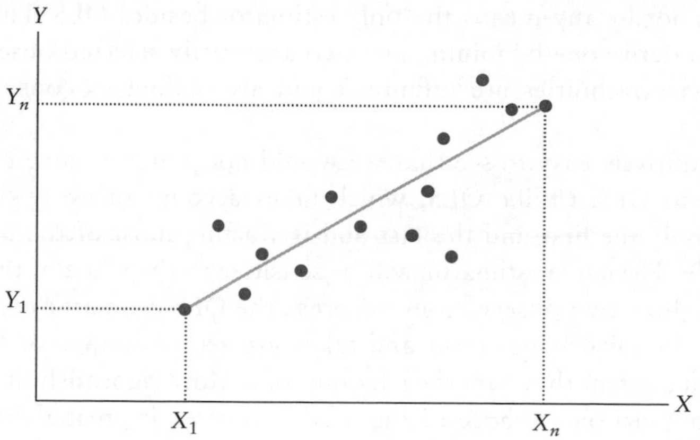

Figure 2.1 Naïve estimation of β_2

We will investigate whether it is biased or unbiased. For the first and last observations, we have

$$Y_1 = \beta_1 + \beta_2 X_1 + u_1 \tag{2.27}$$

and

$$Y_n = \beta_1 + \beta_2 X_n + u_n. \tag{2.28}$$

Hence,

$$\begin{aligned} b_2 &= \frac{\beta_1 + \beta_2 X_n + u_n - \beta_1 - \beta_2 X_1 - u_1}{X_n - X_1} \\ &= \beta_2 + \frac{u_n - u_1}{X_n - X_1}. \end{aligned} \tag{2.29}$$

Thus, we have decomposed this naïve estimator into two components, the true value and an error term. This decomposition is parallel to that for the OLS estimator, but the error term is different. The expected value of the estimator is given by

$$\begin{aligned} E(b_2) &= E(\beta_2) + E\left[\frac{u_n - u_1}{X_n - X_1}\right] \\ &= \beta_2 + \frac{1}{X_n - X_1} E(u_n - u_1) \end{aligned} \tag{2.30}$$

since β_2 is a constant and X_1 and X_n are nonstochastic. If Assumption A.3 is satisfied,

$$E(u_n - u_1) = E(u_n) - E(u_1) = 0. \tag{2.31}$$

Therefore, despite being naïve, this estimator is unbiased.

This is not by any means the only estimator besides OLS that is unbiased. You could derive one by joining any two arbitrarily selected observations, and in fact the possibilities are infinite if you are willing to consider less naïve procedures.

It is intuitively easy to see that we would not prefer a naïve estimator such as (2.26) to OLS. Unlike OLS, which takes account of every observation, it employs only the first and the last and is wasting most of the information in the sample. The naïve estimator will be sensitive to the value of the disturbance term u in those two observations, whereas the OLS estimator combines all the values of the disturbance term and takes greater advantage of the possibility that to some extent they cancel each other out. More rigorously, it can be shown that the population variance of the naïve estimator is greater than that of the OLS estimator, and that the naïve estimator is therefore less efficient. We will discuss efficiency in Section 2.5.

Normal distribution of the regression coefficients

A further implication of the decompositions (2.20) and (2.23) is that the regression coefficients will have normal distributions if the disturbance term in each observation has a normal distribution, as specified in Assumption A.6. This is because a linear combination of normal distributions is itself a normal distribution (a result that we shall take for granted).

Even if Assumption A.6 is invalid and the disturbance term has some other distribution, the distributions of the regression coefficients may be approximately normal. We may be able to invoke a central limit theorem that tells us that the linear combination of the values of the disturbance term may be approximately normal, even if each value has a non-normal distribution, provided that the sample size is large enough.

EXERCISES

2.1* Derive the decomposition of b_1 shown in equation (2.23).

2.2 For the model $Y_i = \beta_2 X_i + u_i$, the OLS estimator of β_2 is $b_2 = \sum_{i=1}^{n} X_i Y_i \Big/ \sum_{j=1}^{n} X_j^2$. Demonstrate that b_2 may be decomposed as

$$b_2 = \beta_2 + \sum_{i=1}^{n} d_i u_i,$$

where $d_i = \dfrac{X_i}{\sum_{j=1}^{n} X_j^2}$, and hence demonstrate that it is an unbiased estimator of β_2.

2.3 For the model $Y_i = \beta_1 + u_i$, the OLS estimator of β_1 is $b_1 = \bar{Y}$. Demonstrate that b_1 may be decomposed into the true value plus a linear combination of the disturbance terms in the sample. Hence, demonstrate that b_1 is an unbiased estimator of β_1.

2.4 An investigator correctly believes that the relationship between two variables X and Y is given by $Y_i = \beta_1 + \beta_2 X_i + u_i$. Given a sample of n observations, the investigator estimates β_2 by calculating it as the average value of Y divided by the average value of X. Discuss the properties of this estimator. What difference would it make if it could be assumed that $\beta_1 = 0$?

2.5* An investigator correctly believes that the relationship between two variables X and Y is given by $Y_i = \beta_1 + \beta_2 X_i + u_i$. Given a sample of observations on Y, X, and a third variable Z (which is not a determinant of Y), the investigator estimates β_2 as

$$\frac{\sum_{i=1}^{n}(Z_i - \bar{Z})(Y_i - \bar{Y})}{\sum_{i=1}^{n}(Z_i - \bar{Z})(X_i - \bar{X})}.$$

Demonstrate that this estimator is unbiased.

2.4 A Monte Carlo experiment

It often happens in econometrics that we can establish the asymptotic properties of estimators analytically but we can say nothing analytically for finite samples. The reason for this is that asymptotically we may be in a position to use plims where we cannot use expectations, and we may be able to invoke a central limit theorem that cannot be applied to finite samples.

In reality, we deal with finite samples, but practitioners typically ignore the issue. If they can demonstrate that an estimator is consistent, they may then (sometimes with justification) assume that any element of bias in a finite sample can be ignored. Similarly, if they can demonstrate that asymptotically the distribution of the estimator is normal, then they may assume that it will be approximately normal for a finite sample and so the usual tests will be approximately valid.

Alternatively, practitioners may undertake a simulation to investigate the finite sample properties directly under controlled conditions. Such simulations are often described as **Monte Carlo experiments**. Nobody seems to know for certain how the term originated. Probably it has something to do with the famous casino, as a symbol of the laws of chance.

An example of a simulation was provided in Section R.14 of the Review chapter. We will undertake many simulations of this type later in the text, particularly in the context of regressions using time series data, where it is often impossible to establish finite-sample properties analytically.

Simulations are often also useful for expository purposes. Even if it is possible to establish the finite-sample properties of an estimator mathematically, it may be helpful to illustrate them graphically. We will do this for the OLS estimators of the parameters of the simple regression model

$$Y_i = \beta_1 + \beta_2 X_i + u_i. \tag{2.32}$$

To perform the simulation, first (step 1),

1. you choose the true values of β_1 and β_2,
2. you choose the value of X in each observation, and
3. you use some random number generating process to provide the random element u in each observation.

Next (step 2), you *generate* the value of Y in each observation, using the relationship (2.32) and the values of β_1, β_2, X, and u. Then (step 3), using only the values of Y thus generated and the data for X, you use regression analysis to obtain estimates b_1 and b_2.

In the first two steps you are preparing a challenge for the regression technique. You are in complete control of the model that you are constructing and you *know* the true values of the parameters because you yourself have determined them. In the third step you see how the regression technique provides estimates of β_1 and β_2 using only the data for Y and X. Note that the inclusion of a stochastic term in the generation of Y is responsible for the element of challenge. If you did not include it, the observations would lie exactly on the straight line $Y_i = \beta_1 + \beta_2 X_i$, and it would be a trivial matter to determine the exact values of β_1 and β_2 from the data for Y and X.

You repeat the process a large number of times, keeping the *same* values of β_1 and β_2, and the *same* values of X, but using a *new* set of random numbers for the random element u each time. Finally, you plot the distributions of b_1 and b_2. If you have been able to determine these analytically, you can check that they conform to what you anticipated. If analysis was not possible, you have gained information otherwise unavailable to you.

Obviously, the distributions of b_1 and b_2 will depend on your choice of β_1 and β_2 and on your choice of the data for X. This may even be a focus of interest, as in the simulations in Chapters 11 and 13. However, as in the present case, we are interested in the qualitative nature of the results and they do not depend on our choices.

Quite arbitrarily, let us put β_1 equal to 2 and β_2 equal to 0.5, so the true relationship is

$$Y_i = 2 + 0.5X_i + u_i. \tag{2.33}$$

To keep things simple, we will assume that we have 20 observations and that the values of X go from 1 to 20. For u, the disturbance term, we will use random numbers drawn from a normally distributed population with zero mean and unit variance. We will need a set of 20 and will denote them rn_1 to rn_{20}. u_1, the disturbance term in the first observation, is simply equal to rn_1, u_2 to rn_2, etc.

Given the values of X_i and u_i in each observation, the values of Y_i are determined by (2.33), and this is done in Table 2.1.

Table 2.1

X	u	Y	X	u	Y
1	−0.59	1.91	11	1.59	9.09
2	−0.24	2.76	12	−0.92	7.08
3	−0.83	2.67	13	−0.71	7.79
4	0.03	4.03	14	−0.25	8.75
5	−0.38	4.12	15	1.69	11.19
6	−2.19	2.81	16	0.15	10.15
7	1.03	6.53	17	0.02	10.52
8	0.24	6.24	18	−0.11	10.89
9	2.53	9.03	19	−0.91	10.59
10	−0.13	6.87	20	1.42	13.42

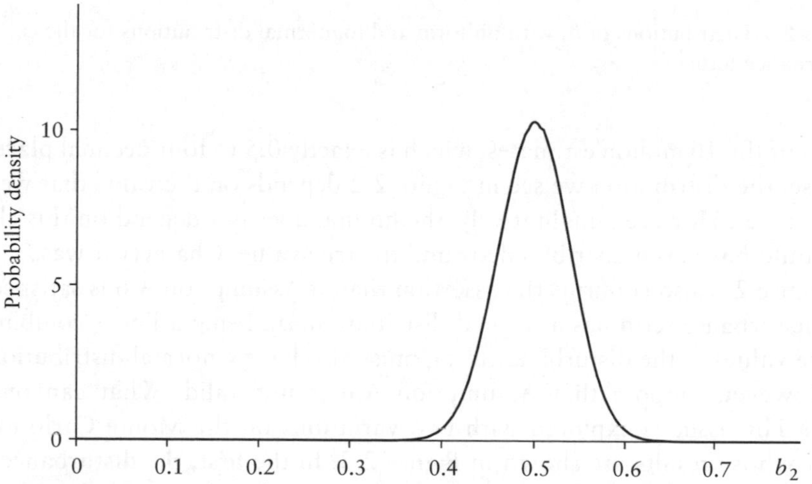

Figure 2.2 Distribution of b_2 in the Monte Carlo experiment

If you now regress Y on X, you obtain

$$\hat{Y}_i = 1.63 + 0.54X_i. \tag{2.34}$$

In this case, b_1 is an underestimate of β_1 (1.63 as opposed to 2.00) and b_2 is a slight overestimate of β_2 (0.54 as opposed to 0.50). The discrepancies are caused by the collective effects of the values of the disturbance term in the 20 observations.

We perform the regression with 10 million samples, each time keeping the same values of β_1, β_2, and the same observations on X, but using a fresh set of 20 random values for the disturbance term each time. The distribution of b_2 is shown in Figure 2.2.

b_2 is symmetrically distributed around the true value, 0.5, confirming that it is an unbiased estimator. We can see this visually, and we can also compute the

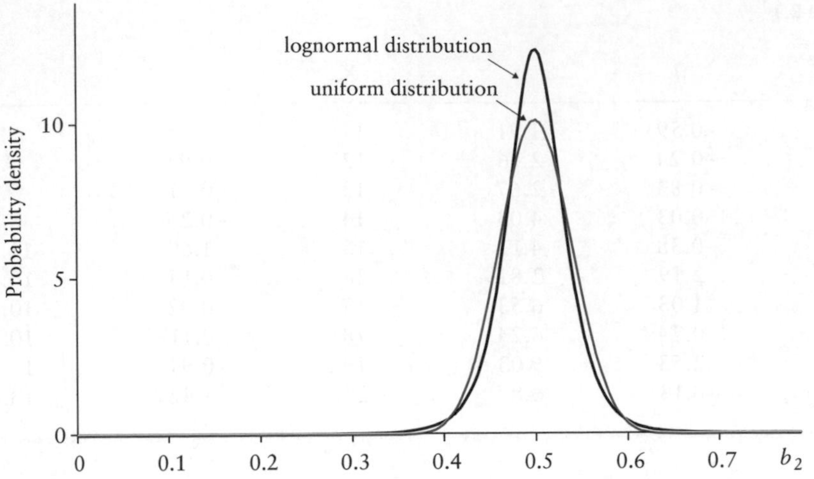

Figure 2.3 Distributions of b_2 with uniform and lognormal distributions for the disturbance term

mean of the 10 million estimates, which is exactly 0.5 to four decimal places. Of course, the distribution we see in Figure 2.2 depends on the value that we have given to β_2. However, qualitatively, the finding does not depend on this choice. b_2 would have been distributed around the true value, whatever it was.

Figure 2.2 also confirms the assertion that, if Assumption A.6 is satisfied and the disturbance term has a normal distribution, b_2, being a linear combination of the values of the disturbance term, must also have a normal distribution.

However, suppose that Assumption A.6 is not valid. What can one say then? This issue is explored with two variations on the Monte Carlo experiment whose results are shown in Figure 2.3. In the first, the disturbance term was generated from a uniform distribution with mean zero and variance 1. We know from the Lindeberg–Levy central limit theorem that the mean of a sample of observations from any distribution with finite mean and variance will have a distribution that converges on the normal distribution as the sample size becomes large. This was demonstrated in the case of the uniform and lognormal distributions in Section R.15 of the Review chapter. For the uniform distribution, the convergence was close to perfect for a sample size as small as 10. In the present context, we are not dealing with the straight mean of a set of observations, but the weighted linear combination $\sum_{i=1}^{n} a_i u_i$ in equation (2.20). However, another central limit theorem, the Lindeberg–Feller CLT, covers this case. Subject to certain conditions, the weighted linear combination will also have a normal distribution. The distribution of b_2 with the disturbance term generated from a uniform distribution is shown in Figure 2.3. It is identical to the normal distribution in Figure 2.2.

A more severe test is provided by the case where the disturbance term has a lognormal distribution, because the lognormal distribution is highly skewed.

When the application of the Lindeberg–Levy CLT to the lognormal distribution was investigated in Section R.15, it was found that the sample size had to be quite large for the distribution of the mean to approach normality. Even for $n = 100$, the shape was noticeably non-normal. Naturally, the outcome is similar in the present context. The value of the disturbance term in each observation was generated by drawing a value from a lognormal distribution with mean 1 and variance 1, and then subtracting 1 to make the mean zero. The distribution of the estimates of β_2 is shown in Figure 2.3. Unsurprisingly, it is distinctly non-normal, with excessively high mode and excessively large tails. However, it should be noted that the sample size is very small and that the lognormal distribution may be considered to be an extreme case.

Returning to Figure 2.2 where the disturbance term had a normal distribution, the standard deviation of the distribution is 0.0388. We have not yet said anything analytically about the determinants of the dispersion of the distribution. To this we now turn.

2.5 Precision of the regression coefficients

Variances of the regression coefficients

The population variances of b_1 and b_2 about their population means, $\sigma_{b_1}^2$ and $\sigma_{b_2}^2$, are given by the following expressions:

$$\sigma_{b_1}^2 = \sigma_u^2 \left(\frac{1}{n} + \frac{\overline{X}^2}{\sum_{i=1}^{n} (X_i - \overline{X})^2} \right) \quad \text{and} \quad \sigma_{b_2}^2 = \frac{\sigma_u^2}{\sum_{i=1}^{n} (X_i - \overline{X})^2}. \tag{2.35}$$

Box 2.3 provides a proof of the expression for $\sigma_{b_2}^2$. The proof of the expression for $\sigma_{b_1}^2$ follows similar lines and is left as an exercise.

We will focus on the implications of the expression for $\sigma_{b_2}^2$. Clearly, the larger is $\sum (X_i - \overline{X})^2$, the smaller is the variance of b_2. However, the size of $\sum (X_i - \overline{X})^2$ depends on two factors: the number of observations and the size of the deviations of X_i about its sample mean. To discriminate between them, it is convenient to define the mean square deviation of X, MSD(X):

$$\text{MSD}(X) = \frac{1}{n} \sum_{i=1}^{n} (X_i - \overline{X})^2. \tag{2.36}$$

Using this to rewrite $\sigma_{b_2}^2$ as

$$\sigma_{b_2}^2 = \frac{\sigma_u^2}{n \, \text{MSD}(X)}, \tag{2.37}$$

it is then obvious that the variance of b_2 is inversely proportional to the number of observations in the sample, holding the mean square deviation constant.

BOX 2.3 Proof of the expression for the population variance of b_2

By definition,

$$\sigma_{b_2}^2 = E\left\{(b_2 - E(b_2))^2\right\} = E\left\{(b_2 - \beta_2)^2\right\}$$

since we have shown that $E(b_2) = \beta_2$. We have seen that

$$b_2 = \beta_2 + \sum_{i=1}^{n} a_i u_i,$$

where

$$a_i = \frac{(X_i - \bar{X})}{\sum_{j=1}^{n}(X_j - \bar{X})^2}.$$

Hence,

$$\sigma_{b_2}^2 = E\left\{\left(\sum_{i=1}^{n} a_i u_i\right)^2\right\}.$$

Expanding the quadratic,

$$\begin{aligned}\sigma_{b_2}^2 &= E\left\{\sum_{i=1}^{n} a_i^2 u_i^2 + \sum_{i=1}^{n}\sum_{j\neq i}^{n} a_i a_j u_i u_j\right\} \\ &= \sum_{i=1}^{n} a_i^2 E(u_i^2) + \sum_{i=1}^{n}\sum_{j\neq i}^{n} a_i a_j E(u_i u_j).\end{aligned}$$

Now, by virtue of Assumption A.4, $E(u_i^2) = \sigma_u^2$, and by virtue of Assumption A.5, $E(u_i u_j) = 0$, for $j \neq i$, so

$$\sigma_{b_2}^2 = \sum_{i=1}^{n} a_i^2 \sigma_u^2 = \sigma_u^2 \sum_{i=1}^{n} a_i^2 = \frac{\sigma_u^2}{\sum_{j=1}^{n}(X_j - \bar{X})^2},$$

using the second of the properties of the a_i coefficients proved in Box 2.2.

This makes good sense. The larger the number of observations, the more closely will the sample resemble the population from which it is drawn, and the more accurate b_2 should be as an estimator of β_2.

It is also obvious that the variance of b_2 is proportional to the variance of the disturbance term. The bigger the variance of the random factor in the relationship, the worse the estimates of the parameters are likely to be, other things being equal. This is illustrated graphically in Figures 2.4a and 2.4b. We will use the same model as in the Monte Carlo experiment in Section 2.4. In both diagrams, the nonstochastic component of the relationship between Y and X, depicted by the dotted line, is given by

$$Y_i = 2.0 + 0.5X_i. \quad \mathbf{(2.38)}$$

There are 20 observations, with the values of X being the integers from 1 to 20. In the two figures, the same random numbers are used to generate the values of the disturbance term, but those in Figure 2.4b have been multiplied by a factor of 5. As a consequence, the regression line, depicted by the solid line, is a much poorer approximation to the nonstochastic relationship in Figure 2.4b than in Figure 2.4a.

From (2.37) it can be seen mathematically that the variance of b_2 is inversely related to the mean square deviation of X. What is the reason for this? The regression coefficients are calculated on the assumption that the observed variations in Y are attributable to variations in X, but in reality the observed variations in Y are *partly* attributable to variations in X and *partly* to variations in u.

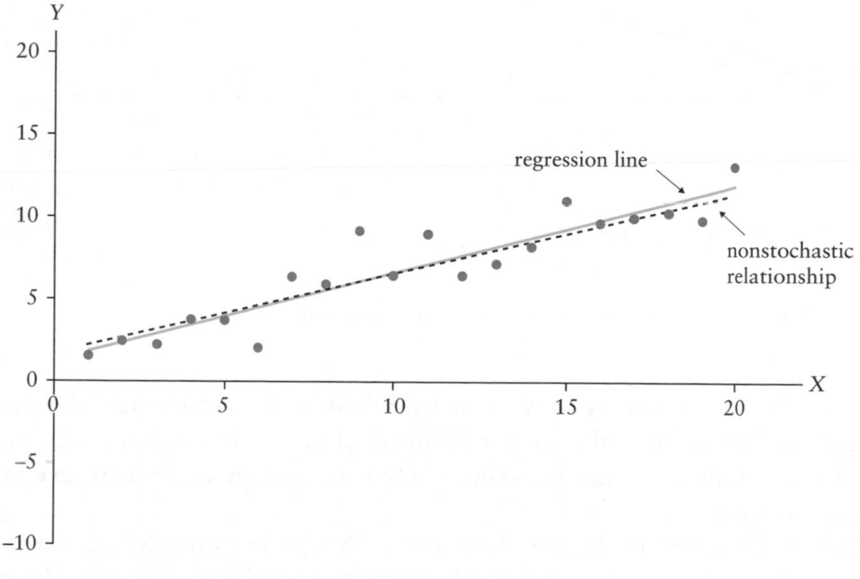

Figure 2.4a Disturbance term with relatively small variance

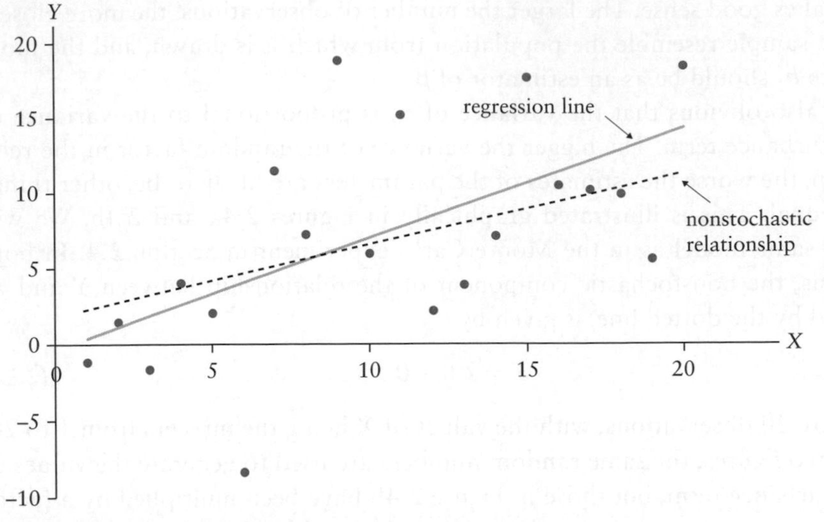

Figure 2.4b Disturbance term with relatively large variance

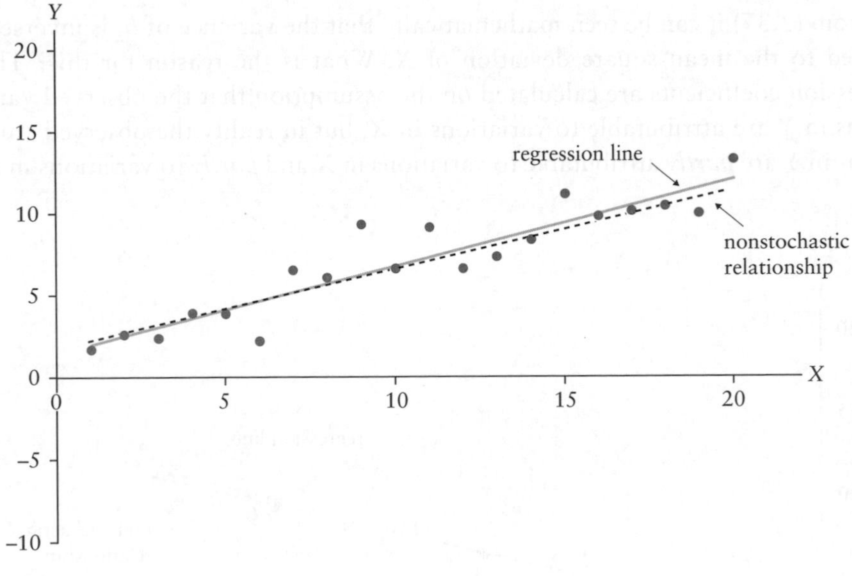

Figure 2.5a X with relatively large mean square deviation

The smaller the variations in X, as summarized by its mean square deviation, the greater is likely to be the relative influence of the random factor in determining the variations in Y and the more likely is regression analysis to give inaccurate estimates.

This is illustrated by Figures 2.5a and 2.5b. The nonstochastic component of the relationship is given by (2.38), and the disturbance terms in the two figures are identical. In Figure 2.5a, the values of X are the integers from 1

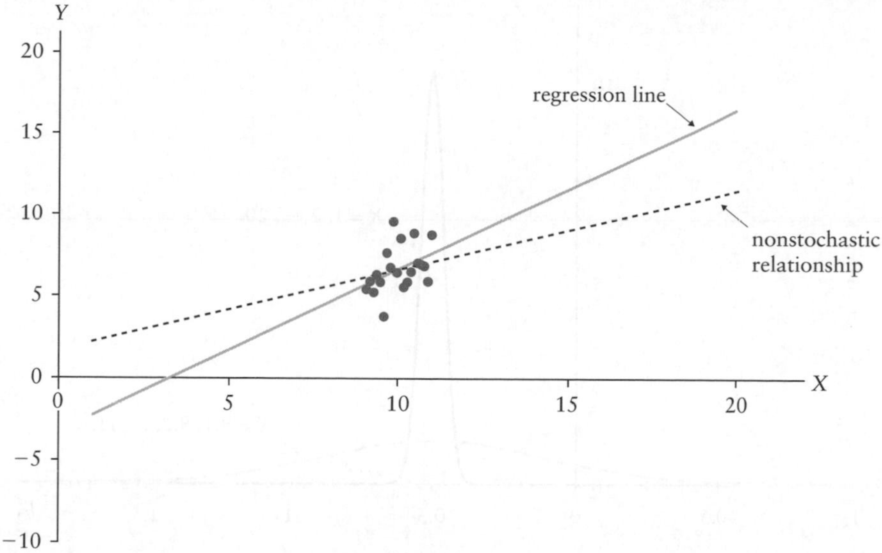

Figure 2.5b X with relatively small mean square deviation

to 20. In Figure 2.5b, the values of X are the numbers 9.1, 9.2, ..., 10.9, 11. In Figure 2.5a, the variations in X are responsible for most of the variations in Y and the relationship between the two variables can be determined relatively accurately. However, in Figure 2.5b, the variations in X are so small that their influence is overwhelmed by the effect of the variance of u. As a consequence, the effect of X is difficult to pick out and the estimates of the regression coefficients are likely to be relatively inaccurate.

Figure 2.5b is sufficient to demonstrate that the slope of the regression line is likely to be sensitive to the actual values of the disturbance term in the sample. We can make the same point more systematically with a simulation. Figure 2.6 shows the distributions of the slope coefficients when regressions similar to those shown in Figures 2.5a and 2.5b are performed with 10 million samples. The variance of the distribution is much greater in the case where X is limited to the range 9–11. Indeed, sometimes it yields estimates with the wrong sign.

Of course, Figures 2.4 and 2.5 make the same point in different ways. As can be seen from (2.37), it is the *relative* size of σ_u^2 and MSD(X) that is important, rather than the *actual* size of either.

Standard errors of the regression coefficients

In practice, one cannot calculate the population variances of either b_1 or b_2 because σ_u^2 is unknown. However, we can derive an estimator of σ_u^2 from the residuals. Clearly the scatter of the residuals around the regression line will reflect the unseen scatter of u about the line $Y_i = \beta_1 + \beta_2 X_i$, although, in general,

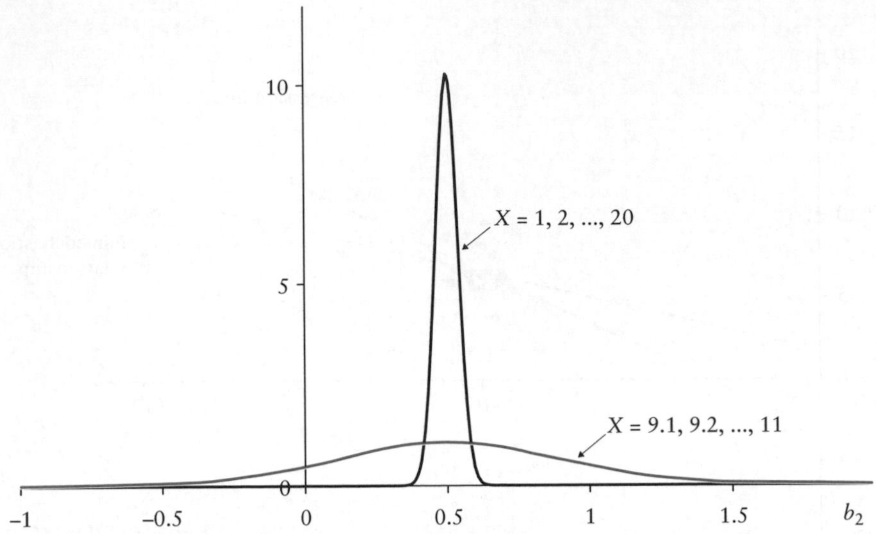

Figure 2.6 Distributions of b_2 with high and low dispersions of X

the residual and the value of the disturbance term in any given observation are not equal to one another. One measure of the scatter of the residuals is their mean square deviation, MSD(e), defined by

$$\text{MSD}(e) = \frac{1}{n}\sum_{i=1}^{n}(e_i - \bar{e})^2 = \frac{1}{n}\sum_{i=1}^{n} e_i^2 \tag{2.39}$$

($\bar{e} = 0$; see Section 1.5). Intuitively MSD(e) should provide a guide to σ_u^2.

Before going any further, one should consider the following question. Which line is likely to be closer to the points representing the sample of observations on X and Y, the true line $Y_i = \beta_1 + \beta_2 X_i$ or the regression line $\hat{Y}_i = b_1 + b_2 X_i$? The answer is the regression line, because by definition it is drawn in such a way as to minimize the sum of the squares of the distances between it and the observations. Hence the spread of the residuals will tend to be smaller than the spread of the values of u, and MSD(e) will tend to underestimate σ_u^2. Indeed, it can be shown that the expected value of MSD(e), when there is just one explanatory variable, is given by

$$E\{\text{MSD}(e)\} = \frac{n-2}{n}\sigma_u^2. \tag{2.40}$$

However, it follows that, if one defines s_u^2 by

$$s_u^2 = \frac{n}{n-2}\text{MSD}(e) = \frac{n}{n-2}\frac{1}{n}\sum_{i=1}^{n} e_i^2 = \frac{1}{n-2}\sum_{i=1}^{n} e_i^2, \tag{2.41}$$

then s_u^2 will be an unbiased estimator of σ_u^2.

Using (2.35) and (2.41), one can obtain estimates of the population variances of b_1 and b_2 and, by taking square roots, estimates of their standard deviations. Rather than talk about the estimate of the standard deviation of the probability density function of a regression coefficient, which is a bit cumbersome, one uses the term standard error of a regression coefficient, which in this text will frequently be abbreviated to s.e. For simple regression analysis, therefore, one has

$$\text{s.e.}(b_1) = \sqrt{s_u^2\left(\frac{1}{n}+\frac{\bar{X}^2}{\sum_{i=1}^{n}(X_i-\bar{X})^2}\right)} \quad \text{and} \quad \text{s.e.}(b_2) = \sqrt{\frac{s_u^2}{\sum_{i=1}^{n}(X_i-\bar{X})^2}}. \tag{2.42}$$

The standard errors of the regression coefficients are automatically calculated as part of the computer output.

Example

These relationships will be illustrated with the Monte Carlo experiment described in Section 2.4. The disturbance term was determined by random numbers drawn from a population with zero mean and unit variance, so $\sigma_u^2 = 1$. X was the set of numbers from 1 to 20. $\bar{X} = 10.5$ and $\sum(X_i - \bar{X})^2 = 665$. Hence,

$$\sigma_{b_1}^2 = \sigma_u^2\left(\frac{1}{n}+\frac{\bar{X}^2}{\sum_{i=1}^{n}(X_i-\bar{X})^2}\right) = \frac{1}{20}+\frac{10.5^2}{665} = 0.2158 \tag{2.43}$$

and

$$\sigma_{b_2}^2 = \frac{\sigma_u^2}{\sum_{i=1}^{n}(X_i-\bar{X})^2} = \frac{1}{665} = 0.001504. \tag{2.44}$$

Therefore, the true standard deviation of the distribution of b_2 shown in Figure 2.2 (and again as the narrower distribution in Figure 2.6) is $\sqrt{0.001504} = 0.0388$. The distribution of the standard error for the 10 million samples is shown in Figure 2.7, with the true standard deviation also marked.

We know that b_2 has a potential distribution around β_2. We would like the standard error to be as accurate as possible as an estimator of the standard deviation of this distribution since it is our main, indeed usually only, guide to the reliability of b_2 as an estimator of β_2. Figure 2.7 suggests that, in this case, the standard error, as a reliability measure, is itself not particularly reliable. But

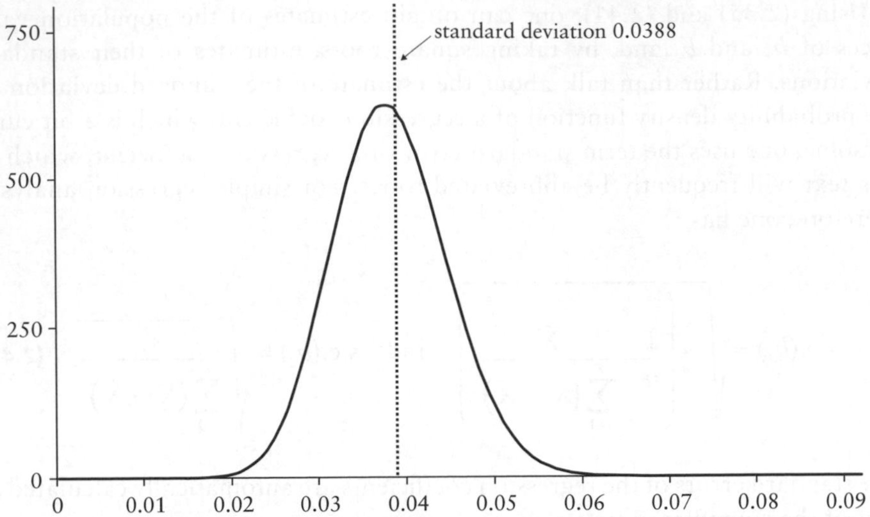

Figure 2.7 Distribution of the standard error of b_2

then, with only 20 observations, the sample is very small. With a larger sample, its distribution would be closer to the actual standard deviation.

One fundamental point must be emphasized. The standard error gives only a general guide to the likely accuracy of a regression coefficient. It enables you to obtain some idea of the width, or narrowness, of its probability density function as represented in Figure 2.2, but it does *not* tell you whether your regression estimate comes from the middle of the function, and is therefore accurate, or from the tails, and is therefore relatively inaccurate.

The higher the variance of the disturbance term, the higher the sample variance of the residuals is likely to be, and hence the higher will be the standard errors of the coefficients in the regression equation, reflecting the risk that the coefficients are inaccurate. However, it is only a *risk*. It is possible that in any particular sample the effects of the disturbance term in the different observations will cancel each other out and the regression coefficients will be accurate after all. The trouble is that in general there is no way of telling whether you happen to be in this fortunate position or not.

The Gauss–Markov theorem

In the Review chapter, we considered estimators of the unknown population mean μ_X of a random variable X, given a sample of observations. Although we instinctively use the sample mean $\bar{X}$ as our estimator, we saw that it was only one of an infinite number of possible unbiased estimators of μ_X. The reason that the sample mean is preferred to any other estimator is that, under certain assumptions, it is the most efficient. Of all unbiased estimators, it has the smallest variance.

Similar considerations apply to regression coefficients. The Gauss–Markov theorem states that, provided that the assumptions in Section 2.2 are satisfied, the OLS estimators are efficient. Sometimes, they are described as BLUE: best (smallest variance) linear (combinations of the Y_i) unbiased estimators of the regression parameters. This is demonstrated for the slope coefficient b_2 in Appendix 2.1.

EXERCISES

2.6* Using the decomposition of b_1 obtained in Exercise 2.1, derive the expression for $\sigma^2_{b_1}$ given in equation (2.35).

2.7* Given the decomposition in Exercise 2.2 of the OLS estimator of β_2 in the model $Y_i = \beta_2 X_i + u_i$, demonstrate that the variance of the slope coefficient is given by

$$\sigma^2_{b_2} = \frac{\sigma^2_u}{\sum_{j=1}^{n} X_j^2}.$$

2.8 Given the decomposition in Exercise 2.3 of the OLS estimator of β_1 in the model $Y_i = \beta_1 + u_i$, demonstrate that the variance of the slope coefficient is given by

$$\sigma^2_{b_1} = \frac{\sigma^2_u}{n}.$$

2.9 Assuming that the true model is $Y_i = \beta_1 + \beta_2 X_i + u_i$, it was demonstrated in Section 2.3 that the naïve estimator of the slope coefficient,

$$b_2 = \frac{Y_n - Y_1}{X_n - X_1},$$

is unbiased. It can be shown that its variance is given by

$$\frac{\sigma^2_u}{(X_1 - \bar{X})^2 + (X_n - \bar{X})^2 - 0.5(X_1 + X_n - 2\bar{X})^2}.$$

Use this information to verify that the estimator is less efficient than the OLS estimator.

2.10* It can be shown that the variance of the estimator of the slope coefficient in Exercise 2.5,

$$\frac{\sum_{i=1}^{n}(Z_i - \bar{Z})(Y_i - \bar{Y})}{\sum_{i=1}^{n}(Z_i - \bar{Z})(X_i - \bar{X})},$$

is given by

$$\sigma_{b_2}^2 = \frac{\sigma_u^2}{\sum_{i=1}^{n}(X_i - \bar{X})^2} \times \frac{1}{r_{XZ}^2},$$

where r_{XZ} is the correlation between X and Z. What are the implications for the efficiency of the estimator?

2.11 Can one come to any conclusions concerning the efficiency of the estimator in Exercise 2.4, for the case $\beta_1 = 0$?

2.12 Suppose that the true relationship between Y and X is $Y_i = \beta_1 + \beta_2 X_i + u_i$ and that the fitted model is $\hat{Y}_i = b_1 + b_2 X_i$. In Section 1.4, it was shown that if $Y_i^* = \lambda_1 + \lambda_2 Y_i$, and Y^* is regressed on X, the slope coefficient $b_2^* = \lambda_2 b_2$. How will the standard error of b_2^* be related to the standard error of b_2?

2.13* Suppose that the true relationship between Y and X is $Y_i = \beta_1 + \beta_2 X_i + u_i$ and that the fitted model is $\hat{Y}_i = b_1 + b_2 X_i$. In Exercise 1.12, it was shown that if $X_i^* = \mu_1 + \mu_2 X_i$, and Y is regressed on X^*, the slope coefficient $b_2^* = b_2/\mu_2$. How will the standard error of b_2^* be related to the standard error of b_2?

2.6 Testing hypotheses relating to the regression coefficients

The principles relating to tests of hypotheses and the construction of confidence intervals have been discussed in Sections R.9–R.12 of the Review chapter. There the context was the estimation of the unknown mean of a random variable X with a normal distribution with mean μ and variance σ^2. We will begin by summarizing what we did there.

The estimator of μ was $\bar{X}$. If a null hypothesis H_0: $\mu = \mu_0$ is true, the potential distribution of $\bar{X}$ is as shown in Figure 2.8, which reproduces Figure R.15. The figure supposes that we know the standard deviation of the distribution. We decided to reject H_0 if the discrepancy between μ_0 and $\bar{X}$ was 'too great'. 'Too great' is, of course, a subjective matter. In the case of a 5 percent significance test, we decided to reject H_0 if $\bar{X}$ fell in either the upper or the lower 2.5 percent tails of the distribution, conditional on H_0: $\mu = \mu_0$ being true. These are the rejection regions in Figure 2.8. They start 1.96 standard deviations above and below μ_0. Thus, a value of $\bar{X}$ represented by the point A would not lead to a rejection of H_0, while a value represented by the point B would lead to rejection. In general, we would reject H_0 if $\bar{X} > \mu_0 + 1.96\,\text{s.d.}$ or if $\bar{X} < \mu_0 - 1.96\,\text{s.d.}$ Equivalently, we could say that we would reject H_0 if $z > 1.96$ or if $z < -1.96$, where $z = (\bar{X} - \mu_0)/\text{s.d.}$

All this supposes that we know the standard deviation of the distribution. In practice, it has to be estimated, and we call the estimate the standard error. As a consequence of using the estimated standard error instead of the true standard deviation, the test statistic has a t distribution instead of a normal distribution, and the decision rule is to reject H_0 if $t > t_{\text{crit}}$ or if $t < -t_{\text{crit}}$,

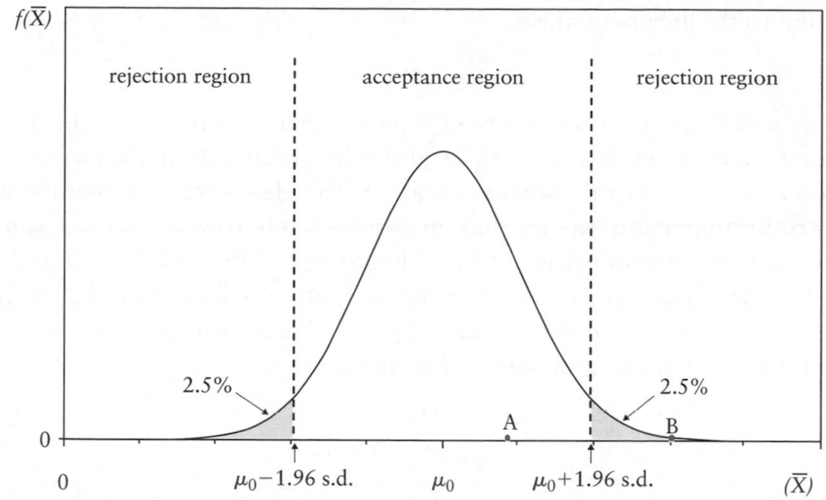

Figure 2.8 Rejection regions, conditional on H_0: $\mu = \mu_0$, 5 percent test

where $t = (\bar{X} - \mu_0)/\text{s.e.}$ and t_{crit} is the critical value of t, given the significance level and the number of degrees of freedom.

Performing tests of hypotheses relating to regression coefficients follows the same pattern in a straightforward manner. Suppose that the true model, as usual, is $Y_i = \beta_1 + \beta_2 X_i + u_i$ and we are fitting the regression equation $\hat{Y}_i = b_1 + b_2 X_i$. Suppose that we have a hypothesis relating to the slope coefficient H_0: $\beta_2 = \beta_2^0$. We will reject H_0 if the discrepancy between b_2 and β_2^0 is too great, measured in terms of standard errors. We define the t statistic

$$t = \frac{b_2 - \beta_2^0}{\text{s.e.}(b_2)} \tag{2.45}$$

and we reject H_0 if $|t| > t_{crit}$, that is, if $t > t_{crit}$ or if $t < -t_{crit}$.

There is one important difference. When we performed t tests of H_0: $\mu = \mu_0$ in Section R.11, the number of degrees of freedom was equal to $n - 1$, where n is the number of observations in the sample. In a regression equation, the estimation of each parameter consumes one degree of freedom in the sample. Hence, the number of degrees of freedom is equal to the number of observations in the sample minus the number of parameters estimated. The parameters are the constant (assuming that this is specified in the regression model) and the coefficients of the explanatory variables. In the present case of simple regression analysis, two parameters, β_1 and β_2, are estimated and hence the number of degrees of freedom is $n - 2$. It should be emphasized that a more general expression will be required when we come to multiple regression analysis.

For instance, suppose that we hypothesize that the percentage rate of price inflation in an economy, p, depends on the percentage rate of wage inflation, w, according to the linear equation

$$p = \beta_1 + \beta_2 w + u, \tag{2.46}$$

where β_1 and β_2 are parameters and u is a disturbance term. We might further hypothesize that, apart from the effects of the disturbance term, the rate of price inflation is equal to the rate of wage inflation. The idea is that if wages increase by a certain proportion, the increase in costs is likely to give rise to a similar proportional increase in prices. The null hypothesis is then $H_0: \beta_2 = 1$ and the alternative hypothesis is $H_1: \beta_2 \neq 1$. Suppose that we take actual observations on average rates of price inflation and wage inflation over the past five years for a sample of 20 countries and the fitted model is

$$\underset{}{\hat{p}} = \underset{(0.05)}{-1.21} + \underset{(0.10)}{0.82}w, \tag{2.47}$$

where the numbers in parentheses are standard errors. The t statistic for testing $H_0: \beta_2 = 1$ is

$$t = \frac{b_2 - \beta_2^0}{\text{s.e.}(b_2)} = \frac{0.82 - 1.00}{0.10} = -1.80. \tag{2.48}$$

Since there are 20 observations in the sample, the number of degrees of freedom is 18 and the critical value of t at the 5 percent significance level is 2.101. The absolute value of the t statistic is less than this, so on this occasion we do not reject the null hypothesis. The estimate 0.82 is below the hypothesized value 1.00, but not so far below as to exclude the possibility that the null hypothesis is correct.

In this example, we tested a particular null hypothesis H_0: $\beta_2 = 1$ that was suggested by theory. In practice, given a theoretical model $Y = \beta_1 + \beta_2 X + u$, we are seldom able to hypothesize that a variable X has a *specific* effect on another variable Y. Usually, the aim of a t test is less ambitious. The aim is to determine whether X has *some* effect on Y. We believe that X does influence Y and that β_2 is therefore nonzero, but we are not able to anticipate the value of the parameter. So we adopt an inverse strategy. We set up the null hypothesis $H_0: \beta_2 = 0$. We then hope to demonstrate that H_0 should be rejected. If we are successful, our interest next turns to the magnitude of the effect and the margin of error of the estimate.

For example, consider the simple earnings function

$$EARNINGS = \beta_1 + \beta_2 S + u, \tag{2.49}$$

where *EARNINGS* is hourly earnings in dollars and S is years of schooling. On very reasonable theoretical grounds, you expect earnings to be influenced by years of schooling, but your theory is not strong enough to enable you to specify a particular value for β_2. You can nevertheless establish the dependence of earnings on schooling by the inverse procedure in which you take as your

Table 2.2

```
.reg EARNINGS S
     Source    |       SS          df             MS        Number of obs =    540
---------------------------------------------------------   F(1, 538)     = 112.15
     Model     |   19321.5589       1         19321.5589    Prob > F      = 0.0000
    Residual   |   92688.6722     538         172.283777    R-squared     = 0.1725
---------------------------------------------------------   Adj R-squared = 0.1710
     Total     |   112010.231     539         207.811189    Root MSE      = 13.126
-------------------------------------------------------------------------------------
   EARNINGS    |       Coef.    Std. Err.      t       P>|t|     [95% Conf.  Interval]
-------------------------------------------------------------------------------------
          S    |    2.455321    .2318512     10.59     0.000      1.999876    2.910765
      _ cons   |   -13.93347    3.219851     -4.33     0.000     -20.25849   -7.608444
-------------------------------------------------------------------------------------
```

null hypothesis the assertion that earnings do *not* depend on schooling, that is, $H_0\colon \beta_2 = 0$. Your alternative hypothesis is $H_1\colon \beta_2 \neq 0$, that is, that schooling *does* affect earnings. If you can reject the null hypothesis, you have established the relationship, at least in general terms.

Table 2.2 reproduces the regression of hourly earnings on years of schooling using data from the United States National Longitudinal Survey of Youth shown in Table 1.2. The first two columns of the lower part of the output give the names of the variables and the estimates of their coefficients. The third column gives the corresponding standard errors. The t statistic for the null hypothesis $H_0\colon \beta_2 = 0$, using (2.45), is simply the estimate of the coefficient divided by its standard error:

$$t = \frac{b_2 - \beta_2^0}{\text{s.e.}(b_2)} = \frac{b_2 - 0}{\text{s.e.}(b_2)} = \frac{2.4553}{0.2319} = 10.59. \qquad \textbf{(2.50)}$$

Since there are 540 observations in the sample and we have estimated two parameters, the number of degrees of freedom is 538. Table A.2 does not give the critical values of t for 538 degrees of freedom, but we know that they must be lower than the corresponding critical values for 500, since the critical value is inversely related to the number of degrees of freedom. The critical value with 500 degrees of freedom at the 5 percent level is 1.965. Hence, we can be sure that we would reject H_0 at the 5 percent level with 538 degrees of freedom and we conclude that schooling does affect earnings.

Of course, since we are using the 5 percent significance level as the basis for the test, there is in principle a 5 percent risk of a Type I error, if the null hypothesis of no effect is true. We could reduce the risk to 1 percent by using the 1 percent significance level instead. The critical value of t at the 1 percent significance level with 500 degrees of freedom is 2.586. Since the t statistic is greater than this, we see that we can easily reject the null hypothesis at this level as well.

Note that when the 5 percent and 1 percent tests lead to the same conclusion, there is no need to report both, and indeed you would look ignorant if you did. See Box 2.4 on reporting test results.

BOX 2.4 Reporting the results of *t* tests

Suppose you have a theoretical relationship

$$Y_i = \beta_1 + \beta_2 X_i + u_i$$

and your null and alternative hypotheses are H_0: $\beta_2 = \beta_2^0$, H_1: $\beta_2 \neq \beta_2^0$. Given an experimental estimate b_2 of β_2, the acceptance and rejection regions for the hypothesis for the 5 percent and 1 percent significance levels can be represented in general terms by the left part of Figure 2.9.

The right side of the figure gives the same regions for a specific example, the price inflation/wage inflation model, the null hypothesis being that β_2 is equal to 1. The null hypothesis will not be rejected at the 5 percent level if b_2 lies within 2.101 standard errors of 1, that is, in the range 0.79 to 1.21, and it will not be rejected at the 1 percent level if b_2 lies within 2.878 standard errors of 1, that is, in the range 0.71 to 1.29.

From Figure 2.9 it can be seen that there are three types of decision zone:

1. where b_2 is so far from the hypothetical β_2 that the null hypothesis is rejected at both the 5 percent and the 1 percent levels,
2. where b_2 is far enough from the hypothetical β_2 for the null hypothesis to be rejected at the 5 percent but not the 1 percent level,
3. where b_2 is close enough to the hypothetical β_2 for the null hypothesis not to be rejected at either level.

From the diagram it can be verified that if the null hypothesis is rejected at the 1 percent level, it is automatically rejected at the 5 percent level. Hence, in case (1) it is only necessary to report the rejection of the hypothesis at the 1 percent level. To report that it is rejected also at the 5 percent level is superfluous and suggests that you are not aware of this. It would be a bit like reporting that a certain high jumper can clear two meters, and then adding that the athlete can also clear one and a half meters.

In case (3), likewise, you only need to make one statement, in this case that the hypothesis is not rejected at the 5 percent level. It automatically follows that it is not rejected at the 1 percent level, and to add a statement to this effect as well would be like saying that the high jumper cannot clear one and a half meters, and also reporting that the athlete cannot clear two meters either.

Only in case (2) is it necessary (and desirable) to report the results of both tests.

Note that if you find that you can reject the null hypothesis at the 5 percent level, you should not stop there. You have established that the null hypothesis can be rejected at that level, but there remains a 5 percent chance of a Type I error. You should also perform the test at the 1 percent level. If you find that you can reject the null hypothesis at this level, this is the outcome that you should report. The risk of a Type I error is now only 1 percent and your conclusion is much more convincing. This is case (1) above. If you cannot reject at the 1 percent level, you have reached case (2) and you should report the results of both tests.

This procedure of establishing a relationship between a dependent and an explanatory variable by setting up, and then refuting, a null hypothesis H_0: $\beta_2 = 0$ is used very frequently indeed. Consequently, all serious regression applications automatically print out the t statistic for this special case: that is,

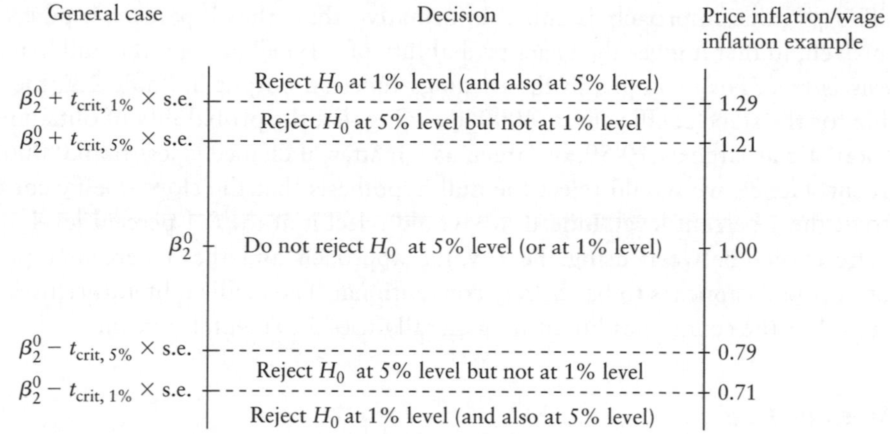

Figure 2.9 Reporting the results of a t test (no need to report conclusions in parentheses)

the coefficient divided by its standard error. The ratio is often denoted 'the' t statistic. In Table 2.2, the t statistics for the constant and slope coefficient appear in the middle column of the regression output.

However, if the null hypothesis specifies some nonzero value of β_2, the more general expression (2.71) has to be used and the t statistic has to be calculated by hand, as in the price inflation/wage inflation example.

0.1 percent tests

If the t statistic is very high, you should check whether you can reject the null hypothesis at the 0.1 percent level. If you can, you should always report the result of the 0.1 percent test in preference to that of the 1 percent test because it demonstrates that you are able to reject the null hypothesis of no effect with an even smaller risk of a Type I error.

p values

The fifth column of the lower half of the output in Table 2.2, headed $P > |t|$, provides an alternative approach to reporting the significance of regression coefficients. The figures in this column give the p value for each coefficient. This is the probability of obtaining the corresponding t statistic as a matter of chance, if the null hypothesis H_0: $\beta_2 = 0$ were true. A p value of less than 0.01 means that the probability is less than 1 percent, which in turn means that the null hypothesis would be rejected at the 1 percent level; a p value between 0.01 and 0.05 means that the null hypothesis would be rejected at the 5 percent, but not the 1 percent level; and a p value of 0.05 or more means that it would not be rejected at the 5 percent level.

The p value approach is more informative than the 5 percent/1 percent approach, in that it gives the exact probability of a Type I error, if the null hypothesis is true. For example, in the earnings function output in Table 2.2, the p value for the slope coefficient is 0.000, meaning that the probability of obtaining a t statistic as large as 10.59, or larger, as a matter of chance is less than 0.0005 percent. Hence, we would reject the null hypothesis that the slope coefficient is zero at the 1 percent level. Indeed, we would reject it at the 0.1 percent level.

The choice between using the p value approach and the 5 percent/1 percent approach appears to be entirely conventional. The medical literature uses p values, but the economics literature generally uses 5 percent/1 percent.

One-sided tests

The logic underlying one-sided tests, and the potential benefits from performing them, have been discussed at length in Section R.13 of the Review chapter. Application to regression analysis is straightforward. For example, in the case of the price inflation/wage inflation model

$$p = \beta_1 + \beta_2 w + u, \tag{2.51}$$

the null hypothesis was that price inflation is equal to wage inflation: H_0: $\beta_2 = 1$ since increases in wages give rise to increases in costs, and subsequently prices. In practice, there is another important element in the relationship, the rate of improvement in productivity. The rates of inflation of wages and prices may differ because improvements in productivity may cause cost inflation, and hence price inflation, to be lower than wage inflation. Certainly, improvements in productivity will not cause price inflation to be greater than wage inflation and so in this case we are justified in ruling out $\beta_2 > 1$. We are left with H_0: $\beta_2 = 1$ and H_1: $\beta_2 < 1$. Given the regression result

$$\hat{p} = -1.21 + 0.82w \tag{2.52}$$
$$(0.05) \quad (0.10)$$

for a sample of 20 countries, the t statistic for the null hypothesis is

$$t = \frac{b_2 - \beta_2^0}{\text{s.e.}(b_2)} = \frac{0.82 - 1}{0.10} = -1.80. \tag{2.53}$$

This is not high enough, in absolute terms, to cause H_0 to be rejected at the 5 percent level using a two-sided test (critical value 2.10 for 18 degrees of freedom). However, if we use a one-sided test, as we are entitled to, the critical value falls to 1.73 and we *can* reject the null hypothesis. In other words, we can conclude that price inflation is significantly lower than wage inflation.

One-sided tests are particularly useful in the very common case where we have adopted the inverse approach to demonstrating that a variable Y is influenced by another variable X. We have set up the model $Y_i = \beta_1 + \beta_2 X_i + u_i$ and we hope to show that H_0: $\beta_2 = 0$ can be rejected. Often, we are in a position to argue either that β_2 cannot be negative or that it cannot be positive. If we can argue that it cannot be negative, the alternative hypothesis is H_1: $\beta_2 > 0$. If we can argue that it cannot be positive, the alternative hypothesis is H_1: $\beta_2 < 0$. In either case, the test statistic is

$$t = \frac{b_2 - \beta_2^0}{\text{s.e.}(b_2)} = \frac{b_2 - 0}{\text{s.e.}(b_2)} = \frac{b_2}{\text{s.e.}(b_2)} \tag{2.54}$$

and we compare it with the critical value of t. At any given significance level, the critical value of t for a one-sided test is smaller in magnitude than that for a two-sided test. This will sometimes make it possible to reject H_0 and establish the relationship with a one-sided test when we could not with a two-sided test.

There are three possibilities. One is that the effect of X on Y is very strong, the t statistic is large, and we reject H_0 at a high significance level, even if we use a two-sided test. Obviously, we would also reject H_0 using a one-sided test. The second is that the effect is weak or non-existent, and we do not reject H_0, even using a one-sided test. Obviously, we would not reject H_0 using a two-sided test. The third possibility is that the t statistic lies between the critical values of t for the one-sided and two-sided tests. Only in this case is there any actual benefit from using a one-sided test.

The earnings–schooling regression in Table 2.2 provides an example. There are 538 degrees of freedom and the critical value of t, using the 0.1 percent significance level and a two-sided test, is 3.31. However, one may reasonably rule out the possibility that, in general, extra schooling will be responsible for a fall in earnings. Hence, one may perform a one-sided test with H_0: $\beta_2=0$ and H_1: $\beta_2 > 0$. For a one-sided test, the critical value is reduced to 3.11. The t statistic is in fact equal to 10.59, so in this case the refinement makes no difference. The estimated coefficient is so large relative to its standard error that we reject the null hypothesis at the 0.1 percent significance level regardless of whether we use a two-sided or a one-sided test.

A final comment on the justification of the use of a one-sided test is in order. In the case of the earnings–schooling example, it is tempting to say that we are justified in using a one-sided test because schooling can be expected to have a positive effect on earnings. However, this is too strong. By assumption, we have excluded the null hypothesis H_0: $\beta_2 = 0$ before we start. There is nothing left to test. The correct justification is that we can exclude the possibility of a negative effect. This leaves us with the null hypothesis H_0: $\beta_2 = 0$ and the alternative hypothesis H_1: $\beta_2 > 0$, and we use the test to discriminate between them.

Similarly, in the case of the price inflation/wage inflation example, it is tempting to say that we can use a one-sided test because improvements in productivity will cause the rate of price inflation to be lower than the rate of wage inflation. Again, this is too strong, because we have excluded H_0: $\beta_2 = 1$ before we start.

We should say that we exclude the possibility that $\beta_2 > 1$, which leaves us to test the null hypothesis against the alternative hypothesis $H_1: \beta_2 < 1$.

Confidence intervals

Confidence intervals were also treated at length in the Review chapter and their application to regression analysis presents no problems. We will briefly provide the mathematical derivation in the context of a regression. For a further graphical explanation, see Section R.12.

From the initial discussion in this section, we saw that, given a theoretical model $Y_i = \beta_1 + \beta_2 X_i + u_i$ and a fitted model $\hat{Y}_i = b_1 + b_2 X_i$, the regression coefficient b_2 and a hypothetical value $\beta_2 = \beta_2^0$ are incompatible if either

$$\frac{b_2 - \beta_2^0}{\text{s.e.}(b_2)} > t_{\text{crit}} \quad \text{or} \quad \frac{b_2 - \beta_2^0}{\text{s.e.}(b_2)} < -t_{\text{crit}}, \tag{2.55}$$

that is, if either

$$b_2 - \beta_2^0 > \text{s.e.}(b_2) \times t_{\text{crit}} \quad \text{or} \quad b_2 - \beta_2^0 < -\text{s.e.}(b_2) \times t_{\text{crit}}, \tag{2.56}$$

that is, if either

$$b_2 - \text{s.e.}(b_2) \times t_{\text{crit}} > \beta_2^0 \quad \text{or} \quad b_2 + \text{s.e.}(b_2) \times t_{\text{crit}} < \beta_2^0. \tag{2.57}$$

It therefore follows that a hypothetical β_2 *is* compatible with the regression result if both

$$b_2 - \text{s.e.}(b_2) \times t_{\text{crit}} \le \beta_2 \quad \text{and} \quad b_2 + \text{s.e.}(b_2) \times t_{\text{crit}} \ge \beta_2, \tag{2.58}$$

that is, if β_2 satisfies the double inequality

$$b_2 - \text{s.e.}(b_2) \times t_{\text{crit}} \le \beta_2 \le b_2 + \text{s.e.}(b_2) \times t_{\text{crit}}. \tag{2.59}$$

This is the confidence interval, in abstract. Any hypothetical value of β_2 that satisfies (2.59) will be compatible with the estimate b_2, that is, will not be rejected by it. To make the confidence interval operational, we need to select a significance level and determine the corresponding critical value of t.

Example

In the earnings function output in Table 2.2, the coefficient of S was 2.455, its standard error was 0.232, and the critical value of t at the 5 percent significance level was about 1.965. The corresponding 95 percent confidence interval is therefore

$$2.455 - 0.232 \times 1.965 \le \beta_2 \le 2.455 + 0.232 \times 1.965, \tag{2.60}$$

that is,

$$1.999 \le \beta_2 \le 2.911. \quad \textbf{(2.61)}$$

We would therefore reject hypothetical values below 1.999 and above 2.911. Any hypotheses within these limits would not be rejected, given the regression result. This confidence interval actually appears as the final column in the Stata output. However, this is not a standard feature of a regression application, so you usually have to calculate the interval yourself.

EXERCISES

2.14 A researcher hypothesizes that years of schooling, S, may be related to the number of siblings (brothers and sisters), $SIBLINGS$, according to the relationship

$$S = \beta_1 + \beta_2 SIBLINGS + u.$$

She is prepared to test the null hypothesis H_0: $\beta_2 = 0$ against the alternative hypothesis H_1: $\beta_2 \neq 0$ at the 5 percent and 1 percent levels. She has a sample of 60 observations. What should she report:

1. if $b_2 = -0.20$, s.e.$(b_2) = 0.07$?

2. if $b_2 = -0.12$, s.e.$(b_2) = 0.07$?

3. if $b_2 = 0.06$, s.e.$(b_2) = 0.07$?

4. if $b_2 = 0.20$, s.e.$(b_2) = 0.07$?

2.15* A researcher with a sample of 50 individuals with similar education but differing amounts of training hypothesizes that hourly earnings, $EARNINGS$, may be related to hours of training, $TRAINING$, according to the relationship

$$EARNINGS = \beta_1 + \beta_2 TRAINING + u.$$

He is prepared to test the null hypothesis H_0: $\beta_2 = 0$ against the alternative hypothesis H_1: $\beta_2 \neq 0$ at the 5 percent and 1 percent levels. What should he report:

1. if $b_2 = 0.30$, s.e.$(b_2) = 0.12$?

2. if $b_2 = 0.55$, s.e.$(b_2) = 0.12$?

3. if $b_2 = 0.10$, s.e.$(b_2) = 0.12$?

4. if $b_2 = -0.27$, s.e.$(b_2) = 0.12$?

2.16 Perform a t test on the slope coefficient and the intercept of the educational attainment function fitted using your *EAEF* data set in Exercise 1.6, and state your conclusions.

2.17 Perform a t test on the slope coefficient and the intercept of the earnings function fitted using your *EAEF* data set in Exercise 1.7, and state your conclusions.

2.18 In Exercise 1.4, the growth rate of employment was regressed on the growth rate of GDP for a sample of 25 OECD countries. Perform t tests on the slope coefficient and the intercept and state your conclusions.

2.19 Explain whether it would have been justifiable to perform one-sided tests instead of two-sided tests in Exercise 2.14. If you think that one-sided tests are justified, perform them and state whether the use of a one-sided test makes any difference.

2.20* Explain whether it would have been justifiable to perform one-sided tests instead of two-sided tests in Exercise 2.15. If you think that one-sided tests are justified, perform them and state whether the use of a one-sided test makes any difference.

2.21 Explain whether it would have been justifiable to perform one-sided tests instead of two-sided tests in Exercise 2.16. If you think that one-sided tests are justified, perform them and state whether the use of a one-sided test makes any difference.

2.22 Explain whether it would have been justifiable to perform one-sided tests instead of two-sided tests in Exercise 2.17. If you think that one-sided tests are justified, perform them and state whether the use of a one-sided test makes any difference.

2.23 In Exercise 1.9, the number of children in the family was regressed on the years of schooling of the mother for a sample of 540 NLSY respondents. Explain whether it would be justifiable to perform a one-sided test instead of a two-sided test on the slope coefficient.

2.24 Suppose that the true relationship between Y and X is $Y_i = \beta_1 + \beta_2 X_i + u_i$ and that the fitted model is $\hat{Y}_i = b_1 + b_2 X_i$. In Section 1.4, it was shown that if $Y_i^* = \lambda_1 + \lambda_2 Y_i$, and Y^* is regressed on X, the slope coefficient $b_2^* = \lambda_2 b_2$. How will the *t* statistic for b_2^* be related to the *t* statistic for b_2? (See also Exercise 2.12.)

2.25* Suppose that the true relationship between Y and X is $Y_i = \beta_1 + \beta_2 X_i + u_i$ and that the fitted model is $\hat{Y}_i = b_1 + b_2 X_i$. In Exercise 1.12, it was shown that if $X_i^* = \mu_1 + \mu_2 X_i$, and Y is regressed on X^*, the slope coefficient $b_2^* = b_2/\mu_2$. How will the *t* statistic for b_2^* be related to the *t* statistic for b_2? (See also Exercise 2.13.)

2.26 Calculate the 99 percent confidence interval for β_2 in the earnings function example in Table 2.2 ($b_2 = 2.455$, s.e.$(b_2) = 0.232$), and explain why it includes some values not included in the 95 percent confidence interval calculated in inequality (2.61).

2.27 Calculate the 95 percent confidence interval for the slope coefficient in the earnings function fitted with your *EAEF* data set in Exercise 1.7.

2.28* Calculate the 95 percent confidence interval for β_2 in the price inflation/wage inflation example:

$$\hat{p} = -1.21 + 0.82w.$$
$$(0.05)\quad(0.10)$$

What can you conclude from this calculation?

2.7 The *F* test of goodness of fit

Even if there is no relationship between *Y* and *X*, in any given sample of observations there may appear to be one, if only a faint one. Only by coincidence will the R^2 from a regression of *Y* on *X* be exactly equal to zero. So how do we know if the R^2 for the regression reflects a true relationship or if it has arisen as a matter of chance?

We could in principle adopt the following procedure. Suppose that the regression model is

$$Y_i = \beta_1 + \beta_2 X_i + u_i. \tag{2.62}$$

We take as our null hypothesis $H_0\text{: } \beta_2 = 0$, that there is no relationship between *Y* and *X*. We calculate the value that R^2 would exceed 5 percent of the time as a matter of chance if H_0 is true. We then take this figure as the critical level of R^2 for a 5 percent significance test. If it is exceeded, we reject the null hypothesis and conclude that $\beta_2 \neq 0$.

Such a test, like the *t* test on a coefficient, would not be error-free. Indeed, at the 5 percent significance level, one would risk making a Type I error (rejecting the null hypothesis when it is in fact true) 5 percent of the time. Of course you could cut down on this risk by using a higher significance level, for example, the 1 percent level. The critical level of R^2 would then be that which would be exceeded by chance only 1 percent of the time if H_0 is true, so it would be higher than the critical level for the 5 percent test.

How does one find the critical level of R^2 at either significance level? There is a problem. There is no such thing as a table of critical levels of R^2. The traditional procedure is to use an indirect approach and perform what is known as an *F* test based on analysis of variance.

We saw in Chapter 1 that the variations in the dependent variable may be decomposed into 'explained' and 'unexplained' components using (1.58):

$$\sum_{i=1}^{n}(Y_i - \bar{Y})^2 = \sum_{i=1}^{n}(\hat{Y}_i - \bar{Y})^2 + \sum_{i=1}^{n} e_i^2. \tag{2.63}$$

The left side is *TSS*, the total sum of squares of the values of the dependent variable about its sample mean. The first term on the right side is *ESS*, the explained sum of squares, and the second term is *RSS*, the unexplained, residual sum of squares:

$$TSS = ESS + RSS. \tag{2.64}$$

R^2 was then defined as the ratio of the explained sum of squares to the total sum of squares:

$$R^2 = \frac{ESS}{TSS} = \frac{\sum_{i=1}^{n}\left(\hat{Y}_i - \bar{Y}\right)^2}{\sum_{i=1}^{n}\left(Y_i - \bar{Y}\right)^2}. \tag{2.65}$$

The F statistic for the goodness of fit of a regression is written as the explained sum of squares, per explanatory variable, divided by the residual sum of squares, per degree of freedom remaining:

$$F = \frac{ESS/(k-1)}{RSS/(n-k)}, \tag{2.66}$$

where k is the number of parameters in the regression equation (intercept and $k-1$ slope coefficients).

The F statistic is an increasing function of R^2. Dividing both the numerator and the denominator of the ratio by TSS, we have

$$F = \frac{(ESS/TSS)/(k-1)}{(RSS/TSS)/(n-k)} = \frac{R^2/(k-1)}{(1-R^2)/(n-k)}. \tag{2.67}$$

An increase in R^2 leads to an increase in the numerator and a decrease in the denominator, and hence unambiguously to an increase in F. In the present context, $k = 2$, so (2.67) becomes

$$F = \frac{R^2}{(1-R^2)/(n-2)}. \tag{2.68}$$

F can be calculated using (2.66) and ESS and RSS or, equivalently, (2.68) and R^2. It is then compared with F_{crit}, the critical level of F, in the appropriate table. If F is greater than F_{crit}, you reject the null hypothesis H_0: $\beta_2 = 0$ and conclude that the 'explanation' of Y is better than is likely to have arisen by chance. In any serious regression application, F is automatically presented as part of the output.

Why do we take this indirect approach? Why not publish a table of critical levels of R^2? The answer is that the F table is useful for testing many forms of analysis of variance, of which R^2 is only one. Rather than have a specialized table for each application, it is more convenient (or, at least, it saves a lot of paper) to have just one general table, and make transformations such as (2.66) when necessary.

Table A.3 gives the critical levels of F at the 5 percent, 1 percent, and 0.1 percent significance levels. In each case, the critical level depends on the number of explanatory variables, $k-1$, which is read from along the top of the table, and the number of degrees of freedom, $n-k$, which is read off down the side. In the present context, we are concerned with simple regression analysis, k is 2, and we should use the first column of the table.

Example

Table 2.2 presents the output for the earnings function example regression. In the top left corner of the output, there is a column headed 'SS', meaning sums of squares. In that column one sees that ESS = 19,322 (Stata refers to ESS as the 'model' sum of squares), $RSS = 92{,}689$, and $TSS = 112{,}010$. The number of observations is 540, $k = 2$, and so the number of degrees of freedom is 538. Hence,

$$F = \frac{ESS/(k-1)}{RSS/(n-k)} = \frac{19{,}322/1}{92{,}689/538} = \frac{19{,}322}{172.28} = 112.15. \qquad \textbf{(2.69)}$$

The F statistic is printed in the top right corner of the output, together with its p value: the probability of obtaining an F statistic as high as that as a matter of chance if H_0: $\beta_2 = 0$ is true and there is no real relationship. (In this case, no chance, at least to four decimal places, so the F statistic is very strong evidence of a genuine relationship.) Looking at Table A.3, at the 0.1 percent significance level, the critical level of F for 1 and 500 degrees of freedom (first column, row 500) is 10.96. The critical value for 1 and 538 degrees of freedom must be lower, so we have no hesitation in rejecting the null hypothesis in this example.

We will verify that we obtain the same value of F using the expression for it as a function of R^2:

$$F = \frac{R^2/(k-1)}{(1-R^2)/(n-k)} = \frac{0.1725/1}{0.8275/538} = \frac{0.1725}{0.001538} = 112.16, \qquad \textbf{(2.70)}$$

which is the same, apart from rounding error on the last digit.

Relationship between the F test and the t test on the slope coefficient in simple regression analysis

In the context of simple regression analysis (and *only* simple regression analysis), the F test and the two-sided t test on the slope coefficient have the same null hypothesis H_0: $\beta_2 = 0$ and the same alternative hypothesis H_1: $\beta_2 \neq 0$. This gives rise to the possibility that they might lead to different conclusions. Fortunately, they are in fact equivalent. The F statistic is equal to the square of the t statistic, and, at any given significance level, the critical value of F is equal to the square of the critical value of t. Starting with the definition of F in (2.66), and putting $k = 2$,

$$F = \frac{ESS}{RSS/(n-2)} = \frac{\sum_{i=1}^{n}\left(\hat{Y}_i - \bar{Y}\right)^2}{\sum_{i=1}^{n} e_i^2 \Big/ (n-2)} = \frac{\sum_{i=1}^{n}\left([b_1 + b_2X_i] - [b_1 + b_2\bar{X}]\right)^2}{s_u^2}$$

$$= \frac{1}{s_u^2}\sum_{i=1}^{n} b_2^2\left(X_i - \bar{X}\right)^2 = \frac{b_2^2}{s_u^2 \Big/ \sum_{i=1}^{n}\left(X_i - \bar{X}\right)^2} = \frac{b_2^2}{(\text{s.e.}(b_2))^2} = t^2. \qquad \textbf{(2.71)}$$

The proof that, at any given significance level, the critical value of F is equal to the critical value of t for a two-sided t test is more complicated and will be omitted. When we come to multiple regression analysis, we will see that the F test and the t tests have different roles and different null hypotheses. However, in simple regression analysis, the fact that they are equivalent means that there is no point in performing both. Indeed, you would look ignorant if you did. Obviously, provided that it is justifiable, a one-sided t test would be preferable to either.

Key terms

- autocorrelation
- cross-sectional data
- F statistic
- F test of goodness of fit
- Gauss–Markov theorem
- homoscedastic disturbance term
- Monte Carlo experiment
- nonstochastic regressor
- p value
- panel data
- standard error of a regression coefficient
- stochastic regressor
- time series data

EXERCISES

2.29 In Exercise 1.4, in the regression of the rate of growth of employment on the rate of growth of real GDP using a sample of 25 OECD countries, ESS = 14.58 and RSS = 10.13. Calculate the corresponding F statistic and check that it is equal to 33.1, the value printed in the output. Also calculate the F statistic using $R^2 = 0.5900$ and verify that it is the same. Perform the F test at the 5 percent, 1 percent, and 0.1 percent significance levels. Is it necessary to report the results of the tests at all three levels?

2.30 Calculate the F statistic from ESS and RSS obtained in the earnings function fitted using your *EAEF* data set and check that it is equal to the value printed in the output. Check that the F statistic derived from R^2 is the same. Perform an appropriate F test.

2.31 Verify that the F statistic in the earnings function regression run by you using your *EAEF* data set is equal to the square of the t statistic for the slope coefficient, and that the critical value of F at the 1 percent significance level is equal to the square of the critical value of t.

2.32 In Exercise 1.16, both researchers obtained a t statistic of 10.59 for the slope coefficient in their regressions. Was this a coincidence?

2.33 Suppose that the true relationship between Y and X is $Y_i = \beta_1 + \beta_2 X_i + u_i$ and that the fitted model is $\hat{Y}_i = b_1 + b_2 X_i$. Suppose that $Y_i^* = \lambda_1 + \lambda_2 Y_i$, and Y^* is regressed on X. How will the F statistic for this regression be related to the F statistic for the original regression? (See also Exercises 1.21, 2.12, and 2.24.)

2.34* Suppose that the true relationship between Y and X is $Y_i = \beta_1 + \beta_2 X_i + u_i$ and that the fitted model is $\hat{Y}_i = b_1 + b_2 X_i$. Suppose that $X_i^* = \mu_1 + \mu_2 X_i$, and Y is regressed on X^*. How will the F statistic for this regression be related to the F statistic for the original regression? (See also Exercises 1.22, 2.13, and 2.25.)

Appendix 2.1 The Gauss–Markov theorem

At the end of Section 2.5, it was asserted that the OLS estimators of the parameters are BLUE (best linear unbiased estimator), if the assumptions for Model A are satisfied. This appendix provides a demonstration for the OLS slope coefficient.

To see the linearity property, note that

$$\begin{aligned}\sum_{i=1}^{n}\left(X_i-\bar{X}\right)\left(Y_i-\bar{Y}\right) &= \sum_{i=1}^{n}\left(X_i-\bar{X}\right)Y_i-\sum_{i=1}^{n}\left(X_i-\bar{X}\right)\bar{Y} \\ &= \sum_{i=1}^{n}\left(X_i-\bar{X}\right)Y_i-\bar{Y}\sum_{i=1}^{n}\left(X_i-\bar{X}\right) \\ &= \sum_{i=1}^{n}\left(X_i-\bar{X}\right)Y_i-\bar{Y}\left\{\sum_{i=1}^{n}X_i-n\bar{X}\right\} \\ &= \sum_{i=1}^{n}\left(X_i-\bar{X}\right)Y_i. \end{aligned} \qquad \textbf{(A2.1)}$$

Then

$$b_2=\frac{\sum_{i=1}^{n}\left(X_i-\bar{X}\right)\left(Y_i-\bar{Y}\right)}{\sum_{j=1}^{n}\left(X_j-\bar{X}\right)^2}=\frac{\sum_{i=1}^{n}\left(X_i-\bar{X}\right)Y_i}{\sum_{j=1}^{n}\left(X_j-\bar{X}\right)^2}=\sum_{i=1}^{n}\frac{\left(X_i-\bar{X}\right)}{\sum_{j=1}^{n}\left(X_j-\bar{X}\right)^2}Y_i=\sum_{i=1}^{n}a_iY_i, \qquad \textbf{(A2.2)}$$

where the a_i are defined as before.

We will demonstrate the efficiency property. Consider any other unbiased estimator

$$\tilde{b}_2=\sum_{i=1}^{n}g_iY_i \qquad \textbf{(A2.3)}$$

that is a linear function of the Y_i. We will show that it has a larger variance unless $g_i = a_i$ for all i. For $\tilde{b}_2$ to be unbiased, we need $E\left(\tilde{b}_2\right)=\beta_2$.

$$\tilde{b}_2=\sum_{i=1}^{n}g_iY_i=\sum_{i=1}^{n}g_i\left(\beta_1+\beta_2X_i+u_i\right)=\sum_{i=1}^{n}\beta_1g_i+\sum_{i=1}^{n}\beta_2g_iX_i+\sum_{i=1}^{n}g_iu_i. \qquad \textbf{(A2.4)}$$

Hence,

$$E\left(\tilde{b}_2\right)=\beta_1\sum_{i=1}^{n}g_i+\beta_2\sum_{i=1}^{n}g_iX_i+E\left\{\sum_{i=1}^{n}g_iu_i\right\}. \qquad \textbf{(A2.5)}$$

The first two terms on the right side are nonstochastic and are therefore unaffected by taking expectations. Now

$$E\left\{\sum_{i=1}^{n}g_iu_i\right\}=\sum_{i=1}^{n}E\left(g_iu_i\right)=\sum_{i=1}^{n}g_iE\left(u_i\right)=0. \qquad \textbf{(A2.6)}$$

The first step used the first expected value rule. Thus,

$$E\left(\tilde{b}_2\right) = \beta_1 \sum_{i=1}^{n} g_i + \beta_2 \sum_{i=1}^{n} g_i X_i. \qquad \textbf{(A2.7)}$$

Hence for $E\left(\tilde{b}_2\right) = \beta_2$, the g_i must satisfy $\sum g_i = 0$ and $\sum g_i X_i = 1$. The variance of $\tilde{b}_2$ is given by

$$\sigma_{\tilde{b}_2}^2 = E\left\{\left(\tilde{b}_2 - E\left(\tilde{b}_2\right)\right)^2\right\} = E\left\{\left[\sum_{i=1}^{n} (g_i u_i)\right]^2\right\} = \sigma_u^2 \sum_{i=1}^{n} g_i^2. \qquad \textbf{(A2.8)}$$

The last step is exactly parallel to that in the proof that $E\left\{\sum (a_i u_i)^2\right\} = \sigma_u^2 \sum a_i^2$ in Box 2.3. Let

$$h_i = g_i - a_i. \qquad \textbf{(A2.9)}$$

Writing $g_i = a_i + h_i$, the first condition for the unbiasedness of $\tilde{b}_2$ becomes

$$\sum_{i=1}^{n} g_i = \sum_{i=1}^{n} (a_i + h_i) = 0. \qquad \textbf{(A2.10)}$$

Since $\sum a_i = 0$ (see Box 2.2), this implies $\sum h_i = 0$. The second condition for the unbiasedness of $\tilde{b}_2$ becomes

$$\sum_{i=1}^{n} g_i X_i = \sum_{i=1}^{n} (a_i + h_i) X_i = \sum_{i=1}^{n} a_i X_i + \sum_{i=1}^{n} h_i X_i = 1. \qquad \textbf{(A2.11)}$$

Since $\sum a_i X_i = 1$ (see Box 2.2 again), this implies $\sum h_i X_i = 0$. The variance of $\tilde{b}_2$ becomes

$$\sigma_{\tilde{b}_2}^2 = \sigma_u^2 \sum_{i=1}^{n} g_i^2 = \sigma_u^2 \sum_{i=1}^{n} (a_i + h_i)^2 = \sigma_u^2 \left\{\sum_{i=1}^{n} a_i^2 + \sum_{i=1}^{n} h_i^2 + 2\sum_{i=1}^{n} a_i h_i\right\}. \qquad \textbf{(A2.12)}$$

Now

$$\sum_{i=1}^{n} a_i h_i = \sum_{i=1}^{n} \frac{\left(X_i - \bar{X}\right) h_i}{\sum_{j=1}^{n} \left(X_j - \bar{X}\right)^2} = \frac{1}{\sum_{j=1}^{n} \left(X_j - \bar{X}\right)^2} \left\{\sum_{i=1}^{n} h_i X_i - \bar{X} \sum_{i=1}^{n} h_i\right\}. \qquad \textbf{(A2.13)}$$

This is zero because, as we have seen, the conditions for unbiasedness of $\tilde{b}_2$ require $\sum h_i = 0$ and $\sum h_i X_i = 0$. Hence,

$$\sigma_{\tilde{b}_2}^2 = \sigma_u^2 \left\{\sum_{i=1}^{n} a_i^2 + \sum_{i=1}^{n} h_i^2\right\}. \qquad \textbf{(A2.14)}$$

This must be greater than $\sigma_u^2 \sum a_i^2$, the variance of the OLS estimator b_2, unless $h_i = 0$ for all i, in which case $\tilde{b}_2$ is the same as b_2.

3. Multiple Regression Analysis

Chapters 1 and 2 were restricted to the simple regression model where it was assumed that the dependent variable in the model was related to only one explanatory variable. In general, there will be several, perhaps many, explanatory variables and we wish to quantify the impact of each, controlling for the effects of the others. In the natural sciences, one may perform controlled experiments, varying each explanatory variable, holding the others constant. In economics, this is usually not possible, but we may address the objective of discriminating between the effects of different explanatory variables using the technique known as **multiple regression analysis** that is treated in this chapter. Much of the discussion will be a straightforward extension of the simple regression model. Most of the issues can be explained within the context of a model with just two explanatory variables and we will start with such a model.

3.1 Illustration: a model with two explanatory variables

We will begin by considering an example, the determinants of earnings. We will extend the earlier model to allow for the possibility that earnings are influenced by years of work experience, as well as education, and we will assume that the true relationship can be expressed as

$$EARNINGS = \beta_1 + \beta_2 S + \beta_3 EXP + u, \quad \textbf{(3.1)}$$

where *EARNINGS* is hourly earnings, *S* is years of schooling (highest grade completed), *EXP* is years spent working after leaving full-time education, and *u* is a disturbance term. This model is still of course a great simplification, both in terms of the explanatory variables included in the relationship and in terms of its mathematical specification.

To illustrate the relationship geometrically, one needs a three-dimensional diagram with separate axes for *EARNINGS, S*, and *EXP* as in Figure 3.1. The base of Figure 3.1 shows the axes for *S* and *EXP*, and, if one neglects the effect of the disturbance term for the moment, the tilted plane above it shows the value of *EARNINGS* corresponding to any (*S, EXP*) combination, measured by the vertical height of the plane above the base at that point. Since earnings may be expected to increase with both schooling and work experience, the diagram

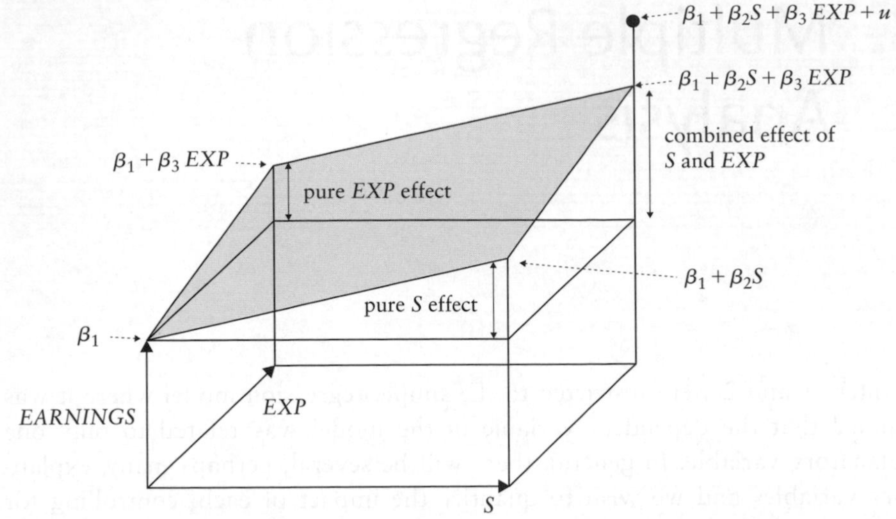

Figure 3.1 True model with two explanatory variables: earnings as a function of schooling and work experience

has been drawn on the assumption that β_2 and β_3 are both positive. Literally, the intercept β_1 gives the predicted earnings for zero schooling and zero work experience. However, such an interpretation would be dangerous because there was nobody with no schooling in the NLSY data set. Indeed very few individuals failed to complete eight years of schooling. Mathematically, (3.1) implies that, if *EXP* were zero, for any positive *S*, earnings would be equal to $\beta_1 + \beta_2 S$, the increase $\beta_2 S$ being marked 'pure *S* effect' in the figure. Keeping *S* at zero, the equation implies that for any positive value of *EXP*, earnings would be equal to $\beta_1 + \beta_3 EXP$, the increase $\beta_3 EXP$ being marked 'pure *EXP* effect'. The combined effect of schooling and work experience, $\beta_2 S + \beta_3 EXP$, is also indicated.

We have thus far neglected the disturbance term. If it were not for the presence of this in (3.1), the values of *EARNINGS* in a sample of observations on *EARNINGS*, *S*, and *EXP* would lie exactly on the tilted plane and it would be a trivial matter to deduce the exact values of β_1, β_2, and β_3 (not trivial geometrically, unless you are a genius at constructing three-dimensional models, but easy enough algebraically).

The disturbance term causes the actual value of earnings to be sometimes above and sometimes below the value indicated by the tilted plane. Consequently, one now has a three-dimensional counterpart to the two-dimensional problem illustrated in Figure 1.2. Instead of locating a line to fit a two-dimensional scatter of points, we now have to locate a plane to fit a three-dimensional scatter. The equation of the fitted plane will be

$$\widehat{EARNINGS} = b_1 + b_2 S + b_3 EXP \qquad \textbf{(3.2)}$$

Table 3.1

```
.reg EARNINGS S EXP

  Source   |       SS           df          MS          Number of obs =    540
-----------+--------------------------------------      F(2, 537)     =  67.54
   Model   |   22513.6473        2     11256.8237       Prob > F      = 0.0000
 Residual  |   89496.5838      537     166.660305       R-squared     = 0.2010
-----------+--------------------------------------      Adj R-squared = 0.1980
   Total   |   112010.231      539     207.811189       Root MSE      =  12.91

------------------------------------------------------------------------------
 EARNINGS  |      Coef.    Std. Err.      t     P>|t|     [95% Conf. Interval]
-----------+------------------------------------------------------------------
        S  |   2.678125    .2336497    11.46    0.000     2.219146    3.137105
      EXP  |   .5624326    .1285136     4.38    0.000     .3099816    .8148837
    _cons  |  -26.48501     4.27251    -6.20    0.000    -34.87789   -18.09213
------------------------------------------------------------------------------
```

and its location will depend on the choice of b_1, b_2, and b_3, the estimates of β_1, β_2, and β_3, respectively. Using *EAEF* Data Set 21, we obtain the regression output shown in Table 3.1.

The equation should be interpreted as follows. For every additional year of schooling, holding work experience constant, hourly earnings increase by \$2.68. For every year of work experience, holding schooling constant, earnings increase by \$0.56. The constant has no meaningful interpretation. Literally, it suggests that a respondent with zero years of schooling (no respondent had fewer than six) and no work experience would earn *minus* \$26.49 per hour.

3.2 Derivation and interpretation of the multiple regression coefficients

We will initially examine the case where a dependent variable Y may be assumed to be determined by two explanatory variables, X_2 and X_3, the true relationship being

$$Y_i = \beta_1 + \beta_2 X_{2i} + \beta_3 X_{3i} + u_i, \tag{3.3}$$

where u is a disturbance term. The X variables now have two subscripts. The first identifies the X variable (years of schooling, years of work experience, etc.) and the second the observation. The fitted model will be written

$$\hat{Y}_i = b_1 + b_2 X_{2i} + b_3 X_{3i}. \tag{3.4}$$

As in the simple regression case, we choose the values of the regression coefficients to make the fit as good as possible in the hope that we will obtain the most satisfactory estimates of the unknown true parameters. As before, our definition of goodness of fit is the minimization of $RSS = \sum_{i=1}^{n} e_i^2$, the sum of squares of the residuals, where e_i is the residual in observation i, the difference

BOX 3.1 Whatever happened to X_1?

You may have noticed that X_1 is missing from the general regression model

$$Y_i = \beta_1 + \beta_2 X_{2i} + \ldots + \beta_k X_{ki} + u_i.$$

Why so? The reason is to make the notation consistent with that found in texts using linear algebra (matrix algebra), and your next course in econometrics will almost certainly use such a text. For analysis using linear algebra, it is essential that every term on the right side of the equation should consist of the product of a parameter and a variable. When there is an intercept in the model, as here, the anomaly is dealt with by writing the equation

$$Y_i = \beta_1 X_{1i} + \beta_2 X_{2i} + \ldots + \beta_k X_{ki} + u_i,$$

where $X_{1i} = 1$ in every observation. In analysis using ordinary algebra, there is usually no point in introducing X_1 explicitly, and so it has been suppressed. One occasion in this text where it can help is in the discussion of the dummy variable trap in Section 5.2.

between the actual value Y_i in that observation and the value $\hat{Y}_i$ predicted by the regression equation:

$$e_i = Y_i - \hat{Y}_i = Y_i - b_1 - b_2 X_{2i} - b_3 X_{3i}. \quad \textbf{(3.5)}$$

Thus,

$$RSS = \sum_{i=1}^{n} (Y_i - b_1 - b_2 X_{2i} - b_3 X_{3i})^2. \quad \textbf{(3.6)}$$

The first-order conditions for a minimum, $\frac{\partial RSS}{\partial b_1} = 0$, $\frac{\partial RSS}{\partial b_2} = 0$, and $\frac{\partial RSS}{\partial b_3} = 0$, yield the following equations:

$$\frac{\partial RSS}{\partial b_1} = -2\sum_{i=1}^{n} (Y_i - b_1 - b_2 X_{2i} - b_3 X_{3i}) = 0 \quad \textbf{(3.7)}$$

$$\frac{\partial RSS}{\partial b_2} = -2\sum_{i=1}^{n} X_{2i}(Y_i - b_1 - b_2 X_{2i} - b_3 X_{3i}) = 0 \quad \textbf{(3.8)}$$

$$\frac{\partial RSS}{\partial b_3} = -2\sum_{i=1}^{n} X_{3i}(Y_i - b_1 - b_2 X_{2i} - b_3 X_{3i}) = 0. \quad \textbf{(3.9)}$$

Hence, we have three equations in the three unknowns, b_1, b_2, and b_3. The first can easily be rearranged to express b_1 in terms of b_2, b_3, and the data on Y, X_2, and X_3:

$$b_1 = \bar{Y} - b_2 \bar{X}_2 - b_3 \bar{X}_3. \quad \textbf{(3.10)}$$

Using this expression and the other two equations, with a little work one can obtain the following expression for b_2:

$$b_2 = \frac{\sum_{i=1}^{n}(X_{2i}-\bar{X}_2)(Y_i-\bar{Y})\sum_{i=1}^{n}(X_{3i}-\bar{X}_3)^2 - \sum_{i=1}^{n}(X_{3i}-\bar{X}_3)(Y_i-\bar{Y})\sum_{i=1}^{n}(X_{2i}-\bar{X}_2)(X_{3i}-\bar{X}_3)}{\sum_{i=1}^{n}(X_{2i}-\bar{X}_2)^2\sum_{i=1}^{n}(X_{3i}-\bar{X}_3)^2 - \left(\sum_{i=1}^{n}(X_{2i}-\bar{X}_2)(X_{3i}-\bar{X}_3)\right)^2}. \quad (3.11)$$

A parallel expression for b_3 can be obtained by interchanging X_2 and X_3 in (3.11).

The intention of this discussion is to make two basic points. First, the principles behind the derivation of the regression coefficients are the same for multiple regression as for simple regression. Second, the expressions, however, are different. The expression for the intercept, b_1, is an extension of that for simple regression analysis, but the expressions for the slope coefficients are more complex.

The general model

When there are more than two explanatory variables, it is not possible to give a geometrical representation of the model, but the extension of the algebra is in principle quite straightforward. We assume that a variable Y depends on $k-1$ explanatory variables $X_2, \ldots, X_k$ according to a true, unknown relationship

$$Y_i = \beta_1 + \beta_2 X_{2i} + \cdots + \beta_k X_{ki} + u_i. \quad (3.12)$$

Given a set of n observations on Y, $X_2, \ldots, X_k$, we use least squares regression analysis to fit the equation

$$\hat{Y}_i = b_1 + b_2 X_{2i} + \ldots + b_k X_{ki}. \quad (3.13)$$

This again means minimizing the sum of the squares of the residuals, which are given by

$$e_i = Y_i - \hat{Y}_i = Y_i - b_1 - b_2 X_{2i} - \ldots - b_k X_{ki}. \quad (3.14)$$

We now choose $b_1, \ldots, b_k$ so as to minimize RSS, the sum of the squares of the residuals, $\sum e_i^2$. We obtain k first-order conditions $\partial RSS/\partial b_1 = 0$, …, $\partial RSS/\partial b_k = 0$, and these provide k equations for solving for the k unknowns. It can readily be shown that the first of these equations yields a counterpart to (3.10) in the case with two explanatory variables:

$$b_1 = \bar{Y} - b_2\bar{X}_2 - \cdots - b_k\bar{X}_k. \quad (3.15)$$

The expressions for $b_2, \ldots, b_k$ become very complicated and the mathematics will not be presented explicitly here. The analysis should be done with linear (matrix) algebra.

Interpretation of the multiple regression coefficients

Multiple regression analysis allows one to discriminate between the effects of the explanatory variables, making allowance for the fact that they may be correlated. The regression coefficient of each X variable provides an estimate of its influence on Y, controlling for the effects of all the other X variables.

This can be demonstrated in two ways. One is to show that the estimators are unbiased, if the model is correctly specified and the assumptions relating to the regression model are valid. We shall do this in the next section for the case where there are only two explanatory variables. A second method is to run a simple regression of Y on one of the X variables, having first purged both Y and the X variable of the components that could be accounted for by the other explanatory variables. The estimate of the slope coefficient and its standard error thus obtained are exactly the same as in the multiple regression, a result that is proved by the **Frisch–Waugh–Lovell theorem** (Frisch and Waugh, 1933; Lovell, 1963). It follows that a scatter diagram plotting the purged Y against the purged X variable will provide a valid graphical representation of their relationship that can be obtained in no other way. This result will not be proved but it will be illustrated using the earnings function in Section 3.1:

$$EARNINGS = \beta_1 + \beta_2 S + \beta_3 EXP + u. \qquad \textbf{(3.16)}$$

Suppose that we are particularly interested in the relationship between earnings and schooling and that we would like to illustrate it graphically. A straightforward plot of $EARNINGS$ on S, as in Figure 1.7, would give a distorted view of the relationship because EXP is negatively correlated with S. Among those of similar age, individuals who have spent more time in school will tend to have spent less time working. As a consequence, as S increases, (1) $EARNINGS$ will tend to increase, because β_2 is positive; (2) EXP will tend to decrease, because S and EXP are negatively correlated; and (3) $EARNINGS$ will be reduced by the decrease in EXP and the fact that β_3 is positive. In other words, the variations in $EARNINGS$ will not fully reflect the influence of the variations in S because in part they will be undermined by the associated variations in EXP. As a consequence, in a simple regression the estimator of β_2 will be biased downwards. We will investigate the bias analytically in Section 6.2.

In this example, there is only one other explanatory variable, EXP. To purge $EARNINGS$ and S of their EXP components, we first regress them on EXP:

$$\widehat{EARNINGS} = c_1 + c_2 EXP \qquad \textbf{(3.17)}$$

$$\hat{S} = d_1 + d_2 EXP. \qquad \textbf{(3.18)}$$

We then subtract the fitted values from the actual values:

$$EEARN = EARNINGS - \widehat{EARNINGS}. \qquad \textbf{(3.19)}$$

Table 3.2

```
.reg EEARN ES
   Source |       SS          df        MS         Number of obs =    540
----------+-------------------------------         F(1, 538)     = 131.63
    Model |  21895.9298        1   21895.9298      Prob > F      = 0.0000
 Residual |  89496.5838      537   166.350527      R-squared     = 0.1966
----------+-------------------------------         Adj R-squared = 0.1951
    Total |  111392.513      539   206.665145      Root MSE      = 12.898

--------------------------------------------------------------------------
    EEARN |      Coef.   Std. Err.      t     P>|t|   [95% Conf. Interval]
----------+---------------------------------------------------------------
       ES |   2.678125   .2334325    11.47    0.000    2.219574   3.136676
    _cons |   8.10e-09   .5550284     0.00    1.000   -1.090288   1.090288
--------------------------------------------------------------------------
```

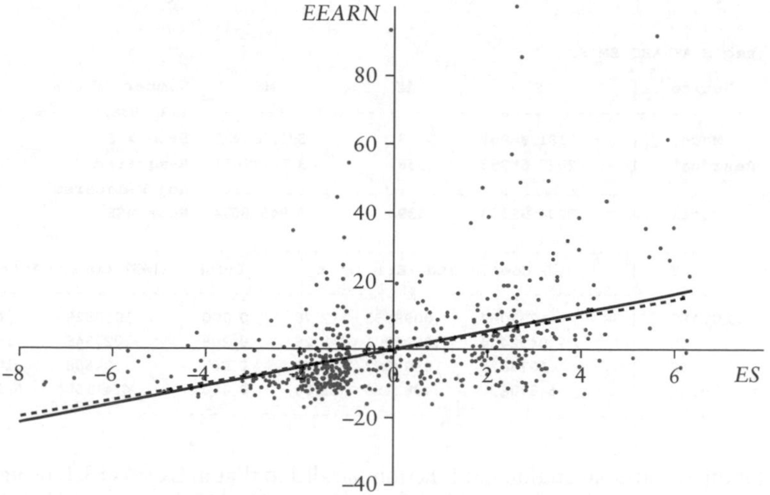

Figure 3.2 Regression of *EARNINGS* residuals on *S* residuals

$$ES = S - \hat{S}. \qquad \textbf{(3.20)}$$

The purged variables *EEARN* and *ES* are of course just the residuals from the regressions (3.17) and (3.18). We now regress *EEARN* on *ES* and obtain the output in Table 3.2.

The estimate of the intercept in the regression uses a common convention for fitting very large numbers or very small ones into a field with a predefined number of digits. e+n indicates that the coefficient should be multiplied by 10^n. Similarly e–n indicates that it should be multiplied by 10^{-n}. Thus, in this regression the intercept is effectively zero.

You can verify that the coefficient of *ES* is identical to that of *S* in the multiple regression in Section 3.1. Figure 3.2 shows the regression line in a scatter diagram. The dotted line in the figure is the regression line from a simple regression of *EARNINGS* on *S*, shown for comparison. The latter is a little flatter than the true relationship between *EARNINGS* and *S* because it does not control for the effect of *EXP*. In this case, the bias is small because the correlation between *S* and *EXP*, –0.22, is small. Even so, the diagram is valuable because it allows a direct inspection of the relationship between earnings and schooling, controlling for experience. The presence of outliers for large values of *S* suggests that the model is misspecified in some way.

EXERCISES

3.1 The output is the result of fitting an educational attainment function, regressing *S* on *ASVABC*, a measure of cognitive ability, *SM*, and *SF*, years of schooling (highest grade completed) of the respondent's mother and father, respectively, using *EAEF* Data Set 21. Give an interpretation of the regression coefficients.

```
.reg S ASVABC SM SF

  Source  |       SS          df           MS        Number of obs =     540
----------+------------------------------------      F(3, 536)     =  104.30
   Model  |  1181.36981        3     393.789935      Prob > F      =  0.0000
Residual  |  2023.61353      536     3.77539837      R-squared     =  0.3686
----------+------------------------------------      Adj R-squared =  0.3651
   Total  |  3204.98333      539     5.94616574      Root MSE      =   1.943

-----------------------------------------------------------------------------
       S  |      Coef.   Std. Err.     t      P>|t|     [95% Conf. Interval]
----------+------------------------------------------------------------------
  ASVABC  |   .1257087   .0098533   12.76     0.000      .1063528   .1450646
      SM  |   .0492424   .0390901    1.26     0.208      -.027546   .1260309
      SF  |   .1076825   .0309522    3.48     0.001        .04688   .1684851
   _cons  |   5.370631   .4882155   11.00     0.000       4.41158   6.329681
-----------------------------------------------------------------------------
```

3.2 Fit an educational attainment function parallel to that in Exercise 3.1, using your *EAEF* data set. First regress *S* on *ASVABC* and *SM* and interpret the regression results. Repeat the regression using *SF* instead of *SM*, and then again, including both *SM* and *SF* as regressors. There is a saying that if you educate a male, you educate an individual, while if you educate a female, you educate a nation. The premise is that the education of a future mother has a beneficial knock-on effect on the educational attainment of her children. Do your regression results support this view?

3.3 Fit an earnings function parallel to that in Section 3.1, using your *EAEF* data set. Regress *EARNINGS* on *S* and *EXP* and interpret the regression results.

3.4 Using your *EAEF* data set, make a graphical representation of the relationship between *S* and *SM* using the Frisch–Waugh–Lovell technique, assuming that the true model is as in Exercise 3.2. To do this, regress *S* on *ASVABC* and *SF* and save the residuals. Do the same with *SM*. Plot the *S* and *SM* residuals. Also regress the former on the latter, and verify that the slope coefficient is the same as that obtained in Exercise 3.2.

3.5* Explain why the intercept in the regression of *EEARN* on *ES* is equal to zero.

3.6 Show that in the general case, with true model (3.12) and fitted regression (3.13), the fitted regression will pass through the point represented by $\bar{Y}$ and the means of the X variables, provided that the equation includes an intercept. (This is a generalization of Exercise 1.1.)

3.7 Two researchers are investigating the effects of time spent studying on the examination marks earned by students on a certain course. For a sample of 100 students, they have the examination mark, M, total hours spent studying, H, hours on primary study, P, and hours spent on revision, R. By definition, $H = P + R$. Researcher A decides to regress M on P and R and fits the following regression:

$$\hat{M} = 45.6 + 0.15\,P + 0.21\,R.$$

Researcher B decides to regress M on H and P, with regression output

$$\hat{M} = 45.6 + 0.21\,H - 0.06\,P.$$

Give an interpretation of the coefficients of both regressions.

3.3 Properties of the multiple regression coefficients

As in the case of simple regression analysis, the regression coefficients should be thought of as special kinds of random variables whose random components are attributable to the presence of the disturbance term in the model. Each regression coefficient is calculated as a function of the values of Y and the explanatory variables in the sample, and Y in turn is determined by the explanatory variables and the disturbance term. It follows that the regression coefficients are really determined by the values of the explanatory variables and the disturbance term and that their properties depend critically upon the properties of the latter.

We are continuing to work within the framework of Model A, where the explanatory variables are nonstochastic. We shall make the following six assumptions, which are a restatement of those in Chapter 2 in terms appropriate for the multiple regression model.

A.1 *The model is linear in parameters and correctly specified.*

$$Y = \beta_1 + \beta_2 X_2 + \cdots + \beta_k X_k + u. \tag{3.21}$$

This is the same as before, except that we have multiple explanatory variables.

A.2 *There does not exist an exact linear relationship among the regressors in the sample.*

This is the only assumption that requires a new explanation. It will be deferred to Section 3.4 on multicollinearity.

Assumptions A.3–A.6 are the same as before.

A.3 *The disturbance term has zero expectation.*

$$E(u_i) = 0 \quad \text{for all } i. \tag{3.22}$$

A.4 The disturbance term is homoscedastic.

$$\sigma_{u_i}^2 = \sigma_u^2 \quad \text{for all } i. \tag{3.23}$$

A.5 The values of the disturbance term have independent distributions.

$$u_i \text{ is distributed independently of } u_j \text{ for all } j \neq i. \tag{3.24}$$

A.6 The disturbance term has a normal distribution.

Unbiasedness

We saw that in the case of the simple regression model

$$b_2 = \beta_2 + \sum_{i=1}^{n} a_i u_i, \tag{3.25}$$

where

$$a_i = \frac{X_i - \overline{X}}{\sum_{j=1}^{n} \left(X_j - \overline{X}\right)^2}. \tag{3.26}$$

Similar relationships obtain in the multiple regression case. The coefficient of X_j can be decomposed as

$$b_j = \beta_j + \sum_{i=1}^{n} a_{ij}^* u_i, \tag{3.27}$$

where the a_{ij}^* terms are functions of the data on the explanatory variables in the model. The difference is that the a_{ij}^* terms are more complex than the a_i terms in the simple regression model and the proof of the decomposition likewise more complex. When one makes the transition to matrix algebra, the results are very easily obtained. We shall take them on trust. Taking (3.27) as given, unbiasedness follows as a formality:

$$E\left(b_j\right) = \beta_j + E\left\{\sum_{i=1}^{n} a_{ij}^* u_i\right\} = \beta_j + \sum_{i=1}^{n} a_{ij}^* E\left(u_i\right) = \beta_j, \tag{3.28}$$

applying Assumption A.3.

It is important to note that the proof of unbiasedness does not require the explanatory variables to be uncorrelated. It is natural to suppose, for example, that if two variables are positively correlated, this will somehow undermine the estimation of their coefficients and give rise to bias. It does not. Even if the variables are highly correlated, the OLS estimators of their coefficients will remain unbiased. As we will see in a moment, correlations will affect the precision of the estimates, but that is another matter. They will not be responsible for a tendency to underestimation or overestimation. This is the reason that multiple regression is such a powerful and popular tool. It enables us to estimate the effect of one variable, controlling for the effects of others, in the non-experimental conditions that characterize the work of most applied economists.

Efficiency

The Gauss–Markov theorem proves that, for multiple regression analysis, as for simple regression analysis, the ordinary least squares (OLS) technique yields the most efficient linear estimators of the parameters, in the sense that it is impossible to find other unbiased estimators with lower variances, using the same sample information, provided that the regression model assumptions are satisfied. We will not attempt to prove this theorem since matrix algebra is required.

Precision of the multiple regression coefficients

We will investigate the factors governing the likely precision of the regression coefficients for the case where there are two explanatory variables. Similar considerations apply in the more general case, but with more than two variables the analysis becomes complex and one needs to switch to matrix algebra.

If the true relationship is

$$Y_i = \beta_1 + \beta_2 X_{2i} + \beta_3 X_{3i} + u_i, \tag{3.29}$$

and the fitted regression line is

$$\hat{Y}_i = b_1 + b_2 X_{2i} + b_3 X_{3i}, \tag{3.30}$$

the population variance of the probability distribution of b_2, $\sigma_{b_2}^2$, is given by

$$\sigma_{b_2}^2 = \frac{\sigma_u^2}{\sum_{i=1}^{n} \left(X_{2i} - \bar{X}_2\right)^2} \times \frac{1}{1 - r_{X_2X_3}^2}, \tag{3.31}$$

where σ_u^2 is the population variance of u and $r_{X_2X_3}$ is the correlation between X_2 and X_3. A parallel expression may be obtained for the population variance of b_3, replacing $\sum \left(X_{2i} - \bar{X}_2\right)^2$ with $\sum \left(X_{3i} - \bar{X}_3\right)^2$. Rewriting this as

$$\sigma_{b_2}^2 = \frac{\sigma_u^2}{n \, \mathrm{MSD}\left(X_2\right)} \times \frac{1}{1 - r_{X_2X_3}^2}, \tag{3.32}$$

where $\mathrm{MSD}\left(X_2\right)$, the mean square deviation of X_2, is given by

$$\mathrm{MSD}\left(X_2\right) = \frac{1}{n} \sum \left(X_{2i} - \bar{X}_2\right)^2, \tag{3.33}$$

we can see that, as in the case of simple regression analysis, it is desirable for n and $\mathrm{MSD}\left(X_2\right)$ to be large and for σ_u^2 to be small. However, we now have the further term $\left(1-r_{X_2X_3}^2\right)$ and clearly it is desirable that the correlation between X_2 and X_3 should be low.

It is easy to give an intuitive explanation of this. The greater the correlation, the harder it is to discriminate between the effects of the explanatory variables on Y, and the less accurate will be the regression estimates. This can be a serious problem and it is discussed in the next section.

The standard deviation of the distribution of b_2 is the square root of the variance. As in the simple regression case, the standard error of b_2 is the estimate of the standard deviation. For this we need to estimate σ_u^2. The sample average of the squared residuals provides a biased estimator:

$$E\left\{\frac{1}{n}\sum_{i=1}^{n}e_i^2\right\}=\frac{n-k}{n}\sigma_u^2, \tag{3.34}$$

where k is the number of parameters in the regression equation. We will not attempt to prove this. In view of (3.34), we can obtain an unbiased estimator, s_u^2, by dividing *RSS* by $n-k$, instead of n, thus neutralizing the bias:

$$s_u^2=\frac{1}{n-k}\sum_{i=1}^{n}e_i^2. \tag{3.35}$$

The standard error is then given by

$$\text{s.e.}(b_2)=\sqrt{\frac{s_u^2}{\sum_{i=1}^{n}\left(X_{2i}-\bar{X}_{2i}\right)^2}\times\frac{1}{1-r_{X_2,X_3}^2}}. \tag{3.36}$$

The determinants of the standard error will be illustrated by comparing them in earnings functions fitted to two subsamples of the respondents in *EAEF* Data Set 21: those who reported that their wages were set by collective bargaining and the remainder. Regression output for the two subsamples is shown in Tables 3.3

Table 3.3

```
.reg EARNINGS S EXP if COLLBARG==1

   Source   |       SS           df            MS        Number of obs =     101
------------+------------------------------------------  F(2, 98)      =    9.72
    Model   |   3076.31726        2       1538.15863     Prob > F       =  0.0001
 Residual   |   15501.9762       98       158.18343      R-squared      =  0.1656
------------+------------------------------------------  Adj R-squared  =  0.1486
    Total   |   18578.2934      100       185.782934     Root MSE       =  12.577

------------------------------------------------------------------------------------
 EARNINGS   |      Coef.    Std. Err.      t      P>|t|     [95% Conf. Interval]
------------+-----------------------------------------------------------------------
        S   |   2.333846    .5492604     4.25    0.000      1.243857    3.423836
      EXP   |   .2235095    .3389455     0.66    0.511     -.4491169    .8961358
    _cons   |  -15.12427    11.38141    -1.33    0.187     -37.71031    7.461779
------------------------------------------------------------------------------------
```

Table 3.4

```
.reg EARNINGS S EXP if COLLBARG==0
```

Source	SS	df	MS		
Model	19540.1761	2	9770.08805	Number of obs =	439
Residual	73741.593	436	169.132094	F(2, 436) =	57.77
				Prob > F =	0.0000
				R-squared =	0.2095
				Adj R-squared =	0.2058
Total	93281.7691	438	212.972076	Root MSE =	13.005

EARNINGS	Coef.	Std. Err.	t	P>|t|	[95% Conf.	Interval]
S	2.721698	.2604411	10.45	0.000	2.209822	3.233574
EXP	.6077342	.1400846	4.34	0.000	.3324091	.8830592
_cons	-28.00805	4.643211	-6.03	0.000	-37.13391	-18.88219

and 3.4. In Stata, subsamples may be selected by adding an 'if' expression to a command. *COLLBARG* is a variable in the data set defined to be 1 for the collective bargaining subsample and 0 for the others. Note that in tests for equality, Stata requires the = sign to be duplicated.

The standard error of the coefficient of *S* in the first regression is 0.5493, twice as large as that in the second, 0.2604. We will investigate the reasons for the difference. It will be convenient to rewrite (3.36) in such a way as to isolate the contributions of the various factors:

$$\text{s.e.}(b_2) = s_u \times \frac{1}{\sqrt{n}} \times \frac{1}{\sqrt{\text{MSD}(X_2)}} \times \frac{1}{\sqrt{1 - r^2_{X_2,X_3}}}. \qquad \textbf{(3.37)}$$

The first element we need, s_u, can be obtained directly from the regression output in any serious regression application. In the Stata output, *RSS* is given in the top left quarter of the regression output, as part of the decomposition of the total sum of squares into the explained ('model') sum of squares and the residual sum of squares. The value of $n-k$ is given to the right of *RSS*, and the ratio $RSS/(n-k)$, the estimator of s_u^2, to the right of that. The square root, s_u, is listed as the Root MSE (root mean square error) in the top right quarter of the regression output, 12.577 for the collective bargaining subsample and 13.005 for the regression with the other respondents.

The number of observations, 101 in the first regression and 439 in the second, is also listed in the top right quarter of the regression output. The mean squared deviations of *S*, 6.2325 and 5.8666, were calculated as the squares of the standard deviations reported using the Stata 'sum' command, multiplied by $(n-1)/n$. The correlations between *S* and *EXP*, –0.4087 and –0.1784 respectively, were calculated using the Stata 'cor' command. The factors of the components of the standard error in equation (3.37) were then derived and are shown in the lower half of Table 3.5.

Table 3.5 Decomposition of the standard error of S

Component	s_u	n	MSD(S)	$r_{S,EXP}$	s.e.
Collective bargaining	12.577	101	6.2325	−0.4087	0.5493
Not collective bargaining	13.005	439	5.8666	−0.1784	0.2604
Factor					
Collective bargaining	12.577	0.0995	0.4006	1.0957	0.5493
Not collective bargaining	13.005	0.0477	0.4129	1.0163	0.2603

It can be seen that, in this example, the reason that the standard error of S in the collective bargaining subsample is relatively large is that the number of observations in that subsample is relatively small. The larger correlation coefficient for S and EXP reinforces the difference while the smaller s_u and the larger MSD(S) reduce it, but these are relatively minor factors.

t tests and confidence intervals

t tests on the regression coefficients are performed in the same way as for simple regression analysis. Note that when you are looking up the critical level of t at any given significance level, it will depend on the number of degrees of freedom, $n - k$: the number of observations minus the number of parameters estimated. The confidence intervals are also constructed in exactly the same way as in simple regression analysis, subject to the above comment about the number of degrees of freedom. As can be seen from the regression output, Stata automatically calculates confidence intervals for the coefficients (95 percent by default, other levels if desired), but this is not a standard feature of regression applications.

EXERCISES

3.8 Perform t tests on the coefficients of the variables in the educational attainment function reported in Exercise 3.1.

3.9 Perform t tests on the coefficients of the variables in the educational attainment and earnings functions fitted by you in Exercises 3.2 and 3.3.

3.10 The following earnings functions were fitted separately for males and females, using *EAEF* Data Set 21 (standard errors in parentheses):

males

$$\widehat{EARNINGS} = \underset{(7.8708)}{-31.5168} + \underset{(0.3693)}{3.1408}\, S + \underset{(0.2382)}{0.6453}\, EXP$$

females

$$\widehat{EARNINGS} = -17.2028 + 2.0772\,S + 0.3179\,EXP.$$
$$\quad(4.5797)\quad(0.2805)\quad(0.1388)$$

Using equation (3.37), explain why the standard errors of the coefficients of *S* and *EXP* are greater for the male subsample than for the female subsample, and why the difference in the standard errors is relatively large for *EXP*.

Further data:

	males	*females*
s_u	14.278	10.548
n	270	270
$r_{S,EXP}$	−0.4029	−0.0632
MSD(*S*)	6.6080	5.2573
MSD(*EXP*)	15.8858	21.4628

3.11* Demonstrate that $\bar{e} = 0$ in multiple regression analysis. (*Note*: The proof is a generalization of the proof for the simple regression model, given in Section 1.5.)

3.12 Investigate whether you can extend the determinants of weight model using your *EAEF* data set, taking *WEIGHT02* as the dependent variable, and *HEIGHT* and other continuous variables in the data set as explanatory variables. Provide an interpretation of the coefficients and perform *t* tests on them.

3.13 In Exercise 3.7, the sample means of *H*, *P*, and *R* are 100 hours, 95 hours, and 5 hours, respectively and the standard deviations of the distributions of *H*, *P*, and *R* are 10.1, 10.1, and 2.1, respectively. The standard errors of the coefficients of the regression of Researcher A are shown in parentheses under the coefficients.

$$\hat{M} = 45.6 + 0.15\,P + 0.21\,R.$$
$$\quad(2.8)\quad(0.03)\quad(0.14)$$

Perform *t* tests of the significance of the coefficients of *P* and *R*. The researcher says that the insignificant coefficient of *R* is to be expected because the students, on average, spent much less time on revision than on primary study. Explain whether this assertion is correct.

3.4 Multicollinearity

In the previous section, in the context of a model with two explanatory variables, it was seen that the higher is the correlation between the explanatory variables, the larger are the population variances of the distributions of their coefficients, and the greater is the risk of obtaining erratic estimates of the coefficients. If the correlation causes the regression model to become unsatisfactory in this respect, it is said to be suffering from **multicollinearity**.

A high correlation does not necessarily lead to poor estimates. If all the other factors determining the variances of the regression coefficients are helpful, that is, if the number of observations and the mean square deviations of the explanatory variables are large, and the variance of the disturbance term small, you may well obtain good estimates after all. Multicollinearity therefore must be caused by a *combination* of a high correlation and one or more of the other factors being unhelpful. And it is a matter of *degree*, not kind. Any regression will suffer from it to some extent, unless all the explanatory variables are uncorrelated. You only start to talk about it when you think that it is affecting the regression results seriously.

It is an especially common problem in time series regressions, that is, where the data consist of a series of observations on the variables over a number of time periods. If two or more of the explanatory variables have strong time trends, they will be highly correlated and this condition may give rise to multicollinearity.

It should be noted that the presence of multicollinearity does not mean that the model is misspecified. Accordingly, the regression coefficients remain unbiased and the standard errors remain valid. The standard errors will be larger than they would have been in the absence of multicollinearity, warning you that the regression estimates are unreliable.

We will consider first the case of exact multicollinearity where the explanatory variables are perfectly correlated. Suppose that the true relationship is

$$Y = 2 + 3X_2 + X_3 + u. \tag{3.38}$$

Suppose that there is a linear relationship between X_2 and X_3:

$$X_3 = 2X_2 - 1, \tag{3.39}$$

and suppose that X_2 increases by one unit in each observation. X_3 will increase by 2 units, and Y by approximately 5 units, for example as shown in Table 3.6 and illustrated in Figure 3.3 (where the effect of the disturbance term has been neglected).

Table 3.6

Observation	X_2	X_3	Y	*Change in* X_2	*Change in* X_3	*Approximate change in* Y
1	10	19	$51+u_1$	1	2	5
2	11	21	$56+u_2$	1	2	5
3	12	23	$61+u_3$	1	2	5
4	13	25	$66+u_4$	1	2	5
5	14	27	$71+u_5$	1	2	5
6	15	29	$76+u_6$	1	2	5

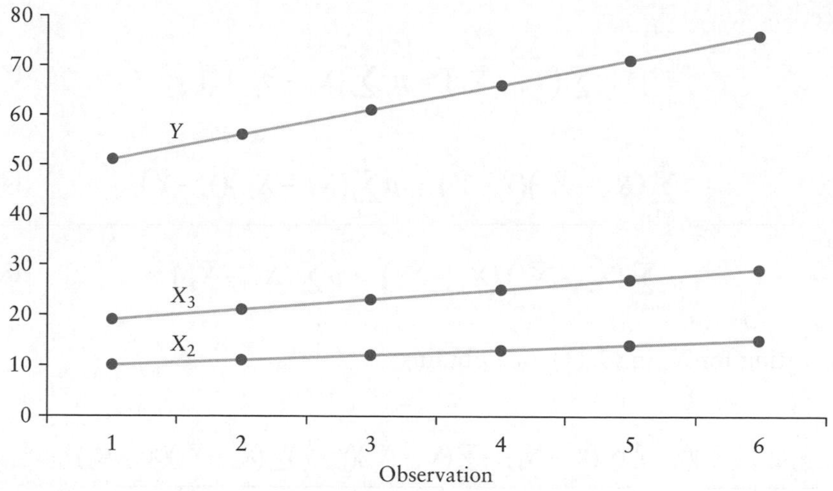

Figure 3.3 Example of exact multicollinearity

Looking at the data, you could come to any of the following conclusions:

1. Y is determined by (3.38).
2. X_3 is irrelevant and Y is determined by the relationship

$$Y = 1 + 5X_2 + u. \tag{3.40}$$

3. X_2 is irrelevant and Y is determined by the relationship

$$Y = 3.5 + 2.5X_3 + u. \tag{3.41}$$

In fact these are not the only possibilities. Any relationship that is a weighted average of (3.40) and (3.41) would also fit the data. For example, (3.38) may be regarded as such a weighted average, being (3.40) multiplied by 0.6 plus (3.41) multiplied by 0.4.

In such a situation, it is impossible for regression analysis, or any other technique for that matter, to distinguish between these possibilities. You would not even be able to calculate the regression coefficients because both the numerator and the denominator of the regression coefficients would collapse to zero. This will be demonstrated with the general two-variable case. Suppose

$$Y = \beta_1 + \beta_2 X_2 + \beta_3 X_3 + u \tag{3.42}$$

and

$$X_3 = \lambda + \mu X_2. \tag{3.43}$$

First note that, given (3.43),

$$\left(X_{3i} - \bar{X}_3\right) = \left([\lambda + \mu X_{2i}] - [\lambda + \mu \bar{X}_2]\right) = \mu\left(X_{2i} - \bar{X}_2\right). \tag{3.44}$$

Hence,

$$\sum_{i=1}^{n}\left(X_{3i}-\bar{X}_3\right)^2=\mu^2\sum_{i=1}^{n}\left(X_{2i}-\bar{X}_2\right)^2 \tag{3.45}$$

$$\sum_{i=1}^{n}\left(X_{3i}-\bar{X}_3\right)\left(Y_i-\bar{Y}\right)=\mu\sum_{i=1}^{n}\left(X_{2i}-\bar{X}_2\right)\left(Y_i-\bar{Y}\right) \tag{3.46}$$

$$\sum_{i=1}^{n}\left(X_{2i}-\bar{X}_2\right)\left(X_{3i}-\bar{X}_3\right)=\mu\sum_{i=1}^{n}\left(X_{2i}-\bar{X}_2\right)^2. \tag{3.47}$$

Substituting for X_3 in (3.11), one obtains

$$\begin{aligned}
b_2 &= \frac{\sum_{i=1}^{n}\left(X_{2i}-\bar{X}_2\right)\left(Y_i-\bar{Y}\right)\sum_{i=1}^{n}\left(X_{3i}-\bar{X}_3\right)^2-\sum_{i=1}^{n}\left(X_{3i}-\bar{X}_3\right)\left(Y_i-\bar{Y}\right)\sum_{i=1}^{n}\left(X_{2i}-\bar{X}_2\right)\left(X_{3i}-\bar{X}_3\right)}{\sum_{i=1}^{n}\left(X_{2i}-\bar{X}_2\right)^2\sum_{i=1}^{n}\left(X_{3i}-\bar{X}_3\right)^2-\left(\sum_{i=1}^{n}\left(X_{2i}-\bar{X}_2\right)\left(X_{3i}-\bar{X}_3\right)\right)^2}\\
&= \frac{\sum_{i=1}^{n}\left(X_{2i}-\bar{X}_2\right)\left(Y_i-\bar{Y}\right)\left(\mu^2\sum_{i=1}^{n}\left(X_{2i}-\bar{X}_2\right)^2\right)-\left(\mu\sum_{i=1}^{n}\left(X_{2i}-\bar{X}_2\right)\left(Y_i-\bar{Y}\right)\right)\left(\mu\sum_{i=1}^{n}\left(X_{2i}-\bar{X}_2\right)^2\right)}{\sum_{i=1}^{n}\left(X_{2i}-\bar{X}_2\right)^2\left(\mu^2\sum_{i=1}^{n}\left(X_{2i}-\bar{X}_2\right)^2\right)-\left(\mu\sum_{i=1}^{n}\left(X_{2i}-\bar{X}_2\right)^2\right)^2}\\
&= \frac{0}{0}.
\end{aligned} \tag{3.48}$$

It is unusual for there to be an exact relationship between the explanatory variables in a regression. When this occurs, it is typically because there is a logical error in the specification. An example is provided by Exercise 3.16. However, it often happens that there is an approximate relationship, and typically this takes the form of high correlations among two or more explanatory variables.

Multicollinearity in models with more than two explanatory variables

The discussion of multicollinearity so far has been restricted to the case where there are two explanatory variables. In models with a greater number of explanatory variables, multicollinearity may be caused by an approximate linear relationship among them. It may be difficult to discriminate between the effects of one variable and those of a linear combination of the remainder. In the model with two explanatory variables, an approximate linear relationship automatically means a high correlation, but when there are three or more, this is not necessarily the case because a linear relationship does not inevitably imply high pairwise correlations between any of the variables. The effects of multicollinearity are the same as in the case with two explanatory variables. As in that case, the problem may not be serious if the population variance of the disturbance term is small, the number of observations large, and the mean square deviations of the explanatory variables large.

Example of multicollinearity

Suppose that one is investigating the determinants of educational attainment. A basic specification, proposed in Exercise 3.1, is

$$S = \beta_1 + \beta_2 SM + \beta_3 SF + \beta_4 ASVABC + u, \tag{3.49}$$

where S is highest grade completed by the respondent, SM and SF are highest grades completed by the respondent's mother and father, and $ASVABC$ is a measure of cognitive ability. $ASVABC$ is a composite of the scores on three tests: $ASVAB02$, arithmetical reasoning; $ASVAB03$, word knowledge; and $ASVAB04$, paragraph comprehension. If we include these separately instead of the composite, the regression results using Data Set 21 are as shown in Table 3.7.

All the regression coefficients are positive, as expected, but those for SM and $ASVAB04$ are not significant, even at the 5 percent level, and that for $ASVAB03$ is significant only at that level. Since maternal education may reasonably be assumed to be a powerful determinant of educational attainment, the lack of significance of the coefficient of SM is surprising. Multicollinearity is the most likely explanation, given that, on account of assortative mating, the correlation between SM and SF is 0.62. The insignificant coefficient of $ASVAB04$ might simply indicate that that variable was not a determinant of educational attainment, but here also multicollinearity must be suspected, for the correlation between $ASVAB03$ and $ASVAB04$, 0.80, is even higher.

What can you do about multicollinearity?

The various ways of trying to alleviate multicollinearity fall into two categories: direct attempts to improve the conditions responsible for the variances of the regression coefficients, and indirect methods.

Table 3.7

.reg S SM SF ASVAB02 ASVAB03 ASVAB04

Source	SS	df	MS
Model	1183.14727	5	236.629455
Residual	2021.83606	534	3.78620985
Total	3204.98333	539	5.94616574

Number of obs	= 540
F(5, 534)	= 62.50
Prob > F	= 0.0000
R-squared	= 0.3692
Adj R-squared	= 0.3633
Root MSE	= 1.9458

S	Coef.	Std. Err.	t	P>|t|	[95% Conf.	Interval]
SM	.04978	.0392495	1.27	0.205	-.0273223	.1268823
SF	.1072127	.0310202	3.46	0.001	.0462762	.1681493
ASVAB02	.0749955	.0127422	5.89	0.000	.0499645	.1000265
ASVAB03	.0354954	.016693	2.13	0.034	.0027034	.0682874
ASVAB04	.0259897	.0149738	1.74	0.083	-.0034251	.0554045
_cons	4.968064	.5140692	9.66	0.000	3.958218	5.97791

Direct methods

The four factors responsible for the variances of the coefficients are the variance of the disturbance term, the number of observations in the sample, the mean square deviations of the explanatory variables, and the correlations among the explanatory variables.

We will start with the number of observations. Table 3.8 shows the result of running the regression with all 2,714 observations in the *EAEF* data set. Comparing this result with that using Data Set 21, we see that the standard errors are much smaller, as expected. As a consequence, the *t* statistics of all of the variables are large and the coefficients significantly different from zero at the 0.1 percent level. The problem of multicollinearity has disappeared.

This example is artificial because the output in Table 3.7 used a subset of the data base. In practice, there would never be any reason to use a subset, unless the entire data base were so enormous, as in the case of a national census of population, that the costs of processing it fully might not be justified.

If you are working with cross-sectional data (individuals, households, enterprises, etc.) and you are undertaking a survey, you could increase the size of the sample by negotiating a bigger budget. Alternatively, you could make a fixed budget go further by using a technique known as clustering. You divide the country geographically into localities. For example, the National Longitudinal Survey of Youth, from which the *EAEF* data are drawn, divides the country into counties, independent cities, and standard metropolitan statistical areas. You select a number of localities randomly, perhaps using stratified random sampling to make sure that metropolitan, other urban, and rural areas are properly represented. You then confine the survey to the localities selected. This reduces the travel time of the fieldworkers, allowing them to interview a greater number of respondents.

Table 3.8

```
.reg S SM SF ASVAB02 ASVAB03 ASVAB04

  Source   |     SS           df          MS             Number of obs =     2714
-----------+-------------------------------------        F(5, 2708)    =   330.75
   Model   |  6294.19353       5      1258.83871         Prob > F      =   0.0000
 Residual  |   10306.567    2708      3.80597008         R-squared     =   0.3792
-----------+-------------------------------------        Adj R-squared =   0.3780
   Total   |  16600.7605    2713      6.11896812         Root MSE      =   1.9509

------------------------------------------------------------------------------
        S  |      Coef.   Std. Err.      t    P>|t|      [95% Conf. Interval]
-----------+------------------------------------------------------------------
       SM  |   .1275844   .0186513     6.84   0.000      .0910122    .1641566
       SF  |   .1187439   .0142069     8.36   0.000      .0908864    .1466014
  ASVAB02  |   .0671771   .0056405    11.91   0.000       .056117    .0782372
  ASVAB03  |   .0283495    .006953     4.08   0.000      .0147157    .0419833
  ASVAB04  |   .0292889   .0064412     4.55   0.000      .0166588    .0419191
    _cons  |   4.549561   .2350241    19.36   0.000      4.088716    5.010406
------------------------------------------------------------------------------
```

If you are working with time series data, you may be able to increase the sample by working with shorter time intervals for the data, for example quarterly or even monthly data instead of annual data. This is such an obvious thing to do that most researchers working with time series almost automatically use quarterly data, if they are available, instead of annual data, even if there does not appear to be a problem of multicollinearity, simply to minimize the population variances of the regression coefficients. There are, however, potential problems. You may introduce, or aggravate, autocorrelation (see Chapter 12), but this can be neutralized. Also you may introduce, or aggravate, measurement error bias (see Chapter 8) if the quarterly data are less accurately measured than the corresponding annual data. This problem is not so easily overcome, but it may be a minor one.

The next direct method that we will consider is the reduction of σ_u^2. The disturbance term is the joint effect of all the variables influencing Y that have not been included explicitly in the regression equation. If you can think of an important variable that you have omitted, and is therefore contributing to u, you will reduce the population variance of the disturbance term if you add it to the regression equation, and hence the variances of the regression coefficients.

In the case of the educational attainment function, we might consider adding *AGE*, the age of the respondent, to the specification. Educational attainment in the population is gradually rising, each new generation tending to be better educated than the last, and so one would anticipate a negative relationship between age and attainment.

Table 3.9 shows the regression output with *AGE* included. Looking at the t statistic, we see that the coefficient of *AGE* is significant at the 5 percent level (p value 0.014), so its inclusion appears to have improved the specification. Comparing Tables 3.7 and 3.9, *RSS* has fallen from 2021.8 to 1999.1.

Table 3.9

```
.reg S SM SF ASVAB02 ASVAB03 ASVAB04 AGE

  Source   |        SS           df          MS            Number of obs =    540
-----------------------------------------------------      F(6, 533)     =  53.58
   Model   |   1205.87487         6     200.979145         Prob > F      = 0.0000
 Residual  |   1999.10846       533     3.75067254         R-squared     = 0.3762
-----------------------------------------------------      Adj R-squared = 0.3692
   Total   |   3204.98333       539     5.94616574         Root MSE      = 1.9367

------------------------------------------------------------------------------
        S  |       Coef.    Std. Err.      t     P>|t|     [95% Conf. Interval]
------------------------------------------------------------------------------
       SM  |    .0426916    .0391708     1.09    0.276     -.0342566    .1196397
       SF  |    .1039566    .0309026     3.36    0.001      .0432509    .1646624
  ASVAB02  |    .0733302    .0127003     5.77    0.000      .0483814     .098279
  ASVAB03  |    .0415514    .0167956     2.47    0.014      .0085577    .0745452
  ASVAB04  |    .0279754    .0149252     1.87    0.061     -.001344     .0572948
      AGE  |   -.0916652    .0372376    -2.46    0.014     -.1648157   -.0185146
    _cons  |    8.522519    1.531916     5.56    0.000      5.513186    11.53185
------------------------------------------------------------------------------
```

As a consequence, s_u^2, the estimator of σ_u^2, has fallen from 3.79 to 3.75 (see the calculation of the residual sum of squares divided by the number of degrees of freedom in the top left quarter of the regression output). Although this is a step in the right direction, it is very small. As a consequence, the reduction of the standard errors of the coefficients of *SM* and *ASVAB04* is very small and those coefficients remain statistically insignificant. This outcome is actually fairly typical. You will probably already have included all of the major variables in your original specification, so those remaining in your data set are likely to be marginal. The approach can even have an effect opposite to that intended. The standard errors of the existing variables in the specification may actually increase if the new variables are correlated with them.

A third possible way of reducing the problem of multicollinearity might be to increase the mean square deviation of the explanatory variables. This is possible only at the design stage of a survey. For example, if you were planning a household survey with the aim of investigating how expenditure patterns vary with income, you should make sure that the sample included relatively rich and relatively poor households as well as middle-income households by stratifying the sample. (For a discussion of sampling theory and techniques, see, for example, Moser and Kalton, 1985, or Fowler, 2009.)

The fourth direct method is the most direct of all. If you are still at the design stage of a survey, you should do your best to obtain a sample where the explanatory variables are less related (more easily said than done, of course).

Indirect methods

Next, we will consider indirect methods. If the correlated variables are similar conceptually, it may be reasonable to combine them into some overall index. That is precisely what has been done with the three cognitive variables in the Armed Services Vocational Aptitude Battery. *ASVABC* has been calculated as a weighted average of *ASVAB02* (arithmetic reasoning), *ASVAB03* (word knowledge), and *ASVAB04* (paragraph comprehension). The three components are highly correlated and by combining them rather than using them individually, one avoids a potential problem of multicollinearity.

However, the *ASVABC* composite is not helpful if one is concerned with determining whether verbal skills or numerical skills are more important for educational attainment. For this purpose, we might leave *ASVAB02* as the indicator of numerical skills and combine *ASVAB03* and *ASVAB04* into an index of verbal skills. In the output shown in Table 3.10, *VERBAL* is defined as the sum of *ASVAB03* and *ASVAB04*. The standard error of its coefficient, 0.00697, is less than half of those of *ASVAB03* and *ASVAB04* in Table 3.7, indicating a large improvement in precision. If one is really interested in the effects of verbal skills, the difference between word knowledge and paragraph comprehension may be unimportant, and using a composite is helpful.

Another possible solution to the problem of multicollinearity is to drop some of the correlated variables if they have insignificant coefficients. Table 3.11 shows

Table 3.10

```
.gen VERBAL = ASVAB03 + ASVAB04
.reg S SM SF ASVAB02 VERBAL

     Source |       SS          df           MS           Number of obs =    540
------------+--------------------------------------       F(4, 535)     =  78.22
      Model |   1182.72356       4       295.68089        Prob > F      = 0.0000
   Residual |   2022.25977     535      3.77992481        R-squared     = 0.3690
------------+--------------------------------------       Adj R-squared = 0.3643
      Total |   3204.98333     539      5.94616574        Root MSE      = 1.9442

----------------------------------------------------------------------------------
          S |      Coef.    Std. Err.      t     P>|t|     [95% Conf. Interval]
------------+---------------------------------------------------------------------
         SM |   .0504512    .0391656     1.29    0.198     -.026486     .1273884
         SF |   .1076162     .030971     3.37    0.001     .0467766     .1684558
    ASVAB02 |   .0754085    .0126717     5.95    0.000      .050516     .1003009
     VERBAL |   .0304221      .00697     4.36    0.000     .0167301     .0441141
      _cons |   4.963665    .5134743     9.67    0.000     3.954992     5.972338
----------------------------------------------------------------------------------
```

Table 3.11

```
.reg S SM SF ASVAB02 ASVAB03

     Source |       SS          df           MS           Number of obs =    540
------------+--------------------------------------       F(4, 535)     =  77.08
      Model |   1171.74101       4      292.935253        Prob > F      = 0.0000
   Residual |   2033.24232     535      3.80045293        R-squared     = 0.3656
------------+--------------------------------------       Adj R-squared = 0.3609
      Total |   3204.98333     539      5.94616574        Root MSE      = 1.9495

----------------------------------------------------------------------------------
          S |      Coef.    Std. Err.      t     P>|t|     [95% Conf. Interval]
------------+---------------------------------------------------------------------
         SM |   .0510298    .0393166     1.30    0.195     -.0262041    .1282636
         SF |   .1072792    .0310784     3.45    0.001      .0462284    .1683299
    ASVAB02 |     .07999    .0124364     6.43    0.000      .0555599    .1044201
    ASVAB03 |   .0531464    .0132626     4.01    0.000      .0270933    .0791996
      _cons |   5.132012    .5062662    10.14    0.000      4.137499    6.126525
----------------------------------------------------------------------------------
```

the output when *ASVAB04* has been dropped. The coefficient of *ASVAB03* is now highly significant. However, the increase in the *t* statistic provides a somewhat misleading indication of the effectiveness of this measure. The increase in precision in the estimation of the coefficient is not dramatic. The standard error does fall, from 0.0167 to 0.0133. But most of the increase in the *t* statistic is attributable to an increase in the size of the estimated coefficient, from 0.0331 to 0.0531. There is always a risk that a variable with an insignificant coefficient does truly belong in the model and that dropping it may distort the results by giving rise to omitted variable bias. We will discuss this in Chapter 6.

A further way of dealing with the problem of multicollinearity is to use extraneous information, if available, concerning the coefficient of one of the variables. For example, suppose that one is relating aggregate demand for a category of consumer expenditure, Y, to aggregate disposable personal income, X, and a price index for the category, P.

$$Y = \beta_1 + \beta_2 X + \beta_3 P + u. \tag{3.50}$$

To fit a model of this type you would use time series data. If X and P possess strong time trends and are therefore highly correlated, which is often the case with time series variables, multicollinearity is likely to be a problem. Suppose, however, that you also have cross-sectional data on Y and X derived from a separate household survey. These variables will be denoted Y' and X' to indicate that the data are household data, not aggregate data. Assuming that all the households in the survey were paying roughly the same price for the commodity, one would fit the simple regression

$$\hat{Y}' = b_1' + b_2' X'. \tag{3.51}$$

Now substitute b_2' for β_2 in the time series model,

$$Y = \beta_1 + b_2' X + \beta_3 P + u, \tag{3.52}$$

subtract $b_2' X$ from both sides,

$$Y - b_2' X = \beta_1 + \beta_3 P + u, \tag{3.53}$$

and regress $Z = Y - b_2' X$ on price. This is a simple regression, so multicollinearity has been eliminated.

There are, however, two possible problems with this technique. First, the estimate of β_3 in (3.53) depends on the accuracy of the estimate of b_2', and this of course is subject to sampling error. Second, you are assuming that the income coefficient has the same meaning in time series and cross-sectional contexts, and this may not be the case. For many commodities, the short-run and long-run effects of changes in income may differ because expenditure patterns are subject to inertia. A change in income can affect expenditure both directly, by altering the budget constraint, and indirectly, through causing a change in lifestyle, and the indirect effect is much slower than the direct one. As a first approximation, it is commonly argued that time series regressions, particularly those using short sample periods, estimate short-run effects, while cross-sectional regressions estimate long-run ones. For a discussion of this and related issues, see Kuh and Meyer (1957).

Last, but by no means least among the indirect methods of alleviating multicollinearity, is the use of a theoretical restriction, which is defined as a hypothetical relationship among the parameters of a regression model. Returning to the educational attainment model,

$$S = \beta_1 + \beta_2 SM + \beta_3 SF + \beta_4 ASVAB02 + \beta_5 ASVAB03 + \beta_6 ASVAB04 + u \tag{3.54}$$

suppose that we hypothesize that word knowledge, *ASVAB03*, and paragraph comprehension, *ASVAB04*, are equally important. We can then impose the restriction $\beta_5 = \beta_6$. This allows us to write the equation as

$$\begin{aligned} S &= \beta_1 + \beta_2 SM + \beta_3 SF + \beta_4 ASVAB02 + \beta_5 (ASVAB03 + ASVAB04) + \\ &= \beta_1 + \beta_2 SM + \beta_3 SF + \beta_4 ASVAB02 + \beta_5 VERBAL + u. \end{aligned} \quad \textbf{(3.55)}$$

Thus, we have returned to the first of the indirect methods that we have considered, the use of a composite. Since the specification is the same, the consequences are the same. The only difference is in the justification for the procedure. Earlier, we decided to use the composite *VERBAL* instead of *ASVAB03* and *ASVAB04* individually as a pragmatic measure. Here we are doing so as a consequence of the use of a restriction.

In the same way, we might hypothesize that mother's and father's education are equally important for educational attainment. We can then impose another restriction, $\beta_2 = \beta_3$, and write the model as

$$\begin{aligned} S &= \beta_1 + \beta_2 (SM + SF) + \beta_4 ASVAB02 + \beta_5 VERBAL + \\ &= \beta_1 + \beta_2 SP + \beta_4 ASVAB02 + \beta_5 VERBAL + u, \end{aligned} \quad \textbf{(3.56)}$$

where $SP = SM + SF$ is total parental education. Table 3.12 gives the corresponding regression output.

The estimate of β_2 is now 0.083. Not surprisingly, this is a compromise between the coefficients of *SM* and *SF* in the previous specification. The standard error of *SP* is much smaller than those of *SM* and *SF*, indicating that, in this case also, the use of the restriction has led to a gain in efficiency.

Two final notes are in order. First, in this example, the two restrictions were of the same type: two parameters were hypothesized to be equal to one another. However, this was a coincidence. We will encounter other types of restriction in

Table 3.12

```
.gen SP - SM + SF
.reg S SP ASVAB02 VERBAL

  Source  |      SS          df         MS            Number of obs =    540
----------+----------------------------------         F(3, 536)     = 104.04
   Model  |  1179.48715       3     393.162385        Prob > F      = 0.0000
Residual  |  2025.49618     536     3.77891078        R-squared     = 0.3680
----------+----------------------------------         Adj R-squared = 0.3645
   Total  |  3204.98333     539     5.94616574        Root MSE      = 1.9439

------------------------------------------------------------------------------
       S  |     Coef.    Std. Err.      t     P>|t|     [95% Conf. Interval]
----------+-------------------------------------------------------------------
      SP  |   .0833379   .0164531     5.07    0.000     .0510174    .1156585
 ASVAB02  |   .0755626   .0126689     5.96    0.000     .0506757    .1004495
  VERBAL  |   .0301108    .006961     4.33    0.000     .0164367    .0437849
  _ cons  |     4.8936   .5077924     9.64    0.000     3.896093    5.891108
------------------------------------------------------------------------------
```

the remainder of this text. Second, restrictions are hypothetical and we cannot assume that they are valid. We need to subject them to formal tests. We shall see how to do this in Chapter 6.

EXERCISES

3.14 Using your *EAEF* data set, regress *S* on *SM*, *SF*, *ASVAB02*, *ASVAB03*, and *ASVAB04*, the three components of the *ASVABC* composite score. Compare the coefficients and their standard errors with those of *ASVABC* in a regression of *S* on *SM*, *SF*, and *ASVABC*. Calculate correlation coefficients for the three *ASVAB* components.

3.15 In Exercise 1.9, the number of children in the respondent's family was regressed on mother's years of schooling. Fit an extended version of the model adding father's years of schooling using your *EAEF* data set. Define *CHILDREN* = *SIBLINGS* + 1 and regress *CHILDREN* on *SM* and *SF*. *SM* and *SF* are likely to be highly correlated (find the correlation in your data set) and the regression may be subject to multicollinearity. Introduce the restriction that the theoretical coefficients of *SM* and *SF* are equal and run the regression a second time, replacing *SM* and *SF* by their sum, *SP*. Evaluate the regression results.

3.16* A researcher investigating the determinants of the demand for public transport in a certain city has the following data for 100 residents for the previous calendar year: expenditure on public transport, *E*, measured in dollars; number of days worked, *W*; and number of days not worked, *NW*. By definition *NW* is equal to 365 – *W*. He attempts to fit the following model:

$$E = \beta_1 + \beta_2 W + \beta_3 NW + u.$$

Explain why he is unable to fit this equation. (Give both intuitive and technical explanations.) How might he resolve the problem?

3.17 Work experience is generally found to be an important determinant of earnings. If a direct measure is lacking in a data set, it is standard practice to use potential work experience, *PWE*, defined by

$$PWE = AGE - S - 5$$

as a proxy. This is the maximum number of years since the completion of full-time education, assuming that an individual enters first grade at the age of six. Using your *EAEF* data set, first regress *EARNINGS* on *S* and *PWE*, and then run the regression a second time adding *AGE* as well. Comment on the regression results.

3.5 Goodness of fit: R^2

As in simple regression analysis, the coefficient of determination, R^2, measures the proportion of the variation in *Y* explained by the regression and is defined equivalently by

$$R^2 = \frac{\sum_{i=1}^{n}\left(\hat{Y}_i - \bar{Y}\right)^2}{\sum_{i=1}^{n}\left(Y_i - \bar{Y}\right)^2}, \tag{3.57}$$

by

$$R^2 = 1 - \frac{\sum_{i=1}^{n} e_i^2}{\sum_{i=1}^{n} (Y_i - \bar{Y})^2}, \tag{3.58}$$

or by the square of the correlation coefficient for Y and $\hat{Y}$. It can never decrease, and generally will increase, if you add another variable to a regression equation, provided that you retain all the previous explanatory variables. To see this, suppose that you regress Y on X_2 and X_3 and fit the equation

$$\hat{Y}_i = b_1 + b_2 X_{2i} + b_3 X_{3i}. \tag{3.59}$$

Next suppose that you regress Y on X_2 only and the result is

$$\hat{Y}_i = b_1^* + b_2^* X_{2i}. \tag{3.60}$$

This can be rewritten

$$\hat{Y}_i = b_1^* + b_2^* X_{2i} + 0 X_{3i}. \tag{3.61}$$

Comparing (3.59) and (3.61), the coefficients in (3.59) have been determined freely by the OLS technique using the data for Y, X_2, and X_3 to give the best possible fit. In (3.61), however, the coefficient of X_3 has arbitrarily been set at zero, and the fit will be suboptimal unless, by coincidence, b_3 happens to be zero, in which case the fit will be the same. (b_1^* will then be equal to b_1, and b_2^* will be equal to b_2). Hence, in general, the level of R^2 will be higher in (3.59) than in (3.61), and it cannot be lower. Of course, if the new variable does not genuinely belong in the equation, the increase in R^2 is likely to be negligible.

You might think that, because R^2 measures the proportion of the variation jointly explained by the explanatory variables, it should be possible to deduce the individual contribution of each explanatory variable and thus obtain a measure of its relative importance. At least it would be very convenient if one could. Unfortunately, such a decomposition is impossible if the explanatory variables are correlated because their explanatory power will overlap. The problem will be discussed further in Section 6.2.

F tests

We saw in Section 2.7 that we could perform an F test of the explanatory power of the simple regression model

$$Y_i = \beta_1 + \beta_2 X_i + u_i, \tag{3.62}$$

the null hypothesis being H_0: $\beta_2 = 0$ and the alternative being H_1: $\beta_2 \neq 0$. The null hypothesis was the same as that for a t test on the slope coefficient and it turned out that the F test was equivalent to a (two-sided) t test. However, in the case of the multiple regression model, the tests have different roles. The t tests test the significance of the coefficient of each variable individually, while the F test tests their joint explanatory power. The null hypothesis, which we hope to reject, is that the model has no explanatory power. The model will have no explanatory power if it turns out that Y is unrelated to any of the explanatory variables. Mathematically, therefore, if the model is

$$Y_i = \beta_1 + \beta_2 X_{2i} + \cdots + \beta_k X_{ki} + u_i, \quad (3.63)$$

the null hypothesis for the F test is that all the slope coefficients $\beta_2, \ldots, \beta_k$ are zero:

$$H_0: \beta_2 = \ldots = \beta_k = 0. \quad (3.64)$$

The alternative hypothesis H_1 is that at least one of the slope coefficients $\beta_2, \ldots, \beta_k$ is different from zero. The F statistic is defined as

$$F(k-1, n-k) = \frac{ESS/(k-1)}{RSS/(n-k)} \quad (3.65)$$

and the test is performed by comparing this with the critical level of F in the column corresponding to $k - 1$ degrees of freedom and the row corresponding to $n - k$ degrees of freedom in the appropriate part of Table A.3 in Appendix A.

This F statistic may also be expressed in terms of R^2 by dividing both the numerator and denominator of (3.65) by TSS, the total sum of squares, and noting that ESS/TSS is R^2 and RSS/TSS is $(1 - R^2)$:

$$F(k-1, n-k) = \frac{R^2/(k-1)}{(1-R^2)/(n-k)}. \quad (3.66)$$

Example

The educational attainment model will be used as an illustration. For simplicity, we will use the composite cognitive ability measure $ASVABC$ instead of any of its components discussed in the previous section. We will suppose that S depends on $ASVABC$, SM, and SF:

$$S = \beta_1 + \beta_2 SM + \beta_3 SF + \beta_4 ASVABC + u. \quad (3.67)$$

The null hypothesis for the F test of goodness of fit is that all three slope coefficients are equal to zero:

$$H_0: \beta_2 = \beta_3 = \beta_4 = 0. \quad (3.68)$$

The alternative hypothesis is that at least one of them is nonzero. The regression output using *EAEF* Data Set 21 is shown in Table 3.13.

In this example, $k - 1$, the number of explanatory variables, is equal to 3 and $n - k$, the number of degrees of freedom, is equal to 536. The numerator of the F statistic is the explained sum of squares divided by $k - 1$. In the Stata output,

Table 3.13

```
.reg S SM SF ASVABC

  Source   |      SS          df         MS              Number of obs =    540
-----------+------------------------------------------   F(3, 536)     = 104.30
   Model   |  1181.36981       3     393.789935          Prob > F      = 0.0000
Residual   |  2023.61353     536     3.77539837          R-squared     = 0.3686
-----------+------------------------------------------   Adj R-squared = 0.3651
   Total   |  3204.98333     539     5.94616574          Root MSE      =  1.943

------------------------------------------------------------------------------
       S   |      Coef.   Std. Err.      t     P>|t|     [95% Conf. Interval]
-----------+------------------------------------------------------------------
      SM   |   .0492424   .0390901     1.26    0.208     -.027546    .1260309
      SF   |   .1076825   .0309522     3.48    0.001       .04688    .1684851
  ASVABC   |   .1257087   .0098533    12.76    0.000     .1063528    .1450646
   _cons   |   5.370631   .4882155    11.00    0.000      4.41158    6.329681
------------------------------------------------------------------------------
```

these numbers, 1181.4 and 3, respectively, are given in the Model row. The denominator is the residual sum of squares divided by the number of degrees of freedom remaining, 2023.6 and 536, respectively. Hence the *F* statistic is

$$F(3,536) = \frac{1181.4/3}{2023.6/536} = 104.3 \qquad \textbf{(3.69)}$$

as in the printed output. All serious regression applications compute this *F* statistic for you as part of the diagnostics in the regression output.

The critical value for *F*(3,536) is not given in the *F* tables, but we know it must be lower than *F*(3,500), which is given. At the 0.1 percent level, this is 5.51. Hence we reject H_0 at that significance level. This result could have been anticipated because both *ASVABC* and *SF* have highly significant *t* statistics. So we knew in advance that both β_2 and β_3 were nonzero.

In practice, the *F* statistic will almost always be significant if any *t* statistic is. In principle, however, it might not be. Suppose that you ran a nonsense regression with 40 explanatory variables, none being a true determinant of the dependent variable. Then the *F* statistic should be low enough for H_0 not to be rejected. However, if you are performing *t* tests on the slope coefficients at the 5 percent level, with a 5 percent chance of a Type I error, on average 2 of the 40 variables could be expected to have 'significant' coefficients.

On the other hand, it can easily happen that the *F* statistic is significant while the *t* statistics are not. Suppose you have a multiple regression model that is correctly specified and R^2 is high. You would be likely to have a highly significant *F* statistic. However, if the explanatory variables are highly correlated and the model is subject to severe multicollinearity, the standard errors of the slope coefficients could all be so large that none of the *t* statistics is significant. In this situation, you would know that your model has high explanatory power, but you are not in a position to pinpoint the contributions made by the explanatory variables individually.

Further analysis of variance

Besides testing the equation as a whole, you can use an F test to see whether or not the joint marginal contribution of a group of variables is significant. Suppose that you first fit the model

$$Y = \beta_1 + \beta_2 X_2 + \cdots + \beta_k X_k + u, \tag{3.70}$$

with explained sum of squares ESS_k. Next you add $m - k$ variables and fit the model

$$Y = \beta_1 + \beta_2 X_2 + \cdots + \beta_k X_k + \beta_{k+1} X_{k+1} + \cdots + \beta_m X_m + u, \tag{3.71}$$

with explained sum of squares ESS_m. You have then explained an additional sum of squares equal to $ESS_m - ESS_k$ using up an additional $m - k$ degrees of freedom, and you want to see whether the increase is greater than is likely to have arisen by chance.

Again an F test is used and the appropriate F statistic may be expressed in verbal terms as

$$F = \frac{\text{improvement in fit/extra degrees of freedom used up}}{\text{residual sum of squares remaining/degrees of freedom remaining}}. \tag{3.72}$$

Since RSS_m, the unexplained sum of squares in the second model, is equal to $TSS - ESS_m$, and RSS_k, the residual sum of squares in the first model, is equal to $TSS - ESS_k$, the improvement in the fit when the extra variables are added, $ESS_m - ESS_k$, is equal to $RSS_k - RSS_m$. Hence, the appropriate F statistic is

$$F(m-k, n-m) = \frac{(RSS_k - RSS_m)/(m-k)}{RSS_m/(n-m)}. \tag{3.73}$$

Under the null hypothesis that the additional variables contribute nothing to the equation,

$$H_0: \beta_{k+1} = \beta_{k+2} = \ldots = \beta_m = 0, \tag{3.74}$$

this F statistic is distributed with $m - k$ and $n - m$ degrees of freedom. The upper half of Table 3.14 gives the analysis of variance for the explanatory power of the original $k - 1$ variables. The lower half gives it for the joint marginal contribution of the new variables.

Example

We will illustrate the test with the educational attainment example. Table 3.15 shows the output from a regression of S on $ASVABC$ using $EAEF$ Data Set 21. We make a note of the residual sum of squares, 2123.0.

Now we add a group of two variables, the years of schooling of each parent, with the output shown in Table 3.16. Do the two new variables jointly make a significant contribution to the explanatory power of the model? Well, we can see

Table 3.14 Analysis of variance, original variables and a group of additional variables

	Sum of squares	Degrees of freedom	Sum of squares divided by degrees of freedom	F statistic
Explained by original variables	ESS_k	$k-1$	$ESS_k/(k-1)$	$\dfrac{ESS_k/(k-1)}{RSS_k/(n-k)}$
Residual	$RSS_k = TSS - ESS_k$	$n-k$	$RSS_k/(n-k)$	
Explained by new variables	$ESS_m - ESS_k = RSS_k - RSS_m$	$m-k$	$(RSS_k - RSS_m)/(m-k)$	$\dfrac{(RSS_k - RSS_m)/(m-k)}{RSS_m/(n-m)}$
Residual	$RSS_m = TSS - ESS_m$	$n-m$	$RSS_m/(n-m)$	

Table 3.15

```
.reg S ASVABC

  Source |       SS          df         MS          Number of obs =     540
---------+-------------------------------------     F(1, 538)     =  274.19
   Model |  1081.97059        1    1081.97059       Prob > F      =  0.0000
Residual |  2123.01275      538    3.94612035       R-squared     =  0.3376
---------+-------------------------------------     Adj R-squared =  0.3364
   Total |  3204.98333      539    5.94616574       Root MSE      =  1.9865

-----------------------------------------------------------------------------
       S |      Coef.   Std. Err.       t     P>|t|     [95% Conf. Interval]
---------+-------------------------------------------------------------------
  ASVABC |    .148084    .0089431    16.56    0.000     .1305165    .1656516
   _cons |   6.066225    .4672261    12.98    0.000     5.148413    6.984036
-----------------------------------------------------------------------------
```

that a t test would show that SF has a highly significant coefficient, but we will perform the F test anyway. We make a note of RSS, 2023.6.

The improvement in the fit on adding the parental schooling variables is the reduction in the residual sum of squares, 2123.0 – 2023.6. The cost is two degrees of freedom because two additional parameters have been estimated. The residual sum of squares remaining unexplained after adding SM and SF is 2023.6. The number of degrees of freedom remaining after adding the new variables is 540 – 4 = 536.

$$F(2,536) = \frac{(2123.0 - 2023.6)/2}{2023.6/536} = 13.16. \tag{3.75}$$

Thus, the F statistic is 13.16. The critical value of $F(2,500)$ at the 0.1 percent level is 7.00. The critical value of $F(2,536)$ must be lower, so we reject H_0 and

Table 3.16

```
.reg S ASVABC SM SF

    Source |       SS       df       MS              Number of obs =     540
-----------+------------------------------           F(3, 536)     =  104.30
     Model |  1181.36981     3  393.789935           Prob > F      =  0.0000
  Residual |  2023.61353   536  3.77539837           R-squared     =  0.3686
-----------+------------------------------           Adj R-squared =  0.3651
     Total |  3204.98333   539  5.94616574           Root MSE      =   1.943

------------------------------------------------------------------------------
         S |      Coef.   Std. Err.      t    P>|t|     [95% Conf. Interval]
-----------+------------------------------------------------------------------
    ASVABC |   .1257087   .0098533   12.76   0.000     .1063528    .1450646
        SM |   .0492424   .0390901    1.26   0.208     -.027546    .1260309
        SF |   .1076825   .0309522    3.48   0.001       .04688    .1684851
     _cons |   5.370631   .4882155   11.00   0.000      4.41158    6.329681
------------------------------------------------------------------------------
```

conclude that the parental education variables do have significant joint explanatory power.

Relationship between *F* statistic and *t* statistic

Suppose that you are considering the following alternative model specifications:

$$Y = \beta_1 + \beta_2 X_2 + \cdots + \beta_{k-1} X_{k-1} + u \qquad \textbf{(3.76)}$$

$$Y = \beta_1 + \beta_2 X_2 + \cdots + \beta_{k-1} X_{k-1} + \beta_k X_k + u, \qquad \textbf{(3.77)}$$

the only difference being the addition of X_k as an explanatory variable in (3.77). You now have two ways to test whether X_k belongs in the model. You could perform a *t* test on its coefficient when (3.77) is fitted. Alternatively, you could perform an *F* test of the type just discussed, treating X_k as a 'group' of just one variable, to test its marginal explanatory power. For the *F* test the null hypothesis will be H_0: $\beta_k = 0$, since only X_k has been added and this is the same null hypothesis as that for the *t* test. Thus, it might appear that there is a risk that the outcomes of the two tests might conflict with each other.

Fortunately, this is impossible, since it can be shown that the *F* statistic for this test must be equal to the square of the *t* statistic and that the critical value of *F* is equal to the square of the critical value of *t* (two-sided test). This result means that the *t* test of the coefficient of a variable is in effect a test of its marginal explanatory power, *after all the other variables have been included in the equation.*

If the variable is correlated with one or more of the other variables, its marginal explanatory power may be quite low, even if it genuinely belongs in the model. If all the variables are correlated, it is possible for all of them to have low marginal explanatory power and for none of the *t* tests to be significant, even

Table 3.17

```
.reg S ASVABC SM
  Source   |      SS          df         MS          Number of obs =    540
-----------+------------------------------------     F(2, 537)     = 147.36
  Model    |  1135.67473       2     567.837363      Prob > F      = 0.0000
 Residual  |  2069.30861     537     3.85346109      R-squared     = 0.3543
-----------+------------------------------------     Adj R-squared = 0.3519
  Total    |  3204.98333     539     5.94616574      Root MSE      =  1.963

------------------------------------------------------------------------------
     S     |     Coef.    Std. Err.      t     P>|t|     [95% Conf. Interval]
-----------+------------------------------------------------------------------
  ASVABC   |  .1328069    .0097389    13.64    0.000     .1136758     .151938
    SM     |  .1235071    .0330837     3.73    0.000     .0585178    .1884963
  _cons    |  5.420733    .4930224    10.99    0.000     4.452244    6.389222
------------------------------------------------------------------------------
```

though the F test for their joint explanatory power is highly significant. If this is the case, the model is said to be suffering from the problem of multicollinearity discussed earlier in this chapter.

No proof of the equivalence will be offered here, but it will be illustrated with the educational attainment model. In Table 3.17, it is hypothesized that S depends on $ASVABC$ and SM. In Table 3.16, it is hypothesized that it depends on SF as well.

Comparing Tables 3.16 and 3.17, the improvement on adding SF is the reduction in the residual sum of squares, 2069.3 – 2023.6. The cost is just the single degree of freedom lost when estimating the coefficient of SF. The residual sum of squares remaining after adding SF is 2023.6. The number of degrees of freedom remaining after adding SF is 540 – 4 = 536. Hence the F statistic is 12.10:

$$F(1,536) = \frac{(2069.3 - 2023.6)/1}{2023.6/536} = 12.10. \tag{3.78}$$

The critical value of F at the 0.1 percent significance level with 500 degrees of freedom is 10.96. The critical value with 536 degrees of freedom must be lower, so we reject H_0 at the 0.1 percent level. The t statistic for the coefficient of SF in the regression with both SM and SF is 3.48. The critical value of t at the 0.1 percent level with 500 degrees of freedom is 3.31. The critical value with 536 degrees of freedom must be lower, so we also reject H_0 with the t test. The square of 3.48 is 12.11, equal to the F statistic, except for rounding error, and the square of 3.31 is 10.96, equal to the critical value of $F(1,500)$. Hence, the conclusions of the two tests must coincide.

'Adjusted' R^2

If you look at regression output, you will almost certainly find near the R^2 statistic something called the 'adjusted' R^2. Sometimes it is called the 'corrected'

R^2. 'Corrected' makes it sound as if it is better than the ordinary one, but this is questionable.

As was noted earlier in this section, R^2 cannot fall, and generally increases, if you add another variable to a regression equation. The adjusted R^2, usually denoted $\bar{R}^2$, attempts to compensate for this automatic upward shift by imposing a penalty for increasing the number of explanatory variables. It is defined as

$$\bar{R}^2 = 1-(1-R^2)\frac{n-1}{n-k} = \frac{n-1}{n-k}R^2 - \frac{k-1}{n-k}$$
$$= R^2 - \frac{k-1}{n-k}(1-R^2), \quad (3.79)$$

where $k - 1$ is the number of explanatory variables. As k increases, $(k - 1)/(n - k)$ increases, and so the negative adjustment to R^2 increases.

It can be shown that the addition of a new variable to a regression will cause $\bar{R}^2$ to rise if and only if the absolute value of its t statistic is greater than 1. Hence, a rise in $\bar{R}^2$ when a new variable is added does not necessarily mean that the coefficient of the new variable is significantly different from zero. It therefore does not follow, as is sometimes suggested, that a rise in $\bar{R}^2$ implies that the specification of an equation has improved.

This is one reason why $\bar{R}^2$ is not widely used as a diagnostic statistic. Another is that small variations in R^2 are not all that critical anyway. Initially, it may seem that R^2 should be regarded as a key indicator of the success of model specification. In practice, however, as will be seen in the following chapters, even a very badly specified regression model may yield a high R^2, and recognition of this fact leads to a reduction in the perceived importance of R^2. R^2 should be regarded as just one of a whole set of diagnostic statistics that should be examined when evaluating a regression model. Consequently, there is little to be gained by fine tuning it with a 'correction' of dubious value.

EXERCISES

3.18 Using your *EAEF* data set, fit an educational attainment function, regressing *S* on *ASVABC*, *SM*, and *SF*. Calculate the *F* statistic using the explained sum of squares and the residual sum of squares in the regression output, verify that it matches the *F* statistic in the output, and perform a test of the explanatory power of the equation as a whole. Also calculate the *F* statistic using R^2 and verify that it is the same.

3.19 Fit an educational attainment function using the specification in Exercise 3.18, adding the ASVAB speed test scores *ASVAB05* and *ASVAB06*. Perform an *F* test of the joint explanatory power of *ASVAB05* and *ASVAB06*, using the results of this regression and that in Exercise 3.18.

3.20 Fit an educational attainment function, regressing *S* on *ASVABC*, *SM*, *SF*, and *ASVAB05*. Perform an *F* test of the explanatory power of *ASVAB06*, using the results of this regression and that in Exercise 3.19. Verify that it leads to the same conclusion as a two-sided *t* test.

3.21* The researcher in Exercise 3.16 decides to divide the number of days not worked into the number of days not worked because of illness, I, and the number of days not worked for other reasons, O. The mean value of I in the sample is 2.1 and the mean value of O is 120.2. He fits the regression (standard errors in parentheses):

$$\hat{E} = \underset{(8.3)}{-9.6} + \underset{(1.98)}{2.10W} + \underset{(1.77)}{0.45O} \qquad R^2 = 0.72.$$

Perform t tests on the regression coefficients and an F test on the goodness of fit of the equation. Explain why the t tests and the F test have different outcomes.

3.6 Prediction

The word prediction is often related to the forecasting of time series, but it is also of practical relevance in a cross-sectional context. One example is hedonic pricing, which we shall use to illustrate the topic.

Hedonic pricing supposes that a good or service has a number of characteristics that individually give it value to the purchaser. The market price of the good is then assumed to be a function, typically a linear combination, of the prices of the characteristics. Thus, one has

$$P_i = \beta_1 + \sum_{j=2}^{k} \beta_j X_{ji} + u_i, \qquad (3.80)$$

where P_i is the price of the good, the X_j are the characteristics, and the β_j are their prices. In principle, the β_j may themselves be market prices, but more often they are implicit.

A common example is the pricing of houses, with the value of a house being related to plot size, floor space, the number of bedrooms, proximity to a metropolitan area, and other details. Another example, responsible for much of the growth of the early literature, is the pricing of automobiles, with value being related to size, weight, engine power, etc. Another is the pricing of computers, value being related to the speed of the processor, the size of the hard drive, etc.

Since a computer is just an assembly of traded components, it might be possible to determine its price from the component prices, but typically the prices of the characteristics have to be inferred, and of course multiple regression analysis is an appropriate tool. Given the prices of automobiles of a roughly similar nature with differing specifications, multiple regression analysis may be used to infer the prices of the latter. In the case of houses, the environment is so important that a hedonic pricing function is never going to explain all the variance, but even so some intuitive kind of multiple regression analysis underlies an assertion that, in a given location, an extra bedroom adds so many extra dollars to the value. More generally, hedonic pricing underlies, if only subjectively, the notion of what is a fair price for a good or a service.

Besides being useful in the marketplace, hedonic pricing is widely used in national accounting. Changes in the money value of output and other aggregates are separated into real changes and changes attributable to inflation. The separation is especially tricky when improvements in technology are causing specifications to change rapidly. In the case of laptop computers, for example, the average price may not seem to change much from year to year, and as a consequence it might seem that changes in volume could be measured in terms of the number of units sold. However, one needs to recognize that the underlying technology, in terms of processor speed, size of hard drive, size of DRAM, etc., is continually being upgraded. Failure to take account of this would lead to underestimation of both the real growth of output and the reduction in prices.

Example

The term 'hedonic price index' was coined in Court (1939), one of the earliest such studies. The study relates to the pricing of automobiles in the 1920s and 1930s and was prompted by the paradox that the price index for automobiles published by the Bureau of Labor Statistics showed an increase of 45 percent from 1925 to 1935, when it was obvious that, in reality, prices had fallen dramatically. The cause of the contradiction was the fact that the Bureau was using a very broad definition of passenger automobile that did not take account of the great improvement in average specification during the period. When one controlled for specification, the conclusion was exactly the opposite.

Table 3.18 presents representative data for eight manufacturers for their cheapest four-passenger vehicles in 1920. Court did not publish his full data set,

Table 3.18 Characteristics and factory price of cheapest four-passenger car, 1920

	Weight (lbs)	Wheelbase (inches)	Brake horsepower	Price ($)
Chrysler	3100	117	45	3170
General Motors	2739	112	44	2435
Graham–Paige	3150	119	43	3260
Hudson	2955	109	55	3010
Hupp	3400	123	45	3400
Nash–Kelvinator	3455	121	35	3285
Studebaker	2900	112	45	2780
Willys–Overland	2152	100	35	1675

Source: Court (1939), p. 106.

but these observations will suffice for illustration. A regression of price on the characteristics yields the following results (standard errors in parentheses):

$$\underset{}{\hat{price}} = \underset{(1667)}{-2441} + \underset{(0.43)}{1.13}\,\text{weight} + \underset{(23.64)}{10.11}\,\text{wheelbase} + \underset{(8.50)}{18.28}\,\text{horsepower} \quad R^2 = 0.97. \tag{3.81}$$

The coefficients indicate that an extra pound of weight adds \$1.13 to the value of a car, an extra inch of wheelbase \$10.11, and one extra horsepower \$18.28, with the weight and horsepower coefficients being significant at the 1 and 5 percent levels, despite the tiny size of the sample. Of course, the regression specification is crude and should be viewed only as a conceptual starting point. For an automobile in this category with the average specification of 2,981 pounds, 114 inch wheelbase, and 43 horsepower, the regression specification indicates a price of \$2,869. By 1939, for an average specification, horsepower had doubled to 85, with wheelbase unchanged and weight increased marginally to 2,934 pounds. The regression indicates a price of \$3,583. In the interval, with the Great Depression, there had been general deflation of 28 percent. Taking this into account, one would anticipate a price of \$2,573. The actual average price was \$795, lower by 70 percent, achieved by improvements in production technology and the exploitation of economies of scale, especially between 1920 and 1925.

Properties of least squares predictors

Suppose that one has fitted a hedonic pricing model

$$\hat{P}_i = b_1 + \sum_{j=2}^{k} b_j X_{ji} \tag{3.82}$$

and one encounters a new variety of the good with characteristics $\{X_2^*, X_3^*, \ldots, X_k^*\}$. Given the sample regression result, it is natural to predict that the price of the new variety should be given by

$$\hat{P}^* = b_1 + \sum_{j=2}^{k} b_j X_j^*. \tag{3.83}$$

What can one say about the properties of this prediction? First, it is natural to ask whether it is fair, in the sense of not systematically overestimating or underestimating the actual price. (It is tempting to talk about an 'unbiased' prediction, but we are reserving this term for the estimation of parameters.) Second, we will be concerned about the likely accuracy of the prediction.

We will start by supposing that the good has only one relevant characteristic and that we have fitted the simple regression model

$$\hat{P}_i = b_1 + b_2 X_i \tag{3.84}$$

and that, given a new variety of the good with characteristic $X = X^*$, the predicted price is

$$\hat{P}^* = b_1 + b_2 X^*. \tag{3.85}$$

We will define the prediction error of the model, *PE*, as the difference between the actual price, P^*, and the predicted price, $\hat{P}^*$:

$$PE = P^* - \hat{P}^*. \tag{3.86}$$

We will assume that the model applies to the new good and therefore the actual price is generated as

$$P^* = \beta_1 + \beta_2 X^* + u^*, \tag{3.87}$$

where u^* is the value of the disturbance term for the new good. Then

$$PE = P^* - \hat{P}^* = \left(\beta_1 + \beta_2 X^* + u^*\right) - \left(b_1 + b_2 X^*\right) \tag{3.88}$$

and the expected value of the prediction error is given by

$$\begin{aligned} E(PE) &= E\left(\beta_1 + \beta_2 X^* + u^*\right) - E\left(b_1 + b_2 X^*\right) \\ &= \beta_1 + \beta_2 X^* + E\left(u^*\right) - E\left(b_1\right) - X^* E\left(b_2\right) \\ &= \beta_1 + \beta_2 X^* - \beta_1 - X^* \beta_2 = 0 \end{aligned} \tag{3.89}$$

Thus, the expected prediction error is zero. Note that we have assumed that the regression model assumptions are satisfied for the sample period, so that $E\left(b_1\right) = \beta_1$ and $E\left(b_2\right) = \beta_2$, and that the disturbance term of the new good satisfies the assumption that the expected value of the disturbance term be zero. The result generalizes to the case where there are multiple characteristics and the new good embodies a new combination of them. The proof is left as an exercise.

The population variance of the prediction error is given by

$$\sigma_{PE}^2 = \left\{1 + \frac{1}{n} + \frac{\left(X^* - \bar{X}\right)^2}{\sum_{i=1}^{n}\left(X_i - \bar{X}\right)^2}\right\}\sigma_u^2, \tag{3.90}$$

where $\bar{X}$ and $\sum\left(X_i - \bar{X}\right)^2$ are the sample mean and sum of squared deviations of *X*. Unsurprisingly, this implies that, the further is the value of X^* from the sample mean, the larger will be the population variance of the prediction error. It also implies, again unsurprisingly, that, the larger is the sample, the smaller will be the population variance of the prediction error, with a lower limit of σ_u^2. Provided that the regression model assumptions are valid, b_1 and b_2 will tend to their true values as the sample becomes large, so the only source of error in the prediction will be u^*, and by definition this has population variance σ_u^2.

We can obtain the standard error of the prediction error by replacing σ_u^2 in (3.90) by s_u^2 and taking the square root. Then $(P^*\_\hat{P}^*)$/standard error follows a t distribution with the number of degrees of freedom when fitting the equation in the sample period, $n - k$. Hence we can derive a confidence interval for the actual outcome, P^*

$$\hat{P}^* - t_{\text{crit}} \times \text{s.e.} < P^* < \hat{P}^* + t_{\text{crit}} \times \text{s.e.}, \qquad \textbf{(3.91)}$$

where t_{crit} is the critical level of t, given the significance level selected and the number of degrees of freedom, and s.e. is the standard error of the prediction. Figure 3.4 depicts in general terms the relationship between the confidence interval for prediction and the value of the explanatory variable.

Naturally, when there are multiple explanatory variables, the expression for the prediction variance becomes complex. One point to note is that multicollinearity may not have an adverse effect on prediction precision, even though the estimates of the coefficients have large variances. The intuitive reason for this is easily explained. For simplicity, suppose that there are two explanatory variables, that both have positive true coefficients, and that they are positively correlated, the model being

$$Y = \beta_1 + \beta_2 X_2 + \beta_3 X_3 + u \qquad \textbf{(3.92)}$$

and that we are predicting the value Y^*, given values X_2^* and X_3^*. Then if the effect of X_2 is overestimated, so that $b_2 > \beta_2$, the effect of X_3 will almost certainly be underestimated, with $b_3 < \beta_3$. As a consequence, the effects of the

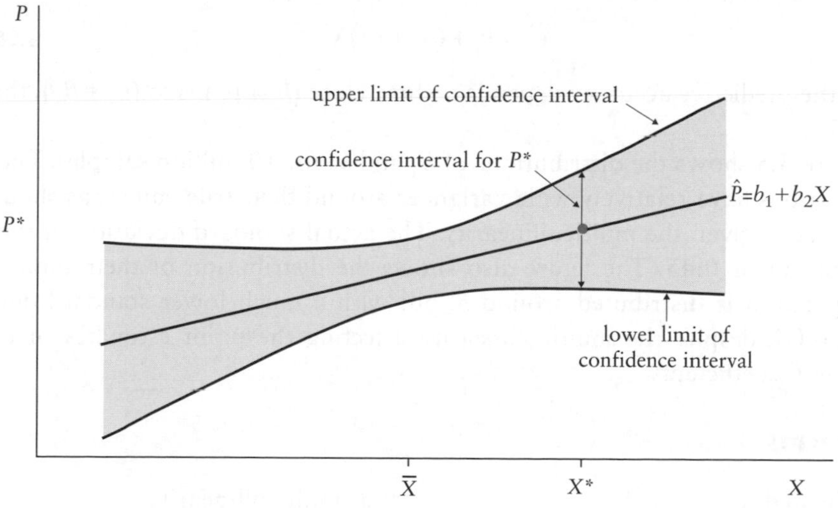

Figure 3.4 Confidence interval for a prediction

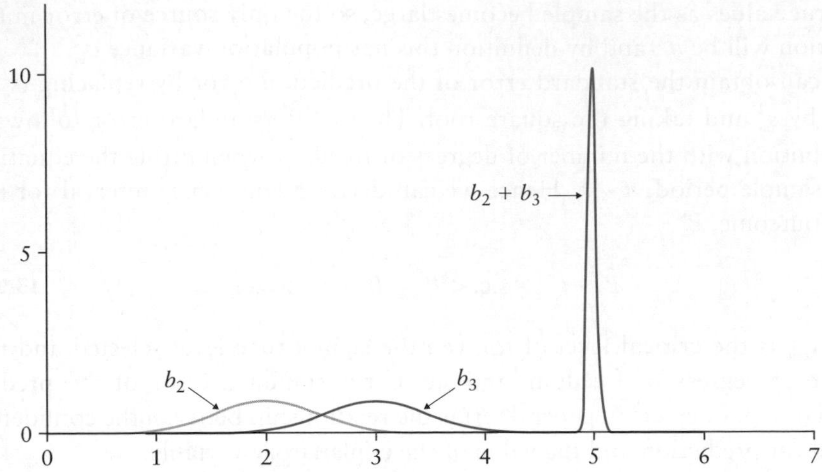

Figure 3.5 Distributions of b_2, b_3, and $b_2 + b_3$

errors may to some extent cancel out, with the result that the linear combination $(b_2X_2^* + b_3X_3^*)$ may be close to $(\beta_2X_2^* + \beta_3X_3^*)$.

This will be illustrated with a simulation, with the model

$$Y = 10 + 2X_2 + 3X_3 + u. \qquad \textbf{(3.93)}$$

X_2 is assigned the numbers 1 to 20, and X_3 is almost identical, being assigned the numbers {2,2,4,4,6,6, …,18,18,20,20}. The correlation between X_2 and X_3 is 0.9962. The disturbance term u is generated as a normal random variable with zero mean and unit variance. We fit the model and make the prediction

$$Y^* = b_1 + b_2X_2^* + b_3X_3^*. \qquad \textbf{(3.94)}$$

Since X_2 and X_3 are virtually identical, this may be approximated as

$$Y^* = b_1 + (b_2 + b_3)X_2^*. \qquad \textbf{(3.95)}$$

Thus, the predictive accuracy depends on how close $(b_2 + b_3)$ is to $(\beta_2 + \beta_3)$, that is, to 5.

Figure 3.5 shows the distributions of b_2 and b_3 for 10 million samples. Their distributions have relatively wide variances around their true values, as should be expected, given the multicollinearity. The actual standard deviation of their distributions is 0.45. The figure also shows the distribution of their sum. As anticipated, it is distributed around 5, but with a much lower standard deviation, 0.04, despite the multicollinearity affecting the point estimates of the individual coefficients.

Key terms

- adjusted R^2
- Frisch–Waugh–Lovell theorem
- hedonic pricing
- multicollinearity
- multiple regression analysis
- restriction

EXERCISES

3.22 It seems that the first study in hedonic pricing was Waugh's investigation of how the prices of vegetables were determined in the Boston wholesale market (Waugh, 1929). Waugh was an economist working for the Bureau of Agricultural Economics and he was surprised to find that one box of cucumbers might sell for \$7 while another for only \$1. Being told that thinner cucumbers had better texture and taste than fat ones, he fitted the following regression (standard errors in parentheses, data from 1925):

$$\hat{P}_i = \underset{(272)}{508} + \underset{(20.1)}{32.3}\, L_i - \underset{(4.45)}{8.80}\, D_i \qquad R^2 = 0.35 \qquad F(2,47) = 12.43$$

where P_i is the price, in cents, of a box of cucumbers and L_i and D_i are the length in inches and the diameter/length ratio, as a percentage, of the cucumbers in the box. The boxes in the market were carefully sorted so that their contents were uniform in terms of these characteristics. Give an interpretation of the regression results.

3.23 The standard deviations of the distributions of b_2 and b_3 for the 10 million samples in Figure 3.5 are both 0.45. Verify that this is what you would expect theoretically, given that the correlation between X_2 and X_3 is 0.9962 and that $\sum_{i=1}^{20}\left(X_2 - \bar{X}_2\right)^2 = 665$ and $\sum_{i=1}^{20}\left(X_3 - \bar{X}_3\right)^2 = 660$.

4. Nonlinear Models and Transformations of Variables

Nonlinear relationships are more plausible than linear ones for many economic processes. In this chapter we will first define what is meant by linear regression analysis and then demonstrate some common methods for extending its use to fit nonlinear relationships. The chapter concludes with a brief outline of the kind of technique used to fit models that cannot be recast in linear form.

4.1 Linearity and nonlinearity

Thus far, when we have used the term 'linear regression analysis', we have not defined exactly what we mean by linearity. It is necessary to do so. Consider the model

$$Y = \beta_1 + \beta_2 X_2 + \beta_3 X_3 + \beta_4 X_4. \tag{4.1}$$

It is linear in two senses. It is linear in variables, because every term consists of a straightforward variable multiplied by a parameter. It is also linear in parameters, because every term consists of a straightforward parameter multiplied by a variable.

For the purpose of linear regression analysis, only the second type of linearity is important. Nonlinearity in the variables can always be sidestepped by using appropriate definitions. For example, suppose that the relationship were of the form

$$Y = \beta_1 + \beta_2 X_2^2 + \beta_3 \sqrt{X_3} + \beta_4 \log X_4 + \cdots \tag{4.2}$$

By defining $Z_2 = X_2^2$, $Z_3 = \sqrt{X_3}$, $Z_4 = \log X_4$, etc., the relationship can be rewritten

$$Y = \beta_1 + \beta_2 Z_2 + \beta_3 Z_3 + \beta_4 Z_4 + \cdots \tag{4.3}$$

and it is now linear in variables as well as in parameters. This type of transformation is only cosmetic, and you will usually see the regression equation presented with the variables written in their original nonlinear form. This avoids the need for explanation and extra notation.

On the other hand, an equation such as

$$Y = \beta_1 X_2^{\beta_2} \tag{4.4}$$

Table 4.1 Average annual percentage rates of growth of employment, *e*, and real GDP, *g*, 1988–97

	e	g	$z = 1/g$		e	g	$z = 1/g$
Australia	1.68	3.04	0.3289	Korea	2.57	7.73	0.1294
Austria	0.65	2.55	0.3922	Luxembourg	3.02	5.64	0.1773
Belgium	0.34	2.16	0.4630	Netherlands	1.88	2.86	0.3497
Canada	1.17	2.03	0.4926	New Zealand	0.91	2.01	0.4975
Denmark	0.02	2.02	0.4950	Norway	0.36	2.98	0.3356
Finland	–1.06	1.78	0.5618	Portugal	0.33	2.79	0.3584
France	0.28	2.08	0.4808	Spain	0.89	2.60	0.3846
Germany	0.08	2.71	0.3690	Sweden	–0.94	1.17	0.8547
Greece	0.87	2.08	0.4808	Switzerland	0.79	1.15	0.8696
Iceland	–0.13	1.54	0.6494	Turkey	2.02	4.18	0.2392
Ireland	2.16	6.40	0.1563	United Kingdom	0.66	1.97	0.5076
Italy	–0.30	1.68	0.5952	United States	1.53	2.46	0.4065
Japan	1.06	2.81	0.3559				

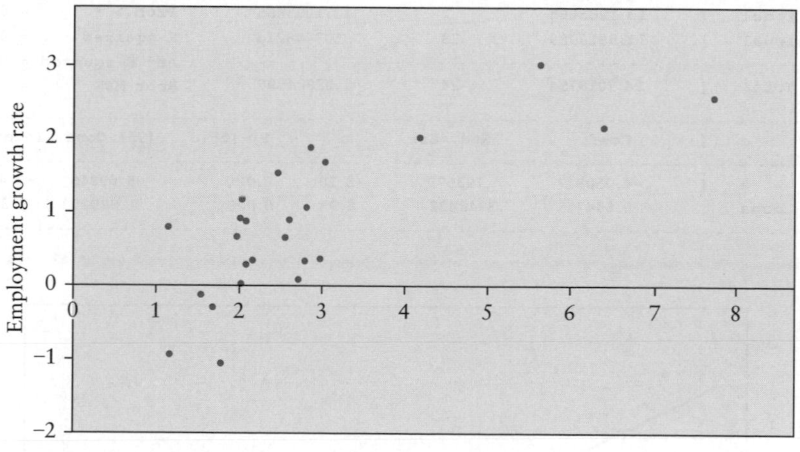

Figure 4.1 Employment and GDP growth rates, 25 OECD countries

is nonlinear in both parameters and variables and cannot be handled by a mere redefinition.

We will begin with an example of a simple model that can be linearized by a cosmetic transformation. Table 4.1 reproduces the data in Exercise 1.4 on average annual rates of growth of employment and GDP for 25 OECD countries. Figure 4.1 plots the data. It is very clear that the relationship is nonlinear. We will consider various nonlinear specifications for the relationship in the course of this chapter, starting with the model

$$e = \beta_1 + \frac{\beta_2}{g} + u. \tag{4.5}$$

This is nonlinear in g, but if we define $z = 1/g$, we can rewrite the model so that it is linear in variables as well as parameters:

$$e = \beta_1 + \beta_2 z + u. \tag{4.6}$$

The data for z are given in Table 4.1. In any serious regression application, one would construct z directly from g. The output for a regression of e on z is shown in Table 4.2 and the regression is plotted in Figure 4.2. The regression is shown in equation form as (4.7). The constant term in the regression is an estimate of β_1 and the coefficient of z is an estimate of β_2.

$$\hat{e} = 2.60 - 4.05z. \tag{4.7}$$

Table 4.2

```
. gen z = 1/g
. reg e z

  Source |       SS          df        MS           Number of obs =      25
---------+---------------------------------------   F(1, 23)      =   26.06
   Model |  13.1203665        1    13.1203665       Prob > F      =  0.0000
Residual |  11.5816089       23    .503548214       R-squared     =  0.5311
---------+---------------------------------------   Adj R-squared =  0.5108
   Total |  24.7019754       24    1.02924898       Root MSE      =  .70961

---------------------------------------------------------------------------
       e |      Coef.     Std. Err.      t     P>|t|   [95% Conf. Interval]
---------+-----------------------------------------------------------------
       z |  -4.050817     .793579     -5.10    0.000   -5.69246   -2.409174
   _cons |   2.604753    .3748822      6.95    0.000    1.82925    3.380256
---------------------------------------------------------------------------
```

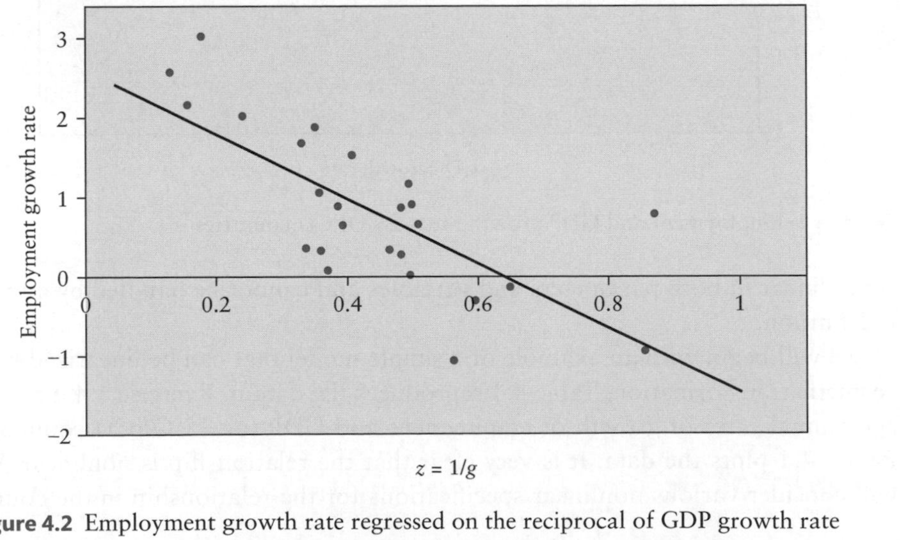

Figure 4.2 Employment growth rate regressed on the reciprocal of GDP growth rate

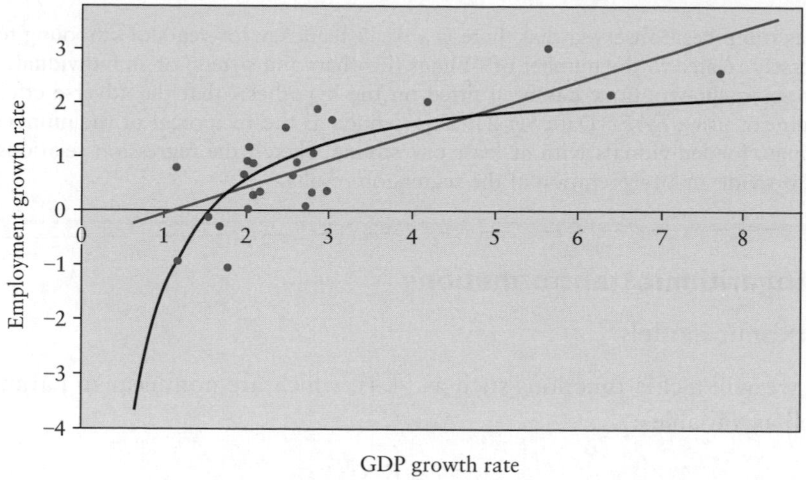

Figure 4.3 Nonlinear and linear regressions of employment growth rate on GDP growth rate

Substituting $z = 1/g$, this becomes

$$\hat{e} = 2.60 - \frac{4.05}{g}. \quad \textbf{(4.8)}$$

Figure 4.3 shows the nonlinear relationship (4.8) plotted in the original diagram. The linear regression reported in Exercise 1.4 is also shown, for comparison.

In this case, it was easy to see that the relationship between e and g was nonlinear. In the case of multiple regression analysis, nonlinearity might be detected using the graphical technique described in Section 3.2.

EXERCISE

4.1

```
. gen Z = 1/SIBLINGS
(11 missing values generated)
. reg S Z

  Source   |       SS          df         MS            Number of obs =    529
-----------+------------------------------------        F(1, 527)     =  30.21
   Model   |  169.838682        1     169.838682        Prob > F      = 0.0000
 Residual  |   2962.9288      527     5.62225579        R-squared     = 0.0542
-----------+------------------------------------        Adj R-squared = 0.0524
   Total   |  3132.76749      528     5.93327175        Root MSE      = 2.3711

-------------------------------------------------------------------------------
      e    |    Coef.     Std. Err.     t       P>|t|     [95% Conf. Interval]
-----------+-------------------------------------------------------------------
      z    |  2.071194    .3768407    5.50     0.000       1.3309     2.811488
   _cons   |   12.7753    .1928491   66.25     0.000     12.39645     13.15415
-------------------------------------------------------------------------------
```

It has often been observed that there is a weak tendency for years of schooling to be inversely related to the number of siblings (brothers and sisters) of an individual. The regression shown above has been fitted on the hypothesis that the adverse effect is nonlinear, using *EAEF* Data Set 21. Z is defined as the reciprocal of the number of siblings, for individuals with at least one sibling. Sketch the regression relationship and provide an interpretation of the regression results.

4.2 Logarithmic transformations

Logarithmic models

Next we will tackle functions such as (4.4), which are nonlinear in parameters as well as variables:

$$Y = \beta_1 X^{\beta_2}. \tag{4.9}$$

When you see such a function, you can immediately say that the elasticity of Y with respect to X is constant and equal to β_2. This is easily demonstrated. Regardless of the mathematical relationship connecting Y and X, or the definitions of Y and X, the elasticity of Y with respect to X is defined to be the proportional change in Y for a given proportional change in X:

$$\text{elasticity} = \frac{dY/Y}{dX/X}. \tag{4.10}$$

Thus, for example, if Y is demand and X is income, the expression defines the income elasticity of demand for the commodity in question.

The expression may be rewritten

$$\text{elasticity} = \frac{dY/dX}{Y/X}. \tag{4.11}$$

In the case of the demand example, this may be interpreted as the marginal propensity to consume the commodity divided by the average propensity to consume it.

If the relationship between Y and X takes the form (4.9),

$$\frac{dY}{dX} = \beta_1 \beta_2 X^{\beta_2 - 1} = \beta_2 \frac{Y}{X}. \tag{4.12}$$

Hence,

$$\text{elasticity} = \frac{dY/dX}{Y/X} = \frac{\beta_2 Y/X}{Y/X} = \beta_2. \tag{4.13}$$

Thus, for example, if you see an Engel curve of the form

$$Y = 0.01X^{0.3} \tag{4.14}$$

this means that the income elasticity of demand is equal to 0.3. If you are trying to explain this to someone who is not familiar with economic jargon, the easiest way to explain it is to say that a 1 percent change in X (income) will cause a 0.3 percent change in Y (demand).

A function of this type can be converted into a linear equation by means of a logarithmic transformation. You will certainly have encountered logarithms in a basic mathematics course. In econometric work they are indispensable. If you are unsure about their use, you should review your notes from that basic math course. The main properties of logarithms are given in Box 4.1.

In the box, it is shown that (4.9) may be linearized as

$$\log Y = \log \beta_1 + \beta_2 \log X. \quad \textbf{(4.15)}$$

This is known as a **logarithmic model** or, alternatively, a **loglinear model**, referring to the fact that it is linear in logarithms. If we write $Y' = \log Y$, $Z = \log X$, and $\beta_1' = \log \beta_1$, the equation may be rewritten

$$Y' = \beta_1' + \beta_2 Z. \quad \textbf{(4.16)}$$

The regression procedure is now as follows. First calculate Y' and Z for each observation, taking the logarithms of the original data. Your regression application will almost certainly do this for you, given the appropriate instructions. Second, regress Y' on Z. The coefficient of Z will be a direct estimate of β_2. The constant term will be an estimate of β_1', that is, of $\log \beta_1$. To obtain an estimate of β_1, you have to take the antilog, that is, calculate $\exp(\beta_1')$.

Example: Engel curve

Figure 4.4 plots annual household expenditure on food eaten at home, *FDHO*, and total annual household expenditure, both measured in dollars, for 869

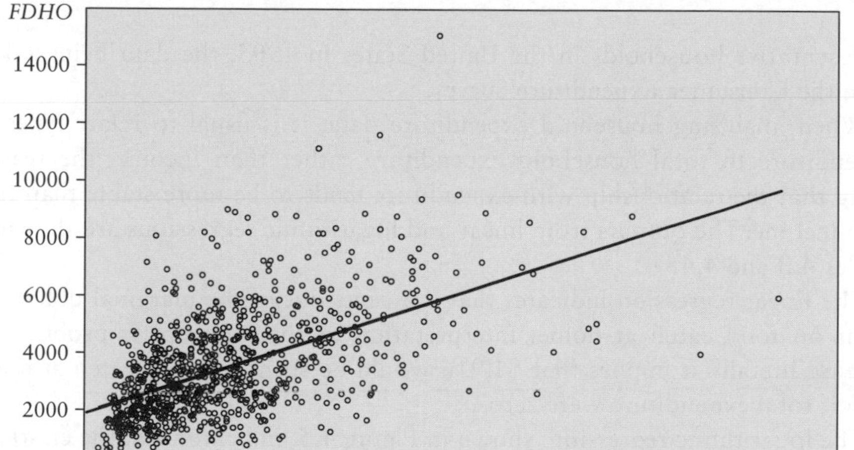

Figure 4.4 Regression of expenditure on food eaten at home on total household expenditure

BOX 4.1 Use of logarithms

First, some basic rules:

1. If $Y = XZ$, $\log Y = \log X + \log Z$
2. If $Y = X/Z$, $\log Y = \log X - \log Z$
3. If $Y = X^n$, $\log Y = n \log X$.

These rules can be combined to transform more complicated expressions. For example, take equation (4.9): if $Y = \beta_1 X^{\beta_2}$,

$$\log Y = \log \beta_1 + \log X^{\beta_2} \quad \text{using rule 1}$$

$$= \log \beta_1 + \beta_2 \log X \quad \text{using rule 3.}$$

Thus far, we have not specified whether we are taking logarithms to base e or to base 10. Throughout this text we shall be using e as the base, and so we shall be using what are known as 'natural' logarithms. This is standard in econometrics. Purists sometimes write ln instead of log to emphasize that they are working with natural logarithms, but this is now unnecessary. Nobody uses logarithms to base 10 any more. They were tabulated in the dreaded log tables that were universally employed for multiplying or dividing large numbers until the early 1970s. When the pocket calculator was invented, they became redundant. They are not missed.

With e as base, we can state another rule:

4. If $Y = e^X$, $\log Y = X$.

e^X, also sometimes written $\exp(X)$, is familiarly known as the antilog of X. One can say that $\log e^X$ is the log of the antilog of X, and since log and antilog cancel out, it is not surprising that $\log e^X$ turns out just to be X. Using rule 2 above, $\log e^X = X \log e = X$ since $\log e$ to base e is 1.

representative households in the United States in 1995, the data being taken from the Consumer Expenditure Survey.

When analyzing household expenditure data, it is usual to relate types of expenditure to total household expenditure rather than income, the reason being that the relationship with expenditure tends to be more stable than that with income. The outputs from linear and logarithmic regressions are shown in Tables 4.3 and 4.4.

The linear regression indicates that 5.3 cents out of the marginal dollar are spent on food eaten at home. Interpretation of the intercept is problematic because literally it implies that \$1,916 would be spent on food eaten at home even if total expenditure were zero.

The logarithmic regression, shown in Figure 4.5, indicates that the elasticity of expenditure on food eaten at home with respect to total household expenditure is 0.48. Is this figure plausible? Yes, because food eaten at home is a

Table 4.3

```
. reg FDHO EXP

      Source |       SS          df        MS            Number of obs =     869
-------------+--------------------------------           F(1, 867)     =  381.47
       Model |   915843574        1     915843574        Prob > F      =  0.0000
    Residual |  2.0815e+09      867    2400831.16        R-squared     =  0.3055
-------------+--------------------------------           Adj R-squared =  0.3047
       Total |  2.9974e+09      868    3453184.55        Root MSE      =  1549.5

------------------------------------------------------------------------------
        FDHO |      Coef.   Std. Err.      t    P>|t|     [95% Conf. Interval]
-------------+----------------------------------------------------------------
         EXP |   .0528427   .0027055   19.531   0.000     .0475325    .0581529
       _cons |   1916.143   96.54591   19.847   0.000     1726.652    2105.634
------------------------------------------------------------------------------
```

Table 4.4

```
. gen LGFDHO = ln(FDHO)
. gen LGEXP = ln(EXP)
. reg LGFDHO LGEXP

      Source |       SS          df        MS            Number of obs =     868
-------------+--------------------------------           F(1, 866)     =  396.06
       Model |  84.4161692        1    84.4161692        Prob > F      =  0.0000
    Residual |  184.579612      866    .213140429        R-squared     =  0.3138
-------------+--------------------------------           Adj R-squared =  0.3130
       Total |  268.995781      867    .310260416        Root MSE      =  .46167

------------------------------------------------------------------------------
      LGFDHO |      Coef.   Std. Err.      t    P>|t|     [95% Conf. Interval]
-------------+----------------------------------------------------------------
       LGEXP |   .4800417   .0241212   19.901   0.000     .4326988    .5273846
       _cons |   3.166271    .244297   12.961   0.000     2.686787    3.645754
------------------------------------------------------------------------------
```

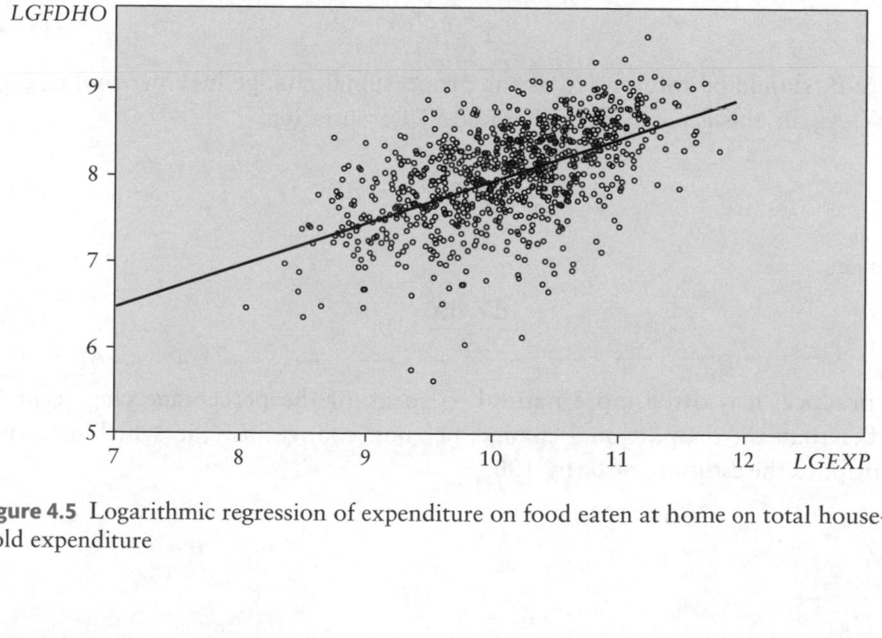

Figure 4.5 Logarithmic regression of expenditure on food eaten at home on total household expenditure

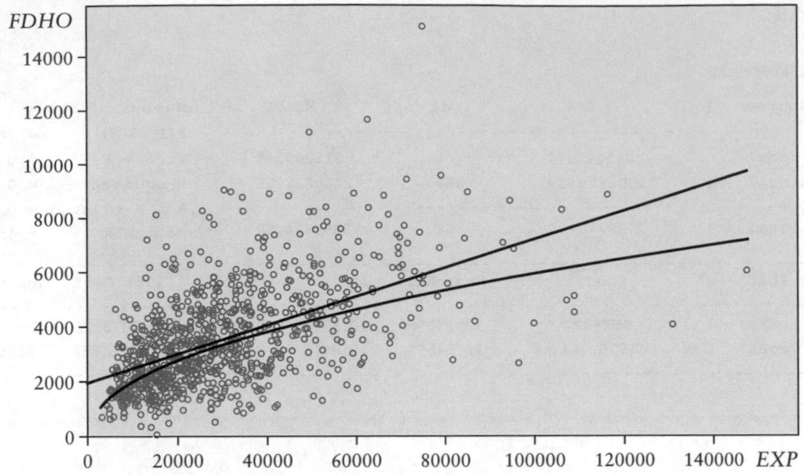

Figure 4.6 Linear and logarithmic regressions of expenditure on food eaten at home on total household expenditure

necessity rather than a luxury, so one would expect the elasticity to be less than 1. The intercept has no economic meaning. Figure 4.6 plots the logarithmic regression line in the original diagram. While there is not much difference between the regression lines over the middle part of the range of observations, it is clear that the logarithmic regression gives a better fit for very low and very high levels of household expenditure.

Semilogarithmic models

Another common functional form is given by equation (4.17):

$$Y = \beta_1 e^{\beta_2 X}. \tag{4.17}$$

Here β_2 should be interpreted as the proportional change in Y per *unit* change in X. Again, this is easily demonstrated. Differentiating,

$$\frac{dY}{dX} = \beta_1 \beta_2 e^{\beta_2 X} = \beta_2 Y. \tag{4.18}$$

Hence,

$$\frac{dY/dX}{Y} = \beta_2 . \tag{4.19}$$

In practice, it is often more natural to speak of the percentage change in Y, rather than the proportional change, per unit change in X, in which case one multiplies the estimate of β_2 by 100.

The function can be converted into a model that is linear in parameters by taking the logarithms of both sides:

$$\begin{aligned}\log Y &= \log \beta_1 e^{\beta_2 X} = \log \beta_1 + \log e^{\beta_2 X} \\ &= \log \beta_1 + \beta_2 X \log e \\ &= \log \beta_1 + \beta_2 X. \end{aligned} \quad (4.20)$$

Note that only the left side is logarithmic in variables, and for this reason (4.20) is described as a semilogarithmic model.

The interpretation of β_2 as the proportional change in Y per *unit* change in X is valid only when β_2 is small. When β_2 is large, the interpretation may be a little more complex. Suppose that Y is related to X by (4.17) and that X increases by one unit to X'. Then Y', the new value of Y is given by

$$\begin{aligned} Y' &= \beta_1 e^{\beta_2 X'} = \beta_1 e^{\beta_2 (X+1)} \\ &= \beta_1 e^{\beta_2 X} e^{\beta_2} = Y e^{\beta_2} \\ &= Y\left(1 + \beta_2 + \frac{\beta_2^2}{2!} + \ldots\right). \end{aligned} \quad (4.21)$$

Thus, the proportional change per unit change in X is actually greater than β_2. However, if β_2 is small (say, less than 0.1), β_2^2 and further terms will be very small and can be neglected. In that case, the right side of the equation simplifies to $Y(1 + \beta_2)$ and the original marginal interpretation of β_2 still applies.

Example: semilogarithmic earnings function

For fitting earnings functions, the semilogarithmic model is generally considered to be superior to the linear model. We will start with the simplest possible version:

$$EARNINGS = \beta_1 e^{\beta_2 S}, \quad (4.22)$$

where *EARNINGS* is hourly earnings, measured in dollars, and S is years of schooling. After taking logarithms, the model becomes

$$LGEARN = \beta_1' + \beta_2 S, \quad (4.23)$$

where *LGEARN* is the natural logarithm of *EARNINGS* and β_1' is the logarithm of β_1.

The model was fitted using *EAEF* Data Set 21, with the output shown in Table 4.5. The coefficient of S indicates that every extra year of schooling increases earnings by a proportion 0.110, that is, 11.0 percent, as a first approximation. Strictly speaking, a whole extra year of schooling is not marginal, so it would be more accurate to calculate $e^{0.110}$, which is 1.116. Thus, a more accurate interpretation is that an extra year of schooling raises earnings by 11.6 percent.

Table 4.5

```
. reg LGEARN S

    Source |       SS       df       MS              Number of obs =     540
-----------+------------------------------           F(1, 538)     =  140.05
     Model |  38.5643833     1  38.5643833           Prob > F      =  0.0000
  Residual |   148.14326   538  .275359219           R-squared     =  0.2065
-----------+------------------------------           Adj R-squared =  0.2051
     Total |  186.707643   539  .34639637            Root MSE      =  .52475

------------------------------------------------------------------------------
    LGEARN |      Coef.   Std. Err.      t    P>|t|     [95% Conf. Interval]
-----------+------------------------------------------------------------------
         S |   .1096934   .0092691   11.83   0.000     .0914853    .1279014
     _cons |   1.292241   .1287252   10.04   0.000     1.039376    1.545107
------------------------------------------------------------------------------
```

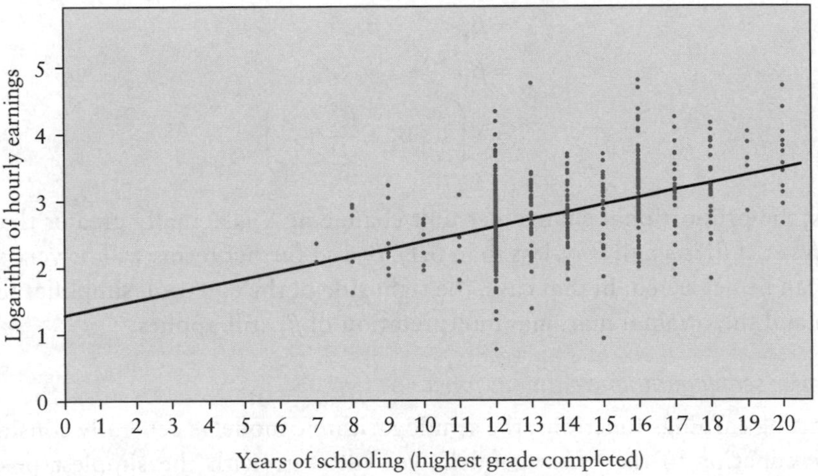

Figure 4.7 Semilogarithmic regression of earnings on schooling

The scatter diagram for the semilogarithmic regression is shown in Figure 4.7. For the purpose of comparison, it is plotted together with the linear regression in a plot with the untransformed variables in Figure 4.8. The two regression lines do not differ greatly in their overall fit, but the semilogarithmic specification has the advantages of not predicting negative earnings for individuals with low levels of schooling and of allowing the increase in earnings per year of schooling to increase with schooling.

The disturbance term

Thus far, nothing has been said about how the disturbance term is affected by these transformations. Indeed, in the discussion above it has been left out altogether.

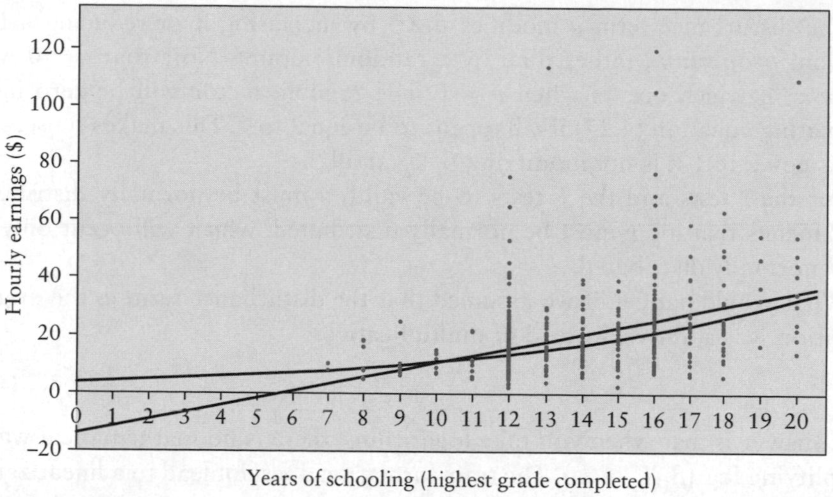

Figure 4.8 Linear and semilogarithmic regressions of earnings on schooling

The fundamental requirement is that the disturbance term should appear in the transformed equation as an additive term (+ u) that satisfies the regression model conditions. If it does not, the least squares regression coefficients will not have the usual properties, and the tests will be invalid.

For example, it is highly desirable that (4.6) should be of the form

$$e = \beta_1 + \beta_2 z + u \qquad \textbf{(4.24)}$$

when we take the random effect into account. Working backwards, this implies that the original (untransformed) equation should be of the form

$$e = \beta_1 + \frac{\beta_2}{g} + u. \qquad \textbf{(4.25)}$$

In this particular case, if it is true that in the original equation the disturbance term is additive and satisfies the regression model conditions, it will also be true in the transformed equation. No problem here.

What happens when we start off with a model such as

$$Y = \beta_1 X_2^{\beta_2}? \qquad \textbf{(4.26)}$$

As we have seen, the regression model, after linearization by taking logarithms, is

$$\log Y = \log \beta_1 + \beta_2 \log X + u \qquad \textbf{(4.27)}$$

when the disturbance term is included. Working back to the original equation, this implies that (4.26) should be rewritten

$$Y = \beta_1 X_2^{\beta_2} v, \qquad \textbf{(4.28)}$$

where v and u are related by $\log v = u$. Hence, to obtain an additive disturbance term in the regression equation for this model, we must start with a multiplicative disturbance term in the original equation.

The disturbance term v modifies $\beta_1 X_2^{\beta_2}$ by increasing it or reducing it by a random *proportion*, rather than by a random amount. Note that $u = 0$ when $\log v = 0$, which occurs when $v = 1$. The random factor will be zero in the estimating equation (4.27) if v happens to be equal to 1. This makes sense, since if v is equal to 1 it is not modifying $\beta_1 X_2^{\beta_2}$ at all.

For the t tests and the F tests to be valid, u must be normally distributed. This means that $\log v$ must be normally distributed, which will occur only if v is lognormally distributed.

What would happen if we assumed that the disturbance term in the original equation was additive, instead of multiplicative?

$$Y = \beta_1 X_2^{\beta_2} + u. \qquad \textbf{(4.29)}$$

The answer is that when you take logarithms, there is no mathematical way of simplifying $\log\left(\beta_1 X_2^{\beta_2} + u\right)$. The transformation does not lead to a linearization. You would have to use a nonlinear regression technique, for example, of the type discussed in the next section.

Example

The central limit theorem suggests that the disturbance term should have a normal distribution. It can be demonstrated that if the disturbance term has a normal distribution, so also will the residuals, provided that the regression equation is correctly specified. An examination of the distribution of the residuals thus provides indirect evidence of the adequacy of the specification of a regression model. Figure 4.9 shows the residuals from linear and semilogarithmic regressions of *EARNINGS* on *S* using *EAEF* Data Set 21, standardized so that they

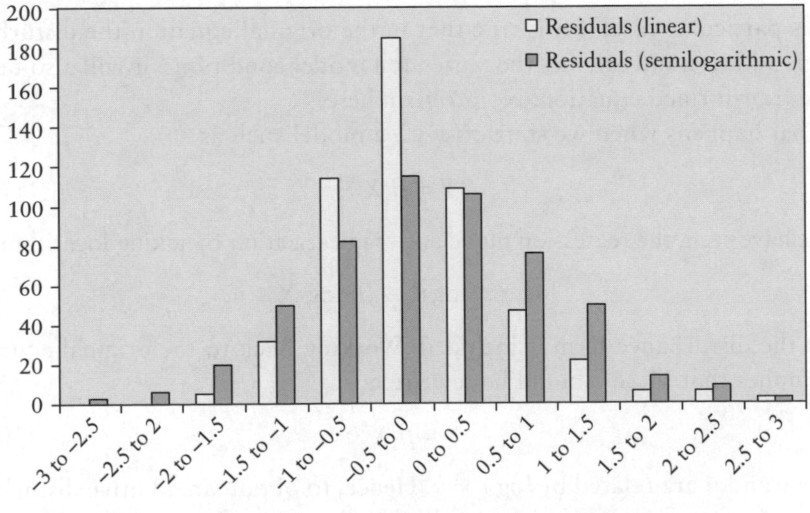

Figure 4.9 Standardized residuals from earnings function regressions

have standard deviation equal to 1, for comparison. The distribution of the residuals from the linear specification is right skewed, while that for the residuals from the semilogarithmic specification is much closer to a normal distribution. This suggests that the semilogarithmic specification is preferable.

Comparing linear and logarithmic specifications

The possibility of fitting nonlinear models, either by means of a linearizing transformation or by the use of a nonlinear regression algorithm, greatly increases the flexibility of regression analysis, but it also makes model specification more complex. You have to ask yourself whether you should start off with a linear relationship or a nonlinear one, and if the latter, what kind.

A graphical inspection of the scatter plot may be sufficient to establish that a relationship is nonlinear. In the case of multiple regression models, the Frisch–Waugh–Lovell technique described in Section 3.2 may be useful. However, it then often happens that several different nonlinear forms might approximately fit the observations if they lie on a curve.

When considering alternative models with the same specification of the dependent variable, the selection procedure is straightforward. The most sensible thing to do is to run regressions based on alternative plausible functions and choose the function that explains the greatest proportion of the variation in the dependent variable. If two or more functions are more or less equally good, you should present the results of each.

However, when alternative models employ different functional forms for the dependent variable, the problem of model selection becomes more complicated because you cannot make direct comparisons of R^2 or the sum of the squares of the residuals. In particular—and this is the most common example of the problem—you cannot compare these statistics for linear and logarithmic dependent variable specifications.

For example, in Section 1.4, the linear regression of earnings on schooling has an R^2 of 0.173, and *RSS* is 92,689. For the semilogarithmic version in Table 4.5, the corresponding figures are 0.207 and 148. *RSS* is much smaller for the logarithmic version, but this means nothing at all. The values of *LGEARN* are much smaller than those of *EARNINGS*, so it is hardly surprising that the residuals are also much smaller. Admittedly, R^2 is unit-free, but it is referring to different concepts in the two equations. In one equation it is measuring the proportion of the variation in earnings explained by the regression, and in the other it is measuring the proportion of the variation in the logarithm of earnings explained. If R^2 is much greater for one model than for the other, you would probably be justified in selecting it without further fuss. But if R^2 is similar for the two models, simple eyeballing will not do.

One procedure under these circumstances, based on Box and Cox (1964), is to scale the observations on Y so that the residual sums of squares in the linear and logarithmic models are rendered directly comparable. The procedure has the following steps:

1. You calculate the geometric mean of the values of Y in the sample. This is equal to the exponential of the mean of log Y, so it is easy to calculate:

$$e^{\frac{1}{n}\sum \log Y_i} = e^{\frac{1}{n}\log(Y_1\times\cdots\times Y_n)} = e^{\log(Y_1\times\cdots\times Y_n)^{\frac{1}{n}}} = (Y_1 \times \cdots \times Y_n)^{\frac{1}{n}}. \quad (4.30)$$

2. You scale the observations on Y by dividing by this figure. So

$$Y_i^* = Y_i \,/\, \text{geometric mean of } Y, \quad (4.31)$$

where Y^* is the scaled value in observation i.

3. You then regress the linear model using Y^* instead of Y as the dependent variable, and the logarithmic model using log Y^* instead of log Y, but otherwise leaving the models unchanged. The residual sums of squares of the two regressions are now comparable, and the model with the lower sum provides the better fit.

Note that the scaled regressions are solely for deciding which model you prefer. You should *not* pay any attention to their coefficients, only to their residual sums of squares. You obtain the coefficients by fitting the unscaled version of the preferred model.

Example

The comparison will be made for the alternative specifications of the earnings function. The mean value of *LGEARN* is 2.7920. The scaling factor is therefore exp(2.7920) = 16.3135. Table 4.6 begins with commands for generating *EARNSTAR*, the scaled version of *EARNINGS*, and its logarithm, *LGEARNST*.

Table 4.6

```
. gen EARNSTAR = EARNINGS/16.3135
. gen LGEARNST = ln(EARNSTAR)
. reg EARNSTAR S EXP
   Source |       SS           df         MS            Number of obs =    540
----------------------------------------------          F(2, 537)     =  67.54
    Model |   84.5963381        2     42.298169         Prob > F      = 0.0000
 Residual |   336.288615      537    .626235783         R-squared     = 0.2010
----------------------------------------------          Adj R-squared = 0.1980
    Total |   420.884953      539    .780862622         Root MSE      = .79135
------------------------------------------------------------------------------
 EARNSTAR |      Coef.    Std. Err.      t     P > |t|    [95% Conf. Interval]
------------------------------------------------------------------------------
        S |   .1641662    .0143225     11.46    0.000     .1360312    .1923011
      EXP |   .0344765    .0078777      4.38    0.000     .0190015    .0499515
    _cons |  -1.623503    .2619003     -6.20    0.000    -2.137977   -1.109028
------------------------------------------------------------------------------
```

Table 4.7

```
. reg LGEARNST S EXP

  Source   |       SS            df          MS            Number of obs =     540
-----------------------------------------------------      F(2, 537)     =  100.86
   Model   |   50.9842589         2      25.4921295        Prob > F      =  0.0000
 Residual  |    135.72339       537      .252743742        R-squared     =  0.2731
-----------------------------------------------------      Adj R-squared =  0.1980
   Total   |   186.707649       539      .346396379        Root MSE      =  .50274

---------------------------------------------------------------------------------
 LGEARNST  |     Coef.        Std. Err.      t      P>|t|     [95% Conf. Interval]
---------------------------------------------------------------------------------
       S   |    .1235911      .0090989    13.58     0.000     .1057173    .141465
     EXP   |    .0350826      .0050046     7.01     0.000     .0252515   .0449137
   _cons   |   -2.282673      .1663823   -13.72     0.000    -2.609513  -1.955833
---------------------------------------------------------------------------------
```

EARNSTAR is then regressed on *S* and *EXP*. The residual sum of squares is 336.29. The corresponding regression of *LGEARNST* on *S* and *EXP* follows in Table 4.7. The residual sum of squares is 135.72. Hence, in this case, the semi-logarithmic specification appears to provide the better fit.

EXERCISES

4.2

```
. gen LGS = ln(S)
. gen LGSM = ln(SM)
(4 missing values generated)
. reg LGS LGSM

  Source   |       SS            df          MS            Number of obs =     536
-----------------------------------------------------      F(1, 534)     =   56.99
   Model   |   1.62650898         1      1.62650898        Prob > F      =  0.0000
 Residual  |   15.2402109       534      .028539721        R-squared     =  0.0964
-----------------------------------------------------      Adj R-squared =  0.0947
   Total   |   16.8667198       535      .031526579        Root MSE      =  .16894

---------------------------------------------------------------------------------
     LGS   |     Coef.        Std. Err.      t      P>|t|     [95% Conf. Interval]
---------------------------------------------------------------------------------
    LGSM   |     .200682      .0265831     7.55     0.000     .1484618   .2529022
   _cons   |     2.11373      .0648636    32.59     0.000     1.986311   2.241149
---------------------------------------------------------------------------------
```

The output shows the result of regressing *LGS*, the logarithm of years of schooling, on *LGSM*, the logarithm of mother's years of schooling, using *EAEF* Data Set 21. Provide an interpretation of the coefficients and evaluate the regression results.

4.3

```
. reg LGS SM

  Source   |       SS          df         MS           Number of obs =    540
-----------+-------------------------------------      F(1, 538)     =  78.13
   Model   |  2.14395934        1     2.14395934       Prob > F      = 0.0000
Residual   |  14.7640299      538    .027442435        R-squared     = 0.1268
-----------+-------------------------------------      Adj R-squared = 0.1252
   Total   |  16.9079893      539    .031369182        Root MSE      = .16566
------------------------------------------------------------------------------
     LGS   |     Coef.    Std. Err.     t     P>|t|    [95% Conf.   Interval]
-----------+------------------------------------------------------------------
      SM   |  .0223929    .0025335    8.84    0.000    .0174162     .0273696
   _cons   |  2.340421    .0301902   77.52    0.000    2.281116     2.399727
------------------------------------------------------------------------------
```

The output shows the result of regressing *LGS*, the logarithm of years of schooling, on *SM*, mother's years of schooling, using *EAEF* Data Set 21. Provide an interpretation of the coefficients and evaluate the regression results.

4.4 Download the *CES* data set from the website (see Appendix B) and fit linear and logarithmic regressions for your commodity on *EXP*, total household expenditure, excluding observations with zero expenditure on your commodity. Interpret the regression results and perform appropriate tests.

4.5 Repeat the logarithmic regression in Exercise 4.4, adding the logarithm of the size of the household as an additional explanatory variable. Interpret the regression results and perform appropriate tests.

4.6 What is the relationship between weight and height? Using your *EAEF* data set, regress the logarithm of *WEIGHT85* on the logarithm of *HEIGHT*. Interpret the regression results and perform appropriate tests.

4.7 Suppose that the logarithm of *Y* is regressed on the logarithm of *X*, the fitted regression being

$$\widehat{\log Y} = b_1 + b_2 \log X.$$

Suppose $Y^* = \lambda Y$, where λ is a constant, and suppose that $\log Y^*$ is regressed on $\log X$. Determine how the regression coefficients are related to those of the original regression. Determine also how the t statistic for b_2 and R^2 for the equation are related to those in the original regression.

4.8* Suppose that the logarithm of *Y* is regressed on the logarithm of *X*, the fitted regression being

$$\widehat{\log Y} = b_1 + b_2 \log X.$$

Suppose $X^* = \mu X$, where λ is a constant, and suppose that $\log Y$ is regressed on $\log X^*$. Determine how the regression coefficients are related to those of the original regression. Determine also how the t statistic for b_2 and R^2 for the equation are related to those in the original regression.

4.9 Using your *EAEF* data set, regress the logarithm of earnings on *S* and *EXP*. Interpret the regression results and perform appropriate tests.

4.10 Using your *EAEF* data set, evaluate whether the dependent variable of an earnings function should be linear or logarithmic. Calculate the geometric mean of *EARNINGS* by taking the exponential of the mean of *LGEARN*. Define

EARNSTAR by dividing *EARNINGS* by this quantity and calculate *LGEARNST* as its logarithm. Regress *EARNSTAR* and *LGEARNST* on *S* and *EXP* and compare the residual sums of squares.

4.11 Evaluate whether a linear or logarithmic specification of the dependent variable is preferable for the expenditure function for your commodity in the *CES* data set. *Note*: Drop households reporting no expenditure on your commodity.

4.3 Models with quadratic and interactive variables

We come now to models with quadratic terms, such as

$$Y = \beta_1 + \beta_2 X_2 + \beta_3 X_2^2 + u \tag{4.32}$$

and models with interactive terms, such as

$$Y = \beta_1 + \beta_2 X_2 + \beta_3 X_3 + \beta_4 X_2 X_3 + u. \tag{4.33}$$

Of course, the quadratic model may be viewed as a special case of the interactive model with $X_3 = X_2$, but it is convenient to treat it separately. These models can be fitted using OLS with no modification. However, the interpretation of their coefficients has to be approached with care. The usual interpretation of a parameter, that it represents the effect of a unit change in its associated variable, holding all other variables constant, cannot be applied. In the case of the quadratic model, it is not possible for X_2 to change without X_2^2 also changing. In the case of the interactive model, it is not possible for X_2 to change without X_2X_3 also changing, if X_3 is kept constant.

Quadratic variables

By differentiating (4.32), one obtains the change in Y per unit change in X_2:

$$\frac{dY}{dX_2} = \beta_2 + 2\beta_3 X_2 . \tag{4.34}$$

Viewed this way, it can be seen that the impact of a unit change in X_2 on Y, $(\beta_2 + 2\beta_3 X_2)$, changes with X_2. This means that β_2 has an interpretation that is different from that in the ordinary linear model

$$Y = \beta_1 + \beta_2 X_2 + u, \tag{4.35}$$

where it is the unqualified effect of a unit change in X_2 on Y. In (4.34), β_2 should be interpreted as the effect of a unit change in X_2 on Y for the special case where $X_2 = 0$. For nonzero values of X_2, the coefficient will be different.

β_3 also has a special interpretation. If we rewrite the model as

$$Y = \beta_1 + (\beta_2 + \beta_3 X_2)X_2 + u, \tag{4.36}$$

β_3 can be interpreted as the rate of change of the coefficient of X_2, per unit change in X_2.

Only β_1 has a conventional interpretation. As usual, it is the value of Y (apart from the random component) when $X_2 = 0$.

There is a further problem. We have already seen that the estimate of the intercept may have no sensible meaning if $X_2 = 0$ is outside the data range. For example, in the case of the linear regression of earnings on schooling reproduced in Figure 4.10, the intercept is negative, implying that an individual with no schooling would have hourly earnings of –\$13.93. If $X_2 = 0$ lies outside the data range, the same type of distortion can happen with the estimate of β_2.

We will illustrate this with the earnings function. Table 4.8 gives the output of a quadratic regression of earnings on schooling (*SSQ* is defined as the square

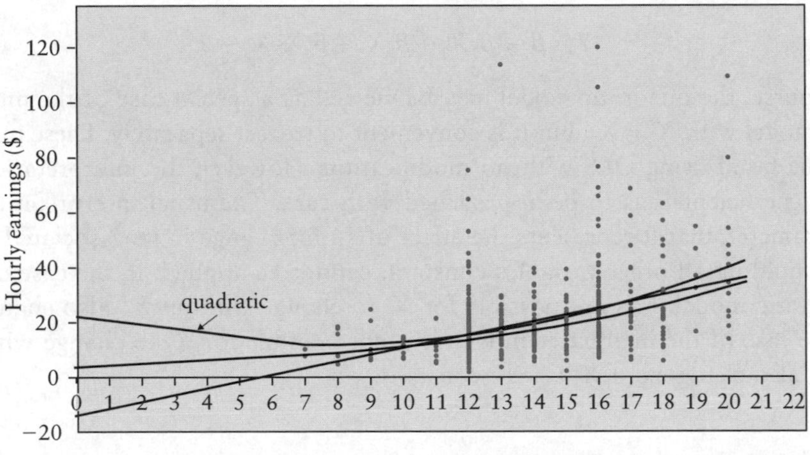

Figure 4.10 Quadratic, linear, and semilogarithmic regressions of earnings on schooling

Table 4.8

```
. gen SSQ = S*S
. reg EARNINGS S SSQ
```

Source	SS	df	MS		
				Number of obs =	540
				F(2, 537) =	59.69
Model	20372.4953	2	10186.2477	Prob > F =	0.0000
Residual	91637.7357	537	170.0647553	R-squared =	0.1819
				Adj R-squared =	0.1788
Total	112010.231	539	207.811189	Root MSE =	13.063

EARNINGS	Coef.	Std. Err.	t	P>|t|	[95% Conf.	Interval]
S	-2.772317	2.119128	-1.31	0.191	-6.935114	1.390481
SSQ	.1829731	.0737308	2.48	0.013	.0381369	.3278092
_cons	22.25089	14.92883	1.49	0.137	-7.075176	51.57695

of schooling). The coefficient of S implies that, for an individual with no schooling, the impact of a year of schooling is to *decrease* hourly earnings by \$2.77. The intercept also has no sensible interpretation. Literally, it implies that an individual with no schooling would have hourly earnings of \$22.25, which is implausibly high.

The quadratic relationship is illustrated in Figure 4.10. Over the range of the actual data, it fits the observations tolerably well. The fit is not dramatically different from those of the linear and semilogarithmic specifications. However, when one extrapolates beyond the data range, the quadratic function increases as schooling decreases, giving rise to implausible estimates of both β_1 and β_2 for $S = 0$. In this example, we would prefer the semilogarithmic specification, as do all wage-equation studies. The slope coefficient of the semilogarithmic specification has a simple interpretation and the specification does not give rise to predictions outside the data range that are obviously nonsensical.

The data on employment growth rate, e, and GDP growth rate, g, for 25 OECD countries in Exercise 1.4 provide a less problematic example of the use of a quadratic function. *gsq* has been defined as the square of g. Table 4.9 shows the output from the quadratic regression. In Figure 4.11, the quadratic regression is compared with that obtained in Section 4.1. The quadratic specification appears to be an improvement on the hyperbolic function fitted in Section 4.1. It is more satisfactory than the latter for low values of g, in that it does not yield implausibly large negative predicted values of e. The only defect is that it predicts that the fitted value of e starts to fall when g exceeds 7.

Higher-order polynomials

Why stop at a quadratic? Why not consider a cubic, or quartic, or a polynomial of even higher order? There are usually several good reasons for not doing so. Diminishing marginal effects are standard in economic theory, justifying

Table 4.9

```
. gen gsq = g*g
. reg e g gsq

   Source |        SS          df          MS          Number of obs =     25
----------+-------------------------------------      F (2, 22)     =  20.15
    Model |   15.9784642        2     7.98923212      Prob > F      = 0.0000
 Residual |    8.7235112       22     .396523236      R-squared     = 0.6468
----------+-------------------------------------      Adj R-squared = 0.6147
    Total |   24.7019754       24     1.02924898      Root MSE      =  .6297

----------------------------------------------------------------------------
        e |     Coef.     Std. Err.     t      P>|t|    [95% Conf. Interval]
----------+-----------------------------------------------------------------
        g |   1.200205    .3862226    3.11     0.005    .3992287    2.001182
      gsq |  -.0838408    .0445693   -1.88     0.073   -.1762719    .0085903
    _cons |  -1.678113    .6556641   -2.56     0.018   -3.037877   -.3183494
----------------------------------------------------------------------------
```

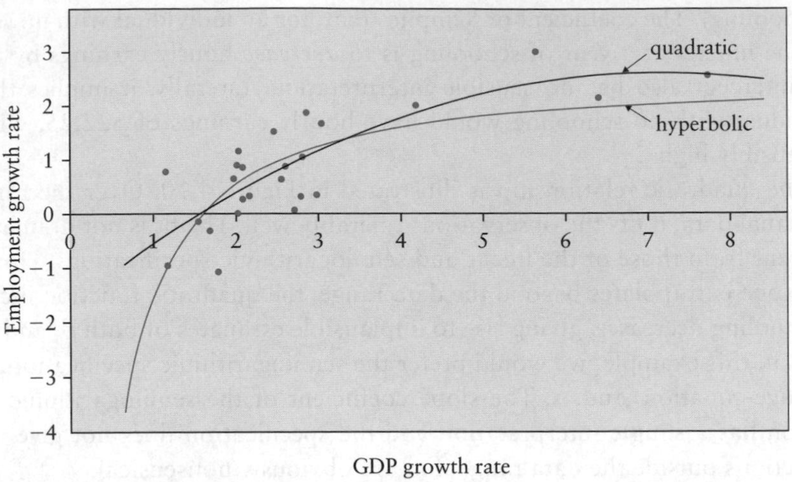

Figure 4.11 Hyperbolic and quadratic regressions of employment growth rate on GDP growth rate

quadratic specifications, at least as an approximation, but economic theory seldom suggests that a relationship might sensibly be represented by a cubic or higher-order polynomial. The second reason follows from the first. There will be an improvement in fit as higher-order terms are added, but because these terms are not theoretically justified, the improvement will be sample-specific. Third, unless the sample is very small, the fits of higher-order polynomials are unlikely to be very different from those of a quadratic over the main part of the data range.

These points are illustrated by Figure 4.12, which shows cubic and quartic regressions with the original linear and quadratic regressions. Over the main

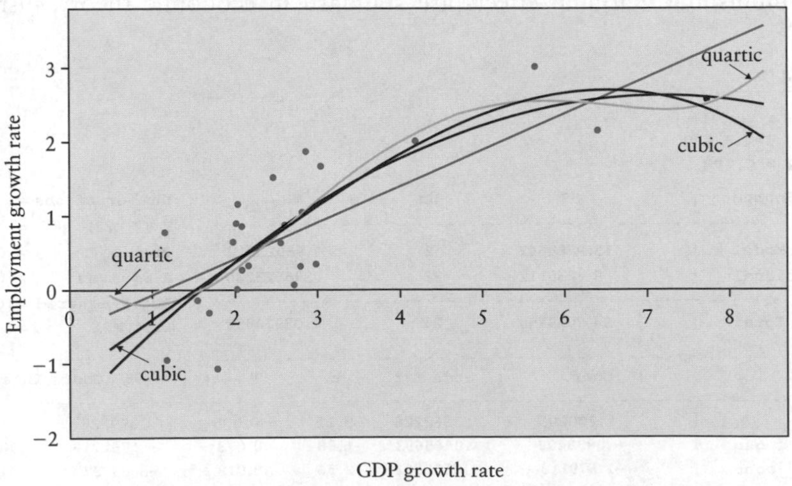

Figure 4.12 Cubic and quartic regressions of employment growth rate on GDP growth rate

data range, from $g = 1.5$ to $g = 4$, the fits of the cubic and quartic are very similar to that of the quadratic. R^2 for the linear specification is 0.590. For the quadratic it improves to 0.647. For the cubic and quartic it is 0.651 and 0.658, relatively small further improvements. Further, the cubic and quartic curves both exhibit implausible characteristics. The cubic declines even more rapidly than the quadratic for high values of g, and the quartic has strange twists at its extremities.

Interactive explanatory variables

We next turn to models with interactive terms, such as

$$Y = \beta_1 + \beta_2 X_2 + \beta_3 X_3 + \beta_4 X_2 X_3 + u. \tag{4.37}$$

This is linear in parameters and so may be fitted using straightforward OLS. However, the fact that it is nonlinear in variables complicates the interpretation of the parameters. It is not possible to interpret β_2 as the effect of X_2 on Y, holding X_3 and X_2X_3 constant, because it is not possible to hold both X_3 and X_2X_3 constant if X_2 changes.

To give a proper interpretation to the coefficients, we can rewrite the model as

$$Y = \beta_1 + (\beta_2 + \beta_4 X_3)X_2 + \beta_3 X_3 + u. \tag{4.38}$$

This representation makes explicit the fact that $(\beta_2 + \beta_4 X_3)$, the marginal effect of X_2 on Y, depends on the value of X_3. From this it can be seen that the interpretation of β_2 has a special interpretation. It gives the marginal effect of X_2 on Y, when $X_3 = 0$.

One may alternatively rewrite the model as

$$Y = \beta_1 + \beta_2 X_2 + (\beta_3 + \beta_4 X_2)X_3 + u. \tag{4.39}$$

From this it may be seen that the marginal effect of X_3 on Y, holding X_2 constant, is $(\beta_3 + \beta_4 X_2)$ and that β_3 may be interpreted as the marginal effect of X_3 on Y, when $X_2 = 0$.

If $X_3 = 0$ is a long way outside the range of X_3 in the sample, the interpretation of the estimate of β_2 as an estimate of the marginal effect of X_2 when $X_3 = 0$ should be treated with caution. Sometimes the estimate will be completely implausible, in the same way as the estimate of the intercept in a regression is often implausible if given a literal interpretation. We have just encountered a similar problem with the interpretation of β_2 in the quadratic specification. Often it is of interest to compare the estimates of the effects of X_2 and X_3 on Y in models excluding and including the interactive term, and the changes in the meanings of β_2 and β_3 caused by the inclusion of the interactive term can make such comparisons difficult.

One way of mitigating the problem is to rescale X_2 and X_3 so that they are measured from their sample means:

$$X_2^* = X_2 - \bar{X}_2 \tag{4.40}$$

$$X_3^* = X_3 - \bar{X}_3. \tag{4.41}$$

Substituting for X_2 and X_3, the model becomes

$$\begin{aligned} Y &= \beta_1 + \beta_2\left(X_2^* + \bar{X}_2\right) + \beta_3\left(X_3^* + \bar{X}_3\right) + \beta_4\left(X_2^* + \bar{X}_2\right)\left(X_3^* + \bar{X}_3\right) + u \\ &= \beta_1^* + \beta_2^* X_2^* + \beta_3^* X_3^* + \beta_4 X_2^* X_3^* + u \end{aligned} \tag{4.42}$$

where $\beta_1^* = \beta_1 + \beta_2\bar{X}_2 + \beta_3\bar{X}_3 + \beta_4\bar{X}_2\bar{X}_3$, $\beta_2^* = \beta_2 + \beta_4\bar{X}_3$, and $\beta_3^* = \beta_3 + \beta_4\bar{X}_2$. The point of doing this is that the coefficients of X_2^* and X_3^* now give the marginal effects of the variables when the other variable is held at its sample mean, which is to some extent a representative value. For example, rewriting the new equation as

$$Y = \beta_1^* + \left(\beta_2^* + \beta_4 X_3^*\right)X_2^* + \beta_3^* X_3^* + u \tag{4.43}$$

it can be seen that β_2^* gives the marginal effect of X_2^*, and hence X_2, when $X_3^* = 0$, that is, when X_3 is at its sample mean. β_3^* has a similar interpretation.

Example

Table 4.10 shows the results of regressing the logarithm of hourly earnings on years of schooling and years of work experience for males using *EAEF* Data Set 21. It implies that an extra year of schooling increases earnings by 13.0 percent and that an extra year of work experience increases them by 3.2 percent. In Table 4.11, the interactive variable *SEXP* is defined as the product of *S* and *EXP* and added to the specification. The schooling coefficient now jumps to 23.7 percent, an extraordinarily high figure. But of course it has now changed its meaning. It now estimates the impact of an extra year of schooling

Table 4.10

```
. reg LGEARN S EXP

  Source   |      SS          df         MS            Number of obs =     270
-----------+-----------------------------------        F(2, 267)     =   50.41
   Model   |  25.4256872       2      12.7128436       Prob > F      =  0.0000
 Residual  |   7.3402828     267      .252210797       R-squared     =  0.2741
-----------+-----------------------------------        Adj R-squared =  0.2686
   Total   |   92.76597      269      .344854907       Root MSE      =  .50221
-------------------------------------------------------------------------------
  LGEARN   |    Coef.      Std. Err.      t     P > |t|    [95% Conf.  Interval]
-------------------------------------------------------------------------------
       S   |   .1303979    .0129905     10.04    0.000     .1048211    .1559747
     EXP   |   .0321614    .0083783      3.84    0.000     .0156655    .0486573
   _cons   |   .5969745    .2768371      2.16    0.032     .0519132    1.142036
-------------------------------------------------------------------------------
```

Table 4.11

```
. gen SEXP = S*EXP
. reg LGEARN S EXP SEXP
```

Source	SS	df	MS		
				Number of obs =	270
				F(3, 266) =	35.58
Model	26.5654376	3	8.85514586	Prob > F =	0.0000
Residual	66.2005325	266	.248874182	R-squared =	0.2864
				Adj R-squared =	0.2783
Total	92.76597	269	.344854907	Root MSE =	.49887

LGEARN	Coef.	Std. Err.	t	P>|t|	[95% Conf.	Interval]
S	.2371066	.0515064	4.60	0.000	.1356944	.3385187
EXP	.1226418	.0430918	2.85	0.005	.0377974	.2074863
SEXP	−.0065695	.0030699	−2.14	0.033	−.0126139	−.0005252
_cons	−.9003565	.7517877	−1.20	0.232	−2.380568	.579855

Table 4.12

```
. egen MEANS = mean(S)
. gen S1 = S - MEANS
. egen MEANEXP = mean(EXP)
. gen EXP1 = EXP - MEANEXP
. gen SEXP1 = S1*EXP1
. reg LGEARN S1 EXP1
```

Source	SS	df	MS		
				Number of obs =	270
				F(2, 267) =	50.41
Model	25.4256872	2	12.7128436	Prob > F =	0.0000
Residual	67.3402828	267	.252210797	R-squared =	0.2741
				Adj R-squared =	0.2686
Total	92.76597	269	.344854907	Root MSE =	.50221

LGEARN	Coef.	Std. Err.	t	P>|t|	[95% Conf.	Interval]
S1	.1303979	.0129905	10.04	0.000	.1048211	.1559747
EXP1	.0321614	.0083783	3.84	0.000	.0156655	.0486573
_cons	2.961112	.0305633	96.88	0.000	2.900936	3.021288

for those individuals who have no work experience. The experience coefficient has also risen sharply. Now it indicates that an extra year increases earnings by a wholly implausible 12.3 percent. But this figure refers to individuals with no schooling, and every individual in the sample had at least 7 years.

To deal with these problems, we define *S1*, *EXP1*, and *SEXP1* as the corresponding schooling, experience, and interactive variables with the means subtracted, and repeat the regressions. We will refer to the original regressions excluding and including the interactive term, with the output shown in Tables 4.10 and 4.11, as Regressions (1) and (2), and the new ones, with the output shown in Tables 4.12 and 4.13, as Regressions (3) and (4).

Table 4.13

```
. reg LGEARN S1 EXP1 SEXP1

   Source |       SS           df        MS         Number of obs =     270
----------+------------------------------------     F(3, 266)     =   35.58
    Model |   26.5654377        3     8.85514589    Prob > F      =  0.0000
 Residual |   66.2005324      266     .248874182    R-squared     =  0.2864
----------+------------------------------------     Adj R-squared =  0.2783
    Total |     92.76597      269     .344854907    Root MSE      =  .49887

------------------------------------------------------------------------------
   LGEARN |      Coef.   Std. Err.      t     P>|t|     [95% Conf. Interval]
----------+-------------------------------------------------------------------
       S1 |   .1196959    .0138394     8.65   0.000     .0924473    .1469446
     EXP1 |   .0324933    .0083241     3.90   0.000     .0161038    .0488829
    SEXP1 |  -.0065695    .0030699    -2.14   0.033    -.0126139   -.0005252
    _cons |   2.933994    .0328989    89.18   0.000     2.869218    2.998769
------------------------------------------------------------------------------
```

Regression (3) is virtually identical to Regression (1). In particular, comparing Tables 4.10 and 4.12, the slope coefficients are the same, as are the standard errors, t statistics, and R^2. The only difference is in the intercept. This now refers to the logarithm of hourly earnings of an individual with mean schooling and mean experience. It implies an hourly rate of $e^{2.96} = 19.32$ dollars, and since it is in the middle of the data range it is perhaps more informative than the intercept in Regression (1), which suggested that the hourly earnings of an individual with no schooling and no work experience would be $e^{0.60} = 1.82$ dollars.

Regressions (2) and (4) also have much in common. The analysis of variance and goodness of fit statistics are the same, and the results relating to the interactive effect are the same. The only differences are in the output relating to the schooling and work experience slope coefficients, which in Regression (4) now relate to an individual with mean schooling and experience. A comparison of Regressions (3) and (4) allows a more meaningful evaluation of the impact of including the interactive term. We see that, for an individual at the mean, it has little effect on the value of work experience, but it suggests that the value of a year of schooling was overestimated by a small amount in Regression (3). The interactive effect itself suggests that the value of education diminishes for all individuals with increasing experience.

Ramsey's RESET test of functional misspecification

Adding quadratic terms of the explanatory variables and interactive terms to the specification is one way of investigating the possibility that the dependent variable in a model may be a nonlinear function of them. However, if there are many explanatory variables in the model, before devoting time to experimentation with quadratic and interactive terms, it may be useful to have some means of detecting whether there is any evidence of nonlinearity in the first place.

Ramsey's RESET test of functional misspecification is intended to provide a simple indicator.

To implement it, one runs the regression in the original form and then saves the fitted values of the dependent variable, which we will denote $\hat{Y}$. Since, by definition,

$$\hat{Y} = b_1 + \sum_{j=2}^{k} b_j X_j, \tag{4.44}$$

$\hat{Y}^2$ is a linear combination of the squares of the X variables and their interactions. If $\hat{Y}^2$ is added to the regression specification, it should pick up quadratic and interactive nonlinearity, if present, without necessarily being highly correlated with any of the X variables and consuming only one degree of freedom. If the t statistic for the coefficient of $\hat{Y}^2$ is significant, this indicates that some kind of nonlinearity may be present.

Of course the test does not indicate the actual form of the nonlinearity and it may fail to detect other types of nonlinearity. However, it does have the virtue of being very easy to implement.

In principle, one could also include higher powers of $\hat{Y}$. However, the consensus appears to be that this is not usually worthwhile.

EXERCISES

4.12

```
. gen SMSQ = SM*SM
. reg S SM SMSQ

  Source   |       SS          df        MS              Number of obs =    540
-----------+-----------------------------------          F(2, 537)     =  51.90
   Model   |   519.131914       2    259.565957          Prob > F      = 0.0000
Residual   |   2685.85142     534    5.00158551          R-squared     = 0.1620
-----------+-----------------------------------          Adj R-squared = 0.1589
   Total   |   3204.98333     539    5.94616574          Root MSE      = 2.2364

---------------------------------------------------------------------------------
       S   |      Coef.   Std. Err.      t     P>|t|     [95% Conf. Interval]
-----------+---------------------------------------------------------------------
      SM   |  -.2564658    .1318583   -1.95    0.052    -.5154872     .0025556
    SMSQ   |   .0271172    .0060632    4.47    0.000     .0152068     .0390277
   _cons   |   12.79121    .7366358   17.36    0.000     11.34416     14.23825
---------------------------------------------------------------------------------
```

The output shows the result of regression of S on SM and its square, $SMSQ$. Evaluate the regression results. In particular, explain why the coefficient of SM is negative.

4.13 Using your *EAEF* data set, perform a regression parallel to that in Exercise 4.12 and evaluate the results. Define a new variable $SM12$ as $SM - 12$. $SM12$ may be interpreted as the number of years of schooling of the mother after completing high school, if positive, and the number of years of schooling lost before completing high school, if negative. Regress S on $SM12$ and its square, and compare the results with those in your original regression.

4.14*

```
. reg LGS LGSM LGSMSQ

  Source  |       SS          df          MS          Number of obs =     536
----------+------------------------------------       F(1, 534)     =   56.99
   Model  |   1.62650898       1      1.62650898      Prob > F      =  0.0000
Residual  |   15.2402109     534      .028539721      R-squared     =  0.0964
----------+------------------------------------       Adj R-squared =  0.0947
   Total  |   16.8667198     535      .031526579      Root MSE      =  .16894

-----------------------------------------------------------------------------
     LGS  |      Coef.     Std. Err.      t      P>|t|     [95% Conf. Interval]
----------+------------------------------------------------------------------
    LGSM  |  (omitted)
  LGSMSQ  |    .100341     .0132915    7.55     0.000     .0742309    .1264511
   _cons  |    2.11373     .0648636   32.59     0.000     1.986311    2.241149
-----------------------------------------------------------------------------
```

The output shows the results of regressing *LGS*, the logarithm of *S*, on *LGSM*, the logarithm of *SM*, and *LGSMSQ*, the logarithm of *SMSQ*. Explain the regression results.

4.15 Perform a RESET test of functional misspecification. Using your *EAEF* data set, regress *WEIGHT02* on *HEIGHT*. Save the fitted values as *YHAT* and define *YHATSQ* as its square. Add *YHATSQ* to the regression specification and test its coefficient.

4.4 Nonlinear regression

Suppose you believe that a variable Y depends on a variable X according to the relationship

$$Y = \beta_1 + \beta_2 X^{\beta_3} + u, \tag{4.45}$$

and you wish to obtain estimates of β_1, β_2, and β_3 given data on Y and X. There is no way of transforming (4.45) to obtain a linear relationship, and so it is not possible to apply the usual regression procedure.

Nevertheless, one can still use the principle of minimizing the sum of the squares of the residuals to obtain estimates of the parameters. We will describe a simple nonlinear regression algorithm that uses the principle. It consists of a series of repeated steps:

1. You start by guessing plausible values for the parameters.
2. You calculate the predicted values of Y from the data on X, using these values of the parameters.
3. You calculate the residual for each observation in the sample, and hence *RSS*, the sum of the squares of the residuals.
4. You then make small changes in one or more of your estimates of the parameters.
5. You calculate the new predicted values of Y, residuals, and *RSS*.
6. If *RSS* is smaller than before, your new estimates of the parameters are better than the old ones and you take them as your new starting point.

7. You repeat steps 4, 5, and 6 again and again until you are unable to make any changes in the estimates of the parameters that would reduce *RSS*.
8. You conclude that you have minimized *RSS*, and you can describe the final estimates of the parameters as the least squares estimates.

Example

We will return to the relationship between employment growth rate, e, and GDP growth rate, g, in Section 4.1, where e and g are hypothesized to be related by

$$e = \beta_1 + \frac{\beta_2}{g} + u. \tag{4.46}$$

According to this specification, as g becomes large, e will tend to a limit of β_1. Looking at the scatter diagram for e and g, we see that the maximum value of e is about 2. So we will take this as our initial value for b_1. We then hunt for the optimal value of b_2, conditional on this guess for b_1. Figure 4.13 shows *RSS* plotted as a function of b_2, conditional on $b_1 = 2$. From this we see that the optimal value of b_2, conditional on $b_1 = 2$, is -2.86.

Next, holding b_2 at -2.86, we look to improve on our guess for b_1. Figure 4.14 shows *RSS* as a function of b_1, conditional on $b_2 = -2.86$. We see that the optimal value of b_1 is 2.08.

We continue to do this until both parameter estimates cease to change. We will then have reached the values that yield minimum *RSS*. These must be the values from the linear regression shown in Table 4.2: $b_1 = 2.60$ and $b_2 = -4.05$. They have been determined by the same criterion, the minimization of *RSS*. All that we have done is to use a different method.

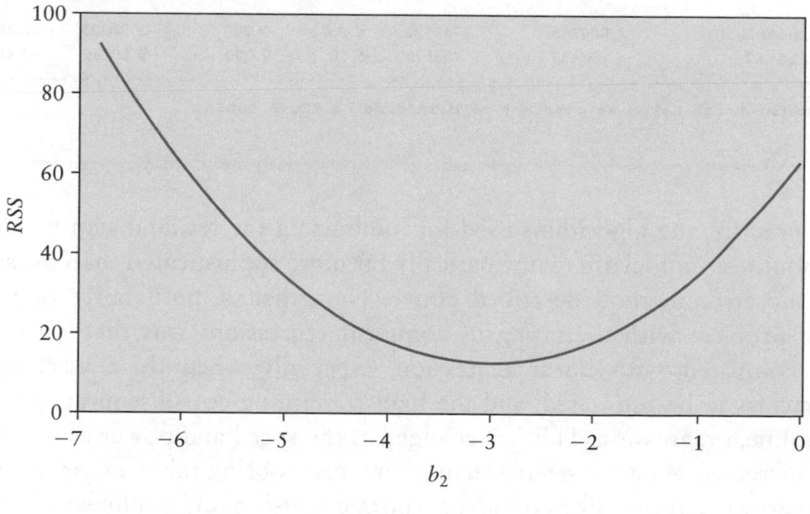

Figure 4.13 *RSS* as a function of b_2, conditional on $b_1 = 2$

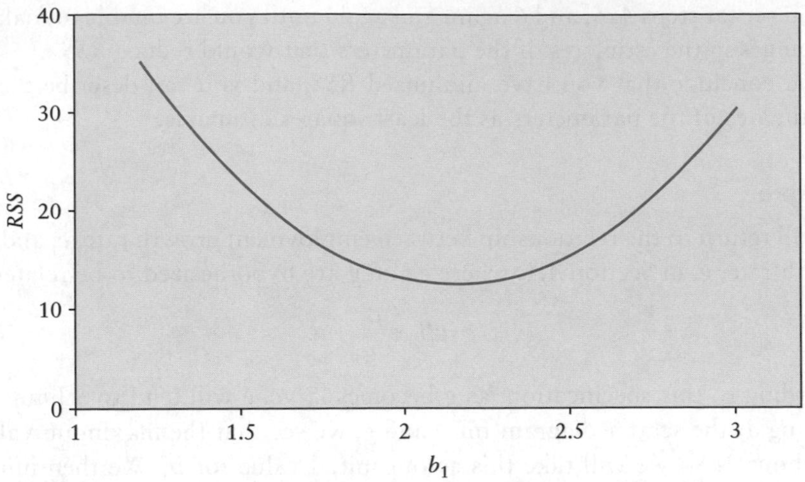

Figure 4.14 *RSS* as a function of b_1, conditional on $b_2 = -2.86$

Table 4.14

```
. nl (e = {beta1} + {beta2}/g)
(obs = 25)
Iteration 0: residual SS = 11.58161
Iteration 1: residual SS = 11.58161
    Source |         SS         df          MS         Number of obs =      25
-----------+------------------------------------       R-squared     =  0.5311
     Model |   13.1203672        1   13.1203672        Adj R-squared =  0.5108
  Residual |   11.5816083       23   .503548186        Root MSE      = .7096113
-----------+------------------------------------       Res. dev.     = 51.71049
     Total |   24.7019754       24   1.02924898
------------------------------------------------------------------------------
         e |       Coef.   Std. Err.      t    P>|t|     [95% Conf. Interval]
-----------+------------------------------------------------------------------
    /beta1 |    2.604753   .3748821    6.95    0.000      1.82925    3.380256
    /beta2 |   -4.050817    .793579   -5.10    0.000     -5.69246   -2.409174
------------------------------------------------------------------------------
Parameter beta1 taken as constant term in model & ANOVA table
```

In practice, the algorithms used for minimizing the residual sum of squares in a nonlinear model are mathematically far more sophisticated than the simple trial-and-error method described above. Nevertheless, until fairly recently a major problem with the fitting of nonlinear regressions was that it was very slow compared with linear regression, especially when there were several parameters to be estimated, and the high computing cost discouraged the use of nonlinear regression. This has changed as the speed and power of computers have increased. As a consequence, more interest is being taken in the technique and regression applications often incorporate user-friendly nonlinear regression features.

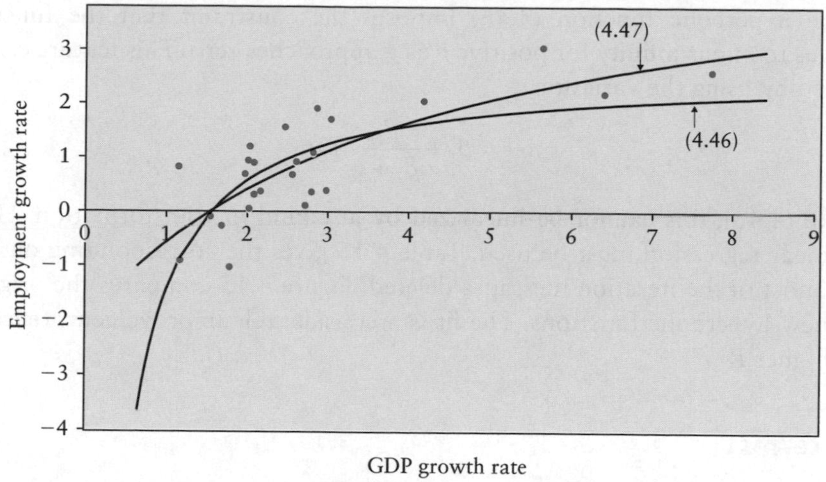

Figure 4.15 Alternative hyperbolic specifications (4.46) and (4.47)

Table 4.15

```
. nl (e = {beta1} + {beta2}/({beta3} + g))
(obs = 25)
Iteration 0:  residual SS = 11.58161
Iteration 1:  residual SS = 11.19238
-----------------------------------------------------------------------------
Iteration 15: residual SS = 9.01051

      Source |       SS          df          MS         Number of obs =      25
-------------+--------------------------------------   R-squared     =  0.6352
       Model |  15.6914659        2     7.84573293     Adj R-squared =  0.6021
    Residual |  9.01050957       22     .409568617     Root MSE      = .6399755
-------------+--------------------------------------   Res. dev.     = 45.43482
       Total |  24.7019754       24     1.02924898

-----------------------------------------------------------------------------
           e |      Coef.    Std. Err.      t    P>|t|     [95% Conf. Interval]
-------------+---------------------------------------------------------------
      /beta1 |   5.467548    2.826401     1.93   0.066     -.3940491   11.32914
      /beta2 |   -31.0764    41.78914    -0.74   0.465     -117.7418   55.58897
      /beta3 |   4.148589    4.870437     0.85   0.404      -5.95208   14.24926
-----------------------------------------------------------------------------
Parameter beta1 taken as constant term in model & ANOVA table
```

Table 4.14 shows such output for the present hyperbolic regression of e on g. It is, as usual, Stata output, but output from other regression applications will look similar. The Stata command for a nonlinear regression is 'nl'. This is followed by the hypothesized mathematical relationship within parentheses. The parameters must be given names placed within braces. Here β_1 is {beta1} and β_2 is {beta2}. The output is effectively the same as the linear regression output in Table 4.2.

The hyperbolic function (4.46) imposes the constraint that the function plunges to minus infinity for positive g as g approaches zero. This feature can be relaxed by using the variation

$$e = \beta_1 + \frac{\beta_2}{\beta_3 + g} + u. \tag{4.47}$$

Unlike (4.46), this cannot be linearized by any kind of transformation. Here, nonlinear regression must be used. Table 4.15 gives the corresponding output, with most of the iteration messages deleted. Figure 4.15 compares the original and new hyperbolic functions. The fit is a considerable improvement, reflected in a higher R^2.

Key terms

- elasticity
- linear in parameters
- linear in variables
- logarithmic model
- logarithmic transformation
- loglinear model
- nonlinear regression algorithm
- semilogarithmic model

EXERCISE

4.16*

```
. nl (S = {beta1} + {beta2}/({beta3} + SIBLINGS)) if SIBLINGS>0
(obs = 529)
Iteration 0: residual SS = 2962.929
Iteration 1: residual SS = 2951.616
-----------------------------------
Iteration 13: residual SS = 2926.201

  Source  |      SS          df          MS           Number of obs =       529
----------+-------------------------------------      R-squared     =    0.0659
   Model  |  206.566702       2     103.283351        Adj R-squared =    0.0624
Residual  |  2926.20078     526     5.56311936        Root MSE      =  2.358627
----------+-------------------------------------      Res. dev.     =  2406.077
   Total  |  3132.76749     528     5.93327175
-------------------------------------------------------------------------------
       s  |     Coef.    Std. Err.      t      P>|t|     [95% Conf. Interval]
-------------------------------------------------------------------------------
  /beta1  |   11.09973    1.363292    8.14     0.000     8.421565     13.7779
  /beta2  |   17.09479    18.78227    0.91     0.363    -19.80268    53.99227
  /beta3  |   3.794949     3.66492    1.04     0.301    -3.404729    10.99463
-------------------------------------------------------------------------------
Parameter beta1 taken as constant term in model & ANOVA table
```

The output above uses *EAEF* Data Set 21 to fit the nonlinear model

$$S = \beta_1 + \frac{\beta_2}{\beta_3 + SIBLINGS} + u,$$

where S is the years of schooling of the respondent and *SIBLINGS* is the number of brothers and sisters. The specification is an extension of that for Exercise 4.1, with the addition of the parameter β_3. Provide an interpretation of the regression results and compare it with that for Exercise 4.1.

5. Dummy Variables

It frequently happens that some of the factors that you would like to introduce into a regression model are qualitative in nature and therefore not measurable in numerical terms. Some examples are the following.

1. You are investigating the relationship between schooling and earnings, and you have both males and females in your sample. You would like to see if the sex of the respondent makes a difference.
2. You are investigating the relationship between income and expenditure in Belgium, and your sample includes both Flemish-speaking and French-speaking households. You would like to find out whether the ethnic difference is relevant.
3. You have data on the growth rate of GDP per capita and foreign aid per capita for a sample of developing countries, of which some are democracies and some are not. You would like to investigate whether the impact of foreign aid on growth is affected by the type of government.

In each of these examples, one solution would be to run separate regressions for the two categories and see if the coefficients are different. Alternatively, you could run a single regression using all the observations together, measuring the effect of the qualitative factor with what is known as a dummy variable. This has the two important advantages of providing a simple way of testing whether the effect of the qualitative factor is significant and, provided that certain assumptions are valid, making the regression estimates more efficient.

5.1 Illustration of the use of a dummy variable

We will illustrate the use of a dummy variable with a series of regressions investigating how the cost of running a secondary school varies with the number of students and the type of school. We will take as our starting point the model

$$COST = \beta_1 + \beta_2 N + u, \qquad (5.1)$$

where $COST$ is the annual recurrent expenditure incurred by a school and N is the number of students attending it. Fitting a regression to a sample of 74 secondary schools in Shanghai in the mid-1980s (for further information, see Appendix B), the Stata output is as shown in Table 5.1.

Table 5.1

```
. reg COST N

  Source   |       SS           df          MS        Number of obs =     74
-----------+----------------------------------        F(1, 72)      =  46.82
  Model    |  5.7974e+11         1     5.7974e+11     Prob > F      = 0.0000
 Residual  |  8.9160e+11        72     1.2383e+10     R-squared     = 0.3940
-----------+----------------------------------        Adj R-squared = 0.3856
  Total    |  1.4713e+12        73     2.0155e+10     Root MSE      = 1.1e+05

-------------------------------------------------------------------------------
   COST    |    Coef.      Std. Err.    t      P>|t|      [95% Conf. Interval]
-----------+-------------------------------------------------------------------
     N     |  339.0432     49.55144   6.842    0.000      240.2642     437.8222
   _cons   |   23953.3     27167.96   0.882    0.381     -30205.04     78111.65
-------------------------------------------------------------------------------
```

The regression equation is thus (standard errors in parentheses)

$$\underset{}{\widehat{COST}} = \underset{(27,000)}{24,000} + \underset{(50)}{339N} \qquad R^2 = 0.39, \tag{5.2}$$

the cost being measured in yuan, one yuan being worth about 20 cents US at the time of the survey. The equation implies that the marginal cost per student is 339 yuan and that the annual overhead cost (administration and maintenance) is 24,000 yuan.

This is just the starting point. Next we will investigate the impact of the type of school on the cost. Occupational schools aim to provide skills for specific occupations and they tend to be relatively expensive to run because they need to maintain specialized workshops. We could model this by having two equations

$$COST = \beta_1 + \beta_2 N + u \tag{5.3}$$

and

$$COST = \beta_1' + \beta_2 N + u, \tag{5.4}$$

the first equation relating to regular schools and the second to the occupational schools. Effectively, we are hypothesizing that the annual overhead cost is different for the two types of school, but the marginal cost is the same. The marginal cost assumption is not very plausible and we will relax it in due course. Let us define δ to be the difference in the intercepts: $\delta = \beta_1' - \beta_1$. Then $\beta_1' = \beta_1 + \delta$ and we can rewrite the cost function for occupational schools as

$$COST = \beta_1 + \delta + \beta_2 N + u. \tag{5.5}$$

The model is illustrated in Figure 5.1. The two lines show the relationship between the cost and the number of students, neglecting the disturbance term. The line for the occupational schools is the same as that for the regular schools, except that it has been shifted up by an amount δ.

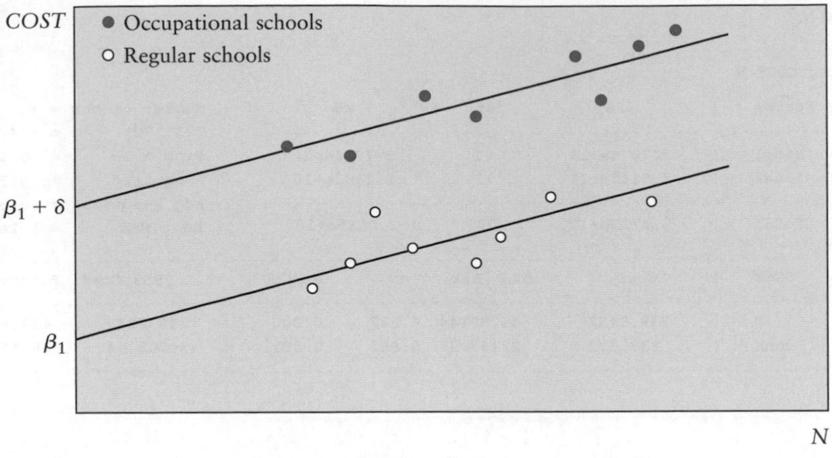

Figure 5.1 Cost functions for regular and occupational schools

The object of the present exercise is to estimate this unknown shift factor. To do this, we rewrite the model as

$$COST = \beta_1 + \delta OCC + \beta_2 N + u, \tag{5.6}$$

where *OCC* is a dummy variable, an artificial variable with two possible values, 0 and 1. If *OCC* is equal to 0, the cost function becomes (5.3), that for regular schools. If *OCC* is equal to 1, the cost function becomes (5.5), that for occupational schools. Hence, instead of two separate regressions for the different types of school, we can run just one regression using the whole sample. Using the whole sample in a single regression will reduce the population variances of the coefficients, and this should be reflected by smaller standard errors. We will also obtain a single estimate of β_2, instead of two separate ones that are likely to conflict. The price we have to pay is that we have to assume that β_2 is the same for both subsamples. We will relax this assumption in due course.

Data for the first 10 schools in the sample are shown in Table 5.2. Note how *OCC* varies with the type of school. Multiple regression is used to regress *COST* on *N* and *OCC*. *OCC* is treated exactly like an ordinary variable, even though it consists only of 0s and 1s.

The Stata output in Table 5.3 gives the results of the regression, using the full sample of 74 schools. In equation form, we have (standard errors in parentheses)

$$\begin{aligned}\widehat{COST} &= \underset{(24{,}000)}{-34{,}000} + \underset{(21{,}000)}{133{,}000}OCC + \underset{(40)}{331}N \qquad R^2 = 0.62.\end{aligned} \tag{5.7}$$

Putting *OCC* equal to 0 and 1, respectively, we can obtain the implicit cost functions for the two types of school:

$$\textit{Regular schools: } \widehat{COST} = -34{,}000 + 331N \tag{5.8}$$

$$\begin{aligned}\textit{Occupational schools: } \widehat{COST} &= -34{,}000 + 133{,}000 + 331N \\ &= 99{,}000 + 331N.\end{aligned} \tag{5.9}$$

Table 5.2 Recurrent expenditure, number of students, and type of school

School	*Type*	*COST*	*N*	*OCC*
1	Occupational	345,000	623	1
2	Occupational	537,000	653	1
3	Regular	170,000	400	0
4	Occupational	526,000	663	1
5	Regular	100,000	563	0
6	Regular	28,000	236	0
7	Regular	160,000	307	0
8	Occupational	45,000	173	1
9	Occupational	120,000	146	1
10	Occupational	61,000	99	1

Table 5.3

```
. reg COST N OCC

  Source  |       SS          df       MS           Number of obs =      74
----------------------------------------------      F(2, 71)      =   56.86
   Model  |   9.0582e+11       2   4.5291e+11       Prob > F      = 0.0000
Residual  |   5.6553e+11      71   7.9652e+09       R-squared     = 0.6156
----------------------------------------------      Adj R-squared = 0.6048
   Total  |   1.4713e+12      73   2.0155e+10       Root MSE      =   89248

---------------------------------------------------------------------------
    COST  |     Coef.      Std. Err.      t     P>|t|    [95% Conf. Interval]
---------------------------------------------------------------------------
       N  |   331.4493     39.75844    8.337   0.000    252.1732    410.7254
     OCC  |   133259.1     20827.59    6.398   0.000    91730.06    174788.1
   _cons  |  -33612.55     23573.47   -1.426   0.158   -80616.71    13391.61
---------------------------------------------------------------------------
```

The regression implies that the marginal cost per student per year is 331 yuan and that the annual overhead cost of a regular school is −34,000 yuan. Obviously having a negative intercept does not make any sense at all and it suggests that the model is misspecified in some way. We will come back to this later. The coefficient of the dummy variable, 133,000, is an estimate of the extra annual overhead cost of an occupational school. The marginal cost of an occupational school is the same as that for a regular school—it must be, given the model specification. Figure 5.2 shows the data and the cost functions derived from the regression results.

Standard errors and hypothesis testing

In addition to the estimates of the coefficients, the regression results include standard errors and the usual diagnostic statistics. We will perform a t test on the coefficient of the dummy variable. Our null hypothesis is H_0: $\delta = 0$ and

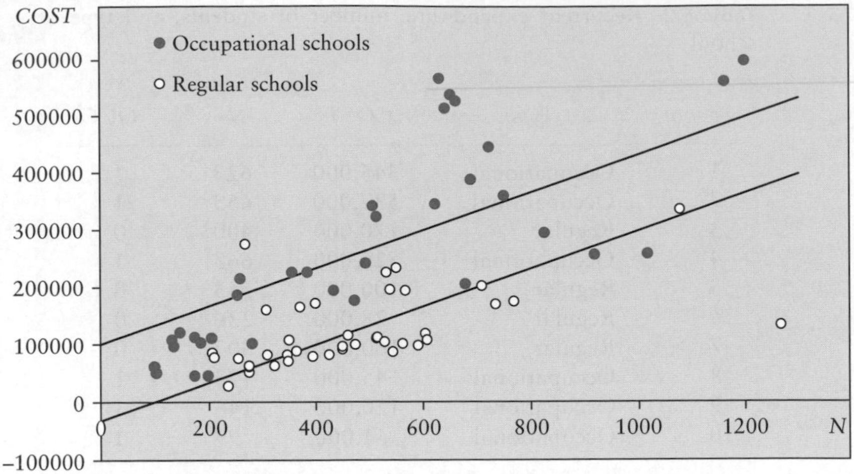

Figure 5.2 Cost functions for regular and occupational schools in Shanghai

our alternative hypothesis is H_1: $\delta \neq 0$. In other words, our null hypothesis is that there is no difference in the overhead costs of the two types of school. The t statistic is 6.40, so it is rejected at the 0.1 percent significance level. We can perform t tests on the other coefficients in the usual way. The t statistic for the coefficient of N is 8.34, so we conclude that the marginal cost is (very) significantly different from zero. In the case of the intercept, the t statistic is -1.43, so we do not reject the null hypothesis H_0: $\beta_1 = 0$. Thus, one explanation of the nonsensical negative overhead cost of regular schools might be that they do not actually have any overheads and our estimate is a random number. A more realistic version of this hypothesis is that β_1 is positive but small (as you can see, the 95 percent confidence interval includes positive values) and the disturbance term is responsible for the negative estimate. As already noted, a further possibility is that the model is misspecified in some way.

EXERCISES

5.1 Does the sex of an individual affect educational attainment? Using your *EAEF* data set, regress *S* on *ASVABC*, *SM*, *SF* and *MALE*, a dummy variable that is 1 for male respondents and 0 for female ones. Interpret the coefficients and perform t tests. Is there any evidence that the educational attainment of males is different from that of females?

5.2* The Stata output shows the result of regressing weight in 1985, measured in pounds, on height, measured in inches, first with a linear specification, then with a logarithmic one, including a dummy variable *MALE*, defined as in Exercise 5.1, in both cases. Give an interpretation of the equations and perform appropriate statistical tests. See Box 5.1 for a guide to the interpretation of dummy variable coefficients in logarithmic regressions.

```
. reg WEIGHT85 HEIGHT MALE

  Source  |       SS           df        MS            Number of obs =     540
----------+-------------------------------------       F(2, 537)     =  191.56
   Model  |   273040.775        2    136520.388        Prob > F      =  0.0000
Residual  |   382702.973      537    712.668479        R-squared     =  0.4164
----------+-------------------------------------       Adj R-squared =  0.4142
   Total  |   655743.748      539    1216.59322        Root MSE      =  26.696
------------------------------------------------------------------------------
WEIGHT85  |      Coef.    Std. Err.     t     P>|t|     [95% Conf. Interval]
----------+-------------------------------------------------------------------
  HEIGHT  |   4.006225    .3971644    10.09   0.000     3.226039    4.786412
    MALE  |    13.7615    3.363568     4.09   0.000     7.154131    20.36886
   _cons  |  -121.2502    25.70087    -4.72   0.000    -171.7367   -70.76363
------------------------------------------------------------------------------

. reg LGWEIGHT LGHEIGHT MALE

  Source  |       SS           df        MS            Number of obs =     540
----------+-------------------------------------       F(2, 537)     =  224.03
   Model  |   11.3390838        2    5.66954189        Prob > F      =  0.0000
Residual  |   13.5897932      537    .025306877        R-squared     =  0.4549
----------+-------------------------------------       Adj R-squared =  0.4528
   Total  |    24.928877      539    .046250236        Root MSE      =  .15908
------------------------------------------------------------------------------
LGWEIGHT  |      Coef.    Std. Err.     t     P>|t|     [95% Conf. Interval]
----------+-------------------------------------------------------------------
LGHEIGHT  |   1.675851    .1581459    10.09   0.000      1.36519    1.986511
    MALE  |   .0975722    .0199191     4.90   0.000     .0584432    .1367012
   _cons  |  -2.077515    .6590635    -3.15   0.002    -3.372173    -.782856
------------------------------------------------------------------------------
```

5.3 Using your *EAEF* data set, regress *LGEARN* on *S*, *EXP*, and *MALE*. Interpret the coefficients and perform *t* tests. See Box 5.1 for a guide to the interpretation of dummy variable coefficients in semilogarithmic regressions.

5.4 Consider the rudimentary educational attainment model

$$S = \beta_1 + \beta_2 MALE + u.$$

Demonstrate that, if it were fitted with a sample of observations, $b_1 = \overline{S}_F$ and $b_2 = \overline{S}_M - \overline{S}_F$, where $\overline{S}_F$ and $\overline{S}_M$ are mean years of schooling of females and males in the sample.

5.5* Suppose that the relationship

$$Y_i = \beta_1 + \beta_2 X_i + u_i$$

is being fitted and that the value of *X* is missing for some observations. One way of handling the missing values problem is to drop those observations. Another is to set $X = 0$ for the missing observations and include a dummy variable *D* defined to be equal to 1 if *X* is missing, 0 otherwise. Demonstrate that the two methods must yield the same estimates of β_1 and β_2. Write down an expression for *RSS* using the second approach, decompose it into the *RSS* for observations with *X* present and *RSS* for observations with *X* missing, and determine how the resulting expression is related to *RSS* when the missing-value observations are dropped.

BOX 5.1 Interpretation of dummy variable coefficients in logarithmic and semi-logarithmic regressions

Suppose that the regression model is

$$\log Y = \beta_1 + \beta_2 \log X + \delta D + u,$$

where D is a dummy variable and δ is its coefficient. Rewriting the model as

$$Y = e^{\beta_1 + \beta_2 \log X + \delta D + u} = e^{\beta_1} e^{\log X^{\beta_2}} e^{\delta D} e^{u} = e^{\beta_1} X^{\beta_2} e^{\delta D} e^{u},$$

it can be seen that the term $e^{\delta D}$ multiplies Y by e^0 when $D = 0$ for the reference category and e^{δ} when $D = 1$ for the other category. e^0 is of course 1, so the dummy variable has no effect on the reference category. For the other category where $D = 1$, the dummy variable multiplies Y by e^{δ}. If δ is small, e^{δ} is approximately equal to $(1 + \delta)$, implying that Y is a proportion δ greater for the other category than for the reference category. If δ is not small, the proportional difference is $\left(e^{\delta} - 1\right)$.

A semilogarithmic model

$$\log Y = \beta_1 + \beta_2 X + \delta D + u$$

can be rewritten

$$Y = e^{\beta_1 + \beta_2 X + \delta D + u} = e^{\beta_1} e^{\beta_2 X} e^{\delta D} e^{u}.$$

The effect of the dummy variable and the interpretation of its coefficient are the same as in the logarithmic model.

5.2 Extension to more than two categories and to multiple sets of dummy variables

In the previous section, we used a dummy variable to differentiate between regular and occupational schools when fitting a cost function. In fact, there are two types of regular secondary school in Shanghai. There are general schools, which provide the usual academic education, and vocational schools. As their name implies, the vocational schools are meant to impart occupational skills as well as give an academic education. However, the vocational component of the curriculum is typically quite small and the schools are similar to the general schools. Often they are just general schools with a couple of workshops added. Likewise, there are two types of occupational school. There are technical schools training technicians and skilled workers' schools training craftsmen.

Thus, now the qualitative variable has four categories and we need to develop a more elaborate set of dummy variables. The standard procedure is to choose one category as the reference category to which the basic equation applies, and then to define dummy variables for each of the other categories. In general, it is good practice to select the dominant or most normal category, if there is one, as the reference category. In the Shanghai sample, it is sensible to choose the general schools. They are the most numerous and the other schools are variations of them.

Accordingly, we will define dummy variables for the other three types. *TECH* will be the dummy variable for the technical schools: *TECH* is equal to 1 if the observation relates to a technical school, 0 otherwise. Similarly, we will define dummy variables *WORKER* and *VOC* for the skilled workers' schools and the vocational schools. The regression model is now

$$COST = \beta_1 + \delta_T TECH + \delta_W WORKER + \delta_V VOC + \beta_2 N + u, \quad (5.10)$$

where δ_T, δ_W, and δ_V are coefficients that represent the extra overhead costs of the technical, skilled workers', and vocational schools, relative to the cost of a general school. Note that you do not include a dummy variable for the reference category, and that is the reason why the reference category is often described as the omitted category. Note that we do not make any prior assumption about the size, or even the sign, of the δ coefficients. They will be estimated from the sample data.

Table 5.4 gives the data for the first 10 of the 74 schools. Note how the values of the dummy variables *TECH*, *WORKER*, and *VOC* are determined by the type of school in each observation.

The Stata output in Table 5.5 gives the regression results for this model. In equation form, we have (standard errors in parentheses)

$$\begin{aligned} \widehat{COST} &= \underset{(27{,}000)}{-55{,}000} + \underset{(27{,}000)}{154{,}000}TECH + \underset{(28{,}000)}{143{,}000}WORKER \\ &\quad + \underset{(31{,}000)}{53{,}000}VOC + \underset{(40)}{343}N \qquad R^2 = 0.63. \end{aligned} \quad (5.11)$$

The coefficient of N indicates that the marginal cost per student per year is 343 yuan. The constant indicates that the annual overhead cost of a general academic school is −55,000 yuan per year. Obviously, this is nonsense and indicates

Table 5.4 Recurrent expenditure, number of students, and type of school

School	*Type*	*COST*	*N*	*TECH*	*WORKER*	*VOC*
1	Technical	345,000	623	1	0	0
2	Technical	537,000	653	1	0	0
3	General	170,000	400	0	0	0
4	Skilled workers'	526,000	663	0	1	0
5	General	100,000	563	0	0	0
6	Vocational	28,000	236	0	0	1
7	Vocational	160,000	307	0	0	1
8	Technical	45,000	173	1	0	0
9	Technical	120,000	146	1	0	0
10	Skilled workers'	61,000	99	0	1	0

Table 5.5

```
. reg COST N TECH WORKER VOC

  Source |        SS       df        MS            Number of obs =     74
---------+------------------------------           F(4, 69)      =  29.63
   Model |  9.2996e+11      4   2.3249e+11         Prob > F      = 0.0000
Residual |  5.4138e+11     69   7.8461e+09         R-squared     = 0.6320
---------+------------------------------           Adj R-squared = 0.6107
   Total |  1.4713e+12     73   2.0155e+10         Root MSE      =  88578

------------------------------------------------------------------------------
    COST |      Coef.   Std. Err.       t     P>|t|     [95% Conf. Interval]
---------+--------------------------------------------------------------------
       N |   342.6335    40.2195     8.519    0.000     262.3978    422.8692
    TECH |   154110.9   26760.41     5.759    0.000     100725.3    207496.4
  WORKER |   143362.4    27852.8     5.147    0.000     87797.57     98927.2
     VOC |   53228.64   31061.65     1.714    0.091    -8737.646    115194.9
   _cons |  -54893.09   23573.47    -2.058    0.043    -108104.4   -1681.748
------------------------------------------------------------------------------
```

that something is wrong with the model. The coefficients of *TECH*, *WORKER*, and *VOC* indicate that the overhead costs of technical, skilled workers', and vocational schools are 154,000 yuan, 143,000 yuan, and 53,000 yuan greater than the cost of a general school.

From this equation we can obtain the implicit cost functions for the four types of school. First, putting the three dummy variables equal to 0, we obtain the cost function for general schools:

$$\textit{General schools: } \widehat{COST} = -55{,}000 + 343N. \quad \textbf{(5.12)}$$

Next, putting *TECH* equal to 1 and *WORKER* and *VOC* to 0, we obtain the cost function for technical schools:

$$\textit{Technical schools: } \widehat{COST} = -55{,}000 + 154{,}000 + 343N = 99{,}000 + 343N. \quad \textbf{(5.13)}$$

And similarly, we obtain the cost functions for skilled workers' and vocational schools:

$$\textit{Skilled workers' schools: } \widehat{COST} = -55{,}000 + 143{,}000 + 343N = 88{,}000 + 343N \quad \textbf{(5.14)}$$

$$\textit{Vocational schools: } \widehat{COST} = -55{,}000 + 53{,}000 + 343N = -2{,}000 + 343N. \quad \textbf{(5.15)}$$

Note that in each case the annual marginal cost per student is estimated at 343 yuan. The model specification assumes that this figure does not differ according to type of school. The four cost functions are illustrated in Figure 5.3.

We can perform *t* tests on the coefficients in the usual way. The *t* statistic for *N* is 8.52, so the marginal cost is (very) significantly different from zero, as we would expect. The *t* statistic for the technical school dummy is 5.76, indicating

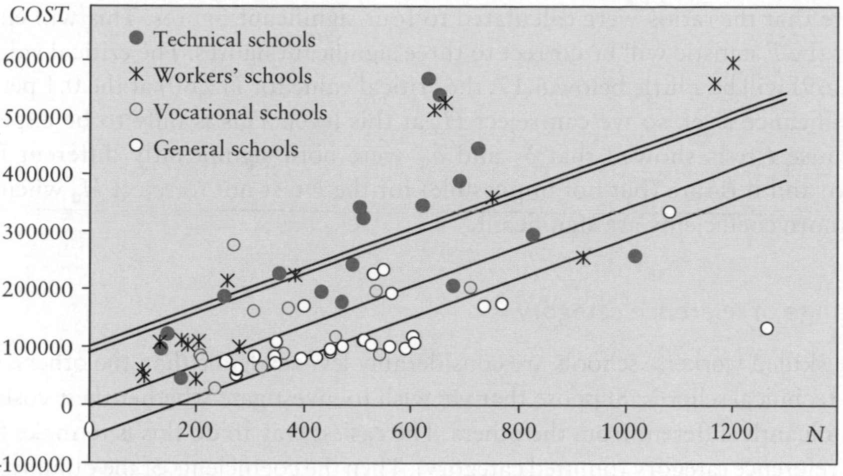

Figure 5.3 Cost functions for four types of school in Shanghai

that the annual overhead cost of a technical school is (very) significantly greater than that of a general school, again as expected. Similarly, for skilled workers' schools, the t statistic being 5.15. In the case of vocational schools, however, the t statistic is only 1.71, indicating that the overhead cost of such a school is not significantly greater than that of a general school. This is not surprising, given that the vocational schools are not much different from the general schools. Note that the null hypotheses for the tests on the coefficients of the dummy variables are that the overhead costs of the other schools are not different from the overhead cost of a general school.

Joint explanatory power of a group of dummy variables

Finally, we will perform an F test of the joint explanatory power of the dummy variables as a group. The null hypothesis is H_0: $\delta_T = \delta_W = \delta_V = 0$. The alternative hypothesis H_1 is that at least one δ is different from zero. The residual sum of squares in the specification including the dummy variables is 5.41×10^{11}. (In the Stata output, it appears as 5.4138e+11. The e+11 means that the coefficient should be multiplied by 10^{11}.) The residual sum of squares in the original specification excluding the dummy variables was 8.92×10^{11} (see Section 5.1). The reduction in RSS when we include the dummies is therefore $(8.92 - 5.41) \times 10^{11}$. We will check whether this reduction is significant with the usual F test.

The numerator in the F ratio is the reduction in RSS divided by the cost, which is the three degrees of freedom given up when we estimate three additional coefficients (the coefficients of the dummies). The denominator is RSS for the specification including the dummy variables, divided by the number of degrees of freedom remaining after they have been added. The F ratio is therefore given by

$$F(3,69) = \frac{(8.9160 \times 10^{11} - 5.4138 \times 10^{11})/3}{5.4138 \times 10^{11}/69} = \frac{1.1674}{0.07846} = 14.9. \qquad \textbf{(5.16)}$$

Note that the ratios were calculated to four significant figures. This will ensure that the F statistic will be correct to three significant figures. The critical value of $F(3,69)$ will be a little below 6.17, the critical value for $F(3,60)$ at the 0.1 percent significance level, so we can reject H_0 at this level. This is only to be expected because t tests showed that δ_T and δ_W were both significantly different from zero, and it is rare (but not impossible) for the F test not to reject H_0 when one or more coefficients are significant.

Change of reference category

The skilled workers' schools are considerably less academic than the others, even the technical schools. Suppose that we wish to investigate whether their costs are significantly different from the others. The easiest way to do this is to make them the reference category (omitted category). Then the coefficients of the dummy variables become estimates of the differences between the overhead costs of the other types of school and those of the skilled workers' schools. Since skilled workers' schools are now the reference category, we need a dummy variable, which will be called GEN, for the general academic schools. The model becomes

$$COST = \beta_1 + \delta_T TECH + \delta_V VOC + \delta_G GEN + \beta_2 N + u, \qquad \textbf{(5.17)}$$

where δ_T, δ_V, and δ_G are the extra costs of technical, vocational, and general schools relative to skilled workers' schools. The data table for the first 10 schools is now as shown in Table 5.6. The Stata output is shown in Table 5.7.

The regression equation is therefore (standard errors in parentheses)

$$\begin{aligned}\widehat{COST} &= \underset{(29{,}000)}{88{,}000} + \underset{(30{,}000)}{11{,}000}TECH - \underset{(28{,}000)}{143{,}000}GEN \\ &\quad - \underset{(34{,}000)}{90{,}000}VOC + \underset{(40)}{343}N \qquad R^2 = 0.63. \end{aligned} \qquad \textbf{(5.18)}$$

Table 5.6 Recurrent expenditure, enrollments, and type of school

School	*Type*	*COST*	*N*	*TECH*	*GEN*	*VOC*
1	Technical	345,000	623	1	0	0
2	Technical	537,000	653	1	0	0
3	General	170,000	400	0	1	0
4	Skilled workers'	526,000	663	0	0	0
5	General	100,000	563	0	1	0
6	Vocational	28,000	236	0	0	1
7	Vocational	160,000	307	0	0	1
8	Technical	45,000	173	1	0	0
9	Technical	120,000	146	1	0	0
10	Skilled workers'	61,000	99	0	0	0

Table 5.7

```
. reg COST N TECH VOC GEN

  Source |       SS       df       MS              Number of obs =      74
---------+------------------------------           F(4, 69)      =   29.63
   Model |  9.2996e+11     4  2.3249e+11           Prob > F      =  0.0000
Residual |  5.4138e+11    69  7.8461e+09           R-squared     =  0.6320
---------+------------------------------           Adj R-squared =  0.6107
   Total |  1.4713e+12    73  2.0155e+10           Root MSE      =   88578

------------------------------------------------------------------------------
    COST |      Coef.   Std. Err.       t     P>|t|     [95% Conf. Interval]
---------+--------------------------------------------------------------------
       N |   342.6335    40.2195     8.519   0.000     262.3978    422.8692
    TECH |   10748.51   30524.87     0.352   0.726    -50146.93    71643.95
     VOC |  -90133.74   33984.22    -2.652   0.010    -157930.4   -22337.07
     GEN |  -143362.4    27852.8    -5.147   0.000    -198927.2   -87797.57
   _cons |   88469.29   28849.56     3.067   0.003     30916.01    146022.6
------------------------------------------------------------------------------
```

From this equation we can again obtain the implicit cost functions for the four types of school. Putting all the dummy variables equal to 0, we obtain the cost function for skilled workers' schools:

$$\text{Skilled workers' schools: } \widehat{COST} = 88{,}000 + 343N. \quad \textbf{(5.19)}$$

Then, putting *TECH*, *WORKER*, and *GEN* equal to 1 and the other two to 0, we derive the cost functions for the other types of school:

$$\begin{aligned}\text{Technical schools: } \widehat{COST} &= 88{,}000 + 11{,}000 + 343N \\ &= 99{,}000 + 343N \quad \textbf{(5.20)}\end{aligned}$$

$$\begin{aligned}\text{Vocational schools: } \widehat{COST} &= 88{,}000 - 90{,}000 + 343N \\ &= -2{,}000 + 343N \quad \textbf{(5.21)}\end{aligned}$$

$$\begin{aligned}\text{General schools: } \widehat{COST} &= 88{,}000 - 143{,}000 + 343N \\ &= -55{,}000 + 343N. \quad \textbf{(5.22)}\end{aligned}$$

Note that these equations are identical to those obtained when general schools were the reference category. The choice of omitted category does not affect the substance of the regression results. The only components that change are the standard errors and the interpretation of the *t* tests. R^2, the coefficients of the other variables, the *t* statistics for the other variables, and the *F* statistic for the equation as a whole do not alter. And of course the diagram representing the four cost functions is the same as before.

The dummy variable trap

What would happen if you included a dummy variable for the reference category? There would be two consequences.

First, were it possible to compute regression coefficients, you would not be able to give them an interpretation. The coefficient b_1 is a basic estimate of the intercept, and the coefficients of the dummies are the estimates of the increase in the intercept from this basic level, but now there is no definition of what is basic, so the interpretation collapses.

The other consequence is that the numerical procedure for calculating the regression coefficients will break down and the computer will simply send you an error message (or possibly, in sophisticated applications, drop one of the dummies for you). Suppose that there are m dummy categories and you define dummy variables $D_1, ..., D_m$. Then, in observation i, $\sum D_{ji} = 1$ because one of the dummy variables will be equal to 1 and all the others will be equal to 0. But the intercept β_1 is really the product of the parameter β_1 and a special variable whose value is 1 in all observations (see Box 3.1). Hence, for all observations, the sum of the dummy variables is equal to this special variable, and one has an exact linear relationship among the variables in the regression model. This is known as the dummy variable trap. As a consequence, the model is subject to a special case of exact multicollinearity, making it impossible to compute regression coefficients.

An alternative procedure for avoiding the dummy variable trap is to drop the intercept from the model. The special unit variable is thereby dropped and there is no longer an exact linear relationship among the variables.

This is illustrated with the school cost data in Table 5.8, where the specification is the same as those for Tables 5.5 and 5.7, except that dummy variables have been included for all the types of school and the intercept has been dropped by adding 'noconstant' to the regression command. In this specification, the dummy variable coefficients may be interpreted as category-specific estimates of the intercept. Thus, we obtain directly the implicit cost functions (5.19)−(5.22).

This alternative procedure is seldom used in practice. The point of including a set of dummy variables is that it enables you to investigate whether, having defined a reference category, the relationship is different for the other categories,

Table 5.8

```
. reg COST N TECH WORKER VOC GEN, noconstant

  Source  |       SS         df       MS          Number of obs =    74
----------+------------------------------         F(5, 69)      = 89.96
   Model  |  3.5293e+12       5   7.0585e+11      Prob > F      = 0.0000
Residual  |  5.4138e+11      69   7.8461e+09      R-squared     = 0.8670
----------+------------------------------         Adj R-squared = 0.8574
   Total  |  4.0706e+12      74   5.5009e+10      Root MSE      =  88578

-------------------------------------------------------------------------
    COST  |      Coef.   Std. Err.      t    P>|t|   [95% Conf. Interval]
-------------------------------------------------------------------------
       N  |   342.6335    40.2195     8.52   0.000   262.3978    422.8692
    TECH  |    99217.8   29494.73     3.36   0.001   40377.43    158058.2
  WORKER  |   88469.29   28849.56     3.07   0.003   30916.01    146022.6
     VOC  |   -1664.45   29757.08    -0.06   0.956  -61028.21    57699.31
     GEN  |  -54893.09   26673.08    -2.06   0.043  -108104.4   -1681.745
-------------------------------------------------------------------------
```

and to test the differences statistically. With this alternative approach, we can still estimate differences in the intercepts, but we have no direct means of testing whether the differences are significant.

There are further complications. When there is no intercept in the model, it is generally not possible to decompose *TSS*, the total sum of squares, into *ESS*, the explained sum of squares, and *RSS*. This means that R^2 cannot be defined in the usual way. Some regression applications nevertheless produce a statistic that is denoted R^2. Stata does this by defining *TSS* as $\sum_{i=1}^{n} Y_i^2$ instead of $\sum_{i=1}^{n} (Y_i - \bar{Y})^2$ and then defining $R^2 = 1 - (RSS/TSS)$. Note the differences in *TSS* and R^2 in Tables 5.7 and 5.8.

Multiple sets of dummy variables

It may happen that you wish to include more than one set of dummy variables in your regression equation. This is especially common when working with cross-sectional data, when you may have gathered data on a number of qualitative as well as quantitative characteristics. There is no problem in extending the use of dummy variables in this way, provided that the framework is defined clearly.

We will illustrate the procedure using the school cost data. Many of the occupational schools and some of the regular schools are residential. We will investigate the extra cost of running a residential school, controlling for number of students and type of school. To do this, we introduce a dummy variable, *RES*, which is equal to 1 for residential schools and 0 for the others. For the sake of simplicity we will revert to the occupational/regular classification of school type. The model now becomes

$$COST = \beta_1 + \delta OCC + \varepsilon RES + \beta_2 N + u, \qquad (5.23)$$

where ε is the extra cost of a residential school. The reference category now has two dimensions, one for each qualitative characteristic. In this case, it is a nonresidential ($RES = 0$), regular ($OCC = 0$) school. Table 5.9 presents the data for the first 10 schools in the sample. The second, fourth, and seventh are residential schools and so *RES* is set equal to 1, while for the others it is 0.

The Stata regression results are shown in Table 5.10. The regression equation is therefore (standard errors in parentheses)

$$\begin{aligned} \widehat{COST} &= \underset{(23{,}000)}{-29{,}000} + \underset{(24{,}000)}{110{,}000\,OCC} + \underset{(31{,}000)}{58{,}000\,RES} \\ &\quad + \underset{(39)}{322N} \qquad R^2 = 0.63. \end{aligned} \qquad (5.24)$$

Using the four combinations of *OCC* and *RES*, one may obtain the following subequations:

$$\textit{Regular, nonresidential}: \widehat{COST} = -29{,}000 + 322N \qquad (5.25)$$

$$\begin{aligned} \textit{Occupational, nonresidential}: \widehat{COST} &= -29{,}000 + 110{,}000 + 322N \\ &= 81{,}000 + 322N \end{aligned} \qquad (5.26)$$

Table 5.9 Recurrent expenditure, number of students, school type, and whether residential

School	*Type*	*COST*	*N*	*OCC*	*RES*
1	Occupational, nonresidential	345,000	623	1	0
2	Occupational, residential	537,000	653	1	1
3	Regular, nonresidential	170,000	400	0	0
4	Occupational, residential	526,000	663	1	1
5	Regular, nonresidential	100,000	563	0	0
6	Regular, nonresidential	28,000	236	0	0
7	Regular, residential	160,000	307	0	1
8	Occupational, nonresidential	45,000	173	1	0
9	Occupational, nonresidential	120,000	146	1	0
10	Occupational, nonresidential	61,000	99	1	0

Table 5.10

```
. reg COST N OCC RES
  Source |       SS          df        MS              Number of obs =     74
---------+------------------------------------         F(3, 70)      =  40.43
   Model |  9.3297e+11        3   7.0585e+11           Prob > F      = 0.0000
Residual |  5.3838e+11       70   7.6911e+09           R-squared     = 0.6341
---------+------------------------------------         Adj R-squared = 0.6184
   Total |  1.4713e+12       73   2.0155e+10           Root MSE      =  87699

------------------------------------------------------------------------------
    COST |      Coef.    Std. Err.       t     P>|t|      [95% Conf. Interval]
---------+--------------------------------------------------------------------
       N |    321.833    39.40225    8.168    0.000      243.2477    400.4183
     OCC |   109564.6    24039.58    4.558    0.000      61619.15      157510
     RES |   57909.01    30821.31    1.879    0.064     -3562.137    119380.2
   _cons |  -29045.27    23291.54   -1.247    0.217     -75498.78    17408.25
------------------------------------------------------------------------------
```

$$\textit{Regular, residential}: \widehat{COST} = -29{,}000 + 58{,}000 + 322N = 29{,}000 + 322N \qquad \textbf{(5.27)}$$

$$\textit{Occupational, residential}: \widehat{COST} = -29{,}000 + 110{,}000 + 58{,}000 + 322N = 139{,}000 + 322N. \qquad \textbf{(5.28)}$$

The cost functions are illustrated in Figure 5.4. Note that the model incorporates the (plausible) assumption that the extra cost of a residential school is the same for regular and occupational schools.

The t statistic for the residential dummy is only 1.88. However, we can perform a one-sided test because it is reasonable to exclude the possibility that residential schools cost less to run than nonresidential ones, and so we can reject the null hypothesis of no difference in the costs at the 5 percent level.

The procedure may be generalized, with no limit on the number of qualitative characteristics in the model or the number of categories defined for each characteristic.

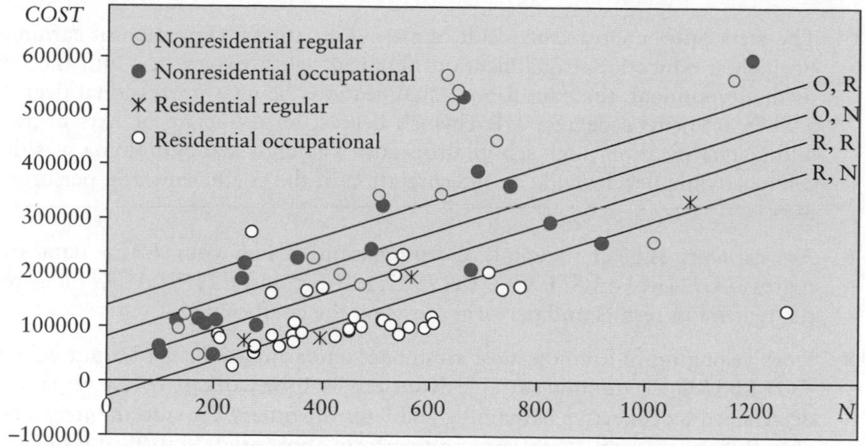

Figure 5.4 Cost functions for residential and nonresidential schools in Shanghai

EXERCISES

5.6 Does ethnicity affect educational attainment? In your *EAEF* data set you will find the following ethnic dummy variables:

ETHHISP	1 if hispanic, 0 otherwise
ETHBLACK	1 if black, 0 otherwise
ETHWHITE	1 if not hispanic or black, 0 otherwise.

Regress *S* on *ASVABC*, *MALE*, *SM*, *SF*, *ETHBLACK*, and *ETHHISP*. (In this specification, *ETHWHITE* has been chosen as the reference category, and so it is omitted.) Interpret the regression results and perform *t* tests on the coefficients.

5.7*

```
. reg LGEARN EDUCPROF EDUCPHD EDUCMAST EDUCBA EDUCAA EDUCDO EXP MALE
    Source  |       SS           df         MS          Number of obs =     540
--------------------------------------------------      F(8, 531)     =   29.64
     Model  |  57.6389757         8     136520.388      Prob > F      =  0.0000
  Residual  |  129.707643       539    .243067171      R-squared     =  0.3087
--------------------------------------------------      Adj R-squared =  0.2983
     Total  |  186.707643       539     .34639637      Root MSE      =  .49302
-----------------------------------------------------------------------------
    LGEARN  |      Coef.    Std. Err.     t    P>|t|    [95% Conf. Interval]
-----------------------------------------------------------------------------
  EDUCPROF  |    1.59193    .2498069   6.37   0.000    1.101199    2.082661
   EDUCPHD  |   .3089521    .4943698   0.62   0.532   -.6622084    1.280113
  EDUCMAST  |   .6280672    .0993222   6.32   0.000    .4329546    .8231798
    EDUCBA  |   .5053643    .0561215   9.00   0.000    .3951168    .6156118
    EDUCAA  |    .170838    .0765684   2.23   0.026    .0204238    .3212522
    EDUCDO  |  -.2527803      .08179  -3.09   0.002    -.413452   -.0921085
       EXP  |   .0230536    .0050845   4.53   0.000    .0130654    .0330419
      MALE  |   .2755451    .0437642   6.30   0.000     .189573    .3615173
     _cons  |   2.125885    .0915997  23.21   0.000    1.945943    2.305828
-----------------------------------------------------------------------------
```

The Stata output shows the result of a semilogarithmic regression of earnings on highest educational qualification obtained, work experience, and the sex of the respondent, the educational qualifications being a professional degree, a PhD, a Master's degree, a Bachelor's degree, an Associate of Arts degree, and no qualification (high school drop-out). The high school diploma was the reference category. Provide an interpretation of the coefficients and perform *t* tests.

5.8 Are earnings subject to ethnic discrimination? Using your *EAEF* data set, regress *LGEARN* on *S*, *EXP*, *MALE*, *ETHHISP*, and *ETHBLACK*. Interpret the regression results and perform *t* tests on the coefficients.

5.9 Does belonging to a union have an impact on earnings? In the output below, *COLLBARG* is a dummy variable defined to be 1 for workers whose wages are determined by collective bargaining and 0 for the others. Provide an interpretation of the regression coefficients and perform appropriate statistical tests.

```
. reg LGEARN S EXP MALE COLLBARG

  Source |       SS       df       MS              Number of obs =     540
---------+------------------------------           F(4, 535)     =   64.84
   Model |  60.9620285     4  15.2405071           Prob > F      =  0.0000
Residual |  125.745615   535  .235038532           R-squared     =  0.3265
---------+------------------------------           Adj R-squared =  0.3215
   Total |  186.707643   539   .34639637           Root MSE      =  .48481

------------------------------------------------------------------------------
  LGEARN |      Coef.   Std. Err.      t     P>|t|     [95% Conf. Interval]
---------+--------------------------------------------------------------------
       S |   .1194004    .008798    13.57   0.000     .1021175    .1366832
     EXP |   .0274958   .0049647     5.54   0.000     .0177431    .0372484
    MALE |    .269056   .0429286     6.27   0.000     .1847267    .3533853
COLLBARG |   .0790935   .0536727     1.47   0.141    -.0263416    .1845287
   _cons |   .5455149   .1606062     3.40   0.001     .2300187    .8610111
------------------------------------------------------------------------------
```

5.10 Evaluate whether the ethnicity dummies as a group have significant explanatory power for educational attainment by comparing the residual sums of squares in the regressions in Exercises 5.1 and 5.6.

5.11 Evaluate whether the ethnicity dummies as a group have significant explanatory power for earnings by comparing the residual sums of squares in the regressions in Exercises 5.3 and 5.8.

5.12 Repeat Exercise 5.6 making *ETHBLACK* the reference category. Evaluate the impact on the interpretation of the coefficients and the statistical tests.

5.13 Repeat Exercise 5.8 making *ETHBLACK* the reference category. Evaluate the impact on the interpretation of the coefficients and the statistical tests.

5.14 Repeat Exercise 5.3 including *FEMALE* as well as *MALE*. Regress *LGEARN* on *S*, *EXP*, *MALE*, and *FEMALE*. Discuss the regression results.

5.3 Slope dummy variables

We have so far assumed that the qualitative variables we have introduced into the regression model are responsible only for shifts in the intercept of the regression line. We have implicitly assumed that the slope of the regression line is the same for each category of the qualitative variables. This is not necessarily a plausible assumption, and we will now see how to relax it, and test it, using the device known as a **slope dummy variable** (also sometimes known as an interactive dummy variable).

To illustrate this, we will return to the school cost example. The assumption that the marginal cost per student is the same for occupational and regular schools is unrealistic because occupational schools incur expenditure on training materials related to the number of students and the staff–student ratio has to be higher in occupational schools because workshop groups cannot be, or at least should not be, as large as academic classes. We can relax the assumption by introducing the slope dummy variable, *NOCC*, defined as the product of *N* and *OCC*:

$$COST = \beta_1 + \delta OCC + \beta_2 N + \lambda NOCC + u. \quad (5.29)$$

Since it is the product of two other variables in the specification, a slope dummy variable is a special case of an interactive variable of the kind discussed in Section 4.3. However, because one of the variables in the interaction is qualitative, the interpretation of a slope dummy variable is generally more straightforward than in the general case. In the present example, if (5.29) is rewritten

$$COST = \beta_1 + \delta OCC + (\beta_2 + \lambda OCC)N + u, \quad (5.30)$$

it can be seen that the effect of the slope dummy variable is to allow the coefficient of *N* for occupational schools to be λ greater than that for regular schools. If *OCC* is 0, so is *NOCC* and the equation becomes

$$COST = \beta_1 + \beta_2 N + u. \quad (5.31)$$

If *OCC* is 1, *NOCC* is equal to *N* and the equation becomes

$$COST = \beta_1 + \delta + (\beta_2 + \lambda)N + u. \quad (5.32)$$

λ is thus the incremental marginal cost associated with occupational schools, in the same way that δ is the incremental overhead cost associated with them. Table 5.11 gives the data for the first 10 schools in the sample.

From the Stata output in Table 5.12 we obtain the regression equation (standard errors in parentheses)

$$\underset{}{\widehat{COST}} = \underset{(31{,}000)}{51{,}000} - \underset{(41{,}000)}{4{,}000OCC} + \underset{(60)}{152N} + \underset{(76)}{284NOCC} \qquad R^2 = 0.68. \quad (5.33)$$

Putting *OCC*, and hence *NOCC*, equal to 0, we get the cost function for a regular school. We estimate that the annual overhead cost is 51,000 yuan and the annual marginal cost per student is 152 yuan:

$$\textit{Regular schools}: \widehat{COST} = 51{,}000 + 152N. \quad (5.34)$$

Table 5.11 Recurrent expenditure, number of students, and type of school

School	*Type*	*COST*	*N*	*OCC*	*NOCC*
1	Occupational	345,000	623	1	623
2	Occupational	537,000	653	1	653
3	Regular	170,000	400	0	0
4	Occupational	526,000	663	1	663
5	Regular	100,000	563	0	0
6	Regular	28,000	236	0	0
7	Regular	160,000	307	0	0
8	Occupational	45,000	173	1	173
9	Occupational	120,000	146	1	146
10	Occupational	61,000	99	1	99

Table 5.12

```
. gen NOCC=N*OCC
. reg COST N OCC NOCC

      Source |       SS       df       MS          Number of obs =      74
-------------+------------------------------         F(3, 70)      =   49.64
       Model |  1.0009e+12     3  3.3363e+11       Prob > F      =  0.0000
    Residual |  4.7045e+11    70  6.7207e+09       R-squared     =  0.6803
-------------+------------------------------         Adj R-squared =  0.6666
       Total |  1.4713e+12    73  2.0155e+10       Root MSE      =   81980

------------------------------------------------------------------------------
        COST |      Coef.   Std. Err.      t    P>|t|     [95% Conf. Interval]
-------------+----------------------------------------------------------------
           N |   152.2982   60.01932    2.537   0.013     32.59349     272.003
         OCC |  -3501.177   41085.46   -0.085   0.932    -85443.55    78441.19
        NOCC |   284.4786   75.63211    3.761   0.000     133.6351    435.3221
       _cons |   51475.25   31314.84    1.644   0.105    -10980.24    113930.7
------------------------------------------------------------------------------
```

Putting *OCC* equal to 1, and hence *NOCC* equal to *N*, we estimate that the annual overhead cost of an occupational school is 47,000 yuan and the annual marginal cost per student is 436 yuan:

$$\text{Occupational schools: } \widehat{COST} = 51{,}000 - 4{,}000 + 152N + 284N$$
$$= 47{,}000 + 436N. \qquad (5.35)$$

The two cost functions are shown in Figure 5.5. You can see that they fit the data much better than before and that the real difference is in the marginal cost, not the overhead cost. We can now see why we had a nonsensical negative estimate of the overhead cost of a regular school in previous specifications. The assumption of the same marginal cost led to an estimate of the marginal cost that was a compromise between the marginal costs of occupational and regular schools. The cost function for regular schools was too steep and as a consequence the intercept was underestimated, actually becoming negative and indicating that something must be wrong with the specification of the model.

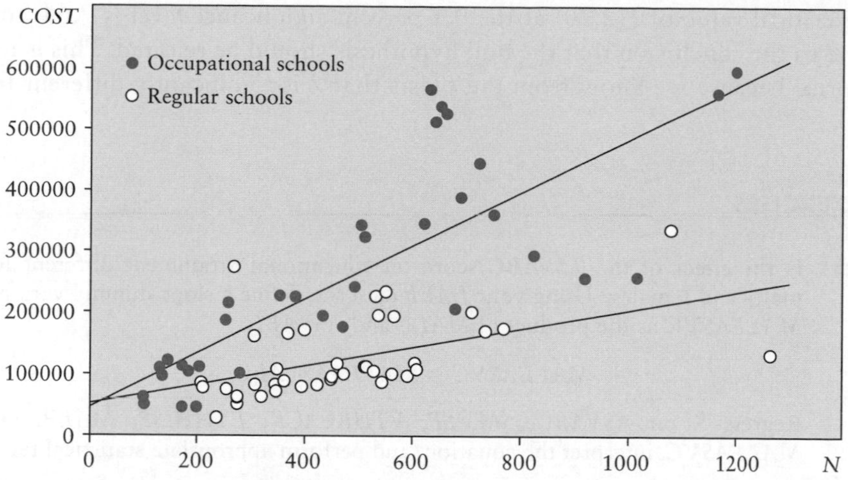

Figure 5.5 School cost functions with a slope dummy variable

We can perform t tests as usual. The t statistic for the coefficient of $NOCC$ is 3.76, so the marginal cost per student in an occupational school is significantly higher than that in a regular school. The coefficient of OCC is now negative, suggesting that the overhead cost of an occupational school is actually lower than that of a regular school. This is unlikely. However, the t statistic is only −0.09, so we do not reject the null hypothesis that the overhead costs of the two types of school are the same.

Joint explanatory power of the intercept and slope dummy variables

The joint explanatory power of the intercept and slope dummies can be tested with the usual F test for a group of variables, comparing RSS when the dummy variables are included with RSS when they are not. The null hypothesis is H_0: $\delta = \lambda = 0$. The alternative hypothesis is that one or both are nonzero. The numerator of the F statistic is the reduction in RSS when the dummies are added, divided by the cost in terms of degrees of freedom. RSS in the regression without the dummy variables was 8.9160×10^{11}, and in the regression with the dummy variables it was 4.7045×10^{11}. The cost is 2 because 2 extra parameters, the coefficients of the dummy variables, have been estimated, and as a consequence the number of degrees of freedom remaining has been reduced from 72 to 70. The denominator of the F statistic is RSS after the dummies have been added, divided by the number of degrees of freedom remaining. This is 70 because there are 74 observations and four parameters have been estimated. The F statistic is therefore

$$F(2,70) = \frac{(8.9160\times10^{11} - 4.7045\times10^{11})/2}{4.7045\times10^{11}/70} = 31.3. \qquad (5.36)$$

The critical value of $F(2,70)$ at the 0.1 percent significance level is 7.64, so we come to the conclusion that the null hypothesis should be rejected. This is not a surprise because we know from the t tests that λ is significantly different from zero.

EXERCISES

5.15 Is the effect of the *ASVABC* score on educational attainment different for males and females? Using your *EAEF* data set, define a slope dummy variable *MALEASVC* as the product of *MALE* and *ASVABC*:

$$MALEASVC = MALE*ASVABC.$$

Regress *S* on *ASVABC*, *SM*, *SF*, *ETHBLACK*, *ETHHISP*, *MALE*, and *MALEASVC*, interpret the equation, and perform appropriate statistical tests.

5.16* Is the effect of education on earnings different for members of a union? In the output below, *COLLBARG* is a dummy variable defined to be 1 for workers whose wages are determined by collective bargaining and 0 for the others. *SBARG* is a slope dummy variable defined as the product of *S* and *COLLBARG*. Provide an interpretation of the regression coefficients, comparing them with those in Exercise 5.9, and perform appropriate statistical tests.

```
. gen SBARG=S*COLLBARG
. reg LGEARN S EXP MALE COLLBARG SBARG
```

Source	SS	df	MS		
				Number of obs	= 540
				F(5, 534)	= 52.06
Model	61.1824375	5	12.2364875	Prob > F	= 0.0000
Residual	125.525206	534	.235065928	R-squared	= 0.3277
				Adj R-squared	= 0.3214
Total	186.707643	539	.34639637	Root MSE	= .48484

LGEARN	Coef.	Std. Err.	t	P>|t|	[95% Conf.	Interval]
S	.1234328	.0097343	12.68	0.000	.1043107	.142555
EXP	.0272315	.0049725	5.48	0.000	.0174635	.0369995
MALE	.2658057	.0430621	6.17	0.000	.1812137	.3503977
COLLBARG	.3669224	.3020525	1.21	0.225	-.2264344	.9602792
SBARG	-.0209955	.0216824	-0.97	0.333	-.0635887	.0215977
_cons	.4964114	.1684306	2.95	0.003	.1655436	.8272792

5.17 Is the effect of education on earnings different for males and females? Using your *EAEF* data set, define a slope dummy variable *MALES* as the product of *MALE* and *S*:

$$MALES = MALE*S.$$

Regress *LGEARN* on *S*, *ASVABC*, *EXP*, *ETHBLACK*, *ETHHISP*, *MALE*, and *MALES*, interpret the equation, and perform appropriate statistical tests.

5.18 Are there ethnic variations in the effect of the sex of a respondent on educational attainment? A special case of a slope dummy variable is the interactive dummy variable defined as the product of two dummy variables. Using your *EAEF* data set, define interactive dummy variables *MALEBLAC* and *MALEHISP* as the product of *MALE* and *ETHBLACK*, and of *MALE* and *ETHHISP*, respectively:

$$MALEBLAC = MALE * ETHBLACK$$
$$MALEHISP = MALE * ETHHISP.$$

Regress *S* on *ASVABC, SM, SF, MALE, ETHBLACK, ETHHISP, MALEBLAC* and *MALEHISP*. Interpret the regression results and perform appropriate statistical tests.

5.4 The Chow test

It sometimes happens that your sample of observations consists of two or more subsamples, and you are uncertain about whether you should run one combined regression or separate regressions for each subsample. Actually, in practice the choice is not usually as stark as this, because there may be some scope for combining the subsamples, using appropriate dummy and slope dummy variables to relax the assumption that all the coefficients must be the same for each subsample. This is a point to which we shall return.

Suppose that we have a sample consisting of two subsamples and that you are wondering whether to combine them in a pooled regression, *P*, or to run separate regressions, *A* and *B*. We will denote the residual sums of squares for the subsample regressions RSS_A and RSS_B. We will denote RSS_A^P and RSS_B^P the sum of the squares of the residuals in the pooled regression for the observations belonging to the two subsamples. Since the subsample regressions minimize *RSS* for their observations, they must fit them at least as well as, and generally better than, the pooled regression. Thus, $RSS_A \leq RSS_A^P$ and $RSS_B \leq RSS_B^P$, and so $(RSS_A + RSS_B) \leq RSS_P$, where RSS_P, the total sum of the squares of the residuals in the pooled regression, is equal to the sum of RSS_A^P and RSS_B^P.

Equality between RSS_P and $(RSS_A + RSS_B)$ will occur only when the regression coefficients for the pooled and subsample regressions coincide. In general, there will be an improvement $(RSS_P - RSS_A - RSS_B)$ when the sample is split up. There is a price to pay, in that *k* extra degrees of freedom are used up, since instead of *k* parameters for the pooled regression we now have to estimate *k* for each subsample, making $2k$ in all. After breaking up the sample, we are still left with $(RSS_A + RSS_B)$ (unexplained) sum of squares of the residuals, and we have $n - 2k$ degrees of freedom remaining.

We are now in a position to see whether the improvement in fit when we split the sample is significant, performing an *F* test known as the Chow test (Chow, 1960). We use the *F* statistic

$$F(k,n-2k) = \frac{\text{improvement in fit / extra degrees of freedom used up}}{\text{residual sum of squares remaining / degrees of freedom remaining}}$$
$$= \frac{(RSS_P - RSS_A - RSS_B)/k}{(RSS_A + RSS_B)/(n-2k)}, \tag{5.37}$$

which is distributed with k and $n - 2k$ degrees of freedom under the null hypothesis of no significant improvement in fit.

We will illustrate the Chow test with reference to the school cost function data, making a simple distinction between regular and occupational schools. We need to run three regressions. In the first, we regress *COST* on *N* using the whole sample of 74 schools. We have already done this in Section 5.1. This is the pooled regression. We make a note of *RSS* for it, 8.9160×10^{11}. In the second and third, we run the same regression for the two subsamples of regular and occupational schools separately and again make a note of *RSS*. The output for the subsample regressions is shown in Tables 5.13 and 5.14 and the regression lines are shown in Figure 5.6.

Table 5.13

```
. reg COST N if OCC==0

  Source  |      SS         df        MS           Number of obs =     40
----------+------------------------------------    F(1, 38)      =  13.53
   Model  |  4.3273e+10      1    4.3273e+10       Prob > F      = 0.0007
Residual  |  1.2150e+11     38    3.1973e+09       R-squared     = 0.2626
----------+------------------------------------    Adj R-squared = 0.2432
   Total  |  1.6477e+11     39    4.2249e+09       Root MSE      =  56545

------------------------------------------------------------------------------
   COST   |    Coef.     Std. Err.     t     P>|t|    [95% Conf. Interval]
----------+-------------------------------------------------------------------
      N   |  152.2982    41.39782    3.679   0.001    68.49275    236.1037
  _cons   |  51475.25    21599.14    2.383   0.022    7750.064    95200.43
------------------------------------------------------------------------------
```

Table 5.14

```
. reg COST N if OCC==1

  Source  |      SS         df        MS           Number of obs =     34
----------+------------------------------------    F(1, 32)      =  55.52
   Model  |  6.0538e+11      1    6.0538e+11       Prob > F      = 0.0007
Residual  |  3.4895e+11     32    1.0905e+10       R-squared     = 0.6344
----------+------------------------------------    Adj R-squared = 0.6229
   Total  |  9.5433e+11     33    2.8919e+10       Root MSE      =1.0e+05

------------------------------------------------------------------------------
   COST   |    Coef.     Std. Err.     t     P>|t|    [95% Conf. Interval]
----------+-------------------------------------------------------------------
      N   |  436.7769    58.62085    7.451   0.000    317.3701    556.1836
  _cons   |  47974.07    33879.03    1.416   0.166   -21035.26    116983.4
------------------------------------------------------------------------------
```

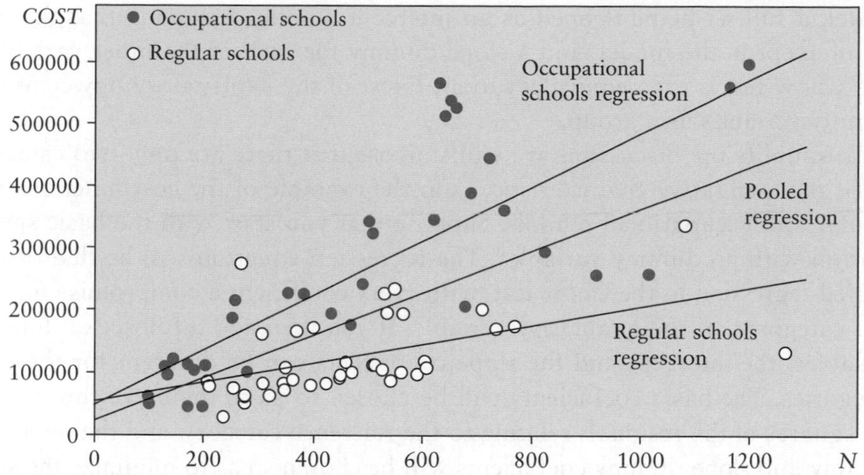

Figure 5.6 Pooled and subsample regression lines

RSS is 1.2150×10^{11} for the regular schools and 3.4895×10^{11} for the occupational schools. The total *RSS* from the subsample regressions is therefore 4.7045×10^{11}. It must be lower than *RSS* for the pooled regression. To see if it is significantly lower, we perform the Chow test. The numerator of the *F* statistic is the improvement in fit on splitting the sample, $(8.9160 - 4.7045)\times10^{11}$, divided by the cost in terms of degrees of freedom. The latter is equal to two because we have had to estimate two intercepts and two slope coefficients, instead of only one of each. The denominator is the joint *RSS* remaining after splitting the sample, 4.7045×10^{11}, divided by the joint number of degrees of freedom remaining. The latter is equal to 70 since there are 74 observations and we have used up four degrees of freedom estimating two parameters in each equation. When we calculate the *F* statistic, the 10^{11} factors cancel out and we have

$$F(2,70) = \frac{(8.9160 - 4.7045)\times10^{11}/2}{4.7045\times10^{11}/70} = 31.3. \tag{5.38}$$

The critical value of $F(2,70)$ at the 0.1 percent significance level is 7.64, so we come to the conclusion that there is a significant improvement in the fit on splitting the sample and that we should not use the pooled regression.

Relationship between the Chow test and the *F* test of the explanatory power of a set of dummy variables

In this chapter, we have used both dummy variables and a Chow test to investigate whether there are significant differences in a regression model for different categories of a qualitative characteristic. Could the two approaches have led to different conclusions? The answer is no, provided that a full set of dummy variables for the qualitative characteristic has been included in the regression model, a full set being defined as an intercept dummy, assuming that there is an intercept in the model, and a slope dummy for each of the other variables. The Chow test is then equivalent to an F test of the explanatory power of the dummy variables as a group.

To simplify the discussion, we will suppose that there are only two categories of the qualitative characteristic, as in the example of the cost functions for regular and occupational schools. Suppose that you start with the basic specification with no dummy variables. The regression equation will be that of the pooled regression in the Chow test, with every coefficient a compromise for the two categories of the qualitative variable. If you then add a full set of dummy variables, the intercept and the slope coefficients can be different for the two categories. The basic coefficients will be chosen so as to minimize the sum of the squares of the residuals relating to the reference category, and the intercept dummy and slope dummy coefficients will be chosen so as to minimize the sum of the squares of the residuals for the other category. Effectively, the outcome of the estimation of the coefficients is the same as if you had run separate regressions for the two categories.

In the school cost function example, the implicit cost functions for regular and occupational schools with a full set of dummy variables (in this case, just an intercept dummy and a slope dummy for N), shown in Figure 5.5, are identical to the cost functions for the subsample regressions in the Chow test, shown in Figure 5.6. It follows that the improvement in the fit, as measured by the reduction in the residual sum of squares, when one adds the dummy variables to the basic specification is identical to the improvement in fit on splitting the sample and running subsample regressions. The cost, in terms of degrees of freedom, is also the same. In the dummy variable approach you have to add an intercept dummy and a slope dummy for each variable, so the cost is k if there are $k - 1$ variables in the model. In the Chow test, the cost is also k because you have to estimate $2k$ parameters instead of k when you split the sample. Thus, the numerator of the F statistic is the same for both tests. The denominator is also the same because in both cases it is the residual sum of squares for the subsample regressions divided by $n - 2k$. In the case of the Chow test, $2k$ degrees of freedom are used up when fitting the separate regressions. In the case of the dummy variable group test, k degrees of freedom are used up when estimating the original intercept and slope coefficients, and a further k degrees of freedom are used up estimating the intercept dummy and the slope dummy coefficients.

What are the advantages and disadvantages of the two approaches? The Chow test is quick. You just run the three regressions and compute the test statistic. But it does not tell you how the functions differ, if they do. The dummy variable approach involves more preparation because you have to define a dummy variable for the intercept and for each slope coefficient. However, it is more informative because you can perform t tests on the individual dummy coefficients and they may indicate where the functions differ, if they do.

Key terms

- Chow test
- dummy variable
- dummy variable trap
- omitted category
- reference category
- slope dummy variable

EXERCISES

5.19 Are educational attainment functions different for males and females? Using your *EAEF* data set, regress *S* on *ASVABC*, *ETHBLACK*, *ETHHISP*, *SM*, and *SF* (do not include *MALE*). Repeat the regression using only the male respondents. Repeat it again using only the female respondents. Perform a Chow test.

5.20 Are earnings functions different for males and females? Using your *EAEF* data set, regress *LGEARN* on *S*, *EXP*, *ETHBLACK*, and *ETHHISP* (do not include *MALE*). Repeat the regression using only the male respondents. Repeat it again using only the female respondents. Perform a Chow test.

5.21 Are there differences in male and female educational attainment functions? This question has been answered by Exercise 5.19 but nevertheless it is instructive to investigate the issue using the dummy variable approach. Using your *EAEF* data set, define the following slope dummies combining *MALE* with the parental education variables:

$$MALESM = MALE*SM$$
$$MALESF = MALE*SF$$

and regress *S* on *ETHBLACK*, *ETHHISP*, *ASVABC*, *SM*, *SF*, *MALE*, *MALEBLAC*, *MALEHISP* (defined in Exercise 5.18), *MALEASVC* (defined in Exercise 5.15), *MALESM*, and *MALESF*. Next regress *S* on *ETHBLACK*, *ETHHISP*, *ASVABC*, *SM*, and *SF* only. Perform an *F* test of the joint explanatory power of *MALE* and the slope dummy variables as a group (verify that the *F* statistic is the same as in Exercise 5.19) and perform *t* tests on the coefficients of the slope dummy variables in the first regression. Calculate the correlations among the dummy variables.

5.22 Where are the differences in male and female earnings functions? Using your *EAEF* data set, regress *LGEARN* on *S*, *EXP*, *ETHBLACK*, *ETHHISP*, *MALE*, *MALES*, *MALEEXP*, *MALEBLAC*, and *MALEHISP*. Next regress *LGEARN* on *S*, *EXP*, *ETHBLACK*, and *ETHHISP* only. Calculate the correlation matrix for *MALE* and the slope dummies. Perform an *F* test of the joint explanatory power of *MALE* and the slope dummies (verify that the *F* statistic is the same as in Exercise 5.20) and perform *t* tests on the coefficients of the dummy variables. *MALEEXP* should be defined as the product of *MALE* and *EXP*:

$$MALEEXP = MALE*EXP.$$

6. Specification of Regression Variables

What are the consequences of including in the regression model a variable that should not be there? What are the consequences of leaving out a variable that should be included? What happens if you have difficulty finding data on a variable and use a proxy instead? This chapter is a preliminary skirmish with these issues in the sense that it focuses on the consequences of variable misspecification, rather than on procedures for model selection, a much more complex subject that is left to later in the text. The chapter concludes by showing how simple restrictions on the parameters can be tested.

6.1 Model specification

The construction of an economic model involves the specification of the relationships that constitute it, the specification of the variables that participate in each relationship, and the mathematical function representing each relationship. The last element was discussed in Chapter 4. In this chapter, we will consider the second element, and we will continue to assume that the model consists of just one equation. We will discuss the application of regression analysis to models consisting of systems of simultaneous relationships in Chapter 9.

If we know exactly which explanatory variables ought to be included in the equation when we undertake regression analysis, our task is limited to calculating estimates of their coefficients, confidence intervals for these estimates, and so on. In practice, however, we can never be sure that we have specified the equation correctly. Economic theory ought to provide a guide, but theory is never perfect. Without being aware of it, we might be including some variables that ought not to be in the model, and we might be leaving out others that ought to be included.

The properties of the regression estimates of the coefficients depend crucially on the validity of the specification of the model. The consequences of misspecification of the variables in a relationship are summarized in Table 6.1.

1. If you leave out a variable that ought to be included, the regression estimates are in general (but not always) biased. The standard errors of the coefficients and the corresponding *t* tests are in general invalid.

Table 6.1 Consequences of variable specification

		True model	
		$Y = \beta_1 + \beta_2 X_2 + u$	$Y = \beta_1 + \beta_2 X_2 + \beta_3 X_3 + u$
Fitted model	$\hat{Y} = b_1 + b_2 X_2$	Correct specification, no problems	Coefficients are biased (in general). Standard errors are invalid
	$\hat{Y} = b_1 + b_2 X_2 + b_3 X_3$	Coefficients are unbiased (in general) but inefficient. Standard errors are valid (in general)	Correct specification, no problems

2. If you include a variable that ought not to be in the equation, the regression coefficients are in general (but not always) inefficient but not biased. The standard errors are in general valid but, because the regression estimation is inefficient, they will be needlessly large.

We will begin by discussing these two cases and then come to some broader issues of model specification.

6.2 The effect of omitting a variable that ought to be included

The problem of bias

Suppose that the dependent variable Y depends on two variables X_2 and X_3 according to a relationship

$$Y = \beta_1 + \beta_2 X_2 + \beta_3 X_3 + u, \tag{6.1}$$

but you are unaware of the importance of X_3. Thinking that the model should be

$$Y = \beta_1 + \beta_2 X_2 + u, \tag{6.2}$$

you use regression analysis to fit

$$\hat{Y} = b_1 + b_2 X_2, \tag{6.3}$$

and you calculate b_2 using the expression

$$b_2 = \frac{\sum_{i=1}^{n}(X_i - \bar{X})(Y_i - \bar{Y})}{\sum_{i=1}^{n}(X_i - \bar{X})^2} \tag{6.4}$$

instead of the correct expression for a regression with two explanatory variables. By definition, b_2 is an unbiased estimator of b_2 if and only if $E(b_2)$ is equal to b_2. In fact, if (6.1) is true,

$$E\left[\frac{\sum_{i=1}^{n}(X_{2i}-\bar{X}_2)(Y_i-\bar{Y})}{\sum_{i=1}^{n}(X_{2i}-\bar{X}_2)^2}\right]=\beta_2+\beta_3\frac{\sum_{i=1}^{n}(X_{2i}-\bar{X}_2)(X_{3i}-\bar{X}_3)}{\sum_{i=1}^{n}(X_{2i}-\bar{X}_2)^2} \qquad \textbf{(6.5)}$$

and b_2 is then described as being subject to omitted variable bias. We shall give first an intuitive explanation of (6.5) and then a formal proof.

If X_3 is omitted from the regression model, X_2 will appear to have a double effect, as illustrated in Figure 6.1. It will have a direct effect and also a proxy effect when it mimics the effect of X_3. The apparent indirect effect of X_2 on Y depends on two factors: the apparent ability of X_2 to mimic X_3, and the effect of X_3 on Y.

The apparent ability of X_2 to explain X_3 is determined by the slope coefficient h in the pseudo-regression

$$\hat{X}_3 = g + hX_2. \qquad \textbf{(6.6)}$$

h of course is given by the usual simple regression formula

$$h=\frac{\sum_{i=1}^{n}(X_{2i}-\bar{X}_2)(X_{3i}-\bar{X}_3)}{\sum_{i=1}^{n}(X_{2i}-\bar{X}_2)^2}. \qquad \textbf{(6.7)}$$

The effect of X_3 on Y is β_3, so the mimic effect via X_3 may be written $\beta_3\frac{\sum(X_{2i}-\bar{X}_2)(X_{3i}-\bar{X}_3)}{\sum(X_{2i}-\bar{X}_2)^2}$. The direct effect of X_2 on Y is β_2, and hence when Y

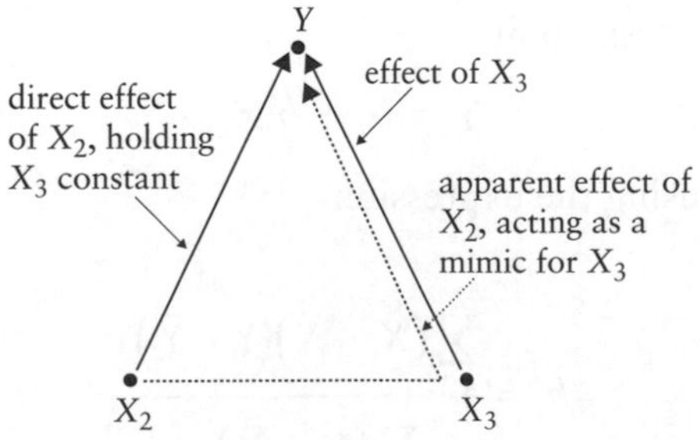

Figure 6.1 Direct and indirect effects of X_2 when X_3 is omitted

is regressed on X_2, omitting X_3, the coefficient of X_2 is given by

$$\beta_2 + \beta_3 \frac{\sum_{i=1}^{n}(X_{2i}-\bar{X}_2)(X_{3i}-\bar{X}_3)}{\sum_{i=1}^{n}(X_{2i}-\bar{X}_2)^2} + \text{sampling error.} \tag{6.8}$$

Provided that X_2 and X_3 are nonstochastic, the expected value of the coefficient will be the sum of the first two terms. The presence of the second term implies that in general the expected value of the coefficient will be different from the true value β_2 and therefore biased.

The formal proof of (6.5) is straightforward. We begin by making a theoretical expansion of the estimator b_2, replacing Y_i and $\bar{Y}$ using (6.1):

$$\begin{aligned}
b_2 &= \frac{\sum_{i=1}^{n}(X_{2i}-\bar{X}_2)(Y_i-\bar{Y})}{\sum_{i=1}^{n}(X_{2i}-\bar{X}_2)^2} \\
&= \frac{\sum_{i=1}^{n}(X_{2i}-\bar{X}_2)\left([\beta_1+\beta_2X_{2i}+\beta_3X_{3i}+u_i]-[\beta_1+\beta_2\bar{X}_2+\beta_3\bar{X}_3+\bar{u}]\right)}{\sum_{i=1}^{n}(X_{2i}-\bar{X}_2)^2} \\
&= \frac{\beta_2\sum_{i=1}^{n}(X_{2i}-\bar{X}_2)^2+\beta_3\sum_{i=1}^{n}(X_{2i}-\bar{X}_2)(X_{3i}-\bar{X}_3)+\sum_{i=1}^{n}(X_{2i}-\bar{X}_2)(u_i-\bar{u})}{\sum_{i=1}^{n}(X_{2i}-\bar{X}_2)^2} \\
&= \beta_2+\beta_3\frac{\sum_{i=1}^{n}(X_{2i}-\bar{X}_2)(X_{3i}-\bar{X}_3)}{\sum_{i=1}^{n}(X_{2i}-\bar{X}_2)^2}+\frac{\sum_{i=1}^{n}(X_{2i}-\bar{X}_2)(u_i-\bar{u})}{\sum_{i=1}^{n}(X_{2i}-\bar{X}_2)^2}.
\end{aligned} \tag{6.9}$$

Provided that X_2 and X_3 are nonstochastic, the first two terms are unaffected when we take expectations and the third is zero. Hence we obtain (6.5). Since $\sum(X_{2i}-\bar{X}_2)^2$ must be positive (except in the case where X_2 is constant in all observations, in which case it would not be possible to run a regression), the direction of the bias will depend on the signs of β_3 and $\sum(X_{2i}-\bar{X}_2)(X_{3i}-\bar{X}_3)$. We note that the latter is the numerator of the sample correlation between X_2 and X_3, $r_{X_2X_3}$:

$$r_{X_2X_3} = \frac{\sum_{i=1}^{n}(X_{2i}-\bar{X}_2)(X_{3i}-\bar{X}_3)}{\sqrt{\sum_{i=1}^{n}(X_{2i}-\bar{X}_2)^2\sum_{i=1}^{n}(X_{3i}-\bar{X}_3)^2}}. \tag{6.10}$$

The denominator of the correlation coefficient must be positive (unless it is zero, in which case it would not be possible to run a regression). Hence, the sign of $\sum(X_{2i} - \bar{X}_2)(X_{3i} - \bar{X}_3)$ is the same as that of the correlation coefficient.

For example, if β_3 is positive and the correlation is positive, the bias will be positive and b_2 will tend to overestimate β_2. There is, however, one exceptional case where b_2 is unbiased after all. That is when the sample correlation between X_2 and X_3 happens to be exactly zero. This would occur if $\sum(X_{2i} - \bar{X}_2)(X_{3i} - \bar{X}_3)$ is zero, and then the bias term disappears. Indeed, the regression coefficient obtained using simple regression will be exactly the same as if you had used a properly specified multiple regression. Of course, the bias term would also be zero if β_3 were zero, but then the model is not misspecified.

Invalidation of the statistical tests

Another serious consequence of omitting a variable that ought to be included in the regression is that the standard errors of the coefficients and the test statistics are in general invalidated. This means of course that you are not in principle able to test any hypotheses with your regression results.

EXAMPLE

The problem of omitted variable bias will first be illustrated with the educational attainment function using *EAEF* Data Set 21. For the present purposes, it will be assumed that the true model is

$$S = \beta_1 + \beta_2 ASVABC + \beta_3 SM + u, \tag{6.11}$$

although obviously this is a great oversimplification. Table 6.2 shows the result of this regression. Tables 6.3 and 6.4 then show the effects of omitting *SM* and *ASVABC*, respectively.

Table 6.2

```
. reg S ASVABC SM

      Source |       SS           df        MS           Number of obs =     540
-----------------------------------------------------    F(2, 537)     =  147.36
       Model |   1135.67473        2    567.837363       Prob > F      =  0.0000
    Residual |   2069.30861      537    3.85346109       R-squared     =  0.3543
-----------------------------------------------------    Adj R-squared =  0.3519
       Total |   3204.98333      539    5.94616574       Root MSE      =   1.963

------------------------------------------------------------------------------
           S |     Coef.     Std. Err.      t     P>|t|     [95% Conf. Interval]
------------------------------------------------------------------------------
      ASVABC |   .1328069    .0097389    13.64    0.000     .1136758    .151938
          SM |   .1235071    .0330837     3.73    0.000     .0585178   .1884963
       _cons |   5.420733    .4930224    10.99    0.000     4.452244   6.389222
------------------------------------------------------------------------------
```

Table 6.3

. reg S ASVABC

Source	SS	df	MS		
				Number of obs	= 540
				F(2, 538)	= 274.19
Model	1081.97059	1	1081.97059	Prob > F	= 0.0000
Residual	2123.01275	538	3.94612035	R-squared	= 0.3376
				Adj R-squared	= 0.3519
Total	3204.98333	539	5.94616574	Root MSE	= 1.9865

S	Coef.	Std. Err.	t	P>|t|	[95% Conf.	Interval]
ASVABC	.148084	.0089431	16.56	0.000	.1305165	.1656516
_cons	6.066225	.4672261	12.98	0.000	5.148413	6.984036

Table 6.4

. reg S SM

Source	SS	df	MS		
				Number of obs	= 540
				F(1, 538)	= 80.93
Model	419.086251	1	419.086251	Prob > F	= 0.0000
Residual	2785.89708	538	5.17824736	R-squared	= 0.1308
				Adj R-squared	= 0.1291
Total	3204.98333	539	5.94616574	Root MSE	= 2.2756

S	Coef.	Std. Err.	t	P>|t|	[95% Conf.	Interval]
SM	.3130793	.0348012	9.00	0.000	.2447165	.3814422
_cons	10.04688	.4147121	24.23	0.000	9.232226	10.86153

When *SM* is omitted,

$$E(b_2) = \beta_2 + \beta_3 \frac{\sum_{i=1}^{n}\left(ASVABC_i - \overline{ASVABC}\right)\left(SM_i - \overline{SM}\right)}{\sum_{i=1}^{n}\left(ASVABC_i - \overline{ASVABC}\right)^2}. \tag{6.12}$$

The correlation between *ASVABC* and *SM* is positive (0.42). Therefore the numerator of the bias term is positive. The denominator must be positive (unless equal to zero, in which case it would not be possible to perform the regression). It is reasonable to assume that β_3 is positive, and the fact that its estimate in the first regression is indeed positive and highly significant provides overwhelming corroborative evidence. One would therefore anticipate that the coefficient of *ASVABC* will be upwards biased when *SM* is omitted, and you can see that it is indeed higher. Not all of the difference should be attributed to bias. Part of it may be attributable to the effects of the disturbance term, which could go either way.

Similarly, when *ASVABC* is omitted,

$$E(b_3) = \beta_3 + \beta_2 \frac{\sum_{i=1}^{n}\left(ASVABC - \overline{ASVABC}\right)\left(SM - \overline{SM}\right)}{\sum_{i=1}^{n}\left(SM - \overline{SM}\right)^2}. \tag{6.13}$$

Since β_2 is also likely to be positive, the coefficient of *SM* in the third regression should be upwards biased. The estimate in the third regression is indeed higher than that in the first.

In this example, the omission of one explanatory variable causes the coefficient of the other to be overestimated. However, the bias could just as easily be negative. The sign of the bias depends on the sign of the true coefficient of the omitted variable and on the sign of the correlation between the included and omitted variables, and these will depend on the nature of the model being investigated.

It should be emphasized that the analysis above applies only to the case where the true model is a multiple regression model with two explanatory variables. When there are more explanatory variables, it may be difficult to predict the impact of omitted variable bias mathematically. Nevertheless, it may be possible to conclude that the estimates of the coefficients of some of the variables may have been inflated or deflated by the bias.

R^2 in the presence of omitted variable bias

In Section 3.5 it was asserted that in general it is impossible to determine the contribution to R^2 of each explanatory variable in multiple regression analysis, and we are now in a position to see why.

We will discuss the issue first with reference to the educational attainment model above. In the regression of *S* on *ASVABC* alone, R^2 was 0.34. In the regression on *SM* alone, it was 0.13. Does this mean that *ASVABC* explains 34 percent of the variation in *S*, and *SM* 13 percent? No, because this would imply that together they would explain 47 percent of the variation, and this conflicts with the finding in the multiple regression that their joint explanatory power is 0.35.

The explanation is that in the simple regression of *S* on *ASVABC*, *ASVABC* is acting partly as a variable in its own right and partly as a proxy for the missing *SM*, as in Figure 6.1. R^2 for that regression therefore reflects the combined explanatory power of *ASVABC* in both of these roles, and not just its direct explanatory power. Hence 0.34 overestimates the latter.

Similarly, in the simple regression of *S* on *SM*, *SM* is acting partly as a proxy for the missing *ASVABC*, and the level of R^2 in that regression reflects the combined explanatory power of *SM* in both those roles, and not just its direct explanatory power.

In this example, the explanatory power of the two variables overlapped, with the consequence that R^2 in the multiple regression was less than the sum of R^2 in the individual simple regressions. However, it is also possible for R^2 in the multiple regression to be greater than the sum of R^2 in the individual simple regressions, as is shown in the regression output in Tables 6.5–6.7 for an earnings function model. It is assumed that the true model is

$$LGEARN = \beta_1 + \beta_2 S + \beta_3 EXP + u. \tag{6.14}$$

Table 6.5 shows the result of fitting (6.14), and Tables 6.6 and 6.7 show the results of omitting, first *EXP*, and then *S*. R^2 in the multiple regression is 0.27, while it is 0.21 and 0.02 in the simple regressions, the sum being 0.23. As in the previous example, it can be assumed that both β_2 and β_3 are positive. However, *S* and *EXP* are negatively correlated, so in this case the coefficients of *S* and *EXP* in the second and third regressions may be expected to be biased downwards. As a consequence, the apparent explanatory power of *S* and *EXP* in the simple regressions is underestimated.

Table 6.5

```
. reg LGEARN S EXP
```

Source	SS	df	MS		
Model	50.9842581	2	25.492129	Number of obs =	540
Residual	135.723385	537	.252743734	F(2, 537)	= 100.86
Total	186.707643	539	.34639637	Prob > F	= 0.0000
				R-squared	= 0.2731
				Adj R-squared	= 0.2704
				Root MSE	= .50274

LGEARN	Coef.	Std. Err.	t	P>|t|	[95% Conf.	Interval]
S	.1235911	.0090989	13.58	0.000	.1057173	.141465
EXP	.0350826	.0050046	7.01	0.000	.0252515	.0449137
_cons	.5093196	.1663823	3.06	0.002	.1824796	.8361596

Table 6.6

```
. reg LGEARN S
```

Source	SS	df	MS		
Model	38.5643833	1	38.5643833	Number of obs =	540
Residual	148.14326	538	.275359219	F(1, 538)	= 140.05
Total	186.707643	539	.34639637	Prob > F	= 0.0000
				R-squared	= 0.2065
				Adj R-squared	= 0.2051
				Root MSE	= .52475

LGEARN	Coef.	Std. Err.	t	P>|t|	[95% Conf.	Interval]
S	.1096934	.0092691	11.83	0.000	.0914853	.1279014
_cons	1.292241	.1287252	10.04	0.000	1.039376	1.545107

Table 6.7

```
. reg LGEARN EXP

      Source |       SS       df       MS              Number of obs =     540
-------------+------------------------------           F(1, 538)     =   12.84
       Model |  4.35309315     1  4.35309315           Prob > F      =  0.0004
    Residual |   182.35455   538  .338948978           R-squared     =  0.0233
-------------+------------------------------           Adj R-squared =  0.0215
       Total |  186.707643   539   .34639637           Root MSE      =  .58219

------------------------------------------------------------------------------
      LGEARN |      Coef.   Std. Err.      t    P>|t|     [95% Conf. Interval]
-------------+----------------------------------------------------------------
         EXP |   .0202708   .0056564     3.58   0.000     .0091595     .031382
       _cons |    2.44941   .0988233    24.79   0.000     2.255284    2.643537
------------------------------------------------------------------------------
```

EXERCISES

6.1 Using your *EAEF* data set, regress *S* (1) on *ASVABC* and *SM*, (2) on *ASVABC* only, and (3) on *SM* only. Calculate the correlation between *ASVABC* and *SM*. Compare the coefficients of *ASVABC* in regressions (1) and (2). Give both mathematical and intuitive explanations of direction of the change. Also compare the coefficients of *SM* in regressions (1) and (3) and explain the direction of the change.

6.2 Using your *EAEF* data set, regress *LGEARN* (1) on *S* and *EXP*, (2) on *S* only, and (3) on *EXP* only. Calculate the correlation between *S* and *EXP*. Compare the coefficients of *S* in regressions (1) and (2). Give both mathematical and intuitive explanations of the direction of the change. Also compare the coefficients of *EXP* in regressions (1) and (3) and explain the direction of the change.

6.3 Using your *EAEF* data set, regress *LGEARN* (1) on *S*, *EXP*, *MALE*, *ETHHISP*, and *ETHBLACK*, and (2) on *S*, *EXP*, *MALE*, *ETHHISP*, *ETHBLACK*, and *ASVABC*. Calculate the correlation coefficients for the explanatory variables and discuss the differences in the regression results. (A detailed mathematical analysis is not expected.)

6.4* The table gives the results of multiple and simple regressions of *LGFDHO*, the logarithm of annual household expenditure on food eaten at home, on *LGEXP*, the logarithm of total annual household expenditure, and *LGSIZE*, the logarithm of the number of persons in the household, using a sample of 868 households in the 1995 Consumer Expenditure Survey. The correlation coefficient for *LGEXP* and *LGSIZE* was 0.45. Explain the variations in the regression coefficients.

	(1)	(2)	(3)
LGEXP	0.29	0.48	–
	(0.02)	(0.02)	
LGSIZE	0.49	–	0.63
	(0.03)		(0.02)
constant	4.72	3.17	7.50
	(0.22)	(0.24)	(0.02)
R^2	0.52	0.31	0.42

6.5 Suppose that Y is determined by X_2 and X_3 according to the relationship

$$Y = \beta_1 + \beta_2 X_2 + \beta_3 X_3 + u,$$

and that the correlation between X_2 and X_3, and hence $\sum (X_{2i} - \bar{X}_2)(X_{3i} - \bar{X}_3)$, is zero. Use this to simplify the multiple regression coefficient b_2 given by

$$b_2 = \frac{\sum_{i=1}^{n}(X_{2i} - \bar{X}_2)(Y_i - \bar{Y})\sum_{i=1}^{n}(X_{3i} - \bar{X}_3)^2 - \sum_{i=1}^{n}(X_{3i} - \bar{X}_3)(Y_i - \bar{Y})\sum_{i=1}^{n}(X_{2i} - \bar{X}_2)(X_{3i} - \bar{X}_3)}{\sum_{i=1}^{n}(X_{2i} - \bar{X}_2)^2\sum_{i=1}^{n}(X_{3i} - \bar{X}_3)^2 - \left(\sum_{i=1}^{n}(X_{2i} - \bar{X}_2)(X_{3i} - \bar{X}_3)\right)^2}$$

and show that it reduces to the simple regression expression. What are the implications for the specification of the regression equation?

6.6 In a Monte Carlo experiment, a variable Y was generated as a linear function of two variables X_2 and X_3:

$$Y = 10.0 + 10.0X_2 + 0.5X_3 + u,$$

where X_2 was the sequence of integers 1, 2, ..., 30, X_3 was generated from X_2 by adding random numbers, and u was a disturbance term with a normal distribution with mean zero and variance 10,000. The correlation between X_2 and X_3 was 0.95. The table shows the result of fitting the following regressions for 10 samples:

Model A $\hat{Y} = b_1 + b_2 X_2 + b_3 X_3$

Model B $\hat{Y} = b_1 + b_2 X_2$.

The figure shows the distributions of b_2 for the two models for 10 million samples. In the case of Model A, the distribution of b_2 had mean 10.001 and standard deviation 6.910. For Model B, the mean was 10.500 and the standard deviation was 2.109.

Comment on all aspects of the regression results, giving full explanations of what you observe.

	Model A					Model B		
Sample	b_2	s.e.(b_2)	b_3	s.e.(b_3)	R^2	b_2	s.e.(b_2)	R^2
1	10.68	6.05	0.60	5.76	0.5800	11.28	1.82	0.5799
2	7.52	7.11	3.74	6.77	0.5018	11.26	2.14	0.4961
3	7.26	6.58	2.93	6.26	0.4907	10.20	1.98	0.4865
4	11.47	8.60	0.23	8.18	0.4239	11.70	2.58	0.4239
5	13.07	6.07	−3.04	5.78	0.5232	10.03	1.83	0.5183
6	16.74	6.63	−4.01	6.32	0.5966	12.73	2.00	0.5906
7	15.70	7.50	−4.80	7.14	0.4614	10.90	2.27	0.4523
8	8.01	8.10	1.50	7.71	0.3542	9.51	2.43	0.3533
9	1.08	6.78	9.52	6.45	0.5133	10.61	2.11	0.4740
10	13.09	7.58	−0.87	7.21	0.5084	12.22	2.27	0.5081

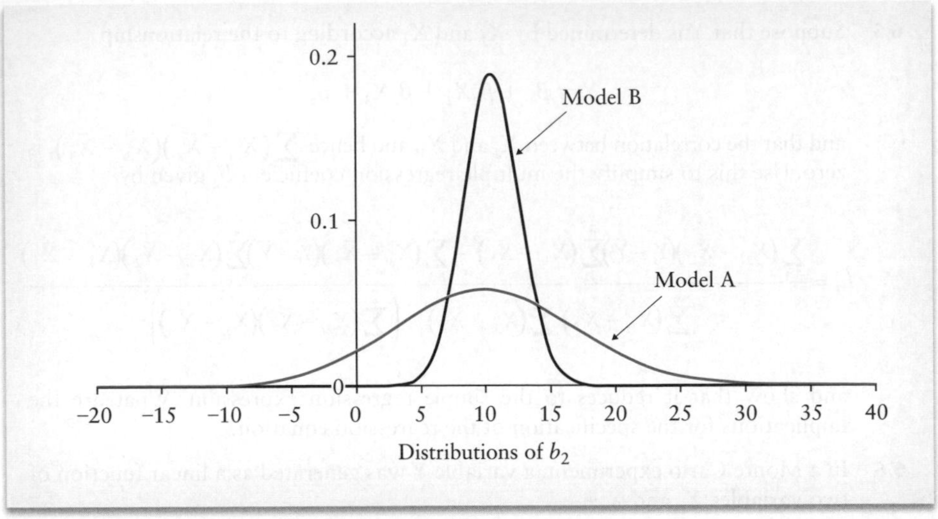

6.3 The effect of including a variable that ought not to be included

Suppose that the true model is

$$Y = \beta_1 + \beta_2 X_2 + u \tag{6.15}$$

and you think it is

$$Y = \beta_1 + \beta_2 X_2 + \beta_3 X_3 + u, \tag{6.16}$$

and you estimate b_2 using

$$b_2 = \frac{\sum_{i=1}^{n}(X_{2i}-\bar{X}_2)(Y_i-\bar{Y})\sum_{i=1}^{n}(X_{3i}-\bar{X}_3)^2 - \sum_{i=1}^{n}(X_{3i}-\bar{X}_3)(Y_i-\bar{Y})\sum_{i=1}^{n}(X_{2i}-\bar{X}_2)(X_{3i}-\bar{X}_3)}{\sum_{i=1}^{n}(X_{2i}-\bar{X}_2)^2\sum_{i=1}^{n}(X_{3i}-\bar{X}_3)^2 - \left(\sum_{i=1}^{n}(X_{2i}-\bar{X}_2)(X_{3i}-\bar{X}_3)\right)^2} \tag{6.17}$$

instead of

$$b_2 = \frac{\sum_{i=1}^{n}(X_i-\bar{X})(Y_i-\bar{Y})}{\sum_{i=1}^{n}(X_i-\bar{X})^2}. \tag{6.18}$$

In general there is no problem of bias if you include a redundant variable in the model, even though b_2 has been calculated incorrectly. $E(b_2)$ will still be equal to β_2, but in general b_2 will be an inefficient estimator. It will be more erratic, in the sense of having a larger variance about β_2, than if it had been calculated correctly. This is illustrated in Figure 6.2.

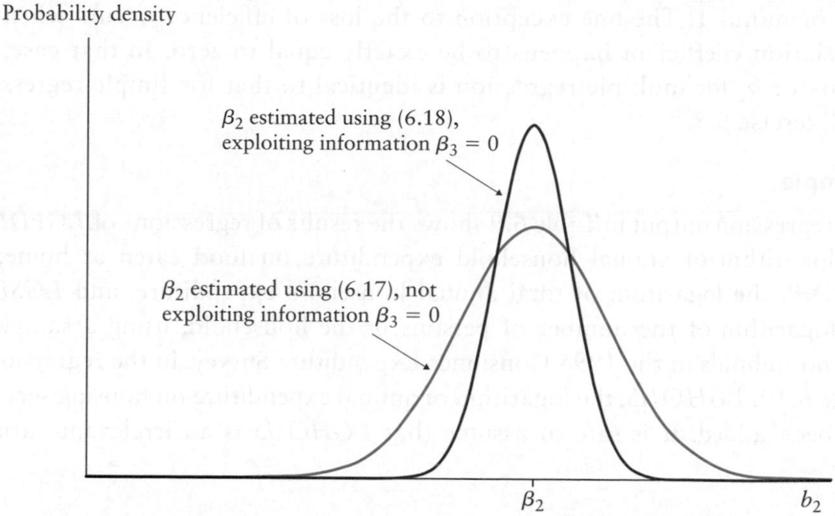

Figure 6.2 Loss of efficiency caused by the inclusion of an irrelevant variable

There is a simple intuitive explanation. The true model may be rewritten

$$Y = \beta_1 + \beta_2 X_2 + 0X_3 + u. \tag{6.19}$$

So if you regress Y on X_2 and X_3, b_2 will be an unbiased estimator of β_2 and b_3 will be an unbiased estimator of zero, provided that the regression model conditions are satisfied. Effectively, you are discovering for yourself that $\beta_3 = 0$. If you realized beforehand that $\beta_3 = 0$, you would be able to exploit this information to exclude X_3 and use simple regression, which in this context is more efficient.

The loss of efficiency caused by including X_3 when it ought not to be included depends on the correlation between X_2 and X_3. Compare the expressions for the variances of b_2 using simple and multiple regression in Table 6.8. The variance will in general be larger in the case of multiple regression, and the difference will be the greater, the closer the correlation coefficient is to

Table 6.8 Slope coefficient variances

Simple regression	*Multiple regression*
$\sigma_{b_2}^2 = \dfrac{\sigma_u^2}{\sum_{i=1}^{n}(X_{2i}-\bar{X}_2)^2}$	$\sigma_{b_2}^2 = \dfrac{\sigma_u^2}{\sum_{i=1}^{n}(X_{21}-\bar{X}_2)^2}\dfrac{1}{(1-r_{X_2X_3}^2)}$

plus or minus 1. The one exception to the loss of efficiency occurs when the correlation coefficient happens to be exactly equal to zero. In that case, the estimator b_2 for multiple regression is identical to that for simple regression. See Exercise 6.5.

Example

The regression output in Table 6.9 shows the results of regressions of *LGFDHO*, the logarithm of annual household expenditure on food eaten at home, on *LGEXP*, the logarithm of total annual household expenditure, and *LGSIZE*, the logarithm of the number of persons in the household, using a sample of 868 households in the 1995 Consumer Expenditure Survey. In the regression in Table 6.10, *LGHOUS*, the logarithm of annual expenditure on housing services, has been added. It is safe to assume that *LGHOUS* is an irrelevant variable

Table 6.9

```
. reg LGFDHO LGEXP LGSIZE

  Source   |       SS          df         MS             Number of obs =      868
-----------------------------------------------------    F(2, 865)     =   460.92
   Model   |   138.776549       2     69.3882747         Prob > F      =   0.0000
Residual   |   130.219231     865     .150542464         R-squared     =   0.5159
-----------------------------------------------------    Adj R-squared =   0.5148
   Total   |   268.995781     867     .310260416         Root MSE      =      388

---------------------------------------------------------------------------------
  LGFDHO   |     Coef.      Std. Err.      t     P>|t|     [95% Conf. Interval]
---------------------------------------------------------------------------------
   LGEXP   |   .2866813     .0226824    12.639   0.000     .2421622     .3312003
  LGSIZE   |   .4854698     .0255476    19.003   0.000     .4353272     .5356124
   _cons   |   4.720269     .2209996    21.359   0.000     4.286511     5.154027
---------------------------------------------------------------------------------
```

Table 6.10

```
. reg LGFDHO LGEXP LGSIZE LGHOUS

  Source   |       SS          df         MS             Number of obs =      868
-----------------------------------------------------    F(3, 864)     =   307.22
   Model   |   138.841976       3     46.2806586         Prob > F      =   0.0000
Residual   |   130.153805     864     .150640978         R-squared     =   0.5161
-----------------------------------------------------    Adj R-squared =   0.5145
   Total   |   268.995781     867     .310260416         Root MSE      =   .38812

---------------------------------------------------------------------------------
  LGFDHO   |     Coef.      Std. Err.      t     P>|t|     [95% Conf. Interval]
---------------------------------------------------------------------------------
   LGEXP   |   .2673552     .0370782     7.211   0.000     .1945813      .340129
  LGSIZE   |   .4868228     .0256383    18.988   0.000     .4365021     .5371434
  LGHOUS   |   .0229611     .0348408     0.659   0.510    -.0454214     .0913436
   _cons   |   4.708772     .2217592    21.234   0.000     4.273522     5.144022
---------------------------------------------------------------------------------
```

and, not surprisingly, its coefficient is not significantly different from zero. It is, however, highly correlated with *LGEXP* (correlation coefficient 0.81), and also, to a lesser extent, with *LGSIZE* (correlation coefficient 0.33). Its inclusion does not cause the coefficients of those variables to be biased but it does increase their standard errors, particularly that of *LGEXP*, as you would expect, given the loss of efficiency.

EXERCISES

6.7* A social scientist thinks that the level of activity in the shadow economy, *Y*, depends either positively on the level of the tax burden, *X*, or negatively on the level of government expenditure to discourage shadow economy activity, *Z*. *Y* might also depend on both *X* and *Z*. International cross-sectional data on *Y*, *X*, and *Z*, all measured in US$ million, are obtained for a sample of 30 industrialized countries and a second sample of 30 developing countries. The social scientist regresses (1) log *Y* on both log *X* and log *Z*, (2) log *Y* on log *X* alone, and (3) log *Y* on log *Z* alone, for each sample, with the following results (standard errors in parentheses):

	Industrialized countries			*Developing countries*		
	(1)	(2)	(3)	(1)	(2)	(3)
log *X*	0.699 (0.154)	0.201 (0.112)	–	0.806 (0.137)	0.727 (0.090)	–
log *Z*	−0.646 (0.162)	–	−0.053 (0.124)	−0.091 (0.117)	–	0.427 (0.116)
constant	−1.137 (0.863)	−1.065 (1.069)	1.230 (0.896)	−1.122 (0.873)	−1.024 (0.858)	2.824 (0.835)
R^2	0.44	0.10	0.01	0.71	0.70	0.33

X was positively correlated with *Z* in both samples. Having carried out the appropriate statistical tests, write a short report advising the social scientist how to interpret these results.

6.8 Using your *EAEF* data set, regress *LGEARN* on *S*, *EXP*, *ASVABC*, *MALE*, *ETHBLACK*, and *ETHHISP*. Repeat the regression, adding *SIBLINGS*. Calculate the correlations between *SIBLINGS* and the other explanatory variables. Compare the results of the two regressions.

6.4 Proxy variables

It frequently happens that you are unable to obtain data on a variable that you would like to include in a regression equation. Some variables, such as socio-economic status and quality of education, are so vaguely defined that it may be impossible even in principle to measure them. Others might be measurable, but require so much time and energy that in practice they have to be abandoned.

Sometimes you are frustrated because you are using survey data collected by someone else, and an important variable (from your point of view) has been omitted.

Whatever the reason, it is usually a good idea to use a proxy variable to stand in for the missing variable, rather than leave it out entirely. For socioeconomic status, you might use income as a substitute, if data on it are available. For quality of education, you might use the staff–student ratio or expenditure per student. For a variable omitted in a survey, you will have to look at the data actually collected to see if there is a suitable substitute.

There are two good reasons for trying to find a proxy. First, if you simply leave the variable out, your regression is likely to suffer from omitted variable bias of the type described in Section 6.2, and the statistical tests will be invalidated. Second, the results from your proxy regression may indirectly shed light on the influence of the missing variable.

Suppose that the true model is

$$Y = \beta_1 + \beta_2 X_2 + \beta_3 X_3 + \cdots + \beta_k X_k + u. \tag{6.20}$$

Suppose that we have no data for X_2, but another variable Z is an ideal proxy for it in the sense that there exists an exact linear relationship between X_2 and Z:

$$X_2 = \lambda + \mu Z, \tag{6.21}$$

λ and μ being fixed, but unknown, constants. (Note that if λ and μ were known, we could calculate X_2 from Z, and so there would be no need to use Z as a proxy. Note further that we cannot estimate λ and μ by regression analysis, because to do that we need data on X_2.)

Substituting for X_2 from (6.21) into (6.20), the model may be rewritten

$$\begin{aligned} Y &= \beta_1 + \beta_2(\lambda + \mu Z) + \beta_3 X_3 + \cdots + \beta_k X_k + u \\ &= \beta_1 + \beta_2\lambda + \beta_2\mu Z + \beta_3 X_3 + \cdots + \beta_k X_k + u. \end{aligned} \tag{6.22}$$

The model is now formally specified correctly in terms of observable variables, and if we fit it, the following results will obtain:

1. The coefficients of $X_3, \ldots, X_k$, their standard errors, and their t statistics will be the same as if X_2 had been used instead of Z.
2. R^2 will be the same as if X_2 had been used instead of Z.
3. The coefficient of Z will be an estimate of $\beta_2\mu$ and so it will not be possible to obtain an estimate of β_2, unless you are able to guess the value of μ.
4. However, the t statistic for Z will be the same as that which would have been obtained for X_2, and so you are able to assess the significance of X_2, even though you are not able to estimate its coefficient.
5. It will not be possible to obtain an estimate of β_1, since the intercept is now $(\beta_1 + \beta_2\lambda)$, but usually the intercept is of secondary interest, anyway.

With regard to the third point, suppose that you are investigating migration from country A to country B and you are using the (very naïve) model

$$M = \beta_1 + \beta_2 W + u, \quad (6.23)$$

where M is the rate of migration of a certain type of worker from A to B, and W is the ratio of the wage rate in B to the wage rate in A. The higher the relative wage rate, you think the higher is migration. But suppose that you only have data on GDP per capita, not wages. You might define a proxy variable G that is the ratio of GDP in B to GDP in A.

In this case, it might be reasonable to assume, as a first approximation, that relative wages are proportional to relative GDP. If that were true, one could write (6.21) with $\lambda = 0$ and $\mu = 1$. In this case, the coefficient of relative GDP would yield a direct estimate of the coefficient of relative wages. Since variables in regression analysis are frequently defined in relative terms, this special case actually has quite a wide application.

In this discussion, we have assumed that Z is an ideal proxy for X_2, and the validity of all the foregoing results depends on this condition. In practice, it is unusual to find a proxy that is exactly linearly related to the missing variable, but if the relationship is close, the results will hold approximately. A major problem is posed by the fact that there is never any means of testing whether the condition is or is not approximated satisfactorily. One has to justify the use of the proxy subjectively.

Example

The main determinants of educational attainment appear to be the cognitive ability of an individual and the support and motivation provided by the family background. The NLSY data set is exceptional in that cognitive ability measures are available for virtually all the respondents, the data being obtained when the Department of Defense, needing to re-norm the Armed Services Vocational Aptitude Battery scores, sponsored the administration of the tests. However, there are no data that bear directly on support and motivation provided by the family background. This factor is difficult to define and probably has several dimensions. Accordingly, it is unlikely that a single proxy could do justice to it. The NLSY data set includes data on parental educational attainment and the number of siblings of the respondent, both of which could be used as proxies, the rationale for the latter being that parents who are ambitious for their children tend to limit the family size in order to concentrate resources. The data set also contains three dummy variables specifically intended to capture family background effects: whether anyone in the family possessed a library card, whether anyone in the family bought magazines, and whether anyone in the family bought newspapers, when the respondent was aged 14. However, the explanatory power of these variables appears to be very limited.

The regression output in Table 6.6 shows the results of regressing *S* on *ASVABC* only. In Table 6.12, parental education, number of siblings, and the library card dummy variable have been added to the specification. *ASVABC* is positively correlated with *SM*, *SF*, and *LIBRARY* (correlation coefficients 0.38, 0.42 and 0.22, respectively), and negatively correlated with *SIBLINGS* (correlation coefficient –0.19). Its coefficient is therefore unambiguously biased upwards in the first regression. However, there may still be an element of bias in the second, given the weakness of the proxy variables.

Unintentional proxies

It sometimes happens that you use a proxy without realizing it. You think that *Y* depends upon *Z*, but in reality it depends upon *X*.

Table 6.11

```
. reg S ASVABC

  Source |       SS        df        MS            Number of obs =    540
---------+------------------------------           F(1, 538)     = 274.19
   Model |  1081.97059      1   1081.97059         Prob > F      = 0.0000
Residual |  2123.01275    538   3.94612035         R-squared     = 0.3376
---------+------------------------------           Adj R-squared = 0.3364
   Total |  3204.98333    539   5.94616574         Root MSE      = 1.9865

------------------------------------------------------------------------
       S |     Coef.    Std. Err.      t     P>|t|   [95% Conf. Interval]
---------+--------------------------------------------------------------
  ASVABC |   .148084    .0089431    16.56   0.000    .1305165    .1656516
   _cons |  6.066225    .4672261    12.98   0.000    5.148413    6.984036
------------------------------------------------------------------------
```

Table 6.12

```
. reg S ASVABC SM SF LIBRARY SIBLINGS

  Source |       SS        df        MS            Number of obs =    540
---------+------------------------------           F(5, 534)     =  63.21
   Model |  1191.57546      5   238.315093         Prob > F      = 0.0000
Residual |  2013.40787    534   3.77042672         R-squared     = 0.3718
---------+------------------------------           Adj R-squared = 0.3659
   Total |  3204.98333    539   5.94616574         Root MSE      = 1.9418

------------------------------------------------------------------------
       S |     Coef.    Std. Err.      t     P>|t|   [95% Conf. Interval]
---------+--------------------------------------------------------------
  ASVABC |  .1245327    .0099875    12.47   0.000     .104913    .1441523
      SM |  .0388414     .039969     0.97   0.332   -.0396743    .1173571
      SF |  .1035001    .0311842     3.32   0.001    .0422413    .1647588
 LIBRARY | -.0355224    .2134634    -0.17   0.868   -.4548534    .3838086
SIBLINGS | -.0665348    .0408795    -1.63   0.104   -.1468392    .0137696
   _cons |  5.846517    .5681221    10.29   0.000    4.730489    6.962546
------------------------------------------------------------------------
```

If the correlation between Z and X is low, the results will be poor, so you may realize that something is wrong but, if the correlation is good, the results may appear to be satisfactory (R^2 up to the anticipated level, etc.) and you may remain blissfully unaware that the relationship is false.

Does this matter? Well, it depends on why you are running the regression in the first place. If the purpose of fitting the regression line is to predict future values of Y, the use of a proxy will not matter much, provided of course that the correlation remains high and was not a statistical fluke in the sample period. However, if your intention is to use the explanatory variable as a policy instrument for influencing the dependent variable, the consequences could be serious. Unless there happens to be a functional connection between the proxy and the true explanatory variable, manipulating the proxy will have no effect on the dependent variable. If the motive for your regression is scientific curiosity, the outcome is equally unsatisfactory.

Unintentional proxies are especially common in time series analysis, particularly in macroeconomic models. If the true explanatory variable is subject to a time trend, you will probably get a good fit if you substitute (intentionally or otherwise) any other variable with a time trend. Even if you relate changes in your dependent variable to changes in your explanatory variable, you are likely to get similar results whether you are using the correct explanatory variable or a proxy, since macroeconomic variables tend to change in concert in periods of economic expansion or recession.

EXERCISES

6.9 Is potential work experience a satisfactory proxy for actual work experience? Length of work experience is generally found to be an important determinant of earnings. Many data sets do not contain this variable. To avoid the problem of omitted variable bias, a standard practice is to use *PWE*, potential years of work experience, as a proxy. *PWE* is defined as *AGE*, less age at completion of full-time education (years of schooling plus 5, assuming that schooling begins at the age of 6):

$$PWE = AGE - S - 5.$$

Using your *EAEF* data set, regress *LGEARN* (1) on *S*, *ASVABC*, *MALE*, *ETHBLACK*, and *ETHHISP*, (2) on *S*, *ASVABC*, *MALE*, *ETHBLACK*, *ETHHISP*, and *PWE* and (3) on *S*, *ASVABC*, *MALE*, *ETHBLACK*, *ETHHISP*, and *EXP*. Compare the results and evaluate whether *PWE* would have been a satisfactory proxy for *EXP* if data for *EXP* had not been available.

Variation: *PWE* is not likely to be a satisfactory proxy for work experience for females because it does not take into account time spent not working while rearing children. Investigate this by running the three regressions for the male and female subsamples separately. You must drop the *MALE* dummy from the specification (explain why).

6.10* A researcher has data on output per worker, Y, and capital per worker, K, both measured in thousands of dollars, for 50 firms in the textiles industry in 2005. She hypothesizes that output per worker depends on capital per worker and perhaps also the technological sophistication of the firm, $TECH$:

$$Y = \beta_1 + \beta_2 K + \beta_3 TECH + u,$$

where u is a disturbance term. She is unable to measure $TECH$ and decides to use expenditure per worker on research and development in 2005, $R\&D$, as a proxy for it. She fits the following regressions (standard errors in parentheses):

$$\hat{Y} = \underset{(0.45)}{1.02} + \underset{(0.04)}{0.32}K \qquad R^2 = 0.749$$

$$\hat{Y} = \underset{(0.61)}{0.34} + \underset{(0.22)}{0.29}K + \underset{(0.15)}{0.05}R\&D \qquad R^2 = 0.750.$$

The correlation coefficient for K and $R\&D$ was 0.92. Discuss these regression results

(1) assuming that Y does depend on both K and $TECH$,
(2) assuming that Y depends only on K.

6.5 Testing a linear restriction

In Section 3.4, it was demonstrated that you may be able to alleviate a problem of multicollinearity in a regression model if you believe that there exists a linear relationship between its parameters. By exploiting the information about the relationship, you will make the regression estimates more efficient. Even if the original model was not subject to multicollinearity, the gain in efficiency may yield a welcome improvement in the precision of the estimates, as reflected by their standard errors.

The example discussed in Section 3.4 was an educational attainment model with S as the dependent variable and $ASVABC$, SM, and SF as explanatory variables. The regression output is shown in Table 6.13.

Somewhat surprisingly, the coefficient of SM is not significant, even at the 5 percent level, using a one-sided test. However, assortative mating leads to a high correlation between SM and SF and the regression appeared to be suffering from multicollinearity.

We then hypothesized that mother's and father's education are equally important for educational attainment, allowing us to impose the restriction $\beta_3 = \beta_4$ and rewrite the equation as

$$\begin{aligned} S &= \beta_1 + \beta_2 ASVABC + \beta_3(SM + SF) + u \\ &= \beta_1 + \beta_2 ASVABC + \beta_3 SP + u, \end{aligned} \tag{6.24}$$

where SP is the sum of SM and SF. The regression output from this specification is shown in Table 6.14.

Table 6.13

```
. reg S ASVABC SM SF

  Source  |      SS          df        MS          Number of obs =    540
----------+-------------------------------         F(3, 536)     = 104.30
   Model  |  1181.36981      3     393.789935      Prob > F      = 0.0000
Residual  |  2023.61353    536     3.77539837      R-squared     = 0.3686
----------+-------------------------------         Adj R-squared = 0.3651
   Total  |  3204.98333    539     5.94616574      Root MSE      =  1.943

------------------------------------------------------------------------
       S  |     Coef.   Std. Err.      t    P>|t|   [95% Conf. Interval]
------------------------------------------------------------------------
  ASVABC  |  .1257087   .0098533   12.76    0.000   .1063528    .1450646
      SM  |  .0492424   .0390901    1.26    0.208   -.027546    .1260309
      SF  |  .1076825   .0309522    3.48    0.001    .04688     .1684851
   _cons  |  5.370631   .4882155   11.00    0.000   4.41158     6.329681
------------------------------------------------------------------------
```

Table 6.14

```
. g SP=SM+SF
. reg S ASVABC SP

  Source  |      SS          df        MS          Number of obs =    540
----------+-------------------------------         F(2, 537)     = 156.04
   Model  |  1177.98338      2     588.991689      Prob > F      = 0.0000
Residual  |  2026.99996    537     3.77467403      R-squared     = 0.3675
----------+-------------------------------         Adj R-squared = 0.3652
   Total  |  3204.98333    539     5.94616574      Root MSE      = 1.9429

------------------------------------------------------------------------
       S  |     Coef.   Std. Err.      t    P>|t|   [95% Conf. Interval]
------------------------------------------------------------------------
  ASVABC  |  .1253106   .0098434   12.73    0.000   .1059743    .1446469
      SP  |  .0828368   .0164247    5.04    0.000   .0505722    .1151014
   _cons  |  5.29617    .4817972   10.99    0.000   4.349731    6.242608
------------------------------------------------------------------------
```

The standard error of *SP* is much smaller than those of *SM* and *SF*, indicating that the use of the restriction has led to a gain in efficiency, and as a consequence the *t* statistic is very high. Thus, the problem of multicollinearity has been eliminated. However, we are obliged to test the validity of the restriction, and there are two equivalent procedures.

Before we do this, we should make a distinction between linear restrictions and nonlinear restrictions. In a linear restriction such as $\beta_2 = \beta_3$ or $\beta_2 + \beta_3 = 1$, the parameters conform to a simple linear equation. In a nonlinear restriction, such as $\beta_2 = \beta_3\beta_4$, they do not. The procedures described here are for linear restrictions only. We shall encounter nonlinear restrictions and tests for them in later chapters.

F test of a linear restriction

One procedure is to perform an *F* test of a linear restriction. We run the regression in both the restricted and the unrestricted forms and denote the sum of the squares of the residuals RSS_R for the restricted model and RSS_U for the unrestricted model. Since the imposition of the restriction makes it more difficult to fit the regression equation to the data, RSS_R cannot be less than RSS_U and will in general be greater. We would like to test whether the improvement in the fit on going from the restricted to the unrestricted model is significant. If it is, the restriction should be rejected.

For this purpose we can use an *F* test whose structure is the same as that described in Section 3.5:

$$F = \frac{\text{improvement in fit / extra degrees of freedom used up}}{\text{residual sum of squares remaining / degrees of freedom remaining}}. \quad \textbf{(6.25)}$$

In this case, the improvement on going from the restricted to the unrestricted model is $(RSS_R - RSS_U)$, one extra degree of freedom is used up in the unrestricted model (because there is one more parameter to estimate), and the residual sum of squares remaining after the shift from the restricted to the unrestricted model is RSS_U. Hence, the *F* statistic in this case is

$$F(1, n-k) = \frac{RSS_R - RSS_U}{RSS_U / (n-k)}, \quad \textbf{(6.26)}$$

where k is the number of parameters in the unrestricted model. It is distributed with 1 and $n - k$ degrees of freedom under the null hypothesis that the restriction is valid. The first argument for the distribution of the *F* statistic is 1 because we are testing just one restriction. If we were simultaneously testing several restrictions, it would be equal to the number of restrictions being tested. The second argument is the number of degrees of freedom in the unrestricted model.

In the case of the educational attainment function, the null hypothesis was H_0: $\beta_3 = \beta_4$, where β_3 is the coefficient of *SM* and β_4 is the coefficient of *SF*. The residual sum of squares was 2027.00 in the restricted model and 2023.61 in the unrestricted model. Hence, the *F* statistic is

$$F(1, n-k) = \frac{2027.00 - 2023.61}{2023.61/536} = 0.90. \quad \textbf{(6.27)}$$

Since the *F* statistic is less than 1, it is not significant at any significance level and we do not reject the null hypothesis that the coefficients of *SM* and *SF* are equal.

The reparameterization of a regression model

We may also perform a *t* test of a linear restriction. Before discussing this, it is convenient to discuss the reparameterization of a regression model. We will start with a simple example and then proceed to the general case.

Suppose the regression model is

$$Y = \beta_1 + \beta_2 X_2 + \beta_3 X_3 + u \tag{6.28}$$

and that we have fitted it as

$$\hat{Y} = b_1 + b_2 X_2 + b_3 X_3 \tag{6.29}$$

and suppose we are interested in estimating the sum of β_2 and β_3. To obtain a point estimate of the sum, it is natural to add the individual estimates, $b_2 + b_3$, and indeed, provided that the regression model assumptions are valid, it can easily be shown that this is unbiased and the most efficient estimator of $\beta_2 + \beta_3$. However, you do not have information on the standard error of the sum and hence you are not able to construct confidence intervals or to perform t tests. There are three ways that you might use to obtain such information:

(1) Some regression applications have a special command that produces an estimate of the combination and associated diagnostics. For example, Stata has the lincom command.

(2) Given the appropriate command, most regression applications will produce the variance-covariance matrix for the estimates of the parameters. This is the complete list of the estimates of their variances and covariances, for convenience arranged in table form. The standard errors in the ordinary regression output are the square roots of the variances. The estimator of the variance of the sum of b_2 and b_3 is given by

$$s_{b_2}^2 + s_{b_3}^2 + 2s_{b_2 b_3}, \tag{6.30}$$

where $s_{b_2}^2$ and $s_{b_3}^2$ are the estimators of the variances of b_2 and b_3, and $s_{b_2 b_3}$ is the estimator of the covariance between b_2 and b_3. The standard error of the sum is the square root of this expression.

(3) The third method is to reparameterize the model, manipulating it so that $\beta_2 + \beta_3$ and its standard error are estimated directly as part of the regression output. To do this, we define

$$\theta = \beta_2 + \beta_3. \tag{6.31}$$

We rewrite this as

$$\beta_3 = \theta - \beta_2. \tag{6.32}$$

It makes no substantive difference which β we take to the left side. Substituting in the original model, we have

$$\begin{aligned} Y &= \beta_1 + \beta_2 X_2 + (\theta - \beta_2) X_3 + u \\ &= \beta_1 + \beta_2 (X_2 - X_3) + \theta X_3 + u. \end{aligned} \tag{6.33}$$

Thus, if we define a new variable $Z = X_2 - X_3$ and regress Y on Z and X_3, the coefficient of Z will be an estimate of β_2 and that of X_3 will be an estimate of θ.

The estimate of θ will be exactly the same as that obtained by summing the estimates of β_2 and β_3 if we fitted (6.29). The difference is that we obtain its standard error directly from the regression results.

We will now consider the general case. Suppose that the regression model is

$$Y = \beta_1 + \sum_{j=2}^{k} \beta_j X_j + u. \tag{6.34}$$

Let the fitted model be

$$\hat{Y} = b_1 + \sum_{j=2}^{k} b_j X_j \tag{6.35}$$

as usual. Suppose that, as well as the individual parameter estimates, you are interested in the estimation of some linear combination:

$$\theta = \sum_{j=1}^{k} \lambda_j \beta_j. \tag{6.36}$$

From (6.35) we can construct the statistic $\sum_{j=1}^{k} \lambda_j b_j$. As in the example of the sum, it can easily be shown that this is unbiased and the most efficient estimator of θ. Next, we need to obtain the standard error of this expression. If the regression application does not have a special command for computing combinations and associated statistics, we will have to compute the standard error from the underlying variances and covariances, or reparameterize. The estimator of the variance of the estimator of θ, the generalization of (6.30), is given by

$$\sum_{j=1}^{k} \lambda_j^2 s_{b_j}^2 + 2\sum_{p \neq j} \lambda_p \lambda_j s_{b_p b_j}, \tag{6.37}$$

where $s_{b_j}^2$ is the estimator of the variance of b_j and $s_{b_p b_j}$ is the estimator of the covariance between b_p and b_j. If there are many coefficients in the linear combination, this can be a laborious task.

The alternative is to perform an appropriate reparameterization so that θ and its standard error are estimated directly as part of the regression output. This may look complicated but in practice is usually quite straightforward. We rewrite (6.36) so that one of the β parameters is expressed in terms of θ and the other β parameters. For example, we can rewrite (6.36) as

$$\beta_k = \frac{1}{\lambda_k}\left(\theta - \sum_{j=1}^{k-1} \lambda_j \beta_j\right). \tag{6.38}$$

We can then rewrite (6.34) as

$$\begin{aligned} Y &= \beta_1 + \sum_{j=2}^{k-1} \beta_j X_j + \frac{1}{\lambda_k}\left(\theta - \sum_{j=1}^{k-1} \lambda_j \beta_j\right) X_k + u \\ &= \beta_1\left(1 - \frac{\lambda_1}{\lambda_k} X_k\right) + \sum_{j=2}^{k-1} \beta_j \left(X_j - \frac{\lambda_j}{\lambda_k} X_k\right) + \frac{\theta}{\lambda_k} X_k + u. \end{aligned} \tag{6.39}$$

We compute the artificial variables $Z_1 = 1 - (\lambda_1/\lambda_k)X_k$ and $Z_j = X_j - (\lambda_j/\lambda_k)X_k$ for j = 2, ..., $k-1$. We regress Y on the Z variables and X_k. The coefficient of X_k is an estimate of θ/λ_k and hence we derive an estimate of θ. We multiply the standard error of the coefficient of X_k by λ_k to obtain the standard error of θ. We are then in a position to construct confidence intervals.

t test of a linear restriction

An obvious application of reparameterization is its use in the testing of linear restrictions. Suppose that your hypothetical restriction is

$$\sum_{j=1}^{k} \lambda_j \beta_j = \alpha, \tag{6.40}$$

where θ is a scalar. Define

$$\theta = \sum_{j=1}^{k} \lambda_j \beta_j - \alpha \tag{6.41}$$

and reparameterize. θ will become the coefficient of one of the variables in the model, and a t test of H_0: $\theta = 0$ is effectively a t test of H_0: $\sum_{j=1}^{k} \lambda_j \beta_j = \alpha$, and hence of the restriction.

As an illustration, we will again use the educational attainment example, relating years of schooling, S, to the cognitive ability score $ASVABC$ and years of schooling of the mother and the father, SM and SF:

$$S = \beta_1 + \beta_2 ASVABC + \beta_3 SM + \beta_4 SF + u. \tag{6.42}$$

It was hypothesized that mother's education and father's education are equally important for educational attainment, implying the restriction $\beta_4 = \beta_3$, or

$$\beta_4 - \beta_3 = 0. \tag{6.43}$$

Define

$$\theta = \beta_4 - \beta_3 \tag{6.44}$$

and rewrite this equation as

$$\beta_4 = \beta_3 + \theta. \tag{6.45}$$

Substitute into the original model:

$$\begin{aligned} S &= \beta_1 + \beta_2 ASVABC + \beta_3 SM + (\beta_3 + \theta) SF + u \\ &= \beta_1 + \beta_2 ASVABC + \beta_3 (SM + SF) + \theta SF + u \\ &= \beta_1 + \beta_2 ASVABC + \beta_3 SP + \theta SF + u, \end{aligned} \tag{6.46}$$

where $SP = SM + SF$, and test the coefficient of SF, which is an estimate of θ.

Table 6.15

```
. reg S ASVABC SP SF

  Source  |       SS          df        MS             Number of obs =    540
----------+-------------------------------------       F(3, 536)     = 104.30
   Model  |  1181.36981        3    393.789935         Prob > F      = 0.0000
Residual  |  2023.61353      536    3.77539837         R-squared     = 0.3686
----------+-------------------------------------       Adj R-squared = 0.3651
   Total  |  3204.98333      539    5.94616574         Root MSE      =  1.943

-------------------------------------------------------------------------------
       S  |     Coef.     Std. Err.      t     P > |t|     [95% Conf. Interval]
----------+--------------------------------------------------------------------
  ASVABC  |   .1257087    .0098533    12.76    0.000     .1063528     .1450646
      SP  |   .0492424    .0390901     1.26    0.208     -.027546     .1260309
      SF  |   .0584401    .0617051     0.95    0.344    -.0627734     .1796536
   _cons  |   5.370631    .4882155    11.00    0.000      4.41158     6.329681
-------------------------------------------------------------------------------
```

Table 6.15 presents the output for this specification. The coefficient of *SF* is not significantly different from zero and so we do not reject the restriction.

The right side of (6.46) consists of the right side of the restricted version of the model plus the term θSF. The term θSF thus can be thought of as a conversion term, a term that converts the restricted version into (a reparameterized form of) the unrestricted version. Effectively, we are testing to see if we need to include this term. If the estimate of θ is not significantly different from zero, we can argue that we can drop the term and use the restricted version. If it is significantly different from zero, we cannot drop it and must stay with the unrestricted model.

This perspective provides an explanation of the equivalence of the F and t tests of the restriction. The F test tests the improvement in fit when you go from the restricted model to the unrestricted model. This is accomplished by adding the conversion term, but, as we know, an F test on the improvement in fit when you add an extra term is equivalent to the t test on the coefficient of that term (see Section 3.5).

Multiple restrictions

The F test approach may be extended to cover the case where we wish to test whether several restrictions are valid simultaneously. Suppose that there are p restrictions. Let RSS_U be RSS for the fully unrestricted model and RSS_R be RSS for the model where all p restrictions have been imposed. The test statistic is then

$$F(p, n-k) = \frac{(RSS_R - RSS_U)/p}{RSS_U/(n-k)}, \qquad (6.47)$$

where k is the number of parameters in the original, unrestricted version. The t test approach can be used to test only one restriction at a time, in isolation.

Zero restrictions

You will often encounter references to zero restrictions. This just means that a particular parameter is hypothesized to be equal to zero. Taken in isolation, the appropriate test is of course the t test. It can be considered to be a special case of the t test of a restriction discussed above where there is no need for reparameterization. Likewise the testing of multiple zero restrictions can be thought of as a special case of the testing of multiple restrictions. The test of the joint explanatory power of a group of explanatory variables discussed in Section 3.5 in the text can be thought of in this way. Even the F statistic for the equation as a whole can be treated as a special case. Here the unrestricted model is

$$Y = \beta_1 + \sum_{j=2}^{k} \beta_j X_j + u. \tag{6.48}$$

The restricted model is

$$Y = \beta_1 + u \tag{6.49}$$

since all the slope coefficients are hypothesized to be zero. If this model is fitted, the OLS estimate of β_1 is $\bar{Y}$, the residual in observation i is $Y_i - \bar{Y}$, and $RSS_R = \sum_{i=1}^{n} (Y_i - \bar{Y})^2$ which is the total sum of squares, TSS, for Y. The F statistic is therefore

$$\begin{aligned} F(k-1, n-k) &= \frac{(RSS_R - RSS_U)/(k-1)}{RSS_U/(n-k)} = \frac{(TSS - RSS_U)/(k-1)}{RSS_U/(n-k)} \\ &= \frac{ESS_U/(k-1)}{RSS_U/(n-k)}, \end{aligned} \tag{6.50}$$

where RSS_U and ESS_U are the residual sum of squares and the explained sum of squares for the original, unrestricted model. This is the definition of F for the equation as a whole given in equation (3.65).

EXERCISES

6.11 Is previous work experience as valuable as experience with the current employer? Using your *EAEF* data set, first regress *LGEARN* on *S*, *EXP*, *MALE*, *ETHBLACK*, *ETHHISP*, and *ASVABC*. Then define

$$PREVEXP = EXP - TENURE.$$

The variable *TENURE* in your data set is the number of years spent working with the current employer. Regress *LGEARN* on *S*, *PREVEXP*, *TENURE*,

ASVABC, *MALE*, *ETHBLACK*, and *ETHHISP*. The estimates of the coefficients of *PREVEXP* and *TENURE* will be different. This raises the issue of whether the difference is due to random factors or whether the coefficients are significantly different. Set up the null hypothesis H_0: $\delta_1 = \delta_2$, where δ_1 is the coefficient of *PREVEXP* and δ_2 is the coefficient of *TENURE*. Explain why the regression with *EXP* is the correct specification if H_0 is true, while the regression with *PREVEXP* and *TENURE* should be used if H_0 is false. Perform an *F* test of the restriction using *RSS* for the two regressions. Do this for the combined sample and also for males and females separately.

6.12 Using your *EAEF* data set, regress *LGEARN* on *S*, *EXP*, *MALE*, *ETHBLACK*, *ETHHISP*, *ASVABC*, and *TENURE*. Demonstrate that a *t* test on the coefficient of *TENURE* is a test of the restriction described in Exercise 6.11. Verify that the same result is obtained. Do this for the combined sample and also for males and females separately.

6.13* The first regression shows the result of regressing *LGFDHO*, the logarithm of annual household expenditure on food eaten at home, on *LGEXP*, the logarithm of total annual household expenditure, and *LGSIZE*, the logarithm of the number of persons in the household, using a sample of 868 households in the 1995 Consumer Expenditure Survey. In the second regression, *LGFDHOPC*, the logarithm of food expenditure per capita (*FDHO*/*SIZE*), is regressed on *LGEXPPC*, the logarithm of total expenditure per capita (*EXP*/*SIZE*). In the third regression, *LGFDHOPC* is regressed on *LGEXPPC* and *LGSIZE*.

```
. reg LGFDHO LGEXP LGSIZE

    Source   |       SS           df           MS             Number of obs =     868
-----------------------------------------------------         F(2, 865)     =  460.92
     Model   |   138.776549        2       69.3882747         Prob > F      =  0.0000
  Residual   |   130.219231      865       .150542464         R-squared     =  0.5159
-----------------------------------------------------         Adj R-squared =  0.5148
     Total   |   268.995781      867       .310260416         Root MSE      =    .388

------------------------------------------------------------------------------------
    LGFDHO   |     Coef.      Std. Err.      t      P > |t|     [95% Conf. Interval]
------------------------------------------------------------------------------------
     LGEXP   |   .2866813     .0226824    12.639     0.000     .2421622     .3312003
    LGSIZE   |   .4854698     .0255476    19.003     0.000     .4353272     .5356124
     _cons   |   4.720269     .2209996    21.359     0.000     4.286511     5.154027
------------------------------------------------------------------------------------
```

```
. reg LGFDHOPC LGEXPPC

    Source   |       SS           df           MS             Number of obs =     868
-----------------------------------------------------         F(1, 866)     =  313.04
     Model   |   51.4364364        1       51.4364364         Prob > F      =  0.0000
  Residual   |   142.293973      866       .164311747         R-squared     =  0.2655
-----------------------------------------------------         Adj R-squared =  0.2647
     Total   |   193.73041       867       .223449146         Root MSE      =  .40535

------------------------------------------------------------------------------------
  LGFDHOPC   |     Coef.      Std. Err.      t      P > |t|     [95% Conf. Interval]
------------------------------------------------------------------------------------
   LGEXPPC   |   .376283      .0212674    17.693     0.000     .3345414     .4180246
     _cons   |   3.700667     .1978925    18.700     0.000     3.312262     4.089072
------------------------------------------------------------------------------------
```

```
. reg LGFDHOPC LGEXPPC LGSIZE

  Source  |      SS          df       MS            Number of obs =    868
----------+------------------------------          F(2, 865)     = 210.94
   Model  |  63.5111811       2   31.7555905        Prob > F      = 0.0000
Residual  |  130.219229     865   .150542461        R-squared     = 0.3278
----------+------------------------------          Adj R-squared = 0.3263
   Total  |   193.73041     867   .223449146        Root MSE      =   .388

-------------------------------------------------------------------------
LGFDHOPC  |     Coef.   Std. Err.     t    P > |t|   [95% Conf. Interval]
----------+--------------------------------------------------------------
 LGEXPPC  |   .2866813  .0226824  12.639    0.000    .2421622   .3312004
  LGSIZE  |  -.2278489  .0254412  -8.956    0.000   -.2777826  -.1779152
   _cons  |   4.720269  .2209996  21.359    0.000    4.286511   5.154027
-------------------------------------------------------------------------
```

1. Explain why the second model is a restricted version of the first, stating the restriction.
2. Perform an F test of the restriction.
3. Perform a t test of the restriction.
4. Summarize your conclusions from the analysis of the regression results.

6.14 The composite measure of cognitive ability, *ASVABC*, in the *EAEF* data sets was constructed as a weighted average of the scores of tests of arithmetic reasoning, *ASVAB02*, word knowledge, *ASVAB03*, and paragraph comprehension, *ASVAB04*, with *ASVAB02* being given double weight. Show mathematically that, when fitting the educational attainment function

$$S = \beta_1 + \beta_2 SM + \beta_3 SF + \beta_4 ASVABC + u$$

instead of the model using the individual scores

$$S = \beta_1 + \beta_2 SM + \beta_3 SF + \gamma_1 ASVAB02 + \gamma_2 ASVAB03 + \gamma_3 ASVAB04 + u$$

one is implicitly imposing the restrictions $\gamma_1 = 2\gamma_2$ and $\gamma_1 = 2\gamma_3$. Perform a test of these restrictions using your *EAEF* data set.

6.15 In his classic article (Nerlove, 1963), Nerlove derives the following cost function for electricity generation:

$$C = \beta_1 Y^{\beta_2} P_1^{\gamma_1} P_2^{\gamma_2} P_3^{\gamma_3} v,$$

where C is total production cost, Y is output (measured in kilowatt hours), P_1 is the price of labor input, P_2 is the price of capital input, P_3 is the price of fuel (all measured in appropriate units), and v is a disturbance term. Theoretically, the sum of the price elasticities should be 1:

$$\gamma_1 + \gamma_2 + \gamma_3 = 1$$

and hence the cost function may be rewritten

$$\frac{C}{P_3} = \beta_1 Y^{\beta_2} \left(\frac{P_1}{P_3}\right)^{\gamma_1} \left(\frac{P_2}{P_3}\right)^{\gamma_2} v.$$

The two versions of the cost function are fitted to the 29 medium-sized firms in Nerlove's sample, with the following results (standard errors in parentheses):

$$\begin{aligned}\widehat{\log C} &= \underset{(1.62)}{-4.93} + \underset{(0.11)}{0.94} \log Y + \underset{(0.23)}{0.31} \log P_1 - \underset{(0.29)}{0.26} \log P_2 \\ &\quad + \underset{(0.07)}{0.44} \log P_3 \qquad RSS = 0.336\end{aligned}$$

$$\widehat{\log \frac{C}{P_3}} = \underset{(0.16)}{-6.55} + \underset{(0.11)}{0.91} \log Y + \underset{(0.23)}{0.51} \log \frac{P_1}{P_3} + \underset{(0.19)}{0.09} \log \frac{P_2}{P_3} \quad RSS = 0.364.$$

Compare the regression results for the two equations and perform a test of the validity of the restriction.

6.16 A researcher has data on *HEALTH*, aggregate expenditure on health, *GDP*, aggregate gross domestic product, and *POP*, total population, for a sample of 70 countries in 1999. *HEALTH* and *GDP* are both measured in US$ billion. *POP* is measured in million. Hypothesizing that expenditure on health per capita depends on GDP per capita, she fits the regression (standard errors in parentheses; *RSS* = residual sum of squares):

$$\log \widehat{\frac{HEALTH}{POP}} = \underset{(0.10)}{-3.74} + \underset{(0.05)}{1.27} \log \frac{GDP}{POP} \qquad R^2 = 0.91 \quad RSS = 14.26$$

She also runs the following regressions:

$$\log \widehat{\frac{HEALTH}{POP}} = \underset{(0.14)}{-3.60} + \underset{(0.05)}{1.27} \log GDP - \underset{(0.07)}{0.33} \log POP \qquad R^2 = 0.95 \quad RSS = 13.90$$

$$\log \widehat{\frac{HEALTH}{POP}} = \underset{(0.14)}{-3.60} + \underset{(0.05)}{1.27} \log \frac{GDP}{POP} - \underset{(0.04)}{0.06} \log POP \qquad R^2 = 0.91 \quad RSS = 13.90$$

Demonstrate that the first specification is a restricted version of the second, stating the restriction. Test the restriction, using an *F* test. Demonstrate that the same restriction may be tested using a *t* test on the coefficient of log *POP* in the third specification.

6.6 Getting the most out of your residuals

There are two ways of looking at the residuals obtained after fitting a regression equation to a set of data. If you are pessimistic and passive, you will simply see them as evidence of failure. The bigger the residuals, the worse is your fit, and the smaller is R^2. The whole object of the exercise is to fit the regression equation in such a way as to minimize the sum of the squares of the residuals. However, if you are enterprising, you will also see the residuals as a potentially fertile source of new ideas, perhaps even new hypotheses. They offer both a challenge and constructive criticism. The challenge is that providing the stimulus for most scientific research: evidence of the need to find a better explanation of the facts. The constructive criticism comes in because the residuals, taken individually, indicate when and where and by how much the existing model is failing to fit the facts.

Taking advantage of this constructive criticism requires patience on the part of the researcher. If the sample is small enough, you should look for **outliers**, observations with large positive or negative residuals, and try to hypothesize explanations for them. Some regression applications actually identify outliers for you, as part of the regression diagnostics. Some of the outliers may be caused by special factors specific to the observations in question. These are not of much use to the theorist. Other factors, however, may appear to be associated with the residuals in several observations. As soon as you detect a regularity of this kind, you have the makings of progress. The next step is to find a sensible way of quantifying the factor and of including it in the model.

Key terms

- *F* test of a restriction
- ideal proxy
- linear restriction
- nonlinear restriction
- omitted variable bias
- outlier
- proxy variable
- redundant variable
- *t* test of a restriction

7. Heteroscedasticity

Medicine is traditionally divided into the three branches of anatomy, physiology, and pathology—what a body is made of, how it works, and what can go wrong with it. It is time to start discussing the pathology of least squares regression analysis. The properties of the estimators of the regression coefficients depend on the properties of the disturbance term in the regression model. In this and following chapters we shall be looking at some of the problems that arise when the regression model assumptions listed in Section 3.3 are not satisfied.

7.1 Heteroscedasticity and its implications

Assumption A.4 in Section 3.3 states that the variance of the disturbance term in each observation should be constant. This sounds peculiar and needs a bit of explanation. The disturbance term in each observation has only *one* value, so what can be meant by its 'variance'?

What we are talking about is its *potential* distribution *before* the sample is generated. When we write the model

$$Y = \beta_1 + \beta_2 X + u, \tag{7.1}$$

Assumptions A.3 and A.4 state that the disturbance terms $u_1, \cdots, u_n$ in the n observations are drawn from probability distributions that have zero mean and the same variance. The *actual* values of the disturbance term in the sample will sometimes be positive, sometimes negative, sometimes relatively far from zero, sometimes relatively close, but there will be no reason to anticipate a particularly erratic value in any given observation. To put it another way, the probability of u reaching a given positive (or negative) value will be the same in all observations. This condition is known as **homoscedasticity**, which means 'same dispersion'.

Figure 7.1 provides an illustration of homoscedasticity. To keep the diagram simple, the sample contains only five observations. Let us start with the first observation, where X has the value X_1. If there were no disturbance term in the model, the observation would be represented by the circle vertically above X_1 on the line $Y = \beta_1 + \beta_2 X$. The effect of the disturbance term is to shift the

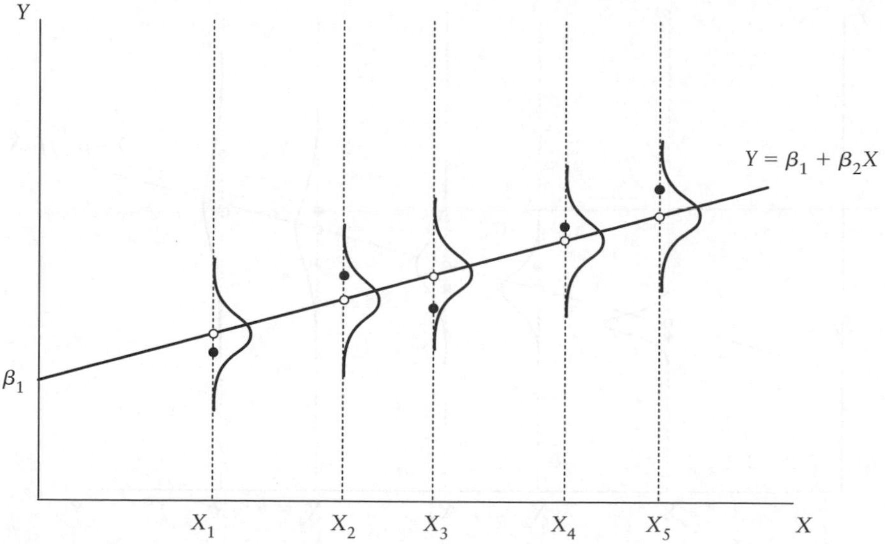

Figure 7.1 Homoscedasticity

observation upwards or downwards vertically. The *potential* distribution of the disturbance term, before the observation has been generated, is shown by the normal distribution above and below the circle. The actual value of the disturbance term for this observation turned out to be negative, the observation being represented by the solid marker. The potential distribution of the disturbance term, and the actual outcome, are shown in a similar way for the other four observations.

Although homoscedasticity is often taken for granted in regression analysis, in some contexts it may be more reasonable to suppose that the potential distribution of the disturbance term is different for different observations in the sample. This is illustrated in Figure 7.2, where the variance of the potential distribution of the disturbance term is increasing as X increases. This does not mean that the disturbance term will *necessarily* have a particularly large (positive or negative) value in an observation where X is large, but it does mean that the *probability* of having an erratic value will be relatively high. This is an example of heteroscedasticity, which means 'differing dispersion'. Mathematically, homoscedasticity and heteroscedasticity may be defined:

Homoscedasticity: $\sigma_{u_i}^2 = \sigma_u^2$, same for all observations;

Heteroscedasticity: $\sigma_{u_i}^2$ not the same for all observations.

Figure 7.3 illustrates how a typical scatter diagram would look if Y were an increasing function of X and the heteroscedasticity were of the type shown in Figure 7.2. You can see that, although the observations are not necessarily further away from the nonstochastic component of the relationship, represented by the line $Y = \beta_1 + \beta_2 X$, there is a tendency for their dispersion to increase as

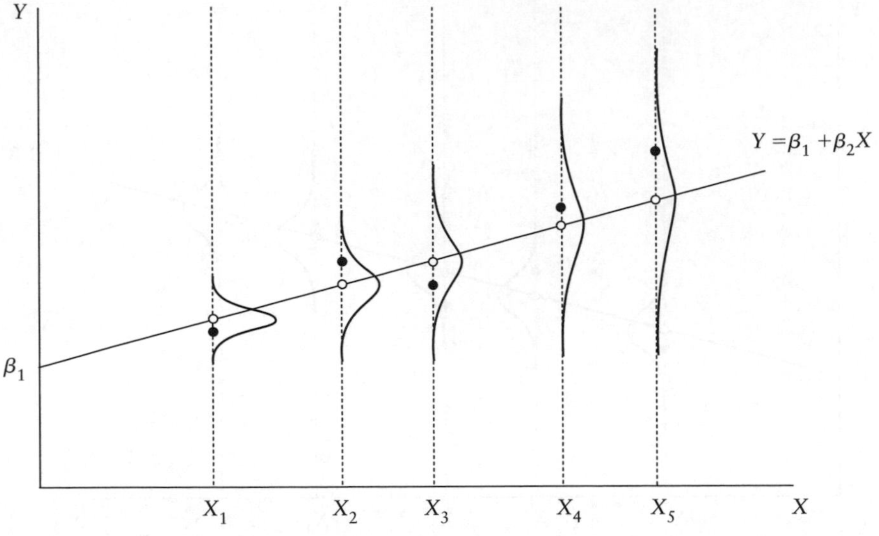

Figure 7.2 Heteroscedasticity

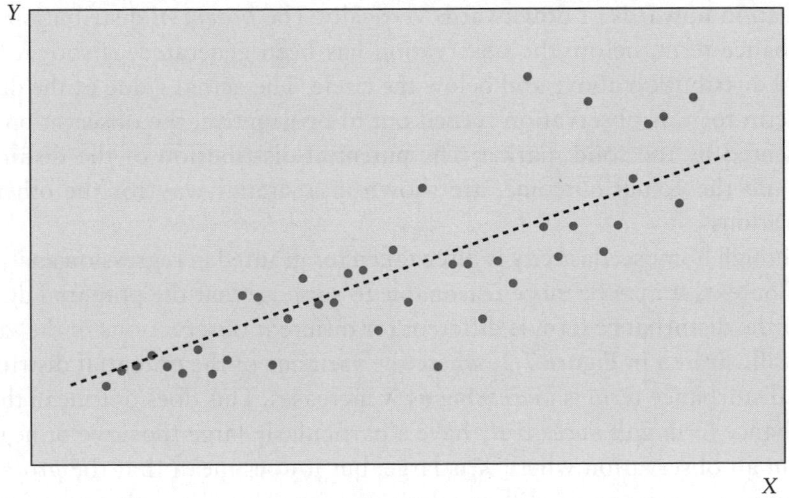

Figure 7.3 Model with a heteroscedastic disturbance term

X increases. (You should be warned that heteroscedasticity is not necessarily of the type shown in Figures 7.2 and 7.3. The term refers to any case in which the variance of the probability distribution of the disturbance term is not the same in all observations.)

Why does heteroscedasticity matter? This particular regression model assumption does not appear to have been used anywhere in the analysis so far, so it might seem almost irrelevant. In particular, the proofs of the unbiasedness of the OLS regression coefficients did not use this assumption.

There are two reasons. The first concerns the variances of the regression coefficients. You want these to be as small as possible so that, in a probabilistic sense, you have maximum precision. If there is no heteroscedasticity, and if the other regression model assumptions are satisfied, the OLS regression coefficients have the lowest variances of all the unbiased estimators that are linear functions of the observations of Y. If heteroscedasticity is present, the OLS estimators are inefficient because you could, at least in principle, find other estimators that have smaller variances and are still unbiased.

The second, equally important, reason is that the estimators of the standard errors of the regression coefficients will be wrong. They are computed on the assumption that the distribution of the disturbance term is homoscedastic. If this is not the case, they are biased, and as a consequence the t tests, and also the usual F tests, are invalid. It is quite likely that the standard errors will be underestimated, so the t statistics will be overestimated and you will have a misleading impression of the precision of your regression coefficients. You may be led to believe that a coefficient is significantly different from zero, at a given significance level, when in fact it is not.

The inefficiency property can be explained intuitively quite easily. Suppose that heteroscedasticity of the type displayed in Figures 7.2 and 7.3 is present. An observation where the potential distribution of the disturbance term has a small standard deviation, like the first observation in Figure 7.2, will tend to lie close to the line $Y = \beta_1 + \beta_2 X$ and hence will be a good guide to the location of the line. By contrast, an observation where the potential distribution has a large standard deviation, like that for the fifth observation in Figure 7.2, will be an unreliable guide to the location of the line. OLS does not discriminate between the quality of the observations, giving equal weight to each, irrespective of whether they are good or poor guides to the location of the line. It follows that if we can find a way of giving more weight to the high-quality observations and less to the unreliable ones, we are likely to obtain a better fit. In other words, our estimators of β_1 and β_2 will be more efficient. We shall see how to do this below.

Possible causes of heteroscedasticity

Heteroscedasticity is likely to be a problem when the values of the variables in the sample vary substantially in different observations. If the true relationship is given by $Y = \beta_1 + \beta_2 X + u$, it may well be the case that the variations in the omitted variables and the measurement errors that are jointly responsible for the disturbance term will be relatively small when Y and X are small and large when they are large, economic variables tending to move in size together.

For example, suppose that you are using the simple regression model to investigate the relationship between value added in manufacturing, *MANU*, and gross domestic product, *GDP*, in cross-country data, and that you have collected the sample of observations given in Table 7.1 and plotted in Figure 7.4. Manufacturing output tends to account for 15 to 25 percent of GDP, variations

Table 7.1 Manufacturing value added, GDP, and population for a sample of countries, 1994

Country	*MANU*	*GDP*	*POP*	*MANU/POP*	*GDP/POP*
Belgium	44517	232006	10.093	4411	22987
Canada	112617	547203	29.109	3869	18798
Chile	13096	50919	13.994	936	3639
Denmark	25927	151266	5.207	4979	29050
Finland	21581	97624	5.085	4244	19199
France	256316	1330998	57.856	4430	23005
Greece	9392	98861	10.413	902	9494
Hong Kong	11758	130823	6.044	1945	21645
Hungary	7227	41506	10.162	711	4084
Ireland	17572	52662	3.536	4970	14893
Israel	11349	74121	5.362	2117	13823
Italy	145013	1016286	57.177	2536	17774
Korea, S.	161318	380820	44.501	3625	8558
Kuwait	2797	24848	1.754	1595	14167
Malaysia	18874	72505	19.695	958	3681
Mexico	55073	420788	89.564	615	4698
Netherlands	48595	334286	15.382	3159	21732
Norway	13484	122926	4.314	3126	28495
Portugal	17025	87352	9.824	1733	8892
Singapore	20648	71039	3.268	6318	21738
Slovakia	2720	13746	5.325	511	2581
Slovenia	4520	14386	1.925	2348	7473
Spain	80104	483652	39.577	2024	12221
Sweden	34806	198432	8.751	3977	22675
Switzerland	57503	261388	7.104	8094	36794
Syria	3317	44753	13.840	240	3234
Turkey	31115	135961	59.903	519	2270
UK	244397	1024609	58.005	4213	17664

Source: UNIDO Yearbook 1997.
Note: *MANU* and *GDP* are measured in US$ million. *POP* is measured in million. *MANU/POP* and *GDP/POP* are measured in US$.

being caused by comparative advantage and historical economic development. The sample includes small economies such as Slovenia and Slovakia as well as large ones such as France, the UK, and Italy. Clearly, when GDP is large, a 1 percent variation will make a great deal more difference, in absolute terms, than when it is small.

South Korea and Mexico are both countries with relatively large GDP. The manufacturing sector is relatively important in South Korea, so its observation is far above the trend line. The opposite was the case for Mexico, at least in 1994. Singapore and Greece are another pair of countries with relatively large and small manufacturing sectors. However, because the GDP of both countries is small, their variations from the trend relationship are also small.

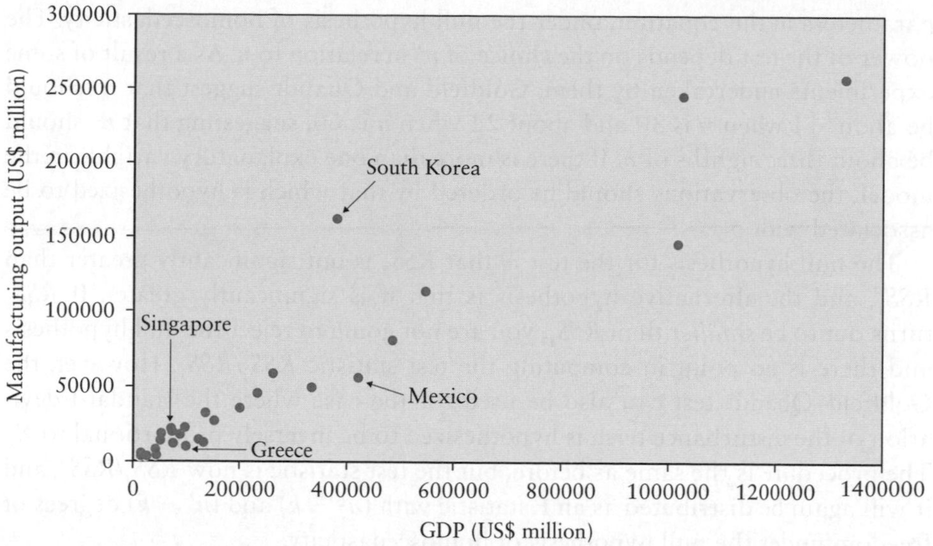

Figure 7.4 Manufacturing output and GDP

7.2 Detection of heteroscedasticity

In principle, there is no limit to the possible different types of heteroscedasticity and accordingly a large number of different tests appropriate for different circumstances have been proposed. They fall into two categories: those that depend on a prior assumption concerning the nature of the heteroscedasticity, and those that do not. We will confine our attention to one of each: the Goldfeld–Quandt test, and the White test.

The Goldfeld–Quandt test

Perhaps the most common formal test for heteroscedasticity is the Goldfeld–Quandt test (Goldfeld and Quandt, 1965). It assumes that σ_{u_i}, the standard deviation of the probability distribution of the disturbance term in observation i, is proportional to the size of X_i. It also assumes that the disturbance term is normally distributed and satisfies the other regression model assumptions.

The n observations in the sample are ordered by the magnitude of X and separate regressions are run for the first n' and for the last n' observations, the middle $(n - 2n')$ observations being dropped entirely. If heteroscedasticity is present, and if the assumption concerning its nature is true, the variance of u in the last n' observations will be greater than that in the first n', and this will be reflected in the residual sums of squares in the two subregressions. Denoting these by RSS_1 and RSS_2 for the subregressions with the first n' and the last n' observations, respectively, the ratio RSS_2/RSS_1 will be distributed as an F statistic with $(n' - k)$ and $(n' - k)$ degrees of freedom, where k is the number of parameters in the equation, under the null hypothesis of homoscedasticity. The power of the test depends on the choice of n' in relation to n. As a result of some experiments undertaken by them, Goldfeld and Quandt suggest that n' should be about 11 when n is 30 and about 22 when n is 60, suggesting that n' should be about three eighths of n. If there is more than one explanatory variable in the model, the observations should be ordered by that which is hypothesized to be associated with σ_i.

The null hypothesis for the test is that RSS_2 is not significantly greater than RSS_1, and the alternative hypothesis is that it is significantly greater. If RSS_2 turns out to be *smaller* than RSS_1, you are not going to reject the null hypothesis and there is no point in computing the test statistic RSS_2/RSS_1. However, the Goldfeld–Quandt test can also be used for the case where the standard deviation of the disturbance term is hypothesized to be inversely proportional to X_i. The procedure is the same as before, but the test statistic is now RSS_1/RSS_2, and it will again be distributed as an F statistic with $(n' - k)$ and $(n' - k)$ degrees of freedom under the null hypothesis of homoscedasticity.

In the case of the data in Table 7.1, OLS regressions were run using the observations for the 11 countries with smallest GDP and for the 11 countries with largest GDP. The residual sum of squares in the first regression was 157×10^6, and in the second it was $13{,}518 \times 10^6$. The ratio RSS_2/RSS_1 was therefore 86.1. The critical value of $F(9, 9)$ at the 0.1 percent level is 10.1, and the null hypothesis of homoscedasticity was therefore rejected.

The White test

The White test for heteroscedasticity (White, 1980) looks more generally for evidence of an association between the variance of the disturbance term and the regressors. Since the variance of the disturbance term in observation i is unobservable, the squared residual for that observation is used as a proxy. The test consists of regressing the squared residuals on the explanatory variables in the model, their squares, and their cross-products, omitting any duplicative variables. (For example, the square of a dummy variable would be duplicative since its values are the same as those of the dummy variable.) The test statistic is nR^2, using R^2 from this regression. Under the null hypothesis of no association, it is distributed as a chi-squared statistic with degrees of freedom equal to the number of regressors, including the constant, minus one, in large samples.

In the case of the data in Table 7.1, the squared residuals were regressed on GDP, its square, and a constant. R^2 was 0.2114 and n was 28. The test statistic was therefore 5.92. The critical value of chi-squared with two degrees of freedom is 5.99 at the 5 percent level and so the null hypothesis of homoscedasticity is not rejected.

Why has the White test failed to detect heteroscedasticity when the Goldfeld–Quandt test concluded that it was present at a high level of significance? One reason is that it is a large-sample test, and the sample is actually quite small. A second is that it tends to have low power—a price that one has to pay for its generality. These problems can be exacerbated by a loss of degrees of freedom if there are many explanatory variables in the original model. In the present example, there was only one explanatory variable, and so only three degrees of freedom were absorbed when fitting the squared residuals regression. If there had been four explanatory variables, 15 degrees of freedom would have been absorbed in the squared residuals regression: five for the constant and the variables, another four for the squares of the variables, and a further six for the cross-product terms, leaving only 13 degrees of freedom in this case for the regression.

EXERCISES

7.1

Country	*I*	*G*	*Y*	*P*	*Country*	*I*	*G*	*Y*	*P*
Australia	94.5	75.5	407.9	18.5	Netherlands	73.0	49.9	360.5	15.6
Austria	46.0	39.2	206.0	8.1	New Zealand	12.9	9.9	65.1	3.8
Canada	119.3	125.1	631.2	30.3	Norway	35.3	30.9	153.4	4.4
Czech Republic	16.0	10.5	52.0	10.3	Philippines	20.1	10.7	82.2	78.5
Denmark	34.2	42.9	169.3	5.3	Poland	28.7	23.4	135.6	38.7
Finland	20.2	25.0	121.5	5.1	Portugal	25.6	19.9	102.1	9.8
France	255.9	347.2	1409.2	58.6	Russia	84.7	94.0	436.0	147.1
Germany	422.5	406.7	2102.7	82.1	Singapore	35.6	9.0	95.9	3.7
Greece	24.0	17.7	119.9	10.5	Spain	109.5	86.0	532.0	39.3
Iceland	1.4	1.5	7.5	0.3	Sweden	31.2	58.8	227.8	8.9
Ireland	14.3	10.1	73.2	3.7	Switzerland	50.2	38.7	256.0	7.1
Italy	190.8	189.7	1145.4	57.5	Thailand	48.1	15.0	153.9	60.6
Japan	1105.9	376.3	3901.3	126.1	Turkey	50.2	23.3	189.1	62.5
Korea	154.9	49.3	442.5	46.0	UK	210.1	230.7	1256.0	58.2
Malaysia	41.6	10.8	97.3	21.0	USA	1517.7	1244.1	8110.9	267.9

The table gives data on government recurrent expenditure, G, investment, I, gross domestic product, Y, and population, P, for 30 countries in 1997 (source: 1999 International Monetary Fund *Yearbook*). G, I, and Y are measured in US$ billion and P in million. A researcher investigating whether government expenditure tends to crowd out investment fits the regression (standard errors in parentheses):

$$\hat{I} = \underset{(7.79)}{18.10} - \underset{(0.14)}{1.07}G + \underset{(0.02)}{0.36}Y \qquad R^2 = 0.99.$$

She sorts the observations by increasing size of Y and runs the regression again for the 11 countries with smallest Y and the 11 countries with largest Y. RSS for these regressions is 321 and 28101, respectively. Perform a Goldfeld–Quandt test for heteroscedasticity.

7.2 The researcher saves the residuals from the full-sample regression in Exercise 7.1 and regresses their squares on G, Y, their squares, and their product. R^2 is 0.9878. Perform a White test for heteroscedasticity.

7.3 Fit an earnings function using your *EAEF* data set, taking *EARNINGS* as the dependent variable and *S*, *EXP*, and *MALE* as the explanatory variables, and perform a Goldfeld–Quandt test for heteroscedasticity in the *S* dimension. Remember to sort the observations by *S* first.

7.4 Fit an earnings function using your *EAEF* data set, using the same specification as in Exercise 7.3 and perform a White test for heteroscedasticity.

7.5* The following regressions were fitted using the Shanghai school cost data introduced in Section 5.1 (standard errors in parentheses):

$$\widehat{COST} = \underset{(27{,}000)}{24{,}000} + \underset{(50)}{339N} \qquad R^2 = 0.39$$

$$\widehat{COST} = \underset{(31{,}000)}{51{,}000} - \underset{(41{,}000)}{4{,}000OCC} + \underset{(60)}{152N} + \underset{(76)}{284NOCC} \qquad R^2 = 0.68,$$

where *COST* is the annual cost of running a school, *N* is the number of students, *OCC* is a dummy variable defined to be 0 for regular schools and 1 for occupational schools, and *NOCC* is a slope dummy variable defined as the product of *N* and *OCC*. There are 74 schools in the sample. With the data sorted by *N*, the regressions are fitted again for the 26 smallest and 26 largest schools, the residual sum of squares being as shown in the table.

	26 smallest	*26 largest*
First regression	7.8×10^{10}	54.4×10^{10}
Second regression	6.7×10^{10}	13.8×10^{10}

Perform a Goldfeld–Quandt test for heteroscedasticity for the two models and, with reference to Figure 5.5, explain why the problem of heteroscedasticity is less severe in the second model.

7.6* The file educ.dta on the website contains international cross-sectional data on aggregate expenditure on education, *EDUC*, gross domestic product, *GDP*, and population, *POP*, for a sample of 38 countries in 1997. *EDUC* and *GDP* are measured in US\$ million and *POP* is measured in thousands. See Appendix B for further information. Download the data set, plot a scatter diagram of *EDUC* on *GDP*, and comment on whether the data set appears to be subject to heteroscedasticity. Sort the data set by *GDP* and perform a Goldfeld–Quandt test for heteroscedasticity, running regressions using the subsamples of 14 countries with the smallest and greatest *GDP*.

7.3 **Remedies for heteroscedasticity**

Suppose that the true relationship is

$$Y_i = \beta_1 + \beta_2 X_i + u_i. \tag{7.2}$$

Let the standard deviation of the disturbance term in observation i be σ_{u_i}. If you happened to know σ_{u_i} for each observation, you could eliminate the heteroscedasticity by dividing each observation by its value of σ. The model becomes

$$\frac{Y_i}{\sigma_{u_i}} = \beta_1 \frac{1}{\sigma_{u_i}} + \beta_2 \frac{X_i}{\sigma_{u_i}} + \frac{u_i}{\sigma_{u_i}}. \tag{7.3}$$

The disturbance term u_i/σ_{u_i} is homoscedastic because the population variance of u_i/σ_{u_i} is

$$E\left\{\left(\frac{u_i}{\sigma_{u_i}}\right)^2\right\} = \frac{1}{\sigma_{u_i}^2} E(u_i^2) = \frac{1}{\sigma_{u_i}^2} \sigma_{u_i}^2 = 1. \tag{7.4}$$

Therefore, every observation will have a disturbance term drawn from a distribution with population variance 1, and the model will be homoscedastic. The revised model may be rewritten

$$Y_i' = \beta_1 H_i + \beta_2 X_i' + u_i', \tag{7.5}$$

where $Y_i' = Y_i/\sigma_{u_i}$, $X_i' = X_i/\sigma_{u_i}$, H is a new variable whose value in observation i is $1/\sigma_{u_i}$, and $u_i' = u_i/\sigma_{u_i}$. Note that there should not be a constant term in the equation. By regressing Y' on H and X', you will obtain efficient estimates of β_1 and β_2 with unbiased standard errors.

A mathematical demonstration that the revised model will yield more efficient estimates than the original one is beyond the scope of this text, but it is easy to give an intuitive explanation. Those observations with the smallest values of σ_{u_i} will be the most useful for locating the true relationship between Y and X because they will tend to have the smallest disturbance terms. We are taking advantage of this fact by performing what is sometimes called weighted least squares (WLS). The fact that observation i is given weight $1/\sigma_{u_i}$ automatically means that the better its quality, the greater the weight that it receives.

The snag with this procedure is that it is most unlikely that you will know the actual values of the σ_{u_i}. However, if you can think of something that is proportional to it in each observation, and divide the equation by that, this will work just as well.

Suppose that you can think of such a variable, which we shall call Z, and it is reasonable to suppose that σ_{u_i} is proportional to Z_i:

$$\sigma_{u_i} = \lambda Z_i \tag{7.6}$$

for some constant, λ. If we divide the original equation through by Z, we have

$$\frac{Y_i}{Z_i} = \beta_1 \frac{1}{Z_i} + \beta_2 \frac{X_i}{Z_i} + \frac{u_i}{Z_i}. \tag{7.7}$$

The model is now homoscedastic because the population variance of u_i/Z_i is

$$E\left\{\left(\frac{u_i}{Z_i}\right)^2\right\} = \frac{1}{Z_i^2} E(u_i^2) = \frac{1}{Z_i^2} \sigma_{u_i}^2 = \frac{\lambda^2 Z_i^2}{Z_i^2} = \lambda^2. \tag{7.8}$$

We do not need to know the value of λ, and indeed in general will not know it. It is enough that it should be constant for all observations.

In particular, it may be reasonable to suppose that σ_{u_i} is roughly proportional to X_i, as in the Goldfeld–Quandt test. If you then divide each observation by its value of X, the model becomes

$$\frac{Y_i}{X_i} = \beta_1 \frac{1}{X_i} + \beta_2 + \frac{u_i}{X_i}, \tag{7.9}$$

and, if the proportionality assumption is true, the new disturbance term u_i/X_i will have constant variance. You now regress Y/X on $1/X$, including a constant term in the regression. The coefficient of $1/X$ will be an efficient estimate of β_1 and the constant will be an efficient estimate of β_2. In the case of the manufacturing output example in the previous section, the dependent variable would be manufacturing output as a proportion of GDP, and the explanatory variable would be the reciprocal of GDP.

Sometimes there may be more than one variable that might be used for scaling the equation. In the case of the manufacturing output example, an alternative candidate would be the size of the population of the country, *POP*. Dividing the original model through by *POP*, one obtains

$$\frac{Y_i}{POP_i} = \beta_1 \frac{1}{POP_i} + \beta_2 \frac{X_i}{POP_i} + \frac{u_i}{POP_i}, \tag{7.10}$$

and again one hopes that the disturbance term, u_i/POP_i, will have constant variance across observations. Thus, now one is regressing manufacturing output per capita on GDP per capita and the reciprocal of the size of the population, this time without a constant term.

Examples

In the previous section it was found that a linear regression of *MANU* on *GDP* using the data in Table 7.1 and the model

$$MANU = \beta_1 + \beta_2 GDP + u \tag{7.11}$$

was subject to severe heteroscedasticity. One possible remedy might be to scale the observations by population, the model becoming

$$\frac{MANU}{POP} = \beta_1 \frac{1}{POP} + \beta_2 \frac{GDP}{POP} + \frac{u}{POP}. \tag{7.12}$$

Figure 7.5 provides a plot of *MANU/POP* on *GDP/POP*. Despite scaling, the plot still looks heteroscedastic. When (7.12) is fitted using the 11 countries with smallest GDP per capita and the 11 countries with the greatest, the residual sums of squares are 5,378,000 and 17,362,000. The ratio, and hence the F statistic, is 3.23. If the subsamples are small, it is possible to obtain high ratios under the null hypothesis of homoscedasticity. In this case, the null hypothesis is just rejected at the 5 percent level, the critical value of $F(9, 9)$ being 3.18.

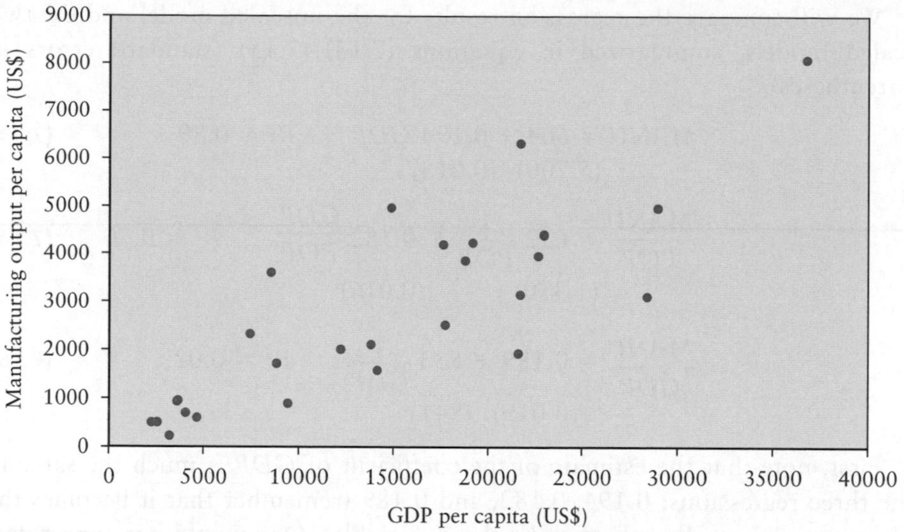

Figure 7.5 Manufacturing output per capita and GDP per capita

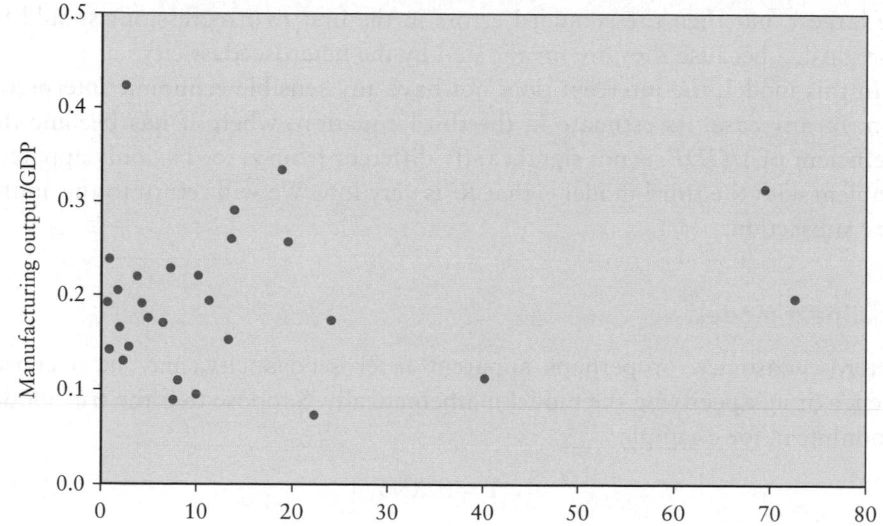

Figure 7.6 Manufacturing as a proportion of GDP and the reciprocal of GDP

Figure 7.6 shows the result of scaling through by GDP itself, manufacturing as a share of GDP being plotted against the reciprocal of GDP. In this case, the residual sums of squares for the subsamples are 0.065 and 0.070, and so finally we have a model where the null hypothesis of homoscedasticity is not rejected.

We will compare the regression results for the unscaled model and the two scaled models, summarized in equations (7.13)–(7.15) (standard errors in parentheses):

$$\widehat{MANU} = \underset{(5{,}700)}{604} + \underset{(0.013)}{0.194}\, GDP \qquad R^2 = 0.89 \tag{7.13}$$

$$\frac{\widehat{MANU}}{POP} = \underset{(1{,}370)}{612}\, \frac{1}{POP} + \underset{(0.016)}{0.182}\, \frac{GDP}{POP} \qquad R^2 = 0.70 \tag{7.14}$$

$$\frac{\widehat{MANU}}{GDP} = \underset{(0.019)}{0.189} + \underset{(841)}{533}\, \frac{1}{GDP} \qquad R^2 = 0.02. \tag{7.15}$$

First, note that the estimate of the coefficient of *GDP* is much the same in the three regressions: 0.194, 0.182, and 0.189 (remember that it becomes the intercept when scaling through by the *X* variable). One would not expect dramatic shifts since heteroscedasticity does not give rise to bias. The estimator in the third estimate should have the smallest variance and therefore ought to have a tendency to be the most accurate. Perhaps surprisingly, its standard error is the largest, but then the standard errors in the first two regressions should be disregarded because they are invalidated by the heteroscedasticity.

In this model, the intercept does not have any sensible economic interpretation. In any case, its estimate in the third equation, where it has become the coefficient of 1/*GDP*, is not significantly different from zero. The only apparent problem with the third model is that R^2 is very low. We will return to this in the next subsection.

Nonlinear models

Heteroscedasticity, or perhaps apparent heteroscedasticity, may be a consequence of misspecifying the model mathematically. Suppose that the true model is nonlinear, for example

$$Y = \beta_1 X^{\beta_2} v, \tag{7.16}$$

with (for sake of argument) β_1 and β_2 positive so that *Y* is an increasing function of *X*. The multiplicative disturbance term v has the effect of increasing or reducing *Y* by a random proportion. Suppose that the probability distribution of v is the same for all observations. This implies, for example, that the probability of a 5 percent increase or decrease in *Y* due to its effects is just the same when *X* is small as when *X* is large. However, in absolute terms a 5 percent increase has a larger effect on *Y* when *X* is large than when *X* is small. If *Y* is plotted against *X*, the scatter of observations will therefore tend to be more widely dispersed about the true relationship as *X* increases, and a linear regression of *Y* on *X* may therefore exhibit heteroscedasticity.

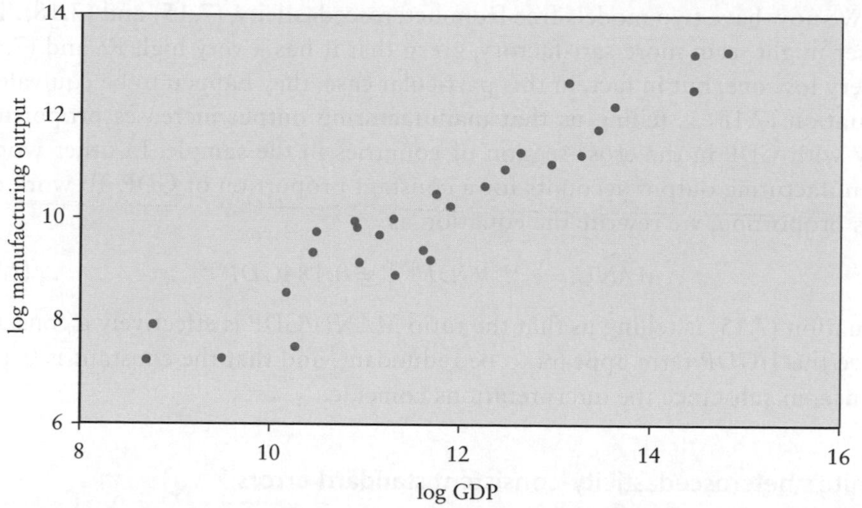

Figure 7.7 The logarithm of manufacturing and the logarithm of GDP

The solution, of course, is to run a logarithmic regression instead:

$$\log Y = \log \beta_1 + \beta_2 \log X + \log v. \quad \textbf{(7.17)}$$

Not only would this be a more appropriate mathematical specification, but it makes the regression model homoscedastic. log v now affects the dependent variable, log Y, additively, so the absolute size of its effect is independent of the magnitude of log X.

Figure 7.7 shows the logarithm of manufacturing output plotted against the logarithm of GDP using the data in Table 7.1. At first sight at least, the plot does not appear to exhibit heteroscedasticity. Logarithmic regressions using the subsamples of 11 countries with smallest and greatest GDP yield residual sums of squares 2.14 and 1.04, respectively. In this case, the conventional Goldfeld–Quandt test is superfluous. Since the second *RSS* is *smaller* than the first, it cannot be significantly *greater*. However, the Goldfeld–Quandt test can also be used to test for heteroscedasticity where the standard deviation of the distribution of the disturbance term is inversely proportional to the size of the X variable. The F statistic is the same, with RSS_1 and RSS_2 interchanged. In the present case, the F statistic if 2.06, which is lower than the critical value of F at the 5 percent level, and we do not reject the null hypothesis of homoscedasticity. Running the regression with the complete sample, we obtain (standard errors in parentheses)

$$\log \widehat{MANU} = \underset{(0.785)}{-1.694} + \underset{(0.066)}{0.999} \log GDP \qquad R^2 = 0.90, \quad \textbf{(7.18)}$$

implying that the elasticity of *MANU* with respect to *GDP* is equal to 1.

We now have two models free from heteroscedasticity, (7.15) and (7.18). The latter might seem more satisfactory, given that it has a very high R^2 and (7.15) a very low one, but in fact, in this particular case, they happen to be equivalent. Equation (7.18) is telling us that manufacturing output increases proportionally with GDP in the cross-section of countries in the sample. In other words, manufacturing output accounts for a constant proportion of GDP. To work out this proportion, we rewrite the equation as

$$\widehat{MANU} = e^{-1.694} GDP^{0.999} = 0.184 GDP^{0.999} . \tag{7.19}$$

Equation (7.15) is telling us that the ratio *MANU*/GDP is effectively a constant, since the $1/GDP$ term appears to be redundant, and that the constant is 0.189. Hence, in substance the interpretations coincide.

White's heteroscedasticity-consistent standard errors

Heteroscedasticity causes OLS standard errors to be biased in finite samples. However, it can be demonstrated that they are nevertheless consistent, provided that their variances are distributed independently of the regressors. Even if a White test demonstrates that this is not the case, it is still possible to obtain consistent estimators. We saw in Section 2.3 that the slope coefficient in a simple OLS regression could be decomposed as

$$b_2^{\mathrm{OLS}} = \beta_2 + \sum_{i=1}^{n} a_i u_i, \tag{7.20}$$

where

$$a_i = \frac{(X_i - \bar{X})}{\sum_{j=1}^{n} (X_j - \bar{X})^2} \tag{7.21}$$

and we saw in Box 2.3 in Section 2.5 that the variance of the estimator is given by

$$\sigma^2_{b_2^{\mathrm{OLS}}} = \sum_{i=1}^{n} a_i^2 E\left(u_i^2\right) = \sum_{i=1}^{n} a_i^2 \sigma^2_{u_i} \tag{7.22}$$

if u_i is distributed independently of u_j for $j \neq i$. White (1980) demonstrates that a consistent estimator of $\sigma^2_{b_2^{\mathrm{OLS}}}$ is obtained if the squared residual in observation i is used as an estimator of $\sigma^2_{u_i}$. Taking the square root, one obtains a **heteroscedasticity-consistent standard error**. Thus, in a situation where heteroscedasticity is suspected, but there is not enough information to identify its nature other than it is of the type detected by a White test, it is possible to overcome the problem of biased standard errors, at least in large samples, and the t tests and F tests are asymptotically valid. Two points need to be kept in mind, however. One is that, although the White estimator is consistent, it may not perform well in finite samples (MacKinnon and White, 1985). The other is that the estimators of the coefficients are unaffected by the procedure and so they remain inefficient.

To illustrate the use of heteroscedasticity-consistent standard errors, the regression of *MANU* on *GDP* in (7.13) was repeated with the 'robust' option available in Stata. The point estimates of the coefficients were exactly the same and so their inefficiency is not alleviated. However, the standard error of the coefficient of *GDP* rose from 0.13 to 0.18, indicating that it was underestimated in the original OLS regression.

How serious are the consequences of heteroscedasticity?

We will undertake a Monte Carlo simulation to illustrate the consequences of heteroscedasticity for the precision of the estimates of the coefficients and for the validity of the standard errors. We will specify the model as

$$Y_i = 10 + 2.0X_i + u_i, \quad \textbf{(7.23)}$$

with the data on X being the integers from 5 to 54 and the disturbance term u generated as

$$u_i = X_i \varepsilon_i, \quad \textbf{(7.24)}$$

where ε_i is IID $N(0, 1)$.

Figure 7.8 shows the relationship, with two lines drawn one standard deviation of u above and below. The divergence of these lines from the relationship provides an indicator of the heteroscedasticity. To eliminate the

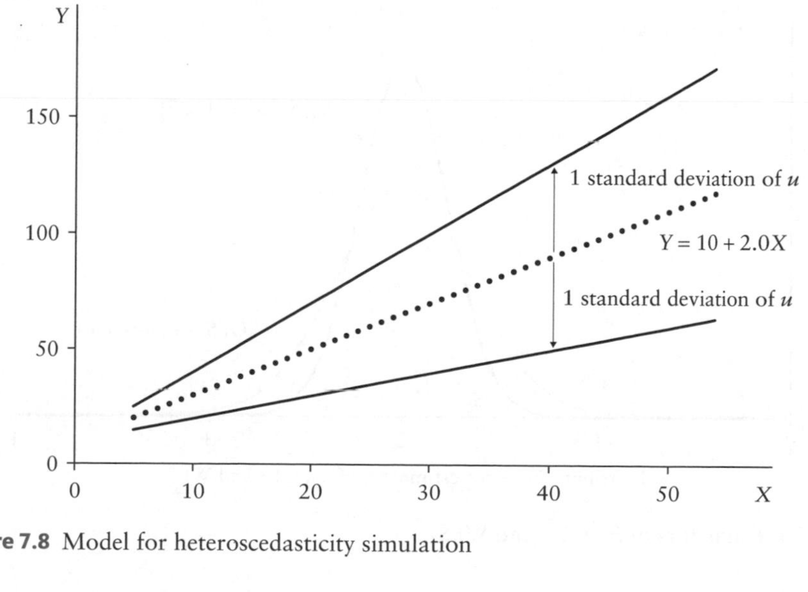

Figure 7.8 Model for heteroscedasticity simulation

heteroscedasticity, we need to use WLS with weight $1/X_i$ for observation i. The model then becomes

$$\frac{Y_i}{X_i} = \frac{10}{X_i} + 2.0 + \frac{u_i}{X_i} = \frac{10}{X_i} + 2.0 + \varepsilon_i \qquad \textbf{(7.25)}$$

and is thus homoscedastic.

Figure 7.9 shows the distribution of b_2 for the OLS regression of (7.23) and of the intercept in the WLS specification (7.25), for 10 million samples. (Note that the intercept is equal to β_2 in the WLS regression.) The means of the distributions are both exactly equal to 2, to three decimal places, confirming that both estimators are unbiased. The standard deviation of the OLS estimator, 0.346, is about 50 percent greater than that of the WLS estimator, 0.227, confirming the greater efficiency of the latter.

We next consider the standard errors. The same considerations apply to standard errors as to the point estimates of the coefficients. We want it to be a reliable indicator of the standard deviation of the distribution of the coefficient. However, like the estimator of the coefficient, it is a random quantity with a distribution of its own. Figure 7.10 shows the distribution of the standard error of the WLS estimator of β_2. The true standard deviation is 0.227 (see Figure 7.9). The WLS standard error is indeed distributed around this number. The mean of the distribution is 0.226, so there is no tendency either to overestimate or to underestimate the standard deviation.

By contrast, the OLS standard error is seriously misleading. The true standard deviation of the OLS estimator is 0.346 (see Figure 7.9, again). As can be seen from Figure 7.10, there is a distinct tendency for it to underestimate

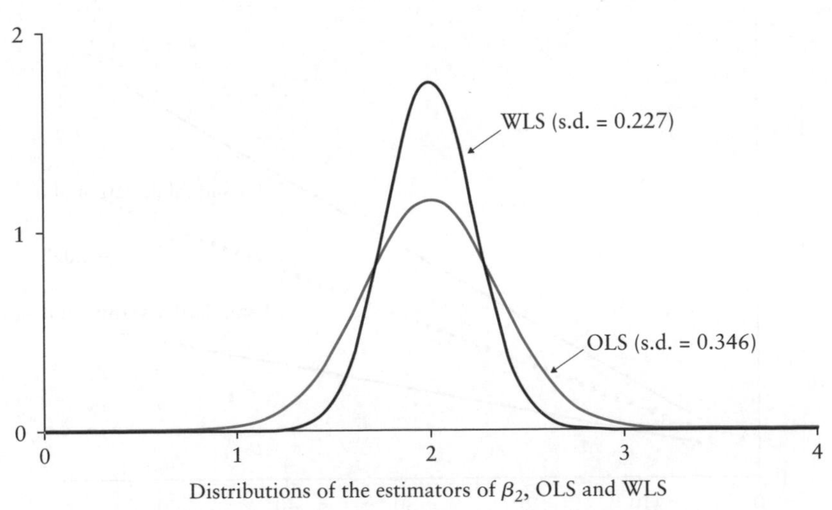

Figure 7.9 Estimators of β_2, OLS and WLS

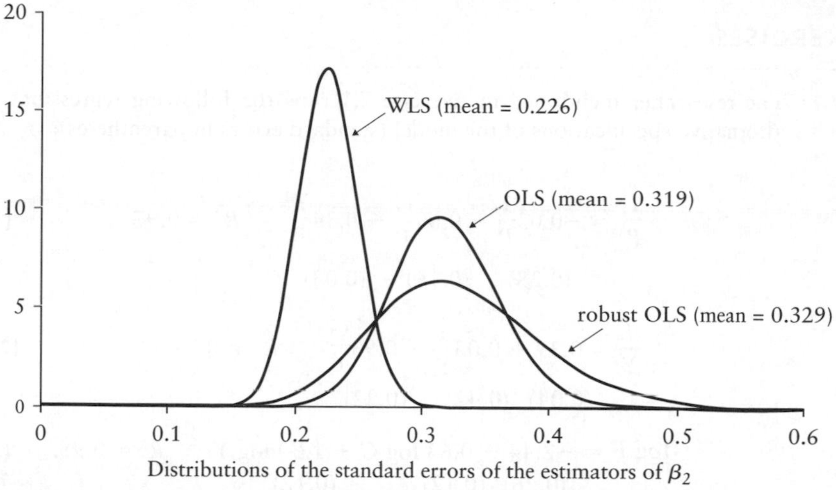

Figure 7.10 Distributions of the standard errors of the estimators of β_2

the true standard deviation. The mean of its distribution is 0.319, which is well below the true standard deviation. If we took it at face value, we would believe the OLS estimator to be more accurate (lower variance) than it actually is.

Finally, we turn to the robust standard error. The estimator of the point estimate is the same as for OLS, so the distribution is that for OLS in Figure 7.9 and the standard deviation is 0.346. However, we hope that the distribution of the standard error will be closer to this figure and so less misleading. The mean of the distribution, 0.329, is indeed closer. Thus, on that criterion, the robust standard error is to be preferred to the ordinary standard error, although there is still a tendency to underestimate the true standard deviation. However, the distribution of the robust standard error has a higher variance than that of the ordinary standard error, and this is an adverse factor. Looking at the distributions in Figure 7.10, it is not obvious that the robust standard error is actually much of an improvement on the OLS standard error. This is not altogether a surprise, since robust standard errors are in theory valid only for large samples. Further, it should be emphasized that this finding applies only to the particular model used for the simulation. If we had had a different type of heteroscedasticity, we might have reached different conclusions.

Key terms

- Goldfeld–Quandt test
- heteroscedasticity
- heteroscedasticity-consistent standard error
- homoscedasticity
- weighted least squares (WLS)
- White test

EXERCISES

7.7 The researcher mentioned in Exercise 7.1 runs the following regressions as alternative specifications of the model (standard errors in parentheses):

$$\frac{\hat{I}}{P} = \underset{(0.28)}{-0.03}\frac{1}{P} - \underset{(0.16)}{0.69}\frac{G}{P} + \underset{(0.03)}{0.34}\frac{Y}{P} \qquad R^2 = 0.97 \qquad \textbf{(1)}$$

$$\frac{\hat{I}}{Y} = \underset{(0.04)}{0.39} + \underset{(0.42)}{0.03}\frac{1}{Y} - \underset{(0.22)}{0.93}\frac{G}{Y} \qquad R^2 = 0.78 \qquad \textbf{(2)}$$

$$\widehat{\log I} = \underset{(0.26)}{-2.44} - \underset{(0.12)}{0.63} \log G + \underset{(0.12)}{1.60} \log Y \qquad R^2 = 0.98. \qquad \textbf{(3)}$$

In each case, the regression is run again for the subsamples of observations with the 11 smallest and 11 greatest values of the sorting variable, after sorting by *Y/P*, *G/Y*, and log *Y*, respectively. The residual sums of squares are as shown in the table.

	11 smallest	*11 largest*
(1)	1.43	12.63
(2)	0.0223	0.0155
(3)	0.573	0.155

Perform a Goldfeld–Quandt test for each model specification and discuss the merits of each specification. Is there evidence that investment is an inverse function of government expenditure?

7.8 Using your *EAEF* data set, repeat Exercises 7.3 and 7.4 with *LGEARN* as the dependent variable. Is there evidence that this is a preferable specification?

7.9* Repeat Exercise 7.6, using the Goldfeld–Quandt test to investigate whether scaling by population or by *GDP*, or whether running the regression in logarithmic form, would eliminate the heteroscedasticity. Compare the results of regressions using the entire sample and the alternative specifications.

7.10* It was reported above that the heteroscedasticity-consistent estimate of the standard error of the coefficient of *GDP* in equation (7.13) was 0.18. Explain why the corresponding standard error in equation (7.15) ought to be lower and comment on the fact that it is not.

7.11* A health economist plans to evaluate whether screening patients on arrival or spending extra money on cleaning is more effective in reducing the incidence of infections by the MRSA bacterium in hospitals. She hypothesizes the following model:

$$MRSA_i = \beta_1 + \beta_2 S_i + \beta_3 C_i + u_i,$$

where, in hospital i, *MRSA* is the number of infections per thousand patients, *S* is expenditure per patient on screening, and *C* is expenditure per patient on cleaning. u_i is a disturbance term that satisfies the usual regression model assumptions. In particular, u_i is drawn from a distribution with mean zero and constant variance σ^2. The researcher would like to fit the relationship using a sample of hospitals. Unfortunately, data for individual hospitals are not available. Instead, she has to use regional data to fit

$$\overline{MRSA}_j = \beta_1 + \beta_2 \overline{S}_j + \beta_3 \overline{C}_j + \overline{u}_j,$$

where $\overline{MRSA}_j$, $\overline{S}_j$, $\overline{C}_j$, and $\overline{u}_j$ are the averages of *MRSA*, *S*, *C*, and *u* for the hospitals in region *j*. There were different numbers of hospitals in the regions, there being n_j hospitals in region *j*.

Show that the variance of $\overline{u}_j$ is equal to σ^2/n_j and that an OLS regression using the grouped regional data to fit the relationship will be subject to heteroscedasticity.

Assuming that the researcher knows the value of n_j for each region, explain how she could re-specify the regression model to make it homoscedastic. State the revised specification and demonstrate mathematically that it is homoscedastic. Give an intuitive explanation of why the revised specification should tend to produce improved estimates of the parameters.

8. Stochastic Regressors and Measurement Errors

So far we have been exploring the regression model within the framework of Model A, in terms of the model classification in Section 2.1, where we assume that the regressors—the explanatory variables—in the regression model are nonstochastic. This means that they do not have random components and that their values in the sample are fixed. Nonstochastic regressors are actually unusual in regression analysis. The reason for making the nonstochasticity assumption has been the technical one of simplifying the analysis of the properties of the regression estimators. We will now progress to Model B and the case of stochastic regressors, where the values of the regressors are assumed to be drawn randomly from defined populations. This is a much more realistic framework for regressions with cross-sectional data.

8.1 Assumptions for models with stochastic regressors

We will begin by re-stating the regression model assumptions and then review the properties of the modified model.

B.1 The model is linear in parameters and correctly specified.

This is the same as Assumption A.1.

B.2 The values of the regressors are drawn randomly from fixed populations.

The values of the regressors in the observations in the sample are drawn randomly from fixed populations with finite means and finite nonzero population variances. Note that we do *not* assume that the regressors are independent of each other. On the contrary, we allow their populations to have joint probability distributions and as a consequence their sample values may be correlated.

B.3 There does not exist an exact linear relationship among the regressors.

This is the counterpart of Assumption A.2. Note that if there is a constant in the model, the assumption includes a requirement that there be some variation in each of the regressors. Strictly speaking, this is a population assumption. However, as a practical matter, it must also be satisfied by the data in a sample. Otherwise there would be exact multicollinearity and it would be impossible to obtain estimates of the parameters of the model.

B.4 The disturbance term has zero expectation.

$$E(u_i) = 0 \quad \text{for all } i. \tag{8.1}$$

This is the same as Assumption A.3.

B.5 The disturbance term is homoscedastic.

$$\sigma^2_{u_i} = \sigma^2_u \quad \text{for all } i. \tag{8.2}$$

This is the same as Assumption A.4.

B.6 The values of the disturbance term have independent distributions.

$$u_i \text{ is distributed independently of } u_{i'} \quad \text{for all } i' \neq i. \tag{8.3}$$

This is the same as Assumption A.5.

B.7 The disturbance term is distributed independently of the regressors.

$$u_i \text{ is distributed independently of } X_{ji'} \quad \text{for all } i' \text{ and all } j. \tag{8.4}$$

This is a new assumption. In Model A, the fact that the regressors had fixed nonstochastic values meant that it was impossible for there to be a distributional relationship between them and the disturbance term. Now that they have random components, the possibility arises. We will see that a violation of the assumption has adverse consequences for the properties of the regression coefficients. Note that the assumption, as stated, means that u_i is distributed independently of the value of every regressor in every observation, not just observation i. In practice, with cross-sectional data it is usually reasonable to suppose that u_i is distributed independently of $X_{ji'}$ for all $i' \neq i$ and so the assumption reduces to u_i being distributed independently of X_{ji}. It can be weakened as follows:

B.7′ The disturbance term has zero conditional expectation.

$$E(u_i \mid \text{values of all the regressors in all observations}) = 0. \tag{8.5}$$

Again, in practice with cross-sectional data it is usually reasonable to suppose that it is sufficient to condition on the values of the regressors in observation i only.

B.8 The disturbance term has a normal distribution.

As with Model A, we need this assumption when we perform tests.

Assumption B.5 and the consequences of its violation have been discussed in the previous chapter. A discussion of Assumption B.6 will be deferred until we come to time series data in Chapter 11. As noted in Chapter 2, Assumption B.4 can be made to be true if we assume that any systematic component of the disturbance term is included in the intercept in the regression model. Note that if we make Assumption B.7′ instead of Assumption B.7, Assumption B.4 is redundant anyway. Under Assumption B.7′, the expectation of u_i, conditional on the specific values of the regressors in the sample, is zero. Since the values of the regressors are generated randomly (Assumption B.2), it follows that the expectation of u_i is zero for *any* values of the regressors, and hence it is zero unconditionally.

8.2 Finite sample properties of the OLS regression estimators

We will start by reviewing the properties of the OLS regression coefficients in our new framework. We will focus on the simple regression model

$$Y_i = \beta_1 + \beta_2 X_i + u_i. \tag{8.6}$$

We have seen in Chapter 2 that the OLS estimator of the slope coefficient can be decomposed as follows:

$$b_2 = \frac{\sum_{i=1}^{n}(X_i - \overline{X})(Y_i - \overline{Y})}{\sum_{i=1}^{n}(X_i - \overline{X})^2} = \beta_2 + \sum_{i=1}^{n} a_i u_i, \tag{8.7}$$

where

$$a_i = \frac{(X_i - \overline{X})}{\sum_{j=1}^{n}(X_j - \overline{X})^2}. \tag{8.8}$$

Hence,

$$E\left(b_2^{\mathrm{OLS}}\right) = \beta_2 + E\left(\sum a_i u_i\right) = \beta_2 + \sum E\left(a_i u_i\right). \tag{8.9}$$

In Model A, where the values of X were nonstochastic, and hence a_i was nonstochastic, we could rewrite $E(a_i u_i)$ as $a_i E(u_i)$, which is zero under Assumption A.3. We cannot do that here because the values of X in the observations are stochastic. Instead we appeal to Assumption B.7. If u_i is distributed independently of every value of X in the sample, it is distributed independently of a_i. Now if X and u are independent, we can make use of the decomposition

$$E\{f(X)g(u)\} = E\{f(X)\}E\{g(u)\}. \tag{8.10}$$

for any functions $f(X)$ and $g(u)$ (see the Review chapter). Put $f(X) = a_i$ and $g(u) = u_i$ and we have

$$E\left(a_i u_i\right) = E(a_i)E\left(u_i\right). \tag{8.11}$$

This allows us to rewrite (8.9) as

$$E\left(b_2^{\mathrm{OLS}}\right) = \beta_2 + \sum E\left(a_i\right)E\left(u_i\right). \tag{8.12}$$

With $E(u_i)$ equal to zero under Assumption B.4, it would appear that the second term on the right side of the equation is equal to zero and hence that we have

BOX 8.1 Proof of the unbiasedness of the estimator of the slope coefficient in a simple regression model under Assumption B.7

Writing the values of X in the sample as $\{X_1, ..., X_n\}$,

$$E\left(b_2^{\text{OLS}} \mid \{X_1,...,X_n\}\right) = \beta_2 + E\left(\sum_{i=1}^{n} a_i u_i \mid \{X_1,...,X_n\}\right) = \beta_2 + \sum_{i=1}^{n} E\left(a_i u_i \mid \{X_1,...,X_n\}\right).$$

Since a_i is a function of the X_i, it may be taken out of the expectation. Hence,

$$E\left(b_2^{\text{OLS}} \mid \{X_1,...,X_n\}\right) = \beta_2 + \sum_{i=1}^{n} a_i E\left(u_i \mid \{X_1,...,X_n\}\right) = \beta_2$$

since

$$E\left(u_i \mid \{X_1,...,X_n\}\right) = 0$$

under Assumption B.7′. Thus, the estimator of the slope coefficient is unbiased, conditional on the actual values of X in the sample. But under Assumption B.2, this is true for any values of X, and hence the estimator is unbiased unconditionally. However, we do need the a_i to be defined, and for this we require Assumption B.3, which we need also to be able to compute the OLS coefficients. Hence, as with Assumption B.7, we conclude that the OLS estimators will be unbiased, if it is possible to compute the coefficients in the first place.

proved unbiasedness. However, we also need to be sure that $E(a_i)$ exists. For this we need Assumption B.3, which in a simple regression model reduces to the requirement that there be some variation in X. Strictly speaking, the assumption relates to the population from which X is drawn. Now even if there is variation in X in the population, it is conceivable that we might be unlucky and draw a sample with constant values. However, if this is the case, it is not possible to compute the OLS regression coefficients anyway. Thus, we can say that the OLS estimators will be unbiased, if it is possible to compute them in the first place. See Box 8.1 for a similarly conditional proof of unbiasedness under the weaker Assumption B.7′.

Precision and efficiency

Provided that they are regarded as being conditional on the sample values of the regressor(s), the expressions for the variances of the regression coefficients for the simple regression model in Chapter 2 and the multiple regression model with two regressors in Chapter 3 remain valid. Likewise the Gauss–Markov theorem remains valid in this conditional sense.

8.3 Asymptotic properties of the OLS regression estimators

We did not investigate the asymptotic properties of the regression estimators—their properties as the sample size becomes large—within the framework of

Model A. Before discussing the reasons for this, we might ask why we should ever be interested in the asymptotic properties of estimators when in practice we have only finite samples.

The main reason is that the expected value rules are weak tools and generally do not allow us to investigate the properties of the regression estimators when the regression model becomes complex. By contrast, the plim rules are robust and often do allow us to predict what would happen if the sample became large. Even though in practice we normally have finite samples, rather than large ones, asymptotic results can be helpful indirectly. Other things being equal, we should prefer consistent estimators to inconsistent ones. A consistent estimator may be biased in finite samples, but often the bias is not serious. (Of course, on this latter point, one would need to undertake a suitable Monte Carlo experiment.) On the other hand, if an estimator is biased in large samples, it follows that it will also be biased in finite ones. Note the qualifying 'other things being equal'. We might prefer an inconsistent estimator to a consistent one after all if the element of bias is small and if the consistent estimator had a larger variance.

We have not needed to concern ourselves with these issues so far because we have been working within the framework of Model A where the regressors are assumed to be nonstochastic. This assumption has allowed us to obtain results using the expected value rules whenever we needed to do so. Indeed, this was the reason that we have been using Model A so far. It is also doubtful if we could have investigated these issues, even if we had so wished. This is because we need to be able to describe how the distribution of the regressors behaves as the sample size becomes large, and Model A is silent on this score. In Model A, we assert that the regressors are nonstochastic, but we have no explanation of how their values are generated.

Now that we have moved to Model B, and the regression model has become more complex, asymptotics will become an important part of our analysis. And with Model B we do have a story to tell with regard to the regressors or, to put it more formally, a data generation process, if only a simple one. We are assuming that for each regressor the sample values are drawn randomly from a defined population. As a consequence, the sample distribution will increasingly resemble the population distribution as the sample size becomes large.

Consistency

We have seen that, for any finite sample of size n, the OLS slope coefficient in a simple regression model may be decomposed as

$$b_2 = \frac{\sum_{i=1}^{n}(X_i - \bar{X})(Y_i - \bar{Y})}{\sum_{i=1}^{n}(X_i - \bar{X})^2} = \beta_2 + \frac{\sum_{i=1}^{n}(X_i - \bar{X})(u_i - \bar{u})}{\sum_{i=1}^{n}(X_i - \bar{X})^2} = \beta_2 + \sum_{i=1}^{n} a_i u_i, \qquad \textbf{(8.13)}$$

where a_i is defined in (8.8). What can we say about plim b_2, its limiting value as n becomes large? To use the plim rules, we have to organize the right side of the relationship so that it consists of constants or elements that have limits as n becomes large. In the present case, we focus on the second part of the equation. Neither $\sum(X_i - \bar{X})(u_i - \bar{u})$ nor $\sum(X_i - \bar{X})^2$ has a limit. In general, both will increase indefinitely with n. However, if we rewrite the relationship as

$$b_2 = \beta_2 + \frac{\frac{1}{n}\sum_{i=1}^{n}(X_i - \bar{X})(u_i - \bar{u})}{\frac{1}{n}\sum_{i=1}^{n}(X_i - \bar{X})^2}, \qquad (8.14)$$

we obtain what we need. As the sample size becomes large, the numerator of the quotient will converge on σ_{Xu}, the population covariance between X and u, and the denominator will converge on σ_X^2, the population variance of X. The former is zero by virtue of Assumption B.7 and the second is nonzero by virtue of Assumption B.3, so we have

$$\text{plim } b_2 = \beta_2 + \frac{\text{plim } \frac{1}{n}\sum_{i=1}^{n}(X_i - \bar{X})(u_i - \bar{u})}{\text{plim } \frac{1}{n}\sum_{i=1}^{n}(X_i - \bar{X})^2} = \beta_2 + \frac{\sigma_{Xu}}{\sigma_X^2} = \beta_2 + \frac{0}{\sigma_X^2} = \beta_2 \qquad (8.15)$$

and we have shown that b_2 is a consistent estimator of β_2.

Asymptotic normality of the regression coefficients

We have shown that, provided that the regression model assumptions are valid, the OLS regression coefficients in the simple regression model can be decomposed into their true values and error terms that are a linear combination of the values of the disturbance terms in the sample. This decomposition generalizes to multiple regression analysis. It follows that if Assumption B.8, which states that the disturbance term should have a normal distribution, is valid, the regression coefficients will also have normal distributions, conditional on the observed values of the explanatory variables. This follows from the fact that a sum of normal distributions is itself a normal distribution. Hence, we may perform t tests and F tests in the usual way. The justification for Assumption B.8 is that it is reasonable to suppose that the disturbance term is jointly generated by a number of minor random factors, and a central limit theorem states that the combination of these factors should approximately have a normal distribution, even if the individual factors do not.

What happens if we have reason to believe that Assumption B.8 is not valid? The central limit theorem comes into the frame a second time. Since the random component of a regression coefficient is a linear combination of the values of the disturbance term in the sample, by virtue of the central limit theorem the combination will have an approximately normal distribution, even if the individual values of the disturbance term do not, provided that the sample is large enough.

EXERCISE

8.1 Demonstrate that $b_1 = \overline{Y} - b_2\overline{X}$ is a consistent estimator of β_1 in the simple regression model. (You may take as given that b_2 is a consistent estimator of β_2.)

8.4 The consequences of measurement errors

We have seen that progressing from Model A to Model B does not lead to any major change in the way that we view the regression model and its properties, provided that the regression model assumptions are satisfied. Assumption B.7, that the disturbance term be distributed independently of the regressors (or alternatively its weaker Assumption B.7′), is particularly important. We will now examine the consequences of its failure in two contexts: measurement error in the rest of this chapter, and simultaneous equations estimation in the next.

It frequently happens in economics that, when you are investigating a relationship, the variables involved have not been measured precisely. For example, most macroeconomic variables, such as gross domestic product, are estimated via sample surveys and the numbers are just approximations. Microeconomic surveys often contain errors caused by the respondent not remembering properly or not understanding a question correctly. However, survey errors are not the only source of inaccuracy. It sometimes happens that you have defined a variable in your model in a certain way, but the available data correspond to a slightly different concept. Friedman's critique of the conventional consumption function, discussed at the end of this section, is a celebrated example.

Measurement errors in the explanatory variable(s)

Let us suppose that a variable Y depends on a variable Z according to the relationship

$$Y_i = \beta_1 + \beta_2 Z_i + v_i, \tag{8.16}$$

where v is a disturbance term with mean zero and variance σ_v^2, distributed independently of Z. We shall suppose that Z cannot be measured absolutely accurately, and we shall use X to denote its measured value. In observation i, X_i

is equal to the true value, Z_i, plus the measurement error, w_i:

$$X_i = Z_i + w_i. \tag{8.17}$$

We shall suppose that w has mean zero and variance σ_w^2, that Z has population variance σ_Z^2, and that w is distributed independently of Z and v.

Substituting from (8.17) into (8.16), we obtain

$$Y_i = \beta_1 + \beta_2(X_i - w_i) + v_i = \beta_1 + \beta_2 X_i + v_i - \beta_2 w_i. \tag{8.18}$$

This equation has two random components, the original disturbance term v and the measurement error (multiplied by $-\beta_2$). Together they form a composite disturbance term, which we shall call u:

$$u_i = v_i - \beta_2 w_i. \tag{8.19}$$

Equation (8.18) may then be written

$$Y_i = \beta_1 + \beta_2 X_i + u_i. \tag{8.20}$$

You have your data on Y (which, for the time being, we shall assume has been measured accurately) and X, and you unsuspectingly regress Y on X. However, by virtue of (8.17) and (8.19), both X_i and u_i depend on w_i. Because they have a component in common, Assumption B.7 is violated and as a consequence b_2 is an inconsistent estimator of β_2. We will demonstrate this.

As usual, the regression coefficient b_2 is given by

$$b_2 = \frac{\sum_{i=1}^{n}(X_i - \bar{X})(Y_i - \bar{Y})}{\sum_{i=1}^{n}(X_i - \bar{X})^2} = \beta_2 + \frac{\sum_{i=1}^{n}(X_i - \bar{X})(u_i - \bar{u})}{\sum_{i=1}^{n}(X_i - \bar{X})^2}. \tag{8.21}$$

Since X and u are not distributed independently of each other, there is no simple way of summarizing the behavior of the error term in finite samples. We cannot even obtain an expression for its expected value. Rewriting it as $\sum a_i u_i$, with the a_i as defined in (8.8), does not help. $E\left(\sum a_i u_i\right) = \sum E(a_i u_i)$ cannot be decomposed as $\sum E(a_i)E(u_i)$ because the a_i are not independent of the u_i. The most we can do is to predict how the error term would behave if the sample were very large. As they stand, neither the numerator nor the denominator of the error term tends to a limit as the sample becomes large. However, if we divide both of them by n, this problem is overcome, since it can be shown that

$$\operatorname{plim}\left(\frac{1}{n}\sum_{i=1}^{n}(X_i - \bar{X})(u_i - \bar{u})\right) = \operatorname{cov}(X, u) \tag{8.22}$$

and

$$\operatorname{plim}\left(\frac{1}{n}\sum_{i=1}^{n}(X_i - \bar{X})^2\right) = \operatorname{var}(X). \tag{8.23}$$

Hence,

$$\text{plim } b_2 = \beta_2 + \frac{\text{cov}(X,u)}{\text{var}(X)}. \tag{8.24}$$

We can analyze the error term in more detail by looking at the components of X and u. To do this, we will use the rules for manipulating population covariances and variances summarized in Section R.4 of the Review chapter. We will start with the numerator of the error term:

$$\begin{aligned} \text{cov}(X,u) &= \text{cov}\left((Z+w),(v-\beta_2 w)\right) \\ &= \text{cov}(Z,v)+\text{cov}(w,v)+\text{cov}(Z,-\beta_2 w)+\text{cov}(w,-\beta_2 w). \end{aligned} \tag{8.25}$$

We will assume that the disturbance term v in the original model satisfies the regression model assumptions and is therefore distributed independently of Z. We will also assume that the measurement error w is distributed independently of Z and v. If this is the case, the first three covariances on the right side of the equation are zero. However, the last covariance is $\beta_2\text{var}(w)$. Hence,

$$\text{cov}(X,u) = -\beta_2 \text{var}(w) = -\beta_2 \sigma_w^2. \tag{8.26}$$

Next, take the denominator:

$$\text{var}(X) = \text{var}(Z+w) = \text{var}(Z) + \text{var}(w) + 2\,\text{cov}(Z,w) = \sigma_Z^2 + \sigma_w^2 \tag{8.27}$$

since we are assuming $\text{cov}(Z, w) = 0$. Hence,

$$\text{plim } b_2 = \beta_2 + \frac{\text{plim } \frac{1}{n}\sum_{i=1}^{n}(X_i-\bar{X})(u_i-\bar{u})}{\text{plim } \frac{1}{n}\sum_{i=1}^{n}(X_i-\bar{X})^2} = \beta_2 - \beta_2\frac{\sigma_w^2}{\sigma_Z^2+\sigma_w^2}. \tag{8.28}$$

Thus, we have shown that in large samples b_2 is subject to measurement error bias that causes the coefficient to be underestimated in absolute size (the bias is negative if β_2 is positive and positive if β_2 is negative). The bigger the population variance of the measurement error, relative to the population variance of Z, the bigger will be the bias.

We have assumed that w is distributed independently of v and Z. The first assumption is usually plausible because in general there is no reason for any measurement error in an explanatory variable to be correlated with the disturbance term. However, we may have to relax the second assumption. If we do, b_2 remains inconsistent, but the expression for the bias becomes more complex. See Exercise 8.5.

The analysis will be illustrated with a simulation. The true model is

$$Y = 2.0 + 0.8Z + u, \tag{8.29}$$

with the values of Z drawn randomly from a normal distribution with mean 10 and variance 4, the values of u being drawn from a normal distribution with mean 0 and variance 4. $X = Z + w$, where w is drawn from a normal distribution with mean 0 and variance 1.

$$\text{plim } b_2 = \beta_2 - \frac{\beta_2 \sigma_w^2}{\sigma_Z^2 + \sigma_w^2} = 0.8 - 0.8\frac{1}{4+1} = 0.8 - 0.16 = 0.64. \quad \textbf{(8.30)}$$

Figure 8.1 shows the distributions of b_2 for sample size 20 and sample size 1,000, for 10 million samples. For both sample sizes, the distributions reveal that the OLS estimator is biased downwards. Further, the figure suggests that, if the sample size were increased, the distribution would contract to the limiting value of 0.64. There remains the question of whether the limiting value provides guidance to the mean of the distribution for a finite sample. In general, the mean will be different from the limiting value, but will approach it as the sample size increases. In the present case, however, the mean of the sample is almost exactly equal to 0.64, even for sample size 20.

Measurement errors in the dependent variable

Measurement errors in the dependent variable do not matter as much. In practice, they can be thought of as contributing to the disturbance term. They are undesirable, because anything that increases the noise in the model will tend to make the regression estimates less accurate, but they will not cause the regression estimates to be biased.

Let the true value of the dependent variable be Q, and the true relationship be

$$Q_i = \beta_1 + \beta_2 X_i + v_i, \quad \textbf{(8.31)}$$

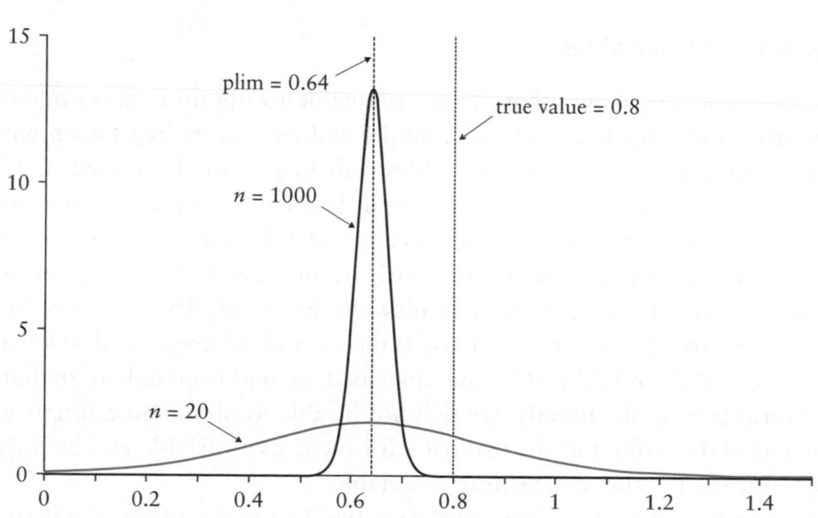

Figure 8.1 Distributions of b_2 for sample sizes 20 and 1,000

where v is a disturbance term. If Y_i is the measured value of the dependent variable in observation i, and r_i is the measurement error,

$$Y_i = Q_i + r_i. \tag{8.32}$$

Hence, the relationship between the observed value of the dependent variable and X is given by

$$Y_i - r_i = \beta_1 + \beta_2 X_i + v_i, \tag{8.33}$$

which may be rewritten

$$Y_i = \beta_1 + \beta_2 X_i + u_i, \tag{8.34}$$

where u is the composite disturbance term $(v + r)$.

The only difference from the usual model is that the disturbance term in (8.34) has two components: the original disturbance term and the error in measuring Y. The important thing is that the explanatory variable X has not been affected. Hence, OLS still yields unbiased estimates provided that X is nonstochastic or that it is distributed independently of v and r. The population variance of the slope coefficient will be given by

$$\sigma_{b_2}^2 = \frac{\sigma_u^2}{\sum_{i=1}^{n}(X_i - \bar{X})^2} = \frac{\sigma_v^2 + \sigma_r^2}{\sum_{i=1}^{n}(X_i - \bar{X})^2} \tag{8.35}$$

and so will be greater than it would have been in the absence of measurement error, reducing the precision of the estimator. The standard errors remain valid but will be larger than they would have been in the absence of the measurement error, reflecting the loss of precision.

Imperfect proxy variables

In Chapter 6 it was shown that, if we are unable to obtain data on one of the explanatory variables in a regression model and we run the regression without it, the coefficients of the other variables will in general be biased and their standard errors will be invalid. However, in Section 6.4 we saw that if we are able to find a perfect proxy for the missing variable, that is, another variable that has an exact linear relationship with it, and use that in its place in the regression, most of the regression results will be saved. Thus, the coefficients of the other variables will not be biased, their standard errors and associated t tests will be valid, and R^2 will be the same as if we had been able to include the unmeasurable variable directly. We will not be able to obtain an estimate of the coefficient of the latter, but the t statistic for the proxy variable will be the same as the t statistic for the unmeasurable variable.

However, it is unusual to find a perfect proxy. Generally, the best that you can hope for is a proxy that is approximately linearly related to the missing variable.

The consequences of using an imperfect proxy instead of a perfect one are parallel to those of using a variable subject to measurement error instead of one that is free from it. It will cause the regression coefficients to be biased, the standard errors to be invalid, and so on, after all.

The use of a proxy may nevertheless be justified if there is reason to believe that the degree of imperfection is not so great as to cause the bias to be serious and the standard errors to be misleading. Since there is normally no way of testing whether the degree of imperfection is great or small, the case for using a proxy has to be made on subjective grounds in the context of the model.

Example: Friedman's permanent income hypothesis

One of the most celebrated applications of measurement error analysis in the whole of economic theory is Friedman's critique of the use of OLS to fit a consumption function (Friedman, 1957). In a sense, it may be considered to be an example of imperfect proxy analysis. We discuss here Friedman's analysis of the problem and in Section 11.4 we will discuss his solution.

In Friedman's permanent income hypothesis model, the consumption of individual (or household) i is related, not to actual (measured) current income Y_i, but to permanent income, which will be denoted Y_i^P. Permanent income is to be thought of as a medium-term notion of income: the amount that the individual can more or less depend on for the foreseeable future, taking into account possible fluctuations. It is subjectively determined by recent experience and by expectations about the future, and because it is subjective it cannot be measured directly. Actual income at any moment may be higher or lower than permanent income depending on the influence of short-run random factors. The difference between actual and permanent income caused by these factors is described as transitory income, Y_i^T. Thus,

$$Y_i = Y_i^P + Y_i^T. \tag{8.36}$$

In the same way, Friedman makes a distinction between actual consumption, C_i, and permanent consumption, C_i^P. Permanent consumption is the level of consumption justified by the level of permanent income. Actual consumption may differ from it as special, unforeseen circumstances arise (unanticipated medical bills, for example) or as a consequence of impulse purchases. The difference between actual and permanent consumption is described as transitory consumption, C_i^T. Thus,

$$C_i = C_i^P + C_i^T. \tag{8.37}$$

Y_i^T and C_i^T are assumed to be random variables with mean zero and constant variance, uncorrelated with Y_i^P and C_i^P and each other. Friedman further hypothesizes that permanent consumption is directly proportional to permanent income:

$$C_i^P = \beta_2 Y_i^P. \tag{8.38}$$

If the Friedman model is correct, what happens if you ignorantly try to fit the usual simple consumption function, relating measured consumption to measured income? Well, both the dependent and the explanatory variables in the regression

$$\hat{C}_i = b_1 + b_2 Y_i \tag{8.39}$$

have been measured inappropriately, C_i^T and Y_i^T being the measurement errors. In terms of the previous discussion,

$$Z_i = Y_i^P, \quad w_i = Y_i^T, \quad Q_i = C_i^P, \quad r_i = C_i^T. \tag{8.40}$$

We have seen that the only effect of the measurement error in the dependent variable is to increase the variance of the disturbance term. The use of the wrong income concept is more serious. It causes the estimate of β_2 to be inconsistent. From (8.28), we can see that in large samples

$$\text{plim } b_2 = \beta_2 - \frac{\sigma_{Y^T}^2}{\sigma_{Y^P}^2 + \sigma_{Y^T}^2}\beta_2, \tag{8.41}$$

where $\sigma_{Y^T}^2$ is the population variance of Y^T and $\sigma_{Y^P}^2$ is the population variance of Y^P. It implies that, even in large samples, the apparent marginal propensity to consume (your estimate b_2) will be lower than the value of β_2 in the true relationship (8.38). The size of the bias depends on the ratio of the variance of transitory income to that of permanent income. It will be highest for those occupations whose earnings are most subject to fluctuations. An obvious example is farming. Friedman's model predicts that, even if farmers have the same β_2 as the rest of the population, an OLS estimate of their marginal propensity to consume will be relatively low, and this is consistent with the facts (Friedman, 1957, pp. 57 ff.).

EXERCISES

8.2 In a certain industry, firms relate their stocks of finished goods, Y, to their expected annual sales, X^e, according to a linear relationship

$$Y = \beta_1 + \beta_2 X^e.$$

Actual sales, X, differ from expected sales by a random quantity u, that is distributed with zero mean and constant variance:

$$X = X^e + u,$$

where u is distributed independently of X^e. An investigator has data on Y and X (but not on X^e) for a cross-section of firms in the industry. Describe the problems that would be encountered if OLS were used to estimate β_1 and β_2, regressing Y on X.

8.3 In a similar industry, firms relate their *intended* stocks of finished goods, Y^*, to their expected annual sales, X^e, according to a linear relationship

$$Y^* = \beta_1 + \beta_2 X^e.$$

Actual sales, X, differ from expected sales by a random quantity u, which is distributed with zero mean and constant variance:

$$X = X^e + u,$$

where u is distributed independently of X^e. Since unexpected sales lead to a reduction in stocks, actual stocks are given by

$$Y = Y^* - u.$$

An investigator has data on Y and X (but not on Y^* or X^e) for a cross-section of firms in the industry. Describe analytically the problems that would be encountered if OLS were used to estimate β_1 and β_2, regressing Y on X. [*Note:* You are warned that the standard expression for measurement error bias is not valid in this case.]

8.4* A variable Q is determined by the model

$$Q = \beta_1 + \beta_2 X + v,$$

where X is a variable and v is a disturbance term that satisfies the regression model conditions. The dependent variable is subject to measurement error and is measured as Y where

$$Y = Q + r$$

and r is the measurement error, distributed independently of v. Describe analytically the consequences of using OLS to fit this model if

(1) the expected value of r is not equal to zero (but r is distributed independently of Q),

(2) r is not distributed independently of Q (but its expected value is zero).

8.5* A variable Y is determined by the model

$$Y = \beta_1 + \beta_2 Z + v,$$

where Z is a variable and v is a disturbance term that satisfies the regression model conditions. The explanatory variable is subject to measurement error and is measured as X where

$$X = Z + w$$

and w is the measurement error, distributed independently of v. Describe analytically the consequences of using OLS to fit this model if

(1) the expected value of w is not equal to zero (but w is distributed independently of Z),

(2) w is not distributed independently of Z (but its expected value is zero).

8.6 Suppose that the true model is $Y = \beta_2 Z + u$, but Z is measured with measurement error w, the observed variable being $X = Z + w$. It may be assumed that w has zero mean and constant variance, and that it is distributed independently of Z. Derive an expression for the limiting value of the usual estimator of the slope coefficient, $\sum_{i=1}^{n} X_i Y_i \Big/ \sum_{i=1}^{n} X_i^2$.

8.7 Suppose that the true model is $Q = \beta_2 X + u$, but Q is measured with measurement error r, the observed variable being $Y = Q + r$. It may be assumed that r has zero mean and constant variance, and that it is distributed independently of Q and X. Determine the consequences of the measurement error for the estimation of β_2.

8.8 Suppose that the true model is $Y = \beta_2 Z + u$, but Z is measured with measurement error w, the observed variable being $X = Z + w$. It may be assumed that w has zero mean and constant variance, and that it is distributed independently of Z. $\bar{Y}/\bar{X}$ is proposed as an estimator of β_2. Derive an expression for its limiting value.

8.9* A researcher investigating the shadow economy using international cross-sectional data for 25 countries hypothesizes that consumer expenditure on shadow goods and services, Q, is related to total consumer expenditure, Z, by the relationship

$$Q = \beta_1 + \beta_2 Z + v,$$

where v is a disturbance term that satisfies the regression model conditions. Q is part of Z and any error in the estimation of Q affects the estimate of Z by the same amount. Hence,

$$Y_i = Q_i + w_i$$

and

$$X_i = Z_i + w_i,$$

where Y_i is the estimated value of Q_i, X_i is the estimated value of Z_i, and w_i is the measurement error affecting both variables in observation i. It is assumed that the expected value of w is zero and that v and w are distributed independently of Z and of each other.

1. Derive an expression for the large-sample bias in the estimate of β_2 when OLS is used to regress Y on X, and determine its sign if this is possible. [*Note*: You are warned that the standard expression for measurement error bias is not valid in this case.]

2. In a Monte Carlo experiment based on the model above, the true relationship between Q and Z is

$$Q = 2.0 + 0.2Z.$$

A sample of 25 observations is generated using the integers 1, 2,..., 25 as data for Z. The variance of Z is 52.0. A normally distributed random variable with mean 0 and variance 25 is used to generate the values of the measurement error in the dependent and explanatory variables. The results with 10 samples are summarized in the table. Comment on the results, stating whether or not they support your theoretical analysis.

3. The graph plots the points (Q, Z) and (Y, X) for the first sample, with each (Q, Z) point linked to the corresponding (Y, X) point. Comment on this graph, given your answers to parts (1) and (2).

Sample	b_1	s.e.(b_1)	b_2	s.e.(b_2)	R^2
1	−0.85	1.09	0.42	0.07	0.61
2	−0.37	1.45	0.36	0.10	0.36
3	−2.85	0.88	0.49	0.06	0.75
4	−2.21	1.59	0.54	0.10	0.57
5	−1.08	1.43	0.47	0.09	0.55
6	−1.32	1.39	0.51	0.08	0.64
7	−3.12	1.12	0.54	0.07	0.71
8	−0.64	0.95	0.45	0.06	0.74
9	0.57	0.89	0.38	0.05	0.69
10	−0.54	1.26	0.40	0.08	0.50

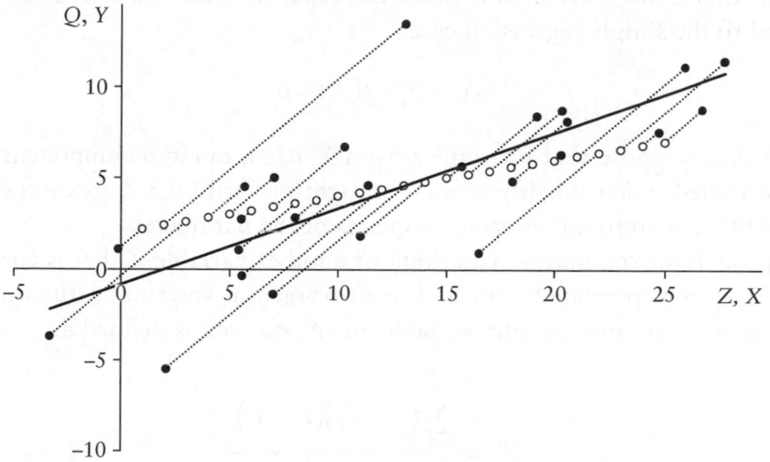

8.10 Within the framework of the permanent income hypothesis, suppose that the variance of transitory income is 0.5 that of permanent income, the propensity to consume nondurables out of permanent income is 0.6, and there is no expenditure on durables. What would be the value of the multiplier derived from a naïve regression of consumption on income, and what would be the true value?

8.11 In his definition of permanent consumption, Friedman includes the consumption of services provided by durables. Purchases of durables are classified as a form of saving. In a model similar to that in Exercise 8.10, the variance of transitory income is 0.5 that of permanent income, the propensity to consume nondurables out of permanent income is 0.6, and half of current saving (actual income minus expenditure on nondurables) takes the form of expenditure on durables. What would be the value of the multiplier derived from a naïve regression of consumption on income, and what would be the true value?

8.5 Instrumental variables

What can be done about measurement errors? If the measurement errors are due to inaccuracy in the recording of the data, not much. If they arise because the variable being measured is conceptually different from the true variable in the relationship, the obvious answer is to attempt to obtain more appropriate data. Often, however, this is not possible. In the case of Friedman's permanent income hypothesis, there is no way of obtaining data directly on permanent income since it is a subjective concept. Sometimes the problem can be sidestepped. Friedman's own approach will be discussed in Section 11.4. Another technique, known as **instrumental variables estimation**, or IV, will be discussed here. IV is a major variation on OLS and it will be of great importance when we come to the fitting of models comprising several simultaneous equations.

Essentially IV consists of semi-replacing a defective explanatory variable with one that is not correlated with the disturbance term. The discussion will be confined to the simple regression case

$$Y_i = \beta_1 + \beta_2 X_i + u_i \tag{8.42}$$

and we shall suppose that for some reason X_i has a random component that is not distributed independently of u_i. A straightforward OLS regression of Y on X would then lead to inconsistent estimates of the parameters.

Suppose, however, that we can think of another variable Z that is correlated with X but not correlated with u. The instrumental variables estimator of β_2 with Z used as an **instrumental variable**, or **instrument**, is defined as

$$b_2^{\mathrm{IV}} = \frac{\sum_{i=1}^{n}(Z_i - \bar{Z})(Y_i - \bar{Y})}{\sum_{i=1}^{n}(Z_i - \bar{Z})(X_i - \bar{X})}. \tag{8.43}$$

We shall show that it is consistent, provided that σ_{ZX}, the population covariance of Z and X, is nonzero.

Before doing this, it is instructive to compare b_2^{IV} with the OLS estimator, which will be denoted b_2^{OLS}:

$$b_2^{\mathrm{OLS}} = \frac{\sum_{i=1}^{n}(X_i - \bar{X})(Y_i - \bar{Y})}{\sum_{i=1}^{n}(X_i - \bar{X})^2} = \frac{\sum_{i=1}^{n}(X_i - \bar{X})(Y_i - \bar{Y})}{\sum_{i=1}^{n}(X_i - \bar{X})(X_i - \bar{X})}. \tag{8.44}$$

The IV estimator, in simple regression analysis, is obtained by substituting the instrument Z for the X in the numerator and for one X factor (but not both) in the denominator.

Substituting for Y from (8.42), we can expand the expression for b_2^{IV}:

$$\begin{aligned} b_2^{\text{IV}} &= \frac{\sum_{i=1}^{n}(Z_i - \bar{Z})\left([\beta_1 + \beta_2 X_i + u_i] - [\beta_1 + \beta_2 \bar{X} + \bar{u}]\right)}{\sum_{i=1}^{n}(Z_i - \bar{Z})(X_i - \bar{X})} \\ &= \frac{\sum_{i=1}^{n}\left(\beta_2 (Z_i - \bar{Z})(X_i - \bar{X}) + (Z_i - \bar{Z})(u_i - \bar{u})\right)}{\sum_{i=1}^{n}(Z_i - \bar{Z})(X_i - \bar{X})} \\ &= \beta_2 + \frac{\sum_{i=1}^{n}(Z_i - \bar{Z})(u_i - \bar{u})}{\sum_{i=1}^{n}(Z_i - \bar{Z})(X_i - \bar{X})} \end{aligned} \tag{8.45}$$

We can see therefore that the instrumental variable estimator is equal to the true value plus an error term. In large samples, the error term will vanish. Dividing the numerator and the denominator of the error term by n so that they both have limits when we take plims,

$$\operatorname{plim} b_2^{\text{IV}} = \beta_2 + \frac{\operatorname{plim} \frac{1}{n}\sum_{i=1}^{n}(Z_i - \bar{Z})(u_i - \bar{u})}{\operatorname{plim} \frac{1}{n}\sum_{i=1}^{n}(Z_i - \bar{Z})(X_i - \bar{X})} = \beta_2 + \frac{\sigma_{Zu}}{\sigma_{ZX}} = \beta_2 + \frac{0}{\sigma_{ZX}} = \beta_2, \tag{8.46}$$

provided that we are correct in supposing that Z is distributed independently of u and so $\sigma_{Zu} = 0$. Hence, in large samples b_2^{IV} will tend to the true value β_2.

Nothing much can be said about the distribution of b_2^{IV} in small samples, but for large samples, we can make an approximative statement. As n increases, the distribution will converge on a normal one with mean β_2 and variance $\sigma^2_{b_2^{\text{IV}}}$ given by

$$\sigma^2_{b_2^{\text{IV}}} = \frac{\sigma_u^2}{\sum_{i=1}^{n}(X_i - \bar{X})^2} \times \frac{1}{r_{XZ}^2}, \tag{8.47}$$

where r_{XZ} is the correlation between X and Z. In the next subsection, the meaning of this assertion will be explained more carefully.

Compare (8.47) with the variance of the OLS estimator:

$$\sigma^2_{b_2^{\text{OLS}}} = \frac{\sigma_u^2}{\sum_{i=1}^{n}(X_i - \bar{X})^2}. \tag{8.48}$$

The difference is that the variance of b_2^{IV} is multiplied by the factor $1/r_{XZ}^2$. The greater the correlation between X and Z, the smaller will be this factor, and hence the smaller will be the variance of b_2^{IV}.

We are now in a position to state the three requirements of an instrument:

1. It should be correlated with the variable being instrumented, and the higher the correlation, the better, provided that the second requirement is satisfied.
2. It should not be correlated with the disturbance term. If it is stochastic, its random component should be distributed independently of the disturbance term. Otherwise plim $\frac{1}{n}\sum(Z_i - \bar{Z})(u_i - \bar{u})$ in (8.46) will not be zero. Thus, it would not be desirable to use an instrument that is perfectly correlated with X, even if you could find one, because then it would automatically be correlated with u as well and you would still obtain inconsistent estimates.
3. It should not be an explanatory variable in its own right.

What should you do if you cannot find an instrumental variable highly correlated with X? Well, you may wish to stick with OLS after all. If, for example, your criterion for selecting an estimator is its mean square error, you may find that the OLS estimator is preferable to an IV estimator, despite the bias, because its variance is smaller.

Asymptotic distribution of the IV estimator

We have shown that the IV estimator is consistent, provided that the instrument is correlated with the variable for which it is acting and that it is distributed independently of the disturbance term. This means that, as the sample size becomes large, the distribution collapses to a spike and the spike is at the true value of the parameter being estimated.

We have also asserted that, for the regression model $Y_i = \beta_1 + \beta_2 X_i + u_i$, with Z acting as an instrument for X, the IV estimator of β_2 asymptotically has a normal distribution with variance

$$\sigma^2_{b_2^{\text{IV}}} = \frac{\sigma_u^2}{\sum_{i=1}^{n}(X_i - \bar{X})^2} \times \frac{1}{r_{XZ}^2}. \tag{8.49}$$

What does this mean? We have just said that the distribution of the IV estimator degenerates to a spike. So how can it have an asymptotic variance?

The contradiction has been caused by compressing several ideas together. We will have to unpick them, taking several small steps. It is important that we do this because we are going to discuss asymptotic limiting distributions again in Chapters 11 (autoregressive processes) and 13 (nonstationary processes).

As might be suspected, the application of a central limit theorem (CLT) underlies the assertion. To use a CLT, we must first show that a variable has a nondegenerate limiting distribution. The CLT will then show that, under appropriate conditions, this limiting distribution is normal.

We cannot apply a CLT to b_2^{IV} directly, because it does not have a nondegenerate limiting distribution. (8.49) may be rewritten as

$$\sigma_{b_2^{\mathrm{IV}}}^2 = \frac{\sigma_u^2}{n\left(\frac{1}{n}\sum_{i=1}^{n}(X_i - \bar{X})^2\right)} \times \frac{1}{r_{XZ}^2} = \frac{\sigma_u^2}{n\mathrm{MSD}(X)} \times \frac{1}{r_{XZ}^2} \tag{8.50}$$

where MSD(X) is the mean square deviation of X. By a law of large numbers, the MSD tends to the population variance of X and so has a well-defined limit. The variance of b_2^{IV} is inversely proportional to n, and so tends to zero. This is the reason that the distribution of b_2^{IV} collapses to a spike.

We can deal with the diminishing-variance problem by considering $\sqrt{n}\, b_2^{\mathrm{IV}}$ instead of b_2^{IV}. This has variance $\frac{\sigma_u^2}{\mathrm{MSD}(X)} \times \frac{1}{r_{XZ}^2}$, which is stable. However, $\sqrt{n}\, b_2^{\mathrm{IV}}$ still does not have a limiting distribution because its mean increases with n.

So instead, consider $\sqrt{n}\,\left(b_2^{\mathrm{IV}} - \beta_2\right)$. Since b_2^{IV} tends to β_2 as the sample size becomes large, this does have a limiting distribution with zero mean and stable variance. Under conditions that are usually satisfied in regressions using cross-sectional data, it can then be shown that we can apply a central limit theorem and demonstrate that

$$\sqrt{n}\left(b_2^{\mathrm{IV}} - \beta_2\right) \xrightarrow{d} \mathrm{N}\left(0, \frac{\sigma_u^2}{\sigma_X^2} \times \frac{1}{\rho_{XZ}^2}\right), \tag{8.51}$$

where ρ_{XZ} is the population correlation between X and Z ($\xrightarrow{d}$ means 'has limiting distribution').

Having established this, we can now start working backwards and say that, for sufficiently large samples, as an approximation,

$$\left(b_2^{\mathrm{IV}} - \beta_2\right) \sim \mathrm{N}\left(0, \frac{\sigma_u^2}{n\mathrm{MSD}(X)} \times \frac{1}{r_{XZ}^2}\right) \tag{8.52}$$

(~ means 'is distributed as'). We can then say

$$b_2^{\mathrm{IV}} \sim \mathrm{N}\left(\beta_2, \frac{\sigma_u^2}{n\mathrm{MSD}(X)} \times \frac{1}{r_{XZ}^2}\right) \tag{8.53}$$

as an approximation, for sufficiently large samples, and use this assertion as justification for performing the usual tests. This is what was intended by equation (8.47).

Of course, we need to be more precise about what we mean by a 'sufficiently large' sample, and 'as an approximation'. We cannot do this mathematically. This was why we resorted to asymptotic analysis in the first place. Instead, the usual procedure is to set up a Monte Carlo experiment using a model appropriate to the context. The answers will depend on the nature of the model, the correlation between X and u, and the correlation between X and Z.

Monte Carlo illustration

Suppose that

$$Y = \beta_1 + \beta_2 X + u, \tag{8.54}$$

where

$$X = \lambda_1 Z + \lambda_2 V + u \tag{8.55}$$

and the observations on Z, V, and u are drawn independently from a normal distribution with mean zero and unit variance. We will think of Z and V as variables and of u as a disturbance term in the model. λ_1 and λ_2 are constants. By construction, X is not independent of u and so Assumption B.7 is violated when we fit (8.54). OLS will yield inconsistent estimates and the standard errors and other diagnostics will be invalid. Z is correlated with X, but independent of u, and so can serve as an instrument. (V is included as a component of X in order to provide some variation in X not connected with either the instrument or the disturbance term.) We will set $\beta_1 = 10$, $\beta_2 = 5$, $\lambda_1 = 2$, and $\lambda_2 = 0.5$.

Figure 8.2 shows the distributions of the OLS and IV estimators of β_2 for $n = 25$ and $n = 100$, for 10 million samples in both cases. Given the information above, it is easy to verify that plim $b_2^{\text{OLS}} = 5.19$. Of course, plim $b_2^{\text{IV}} = 5.00$. The IV estimator has a greater variance than the OLS estimator and for $n = 25$ one might prefer the latter. It is biased, but the smaller variance could make it superior, using some criterion such as the mean square error (see the Review chapter). For $n = 100$, the IV estimator looks better.

Figure 8.3 shows the distributions for $n = 3{,}200$. Both estimators are tending to the predicted limits (the IV estimator more slowly than the OLS, because it has a larger variance). Here the IV estimator is definitely superior.

Figure 8.4 shows the distribution of $\sqrt{n}\,\left(b_2^{\text{IV}} - \beta_2\right)$ for $n = 25$, 100, and 400. It also shows, as the dashed line, the limiting normal distribution predicted by the central limit theorem. It can be seen that the distribution for $n = 25$ is far from normal. Its tails are too fat, its body too thin, and its mode too high. The distributions for $n = 100$ and 400 are better, but even that for 400 is visibly non-normal, with a left tail that is too fat.

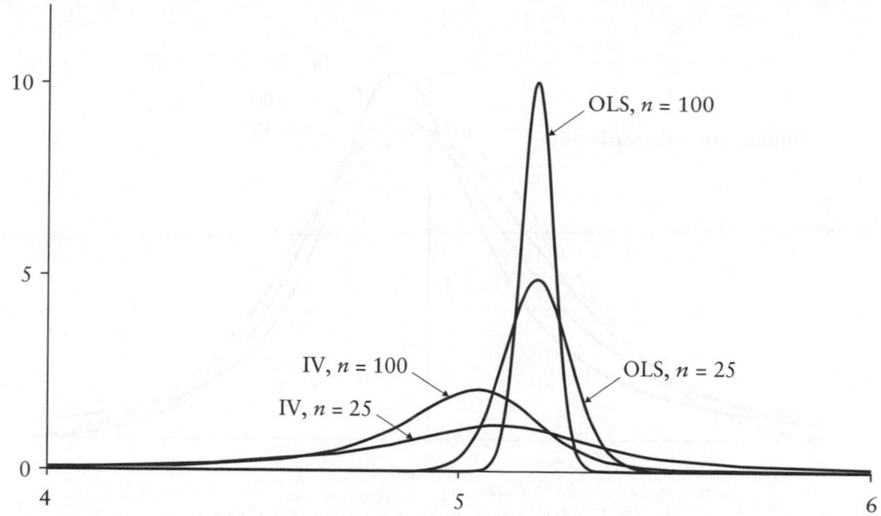

Figure 8.2 Distributions of the OLS and IV estimators of β_2 for $n = 25$ and 100

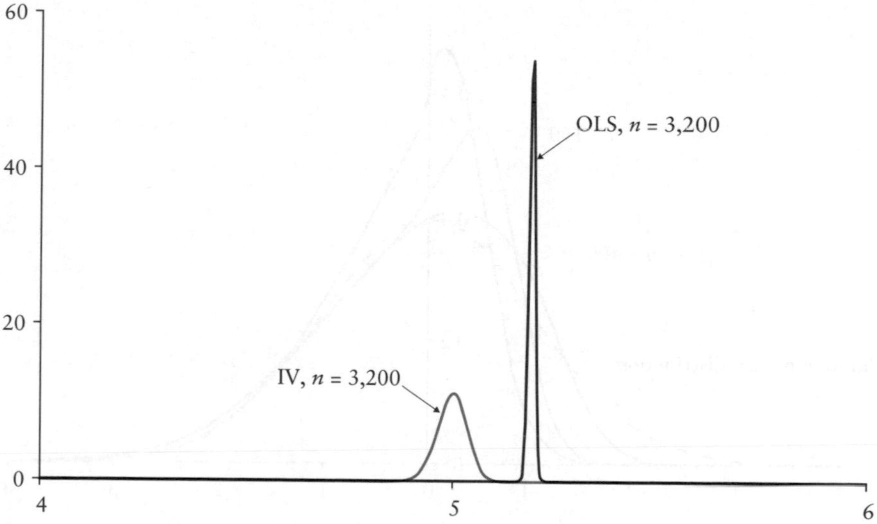

Figure 8.3 Distributions of the OLS and IV estimators of β_2 for $n = 3{,}200$

Figure 8.5 shows the distributions of the t statistic for b_2^{IV} for the three sample sizes, along with the limiting normal distribution. For high values of t, the distributions are close to the normal distribution and inference based on the conventional critical values of t would be approximately correct. However, for negative values of t, the use of the conventional critical values would be seriously misleading. For example, for $n = 25$, with 23 degrees of freedom, the critical value of t is 2.069. The simulation shows that, under H_0, the probability that $t < -2.069$ is far less than 0.025. Indeed, it is almost zero. This means that

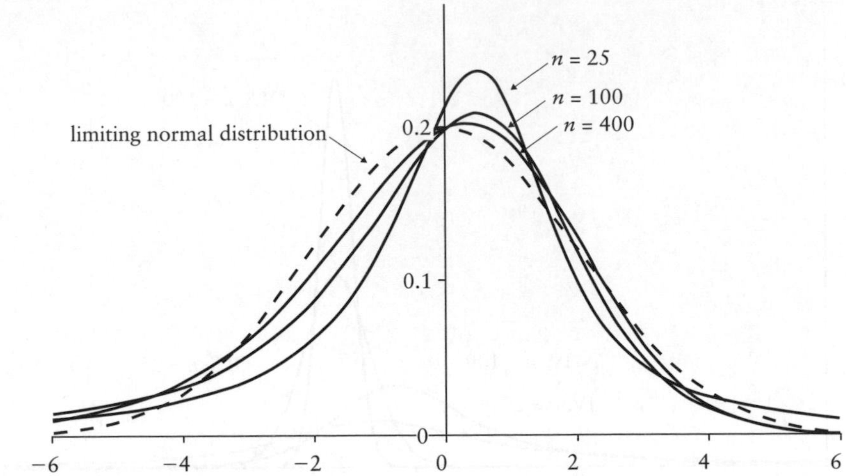

Figure 8.4 Distributions of $\sqrt{n}\,\left(b_2^{\mathrm{IV}} - \beta_2\right)$ for n = 25, 100, and 400

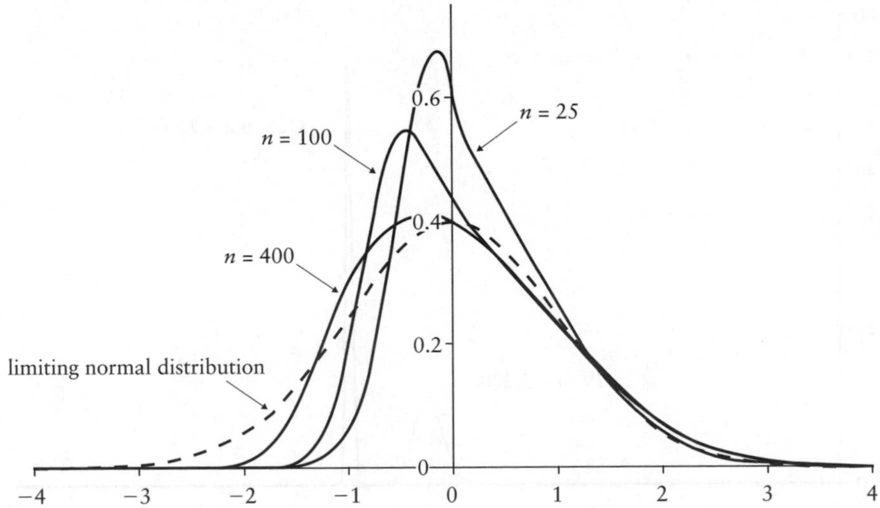

Figure 8.5 Distributions of the t statistic for b_2^{IV} for n = 25, 100, and 400

values of b_2 lower than β_2 will almost never lead to the rejection of H_0. This would reduce the power of the test if H_0 happened to be false.

This simulation has illustrated the theoretical advantage of IV over OLS in this model. The IV estimator is consistent, while the OLS is not. It also illustrates two potential negative aspects of IV estimation, the greater variance of the estimator and the nonstandard distribution of the t statistic for finite samples. The greater variance is commonly acknowledged. The adverse effect on inference is not, perhaps because it is not so easily detected. Both negative aspects tend to be the more severe, the smaller is the sample and the lower is the correlation between the variable and its instrument. In this simulation, the correlation between X and Z was only 0.22, so the negative aspects were readily apparent, even for $n = 400$. Unfortunately, low correlations ('weak instruments') are common in IV estimation. It is difficult to find an instrument that is correlated with X but not the disturbance term. Indeed, it is often difficult to find any credible instrument at all.

Example: Use of IV to fit the Friedman consumption function

The pioneering use of IV in the context of the Friedman permanent income hypothesis is Liviatan (1963). Liviatan had data on the consumption and income of the same 883 households for two consecutive years. We will denote consumption and income in the first year C_1 and Y_1, and in the second year C_2 and Y_2.

Liviatan observed that if Friedman's theory is correct, Y_2 can act as an instrument for Y_1. Obviously it is likely to be highly correlated with Y_1, so the first requirement of a good instrument is satisfied. If the transitory component of measured income is uncorrelated from one year to the next, as hypothesized by Friedman, Y_2 will be uncorrelated with the disturbance term in the relationship between C_1 and Y_1, and so the second condition is satisfied. Finally, C_1 is likely to be related to Y_1 rather than Y_2, so the third condition is satisfied. The instrumental variable estimator is then given by

$$b_2^{\mathrm{IV}} = \frac{\sum_{i=1}^{n}\left(Y_{2i} - \bar{Y}_2\right)\left(C_{1i} - \bar{C}_1\right)}{\sum_{i=1}^{n}\left(Y_{2i} - \bar{Y}_2\right)\left(Y_{1i} - \bar{Y}_1\right)}. \tag{8.56}$$

Alternatively, one could use C_2 as an instrument for Y_1. It will be highly correlated with Y_2, and therefore with Y_1, and also not correlated with the disturbance term in the relationship between C_1 and Y_1 if, as Friedman hypothesized, the transitory components of consumption are uncorrelated.

Similarly, one could run regressions using the data for year 2, using Y_1 and C_1 as instruments for Y_2. Liviatan tried all four combinations, separating his sample into employees and self-employed. He found that four of the estimates of the marginal propensity to consume were significantly greater than those obtained by straightforward OLS at the 1 percent level; one was significantly greater at the 5 percent level, and in the other three cases the difference was not significant, evidence that on the whole corroborates the permanent income hypothesis. However, the marginal propensity to consume was generally not as high as the average propensity; therefore, his results did not support the hypothesis of a unit elasticity of consumption with respect to permanent income, which is implicit in equation (8.38).

Example: Use of IV to fit an earnings function

In some data sets, up to 10 percent of the variance of measured years of schooling is thought to be attributable to measurement error. Accordingly, the coefficient of schooling in an earnings function may be underestimated. Table 8.1 presents the output from an OLS regression of the logarithm of hourly earnings on years of schooling and work experience, and Table 8.2 presents the output from an IV regression with mother's years of schooling used as an instrument for years of schooling. *SM* is likely to be a suitable instrument because it is correlated with *S*, unlikely to be correlated with the disturbance term, and unlikely to be a direct determinant of earnings.

The coefficient of schooling is larger in the IV regression, suggesting that measurement error may have led to a downwards bias in its coefficient in the OLS regression. However, note that its standard error is much larger than in the OLS regression. This is because the correlation between *S* and *SM*, 0.36, is not

Table 8.1

```
.reg LGEARN S EXP

   Source  |        SS          df         MS            Number of obs =     540
-------------------------------------------------        F(2, 537)     =  100.86
    Model  |   50.9842581        2     25.492129         Prob > F      =  0.0000
 Residual  |   135.723385      537    .252743734         R-squared     =  0.2731
-------------------------------------------------        Adj R-squared =  0.2704
    Total  |   186.707643      539    .34639637          Root MSE      =  .50274

-------------------------------------------------------------------------------------
   LGEARN  |       Coef.     Std. Err.      t     P>|t|     [95% Conf. Interval]
-------------------------------------------------------------------------------------
        S  |    .1235911     .0090989    13.58    0.000      .1057173     .141465
      EXP  |    .0350826     .0050046     7.01    0.000      .0252515    .0449137
    _cons  |    .5093196     .1663823     3.06    0.002      .1824796    .8361597
-------------------------------------------------------------------------------------
```

Table 8.2

```
.ivregress 2sls LGEARN EXP (S=SM)
Instrumental variables (2SLS) regression                 Number of obs =     540
                                                         Wald chi2(2)  =   57.08
                                                         Prob > chi2   =  0.0000
                                                         R-squared     =  0.2514
                                                         Root MSE      =  .50874
-------------------------------------------------------------------------------------
   LGEARN  |       Coef.     Std. Err.      z     P>|z|     [95% Conf. Interval]
-------------------------------------------------------------------------------------
        S  |    .1599676     .0252098     6.35    0.000      .1105574    .2093779
      EXP  |    .0394422      .005793     6.81    0.000       .028088    .0507963
    _cons  |   -.0617062      .405047    -0.15    0.879      .1824796    .8361597
-------------------------------------------------------------------------------------
Instrumented: S
Instruments: EXP SM
-------------------------------------------------------------------------------------
```

very high. It is possible that the difference in the OLS and IV estimates of the coefficient may be due to chance. We will improve the IV estimation by drawing on a group of family background variables, instead of just *SM*, to instrument for *S*, and then we will perform a formal test of the difference in the coefficients.

First, however, some practical notes. The example used here is a multiple regression model, and you should be aware that the expressions for IV coefficients in a multiple regression model are more complex than those in a simple regression model, in the same way that OLS multiple regression coefficients are more complex than OLS simple regression coefficients. However, the expressions are straightforward in a treatment using matrix algebra. A facility for performing IV regressions is a standard feature of all regression applications. A typical procedure is to state the variables for the regression in the usual way and append a list of noninstrumented variables and instrument(s) in parentheses. The Stata (version 11) command for IV regressions in Table 8.2 departs from this convention in two ways. It is different from that for OLS regressions (`ivregress 2sls` instead of `reg`), and the list of variables in parentheses is in the form of an equation with the instrumented variable(s) to the left of the = sign and the instruments to the right of it.

Multiple instruments

Father's years of schooling, number of siblings, and possession of a library card are other factors that may be associated with years of schooling of the respondent but are not likely to be direct determinants of earnings. Thus, we have four potential instruments for *S* and, for reasons that will be explained in the next chapter, IV estimation is more efficient if they are used as a group rather than individually. To do this, you include all of them in the list of instruments in the regression command. The corresponding regression output is shown in Table 8.3.

Table 8.3

```
.ivregress 2sls LGEARN EXP (S=SM SF SIBLINGS LIBRARY)
Instrumental variables (2SLS) regression               Number of obs =      540
                                                       Wald chi2(2)  =    74.64
                                                       Prob > chi2   =   0.0000
                                                       R-squared     =   0.2482
                                                       Root MSE      =   .50986
------------------------------------------------------------------------------
  LGEARN   |     Coef.     Std. Err.      z     P>|z|    [95% Conf. Interval]
------------------------------------------------------------------------------
       S   |   .162629     .0213732     7.61    0.000     .1207384    .2045196
     EXP   |  .0397611     .0055767     7.13    0.000      .028831    .0506912
   _cons   | -.1034832     .3464908    -0.30    0.765    -.7825927    .5756262
------------------------------------------------------------------------------
Instrumented: S
Instruments: EXP SM SF SIBLINGS LIBRARY
------------------------------------------------------------------------------
```

The smaller standard error indicates that there has been a gain in efficiency, but it is still much larger than that for the original OLS regression and it is possible that the difference in the OLS and IV estimates of the coefficient of S is purely random. We will perform a formal test.

The Durbin–Wu–Hausman specification test

Most economic data are subject to some element of measurement error and a recurring issue, as in the present case, is whether it is potentially serious enough to require the use of IV instead of OLS to fit a model. It has been shown that if measurement error is serious, OLS estimates will be inconsistent and IV is to be preferred. However, if there is no measurement error, both OLS and IV will be consistent and OLS will be preferred because it is more efficient. The **Durbin–Wu–Hausman (DWH) specification test** (sometimes described as the Hausman test: the standard reference is Hausman (1978), but Durbin (1954) and Wu (1973) made important contributions to its development) can be used in this context to discriminate between the two possibilities. We will assume that the regression model is given by

$$Y = \beta_1 + \beta_2 X_2 + \cdots + \beta_k X_k + u, \tag{8.57}$$

where one or more of the explanatory variables are potentially subject to measurement error. Under the null hypothesis that there is no measurement error, the OLS and IV coefficients will not be systematically different. The test statistic is based on the differences between the OLS and IV coefficients (all of them, not just those of the variables potentially subject to measurement error). Under the null hypothesis of no significant difference, it has a chi-squared distribution with degrees of freedom in principle equal to the number of coefficients being compared. In practice, for technical reasons, the actual number of degrees of freedom may be smaller. The regression application should compute the number for you. The computation of the test statistic is too complex to be described here and in practice one employs a regression application such as Stata or EViews that supports the test.

Tables 8.4–8.6 give the Stata output from performing the test for the earnings function example. Table 8.4 gives the output from the IV regression of the logarithm of earnings on work experience, *ASVABC*, dummy variables for male sex and black and Hispanic ethnicity, and years of schooling. Years of schooling is instrumented with multiple instruments: mother's and father's years of schooling, number of siblings, and a dummy variable equal to 1 if anyone in the family possessed a library card, 0 otherwise, when the respondent was 14. The IV regression is followed by the command '`estimates store name1`' where '`name1`' is a name identifying this regression. In this case, the IV regression has been named '`EARNIV`'.

Table 8.5 gives the output from the corresponding OLS regression, followed by the command '`estimates store name2`' where '`name2`' is a name identifying the OLS regression. It has been called '`EARNOLS`'.

Table 8.4

```
.ivregress 2sls LGEARN EXP ASVABC MALE ETHBLACK ETHHISP (S=SM SF SIBLINGS LIBRARY)

Instrumental variables (2SLS) regression              Number of obs =      540
                                                      Wald chi2(6)  =   230.09
                                                      Prob > chi2   =   0.0000
                                                      R-squared     =   0.3454
                                                      Root MSE      =   .47574
------------------------------------------------------------------------------
    LGEARN |      Coef.   Std. Err.      z    P>|z|     [95% Conf. Interval]
------------------------------------------------------------------------------
         S |    .111379   .0473785     2.35   0.019     .0185189    .2042391
       EXP |   .0258798   .0080659     3.21   0.001      .010071    .0416887
    ASVABC |   .0092263    .007939     1.16   0.245    -.0063339    .0247866
      MALE |   .2619787   .0426492     6.14   0.000     .1783878    .3455696
  ETHBLACK |  -.0121846   .0817591    -0.15   0.882     .1724295    .1480604
   ETHHISP |   .0457639   .0948904     0.48   0.630    -.1402179    .2317457
     _cons |   .2258512   .3862189     0.58   0.559      5311239    .9828263
------------------------------------------------------------------------------
Instrumented: S
Instruments:  EXP ASVABC MALE ETHBLACK ETHHISP SM SF SIBLINGS LIBRARY
------------------------------------------------------------------------------
. estimates store EARNIV
```

Table 8.5

```
.reg LGEARN S EXP ASVABC MALE ETHBLACK ETHHISP

    Source |       SS         df        MS            Number of obs =      540
-------------------------------------------------     F(6, 533)     =    47.99
     Model |   65.490707       6   10.9151178         Prob > F      =   0.0000
  Residual |  121.216936     533   .227423895         R-squared     =   0.3508
-------------------------------------------------     Adj R-squared =   0.3435
     Total |  186.707643     539   .34639637          Root MSE      =   .47689

------------------------------------------------------------------------------
    LGEARN |      Coef.   Std. Err.      t    P>|t|     [95% Conf. Interval]
------------------------------------------------------------------------------
         S |   .0883257   .0109987     8.03   0.000     .0667196    .1099318
       EXP |   .0227131   .0050095     4.53   0.000     .0128724    .0325538
    ASVABC |   .0129274   .0028834     4.48   0.000     .0072633    .0185916
      MALE |   .2652878    .042235     6.28   0.000     .1823203    .3482552
  ETHBLACK |   .0077265   .0715863     0.11   0.914    -.1328994    .1483524
   ETHHISP |   .0536544   .0937966     0.57   0.568     -.130602    .2379107
     _cons |   .4002952   .1663149     2.41   0.016     .0735821    .7270083
------------------------------------------------------------------------------
. estimates store EARNOLS
```

Table 8.6 presents the output for the DWH test. The command for performing the DWH test is '`hausman name1 name2, constant`'—in our case, '`hausman EARNIV EARNOLS`, constant'. The qualifier, '`constant`', should be omitted if for some reason the constant has different meanings in the two regressions being compared. In the present case, it has the same (uninteresting) meaning in both regressions, so it is included.

Table 8.6

```
. hausman EARNIV EARNOLS, constant
Note: the rank of the differenced variance matrix (6) does not equal the number of
      coefficients being tested (7); be sure this is what you expect, or there may be
      problems computing the test. Examine the output of your estimators for anything
      unexpected and possibly consider scaling your variables so that the coefficients
      are on a similar scale.

                         Coefficients
                 ----------------------------------------------------------------
                     (b)            (B)            (b-B)     sqrt(diag(V_b-V_B))
                    EARNIV        EARNOLS       Difference          S.E.
-------------------------------------------------------------------------------------
           S        .111379       .0883257       .0230533          .0460842
         EXP       .0258798       .0227131       .0031667          .0063217
      ASVABC       .0092263       .0129274      -.0037011          .0073969
        MALE       .2619787       .2652878      -.0033091          .0059295
    ETHBLACK      -.0121846       .0077265      -.019911           .0394963
     ETHHISP       .0457639       .0536544      -.0078904          .0143664
       _cons       .2258512       .4002952      -.174444           .3485748
-------------------------------------------------------------------------------------
                        b = consistent under Ho and Ha; obtained from ivregress
            B = inconsistent under Ha, efficient under Ho; obtained from regress

Test: Ho: difference in coefficients not systematic
                chi2(6) = (b-B)'[(V_b-V_B) ^ (-1)](b-B)
                        = 0.25
              Prob>chi2 = 0.9997
                 (V_b-V_B is not positive definite)
```

The top half of Table 8.6 begins with a warning that this is one of those occasions where there is a technical problem with the test and the number of degrees of freedom in the test statistic will be six, rather than the number of coefficients, seven. The output then reproduces the IV coefficients in the column headed (b) and the OLS coefficients in that headed (B). The bottom half computes the chi-squared statistic. This is 0.25, lower than 12.59, the critical value of chi-squared at the 5 percent significance level with six degrees of freedom, and so we do not reject the null hypothesis of no difference in the OLS and IV estimates. We infer that it is safe to use OLS rather than IV, and we are happy to do so because the OLS standard errors, particularly those of the coefficients of *S*, *EXP*, and *ASVABC*, are smaller than their IV counterparts. This is likely to be the correct conclusion. The schooling histories are recorded in great detail in the NLSY data set and accordingly measurement error is almost certainly minimal.

The DWH test can be used in any comparison of OLS and IV estimators where both are consistent, but OLS more efficient, under a null hypothesis, and OLS is inconsistent under the alternative hypothesis. We will encounter another application in the next chapter. With the usage of the test becoming more common, a facility for performing it is now a standard feature of regression applications.

Key terms

- Durbin–Wu–Hausman (DWH) test
- imperfect proxy variable
- instrument
- instrumental variable
- instrumental variable estimation (IV)
- measurement error
- measurement error bias

EXERCISES

8.12 For the model $Y_i = \beta_1 + \beta_2 X_i + u_i$, with Z being used as an instrument for X, the IV estimator of β_1 is $b_1^{IV} = \bar{Y} - b_2^{IV}\bar{X}$. Demonstrate that it is consistent. (You may assume that b_2^{IV} is a consistent estimator of β_2.)

8.13 In Exercise 8.2, the amount of labor, L, employed by the firms is also a linear function of expected sales:

$$L = \delta_1 + \delta_2 X^e.$$

Explain how this relationship might be exploited by the investigator to counter the problem of measurement error bias.

8.14* It is possible that the *ASVABC* test score is a poor measure of the kind of ability relevant for earnings. Accordingly, perform an OLS regression of the logarithm of hourly earnings on *S*, *EXP*, *ASVABC*, *MALE*, *ETHBLACK*, and *ETHHISP* using your *EAEF* data set and an IV regression using *SM*, *SF*, *SIBLINGS*, and *LIBRARY* as instruments for *ASVABC*. Perform a Durbin–Wu–Hausman test to evaluate whether *ASVABC* appears to be subject to measurement error.

8.15* What is the difference between an instrumental variable and a proxy variable (as described in Section 6.4)? When would you use one and when would you use the other?

8.16 Consider the regression model $Y = \beta_1 + \beta_2 X + u$, where X is stochastic and not distributed independently of u. Suppose that a third variable Z is a valid instrument for X., being correlated with X but distributed independently of u. Show that $Z^* = \lambda_1 + \lambda_2 Z$, where λ_1 and λ_2 are arbitrary constants, is also a valid instrument for X. What difference would it make to the regression results if Z^* were used as an instrument for X instead of Z?

8.17 A variable Y is determined by a variable X, the relationship being

$$Y = \beta_1 + \beta_2 X + u,$$

where u is a disturbance term that satisfies the regression model assumptions. The values of X are drawn randomly from a population with variance σ_X^2. A researcher makes a mistake and regresses X on Y, fitting the equation

$$\hat{X} = d_1 + d_2 Y,$$

where $d_2 = \dfrac{\sum(X_i - \bar{X})(Y_i - \bar{Y})}{\sum(Y_i - \bar{Y})^2}$. When he realizes his mistake, he points out that the original relationship could be rewritten

$$X = -\frac{\beta_1}{\beta_2} + \frac{1}{\beta_2}Y - \frac{1}{\beta_2}u$$

and hence d_2 will be an estimator of $1/\beta_2$. From this he could obtain an estimate of β_2.

Explain why it is not possible to derive a closed-form expression for the expected value of d_2 for a finite sample.

Demonstrate that d_2 is an inconsistent estimator of $1/\beta_2$ and determine the direction of the large-sample bias, if this is possible.

Suppose that there exists a third variable Z that is correlated with Y but independent of u. Demonstrate that if the researcher had regressed X on Y using Z as an instrument for Y, the slope coefficient d_2^{IV} would have been a consistent estimator of $1/\beta_2$.

Explain, with reference to the regression model assumptions, why d_2 yielded an inconsistent estimate of $1/\beta_2$ while d_2^{IV} yielded a consistent one.

Is it possible that X might be a valid instrument?

9. Simultaneous Equations Estimation

If you employ OLS to estimate the parameters of an equation that is embedded in a simultaneous equations model, it is likely that the estimates will be biased and inconsistent and that the statistical tests will be invalid. This is demonstrated in the first part of this chapter. The second part discusses how these problems may be overcome by using instrumental variables estimation.

9.1 Simultaneous equations models: structural and reduced form equations

When we progressed from Model A to Model B in Chapter 8, replacing the assumption that the explanatory variables are nonstochastic by the more realistic assumption for cross-sectional data that their sample values are randomly drawn from defined populations, it was noted that Assumption B.7 was particularly important. This stated that the disturbance term be distributed independently of the explanatory variables. Subsequently in that chapter we saw that measurement errors in the explanatory variables would cause the assumption to be violated and that as a consequence OLS estimators would be inconsistent. However, measurement error is not the only possible reason why that assumption may be violated. Simultaneous equations bias is another, and it is best explained with an example.

Suppose that you are investigating the determinants of price inflation and wage inflation. We will start with a very simple model that supposes that p, the annual rate of growth of prices, is related to w, the annual rate of growth of wages, it being hypothesized that increases in wage costs force prices upwards:

$$p = \beta_1 + \beta_2 w + u_p. \qquad \textbf{(9.1)}$$

At the same time, w is related to p and U, the rate of unemployment, workers protecting their real wages by demanding increases in wages as prices rise, but their ability to do so being the weaker, the higher the rate of unemployment ($\alpha_3 < 0$):

$$w = \alpha_1 + \alpha_2 p + \alpha_3 U + u_w, \qquad \textbf{(9.2)}$$

where u_p and u_w are disturbance terms.

By its very specification, this simultaneous equations model involves a certain amount of circularity: w determines p in the first equation, and in turn p helps to determine w in the second. To cut through the circularity we need to make a distinction between endogenous and exogenous variables. Endo- and exo- are Greek prefixes that mean within and outside, respectively. Endogenous variables are variables whose values are determined by the interaction of the relationships in the model. Exogenous ones are those whose values are determined externally. Thus, in the present case, p and w are both endogenous and U is exogenous. The exogenous variables and the disturbance terms ultimately determine the values of the endogenous variables, once one has cut through the circularity. The mathematical relationships expressing the endogenous variables in terms of the exogenous variables and disturbance terms are known as the **reduced form equations**. The original equations that we wrote down when specifying the model are described as the **structural equations**. We will derive the reduced form equations for p and w. To obtain that for p, we take the structural equation for p and substitute for w from the second equation:

$$\begin{aligned} p &= \beta_1 + \beta_2 w + u_p \\ &= \beta_1 + \beta_2(\alpha_1 + \alpha_2 p + \alpha_3 U + u_w) + u_p. \end{aligned} \tag{9.3}$$

Hence,

$$(1 - \alpha_2\beta_2)p = \beta_1 + \alpha_1\beta_2 + \alpha_3\beta_2 U + u_p + \beta_2 u_w \tag{9.4}$$

and so

$$p = \frac{\beta_1 + \alpha_1\beta_2 + \alpha_3\beta_2 U + u_p + \beta_2 u_w}{1 - \alpha_2\beta_2}. \tag{9.5}$$

Similarly, we obtain the reduced form equation for w:

$$\begin{aligned} w &= \alpha_1 + \alpha_2 p + \alpha_3 U + u_w \\ &= \alpha_1 + \alpha_2(\beta_1 + \beta_2 w + u_p) + \alpha_3 U + u_w. \end{aligned} \tag{9.6}$$

Hence,

$$(1 - \alpha_2\beta_2)w = \alpha_1 + \alpha_2\beta_1 + \alpha_3 U + u_w + \alpha_2 u_p \tag{9.7}$$

and so

$$w = \frac{\alpha_1 + \alpha_2\beta_1 + \alpha_3 U + u_w + \alpha_2 u_p}{1 - \alpha_2\beta_2}. \tag{9.8}$$

EXERCISES

9.1* A simple macroeconomic model consists of a consumption function and an income identity:

$$\begin{aligned} C &= \beta_1 + \beta_2 Y + u \\ Y &= C + I, \end{aligned}$$

where C is aggregate consumption, I is aggregate investment, Y is aggregate income, and u is a disturbance term. On the assumption that I is exogenous, derive the reduced form equations for C and Y.

9.2* It is common to write an earnings function with the logarithm of the hourly wage as the dependent variable and characteristics such as years of schooling, cognitive ability, years of work experience, etc. as the explanatory variables. Explain whether such an equation should be regarded as a reduced form equation or a structural equation.

9.2 Simultaneous equations bias

In many (but by no means all) simultaneous equations models, the reduced form equations express the endogenous variables in terms of all the exogenous variables and all the disturbance terms. You can see that this is the case with the price inflation/wage inflation model. In this model, there is only one exogenous variable, U. w depends on it directly; p does not depend on it directly but does so indirectly because it is determined by w. Similarly, both p and w depend on u_p, p directly and w indirectly. And both depend on u_w, w directly and p indirectly.

The dependence of w on u_p means that OLS would yield inconsistent estimates if used to fit equation (9.1), the structural equation for p. w is a stochastic regressor and its random component is not distributed independently of the disturbance term u_p. Similarly, the dependence of p on u_w means that OLS would yield inconsistent estimates if used to fit (9.2). Since (9.1) is a simple regression equation, it is easy to analyze the large-sample bias in the OLS estimator of β_2 and we will do so. After writing down the expression for b_2^{OLS}, the first step, as usual, is to substitute for p. Here we have to make a decision. We now have two equations for p, the structural equation (9.1) and the reduced form equation (9.5). Ultimately, it does not matter which we use, but the algebra is a little more straightforward if we use the structural equation because the expression for b_2^{OLS} decomposes immediately into the true value and the error term. We can then concentrate on the error term:

$$
\begin{aligned}
b_2^{\text{OLS}} &= \frac{\sum_{i=1}^{n}(p_i-\bar{p})(w_i-\bar{w})}{\sum_{i=1}^{n}(w_i-\bar{w})^2} \\
&= \frac{\sum_{i=1}^{n}\left([\beta_1+\beta_2 w_i+u_{pi}]-[\beta_1+\beta_2\bar{w}+\bar{u}_p]\right)(w_i-\bar{w})}{\sum_{i=1}^{n}(w_i-\bar{w})^2} \\
&= \frac{\sum_{i=1}^{n}\left(\beta_2(w_i-\bar{w})(w_i-\bar{w})+(u_{pi}-\bar{u}_p)(w_i-\bar{w})\right)}{\sum_{i=1}^{n}(w_i-\bar{w})^2} \\
&= \beta_2+\frac{\sum_{i=1}^{n}(u_{pi}-\bar{u}_p)(w_i-\bar{w})}{\sum_{i=1}^{n}(w_i-\bar{w})^2}.
\end{aligned}
\tag{9.9}
$$

The error term is a nonlinear function of both u_p and u_w (remember that w depends on both) and it is not possible to obtain an analytical expression for its expected value. Instead we will investigate its probability limit, using the rule that the probability limit of a ratio is equal to the probability limit of the numerator divided by the probability limit of the denominator, provided that both exist. As written in (9.9), neither the numerator nor the denominator has a probability limit. However, it can be shown that if we divide both of them by n, they will tend to the population covariance of u_p and w, and the population variance of w, respectively:

$$\text{plim } b_2^{\text{OLS}} = \beta_2 + \frac{\text{plim } \frac{1}{n}\sum_{i=1}^{n}\left(u_{pi}-\bar{u}_p\right)\left(w_i-\bar{w}\right)}{\text{plim } \frac{1}{n}\sum_{i=1}^{n}\left(w_i-\bar{w}\right)^2} = \beta_2 + \frac{\text{cov}\left(u_p, w\right)}{\text{var}\left(w\right)}. \tag{9.10}$$

We will first focus on $\text{cov}(u_p, w)$. We need to substitute for w and again have two choices, the structural equation (9.2) and the reduced form equation (9.8). We choose (9.8) because (9.2) would reintroduce p and we would find ourselves going round in circles.

$$\begin{aligned}\text{cov}(u_p, w) &= \text{cov}\left(u_p, \frac{1}{1-\alpha_2\beta_2}(\alpha_1+\alpha_2\beta_1+\alpha_3 U+u_w+\alpha_2 u_p)\right)\\ &= \frac{1}{1-\alpha_2\beta_2}\left(\begin{aligned}&\text{cov}(u_p,[\alpha_1+\alpha_2\beta_1])+\alpha_3\text{cov}(u_p,U)\\ &+\text{cov}(u_p,u_w)+\alpha_2\text{cov}(u_p,u_p)\end{aligned}\right).\end{aligned} \tag{9.11}$$

$\text{cov}(u_p, [\alpha_1 + \alpha_2\beta_1]) = 0$ because $[\alpha_1 + \alpha_2\beta_1]$ is a constant. $\text{cov}(u_p, U) = 0$ if U is truly exogenous, as we have assumed. $\text{cov}(u_p, u_w) = 0$ provided that the disturbance terms in the structural equations are independent. But $\text{cov}(u_p, u_p)$ is nonzero because it is $\text{var}(u_p)$. Hence,

$$\text{cov}(u_p, w) = \frac{\alpha_2}{1-\alpha_2\beta_2}\text{ var}\left(u_p\right) = \frac{\alpha_2\sigma_{u_p}^2}{1-\alpha_2\beta_2}. \tag{9.12}$$

Now for $\text{var}(w)$:

$$\begin{aligned}\text{var}(w) &= \text{var}\left(\frac{\alpha_1+\alpha_2\beta_1}{1-\alpha_2\beta_2}+\frac{\alpha_3 U+u_w+\alpha_2 u_p}{1-\alpha_2\beta_2}\right)\\ &= \text{var}\left(\frac{\alpha_3 U+u_w+\alpha_2 u_p}{1-\alpha_2\beta_2}\right)\end{aligned} \tag{9.13}$$

since $\dfrac{\alpha_1+\alpha_2\beta_1}{1-\alpha_2\beta_2}$ is an additive constant. So

$$\text{var}(w) = \frac{1}{(1-\alpha_2\beta_2)^2}\left(\begin{aligned}&\text{var}(\alpha_3 U)+\text{var}(u_w)+\text{var}(\alpha_2 u_p)\\ &+2\text{cov}(\alpha_3 U,u_w)+2\text{cov}(\alpha_3 U,\alpha_2 u_p)\\ &+2\text{cov}(u_w,\alpha_2 u_p)\end{aligned}\right). \tag{9.14}$$

Now if U, u_p and u_w are independently distributed, the three covariance terms are equal to zero. Hence,

$$\begin{aligned}\operatorname{var}(w) &= \frac{1}{(1-\alpha_2\beta_2)^2}\left(\alpha_3^2\operatorname{var}(U)+\operatorname{var}(u_w)+\alpha_2^2\operatorname{var}(u_p)\right)\\ &= \frac{1}{(1-\alpha_2\beta_2)^2}\left(\alpha_3^2\sigma_U^2+\sigma_{u_w}^2+\alpha_2^2\sigma_{u_p}^2\right).\end{aligned} \tag{9.15}$$

Thus,

$$\operatorname{plim} b_2^{\text{OLS}} = \beta_2 + (1-\alpha_2\beta_2)\frac{\alpha_2\sigma_{u_p}^2}{\alpha_3^2\sigma_U^2+\sigma_{u_w}^2+\alpha_2^2\sigma_{u_p}^2} \tag{9.16}$$

and so b_2^{OLS} is an inconsistent estimator of β_2.

The direction of simultaneous equations bias depends on the structure of the model being fitted. Can one say anything about it in this case? Variances are always positive, if not zero, and α_2 should be positive, so it depends on the sign of $(1 - \alpha_2\beta_2)$. Looking at the reduced form equation (9.8), it is reasonable to suppose that w will be negatively influenced by U. Since it is also reasonable to suppose that α_3 is negative, one may infer that $(1 - \alpha_2\beta_2)$ is positive. Actually, this is a condition for equilibrium in this model. Consider the effect of a change ΔU in U. In view of (9.2), its immediate effect is to change w, in the opposite direction, by an amount $\alpha_3\Delta U$. Looking at (9.1), this in turn changes p by an amount $\alpha_3\beta_2\Delta U$. Returning to (9.2), this causes a secondary change in w of $\alpha_2\alpha_3\beta_2\Delta U$, and hence, returning to (9.1), a secondary change in p equal to $\alpha_2\alpha_3\beta_2^2\,\Delta U$. Returning again to (9.2), this causes a further change in w equal to $\alpha_2^2\alpha_3\beta_2^2\,\Delta U$. The total change in w, after taking account of all secondary effects, will therefore be

$$\Delta w = (1+\alpha_2\beta_2+\alpha_2^2\beta_2^2+\alpha_2^3\beta_2^3+\cdots)\,\alpha_3\Delta U \tag{9.17}$$

and this will be finite only if $\alpha_2\beta_2 < 1$.

A Monte Carlo experiment

The rest of this section reports on a Monte Carlo experiment that investigates the performance of OLS and, later, IV when fitting the price inflation equation in the price inflation/wage inflation model. Numerical values were assigned to the parameters of the equations as follows:

$$p = 1.5 + 0.5w + u_p \tag{9.18}$$

$$w = 2.5 + 0.5p - 0.4U + u_w. \tag{9.19}$$

The sample size was 20, with U being assigned the values 2, 2.25, increasing by steps of 0.25 to 6.75. u_p was generated as a normal random variable with zero mean and unit variance, scaled by a factor 0.8. The disturbance term u_w is

Table 9.1 Parameter estimates for 10 samples

Sample	b_1	$s.e.(b_1)$	b_2	$s.e.(b_2)$
1	0.36	0.39	1.11	0.22
2	0.45	0.38	1.06	0.17
3	0.65	0.27	0.94	0.12
4	0.41	0.39	0.98	0.19
5	0.92	0.46	0.77	0.22
6	0.26	0.35	1.09	0.16
7	0.31	0.39	1.00	0.19
8	1.06	0.38	0.82	0.16
9	−0.08	0.36	1.16	0.18
10	1.12	0.43	0.69	0.20

not responsible for the inconsistency of the regression coefficients when OLS is used to fit the price inflation equation and so, to keep things simple, it was suppressed. Using the expression derived above, plim b_2^{OLS} is equal to 0.99 when the price inflation equation is fitted with OLS. The results of 10 regressions, each using the same values of U, but different random numbers for u_p, are shown in Table 9.1.

It is evident that the estimates are heavily biased. Every estimate of the slope coefficient is above the true value of 0.5, and every estimate of the intercept is below the true value of 1.5. The mean of the slope coefficients is 0.96, not far from the theoretical plim for the OLS estimate. The standard errors are invalidated by the violation of the regression model assumption that the disturbance term be distributed independently of the explanatory variable.

Next, the experiment was repeated with 10 million samples, again keeping the same values of U but generating different random numbers for u_p. The distribution of the OLS estimates of the slope coefficient is shown in Figure 9.1. Almost all the estimates of the slope coefficient are above the true value of 0.5, confirming the conclusion of the large-sample analysis that there is a positive bias. Moreover, since the mean of the distribution is 0.95, the plim (0.99) provides quite a good guide to the magnitude of the bias.

Figure 9.2 shows how the bias arises. The hollow circles show what the relationship between p and w would look like in the absence of the disturbance terms, for 20 observations. The disturbance term u_p alters the values of both p and w in each observation when it is introduced. As can be seen from the reduced form equations, it increases p by an amount $u_p/(1-\alpha_2\beta_2)$ and w by an amount $\alpha_2 u_p/(1-\alpha_2\beta_2)$. It follows that the shift is along a line with slope $1/\alpha_2$. The solid circles are the actual observations, after u_p has been introduced. The shift line has been drawn for each observation. As can be seen, the overall effect is to skew the pattern of observations, with the result that the OLS slope coefficient is a compromise between the slope of the true relationship, β_2, and the slope of the shift lines,

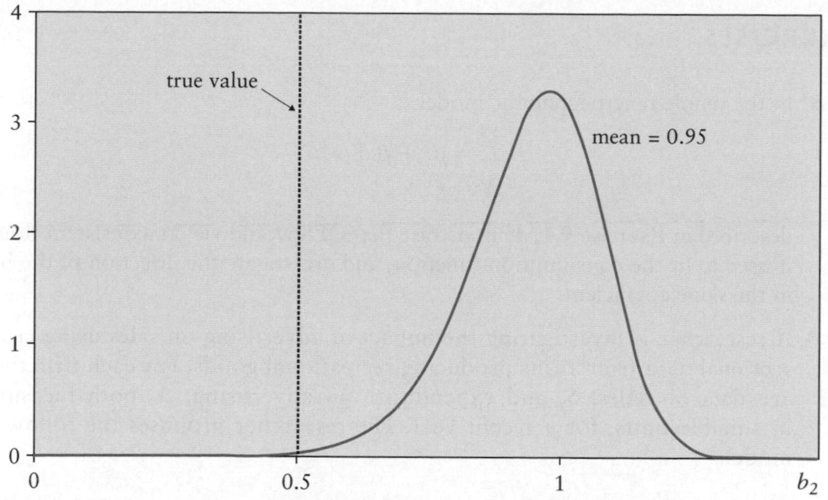

Figure 9.1 Distribution of the OLS estimator of β_2

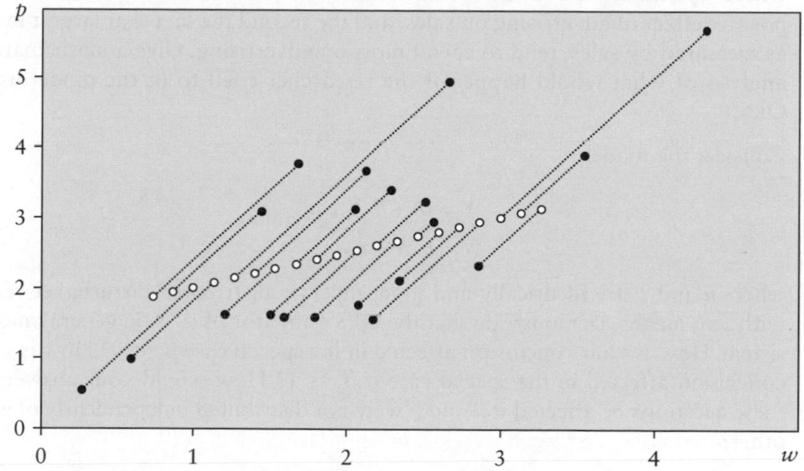

Figure 9.2 Effect on p and w of joint dependence on u_p

$1/\alpha_2$. This can be demonstrated mathematically by rewriting equation (9.16):

$$\begin{aligned}
\text{plim } b_2^{\text{OLS}} &= \beta_2 + (1-\alpha_2\beta_2)\frac{\alpha_2\sigma_{u_p}^2}{\alpha_3^2\sigma_U^2 + \sigma_{u_w}^2 + \alpha_2^2\sigma_{u_p}^2} \\
&= \beta_2 + \left(\frac{1}{\alpha_2} - \beta_2\right)\frac{\alpha_2^2\sigma_{u_p}^2}{\alpha_3^2\sigma_U^2 + \sigma_{u_w}^2 + \alpha_2^2\sigma_{u_p}^2} \\
&= \beta_2\left(\frac{\alpha_3^2\sigma_U^2 + \sigma_{u_w}^2}{\alpha_3^2\sigma_U^2 + \sigma_{u_w}^2 + \alpha_2^2\sigma_{u_p}^2}\right) + \frac{1}{\alpha_2}\left(\frac{\alpha_2^2\sigma_{u_p}^2}{\alpha_3^2\sigma_U^2 + \sigma_{u_w}^2 + \alpha_2^2\sigma_{u_p}^2}\right). \qquad \textbf{(9.20)}
\end{aligned}$$

plim b_2^{OLS} is thus a weighted average of β_2 and $1/\alpha_2$, the bias being proportional to the variance of u_p.

EXERCISES

9.3* In the simple macroeconomic model

$$C = \beta_1 + \beta_2 Y + u$$
$$Y = C + I$$

described in Exercise 9.1, demonstrate that OLS would yield inconsistent results if used to fit the consumption function, and investigate the direction of the bias in the slope coefficient.

9.4 A researcher is investigating the impact of advertising on sales using cross-sectional data from firms producing recreational goods. For each firm there are data on sales, S, and expenditure on advertising, A, both measured in suitable units, for a recent year. The researcher proposes the following model:

$$S = \beta_1 + \beta_2 A + u_S$$
$$A = \alpha_1 + \alpha_2 S + u_A,$$

where u_S and u_A are disturbance terms. The first relationship reflects the positive effect of advertising on sales, and the second the fact that largest firms, as measured by sales, tend to spend most on advertising. Give a mathematical analysis of what would happen if the researcher tried to fit the model using OLS.

9.5 Consider the model

$$Y = \beta_1 + \beta_2 X + u$$
$$X = \alpha_2 Y + v,$$

where u and v are identically and independently distributed disturbance terms with zero means. Demonstrate that the OLS estimator of α_2 is, in general, inconsistent. How is your conclusion affected in the special case $\beta_2 = 0$? How is your conclusion affected in the special case $\alpha_2\beta_2 = 1$? How would your answers to these questions be affected if u and v were not distributed independently of each other?

9.3 Instrumental variables estimation

As we saw in the discussion of measurement error, the instrumental variables approach may offer a solution to the problems caused by a violation of the regression model assumption that the disturbance term be distributed independently of the explanatory variables. In the present case, when we fit the structural equation for p, this condition is violated because w is not distributed independently of u_p. We need a variable that is correlated with w but not with u_p, and does not already appear in the equation in its own right. The reduced form equation for w gave us some bad news—it revealed that w was dependent on u_p. But it also gives us some good news—it shows that w is correlated with U, which is exogenous and thus independent of u_p. So we can fit the equation using U as an instrument for w. Using equation (8.43), the IV estimator of β_2 is given by

$$b_2^{\mathrm{IV}} = \frac{\sum_{i=1}^{n}(U_i - \bar{U})(p_i - \bar{p})}{\sum_{i=1}^{n}(U_i - \bar{U})(w_i - \bar{w})}. \tag{9.21}$$

We will demonstrate that it is consistent. Substituting from the structural equation for p,

$$\begin{aligned} b_2^{\mathrm{IV}} &= \frac{\sum_{i=1}^{n}(U_i - \bar{U})\left([\beta_1 + \beta_2 w_i + u_{pi}] - [\beta_1 + \beta_2 \bar{w} + \bar{u}_p]\right)}{\sum_{i=1}^{n}(U_i - \bar{U})(w_i - \bar{w})} \\ &= \frac{\sum_{i=1}^{n}\beta_2 (U_i - \bar{U})(w_i - \bar{w}) + (U_i - \bar{U})(u_{pi} - \bar{u}_p)}{\sum_{i=1}^{n}(U_i - \bar{U})(w_i - \bar{w})} \\ &= \beta_2 + \frac{\sum_{i=1}^{n}(U_i - \bar{U})(u_{pi} - \bar{u}_p)}{\sum_{i=1}^{n}(U_i - \bar{U})(w_i - \bar{w})}. \end{aligned} \tag{9.22}$$

We cannot take the expectation of the error term because it contains random quantities in the denominator as well as the numerator (remember that the reduced form equation for w_i shows that it is a function of both u_{pi} and u_{wi}). Instead we take plims:

$$\begin{aligned} \operatorname{plim} b_2^{\mathrm{IV}} &= \beta_2 + \frac{\operatorname{plim} \frac{1}{n}\sum_{i=1}^{n}(U_i - \bar{U})(u_{pi} - \bar{u}_p)}{\operatorname{plim} \frac{1}{n}\sum_{i=1}^{n}(U_i - \bar{U})(w_i - \bar{w})} = \beta_2 + \frac{\operatorname{cov}(U, u_p)}{\operatorname{cov}(U, w)} \\ &= \beta_2 + \frac{0}{\operatorname{cov}(U, w)} = \beta_2. \end{aligned} \tag{9.23}$$

Note that we had to divide both the numerator and the denominator of the error term by n in order for them to have probability limits. $\operatorname{cov}(U, u_p) = 0$ because U is exogenous and therefore distributed independently of u_p. $\operatorname{cov}(U, w)$ is nonzero because U is a determinant of w. Hence, the instrumental variable estimator is a consistent estimate of β_2.

Table 9.2 shows the results when IV is used to fit the model described in Section 9.2. In contrast to the OLS estimates, the IV estimates are distributed around the true values, the mean of the estimates of the slope coefficient (true value 0.5) being 0.37 and of those of the intercept (true value 1.5) being 1.69. There is no point in comparing the standard errors using the two approaches. Those for OLS may appear to be slightly smaller, but the simultaneous equations bias renders them invalid. The standard errors of the IV estimates are valid only for large samples, but they may be approximately valid in finite samples.

The experiment was repeated with 10 million samples, keeping the same values of U but generating different random numbers for u_p. The distribution of the OLS and IV estimates of the slope coefficient is shown in Figure 9.3. The mean of the IV estimates is 0.46. It should be remembered that the IV estimator is consistent, meaning that it will tend to the true value in large samples,

Table 9.2 OLS and IV estimates, 10 samples

	OLS				IV			
Sample	b_1	s.e.(b_1)	b_2	s.e.(b_2)	b_1	s.e.(b_1)	b_2	s.e.(b_2)
1	0.36	0.39	1.11	0.22	2.33	0.97	0.16	0.45
2	0.45	0.38	1.06	0.17	1.53	0.57	0.53	0.26
3	0.65	0.27	0.94	0.12	1.13	0.32	0.70	0.15
4	0.41	0.39	0.98	0.19	1.55	0.59	0.37	0.30
5	0.92	0.46	0.77	0.22	2.31	0.71	0.06	0.35
6	0.26	0.35	1.09	0.16	1.24	0.52	0.59	0.25
7	0.31	0.39	1.00	0.19	1.52	0.62	0.33	0.32
8	1.06	0.38	0.82	0.16	1.95	0.51	0.41	0.22
9	−0.08	0.36	1.16	0.18	1.11	0.62	0.45	0.33
10	1.12	0.43	0.69	0.20	2.26	0.61	0.13	0.29

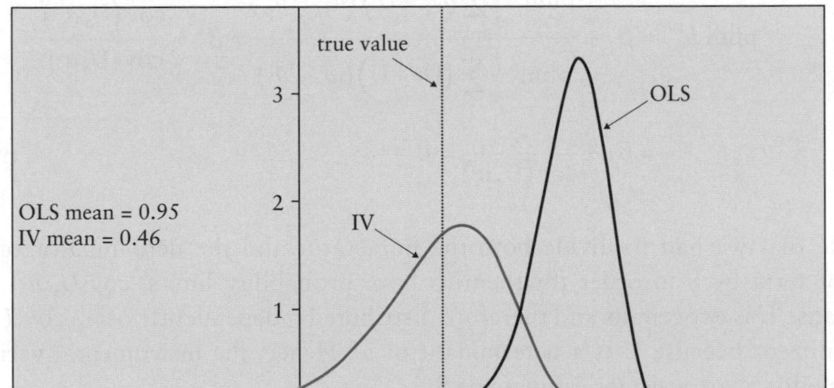

Figure 9.3 Distributions of the OLS and IV estimators of β_2

but there is no claim that it is unbiased in finite samples. In this example, it turned out to be biased downwards, at least for sample size 20, but the bias is quite small and certainly it is much smaller than the upwards bias in the OLS estimates. The standard deviation of the IV estimates is 0.26. The standard errors of the IV estimates in Table 9.2 do appear to be distributed around this figure.

In this example, IV definitely gave better results than OLS, but that outcome was not inevitable. The variance of an IV estimator will in general be greater than that of a corresponding OLS estimator. If the instrument is weak, in the sense of not being highly correlated with the variable for which it is acting, the IV variance may be much greater. So if the bias in the OLS estimator is small, it is possible that OLS might yield superior estimates according to a criterion such as the mean square error that allows a trade-off between bias and variance.

Underidentification

If OLS were used to fit the wage inflation equation

$$w = \alpha_1 + \alpha_2 p + \alpha_3 U + u_w, \tag{9.24}$$

the estimates would be subject to simultaneous equations bias caused by the (indirect) dependence of p on u_w. However, in this case it is not possible to use the instrumental variables approach to obtain consistent estimates, and the relationship is said to be **underidentified**. The only determinant of p, apart from the disturbance terms, is U, and it is already in the model in its own right. An attempt to use it as an instrument for p would lead to a form of exact multicollinearity and it would be impossible to obtain estimates of the parameters. Using the expression in Box 9.1, we would have

$$\begin{aligned} a_2^{\mathrm{IV}} &= \frac{\sum_{i=1}^{n}(Z_i-\bar{Z})(w_i-\bar{w})\sum_{i=1}^{n}(U_i-\bar{U})^2-\sum_{i=1}^{n}(U_i-\bar{U})(w_i-\bar{w})\sum_{i=1}^{n}(Z_i-\bar{Z})(U_i-\bar{U})}{\sum_{i=1}^{n}(Z_i-\bar{Z})(p_i-\bar{p})\sum_{i=1}^{n}(U_i-\bar{U})^2-\sum_{i=1}^{n}(p_i-\bar{p})(U_i-\bar{U})\sum_{i=1}^{n}(Z_i-\bar{Z})(U_i-\bar{U})} \\ &= \frac{\sum_{i=1}^{n}(U_i-\bar{U})(w_i-\bar{w})\sum_{i=1}^{n}(U_i-\bar{U})^2-\sum_{i=1}^{n}(U_i-\bar{U})(w_i-\bar{w})\sum_{i=1}^{n}(U_i-\bar{U})(U_i-\bar{U})}{\sum_{i=1}^{n}(U_i-\bar{U})(p_i-\bar{p})\sum_{i=1}^{n}(U_i-\bar{U})^2-\sum_{i=1}^{n}(p_i-\bar{p})(U_i-\bar{U})\sum_{i=1}^{n}(U_i-\bar{U})(U_i-\bar{U})} \end{aligned} \tag{9.25}$$

and the numerator and denominator both reduce to zero.

However, suppose that the rate of price inflation were hypothesized to be determined by the rate of growth of the money supply, m, as well as the rate of growth of wages, and that m were assumed to be exogenous:

$$p = \beta_1 + \beta_2 w + \beta_3 m + u_p. \tag{9.26}$$

BOX 9.1 Instrumental variables estimation in a model with two explanatory variables

Suppose that the true model is

$$Y = \beta_1 + \beta_2 X_2 + \beta_3 X_3 + u,$$

that X_2 is not distributed independently of u, and that Z is being used as an instrument for X_2. Then the IV estimator of β_2 is given by

$$b_2^{\mathrm{IV}} = \frac{\sum_{i=1}^{n}(Z_i - \bar{Z})(Y_i - \bar{Y})\sum_{i=1}^{n}(X_{3i} - \bar{X}_3)^2 - \sum_{i=1}^{n}(X_{3i} - \bar{X}_3)(Y_i - \bar{Y})\sum_{i=1}^{n}(Z_i - \bar{Z})(X_{3i} - \bar{X}_3)}{\sum_{i=1}^{n}(Z_i - \bar{Z})(X_{2i} - \bar{X}_2)\sum_{i=1}^{n}(X_{3i} - \bar{X}_3)^2 - \sum_{i=1}^{n}(X_{2i} - \bar{X}_2)(X_{3i} - \bar{X}_3)\sum_{i=1}^{n}(Z_i - \bar{Z})(X_{3i} - \bar{X}_3)}.$$

The IV estimator of β_3 is the same, with the subscripts 2 and 3 interchanged.

The reduced form equations become

$$p = \frac{\beta_1 + \alpha_1\beta_2 + \alpha_3\beta_2 U + \beta_3 m + u_p + \beta_2 u_w}{1 - \alpha_2\beta_2} \tag{9.27}$$

$$w = \frac{\alpha_1 + \alpha_2\beta_1 + \alpha_3 U + \alpha_2\beta_3 m + u_w + \alpha_2 u_p}{1 - \alpha_2\beta_2}. \tag{9.28}$$

U may be used as an instrument for w in the price inflation equation, as before, and m can be used as an instrument for p in the wage inflation equation because it satisfies the three conditions required of an instrument. It is correlated with p, by virtue of being a determinant; it is not correlated with the disturbance term, by virtue of being assumed to be exogenous; and it is not already in the structural equation in its own right. Both structural equations are now said to be exactly identified, **exact identification** meaning that the number of exogenous variables available as instruments (that is, not already in the equation in their own right) is equal to the number of endogenous variables requiring instruments.

Overidentification

Next consider the model

$$p = \beta_1 + \beta_2 w + u_p \tag{9.29}$$

$$w = \alpha_1 + \alpha_2 p + \alpha_3 U + \alpha_4 x + u_w, \tag{9.30}$$

where x is the rate of growth of productivity. The corresponding reduced form equations are

$$p = \frac{\beta_1 + \alpha_1\beta_2 + \alpha_3\beta_2 U + \alpha_4\beta_2 x + u_p + \beta_2 u_w}{1 - \alpha_2\beta_2} \qquad (9.31)$$

$$w = \frac{\alpha_1 + \alpha_2\beta_1 + \alpha_3 U + \alpha_4 x + u_w + \alpha_2 u_p}{1 - \alpha_2\beta_2}. \qquad (9.32)$$

The wage inflation equation is underidentified because there is no exogenous variable available to act as an instrument for p. p is correlated with both U and x, but both these variables appear in the wage equation in their own right.

However, the price inflation equation is now said to be overidentified because we have two potential instruments for w. We could use U as an instrument for w, as before:

$$b_2^{\mathrm{IV}} = \frac{\sum_{i=1}^{n}(U_i - \bar{U})(p_i - \bar{p})}{\sum_{i=1}^{n}(U_i - \bar{U})(w_i - \bar{w})}. \qquad (9.33)$$

Alternatively, we could use x as an instrument:

$$b_2^{\mathrm{IV}} = \frac{\sum_{i=1}^{n}(x_i - \bar{x})(p_i - \bar{p})}{\sum_{i=1}^{n}(x_i - \bar{x})(w_i - \bar{w})}. \qquad (9.34)$$

Both are consistent estimators, so they would converge to the true value, and therefore to each other, as the sample size became large, but for finite samples they would give different estimates. Suppose that you had to choose between them (you do not, as we will see). Which would you choose? The population variance of the first is given by

$$\sigma^2_{b_2^{\mathrm{IV}}} = \frac{\sigma^2_{u_p}}{\sum_{i=1}^{n}(w_i - \bar{w})^2} \times \frac{1}{r^2_{w,U}}. \qquad (9.35)$$

The population variance of the second estimator is given by a similar expression with the correlation coefficient replaced by that between w and x. We want the population variance to be as small as possible, so we would choose the instrument with the higher correlation coefficient.

Two-stage least squares

In practice, rather than choose between the instruments in this situation, we would construct a linear function of them and use that instead. The main reason for this is that in general a linear function, with suitably chosen weights, will be more efficient than either instrument individually. A secondary consideration is that using a linear function eliminates the problem of conflicting estimates. Let the linear function be Z, where

$$Z = h_1 + h_2 U + h_3 x. \quad \textbf{(9.36)}$$

How do we choose the h coefficients? Very straightforward. Using OLS, regress w on U and x, save the fitted values, and call the saved variable Z:

$$Z = \hat{w} = h_1 + h_2 U + h_3 x. \quad \textbf{(9.37)}$$

The fitted values are automatically linear functions of U and x and the h coefficients will have been chosen in such a way as to maximize the correlation between the fitted values and w. As we saw in Chapter 1, OLS yields estimates that are optimal according to three mutually equivalent criteria: minimizing the sum of the squares of the residuals, maximizing R^2, and (the criterion that is relevant here) maximizing the correlation between the actual and the fitted values. This is the first stage of the two-stage least squares (TSLS) estimator. The second stage is the calculation of the estimate of β_2 using Z as an instrument:

$$b_2^{\mathrm{TSLS}} = \frac{\sum_{i=1}^{n}(Z_i - \bar{Z})(p_i - \bar{p})}{\sum_{i=1}^{n}(Z_i - \bar{Z})(w_i - \bar{w})} = \frac{\sum_{i=1}^{n}(\hat{w}_i - \bar{\hat{w}})(p_i - \bar{p})}{\sum_{i=1}^{n}(\hat{w}_i - \bar{\hat{w}})(w_i - \bar{w})}. \quad \textbf{(9.38)}$$

The population variance of b_2^{TSLS} is given by

$$\sigma^2_{b_2^{\mathrm{TSLS}}} = \frac{\sigma^2_{u_p}}{\sum_{i=1}^{n}(w_i - \bar{w})^2} \times \frac{1}{r^2_{w,\hat{w}}} \quad \textbf{(9.39)}$$

and in general this will be smaller than the population variances of the IV estimators using U or x because the correlation coefficient will be higher.

The order condition for identification

We have observed that in general an equation will be identified if there are enough exogenous variables not appearing in it to act as instruments for the endogenous variables that do appear in it. In a fully specified model, there will be as many equations as there are endogenous variables. Let us suppose that there are G of each. The maximum number of endogenous variables that can appear on the right side of an equation is $G - 1$ (the other is the dependent variable of that equation). In such a case, we would need at least $G - 1$ exogenous variables not appearing in the equation to have enough instruments.

Suppose, however, that j endogenous variables are also missing from the equation. We would then need only $G - 1 - j$ instruments, so only $G - 1 - j$ exogenous variables would have to be missing from the equation. The total number of variables missing, however, remains the same: j endogenous variables and $G - 1 - j$ exogenous variables make a total of $G - 1$.

Thus, we come to the general conclusion that an equation in a simultaneous equations model is likely to be identified if $G - 1$ or more variables are missing from it. If exactly $G - 1$ are missing, it is likely to be exactly identified, and if more than $G - 1$ are missing, it is likely to be overidentified, calling for the use of TSLS.

This is known as the **order condition for identification**. It must be stressed that this is a necessary condition for identification but not a sufficient one. There are cases, which we will not discuss here, in which an equation is in fact underidentified even if the order condition is satisfied.

Unobserved heterogeneity

In the examples above, simultaneous equations bias and instrumental variables estimation were discussed in the context of fully specified multi-equation models. However, it is common to find these issues discussed in the context of a single-equation model, where the equation is implicitly embedded in a simultaneous equations model where the other relationships are unspecified. For example, in the case of the earnings function

$$LGEARN = \beta_1 + \beta_2 S + \cdots + u, \tag{9.40}$$

it is often asserted that '**unobserved heterogeneity**' will cause the OLS estimate of β_2 to be biased. In this case, unobserved heterogeneity refers to unobserved variations in the characteristics of the respondents, such as ambition and various types of intelligence and ability, which influence both educational attainment and earnings. Because they are unobserved, their influence on earnings is captured by the disturbance term, and thus S and u are positively correlated. As a consequence, the OLS estimate of β_2 will be subject to a positive bias. If this is the case, S needs to be instrumented with a suitable instrument.

However, it requires ingenuity to find a credible instrument, for most factors affecting educational attainment are also likely to affect earnings. One such example is the use of proximity to a four-year college by Card (1995), who argued that this could have a positive effect on educational attainment but was unlikely to be a determinant of earnings.

Table 9.3 presents the results of OLS and IV regressions using a sample of 3,010 males derived from the National Longitudinal Survey of Young Men, a panel study that was a precursor to the NLSY. The earnings data relate to 1976. The regressions included personal, family, and regional characteristics not shown. As can be seen, using college proximity to instrument for educational attainment does make a difference—but it is in a direction opposite

Table 9.3 Schooling effect, OLS and IV

	OLS	*IV*
Coefficient of *S*	0.073	0.140
Standard error	0.004	0.055

to that expected, for if the OLS estimate is upwards biased, the IV estimate ought to be smaller, not larger. Measurement error in *S*, which would cause a downwards bias in the OLS estimate, could account for part of the perverse effect, but not all of it. Card sought an explanation in terms of a higher-than-average return to education for those with relatively poorly educated parents, combined with a higher responsiveness of educational attainment to college proximity for such respondents. However, although educational attainment is positively correlated with college proximity, the correlation is weak and accordingly the standard error of the IV estimate large. It is thus possible that the apparent increase occurred as a matter of chance and that a Durbin–Wu–Hausman test would have shown that the OLS and IV estimates were not significantly different.

Durbin–Wu–Hausman test

In Chapter 8, it was shown that measurement error causes a violation of the regression model assumption that the disturbance term be distributed independently of the regressors, and that one can use the Durbin–Wu–Hausman test, which compares the OLS and IV coefficients, to test for suspected measurement error. The test can be used in the same way more broadly for suspected violations of this regression model assumption and in particular for violations caused by simultaneous equations bias. To illustrate this, we will return to the Monte Carlo experiment described above. The regression output in Tables 9.4–9.6 shows the result of performing the test for the first of the 10 replications of the experiment summarized in Table 9.2. Table 9.4 shows the output from the IV regression of p on w, using U as an instrument for w. Table 9.5 shows the output of the corresponding OLS regression. Table 9.6 shows the result of the DWH test.

Under the null hypothesis that there is no simultaneous equations bias, both OLS and IV will be consistent estimators, but OLS will be more efficient. Under the alternative hypothesis, OLS will be inconsistent. As can be seen from the output, the chi-squared statistic summarizing the differences in the coefficients is 6.77. In principle there should be two degrees of freedom because we are comparing two parameters. This is confirmed by the output. The critical values of chi-squared with two degrees of freedom at the 5 percent and 1 percent levels

Table 9.4

```
. ivregress 2sls p (w=U)
Instrumental variables (2SLS) regression              Number of obs =      20
                                                      Wald chi2(1)  =    0.15
                                                      Prob > chi2   =  0.7018
                                                      R-squared     =  0.1606
                                                      Root MSE      =   1.187
------------------------------------------------------------------------------
           p |      Coef.   Std. Err.      t     P > |z|   [95% Conf. Interval]
-------------+----------------------------------------------------------------
           w |   .1619431   .4230184    0.38    0.702   -.6671577    .9910439
       _cons |   2.328433   .9202004    2.53    0.011    .5248734    4.131993
------------------------------------------------------------------------------
Instrumented: w
Instruments: U
. estimates store REGIV
```

Table 9.5

```
. reg p w
      Source |       SS         df        MS           Number of obs =     20
-------------+------------------------------           F(1, 18)      =  26.16
       Model |  19.8854938       1    19.8854938       Prob > F      = 0.0001
    Residual |   13.683167      18    .760175945       R-squared     = 0.5924
-------------+------------------------------           Adj R-squared = 0.5697
       Total |  33.5686608      19    1.76677162       Root MSE      = .87188
------------------------------------------------------------------------------
           p |      Coef.   Std. Err.      t     P > |t|   [95% Conf. Interval]
-------------+----------------------------------------------------------------
           w |   1.107448   .2165271    5.11    0.000    .6525417    1.562355
       _cons |   .3590688   .4913327    0.73    0.474   -.673183     1.391321
------------------------------------------------------------------------------
. estimates store REGOLS
```

Table 9.6

```
. hausman REGIV REGOLS, constant
                     ----- Coefficients ----
             |      (b)          (B)           (b-B)      sqrt(diag(V_b-V_B))
             |     REGIV        REGOLS       Difference          S.E.
-------------+----------------------------------------------------------------
           w |   .1619431     1.107448      -.9455052          .3634014
       _cons |   2.328433     .3590688       1.969364          .7780495
------------------------------------------------------------------------------
               b = consistent under Ho and Ha; obtained from ivregress
        B = inconsistent under Ha, efficient under Ho; obtained from regress
Test: Ho: difference in coefficients not systematic
          chi2(2) = (b-B)'[(V_b-V_B)^(-1)](b-B)
                  = 6.77
        Prob>chi2 = 0.0339
```

BOX 9.2 Indirect least squares

Indirect least squares (ILS), an alternative procedure for obtaining consistent estimates of parameters in a simultaneous equations model, is no longer used in practice but it retains some pedagogical interest. Returning to the price inflation/wage inflation model

$$p = \beta_1 + \beta_2 w + u_p$$

$$w = \beta_1 + \beta_2 p + \beta_3 U + u_w,$$

the reduced form equations for p and w were

$$p = \frac{\beta_1 + \alpha_1\beta_2 + \alpha_3\beta_2 U + u_p + \beta_2 u_w}{1 - \alpha_2\beta_2}$$

$$w = \frac{\alpha_1 + \alpha_2\beta_1 + \alpha_3 U + u_w + \alpha_2 u_p}{1 - \alpha_2\beta_2}.$$

On the assumption that U is exogenous, it is independent of u_p and u_w and so OLS will give unbiased estimates of the parameters of the equations. The parameters of these equations are of course functions of the parameters of the structural equations, but it may be possible to derive estimates of the structural parameters from them. For example, using the data for the first replication of the Monte Carlo experiment, the fitted reduced form equations are

$$\hat{p} = 2.9741 - 0.0705U$$

$$\hat{w} = 3.9871 - 0.4352U.$$

Hence, linking the numerical estimates to the theoretical coefficients, one has four equations

$$\frac{b_1 + a_1 b_2}{1 - a_2 b_2} = 2.9741 \qquad \frac{a_3 b_2}{1 - a_2 b_2} = -0.0705$$

$$\frac{a_1 + a_2 b_1}{1 - a_2 b_2} = 3.9871 \qquad \frac{a_3}{1 - a_2 b_2} = -0.4352.$$

Substituting the fourth equation into the second, one has $-0.4352b_2 = -0.0705$, and so $b_2 = 0.1620$. Further, since

$$\frac{b_1 + a_1 b_2}{1 - a_2 b_2} - b_2 \frac{a_1 + a_2 b_1}{1 - a_2 b_2} = b_1,$$

one has $b_1 = 2.9741 - 0.1620 \times 3.9871 = 2.3282$. There is no way of deriving estimates of the three remaining parameters. Indeed, since we had four equations in five unknowns, we were lucky to pin down two of the parameters. Since we have obtained (unique) estimates of the parameters of the structural price equation, that equation is said to be exactly identified, while the structural wage equation is said to be underidentified.

BOX 9.2 (continued)

Next consider the model

$$p = \beta_1 + \beta_2 w + u_p$$
$$w = \alpha_1 + \alpha_2 p + \alpha_3 U + \alpha_4 x + u_w$$

where x is the rate of growth of productivity. The corresponding reduced form equations are

$$p = \frac{\beta_1 + \alpha_1\beta_2 + \alpha_3\beta_2 U + \alpha_4\beta_2 x + u_p + \beta_2 u_w}{1 - \alpha_2\beta_2}$$

$$w = \frac{\alpha_1 + \alpha_2\beta_1 + \alpha_3 U + \alpha_4 x + u_w + \alpha_2 u_p}{1 - \alpha_2\beta_2}.$$

Suppose that when these are fitted we obtain, in abstract form,

$$\hat{p} = B_1 + B_2 U + B_3 x$$
$$\hat{w} = A_1 + A_2 U + A_3 x$$

where the B_i and the A_i are numerical regression coefficients. Linking these numerical coefficients to their theoretical counterparts, we obtain six equations in six unknowns:

$$\frac{b_1 + a_1 b_2}{1 - a_2 b_2} = B_1 \qquad \frac{a_3 b_2}{1 - a_2 b_2} = B_2 \qquad \frac{a_4 b_2}{1 - a_2 b_2} = B_3$$

$$\frac{a_1 + a_2 b_1}{1 - a_2 b_2} = A_1 \qquad \frac{a_3}{1 - a_2 b_2} = A_2 \qquad \frac{a_4}{1 - a_2 b_2} = A_3.$$

Substituting the fifth equation into the second, we have $A_2 b_2 = B_2$, and so B_2/A_2 provides an estimate of β_2. However, substituting the sixth equation into the third, we have $A_3 b_2 = B_3$, and so B_3/A_3 also provides an estimate of β_2. Thus we have more than one way of obtaining an estimate and the model is said to be overidentified. This is the counterpart of having alternative instruments in IV estimation. The estimates would both be consistent, and so in large samples they would converge to the true value, but in finite samples they would differ. One would also be able to obtain conflicting estimates of β_1. However, it would not be possible to obtain estimates of the remaining parameters and the wage equation is said to be underidentified.

ILS has no advantages over IV and has the disadvantage of requiring more computation. If an equation is underidentified for IV, it is underidentified for ILS; if it exactly identified, IV and ILS yield identical estimates; if it is overidentified, ILS yields conflicting estimates, a problem that is resolved with IV by using TSLS.

are 5.99 and 9.21, and hence we reject the null hypothesis at the 5 percent level. Given that the Monte Carlo experiment involved a simultaneous equations model designed to demonstrate that OLS would yield inconsistent estimates, it may seem surprising that the null hypothesis was rejected only at the 5 percent level and not at the 1 percent level. This is probably attributable to the small size of the sample and the imprecision of the IV estimates.

Key terms

- endogenous variable
- exact identification
- exogenous variable
- overidentification
- reduced form equation
- simultaneous equations bias
- structural equation
- identification
- indirect least squares
- order condition for identification
- two-stage least squares (TSLS)
- underidentification
- unobserved heterogeneity

EXERCISES

9.6* The table gives consumption per capita, C, gross investment per capita, I, and gross domestic product per capita, Y, all measured in US$, for 33 countries in 1998. The output from an OLS regression of C on Y, and an IV regression using I as an instrument for Y, are shown. Comment on the differences in the results.

	C	I	Y		C	I	Y
Australia	15024	4749	19461	South Korea	4596	1448	6829
Austria	19813	6787	26104	Luxembourg	26400	9767	42650
Belgium	18367	5174	24522	Malaysia	1683	873	3268
Canada	15786	4017	20085	Mexico	3359	1056	4328
China–PR	446	293	768	Netherlands	17558	4865	24086
China–HK	17067	7262	24452	New Zealand	11236	2658	13992
Denmark	25199	6947	32769	Norway	23415	9221	32933
Finland	17991	4741	24952	Pakistan	389	79	463
France	19178	4622	24587	Philippines	760	176	868
Germany	20058	5716	26219	Portugal	8579	2644	9976
Greece	9991	2460	11551	Spain	11255	3415	14052
Iceland	25294	6706	30622	Sweden	20687	4487	26866
India	291	84	385	Switzerland	27648	7815	36864
Indonesia	351	216	613	Thailand	1226	479	1997
Ireland	13045	4791	20132	UK	19743	4316	23844
Italy	16134	4075	20580	USA	26387	6540	32377
Japan	21478	7923	30124				

```
. reg C Y

     Source  |        SS            df          MS             Number of obs =      33
-------------+------------------------------------------       F(1, 31)      = 1192.18
      Model  |   2.5686e+09          1     2.5686e+09          Prob > F      =  0.0000
   Residual  |   59810749.2         31     1929379.01          R-squared     =  0.9772
-------------+------------------------------------------       Adj R-squared =  0.9765
      Total  |   2.6284e+09         32     82136829.4          Root MSE      =    1389

------------------------------------------------------------------------------
           C |      Coef.   Std. Err.      t     P > |t|     [95% Conf. Interval]
-------------+----------------------------------------------------------------
           Y |   .7303066    .0200156    36.49   0.000      .6894845    .7711287
       _cons |   379.4871    443.6764     0.86   0.399      -525.397    1284.371
------------------------------------------------------------------------------

. ivreg C (Y=I)
Instrumental variables (2SLS) regression

     Source  |        SS            df          MS             Number of obs =      33
-------------+------------------------------------------       F(1, 31)      = 1331.29
      Model  |   2.5679e109          1     2.5679e109          Prob > F      =  0.0000
   Residual  |   60494538.1         31     1951436.71          R-squared     =  0.9770
-------------+------------------------------------------       Adj R-squared =  0.9762
      Total  |   2.6284e109         32     82136829.4          Root MSE      =  1396.9

------------------------------------------------------------------------------
           C |      Coef.   Std. Err.      t     P > |t|     [95% Conf. Interval]
-------------+----------------------------------------------------------------
           Y |   .7183909    .0208061    34.53   0.000      .6759566    .7608252
       _cons |    600.946    456.7973     1.32   0.198     -330.6982     1532.59
------------------------------------------------------------------------------
Instrumented: Y
Instruments: I
------------------------------------------------------------------------------
```

9.7 The researcher in Exercise 9.4 discovers that last year's advertising budget, $A(-1)$, is also an important determinant of A, so that the model is

$$S = \beta_1 + \beta_2 A + u_S$$
$$A = \alpha_1 + \alpha_2 S + \alpha_3 A(-1) + u_A.$$

Explain how this information could be used to obtain a consistent estimator of β_2, and prove that it is consistent.

9.8 Suppose that $A(-1)$ in Exercise 9.7 also has an influence on S. How would this affect the fitting of the model?

9.9 The researcher in Exercise 9.4 finds out that the average price of the product, P, and last year's sales, $S(-1)$, are important determinants of S, so that the model is

$$S = \beta_1 + \beta_2 A + \beta_3 P + \beta_4 S(-1) + u_S$$
$$A = \alpha_1 + \alpha_2 S + u_A.$$

How would this affect the fitting of the model?

9.10 In principle, $ASVABC$ might be a positive function of S, in which case the educational attainment model should have two equations:

$$S = \beta_1 + \beta_2 ASVABC + \beta_3 SM + u_S$$
$$ASVABC = \alpha_1 + \alpha_2 S + u_A.$$

Using your *EAEF* data set, fit the second equation, first using OLS, second using instrumental variables estimation with *SM* as an instrument. Demonstrate that in principle IV should yield consistent estimates. Investigate analytically the likely direction of the bias in the slope coefficient in the OLS regression, and check whether a comparison of the OLS and IV estimates confirms your analysis.

9.11* Consider the price inflation/wage inflation model given by equations (9.1) and (9.2):

$$p = \beta_1 + \beta_2 w + u_p.$$
$$w = \alpha_1 + \alpha_2 p + \alpha_3 U + u_w.$$

We have seen that the first equation is exactly identified, U being used as an instrument for w. Suppose that TSLS is applied to this model, despite the fact that it is exactly identified, rather than overidentified. How will the results differ?

9.12 A researcher believes that a model consists of the following relationships:

$$Y = \alpha_1 + \alpha_2 X + u \quad (1)$$
$$X = \beta_1 + \beta_2 Y + v \quad (2)$$
$$Z = \gamma_1 + \gamma_2 Y + \gamma_3 X + \gamma_4 Q + w, \quad (3)$$

where u, v, and w, are disturbance terms that are drawn from fixed distributions with zero mean. It may be assumed that they are distributed independently of Q and of each other. All the parameters may be assumed to be positive and it may be assumed that $\alpha_2\beta_2 < 1$. It may be assumed that the model is correctly specified.

State which variables in this model are endogenous and which are exogenous.

The researcher fits (2) using ordinary least squares (OLS). Evaluate whether the estimate of β_2 is likely to be biased. If it is biased, determine the direction of the bias.

The researcher fits (3) using OLS. Determine whether the parameter estimates are likely to be biased. (You are not expected to evaluate the direction of the bias, if any.)

The researcher decides to fit (2) using instrumental variables (IV), with Q_i as an instrument for Y_i. Determine whether he is likely to obtain a consistent estimate of β_2.

9.13 Consider the model in Exercise 9.5:

$$Y = \beta_1 + \beta_2 X + u$$
$$X = \alpha_2 Y + v,$$

where u and v are identically and independently distributed disturbance terms with zero means.

Determine whether $\overline{X}/\overline{Y}$, where $\overline{X}$ and $\overline{Y}$ are the sample means of X and Y, is (a) an unbiased estimator of α_2, and (b) a consistent estimator of α_2. Do your conclusions depend on the independence of u and v?

9.14 The output from a Durbin–Wu–Hausman test using the regressions in Exercise 9.6 is shown. CGIV and CGOLS are the names given to the IV and OLS regressions, respectively. Perform the test and state whether or not it supports your discussion in Exercise 9.6.

```
. hausman CGIV CGOLS, constant
                    ----- Coefficients ----

             |     (b)          (B)           (b-B)      sqrt(diag(V_b-V_B))
             |     CGIV        CGOLS        Difference          S.E.
------------------------------------------------------------------------------
           Y |  .7183909      .7303066      -.0119157         .0056807
       _cons |   600.946      379.4871       221.4589         108.6968
------------------------------------------------------------------------------
           b = consistent under Ho and Ha; obtained from ivreg
  B = inconsistent under Ha, efficient under Ho; obtained from regress
Test: Ho: difference in coefficients not systematic
    chi2(2) = (b-B)'[(V_b-V_B)^(-1)](b-B)
            = 4.15
  Prob>chi2 = 0.0416
```

10 Binary Choice and Limited Dependent Variable Models, and Maximum Likelihood Estimation

Economists are often interested in the factors behind the decision-making of individuals or enterprises. Examples are:

- Why do some people go to college while others do not?
- Why do some women enter the labor force while others do not?
- Why do some people buy houses while others rent?
- Why do some people migrate while others stay put?

The models that have been developed are known as binary choice or qualitative response models with the outcome, which we will denote Y, being assigned a value of 1 if the event occurs and 0 otherwise. Models with more than two possible outcomes have been developed, but we will restrict our attention to binary choice. The linear probability model apart, binary choice models are fitted using maximum likelihood estimation. The chapter ends with an introduction to this topic.

10.1 The linear probability model

The simplest binary choice model is the linear probability model where, as the name implies, the probability of the event occurring, p, is assumed to be a linear function of a set of explanatory variable(s):

$$p_i = p(Y_i = 1) = \beta_1 + \beta_2 X_i. \qquad \textbf{(10.1)}$$

Graphically, the relationship is as shown in Figure 10.1, if there is just one explanatory variable. Of course p is unobservable. One has data only on the outcome, Y. In the linear probability model this is used as a dummy variable for the dependent variable.

As an illustration, we investigate the factors influencing graduating from high school. We will define a variable *GRAD* that is equal to 1 for those individuals

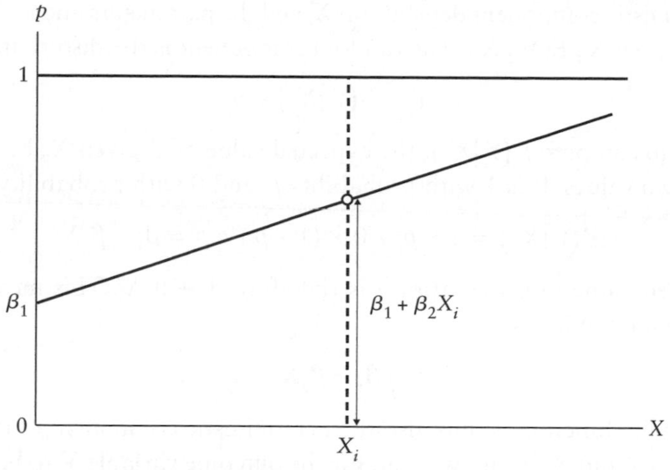

Figure 10.1 Linear probability model

who graduated ($S > 12$), and 0 for those who dropped out ($S < 12$), and we will regress it on *ASVABC*, the composite cognitive ability test score. The regression output in Table 10.1 shows the result of fitting this linear probability model, using *EAEF* Data Set 21.

The regression result suggests that the probability of graduating from high school increases by a proportion 0.007, that is, 0.7 percent, for every point increase in the *ASVABC* score. *ASVABC* is scaled so that it has mean 50 and standard deviation 10, so a one-standard deviation increase in the score would increase the probability of graduating by 7 percent. The intercept implies that if *ASVABC* were zero, the probability of graduating would be 58 percent. However, the *ASVABC* score is scaled in such a way as to make its minimum about 20, and accordingly it is doubtful whether the interpretation should be taken at face value.

Unfortunately, the linear probability model has some serious defects. First, there are problems with the disturbance term. As usual, the value of the dependent variable Y_i in observation i has a deterministic component and a random component.

Table 10.1

```
reg GRAD ASVABC
  Source  |        SS           df           MS             Number of obs  =    540
----------------------------------------------------        F(1, 538)      =  49.59
   Model  |  2.46607893          1      2.46607893          Prob > F       = 0.0000
Residual  |  26.7542914        538      .049729166          R-squared      = 0.0844
----------------------------------------------------        Adj R-squared  = 0.0827
   Total  |  29.2203704        539      .05421219           Root MSE       =   .223
-----------------------------------------------------------------------------------
    GRAD  |      Coef.     Std. Err.       t    P>|t|      [95% Conf.  Interval]
-----------------------------------------------------------------------------------
  ASVABC  |   .0070697     .0010039     7.04    0.000      .0050976     .0090419
   _cons  |   .5794711     .0524502    11.05    0.000      .4764387     .6825035
-----------------------------------------------------------------------------------
```

The deterministic component depends on X_i and the parameters and is the expected value of Y_i given X_i, $E(Y_i \mid X_i)$. The random component is the disturbance term:

$$Y_i = E(Y_i|X_i) + u_i. \tag{10.2}$$

It is simple to compute $E(Y_i|X_i)$, the expected value of Y_i given X_i, because Y can take only two values. It is 1 with probability p_i and 0 with probability $(1 - p_i)$:

$$E(Y_i|X_i) = 1 \times p_i + 0 \times (1 - p_i) = p_i = \beta_1 + \beta_2 X_i. \tag{10.3}$$

The expected value in observation i is therefore $\beta_1 + \beta_2 X_i$. This means that we can rewrite the model as

$$Y_i = \beta_1 + \beta_2 X_i + u_i. \tag{10.4}$$

The probability function is thus also the deterministic component of the relationship between Y and X. It follows that, for the outcome variable Y_i to be equal to 1, as represented by the point A in Figure 10.2, the disturbance term must be equal to $(1 - \beta_1 - \beta_2 X_i)$. For the outcome to be 0, as represented by the point B, the disturbance term must be $(-\beta_1 - \beta_2 X_i)$. Thus, the distribution of the disturbance term consists of just two specific values. It is not even continuous, never mind normal. This means that the standard errors and the usual test statistics are invalidated. For good measure, the two possible values of the disturbance term change with X, so the distribution is heteroscedastic as well. It can be shown that the population variance of u_i is $(\beta_1 + \beta_2 X_i)(1 - \beta_1 - \beta_2 X_i)$, and this varies with X_i.

Another problem is that the predicted probability may be greater than 1 or less than 0 for extreme values of X. In the example of graduating from high school, the regression equation predicts a probability greater than 1 for the 176 respondents with *ASVABC* scores greater than 56.

The first problem is dealt with by fitting the model with a technique known as maximum likelihood estimation, described in Section 10.6, instead of least

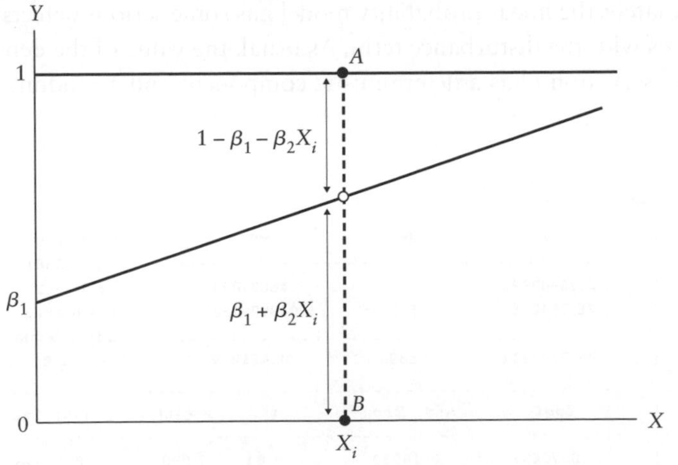

Figure 10.2 Disturbance term in the linear probability model

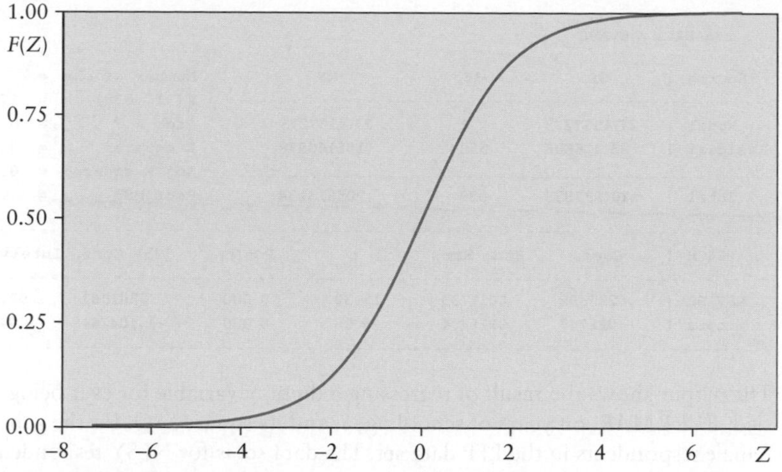

Figure 10.3 Logistic function

squares. The second problem involves elaborating the model as follows. Define a variable Z that is a linear function of the explanatory variables. In the present case, since we have only one explanatory variable, this function is

$$Z_i = \beta_1 + \beta_2 X_i. \tag{10.5}$$

Next, suppose that p is a sigmoid (S-shaped) function of Z, for example as shown in Figure 10.3. Below a certain value of Z, there is very little chance of the individual graduating from high school. Above a certain value, the individual is almost certain to graduate. In between, the probability is sensitive to the value of Z.

This deals with the problem of nonsense probability estimates, but then there is the question of what should be the precise mathematical form of this function. There is no definitive answer to this. The two most popular forms are the logistic function, which is used in logit estimation, and the cumulative normal distribution, which is used in probit estimation. According to one of the leading authorities on the subject, Amemiya (1981), both give satisfactory results most of the time and neither has any particular advantage. We will start with the former.

EXERCISES

10.1 The output shows the result of an investigation of how the probability of a respondent obtaining a bachelor's degree from a four-year college is related to the score on *ASVABC*, using *EAEF* Data Set 21. *BACH* is a dummy variable equal to 1 for those with bachelor's degrees (years of schooling at least 16) and 0 otherwise. *ASVABC* ranged from 22 to 65, with mean value 50.2, and most scores were in the range 40 to 60. Provide an interpretation of the coefficients. Explain why OLS is not a satisfactory estimation method for this kind of model.

```
. reg BACH ASVABC

  Source |       SS         df         MS              Number of obs =     540
---------+------------------------------              F( 1, 538)    =  176.96
   Model |  27.4567273       1    27.4567273           Prob > F      =  0.0000
Residual |   83.476606     538    .155160978           R-squared     =  0.2475
---------+------------------------------              Adj R-squared =  0.2461
   Total |  110.933333     539    .205813234           Root MSE      =   .3939

------------------------------------------------------------------------------
    BACH |     Coef.   Std. Err.       t     P>|t|     [95% Conf. Interval]
---------+--------------------------------------------------------------------
  ASVABC |  .0235898    .0017733    13.30    0.000     .0201063     .0270734
   _cons |  -.922749    .0926474    -9.96    0.000    -1.104744     -.740754
------------------------------------------------------------------------------
```

10.2 The output shows the result of regressing a dummy variable for ever being married, *EVERMAR*, on years of schooling, *S*, and its square *SSQ*, for the subset of female respondents in the LFP data set. The data set is for NLSY respondents in 1994, when they were aged 29–36. Provide an interpretation of the coefficients. The figure plots the function and shows the actual proportion who were ever married by year of schooling. *EVERMAR* was defined to be equal to 1 if marital status, *MARISTAT*, was equal to 2 (married) or 3 (separated or divorced). *EVERMAR* = 0 otherwise.

```
. reg EVERMAR S SSQ if MALE==0

  Source |       SS         df         MS              Number of obs =    2726
---------+------------------------------              F( 2, 2723)   =   10.81
   Model |  3.02632845       2    1.51316423           Prob > F      =  0.0000
Residual |  381.335007    2723    .140042235           R-squared     =  0.0079
---------+------------------------------              Adj R-squared =  0.0071
   Total |  384.361335    2725    .141050031           Root MSE      =  .37422

------------------------------------------------------------------------------
 EVERMAR |     Coef.   Std. Err.       t     P>|t|     [95% Conf. Interval]
---------+--------------------------------------------------------------------
       S |   .071114      .01814     3.92    0.000     .0355445     .1066835
     SSQ |   -.00285     .000667    -4.27    0.000     -.004158     -.001542
   _cons |  .4055487    .1227049     3.31    0.001     .1649445     .6461528
------------------------------------------------------------------------------
```

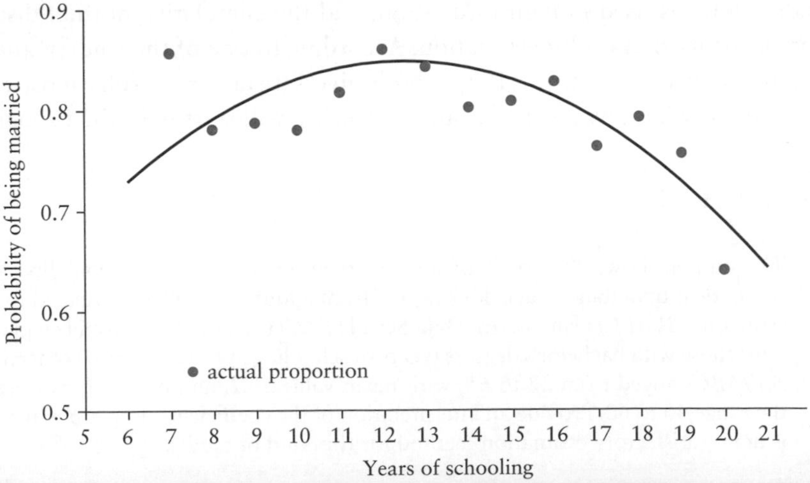

10.2 Logit analysis

In the logit model one hypothesizes that the probability of the occurrence of the event is determined by the function

$$p_i = F(Z_i) = \frac{1}{1+e^{-Z_i}}. \tag{10.6}$$

This is the function shown in Figure 10.3. As Z tends to infinity, e^{-Z} tends to 0 and p has a limiting upper bound of 1. As Z tends to minus infinity, e^{-Z} tends to infinity and p has a limiting lower bound of 0. Hence, there is no possibility of getting predictions of the probability being greater than 1 or less than 0.

The marginal effect of Z on the probability, which will be denoted $f(Z)$, is given by the derivative of this function with respect to Z:

$$f(Z) = \frac{dp}{dZ} = \frac{e^{-Z}}{\left(1+e^{-Z}\right)^2}. \tag{10.7}$$

The function is shown in Figure 10.4. You can see that the effect of changes in Z on the probability is very small for large positive or large negative values of Z, and that the sensitivity of the probability to changes in Z is greatest at the midpoint value of 0.

In the case of the example of graduating from high school, the function is

$$p_i = \frac{1}{1+e^{-\beta_1-\beta_2 ASVABC_i}}. \tag{10.8}$$

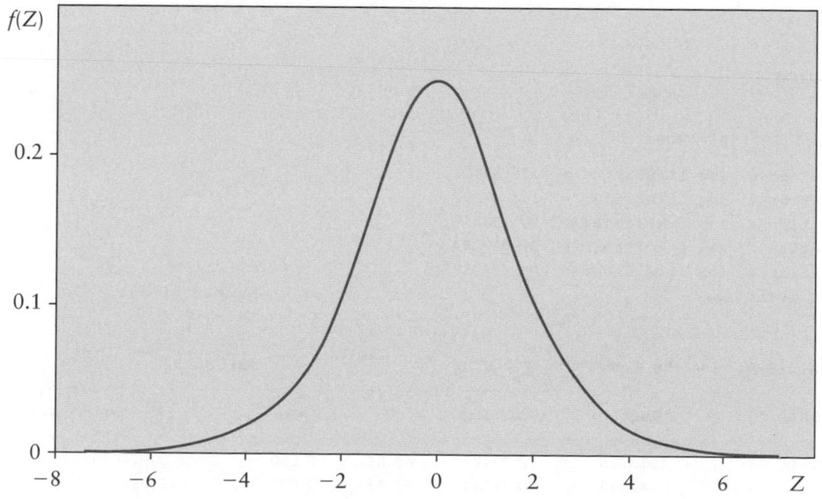

Figure 10.4 Marginal effect of Z on the probability

If we fit the model, we get the output shown in Table 10.2.

The model is fitted by maximum likelihood estimation and, as the output in Table 10.2 indicates, this uses an iterative process to estimate the parameters. How should one interpret the coefficients? To calculate the marginal effect of *ASVABC* on p we need to calculate $dp/dASVABC$. You could calculate the differential directly, but the best way to do this, especially if Z is a function of more than one variable, is to break it up into two stages. p is a function of Z, and Z is a function of *ASVABC*, so

$$\frac{dp}{dASVABC} = \frac{dp}{dZ}\frac{dZ}{dASVABC} = f(Z)\beta_2, \tag{10.9}$$

where $f(Z)$ is as defined in (10.7). The probability of graduating from high school, and the marginal effect, are plotted as functions of *ASVABC* in Figure 10.5.

How can you summarize the effect of the *ASVABC* score on the probability of graduating? The usual method is to calculate the marginal effect at the mean value of the explanatory variables. In this sample, the mean value of *ASVABC* was 51.36. For this value, Z is equal to 3.5085 and e^{-Z} is equal to 0.0299. Using this, $f(Z)$ is 0.0282 and the marginal effect is 0.0037:

$$f(Z)\beta_2 = \frac{e^{-Z}}{\left(1+e^{-Z}\right)^2}\beta_2 = \frac{0.0299}{(1.0299)^2} \times 0.1314 = 0.0037. \tag{10.10}$$

In other words, at the sample mean, a one-point increase in *ASVABC* increases the probability of going to college by 0.4 percent. This is a very small amount and the reason is that, for those with the mean *ASVABC*, the estimated probability

Table 10.2

```
.logit GRAD ASVABC

Iteration 0: log likelihood = -118.67769
Iteration 1: log likelihood = -104.45292
Iteration 2: log likelihood = -97.135677
Iteration 3: log likelihood = -96.887294
Iteration 4: log likelihood = -96.886017
Logit estimates                                  Number of obs   =      540
                                                 LR chi2 (1)     =    43.58
                                                 Prob > chi2     =   0.0000
Log likelihood = -96.886017                      Pseudo R2       =   0.1836
------------------------------------------------------------------------------
    GRAD  |      Coef.     Std. Err.      z     P>|z|    [95% Conf. Interval]
------------------------------------------------------------------------------
  ASVABC  |    .1313626     .022428     5.86    0.000    .0874045   .1753206
   _cons  |   -3.240218    .9444844    -3.43    0.001   -5.091373  -1.389063
------------------------------------------------------------------------------
```

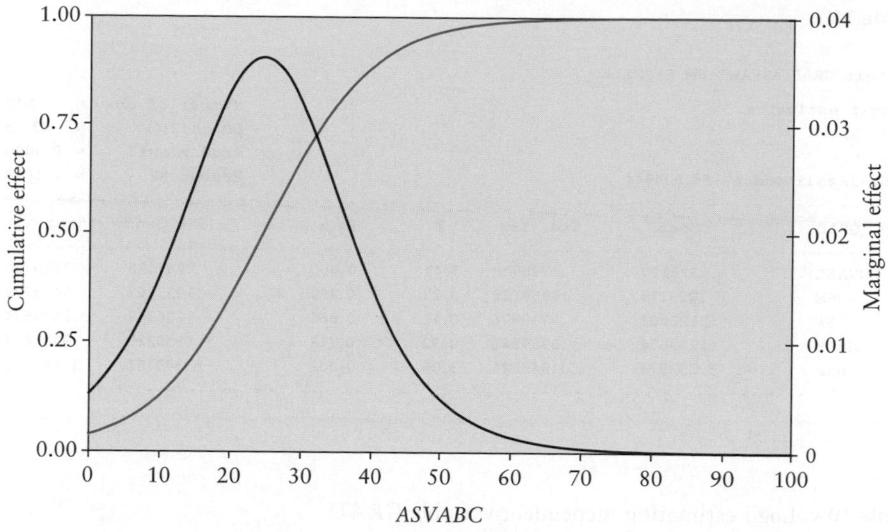

Figure 10.5 Cumulative and marginal effects of *ASVABC*

of graduating is already so high that an increase in *ASVABC* can make little difference:

$$p = \frac{1}{1+e^{-Z}} = \frac{1}{1+0.0299} = 0.9709. \quad \textbf{(10.11)}$$

See also Figure 10.5. Of course we could calculate the marginal effect for other values of *ASVABC* if we wished and in this particular case it may be of interest to evaluate it for low *ASVABC*, where individuals are at greater risk of not graduating. For example, when *ASVABC* is 30, Z is 0.7018, e^{-Z} is 0.4957, $f(Z)$ is 0.2216, and the marginal effect is 0.0291, or 2.9 percent. It is much higher because an individual with such a low score has only a 67 percent chance of graduating and an increase in *ASVABC* can make a substantial difference.

Generalization to more than one explanatory variable

Logit analysis is easily extended to the case where there is more than one explanatory variable. Suppose that we decide to relate graduating from high school to *ASVABC*, *SM*, the number of years of schooling of the mother, *SF*, the number of years of schooling of the father, and a dummy variable *MALE* that is equal to 1 for males, 0 for females. The Z variable becomes

$$Z = \beta_1 + \beta_2 ASVABC + \beta_3 SM + \beta_4 SF + \beta_5 MALE. \quad \textbf{(10.12)}$$

The corresponding regression output (with iteration messages deleted) is shown in Table 10.3.

Table 10.3

```
. logit GRAD ASVABC SM SF MALE

Logit estimates                                   Number of obs   =        540
                                                  LR chi2(4)      =      43.75
                                                  Prob > chi2     =     0.0000
Log likelihood = -96.804844                       Pseudo R2       =     0.1843

------------------------------------------------------------------------------
    GRAD |      Coef.   Std. Err.      z     P>|z|     [95% Conf. Interval]
------------------------------------------------------------------------------
  ASVABC |   .1329127   .0245718    5.41    0.000       .0847528    .1810726
      SM |   .023178    .0868122   -0.27    0.789      -.1933267    .1469708
      SF |   .0122663   .0718876    0.17    0.865      -.1286307    .1531634
    MALE |   .1279654   .3989345    0.32    0.748      -.6539318    .9098627
   _cons |  -3.252373   1.065524   -3.05    0.002      -5.340761   -1.163985
------------------------------------------------------------------------------
```

Table 10.4 Logit estimation, dependent variable *GRAD*

Variable	*Mean*	*b*	*Mean* × *b*	*f(Z)*	*bf(Z)*
ASVABC	51.36	0.1329	6.8257	0.0281	0.0037
SM	11.58	−0.0231	−0.2687	0.0281	−0.0007
SF	11.84	0.0123	0.1456	0.0281	0.0003
MALE	0.50	0.1280	0.0640	0.0281	0.0036
constant	1.000	−3.2524	−3.2524		
Total			3.5143		

The mean values of *ASVABC, SM, SF,* and *MALE* were as shown in Table 10.4, and hence the value of Z at the mean was 3.5143. From this one obtains 0.0298 for e^{-Z} and 0.0281 for $f(Z)$. The table shows the marginal effects, calculated by multiplying $f(Z)$ by the estimates of the coefficients of the logit regression.

According to the computations, a one-point increase in the *ASVABC* score increases the probability of graduating from high school by 0.4 percent, and being male increases it by the same amount. Variations in parental education appear to have negligible effects. From the regression output it can be seen that the effect of *ASVABC* was significant at the 0.1 percent level but the effects of the other variables were insignificant.

Goodness of fit and statistical tests

There is no measure of goodness of fit equivalent to R^2 in maximum likelihood estimation. In default, numerous measures have been proposed for comparing alternative model specifications. Denoting the actual outcome in observation i as Y_i, with $Y_i = 1$ if the event occurs and 0 if it does not, and denoting the predicted probability of the event occurring $\hat{p}$, the measures include the following:

- the number of outcomes correctly predicted, taking the prediction in observation i as 1 if $\hat{p}_i$ is greater than 0.5 and 0 if it is less;
- the sum of the squared residuals $\sum(Y_i - \hat{p}_i)^2$;
- the correlation between the outcomes and predicted probabilities, $r_{Y_i \hat{p}_i}$;
- the pseudo-R^2 in the logit output, explained in Section 10.6.

Each of these measures has its shortcomings and Amemiya (1981) recommends considering more than one and comparing the results.

Nevertheless, the standard significance tests are similar to those for the standard regression model. The significance of an individual coefficient can be evaluated via its t statistic. However, since the standard error is valid only asymptotically (in large samples), the same goes for the t statistic, and since the t distribution converges on the normal distribution in large samples, the critical values of the latter should be used. This is emphasized in Stata by replacing 't' by 'z' in the output. The counterpart of the F test of the explanatory power of the model (H_0: all the slope coefficients are zero, H_1: at least one is nonzero) is a chi-squared test with the chi-squared statistic in the logit output distributed under H_0 with degrees of freedom equal to the number of explanatory variables. Details are provided in Section 10.6.

EXERCISES

10.3* The output shows the results of fitting a logit regression to the data set described in Exercise 10.1 (with four of the iteration messages deleted). 26.7 percent of the respondents earned bachelor's degrees.

```
. logit BACH ASVABC

Iteration 0:  log likelihood = -324.62306
---------------------------------------
Iteration 5:  log likelihood = -238.70933

Logistic regression                              Number of obs   =     540
                                                 LR chi2(1)      =  171.83
                                                 Prob > chi2     =  0.0000
Log likelihood = -238.70933                      Pseudo R2       =  0.2647
------------------------------------------------------------------------------
    BACH |     Coef.     Std. Err.     z     P>|z|     [95% Conf.   Interval]
------------------------------------------------------------------------------
  ASVABC |   .1891621   .0192466    9.83    0.000     .1514395     .2268847
   _cons |   1.096405   .0868122  -10.23    0.000    -13.36089    .-9.063065
------------------------------------------------------------------------------
```

The diagram shows the probability of earning a bachelor's degree as a function of *ASVABC*. It also shows the marginal effect function.

With reference to the diagram, discuss the variation of the marginal effect of the *ASVABC* score implicit in the logit regression.

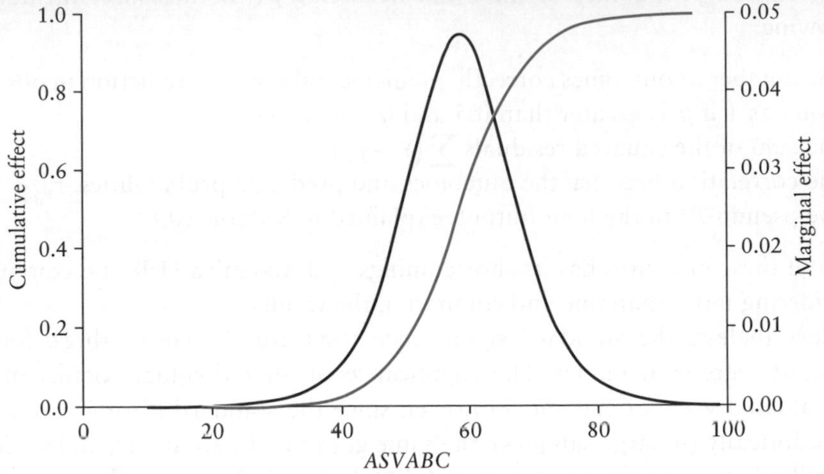

Sketch the probability and marginal effect diagrams for the OLS regression in Exercise 10.1 and compare them with those for the logit regression.

10.4 What are the factors influencing going to college? Using your *EAEF* data set, define a binary variable *COLLEGE* to be equal to 1 if $S > 12$ and 0 otherwise. Regress *COLLEGE* on *ASVABC*, *SM*, *SF*, and *MALE* (1) using ordinary least squares, and (2) using logit analysis. Calculate the marginal effects in the logit analysis and compare them with those obtained using OLS.

10.5 The output shows the results of a logit regression of *EVERMAR*, ever being married, on years of schooling and its square, using the data set described in Exercise 10.2. The figure plots the probability of being ever married against years of schooling for the linear probability model and logit regressions. The table gives the marginal effects for $S = 8$ (completion of grade school), $S = 12$ (completion of high school), and $S = 16$ (completion of four-year college), together with that for $S = 13.31$ (sample mean). Compare the regression results.

```
.logit EVERMAR S SSQ if MALE==0

Iteration 0: log likelihood = -1242.0796
-----------------------------------------
Iteration 4: log likelihood = -1232.8322

Logistic regression                             Number of obs   =    2726
                                                LR chi2(2)      =   18.49
                                                Prob > chi2     =  0.0001
Log likelihood = -1232.8322                     Pseudo R2       =  0.0074
----------------------------------------------------------------------------
 EVERMAR |     Coef.    Std. Err.      z     P>|z|     [95% Conf. Interval]
----------------------------------------------------------------------------
       S |   .3942057    .1100552    3.58    0.000     .1785014    .6099099
     SSQ |   .0160798    .0040493   -3.97    0.000    -.0240164   -.0081433
   _cons |  -.7033118     .745236   -0.94    0.345    -2.163948    .7573238
----------------------------------------------------------------------------
```

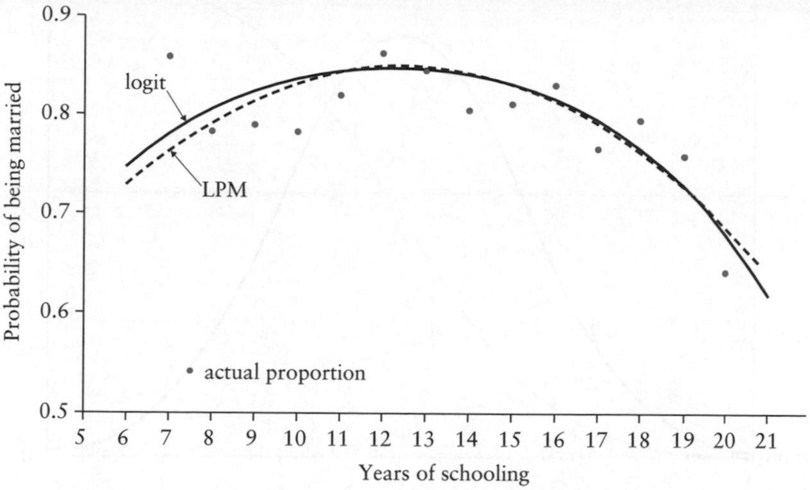

S	Marginal effect
8	0.021
12	0.001
13.31	−0.004
16	−0.018

10.3 Probit analysis

The probit model provides an alternative approach to binary choice. It uses the cumulative standardized normal distribution to model the sigmoid relationship $F(Z)$. (A standardized normal distribution is one with zero mean and unit variance). As with the logit model, you start by defining a variable Z that is a linear function of the variables that determine the probability:

$$Z = \beta_1 + \beta_2 X_2 + \cdots + \beta_k X_k. \qquad \textbf{(10.13)}$$

$F(Z)$, the cumulative standardized normal distribution, gives the probability of the event occurring for any value of Z:

$$p_i = F(Z_i). \qquad \textbf{(10.14)}$$

Maximum likelihood analysis is used to obtain estimates of the parameters. The marginal effect of X_i is $\partial p/\partial X_i$ which, as in the case of logit analysis, is best computed as

$$\frac{\partial p}{\partial X_i} = \frac{dp}{dZ}\frac{\partial Z}{\partial X_i} = f(Z)\beta_i. \qquad \textbf{(10.15)}$$

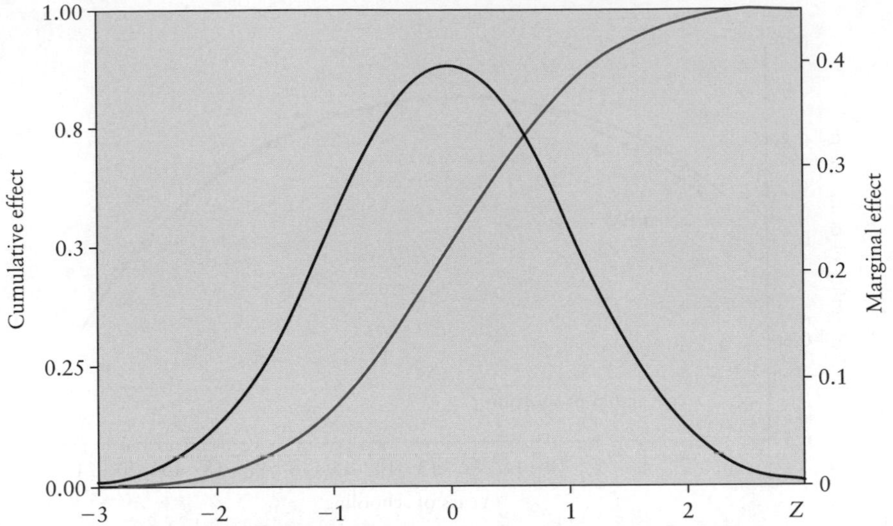

Figure 10.6 Cumulative and marginal normal effects of Z

Now since $F(Z)$ is the cumulative standardized normal distribution, $f(Z)$, its derivative, is just the standardized normal distribution itself:

$$f(Z) = \frac{1}{\sqrt{2\pi}} e^{-\frac{1}{2}Z^2}. \quad \textbf{(10.16)}$$

Figure 10.6 plots $F(Z)$ and $f(Z)$ for probit analysis. As with logit analysis, the marginal effect of any variable is not constant. It depends on the value of $f(Z)$, which in turn depends on the values of each of the explanatory variables. To obtain a summary statistic for the marginal effect, the usual procedure is parallel to that used in logit analysis. You calculate Z for the mean values of the explanatory variables. Next you calculate $f(Z)$, as in (10.16). Then you calculate $f(Z)\beta_i$ to obtain the marginal effect of X_i.

This will be illustrated with the example of graduating from high school, using the same specification as in the logit regression. The regression output, with iteration messages deleted, is shown in Table 10.5.

The computation of the marginal effects at the sample means is shown in Table 10.6. Z is 1.8814 when evaluated at the mean values of the variables and $f(Z)$ is 0.0680. The estimates of the marginal effects are virtually the same as those obtained using logit analysis. Generally, logit and probit analysis yield similar marginal effects. However, the shapes of the tails of the logit and probit distributions are different and so logit and probit can give different results if the sample is unbalanced, with most of the outcomes similar and only a small minority different. The present example is unbalanced because only 6 percent of the respondents failed to graduate, but even so the differences in the estimates of the marginal effects are small.

Table 10.5

```
. probit GRAD ASVABC SM SF MALE
Probit estimates                                  Number of obs   =        540
                                                  LR chi2(4)      =      44.11
                                                  Prob > chi2     =     0.0000
      Log likelihood = -96.624926                 Pseudo R2       =     0.1858
------------------------------------------------------------------------------
    GRAD |      Coef.   Std. Err.      z     P>|z|     [95% Conf.  Interval]
------------------------------------------------------------------------------
  ASVABC |   .0648442   .0120378    5.39     0.000      .0412505    .0884379
      SM |  -.0081163   .0440399    0.18     0.854      -.094433    .0782004
      SF |   .0056041   .0359557    0.16     0.876     -.0648677    .0760759
    MALE |   .0630588   .1988279    0.32     0.751     -.3266368    .4527544
   _cons |  -1.450787   .5470608   -2.65     0.008     -2.523006   -.3785673
------------------------------------------------------------------------------
```

Table 10.6 Probit estimation, dependent variable *GRAD*

Variable	*Mean*	*b*	*Mean × b*	*f(Z)*	*bf(Z)*
ASVABC	51.36	0.0648	3.3281	0.0680	0.0044
SM	11.58	−0.0081	−0.0938	0.0680	−0.0006
SF	11.84	0.0056	0.0663	0.0680	0.0004
MALE	0.50	0.0631	0.0316	0.0680	0.0043
constant	1.00	−1.4508	−1.4508		
Total			1.8814		

EXERCISES

10.6 Regress the variable *COLLEGE* defined in Exercise 10.4 on *ASVABC*, *MALE*, *SM*, and *SF* using probit analysis. Calculate the marginal effects and compare them with those obtained using OLS and logit analysis.

10.7* The following probit regression, with iteration messages deleted, was fitted using 2,726 observations on females in the National Longitudinal Survey of Youth using the *LFP* data set described in Appendix B. The data are for 1994, when the respondents were aged 29 to 36 and many of them were raising young families.

WORKING is a binary variable equal to 1 if the respondent was working in 1994, 0 otherwise. *CHILDL06* is a dummy variable equal to 1 if there was a child aged less than 6 in the household, 0 otherwise. *CHILDL16* is a dummy variable equal to 1 if there was a child aged less than 16, but no child less than 6, in the household, 0 otherwise. *MARRIED* is equal to 1 if the

```
.probit WORKING S AGE CHILDL06 CHILDL16 MARRIED ETHBLACK ETHHISP if MALE==0

Probit estimates                                  Number of obs =    2726
                                                  LR chi2(7)    =  165.08
                                                  Prob > chi2   =  0.0000
Log likelihood = -1403.0835                       Pseudo R2     =  0.0556
------------------------------------------------------------------------------
 WORKING  |    Coef.    Std. Err.     z     P>|z|     [95% Conf. Interval]
------------------------------------------------------------------------------
       S  |  .0892571   .0120629    7.399   0.000     .0656143      .1129
     AGE  | -.0438511    .012478   -3.514   0.000    -.0683076   -.0193946
CHILDL06  | -.5841503   .0744923   -7.842   0.000    -.7301525   -.4381482
CHILDL16  | -.1359097   .0792359   -1.715   0.086    -.2912092    .0193897
 MARRIED  | -.0076543   .0631618   -0.121   0.904    -.1314492    .1161407
ETHBLACK  | -.2780887    .081101   -3.429   0.001    -.4370436   -.1191337
 ETHHISP  | -.0191608   .1055466   -0.182   0.856    -.2260284    .1877068
   _cons  |   .673472   .2712267    2.483   0.013     .1418775    1.205066
------------------------------------------------------------------------------
```

respondent was married with spouse present, 0 otherwise. The remaining variables are as described in Appendix B. The mean values of the variables are given in the output from the sum command:

```
. sum WORKING S AGE CHILDL06 CHILDL16 MARRIED ETHBLACK ETHHISP if MALE==0

Variable  |     Obs        Mean      Std. Dev.       Min        Max
------------------------------------------------------------------------
 WORKING  |    2726     .7652238     .4239366         0          1
       S  |    2726     13.30998     2.444771         0         20
     AGE  |    2726     17.64637      2.24083        14         22
CHILDL06  |    2726     .3991196     .4898073         0          1
CHILDL16  |    2726     .3180484     .4658038         0          1
 MARRIED  |    2726     .6228907     .4847516         0          1
ETHBLACK  |    2726     .1305943     .3370179         0          1
 ETHHISP  |    2726     .0722671     .2589771         0          1
------------------------------------------------------------------------
```

Calculate the marginal effects and discuss whether they are plausible.

10.8 The output in Exercise 10.7 confirms that having a child aged less than 6 in the household has an adverse affect on the probability of the mother working. Determine whether this effect is different for married and unmarried women. Download the *LFP* data set, define an interactive dummy variable *MARL06* as the product of *MARRIED* and *CHILDL06*, and include it as an explanatory variable in the probit regression. Interpret the coefficients of *MARRIED*, *CHILDL06*, and *MARL06*, and comment on the differences between your output and that in Exercise 10.7. See Appendix B for further information relating to the data set.

10.4 Censored regressions: tobit analysis

Suppose that one hypothesizes the relationship

$$Y^* = \beta_1 + \beta_2 X + u, \qquad (10.17)$$

with the dependent variable subject to either a lower bound Y_L or an upper bound Y_U. In the case of a lower bound, the model can be characterized as

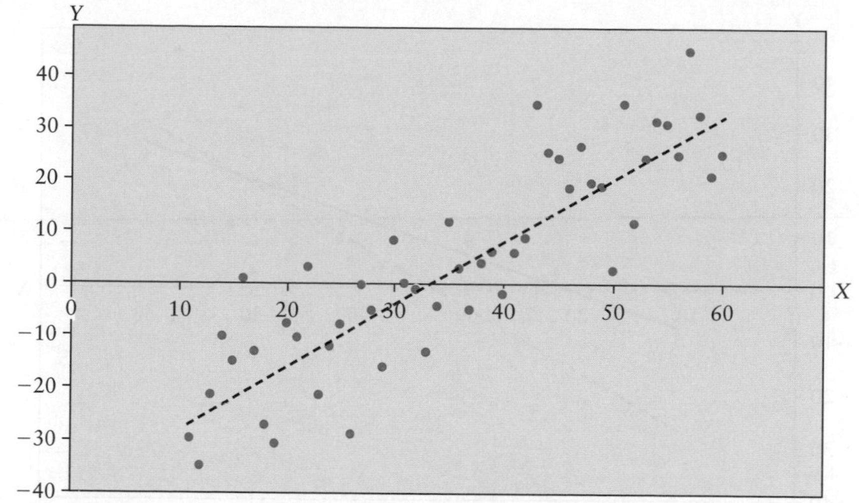

Figure 10.7 Potential distribution, not taking account of contraint

$$Y^* = \beta_1 + \beta_2 X + u$$
$$Y = Y^* \quad \text{for } Y^* > Y_L,$$
$$Y = Y_L \quad \text{for } Y^* \le Y_L \qquad \textbf{(10.18)}$$

and similarly for a model with an upper bound. Such a model is known as a censored regression model because Y^* is unobserved for $Y^* < Y_L$ or $Y^* > Y_U$. It is effectively a hybrid between a standard regression model and a binary choice model, and OLS would yield inconsistent estimates if used to fit it.

To see this, consider the relationship illustrated in Figure 10.7, a one-shot Monte Carlo experiment where the true relationship is

$$Y = -40 + 1.2X + u, \qquad \textbf{(10.19)}$$

the data for X are the integers from 11 to 60, and u is a normally distributed random variable with mean zero and variance 100. If Y were unconstrained, the observations would be as shown in Figure 10.7. However we will suppose that Y is constrained to be non-negative, in which case the observations will be as shown in Figure 10.8. For such a sample, it is obvious that an OLS regression that included those observations with Y constrained to be zero would yield inconsistent estimates, with the estimator of the slope downwards biased and that of the intercept upwards biased.

The remedy, you might think, would be to use only the subsample of unconstrained observations, as in Figure 10.9, but even then the OLS estimators would be biased. In the case of a low value of X, the observation will be unconstrained, and therefore be present in the sample, only if the value of u is positive. Further, the lower the value of X, the larger must be this positive value. This requirement gives rise to a negative association between X and u for observations that are present in the sample. This is illustrated in Figure 10.9. The observations with the

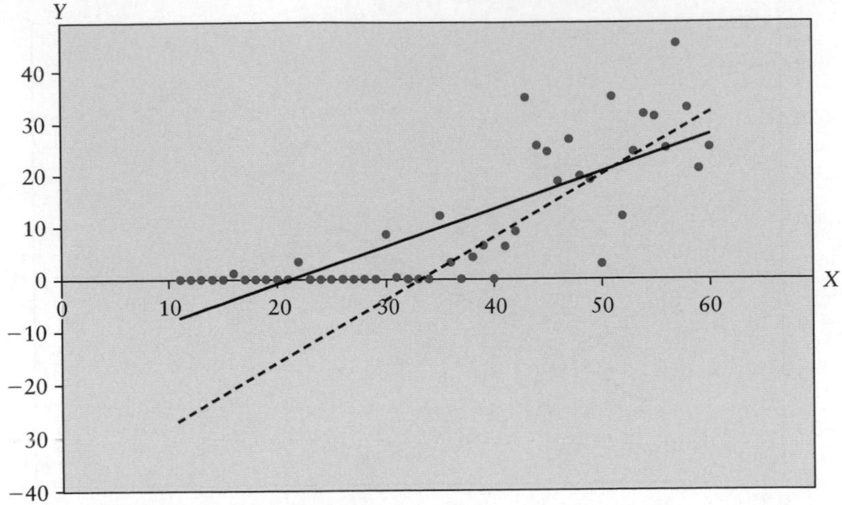

Figure 10.8 Sample with constrained observations

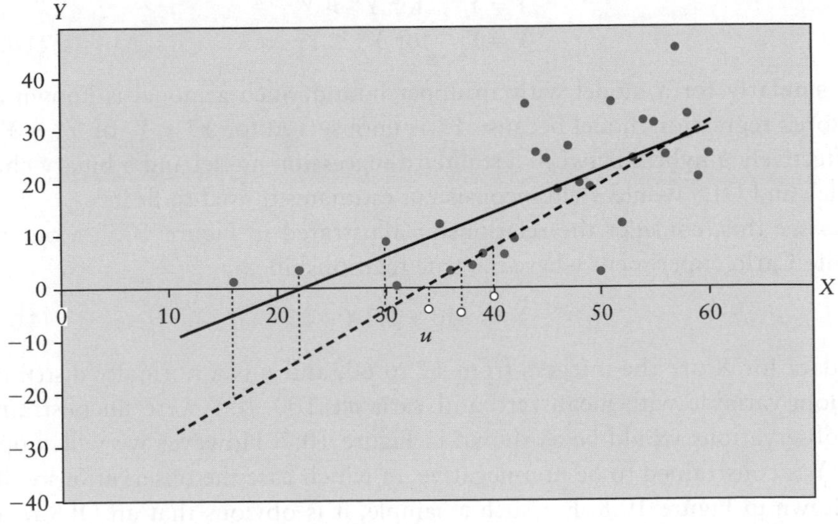

Figure 10.9 Unconstrained observations

four lowest values of X appear in the sample only because their disturbance terms (marked) are positive and large enough to make Y positive. The other observations for X in that range have been deleted because they were constrained, their values of u either being negative, or positive but not large enough.

In mathematical terms, an observation i will appear in the subsample only if $Y_i > 0$, that is, if

$$-40 + 1.2X_i + u_i > 0. \qquad \textbf{(10.20)}$$

This requires

$$u_i > 40 - 1.2X_i \tag{10.21}$$

and so u_i must have a truncated distribution.

This is illustrated for $X = 30$ in Figure 10.10. The disturbance term must lie in the tinted part of the distribution if the observation is to be unconstrained and appear in the sample. The expected value of u for this truncated distribution is 10.7. Figure 10.11 does the same for $X = 20$. Here u must be positive and at least 16 for the observation to be unconstrained. The figure shows the truncated

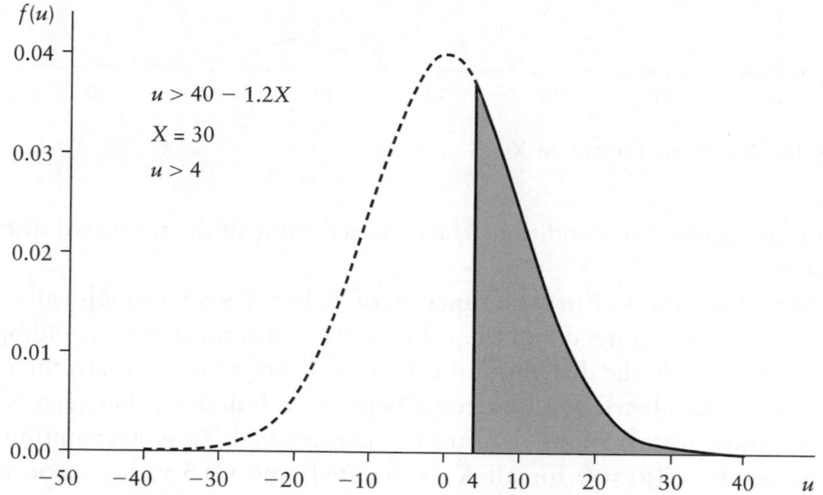

Figure 10.10 Conditional distribution for the disturbance term, $X = 30$

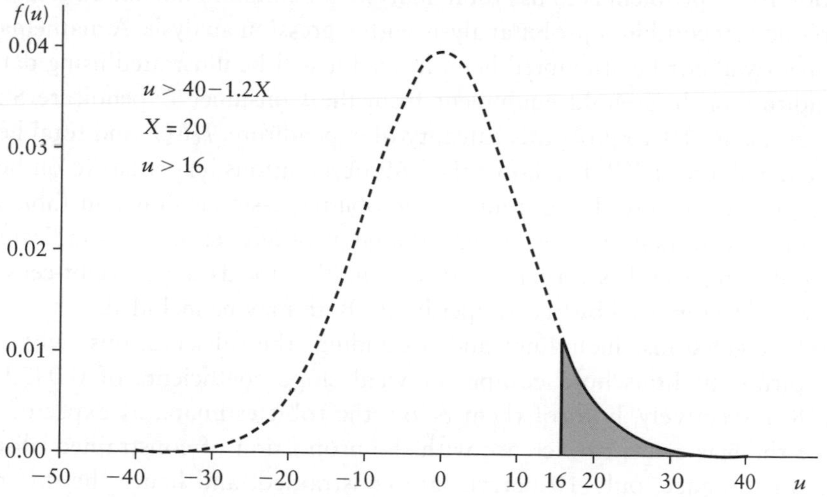

Figure 10.11 Conditional distribution for the disturbance term, $X = 20$

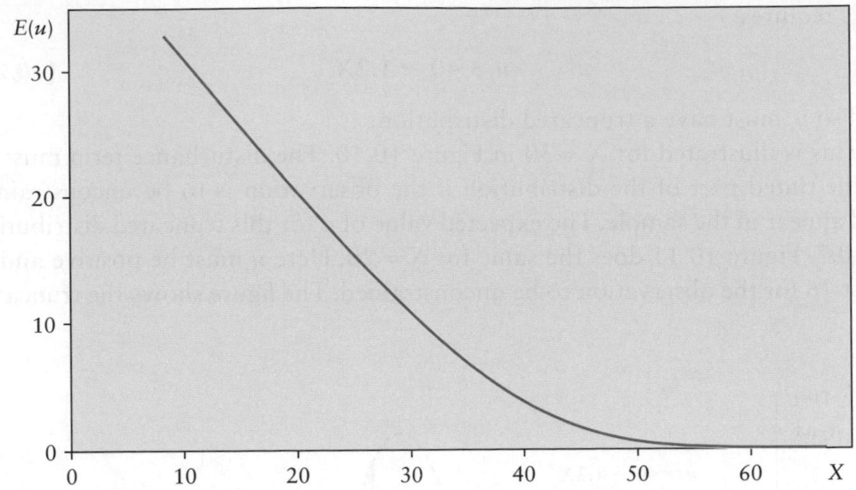

Figure 10.12 $E(u)$ conditional on X

distribution, given this condition. The expected value of the truncated distribution is 20.2.

Figure 10.12 shows $E(u)$ as a function of X. For $X > 60$, virtually all observations are unconstrained and the value of the disturbance term is unimportant. Below $X = 60$, the distribution is truncated, the more severely, the lower the value of X. Hence, we observe a negative relationship between X and $E(u)$ for those observations that are not constrained. Thus Assumption B.7, which requires $E(u) = 0$ for all X, is violated, and OLS yields inconsistent estimates.

If it can be assumed that the disturbance term has a normal distribution, one solution to the problem is to use tobit analysis, a maximum likelihood estimation technique that combines probit analysis with regression analysis. A mathematical treatment will not be attempted here. Instead it will be illustrated using data on expenditure on household equipment from the Consumer Expenditure Survey data set. Figure 10.13 plots this category of expenditure, *HEQ*, and total household expenditure, *EXP*. For 86 of the 869 observations, expenditure on household equipment is zero. The output from a tobit regression is shown in Table 10.7. In Stata the command is '`tobit`' and the point of left-censoring is indicated by the number in parentheses after '`ll`' (lower limit). If the data were right-censored, '`ll`' would be replaced by '`ul`' (upper limit). Both may be included.

OLS regressions including and excluding the observations with zero expenditure on household equipment yield slope coefficients of 0.0472 and 0.0468, respectively, both of them below the tobit estimate, as expected. The size of the bias tends to increase with the proportion of constrained observations. In this case, only 10 percent are constrained, and hence the difference between the tobit and OLS estimates is small.

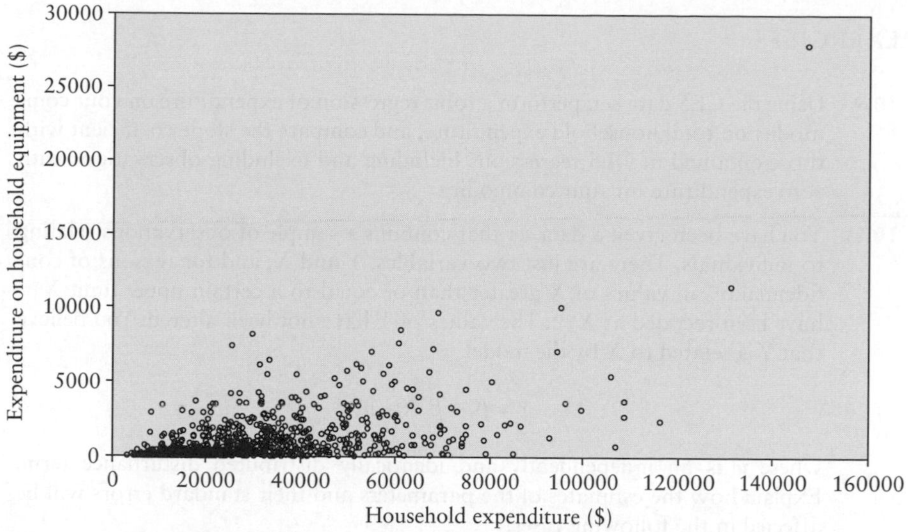

Figure 10.13 Expenditure on household equipment and total household expenditure

Table 10.7

```
.tobit HEQ EXP, ll(0)

Tobit Estimates                                    Number of obs   =        869
                                                   LR chi2(1)      =     315.41
                                                   Prob > chi2     =     0.0000
Log likelihood = -6911.0175                        Pseudo R2       =     0.0223
------------------------------------------------------------------------------
     HEQ |      Coef.   Std. Err.       t     P>|z|     [95% Conf. Interval]
------------------------------------------------------------------------------
     EXP |   .0520828   .0027023    19.273    0.000      .0467789    .0573866
   _cons |  -661.8156   97.95977    -6.756    0.000     -854.0813   -469.5499
------------------------------------------------------------------------------
     _se |   1521.896    38.6333         (Ancillary parameter)
------------------------------------------------------------------------------

Obs. summary:  86 left-censored observations at HEQ<50
              783 uncensored observations
```

Tobit regression yields inconsistent estimates if the disturbance term does not have a normal distribution or if it is subject to heteroscedasticity (Amemiya, 1984). Judging by the plot in Figure 10.13, the observations in the example are subject to heteroscedasticity and it may be preferable to use expenditure on household equipment as a proportion of total expenditure as the dependent variable, in the same way that in his seminal study, which investigated expenditure on consumer durables, Tobin (1958) used expenditure on durables as a proportion of disposable personal income.

EXERCISES

10.9 Using the *CES* data set, perform a tobit regression of expenditure on your commodity on total household expenditure, and compare the slope coefficient with those obtained in OLS regressions including and excluding observations with zero expenditure on your commodity.

10.10 You have been given a data set that contains a sample of observations relating to individuals. There are just two variables, Y and X, and for reasons of confidentiality, all values of X greater than or equal to a certain upper limit X^{max} have been recoded as X^{max}. The values of Y have not been altered. You believe that Y is related to X by the model

$$Y = \beta_1 + \beta_2 X + u,$$

where u is an independently and identically distributed disturbance term. Explain how the estimates of the parameters and their standard errors will be affected in the following cases.

1. If you regress Y on X, including the observations where $X = X^{max}$, using OLS.
2. If you regress Y on X, excluding the observations where $X = X^{max}$, using OLS.

In both cases, you should compare the regression results with those you would have obtained if you had been able to use the original, unmodified data.

10.5 Sample selection bias

In the tobit model, whether or not an observation falls into the regression category ($Y > Y_L$ or $Y < Y_U$) or the constrained category ($Y = Y_L$ or $Y = Y_U$) depends entirely on the values of the regressors and the disturbance term. However, it may well be that participation in the regression category may depend on factors other than those in the regression model, in which case a more general model specification with an explicit two-stage process may be required. The first stage, participation in the regression category, or being constrained, depends on the net benefit of participating, B^*, a latent (unobservable) variable that depends on a set of $m - 1$ variables Q_j and a random term ε:

$$B_i^* = \delta_1 + \sum_{j=2}^{m} \delta_j Q_{ji} + \varepsilon_i . \tag{10.22}$$

The second stage, the regression model, is parallel to that for the tobit model:

$$Y_i^* = \beta_1 + \sum_{j=2}^{k} \beta_j X_{ji} + u_i$$

$$\begin{aligned} &Y_i = Y_i^* && \text{for } B_i^* > 0, \\ &Y_i \text{ is not observed} && \text{for } B_i^* \le 0. \end{aligned} \tag{10.23}$$

For an observation in the sample,

$$E\left(u_i \middle| B_i^* > 0\right) = E\left(u_i \middle| \varepsilon_i > -\delta_1 - \sum_{j=2}^{m} \delta_j Q_{ji}\right). \tag{10.24}$$

If ε_i and u_i are distributed independently, $E\left(u_i \middle| \varepsilon_i > -\delta_1 - \sum \delta_j Q_{ji}\right)$ reduces to the unconditional $E(u_i)$ and the selection process does not interfere with the regression model. However, if ε_i and u_i are correlated, $E(u_i)$ will be nonzero and problems parallel to those in the tobit model arise, with the consequence that OLS estimates are inconsistent and are described as being subject to sample selection bias (see Box 10.1 on the Heckman two-step procedure). If it can be assumed that ε_i and u_i are jointly normally distributed with correlation ρ, the model may be fitted by maximum likelihood estimation, with null hypothesis of no selection bias H_0: $\rho = 0$. The Q and X variables may overlap, identification requiring in practice that at least one Q variable is not also an X variable.

The procedure will be illustrated by fitting an earnings function for females on the lines of Gronau (1974), the earliest study of this type, using the *LFP* subsample from the NLSY data set described in Exercise 10.7. *CHILDL06* is a dummy variable equal to 1 if there was a child aged less than 6 in the household, 0 otherwise. *CHILDL16* is a dummy variable equal to 1 if there was a child aged less than 16, but no child less than 6, in the household, 0 otherwise. *MARRIED* is equal to 1 if the respondent was married with spouse present, 0 otherwise. The other variables have the same definitions as in the *EAEF* data sets. The Stata command for this type of regression is 'heckman' and as usual it is followed by the dependent variable and the explanatory variables and qualifier, if any (here the sample is restricted to females). The variables in parentheses after 'select' are those hypothesized to influence whether the dependent variable is observed. In this example, the dependent variable is observed for the 2,021 females who were working in 1994 and is missing for the remaining 640 who were not working. Seven iteration messages have been deleted from the output shown in Table 10.8.

First, we will check whether there is evidence of selection bias, that is, that $\rho \neq 0$. For technical reasons, ρ is estimated indirectly through atanh $\rho = \frac{1}{2}\log\left(\frac{1+\rho}{1-\rho}\right)$, but the null hypothesis H_0: atanh $\rho = 0$ is equivalent to H_0: $\rho = 0$. atanh ρ is denoted 'athrho' in the output and, with an asymptotic t statistic of 10.92, the null hypothesis is rejected. A second test of the same null hypothesis that can be performed by comparing likelihood ratios is described in Section 10.6.

The regression results indicate that schooling and the *ASVABC* score have highly significant effects on earnings, that schooling has a positive effect on the probability of working, and that age, having a child aged less than 6, and being black have negative effects. The probit coefficients are different from those reported in Exercise 10.7, the reason being that, in a model of this type, probit analysis in isolation yields inefficient estimates.

BOX 10.1 The Heckman two-step procedure

The problem of selection bias arises because the expected value of u is nonzero for observations in the selected category if u and ε are correlated. It can be shown that, for these observations,

$$E\left(u_i \middle| \varepsilon_i > -\delta_1 - \sum_{j=2}^{m} \delta_j Q_{ji}\right) = \frac{\sigma_{u\varepsilon}}{\sigma_\varepsilon} \lambda_i,$$

where $\sigma_{u\varepsilon}$ is the population covariance of u and ε, σ_ε is the standard deviation of ε, and λ_i, the inverse of Mills' ratio, is given by

$$\lambda_i = \frac{f(v_i)}{F(v_i)},$$

where

$$v_i = \frac{\varepsilon_i}{\sigma_\varepsilon} = \frac{-\delta_1 - \sum_{j=2}^{m} \delta_j Q_{ji}}{\sigma_\varepsilon}$$

and the functions f and F are as defined in the section on probit analysis: $f(v_i)$ is the density function for ε normalized by its standard deviation and $F(v_i)$ is the probability of being positive. It follows that

$$E\left(Y_i \middle| \varepsilon_i > -\delta_1 - \sum_{j=2}^{m} \delta_j Q_{ji}\right) = E\left(\beta_1 + \sum_{j=2}^{k} \beta_j X_{ji} + u_i \middle| \varepsilon_i > -\delta_1 - \sum_{j=2}^{m} \delta_j Q_{ji}\right)$$
$$= \beta_1 + \sum_{j=2}^{k} \beta_j X_{ji} + \frac{\sigma_{u\varepsilon}}{\sigma_\varepsilon} \lambda_i.$$

The sample selection bias arising in a regression of Y on the X variables using only the selected observations can therefore be regarded as a form of omitted variable bias, with λ the omitted variable. However, since its components depend only on the selection process, λ can be estimated from the results of probit analysis of selection (the first step). If it is included as an explanatory variable in the regression of Y on the X variables, least squares will then yield consistent estimates.

As Heckman (1976) acknowledges, the procedure was first employed by Gronau (1974), but it is known as the Heckman two-step procedure in recognition of its development by Heckman into an everyday working tool, its attraction being that it is computationally far simpler than maximum likelihood estimation of the joint model. However, with the improvement in computing speeds and the development of appropriate procedures in regression applications, maximum likelihood estimation of the joint model is no more burdensome than the two-step procedure and it has the advantage of being more efficient.

It is instructive to compare the regression results with those from an OLS regression not correcting for selection bias. The results, shown in Table 10.9, are in fact quite similar, despite the presence of selection bias. The main difference is in the coefficient of *ETHBLACK*. The probit regression indicates that black

Table 10.8

.heckman LGEARN S ASVABC ETHBLACK ETHHISP if MALE == 0, select(S AGE CHILDL06
> CHILDL16 MARRIED ETHBLACK ETHHISP)
Iteration 0: log likelihood 5 -2683.5848 (not concave
Iteration 8: log likelihood 5 -2668.8105
Logit estimates
Heckman selection model
(regression model with sample selection)

Log likelihood 5 -2668.81

Number of obs	= 2661
Censored obs	= 640
Uncensored obs	= 2021
Wald chi2(4)	= 714.73
Prob > chi2	= 0.0000

	Coef.	Std. Err.	z	P > |z|	[95% Conf.	Interval]
LGEARN						
S	.095949	.0056438	17.001	0.000	.0848874	.1070106
ASVABC	.0110391	.0014658	7.531	0.000	.0081663	.0139119
ETHBLACK	-.066425	.0381626	-1.741	0.082	-.1412223	.0083722
ETHHISP	.0744607	.0450095	1.654	0.098	-.0137563	.1626777
_cons	4.901626	.0768254	63.802	0.000	4.751051	5.052202
select						
S	.1041415	.0119836	8.690	0.000	.0806541	.1276288
AGE	-.0357225	.011105	-3.217	0.001	-.0574879	-.0139572
CHILDL06	-.3982738	.0703418	-5.662	0.000	-.5361412	-.2604064
CHILDL16	.0254818	.0709693	0.359	0.720	-.1136155	.164579
MARRIED	.0121171	.0546561	0.222	0.825	-.0950069	.1192412
ETHBLACK	-.2941378	.0787339	-3.736	0.000	-.4484535	-.1398222
ETHHISP	-.0178776	.1034237	-0.173	0.863	-.2205843	.1848292
_cons	.1682515	.2606523	0.646	0.519	-.3426176	.6791206
/athrho	1.01804	.0932533	10.917	0.000	.8352669	1.200813
/lnsigma	-.6349788	.0247858	-25.619	0.000	-.6835582	-.5863994
rho	.769067	.0380973			.683294	.8339024
sigma	.5299467	.0131352			.5048176	.5563268
lambda	.4075645	.02867			.3513724	.4637567

LR test of indep. eqns. (rho = 0): chi2(1) = 32.90 Prob > chi2 = 0.0000

Table 10.9

.reg LGEARN S ASVABC ETHBLACK ETHHISP if MALE == 0

Source	SS	df	MS
Model	143.231149	4	35.8077873
Residual	428.301239	2016	.212451012
Total	571.532389	2020	.282936826

Number of obs	= 2021
F(4, 2016)	= 168.55
Prob > F	= 0.0000
R-squared	= 0.2506
Adj R-squared	= 0.2491
Root MSE	= .46092

LGEARN	Coef.	Std. Err.	t	P > |t|	[95% Conf.	Interval]
S	.0807836	.005244	15.405	0.000	.0704994	.0910677
ASVABC	.0117377	.0014886	7.885	0.000	.0088184	.014657
ETHBLACK	-.0148782	.0356868	-0.417	0.677	-.0848649	.0551086
ETHHISP	.0802266	.041333	1.941	0.052	-.0008333	.1612865
_cons	5.223712	.0703534	74.250	0.000	5.085739	5.361685

females are significantly less likely to work than whites, controlling for other characteristics. If this is the case, black females, controlling for other characteristics, may require higher wage offers to be willing to work. This would reduce the apparent earnings discrimination against them, accounting for the smaller negative coefficient in the OLS regression. The other difference in the results is that the schooling coefficient in the OLS regression is 0.081, a little lower than that in the selection bias model, indicating that selection bias leads to a modest underestimate of the effect of education on female earnings.

One of the problems with the selection bias model is that it is often difficult to find variables that belong to the selection process but not the main regression. Having a child aged less than 6 is an excellent variable because it clearly affects the willingness to work of a female but not her earning power while working, and for this reason the example discussed here is very popular in expositions of the model.

One final point, made by Heckman (1976): if a selection variable is illegitimately included in a least squares regression, it may appear to have a significant effect. In the present case, if *CHILDL06* is included in the earnings function, it has a *positive* coefficient significant at the 5 percent level. The explanation would appear to be that females with young children tend to require an especially attractive wage offer, given their education and other endowments, to be induced to work.

EXERCISES

10.11 Does sample selection bias affect the OLS estimate of the return to college education? Using your *EAEF* data set, investigate whether there is evidence that selection bias affects the least squares estimate of the returns to college education. Define $COLLYEAR = S - 12$ if $S > 12$, 0 otherwise, and $LGEARNCL = LGEARN$ if $COLLYEAR > 0$, missing otherwise. Use the Heckman procedure to regress *LGEARNCL* on *COLLYEAR*, *EXP*, *ASVABC*, *MALE*, *ETHBLACK*, and *ETHHISP*, with *ASVABC*, *MALE*, *ETHBLACK*, *ETHHISP*, *SM*, *SF*, and *SIBLINGS* being used to determine whether the respondent attended college. Run the equivalent regression using least squares. Comment on your findings.

10.12* Show that the tobit model may be regarded as a special case of a selection bias model.

10.13 Investigate whether the interaction between having a child aged less than 6 and marital status has an effect on sample selection bias. Download the *LFP* data set from the website and repeat the regressions in this section adding an interactive dummy variable *MARL06* defined as the product of *MARRIED* and *CHILDL06* to the selection part of the model. Note that you will need to define *LGEARN* as the logarithm of *EARNINGS*. See Appendix B for further information relating to the data set.

10.6 An introduction to maximum likelihood estimation

Suppose that a random variable X has a normal distribution with unknown mean μ and standard deviation σ. For the time being we will assume that we know that σ is equal to 1. We will relax this assumption later. You have a sample of two observations, values 4 and 6, and you wish to obtain an estimate of μ. The common sense answer is 5, and we have seen that this is scientifically respectable as well since the sample mean is the least squares estimator and as such it is an unbiased and efficient estimator of the population mean, provided the regression model assumptions are valid.

However, we have seen that in practice in econometrics the assumptions are often not satisfied and as a consequence least squares estimators lose one or more of their desirable properties. We have seen that in some circumstances they may be inconsistent and we have been concerned to develop alternative estimators that are consistent. Typically, we are not able to analyze the finite sample properties of these estimators and we just hope that the estimators are well behaved.

Once we are dealing with consistent estimators, there is no guarantee that those based on the least squares criterion of goodness of fit are optimal. Indeed it can be shown that, under certain assumptions, a different approach, maximum likelihood (ML) estimation, will yield estimators that, besides being consistent, are asymptotically efficient (efficient in large samples).

To return to the numerical example, suppose for a moment that the true value of μ is 3.5. The probability density function of the normal distribution is given by

$$f(X) = \frac{1}{\sqrt{2\pi\sigma^2}} e^{-\frac{1}{2}\frac{(X-\mu)^2}{\sigma^2}}. \qquad \textbf{(10.25)}$$

Figure 10.14 shows the distribution of X conditional on $\mu = 3.5$ and $\sigma = 1$. In particular, the probability density is 0.3521 when $X = 4$ and 0.0175 when

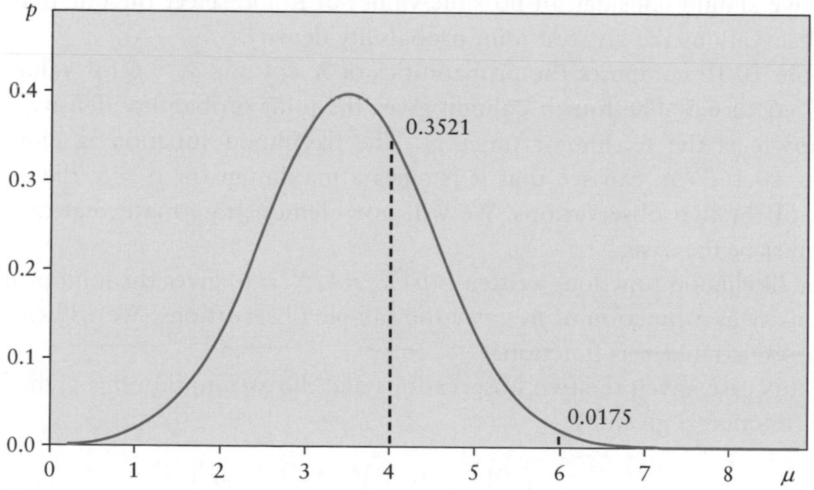

Figure 10.14 Probability densities at $X_1 = 4$ and $X_2 = 6$ conditional on $\mu = 3.5$

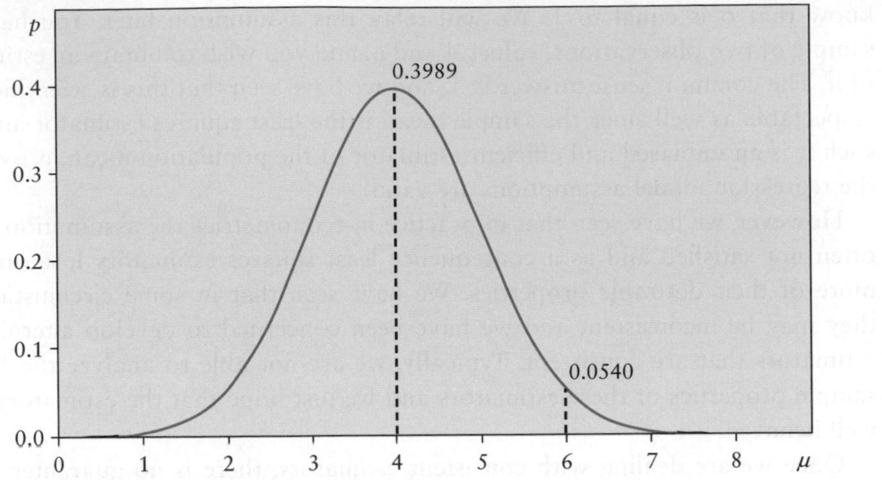

Figure 10.15 Probability densities at $X_1 = 4$ and $X_2 = 6$ conditional on $\mu = 4.0$

$X = 6$. The joint probability density for the two observations is the product, 0.0062.

Now suppose that the true value of μ is 4. Figure 10.15 shows the distribution of X conditional on this value. The probability density is 0.3989 when $X = 4$ and 0.0540 when $X = 6$. The joint probability density for the two observations is now 0.0215. We conclude that the probability of getting values 4 and 6 for the two observations would be three times as great if μ were 4 than it would be if μ were 3.5. In that sense, $\mu = 4$ is more likely than $\mu = 3.5$. If we had to choose between these estimates, we should therefore choose 4. Of course we do not have to choose between them. According to the maximum likelihood principle, we should consider all possible values of μ and select the one that gives the observations the greatest joint probability density.

Table 10.10 computes the probabilities of $X = 4$ and $X = 6$ for values of μ from 3.5 to 6.5. The fourth column gives the joint probability density, which is known as the **likelihood function**. The likelihood function is plotted in Figure 10.16. You can see that it reaches a maximum for $\mu = 5$, the average value of the two observations. We will now demonstrate mathematically that this must be the case.

The likelihood function, written $L(\mu \mid X_1 = 4, X_2 = 6)$ gives the joint probability density as a function of μ, given the sample observations. We will choose μ so as to maximize this function.

In this case, given the two observations and the assumption $\sigma = 1$, the likelihood function is given by

$$L(\mu) = \left(\frac{1}{\sqrt{2\pi}} e^{-\frac{1}{2}(4-\mu)^2} \right) \left(\frac{1}{\sqrt{2\pi}} e^{-\frac{1}{2}(6-\mu)^2} \right). \tag{10.26}$$

Table 10.10 Loglikelihood as a function of μ

μ	$p(4 \mid \mu)$	$p(6 \mid \mu)$	L	$\log L$
3.5	0.3521	0.0175	0.0062	−5.0879
4.0	0.3989	0.0540	0.0215	−3.8379
4.5	0.3521	0.1295	0.0456	−3.0879
4.6	0.3332	0.1497	0.0499	−2.9979
4.7	0.3123	0.1714	0.0535	−2.9279
4.8	0.2897	0.1942	0.0563	−2.8779
4.9	0.2661	0.2179	0.0580	−2.8479
5.0	0.2420	0.2420	0.0585	−2.8379
5.1	0.2179	0.2661	0.0580	−2.8479
5.2	0.1942	0.2897	0.0563	−2.8779
5.3	0.1714	0.3123	0.0535	−2.9279
5.4	0.1497	0.3332	0.0499	−2.9979
5.5	0.1295	0.3521	0.0456	−3.0879
6.0	0.0540	0.3989	0.0215	−3.8379
6.5	0.0175	0.3521	0.0062	−5.0879

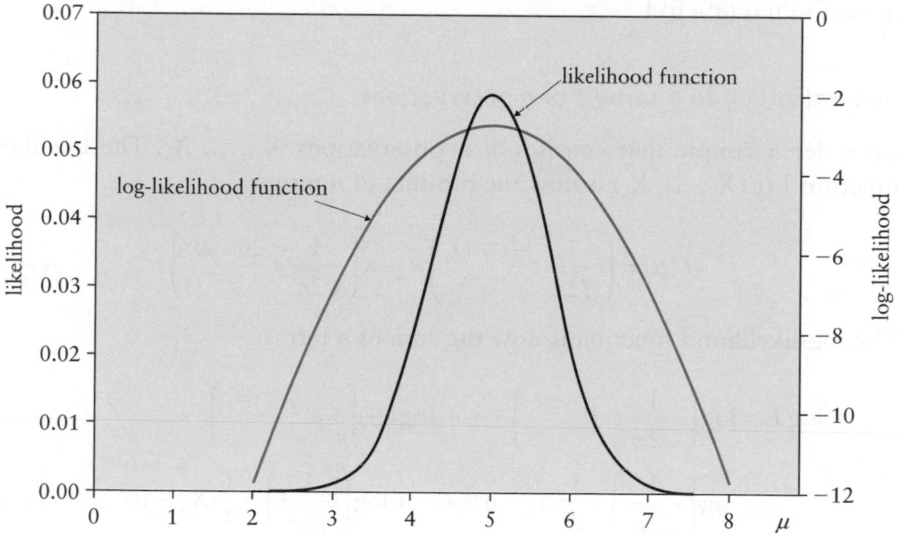

Figure 10.16 Likelihood and log-likelihood functions for μ

We will now differentiate this with respect to μ and set the result equal to zero to obtain the first-order condition for a maximum. We will then differentiate a second time to check the second-order condition. Well, actually we won't. Even with only two observations in the sample, this would be laborious, and when we generalize to n observations, it would be very messy. We will use a trick to simplify the proceedings. The log-likelihood, $\log L$, is a monotonically increasing function of L. So the value of μ that maximizes L also maximizes log L, and vice versa. log L is much easier to work with, since

$$\begin{aligned}\log L &= \log\left[\left(\frac{1}{\sqrt{2\pi}}e^{-\frac{1}{2}(4-\mu)^2}\right)\left(\frac{1}{\sqrt{2\pi}}e^{-\frac{1}{2}(6-\mu)^2}\right)\right]\\ &= \log\left(\frac{1}{\sqrt{2\pi}}e^{-\frac{1}{2}(4-\mu)^2}\right)+\log\left(\frac{1}{\sqrt{2\pi}}e^{-\frac{1}{2}(6-\mu)^2}\right)\\ &= \log\left(\frac{1}{\sqrt{2\pi}}\right)-\frac{1}{2}(4-\mu)^2+\log\left(\frac{1}{\sqrt{2\pi}}\right)-\frac{1}{2}(6-\mu)^2. \end{aligned} \quad \textbf{(10.27)}$$

The maximum likelihood estimator, which we will denote $\hat{\mu}$, is the value of μ that maximizes this function, given the data for X. It is given by the first-order condition

$$\frac{d\log L}{d\mu} = (4-\hat{\mu})+(6-\hat{\mu}) = 0. \quad \textbf{(10.28)}$$

Thus $\hat{\mu} = 5$. The second derivative is –2, so this gives a maximum value for log L, and hence L. [Note that $-(a-\mu)^2/2 = -a^2/2 + a\mu - \mu^2/2$. Hence, the differential with respect to μ is $(a-\mu)$.]

Generalization to a sample of n *observations*

Consider a sample that consists of n observations $X_1, \ldots, X_n$. The likelihood function $L(\mu \mid X_1, \ldots, X_n)$ is now the product of n terms:

$$L(\mu) = \left(\frac{1}{\sqrt{2\pi}}e^{-\frac{1}{2}(X_1-\mu)^2}\right)\times\cdots\times\left(\frac{1}{\sqrt{2\pi}}e^{-\frac{1}{2}(X_n-\mu)^2}\right). \quad \textbf{(10.29)}$$

The log-likelihood function is now the sum of n terms:

$$\begin{aligned}\log L &= \log\left(\frac{1}{\sqrt{2\pi}}e^{-\frac{1}{2}(X_1-\mu)^2}\right)+\cdots+\log\left(\frac{1}{\sqrt{2\pi}}e^{-\frac{1}{2}(X_n-\mu)^2}\right)\\ &= \log\left(\frac{1}{\sqrt{2\pi}}\right)-\frac{1}{2}(X_1-\mu)^2+\cdots+\log\left(\frac{1}{\sqrt{2\pi}}\right)-\frac{1}{2}(X_n-\mu)^2. \end{aligned} \quad \textbf{(10.30)}$$

Hence, the maximum likelihood estimator of μ is given by

$$\frac{d\log L}{d\mu} = (X_1-\hat{\mu})+\cdots+(X_n-\hat{\mu}) = 0. \quad \textbf{(10.31)}$$

Thus,

$$\sum_{i=1}^{n} X_i - n\hat{\mu} = 0 \quad \textbf{(10.32)}$$

and the maximum likelihood estimator of μ is the sample mean. Note that the second derivative is $-n$, confirming that the log-likelihood has been maximized.

Generalization to the case where σ is unknown

We will now relax the assumption that σ is equal to 1 and accept that in practice it would be unknown, like μ. We will investigate the determination of its maximum likelihood graphically using the two-observation example and then generalize to a sample of n observations.

Figure 10.17 shows the probability distribution for X conditional on μ being equal to 5 and σ being equal to 2. The probability density at $X_1 = 4$ and $X_2 = 6$ is 0.1760 and the joint density 0.0310. Clearly we would obtain higher densities, and higher joint density, if the distribution had smaller variance. If we try σ equal to 0.5, we obtain the distribution shown in Figure 10.18. Here the

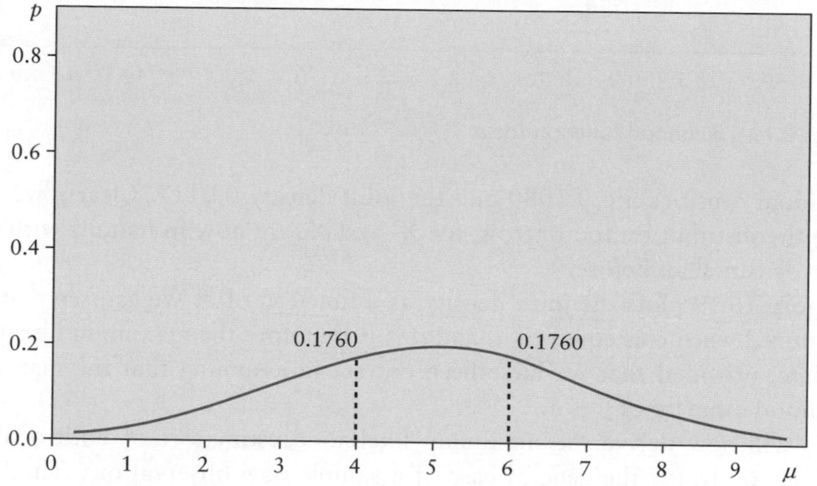

Figure 10.17 Probability densities at $X_1 = 4$ and $X_2 = 6$ conditional on $\sigma = 2$

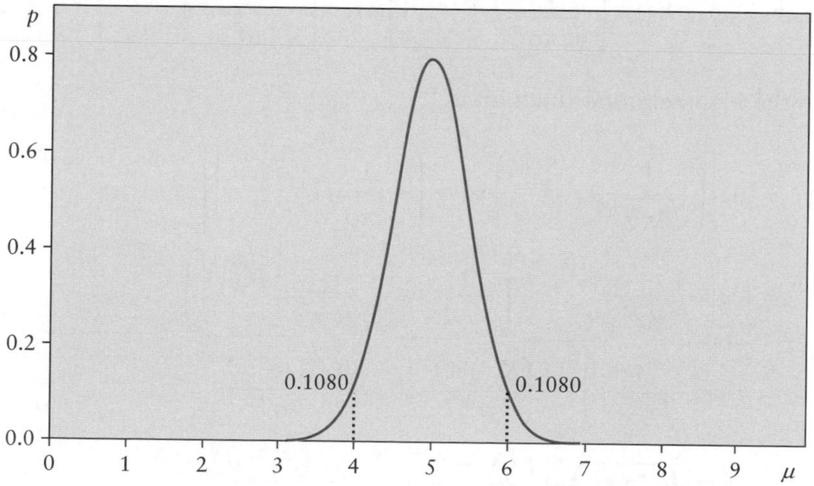

Figure 10.18 Probability densities at $X_1 = 4$ and $X_2 = 6$ conditional on $\sigma = 0.5$

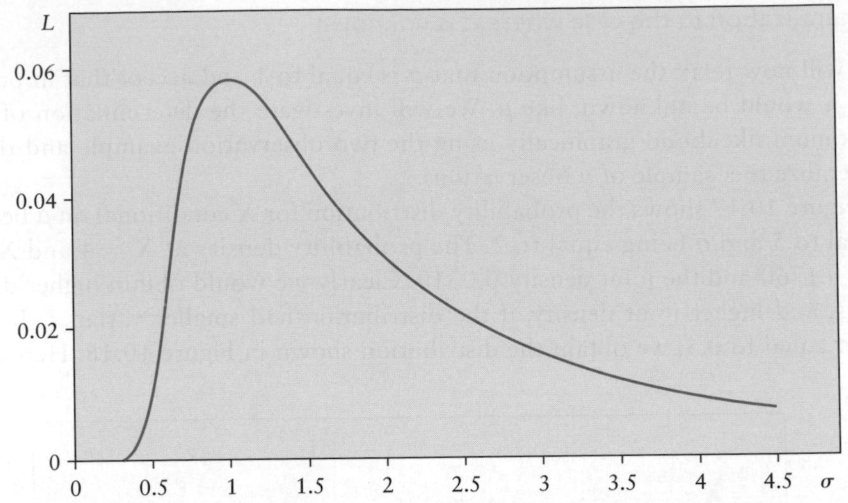

Figure 10.19 Likelihood function for σ

individual densities are 0.1080 and the joint density 0.0117. Clearly we have made the distribution too narrow, for X_1 and X_2 are now in its tails with even lower density than before.

Figure 10.19 plots the joint density as a function of σ. We can see that it is maximized when σ is equal to 1, and this is therefore the maximum likelihood estimate, provided that we have been correct in assuming that the maximum likelihood estimate of μ is 5.

We will now derive the maximum likelihood estimators of both σ and μ simultaneously, for the general case of a sample of n observations. The likelihood function is

$$L(\mu, \sigma \mid X_1,\ldots,X_n) = \left(\frac{1}{\sqrt{2\pi\sigma^2}} e^{-\frac{1}{2}\frac{(X_1-\mu)^2}{\sigma^2}}\right) \times \cdots \times \left(\frac{1}{\sqrt{2\pi\sigma^2}} e^{-\frac{1}{2}\frac{(X_n-\mu)^2}{\sigma^2}}\right) \qquad \textbf{(10.33)}$$

and so the log-likelihood function is

$$\begin{aligned}
\log L &= \log\left[\left(\frac{1}{\sqrt{2\pi\sigma^2}} e^{-\frac{1}{2}\frac{(X_1-\mu)}{\sigma^2}}\right) \times \cdots \times \left(\frac{1}{\sqrt{2\pi\sigma^2}} e^{-\frac{1}{2}\frac{(X_n-\mu)}{\sigma^2}}\right)\right] \\
&= \log\left(\frac{1}{\sqrt{2\pi\sigma^2}} e^{-\frac{1}{2}\frac{(X_1-\mu)}{\sigma^2}}\right) + \cdots + \log\left(\frac{1}{\sqrt{2\pi\sigma^2}} e^{-\frac{1}{2}\frac{(X_n-\mu)}{\sigma^2}}\right) \\
&= n\log\left(\frac{1}{\sqrt{2\pi\sigma^2}}\right) - \frac{1}{2}\frac{(X_1-\mu)^2}{\sigma^2} - \cdots - \frac{1}{2}\frac{(X_n-\mu)^2}{\sigma^2} \\
&= -n\log\left(\sqrt{2\pi\sigma^2}\right) - \frac{1}{2}\frac{(X_1-\mu)^2}{\sigma^2} - \cdots - \frac{1}{2}\frac{(X_n-\mu)^2}{\sigma^2} \\
&= -\frac{n}{2}\log 2\pi - \frac{n}{2}\log\sigma^2 + \frac{1}{\sigma^2}\left(-\frac{1}{2}(X_1-\mu)^2 - \cdots - \frac{1}{2}(X_n-\mu)^2\right).
\end{aligned} \qquad \textbf{(10.34)}$$

The partial derivative of this with respect to μ is

$$\frac{\partial \log L}{\partial \mu} = \frac{1}{\sigma^2}\left[(X_1 - \mu) + \ldots + (X_n - \mu)\right]. \tag{10.35}$$

Setting this equal to zero, one finds that the maximum likelihood estimator of μ is the sample mean, as before. The partial derivative with respect to σ is

$$\frac{\partial \log L}{\partial \sigma} = -\frac{n}{\sigma} + \frac{1}{\sigma^3}\sum_{i=1}^{n}(X_i - \mu)^2. \tag{10.36}$$

Substituting its maximum likelihood estimator for μ, and putting the expression equal to zero, we obtain

$$\hat{\sigma}^2 = \frac{1}{n}\sum_{i=1}^{n}(X_i - \bar{X})^2. \tag{10.37}$$

Note that this is actually biased downwards in finite samples, the unbiased estimator being given by the same expression with n replaced by $n - 1$. However, it is asymptotically more efficient using the mean square error criterion, its smaller variance more than compensating for the bias. The bias in any case attenuates as the sample size becomes large.

Application to the simple regression model

Suppose that Y_i depends on X_i according to the simple relationship

$$Y_i = \beta_1 + \beta_2 X_i + u_i. \tag{10.38}$$

Potentially, before the observations are generated, Y_i has a distribution around $(\beta_1 + \beta_2 X_i)$, according to the value of the disturbance term. We will assume that the disturbance term is normally distributed with mean zero and standard deviation σ, so

$$f(u) = \frac{1}{\sigma\sqrt{2\pi}} e^{-\frac{1}{2}\left(\frac{u}{\sigma}\right)^2}. \tag{10.39}$$

The probability that Y will take a specific value Y_i in observation i is determined by the probability that u_i is equal to $(Y_i - \beta_1 - \beta_2 X_i)$. Given (10.39), the probability density is

$$\frac{1}{\sigma\sqrt{2\pi}} e^{-\frac{1}{2}\left(\frac{Y_i - \beta_1 - \beta_2 X_i}{\sigma}\right)^2}. \tag{10.40}$$

The joint probability density function for the observations in the sample is the product of the terms for each observation. Taking the observations as given, and treating the unknown parameters as variables, we say that the likelihood function for β_1, β_2 and σ is given by

$$L(\beta_1, \beta_2, \sigma \mid Y_1, \ldots, Y_n) = \left(\frac{1}{\sigma\sqrt{2\pi}} e^{-\frac{1}{2}\left(\frac{Y_1 - \beta_1 - \beta_2 X_1}{\sigma}\right)^2}\right) \times \ldots \times \left(\frac{1}{\sigma\sqrt{2\pi}} e^{-\frac{1}{2}\left(\frac{Y_n - \beta_1 - \beta_2 X_n}{\sigma}\right)^2}\right). \tag{10.41}$$

The log-likelihood function is thus given by

$$\begin{aligned}\log L &= n\log\left(\frac{1}{\sigma\sqrt{2\pi}}\right) - \frac{1}{2\sigma^2}\left[\left(Y_1 - \beta_1 - \beta_2 X_1\right)^2 + \dots + \left(Y_n - \beta_1 - \beta_2 X_n\right)^2\right] \\ &= -\frac{n}{2}\log 2\pi - \frac{n}{2}\log\sigma^2 - \frac{1}{2\sigma^2}RSS,\end{aligned} \qquad \textbf{(10.42)}$$

where RSS as usual is the residual sum of squares. Thus, to maximize log L, we choose our estimates of β_1 and β_2 so as to minimize RSS. It follows that the maximum likelihood estimators are identical to the OLS estimators.

Differentiating (10.42) with respect to σ, we obtain the first-order condition

$$-\frac{n}{\sigma} + \frac{1}{\sigma^3}RSS = 0 \qquad \textbf{(10.43)}$$

from which we obtain

$$\hat{\sigma}^2 = \frac{1}{n}RSS. \qquad \textbf{(10.44)}$$

Thus, the maximum likelihood of the estimator of the variance of u is the residual sum of squares divided by n, rather than $n - 2$.

Goodness of fit and statistical tests

As noted in the discussion of logit analysis, there is no measure of goodness of fit equivalent to R^2 in maximum likelihood estimation. The pseudo-R^2 seen in some regression output, including that of Stata, compares its log-likelihood, log L, with the log-likelihood that would have been obtained with only the intercept in the regression, log L_0. A likelihood, being a joint probability, must lie between 0 and 1, and as a consequence a log-likelihood must be negative. The pseudo-R^2 is the proportion by which log L is smaller, in absolute size, than log L_0:

$$\text{pseudo-}R^2 = 1 - \frac{\log L}{\log L_0}. \qquad \textbf{(10.45)}$$

While it has a minimum value of 0, its maximum value must be less than 1 and unlike R^2 it does not have a natural interpretation. However, variations in the likelihood, like variations in the residual sum of squares in a standard regression, can be used as a basis for tests. In particular, the explanatory power of the model can be tested via the likelihood ratio statistic

$$2\log\frac{L}{L_0} = 2(\log L - \log L_0). \qquad \textbf{(10.46)}$$

This is distributed as a chi-squared statistic with $k - 1$ degrees of freedom, where $k - 1$ is the number of explanatory variables, under the null hypothesis that the coefficients of the variables are all jointly equal to zero. Further, the validity of a restriction can be tested by comparing the constrained and unconstrained likelihoods, in the same way that it can be tested by comparing the constrained and unconstrained residual sum of squares in a least squares regression model. For example, the null hypothesis H_0: $\rho = 0$ in the selection bias model can be tested by comparing the unconstrained likelihood L_U with the likelihood L_R when the model is fitted assuming that u and ε are distributed independently. Under the null hypothesis H_0: $\rho = 0$, the test statistic $2\log(L_U / L_R)$ is distributed as a chi-squared statistic with one degree of freedom. In the sample selection example in Section 10.5, the test statistic, 32.90, appears in the last line of the output and the null hypothesis is rejected, the critical value of $\chi^2(1)$ being 10.83 at the 0.1 percent level.

As was noted in Section 10.2, the significance of an individual coefficient can be evaluated via its asymptotic t statistic, so-called because the standard error is valid only in large samples. Since the t distribution converges on the normal distribution in large samples, the critical values of the latter should be used.

Key terms

- binary choice model
- likelihood function
- likelihood ratio statistic
- linear probability model
- logit model
- log-likelihood
- maximum likelihood (ML) estimation
- probit model
- qualitative response model
- sample selection bias
- tobit model

EXERCISES

10.14* An event is hypothesized to occur with probability p. In a sample of n observations, it occurred m times. Demonstrate that the maximum likelihood estimator of p is m/n.

10.15 A random variable X can take the positive integer values 0, 1, 2, 3, ... The probability of it being equal to a specific value x, $p(x)$, is given by

$$p(x) = \frac{e^{-\lambda}\lambda^x}{x!},$$

where λ is an unknown parameter and $x!$ is the product of the terms $x(x-1)(x-2)\ldots(3)(2)(1)$. In a sample of three observations, the values of the random variable are 2, 5, and 2. Write down the likelihood function for λ and derive the maximum likelihood estimate of λ.

10.16 The probability density function of a random variable X is the exponential distribution

$$f(X) = \lambda e^{-\lambda X} \quad \text{for } X > 0$$

with unknown parameter λ. Derive the maximum likelihood estimator of λ, given a sample of n observations on X.

10.17 A random variable X can be equal to any of the positive integers in the range 1 to n with equal probability. n is unknown. In a sample of two observations, the values of X were 2 and 3. Derive the maximum likelihood estimate of n.

10.18* Returning to the example of the random variable X with unknown mean λ and variance σ^2, the log-likelihood for a sample of n observations was given by equation (10.34):

$$\log L = -\frac{n}{2}\log 2\pi - \frac{n}{2}\log\sigma^2 + \frac{1}{\sigma^2}\left(-\frac{1}{2}(X_1-\mu)^2 - \ldots - \frac{1}{2}(X_n-\mu)^2\right).$$

The first-order condition for μ produced the ML estimator of μ and the first-order condition for σ then yielded the ML estimator for σ. Often, the variance is treated as the primary dispersion parameter, rather than the standard deviation. Show that such a treatment yields the same results in the present case. Treat σ^2 as a parameter, differentiate $\log L$ with respect to it, and solve.

10.19* In Exercise 10.7, $\log L_0 = -1485.62$. Compute the pseudo-R^2 and confirm that it is equal to that reported in the output.

10.20* In Exercise 10.7, compute the likelihood ratio statistic $2(\log L - \log L_0)$, confirm that it is equal to that reported in the output, and perform the likelihood ratio test.

Appendix 10.1 Comparing linear and logarithmic specifications

In Chapter 4, it was asserted that one could use the residual sum of squares to compare the fits of model specifications with linear and logarithmic versions of the dependent variable, provided that the dependent variable had first been scaled by dividing the observations by the geometric mean. A proof is provided here. The comparison actually involves the log-likelihood functions. We are asserting that the specification with the greater log-likelihood is superior. In what follows, we assume that we have already performed the geometric mean scaling, so Y in this exposition corresponds to Y^* in Chapter 4. We note that the effect of the scaling is to make the product of the observations on Y equal to 1, so that the logarithm of the product is 0. As a consequence,

$$\sum_i \log Y_i = \log\left(\prod_i Y_i\right) = \log 1 = 0.$$

The log-likelihood function for the linear specification is given by equation (10.42). Substituting for $\hat{\sigma}^2$ from (10.44), we have

$$\begin{aligned}\log L &= -\frac{n}{2}\log 2\pi - \frac{n}{2}\log\sigma^2 - \frac{1}{2\sigma^2}RSS \\ &= -\frac{n}{2}\log 2\pi - \frac{n}{2}\log\left(\frac{1}{n}RSS\right) - \frac{1}{2\left(\frac{1}{n}RSS\right)}RSS \\ &= -\frac{n}{2}\log 2\pi + \frac{n}{2}\log n - \frac{n}{2}\log RSS - \frac{n}{2}.\end{aligned}$$

We will compare this with the log-likelihood of the semilogarithmic specification with the same right side but $Z = \log Y$ as the dependent variable:

$$Z = \log Y = \beta_1 + \beta_2 X + u,$$

where we again assume that the disturbance term u is $N\left(0, \sigma^2\right)$. Then the distribution for Z_i, conditional on X_i, is $N\left(\left[\beta_1 + \beta_2 X_i\right], \sigma^2\right)$ and

$$g\left(Z_i\right) = \frac{1}{\sqrt{2\pi\sigma^2}} e^{-\frac{1}{2\sigma^2}\left(Z_i - \beta_1 - \beta_2 X_i\right)^2}.$$

For comparability with the linear specification, we need to express the log-likelihood in terms of the joint density of the Y_i, not the Z_i. For the density function of a transformed variable, see Appendix R.2. The example at the end covers the present case. The density function for Y_i, $f(Y_i)$, is given by

$$f\left(Y_i\right) = \frac{1}{Y_i} g\left(Z_i\right) = \frac{1}{Y_i} \frac{1}{\sqrt{2\pi\sigma^2}} e^{-\frac{1}{2\sigma^2}\left(\log Y_{ii} - \beta_1 - \beta_2 X_i\right)^2}$$

and the joint density function for the Y observations is

$$\prod_i f\left(Y_i\right) = \prod_i \frac{1}{Y_i} \frac{1}{\sqrt{2\pi\sigma^2}} e^{-\frac{1}{2\sigma^2}\left(\log Y_{ii} - \beta_1 - \beta_2 X_i\right)^2}$$

Re-interpreting this as the likelihood function for β_1, β_2, and σ^2, given the sample data on Y and X, and taking the logarithm,

$$\log L\left(\beta_1, \beta_2, \sigma^2 \mid Y, X\right) = \sum_i \log\left(\frac{1}{Y_i} \frac{1}{\sqrt{2\pi\sigma^2}} e^{-\frac{1}{2\sigma^2}\left(\log Y_{ii} - \beta_1 - \beta_2 X_i\right)^2}\right)$$
$$= -\sum_i \log Y_i - \frac{n}{2}\log 2\pi - \frac{n}{2}\log\sigma^2 - \frac{1}{2\sigma^2}\sum_i \left(\log Y_i - \beta_1 - \beta_2 X_i\right)^2.$$

The first-order condition for σ yields

$$-\frac{n}{\sigma} + \frac{1}{\sigma^3}\sum_i \left(\log Y_i - \beta_1 - \beta_2 X_i\right)^2 = 0$$

and so

$$\sigma^2 = \frac{1}{n}\sum_i \left(\log Y_i - \beta_1 - \beta_2 X_i\right)^2.$$

Substituting for σ^2 in the log-likelihood function,

$$\log L\left(\beta_1, \beta_2, \sigma^2 \mid Y, X\right) = \sum_i \log\left(\frac{1}{Y_i} \frac{1}{\sqrt{2\pi\sigma^2}} e^{-\frac{1}{2\sigma^2}\left(\log Y_{ii} - \beta_1 - \beta_2 X_i\right)^2}\right)$$
$$= -\sum_i \log Y_i - \frac{n}{2}\log 2\pi - \frac{n}{2}\log\left(\frac{1}{n}\sum_i \left(\log Y_i - \beta_1 - \beta_2 X_i\right)^2\right) - \frac{n}{2}.$$

Now

$$\sum_i \log Y_i = 0$$

since the data for Y have been pre-scaled by dividing by the geometric mean. Hence,

$$\log L\left(\beta_1, \beta_2, \sigma^2 \,|\, Y, X\right) = -\frac{n}{2}\log 2\pi + \frac{n}{2}\log n - \frac{n}{2}\log RSS_{\log} - \frac{n}{2},$$

where $RSS_{\log}$ is the residual sum of squares from the OLS regression of log Y on X. As a consequence of the elimination of the $\sum \log Y_i$ term, this expression is identical to that for the linear specification, except that $RSS_{\log}$ has replaced RSS. Hence, the specification with the lower RSS has the higher log-likelihood.

11. Models Using Time Series Data

11.1 Assumptions for regressions with time series data

Hitherto the analysis has been confined to cross-sectional data, first within the framework of Model A and then, more realistically, within that of Model B. We now switch to time series data and the framework of Model C. A crucial difference between Model C and Model B lies in the characterization of the data generation process (DGP), the explanation that we give concerning the way the observations in the sample come into being.

With cross-sectional data, as in Models A and B, the DGP is very simple: the observations relate to discrete units—individuals, households, enterprises, or countries, for example—and a variable is some characteristic of these units. Thus, if the units are individuals, and the characteristic is years of schooling, a random sample of individuals from some population will give us a random sample of values of schooling from the population. The ordering of the observations in the sample does not matter.

Time series data differ in two crucial respects. First, the time dimension imposes a natural ordering. To emphasize the time ordering, the observations will be indexed using t rather than i, and the number of observations in a sample will be denoted T rather than n.

Second, the underlying process is typically continuous, not discrete. Because it is not usually possible to work in continuous time, the data for a time series variable are converted into discrete form by taking readings at regular intervals. The interval between readings is normally constant, the frequency being determined by practical considerations. Thus, r_t might be the rate of interest at time t, and K_t might be the value of the stock of capital. Where a variable is a flow, its value might be the rate of flow per unit time or the total flow since the last reading. Whether a stock or a flow, a continuous variable X_t will be represented as a sequence $\{..., X_1, X_2, ..., X_T, ...\}$ where the subscript indicates the time period of the observation, here 1 being the first period and T the last in our data set. The dots before X_1 and after X_T indicate that the series may have had values in time periods prior to period 1 and that it may continue to exist after the last time period in our sample.

It is important to keep in mind the double structure of a random variable discussed in Section R.5 of the Review chapter. We talk about the variable X taking the form of a sequence of observations $\{..., X_1, X_2, ..., X_T, ...\}$. The individual observations are themselves random variables with their own potential distributions, at least before the sample is generated. Once a sample is generated, the set of actual values is described as a realization. Statisticians distinguish between the potential values of a process and a realization by writing the potential values in upper case as $\{X_1, X_2, ..., X_T\}$, to emphasize that potentially, before the sample is observed, the components are all random variables, and a realization in lower case as $\{x_1, x_2, ..., x_T\}$. Econometricians do not do this because the distinction is usually obvious from the context and the extra notation can cause problems.

As a consequence of their continuous nature, many regressors in time series models exhibit what is known as persistence or dependence, the DGP being characterized by evolution through time and successive observations being correlated, often highly correlated. Thus, for example, the level of aggregate GDP in any country in any year will be closely related to its level in the previous year. As a consequence, the properties of the regression model differ from those of Model B. They depend on the regression model assumptions, and we will need to restate the assumptions for time series regressions.

C.1 The model is linear in parameters and correctly specified.

This is the same as Assumption B.1.

C.2 The time series for the regressors are at most weakly persistent.

This assumption replaces Assumption B.2, that the values of the regressors in the observations in the sample are drawn randomly from fixed populations. That assumption is wholly unrealistic in a time series setting because the values of many time series variables are correlated, often strongly so, from one time period to the next. A discussion of the meaning of 'weakly persistent' and the importance of this assumption leads us to relatively advanced technical issues and will be deferred to Chapter 13.

Assumptions C.3–C.5 are the same as Assumptions B.3–B.5.

C.3 There does not exist an exact linear relationship among the regressors in the sample.

C.4 The disturbance term has zero expectation.

$$E(u_t) = 0 \quad \text{for all } t. \tag{11.1}$$

C.5 The disturbance term is homoscedastic.

$$\sigma_{u_t}^2 = \sigma_u^2 \quad \text{for all } t. \tag{11.2}$$

C.6 The values of the disturbance term have independent distributions.

$$u_t \text{ is distributed independently of } u_t' \quad \text{for } t' \neq t. \tag{11.3}$$

This assumption is the same as Assumption B.6. However, in Model B, it was hardly an issue because violations are unusual in regressions using cross-sectional data. When observations are generated randomly, there is no reason to suppose that there should be any connection between the value of the disturbance term in one observation and its value in any other.

By contrast, with time series data, violations are common because it often happens that the value of the disturbance term in one observation is correlated with its value in the next. The reasons for this and its consequences are discussed in Chapter 12.

C.7 The disturbance term is distributed independently of the regressors.

$$u_t \text{ is distributed independently of } X_{jt'} \quad \text{for all } t' \text{ (including } t\text{) and } j. \qquad \textbf{(11.4)}$$

We have already seen, in the context of cross-sectional data, how violations of this assumption can lead to inconsistent estimates (measurement error bias in Chapter 8 and simultaneous equations bias in Chapter 9). This assumption is of even greater practical importance in the context of time series regressions. As with Assumption B.7, the assumption can be expressed in the weaker form of a conditional expectation:

C.7′ The disturbance term has zero conditional expectation.

$$E(u_t \mid \text{values of all the regressors in all observations}) = 0. \qquad \textbf{(11.5)}$$

C.8 The disturbance term has a normal distribution.

This is the same as Assumption B.8.

We will initially, in Sections 11.2–11.4, discuss simple time series regressions without being concerned with the validity of the assumptions. This will allow us to introduce time series concepts such as lags and dynamics. In Section 11.5, we will begin the main task of this chapter, which is to address the issues that arise relating to Assumption C.7. The other main changes, to Assumptions C.6 and C.2, will be treated in Chapters 12 and 13, respectively.

11.2 Static models

Much of the analysis will be illustrated with a core data set for fitting demand functions. The Demand Functions data set is drawn from national accounts data published by the US Bureau of the Census and consists of annual aggregate data on 20 different categories of consumer expenditure for the period 1959–2003, along with data on disposable personal income, *DPI*, and price index numbers for the 20 categories. A detailed description is provided in Appendix B, with information on how to download the data set from the website. Two of the categories, *FOOD* and *HOUS* (consumer expenditure on food and housing services, respectively) are used as examples in the text and exercises. The other categories are intended for practical work by a small group of students, each student working with a different category, starting with a simple regression specification and gradually developing a more sophisticated one. We will start with a very simple specification for the demand equation for housing services, regressing consumer expenditure on this category, *HOUS*, on *DPI* and a price index for housing, *PRELHOUS*:

$$HOUS_t = \beta_1 + \beta_2 DPI_t + \beta_3 PRELHOUS_t + u_t. \qquad \textbf{(11.6)}$$

HOUS and *DPI* are measured in $ billion at 2000 constant prices. *PRELHOUS* is an index constructed by dividing the nominal price deflator for housing, *PHOUS*, by the price deflator for total personal expenditure, *PTPE*, and multiplying by 100. *PRELHOUS* thus is a real or relative price index that keeps track of whether housing is becoming more or less expensive relative to other types of expenditure. It is plotted in Figure 11.1, which shows that the relative price declined by about 10 percent from the early 1960s to the late 1970s and since then has been rising slowly. A straightforward linear regression using EViews gives the output shown in Table 11.1.

The regression implies that an increase of $1 billion in disposable personal income leads to an increase of $0.15 billion in expenditure on housing. In other words, out of the marginal dollar, 15 cents is spent on housing. Is this a plausible figure? It is a bit difficult to tell, but certainly housing is the largest category of consumer expenditure and one would expect a substantial coefficient. Note that we are talking about housing services, and not investment in housing. Housing services is the value of the services provided by the existing housing stock. In the case of rented housing, rents are taken as a measure of the value of the services. In the case of owner-occupied housing and housing rented at a subsidized rate, imputed rents, that is, the market rents the housing could command, are used instead. The coefficient of *PRELHOUS* implies that a one-point increase in the price index leads to a reduction of $3.83 billion in expenditure on housing. The constant term literally indicates the amount that would be spent on housing if *DPI* and *PRELHOUS* were both zero, but

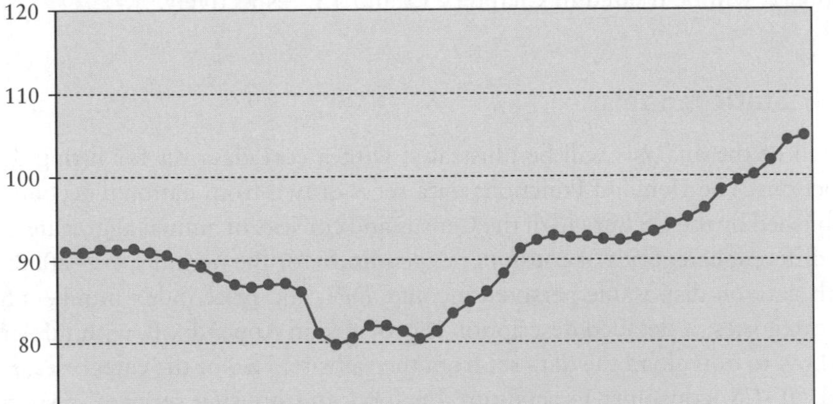

Figure 11.1 Relative price series for housing services, 1959–2003 (2000 = 100)

obviously any such interpretation is nonsense. If the observations referred to households, there might be some that had no income and yet purchased housing services and other essentials with transfer payments, but here we are talking about aggregate data for the whole of the United States and that kind of interpretation is not sensible.

It is common to hypothesize that a constant elasticity function of the type

$$HOUS = \beta_1 DPI^{\beta_2} PRELHOUS^{\beta_3} v \qquad \textbf{(11.7)}$$

is mathematically more appropriate for demand functions. Linearizing it by taking logarithms, one obtains

$$LGHOUS = \beta_1' + \beta_2 LGDPI + \beta_3 LGPRHOUS + u, \qquad \textbf{(11.8)}$$

where *LGHOUS*, *LGDPI* and *LGPRHOUS* are the (natural) logarithms of *HOUS*, *DPI* and *PRELHOUS*, respectively, u is the natural logarithm of the disturbance term v, β_1' is the logarithm of β_1, and β_2 and β_3 are income and price elasticities. The regression result is shown in Table 11.2.

The coefficients of *LGDPI* and *LGPRHOUS* are direct estimates of the income and price elasticities. Is 1.03 a plausible income elasticity? Probably. It is conventional to classify consumer expenditure into normal goods and inferior goods, types of expenditure whose income elasticities are positive and negative, respectively, and to subdivide normal goods into necessities and luxuries, types of expenditure whose income elasticities are less than 1 and greater than 1. Housing is obviously a necessity, so you might expect the elasticity to be positive but less than 1. However, it also has a luxury element, since people spend more on better quality housing as their income rises. Overall, the elasticity seems to work out at about 1, so the present estimate seems reasonable.

Table 11.1

```
Dependent Variable: HOUS
Method: Least Squares
Sample: 1959 2003
Included observations: 45
```

Variable	Coefficient	Std. Error	t-Statistic	Prob.
C	334.6657	37.26625	8.980396	0.0000
DPI	0.150925	0.001665	90.65785	0.0000
PRELHOUS	-3.834387	0.460490	-8.326764	0.0000

R-squared	0.996722	Mean dependent var	630.2830
Adjusted R-squared	0.996566	S.D. dependent var	249.2620
S.E. of regression	14.60740	Akaike info criteri	8.265274
Sum squared resid	8961.801	Schwarz criterion	8.385719
Log likelihood	-182.9687	F-statistic	6385.025
Durbin-Watson stat	0.337638	Prob(F-statistic)	0.000000

Table 11.2

Dependent Variable: LGHOUS
Method: Least Squares
Sample: 1959 2003
Included observations: 45

Variable	Coefficient	Std. Error	t-Statistic	Prob.
C	0.005625	0.167903	0.033501	0.9734
LGDPI	1.031918	0.006649	155.1976	0.0000
LGPRHOUS	-0.483421	0.041780	-11.57056	0.0000

R-squared	0.998583	Mean dependent var	6.359334
Adjusted R-squared	0.998515	S.D. dependent var	0.437527
S.E. of regression	0.016859	Akaike info criter	-5.263574
Sum squared resid	0.011937	Schwarz criterion	-5.143130
Log likelihood	121.4304	F-statistic	14797.05
Durbin-Watson stat	0.633113	Prob(F-statistic)	0.000000

EXERCISES

11.1 The results of linear and logarithmic regressions of consumer expenditure on food, *FOOD*, on *DPI* and a relative price index series for food, *PRELFOOD*, using the Demand Functions data set, are shown. Provide an economic interpretation of the coefficients and perform appropriate statistical tests.

$$\widehat{FOOD} = \underset{(43.2)}{139.4} + \underset{(0.001)}{0.053}\, DPI + \underset{(0.372)}{0.536}\, PRELFOOD \qquad R^2 = 0.987$$

$$\widehat{LGFOOD} = \underset{(0.39)}{2.24} + \underset{0.01)}{0.50}\, LGDPI - \underset{(0.07)}{0.07}\, LGPRFOOD \qquad R^2 = 0.992.$$

11.2 Download the Demand Functions data set from the website (see Appendix B). You should choose, or be assigned by your instructor, one category of expenditure, and it may be helpful to simplify the data set by deleting the expenditure and price variables relating to the other categories. Construct a relative price index series for your category by dividing its nominal price series by *PTPE*, the price series for total consumer expenditure, and multiplying by 100. Plot the series and try to explain why it has changed over the time period.

11.3 Regress your category of expenditure on *DPI* and the relative price index series constructed in Exercise 11.2. Give an economic interpretation of the regression coefficients and perform appropriate statistical tests.

11.4 Regress the logarithm of expenditure on your category on *LGDPI* and the logarithm of the relative price series. Give an economic interpretation of the regression coefficients and perform appropriate statistical tests.

11.5 Sometimes a time trend is included in a regression as an explanatory variable, acting as a proxy for some gradual change not associated with income or price.

Changing tastes might be an example. However, in the present case, the addition of a time trend might give rise to a problem of multicollinearity because it will be highly correlated with the income series and perhaps also the price series. Calculate the correlations between the *TIME* variable in the data set, *LGDPI*, and the logarithm of the relative price of your category. Regress the logarithm of expenditure on your category on *LGDPI*, the logarithm of the relative price series, and *TIME* (not the logarithm of *TIME*). Provide an interpretation of the regression coefficients, perform appropriate statistical tests, and compare the regression results with those of the same regression without *TIME*.

11.6*

Year	*Y*	*K*	*L*	*Year*	*Y*	*K*	*L*
1899	100	100	100	1911	153	216	145
1900	101	107	105	1912	177	226	152
1901	112	114	110	1913	184	236	154
1902	122	122	118	1914	169	244	149
1903	124	131	123	1915	189	266	154
1904	122	138	116	1916	225	298	182
1905	143	149	125	1917	227	335	196
1906	152	163	133	1918	223	366	200
1907	151	176	138	1919	218	387	193
1908	126	185	121	1920	231	407	193
1909	155	198	140	1921	179	417	147
1910	159	208	144	1922	240	431	161

Source: Cobb and Douglas (1928).

The table gives the data used by Cobb and Douglas (1928) to fit the original Cobb–Douglas production function:

$$Y_t = \beta_1 K_t^{\beta_2} L_t^{\beta_3} v_t,$$

Y_t, K_t, and L_t, being index number series for real output, real capital input, and real labor input, respectively, for the manufacturing sector of the United States for the period 1899–1922 (1899 = 100). The model was linearized by taking logarithms of both sides and the following regression was run (standard errors in parentheses):

$$\widehat{\log Y} = -0.18 + 0.23 \log K + 0.81 \log L \quad R^2 = 0.96.$$
$$0.43) \; (0.06) \qquad (0.15)$$

Provide an interpretation of the regression coefficients.

11.7* The Cobb–Douglas model in Exercise 11.6 makes no allowance for the possibility that output may be increasing as a consequence of technical progress, independently of *K* and *L*. Technical progress is difficult to quantify and a common way of allowing for it in a model is to include an exponential time trend:

$$Y_t = \beta_1 K_t^{\beta_2} L_t^{\beta_3} e^{\rho t} v_t,$$

where ρ is the rate of technical progress and t is a time trend defined to be 1 in the first year, 2 in the second, etc. The correlations between log K, log L and t are shown in the table. Comment on the regression results.

$$\widehat{\log Y} = \underset{(1.38)}{2.81} - \underset{(0.34)}{0.53} \log K + \underset{(0.14)}{0.91} \log L + \underset{(0.021)}{0.047}\, t \quad R^2 = 0.97.$$

Correlation

	LGK	LGL	TIME
LGK	1.000000	0.909562	0.996834
LGL	0.909562	1.000000	0.896344
TIME	0.996834	0.896344	1.000000

11.3 Models with lagged explanatory variables

Next, we will introduce some simple dynamics. One might suppose that some types of consumer expenditure are largely determined by current income and price, but this is not so for a category such as housing that is subject to substantial inertia. We will consider specifications in which expenditure on housing depends on lagged values of income and price and we will attempt to determine the lag structure, that is, the sizes of the coefficients of the current and lagged values of the explanatory variables. A variable X lagged one time period has values that are simply the previous values of X, and it is conventionally referred to as $X(-1)$. Generalizing, a variable lagged s time periods has the X values s periods previously, and is denoted $X(-s)$. Major regression applications adopt this convention and for these there is no need to define lagged variables separately. Table 11.3 shows the data for *LGDPI*, *LGDPI*(−1), and *LGDPI*(−2). Note that obviously there is a very high correlation between *LGDPI*, *LGDPI*(−1), and *LGDPI*(−2), and this is likely to cause problems.

The first column of Table 11.4 presents the results of a logarithmic regression using current income and price. The second and third columns show the results of regressing expenditure on housing on income and price lagged one and two time periods, respectively. It is reasonable to hypothesize that expenditure on a category of consumer expenditure might depend on both current and lagged income and price. The fourth column shows the results of a regression using current income and price and the same variables lagged one time period. The fifth column adds the same variables lagged two time periods, as well.

The first three regressions are almost identical. This is because *LGDPI*, *LGDPI*(−1), and *LGDPI*(−2) are very highly correlated. The last two regressions display the classic symptoms of multicollinearity. The point estimates are unstable and the standard errors become much larger when current and lagged values of income and price are simultaneously included as regressors. Multicollinearity is preventing us from discriminating between their current

Table 11.3 Current and lagged values of the logarithm of disposable personal income

Year	*LGDPI*	*LGDPI*(−1)	*LGDPI*(−2)
1959	7.4474	—	—
1960	7.4729	7.4474	—
1961	7.5062	7.4729	7.4474
1962	7.5539	7.5062	7.4729
1963	7.5904	7.5539	7.5062
1964	7.6605	7.5904	7.5539
1965	7.7202	7.6605	7.5904
......	......	......	......
......	......	......	......
1996	8.7129	8.6837	8.6563
1997	8.7476	8.7129	8.6837
1998	8.8045	8.7476	8.7129
1999	8.8337	8.8045	8.7476
2000	8.8810	8.8337	8.8045
2001	8.9002	8.8810	8.8337
2002	8.9306	8.9002	8.8810
2003	8.9534	8.9306	8.9002

Table 11.4 Alternative dynamic specifications, expenditure on housing services

Variable	(1)	(2)	(3)	(4)	(5)
LGDPI	1.03	—	—	0.33	0.29
	(0.01)			(0.15)	(0.14)
LGDPI(−1)	—	1.01	—	0.68	0.22
		(0.01)		(0.15)	(0.20)
LGDPI(−2)	—	—	0.98	—	0.49
			(0.01)		(0.13)
LGPRHOUS	−0.48	—	—	−0.09	−0.28
	(0.04)			(0.17)	(0.17)
LGPRHOUS(−1)	—	−0.43	—	−0.36	0.23
		(0.04)		(0.17)	(0.30)
LGPRHOUS(−2)	—	—	−0.38	—	−0.38
			(0.04)		(0.18)
R^2	0.999	0.999	0.999	0.999	0.999

and lagged effects. For a type of expenditure such as housing, where one might expect long lags, simply adding lags to a static model is unlikely to help us determine the lag structure.

Estimating long-run effects

Despite the problem of multicollinearity, we may be able to obtain relatively precise estimates of the long-run elasticities with respect to income and price. The usual way of investigating the long-run relationship between Y and X is to perform an exercise in comparative statics. One first determines how equilibrium Y is related to equilibrium X, if the process ever reached equilibrium, and then one evaluates the effect of a change in equilibrium X on equilibrium Y.

Suppose that you have a regression model

$$Y_t = \beta_1 + \beta_2 X_t + \beta_3 X_{t-1} + \beta_4 X_{t-2} + u_t. \tag{11.9}$$

In equilibrium, we would have

$$\bar{Y} = \beta_1 + \beta_2 \bar{X} + \beta_3 \bar{X} + \beta_4 \bar{X} = \beta_1 + (\beta_2 + \beta_3 + \beta_4)\bar{X}, \tag{11.10}$$

where $\bar{Y}$ and $\bar{X}$ are the equilibrium values of Y and X. Hence $(\beta_2 + \beta_3 + \beta_4)$ is a measure of the long-run effect of X. We contrast this with the short-run effect, which is simply β_2, the impact of current X_t on Y_t. We can calculate the long-run effect from the point estimates of β_2, β_3, and β_4 in the original specification. The estimate of the sum may be quite stable, even though the estimates of the individual coefficients may be subject to multicollinearity.

Table 11.5 presents an example of this. It gives the sum of the income and price elasticities for the five specifications of the logarithmic housing demand function in Table 11.4. These estimates of the long-run elasticities are very similar.

If we are estimating long-run effects, we need standard errors as well as point estimates. The most straightforward way of obtaining the standard error is to reparameterize the model. In the case of (11.9), we could rewrite it as

$$Y_t = \beta_1 + (\beta_2 + \beta_3 + \beta_4)X_t - \beta_3 (X_t - X_{t-1}) - \beta_4 (X_t - X_{t-2}) + u_t. \tag{11.11}$$

Table 11.5 Estimates of long-run income and price elasticities

Specification	(1)	(2)	(3)	(4)	(5)
Sum of income elasticities	1.03	1.01	0.98	1.01	1.00
Sum of price elasticities	−0.48	−0.43	−0.38	−0.45	−0.43

The point estimate of the coefficient of X_t will be the sum of the point estimates of β_2, β_3, and β_4 in the original specification and so the standard error of that coefficient is the standard error of the estimate of the long-run effect. Since X_t may well not be highly correlated with $(X_t - X_{t-1})$ or $(X_t - X_{t-2})$, there may not be a problem of multicollinearity and the standard error may be relatively small.

When the model in column 5 of Table 11.4 is rewritten in this way and fitted, the coefficient of $LGDPI_t$ is 1.00 with standard error 0.01 and the coefficient of $LGPRHOUS_t$ is –0.41 with standard error 0.01. As expected, the standard errors are much lower than those of the individual coefficients in the original specification.

EXERCISES

11.8 Give an economic interpretation of the coefficients of *LGDPI*, *LGDPI*(–1), and *LGDPI*(–2), in column 5 of Table 11.4.

11.9 To allow for the possibility that expenditure on your category is partly subject to a one-period lag, regress the logarithm of expenditure on your commodity on *LGDPI*, the logarithm of your relative price series, and those two variables lagged one period. Repeat the experiment adding *LGDPI*(–2) and the logarithm of the price series lagged two periods. Compare the regression results, paying attention to the changes in the regression coefficients and their standard errors.

11.4 Models with a lagged dependent variable

For many applications, a widely used solution to the problem of including dynamics in a model while mitigating the problem of multicollinearity is to employ an autoregressive distributed lag model, often written ADL(p, q). The 'autoregressive' part of the name refers to the fact that lagged values of the dependent variable are included on the right side as explanatory variables. p is the maximum number of lags of the dependent variable used in this way. q is the maximum lag of the X variable, or variables if there are several.

The ADL model is particularly appealing when the dependent variable exhibits a high degree of dependence because then, as a matter of common sense, its value in one observation is likely to be influenced by its value in the previous one. It is econometrically attractive because it can accommodate a broad range of dynamic patterns with relatively few lag terms and parameters. (It is parsimonious, to use the technical term.) This is likely to reduce (but obviously, not eliminate) the problem of multicollinearity.

We will start with the simplest model of all, the ADL(1,0) model where the only lagged variable is the lagged dependent variable. Given the continuity of many time series processes, Y_{t-1}, the value of a time series at time $t - 1$, is often a good guide to its value Y_t at time t. When this is the case, it makes sense to include Y_{t-1} explicitly in the model as an explanatory variable:

$$Y_t = \beta_1 + \beta_2 X_t + \beta_3 Y_{t-1} + u_t. \tag{11.12}$$

The use of the lagged dependent variable as an explanatory variable in the model, very widespread in practice, is often a matter of common sense. However, it is sometimes justified as the theoretical outcome of particular models, such as the partial adjustment model and the adaptive expectations model described below.

As will be seen in this section, a model with a lagged dependent variable is often attractive because it permits the representation of the process to have plausible dynamic properties without necessarily giving rise to the problem of multicollinearity. X_t and Y_{t-1} in (11.12) will be correlated, but not to the same extent as X_t with its own lagged values.

We will begin by investigating the dynamics implicit in the model graphically. We will suppose, for convenience, that β_2 is positive and that X increases with time, and we will neglect the effect of the disturbance term. We shall suppose throughout this section that $|\beta_3| < 1$. This is a stability condition for the process. We will discuss the consequences of violations of this condition in Chapter 13. We will in fact assume $0 < \beta_3 < 1$ because Y_t and Y_{t-1} are typically positively correlated.

At time t, Y_t is given by (11.12). Y_{t-1} has already been determined at time t, so the term $\beta_3 Y_{t-1}$ is fixed. (11.12) thus may be viewed as giving the short-run relationship between Y_t and X_t for period t. For period t, it is represented by the bottom line in Figure 11.2, the value of Y_t indicated by the marker being that corresponding to the actual value of X_t. $[\beta_1 + \beta_3 Y_{t-1}]$ is effectively the intercept and β_2, the slope coefficient, gives the short-run effect of X on Y.

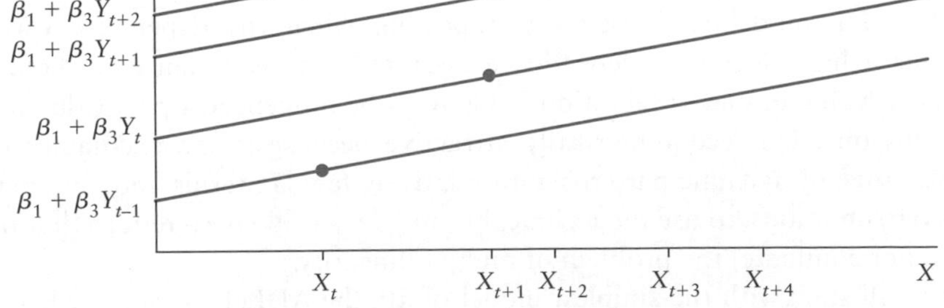

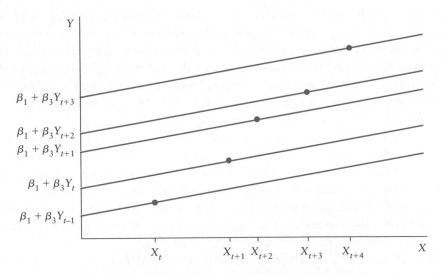

Figure 11.2 Short-run and long-run dynamics in a model with a lagged dependent variable

When we come to time $t + 1$, Y_{t+1} is given by

$$Y_{t+1} = \beta_1 + \beta_2 X_{t+1} + \beta_3 Y_t \tag{11.13}$$

and the effective intercept is now $[\beta_1 + \beta_3 Y_t]$. Since X is increasing, Y is increasing, so the intercept is larger than that for Y_t and the short-run relationship has shifted upwards. The slope is the same as before, β_2. Thus, two factors are responsible for the growth of Y over time: the direct effect of the increase in X, and the gradual upward shift of the short-run relationship. Figure 11.2 shows the outcomes for time t as far as time $t + 4$. You can see that the actual relationship between Y and X, traced out by the markers representing the observations, is steeper than the short-run relationship for each time period.

We will determine the long-run relationship between Y and X by performing the comparative statics analysis described in Section 11.3. Denoting equilibrium Y and X by $\bar{Y}$ and $\bar{X}$, $Y_t = Y_{t-1} = \bar{Y}$ and $X_t = \bar{X}$ in equilibrium. Hence, using (11.12) and ignoring the transient effect of the disturbance term, the equilibrium relationship is given by

$$\bar{Y} = \beta_1 + \beta_2 \bar{X} + \beta_3 \bar{Y}. \tag{11.14}$$

Re-arranging, one has

$$\bar{Y} = \frac{\beta_1}{1-\beta_3} + \frac{\beta_2}{1-\beta_3}\bar{X}. \tag{11.15}$$

$\beta_2/(1-\beta_3)$ gives the effect of a one-unit change in equilibrium X on equilibrium Y. We will describe this as the long-run effect. In the present context, with $0 < \beta_3 < 1$, it will be greater than β_2 because $1-\beta_3$ will also lie between 0 and 1.

Contrasting the short-run and long-run effects of X on Y is one way of looking at the dynamics implicit in (11.12). Another is to look at the implicit relationship between Y_t and current and lagged values of X. If (11.12) is true for time period t, it is also true for time period $t - 1$:

$$Y_{t-1} = \beta_1 + \beta_2 X_{t-1} + \beta_3 Y_{t-2} + u_{t-1}. \tag{11.16}$$

Substituting for Y_{t-1} in (11.9), one then has

$$\begin{aligned} Y_t &= \beta_1 + \beta_2 X_t + \beta_3 (\beta_1 + \beta_2 X_{t-1} + \beta_3 Y_{t-2} + u_{t-1}) + u_t \\ &= \beta_1 (1 + \beta_3) + \beta_2 X_t + \beta_2 \beta_3 X_{t-1} + \beta_3^2 Y_{t-2} + u_t + \beta_3 u_{t-1}. \end{aligned} \tag{11.17}$$

Continuing to lag and substitute, one obtains

$$\begin{aligned} Y_t = {} & \beta_1 (1 + \beta_3 + \beta_3^2 \cdots) + \beta_2 X_t + \beta_2 \beta_3 X_{t-1} + \beta_2 \beta_3^2 X_{t-2} \\ & + \cdots + u_t + \beta_3 u_{t-1} + \beta_3^2 u_{t-2} + \cdots \end{aligned} \tag{11.18}$$

Hence, Y_t can be viewed as a linear combination of current and lagged values of X with geometrically declining weights: $\beta_2, \beta_2\beta_3, \beta_2\beta_3^2, \ldots$ We have thus found a way of allowing lagged values of X to influence Y without introducing them into the model explicitly and giving rise to multicollinearity. One should, however, note that this pattern of weights, known as a lag distribution, embodies the assumption that more recent values of X have more influence than older ones, and that the rate of decline in the weights is constant. We will see in due course that we can relax both of these constraints.

From (11.18) it can be seen that, at time t, with X_{t-1}, X_{t-2}, etc. already determined, the only influence of X on Y is via X_t. For this reason, again, we describe β_2 as the short-run effect. This representation of the model also yields the same long-run effect, as before. The proof is left as an exercise.

The partial adjustment model

The idea behind the partial adjustment model is that, while a dependent variable Y may be related to an explanatory variable X, there is inertia in the system and the actual value of Y_t is a compromise between its value in the previous time period, Y_{t-1}, and the value justified by the current value of the explanatory variable. Let us denote the justified value of Y (or target, desired, or appropriate value, however you want to describe it) as Y_t^*, given by

$$Y_t^* = \gamma_1 + \gamma_2 X_t + u_t. \tag{11.19}$$

In the partial adjustment model, it is assumed that the actual increase in the dependent variable from time $t-1$ to time t, $Y_t - Y_{t-1}$, is proportional to the discrepancy between the justified value and the previous value, $Y_t^* - Y_{t-1}$:

$$Y_t - Y_{t-1} = \lambda(Y_t^* - Y_{t-1}) \quad (0 \le \lambda \le 1). \tag{11.20}$$

λ is usually described as the speed of adjustment. This relationship may be rewritten

$$Y_t = \lambda Y_t^* + (1-\lambda)Y_{t-1}, \tag{11.21}$$

so it can be seen that Y_t is a weighted average of the current justified value and the previous actual value. The higher is the value of λ, the more rapid is the adjustment process. If λ is equal to 1, Y_t is equal to Y_t^* and there is full adjustment in one period. At the other extreme, if λ is equal to 0, Y_t does not adjust at all.

Substituting for Y_t^* from (11.19), one obtains

$$\begin{aligned} Y_t &= \lambda(\gamma_1 + \gamma_2 X_t + u_t) + (1-\lambda)Y_{t-1} \\ &= \gamma_1\lambda + \gamma_2\lambda X_t + (1-\lambda)Y_{t-1} + \lambda u_t. \end{aligned} \tag{11.22}$$

The relationship is now expressed entirely in terms of observable variables and is of the ADL(1,0) form (11.12) with $\beta_1 = \gamma_1\lambda$, $\beta_2 = \gamma_2\lambda$, and $\beta_3 = 1-\lambda$.

Example: Brown's habit persistence model of aggregate consumption

Brown's habit persistence model (Brown, 1952) was one of the earliest examples of a macroeconomic consumption function with dynamics. Brown hypothesized that desired aggregate consumption, C_t^*, was related to wage income, W_t, and nonwage income, NW_t:

$$C_t^* = \beta_1 + \beta_2 W_t + \beta_3 NW_t + \delta A + u_t. \tag{11.23}$$

Brown used aggregate data for Canada for the years 1926–49, omitting the war years 1942–45 and A was a dummy variable equal to 0 for the pre-war period and 1 for the post-war period. The division of income into wage income and nonwage income follows the observation of Michael Kalecki that the marginal propensity to consume out of wage income was likely to be higher than that out of nonwage income.

Because households are slow to adapt their spending patterns in response to changes in income, Brown hypothesized a partial adjustment process for actual consumption:

$$C_t - C_{t-1} = \lambda\left(C_t^* - C_{t-1}\right). \tag{11.24}$$

Substituting for C_t^* from (11.23) and rearranging, one obtains an equation in observable variables:

$$C_t = \beta_1\lambda + \beta_2\lambda W_t + \beta_3\lambda NW_t + (1-\lambda)C_{t-1} + \lambda\delta A + \lambda u_t. \tag{11.25}$$

Fitting the model with a simultaneous equations technique, Brown obtained (t statistics in parentheses)

$$\underset{(4.8)}{\hat{C}_t = 0.90} + \underset{(7.4)}{0.61W_t} + \underset{(4.2)}{0.28NW_t} + \underset{(2.8)}{0.22C_{t-1}} + \underset{(4.8)}{0.69A}. \tag{11.26}$$

The variables were all measured in Canadian \$ billion at constant prices of the 1935–39 period. From the regression one obtains short-run marginal propensities to consume of 0.61 and 0.28 for wage income and nonwage income, respectively. The coefficient of C_{t-1} indicates that 0.78 of the discrepancy between desired and actual consumption is eliminated in one year. Dividing the short-run marginal propensities by the speed of adjustment, one obtains long-run propensities to consume of 0.78 and 0.36 for wage income and nonwage income, respectively.

The error correction model

The error correction model is a variant of the partial adjustment model. As with the partial adjustment model, we assume that there is a long-run relationship between Y and X given by

$$Y_t^* = \gamma_1 + \gamma_2 X_t + u_t, \tag{11.27}$$

where Y_t^* is the level of Y that would correspond to the level of X_t in a long-run relationship. In the short run, ΔY_t, the change in Y_t from Y_{t-1}, is determined by two components: a partial closing of the discrepancy between its previous appropriate and actual values, $Y_{t-1}^* - Y_{t-1}$, and a straightforward response to the rate of change in X, ΔX_t:

$$\begin{aligned}\Delta Y_t &= \lambda\left(Y_{t-1}^* - Y_{t-1}\right) + \delta \Delta X_t + u_t \\ &= \lambda\left(\gamma_1 + \gamma_2 X_{t-1} - Y_{t-1}\right) + \delta\left(X_t - X_{t-1}\right) + u_t \\ &= \lambda\gamma_1 + \delta X_t + \left(\lambda\gamma_2 - \delta\right)X_{t-1} - \lambda Y_{t-1} + u_t. \end{aligned} \qquad \textbf{(11.28)}$$

Hence,

$$Y_t = \beta_1 + \beta_2 X_t + \beta_3 Y_{t-1} + \beta_4 X_{t-1} + u_t, \qquad \textbf{(11.29)}$$

where $\beta_1 = \gamma_1\lambda$, $\beta_2 = \delta$, $\beta_3 = 1 - \lambda$, and $\beta_4 = \lambda\gamma_2 - \delta$. $\delta = \beta_2$ is the short-run effect of X on Y, and $\lambda = \left(1 - \beta_3\right)$ is the speed of adjustment relating to the discrepancy. In this form, it is an ADL(1,1) model since it includes X_{t-1} as an explanatory variable. The ADL(1,0) model is a special case with the testable restriction $\beta_4 = \lambda\gamma_2 - \delta = 0$. This way of representing the process will be particularly useful when we come to cointegration in Chapter 13.

The adaptive expectations model

The dynamics in the partial adjustment model are attributable to inertia, the drag of the past. Another, completely opposite, source of dynamics, is the effect of anticipations. On the basis of information currently available, agents—individuals, households, enterprises—form expectations about the future values of key variables and adapt their plans accordingly. In its simplest form, the dependent variable Y_t is related, not to the current value of the explanatory variable, X_t, but to the value anticipated in the next time period, X_{t+1}^e:

$$Y_t = \beta_1 + \beta_2 X_{t+1}^e + u_t. \qquad \textbf{(11.30)}$$

X_{t+1}^e in general will be subjective and unobservable. To make the model operational, we hypothesize that expectations are updated in response to the discrepancy between what had been anticipated for the current time period, X_{t+1}^e, and the actual outcome, X_t:

$$X_{t+1}^e - X_t^e = \lambda\left(X_t - X_t^e\right). \qquad \textbf{(11.31)}$$

As in the partial adjustment model, λ may be interpreted as a speed of adjustment and should lie between 0 and 1. We can rewrite (11.31) as

$$X_{t+1}^e = \lambda X_t + (1 - \lambda)X_t^e. \qquad \textbf{(11.32)}$$

This indicates that, according to this model, the expected level of X in the next time period is a weighted average of what had been expected for the current time period and the actual outcome for the current time period. Substituting from (11.32) into (11.30), we have

$$Y_t = \beta_1 + \beta_2 \lambda X_t + \beta_2 (1 - \lambda) X_t^e + u_t. \tag{11.33}$$

Now, if (11.30) is valid for time period t, it is also valid for time period $t - 1$:

$$Y_{t-1} = \beta_1 + \beta_2 X_t^e + u_{t-1}. \tag{11.34}$$

From this one obtains the relationship

$$\beta_2 X_t^e = Y_{t-1} - \beta_1 - u_{t-1}. \tag{11.35}$$

Substituting for $\beta_2 X_t^e$ in (11.33), one obtains a model in ADL(1,0) form:

$$\begin{aligned} Y_t &= \beta_1 + \beta_2 \lambda X_t + (1 - \lambda)(Y_{t-1} - \beta_1 - u_{t-1}) + u_t \\ &= \beta_1 \lambda + \beta_2 \lambda X_t + (1 - \lambda) Y_{t-1} + u_t - (1 - \lambda) u_{t-1}. \end{aligned} \tag{11.36}$$

The model is now entirely in terms of observable variables and is therefore operational. Note that, apart from the compound disturbance term, it is mathematically the same as that for the partial adjustment model. Hence, if one fitted the model to a sample of data, it would be difficult to tell whether the underlying process were partial adjustment or adaptive expectations, despite the fact that the approaches are opposite in spirit. This is an example of observational equivalence of two theories.

Example: Friedman's permanent income hypothesis

Without doubt the most celebrated application of the adaptive expectations model is Friedman's use of it when fitting an aggregate consumption function using time series data and his **permanent income hypothesis**. In the early years after the Second World War, econometricians working with macroeconomic data were puzzled by the fact that the long-run average propensity to consume seemed to be roughly constant, despite the marginal propensity to consume being much lower. A model in which current consumption was a function of current income could not explain this phenomenon and was therefore clearly too simplistic. Several more sophisticated models that could explain this apparent contradiction were developed, notably Friedman's permanent income hypothesis, Brown's habit persistence model (discussed above), Duesenberry's relative income hypothesis, and the Modigliani–Ando–Brumberg life cycle model.

Under the permanent income hypothesis, permanent consumption, C_t^P, is proportional to permanent income, Y_t^P:

$$C_t^P = \beta_2 Y_t^P. \tag{11.37}$$

Actual consumption, C_t, and actual income, Y_t, also contain transitory components, C_t^T and Y_t^T respectively:

$$C_t = C_t^P + C_t^T \tag{11.38}$$

$$Y_t = Y_t^P + Y_t^T. \tag{11.39}$$

It is assumed, at least as a first approximation, that the transitory components of consumption and income have expected value zero and are distributed independently of their permanent counterparts and of each other. Substituting for C_t^P in (11.37) using (11.38) one has

$$C_t = \beta_2 Y_t^P + C_t^T. \tag{11.40}$$

We thus obtain a relationship between actual consumption and permanent income in which C_t^T plays the role of a disturbance term, previously lacking in the model.

Earlier, when we discussed the permanent income hypothesis in the context of cross-sectional data, the observations related to households. When Friedman fitted the model, he actually used aggregate time series data. To solve the problem that permanent income is unobservable, he hypothesized that it was subject to an adaptive expectations process in which the notion of permanent income was updated by a proportion of the difference between actual income and the previous period's permanent income:

$$Y_t^P - Y_{t-1}^P = \lambda\left(Y_t - Y_{t-1}^P\right). \tag{11.41}$$

Hence, permanent income at time t is a weighted average of actual income at time t and permanent income at time $t - 1$:

$$Y_t^P = \lambda Y_t + (1-\lambda)Y_{t-1}^P. \tag{11.42}$$

(11.42) cannot be used directly to measure permanent income in year t because we do not know λ and we have no way of measuring Y_{t-1}^P. We can solve the second difficulty by noting that, if (11.42) holds for time t, it also holds for time $t - 1$:

$$Y_{t-1}^P = \lambda Y_{t-1} + (1-\lambda)Y_{t-2}^P. \tag{11.43}$$

Substituting this into (11.42), we obtain

$$Y_t^P = \lambda Y_t + \lambda(1-\lambda)Y_{t-1} + (1-\lambda)^2 Y_{t-2}^P. \tag{11.44}$$

This includes the unobservable term Y_{t-2}^P, but we can deal with it by lagging (11.42) two periods and substituting, thus obtaining Y_t^P in terms of Y_t, Y_{t-1}, Y_{t-2}, and Y_{t-3}^P. Continuing this process indefinitely, we can write Y_t^P as a weighted sum of current and past measured income:

$$Y_t^P = \lambda Y_t + \lambda(1-\lambda)Y_{t-1} + \lambda(1-\lambda)^2 Y_{t-2} + \lambda(1-\lambda)^3 Y_{t-3} + \cdots. \tag{11.45}$$

Provided that λ lies between 0 and 1, a reasonable assumption, $(1-\lambda)^s$ is a decreasing function of s and eventually the weights attached to the lagged values of Y become so small that they can be neglected.

This still leaves us with the problem of estimating λ. Friedman's solution was to use a grid search, calculating the permanent income time series for a range of values of λ between 0 and 1, and regressing consumption on each permanent income series. He then chose that value of λ that produced the series for Y^P that gave him the best fit. Effectively, of course, he was fitting the nonlinear model

$$C_t = \beta_2 \lambda Y_t + \beta_2 \lambda (1-\lambda) Y_{t-1} + \beta_2 \lambda (1-\lambda)^2 Y_{t-2} + \cdots + C_t^T. \tag{11.46}$$

Alternatively, the model may be represented in ADL(1,0) form. This could be done on the lines of equations (11.34)–(11.36), or by lagging (11.46) one period and multiplying through by $1-\lambda$:

$$\begin{aligned}(1-\lambda)C_{t-1} = {} & \beta_2 \lambda (1-\lambda) Y_{t-1} + \beta_2 \lambda (1-\lambda)^2 Y_{t-2} \\ & + \beta_2 \lambda (1-\lambda)^3 Y_{t-3} + \cdots + (1-\lambda)\, C_{t-1}^T. \end{aligned} \tag{11.47}$$

Subtracting (11.47) from (11.46), one has

$$C_t - (1-\lambda)C_{t-1} = \beta_2 \lambda Y_t + C_t^T - (1-\lambda)C_{t-1}^T \tag{11.48}$$

and so

$$C_t = \beta_2 \lambda Y_t + (1-\lambda)C_{t-1} + C_t^T - (1-\lambda)C_{t-1}^T. \tag{11.49}$$

The short-run marginal propensity to consume is $\beta_2\lambda$ and the long-run propensity is β_2. Since λ is less than 1, the model is able to reconcile a low short-run marginal propensity to consume with a higher long-run average propensity.

More general autoregressive models

The ADL(1,0) model (for example, the partial adjustment and adaptive expectations models) is often a reasonable first approximation for the specification of a lag structure. However, it has features that may make it unrealistic in some contexts. In particular, it requires the current value of the explanatory variable to have greater impact than its lagged values on the dependent variable.

The ADL(1,1) model (for example, the error correction model),

$$Y_t = \beta_1 + \beta_2 Y_{t-1} + \beta_3 X_t + \beta_4 X_{t-1} + u_t, \tag{11.50}$$

where there is a lagged value of the explanatory variable (or lagged values of some or all, if there are several), is a little more flexible in this respect. For suitable choice of the parameters, the weight of the first lag can be greater than that of the current value. After the first lag, the weights decline geometrically, as in the ADL(1,0) model.

Greater flexibility is afforded by including further lagged values of the dependent variable among the explanatory variables. However, the flexibility comes at the cost of mathematical complexity. Most of the issues that we wish to discuss in the rest of this chapter and the next can be treated within the context of the relatively straightforward ADL(1,1) model, and for that reason the analysis will be confined to it.

EXERCISES

11.10 Expenditure on housing services, *HOUS*, was regressed on *DPI*, the relative price index for housing, *PRELHOUS*, and the lagged value of *HOUS*, *HOUS*(−1), for the period 1959–2003 for the United States using the Demand Functions data set. The regression was repeated in logarithmic form, *LGHOUS* being regressed on *LGDPI*, *LGPRHOUS*, and *LGHOUS*(−1), with the results shown. Give an interpretation of the regression coefficients, paying attention to the dynamics implicit in the model.

$$\widehat{HOUS} = \underset{(17.78)}{75.35} + \underset{(0.01)}{0.03}\,DPI - \underset{(0.22)}{0.75}\,PRELHOUS + \underset{(0.04)}{0.81}\,HOUS(-1) \qquad R^2 = 0.9997$$

$$\widehat{LGHOUS} = \underset{(0.06)}{0.07} + \underset{(0.05)}{0.28}\,LGDPI - \underset{0.03)}{0.12}\,LGPRHOUS + \underset{(0.04)}{0.71}\,LGHOUS(-1) \qquad R^2 = 0.9998.$$

11.11 Perform regressions parallel to those reported in Exercise 11.10 for your category of expenditure in the Demand Functions data set. Give an interpretation of the regression coefficients, paying attention to the dynamics implicit in the model.

11.12 Brown's habit persistence model allows the marginal propensity to consume out of nonwage income to be different from that of wage income. Explain why this might be the case, and explain how one would test whether the propensities are actually different.

11.13 In an early application of the partial adjustment model, Lintner (1956) hypothesized that the target (or long-run) level of corporate dividends, D_t^*, would be a constant fraction of profits, P_t. However, for various reasons, actual dividends would adjust by only a proportion of the difference between D_t^* and dividends in the previous time period, D_{t-1}. He fitted the relationship

$$\hat{D}_t = 352.3 + 0.15P_t + 0.70D_{t-1}$$

using US corporate data for the period 1918–1951. Standard errors are not reported, but he does report that the *t* statistics were all greater than 4. Determine the target pay-out ratio and the speed of adjustment implicit in the fitted equation. If you have some knowledge of financial markets, explain why a partial adjustment model may be more plausible than a static model with no lags.

11.14* The compound disturbance term in the adaptive expectations model (11.36) does potentially give rise to a problem that will be discussed in Chapter 12 when we come to the topic of autocorrelation. It can be sidestepped by representing the model in the alternative form.

$$Y_t = \beta_1 + \beta_2\lambda X_t + \beta_2\lambda(1-\lambda)X_{t-1} + \cdots + \beta_2\lambda(1-\lambda)^s X_{t-s} + \beta_2(1-\lambda)^{s+1}X_{t-s}^e + u_t.$$

Show how this form might be obtained, and discuss how it might be fitted.

11.15 Explain whether the adaptive expectations process is likely to be a plausible representation of dynamics in financial markets.

11.16* The output shows the result of fitting the model

$$LGFOOD = \beta_1 + \beta_2\lambda LGDPI + \beta_2\lambda(1-\lambda)LGDPI(-1)$$
$$+ \beta_2\lambda(1-\lambda)^2 LGDPI(-2) + \beta_3 LGPRFOOD + u,$$

using the data on expenditure on food in the Demand Functions data set. *LGFOOD* and *LGPRFOOD* are the logarithms of expenditure on food and the relative price index series for food. C(1), C(2), C(3), and C(4) are estimates of β_1, β_2, λ, and β_3, respectively. Explain how the regression equation could be interpreted as an adaptive expectations model and discuss the dynamics implicit in it, both short-run and long-run. Should the specification have included further lagged values of *LGDPI*?

```
============================================================
Dependent Variable: LGFOOD
Method: Least Squares
Sample(adjusted): 1962 2003
Included observations: 42 after adjusting endpoints
Convergence achieved after 25 iterations
LGFOOD = C(1)+C(2)*C(3)*LGDPI + C(2)*C(3)*(1-C(3))*LGDPI(-1) +
         C(2)*C(3)*(1-C(3))^2*LGDPI(-2) + C(2)*C(3)*(1-C(3))^3*LGDPI(-3)
         +C(4)*LGPRFOOD
============================================================
                  Coefficient   Std. Error  t-Statistic      Prob.
============================================================
          C(1)     2.339513     0.468550     4.993091      0.0000
          C(2)     0.496425     0.012264     40.47818      0.0000
          C(3)     0.915046     0.442851     2.066264      0.0457
          C(4)    -0.089681     0.083250    -1.077247      0.2882
============================================================
R-squared           0.989621    Mean dependent var      6.049936
Adjusted R-squared  0.988802    S.D. dependent var      0.201706
S.E. of regression  0.021345    Akaike info criter     -4.765636
Sum squared resid   0.017313    Schwarz criterion      -4.600143
Log likelihood      104.0784    Durbin-Watson stat      0.449978
============================================================
```

11.5 Assumption C.7 and the properties of estimators in autoregressive models

Assumption C.7, like its counterpart B.7 in Model B, is required for the unbiasedness of the OLS regression coefficients. We will outline the proof for the slope coefficient of the simple regression model

$$Y_t = \beta_1 + \beta_2 X_t + u_t, \tag{11.51}$$

with $t = 1, \ldots, T$. The OLS slope coefficient can be decomposed as

$$b_2^{\text{OLS}} = \beta_2 + \sum_{t=1}^{T} a_t u_t, \tag{11.52}$$

where

$$a_t = \frac{X_t - \bar{X}}{\sum_{s=1}^{T}(X_s - \bar{X})^2}. \tag{11.53}$$

Hence,

$$\begin{aligned} E\left(b_2^{\text{OLS}}\right) &= E\left(\beta_2 + \sum_{t=1}^{T} a_t u_t\right) = \beta_2 + \sum_{t=1}^{T} E(a_t u_t) = \beta_2 + \sum_{t=1}^{T} E(a_t)E(u_t) \\ &= \beta_2 + \sum_{t=1}^{T} E(a_t) \times 0 = \beta_2. \end{aligned} \tag{11.54}$$

Note that we use Assumption C.7 in the decomposition $E(a_t u_t) = E(a_t)E(u_t)$. For the decomposition to be valid, u_t must be distributed independently of a_t, and since a_t depends on all of the observations on X in the sample, this means that u_t must be distributed independently of all of the observations on X, not just X_t. For the purposes of our discussion it is convenient to break down Assumption C.7 into two components:

1. the disturbance term in any observation is distributed independently of the values of the regressors in the same observation, and
2. the disturbance term in any observation is distributed independently of the values of the regressors in the other observations.

For cross-sectional regressions, part (2) is seldom an issue. Since the observations are generated randomly, there is almost never any reason to suppose that the disturbance term in one observation is not independent of the values of the regressors in the other observations. Hence, unbiasedness really depends on part (1). Of course, this may be violated, as we saw with measurement errors in the regressors and with simultaneous equations estimation.

With time series regressions, part (2) becomes a major concern. Consider, for example, the model with a lagged dependent variable that we investigated in Section 11.4:

$$Y_t = \beta_1 + \beta_2 X_t + \beta_3 Y_{t-1} + u_t. \tag{11.55}$$

Suppose that u_t is well behaved in the sense that it is IID. It is then distributed independently of X_t and Y_{t-1} and there is no violation of part (1) of Assumption C.7. However, in the next observation, Y_{t+1} is determined by

$$Y_{t+1} = \beta_1 + \beta_2 X_{t+1} + \beta_3 Y_t + u_{t+1}. \tag{11.56}$$

For this observation, u_t is correlated with the regressor Y_t, violating part (2) of the assumption. In fact, u_t will be correlated with every value of Y from time t onwards.

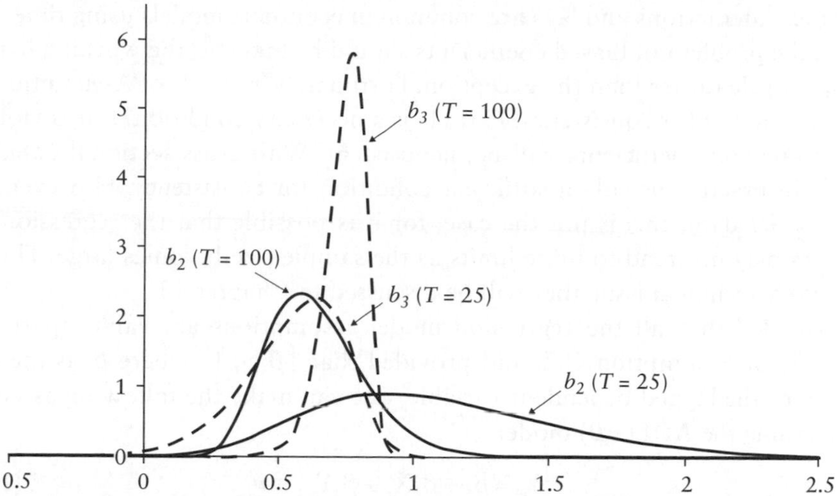

Figure 11.3 Distributions of the coefficients in a model with a lagged dependent variable

The following simulation illustrates the finite-sample bias caused by the violation of part (2) that is inevitable in a model of this kind. The true model is

$$Y_t = 10 + 0.5X_t + 0.8Y_{t-1} + u_t, \qquad \textbf{(11.57)}$$

with X_t being assigned the values 1, 2, ..., T for sample size T. The values of the disturbance term are drawn independently from a normal distribution with zero mean and unit variance. Figure 11.3 shows the distributions of b_2 (solid lines) and b_3 (dashed lines) for sample sizes 25 and 100, for 10 million samples in each case. For sample size 25, b_2 is severely upwards biased, the mean of its distribution being 1.10. b_3 is severely downwards biased, its mean being 0.56.

When the sample size is increased to 100, the biases become smaller, but are still a matter of concern. The means of the distributions are 0.64 and 0.74.

Of course, if the sample size becomes very large, the problem disappears because OLS estimators are consistent, even if part (2) of Assumption C.7 is violated. In the present case, the distributions of the coefficients collapse to spikes at the true values of 0.5 and 0.8.

Consider next the two-equation model

$$Y_t = \beta_1 + \beta_2 X_{t-1} + u_t \qquad \textbf{(11.58)}$$

$$X_t = \alpha_1 + \alpha_2 Y_{t-1} + v_t. \qquad \textbf{(11.59)}$$

Neither equation possesses a lagged dependent variable as a regressor. However, u_t is a determinant of Y_t, and hence of X_{t+1}. This means that u_t is correlated with the X regressor in (11.58) in the observations for Y_{t+2}, Y_{t+4}, ... etc. Again, part (2) of Assumption C.7 is violated and the OLS estimators are biased.

Since interactions and lags are common in economic models using time series data, the problem of biased coefficients should be taken as the working hypothesis, the rule rather than the exception. Fortunately, part (2) of Assumption C.7 is not required for consistency. Part (1) is a necessary condition. If it is violated, the regression coefficients will be inconsistent. With cross-sectional data, part (1) is in practice usually a sufficient condition for consistency. However, with time series data, this is not the case, for it is possible that the regression estimators may not tend to finite limits as the sample size becomes large. This is a relatively technical issue that will be discussed in Chapter 13.

Provided that all the regression model assumptions are valid, apart from part (2) of Assumption C.7, and provided that $|\beta_3| < 1$, where β_3 is the coefficient of the lagged dependent variable, one can make the following assertions concerning the ADL(1,0) model

$$Y_t = \beta_1 + \beta_2 X_t + \beta_3 Y_{t-1} + u_t \tag{11.60}$$

1. OLS estimators of the parameters are consistent and asymptotically normally distributed, and
2. inference, such as *t* and *F* tests, is asymptotically valid,

provided that certain conditions are satisfied with respect to the data for X. We will take a closer look at these statements, both for their own sake, and because it provides an opportunity to review and reinforce some important technical concepts and tools.

Consistency

The presence of lagged value(s) of Y among the explanatory variables in the model means that it is not possible to undertake exact mathematical analysis of the properties of the estimators for finite samples. Instead, in situations such as this, we can take two approaches, usually in combination. One is to look at the asymptotic properties of the estimators. It will typically be possible to analyze these mathematically. The other is to perform Monte Carlo simulations.

For most of this discussion, we will be content to examine the special case

$$Y_t = \beta_2 Y_{t-1} + u_t, \tag{11.61}$$

where $|\beta_2| < 1$ and u is IID with mean 0 and finite variance σ_u^2. We will briefly return to a more general model towards the end. Note that the mean of this process is zero.

The OLS estimator of β_2 is

$$b_2 = \frac{\sum_{t=1}^{T} Y_{t-1} Y_t}{\sum_{t=1}^{T} Y_{t-1}^2} = \beta_2 + \frac{\sum_{t=1}^{T} Y_{t-1} u_t}{\sum_{t=1}^{T} Y_{t-1}^2}. \tag{11.62}$$

We cannot take expectations of the second term because u_s, the value of the disturbance term in period s, is correlated with Y_{t-1} for all $t > s$. Instead, we resort to asymptotic analysis:

$$\operatorname{plim} b_2 = \beta_2 + \operatorname{plim}\left(\frac{\sum_{t=1}^{T} Y_{t-1}u_t}{\sum_{t=1}^{T} Y_{t-1}^2}\right) = \beta_2 + \operatorname{plim}\left(\frac{\frac{1}{T}\sum_{t=1}^{T} Y_{t-1}u_t}{\frac{1}{T}\sum_{t=1}^{T} Y_{t-1}^2}\right)$$

$$= \beta_2 + \frac{\operatorname{plim} \frac{1}{T}\sum_{t=1}^{T} Y_{t-1}u_t}{\operatorname{plim} \frac{1}{T}\sum_{t=1}^{T} Y_{t-1}^2} = \beta_2 + \frac{\operatorname{cov}(Y_{t-1}, u_t)}{\operatorname{var}(Y_{t-1})}. \qquad (11.63)$$

The final step from plims to $\operatorname{cov}(Y_{t-1}, u_t)$ and $\operatorname{var}(Y_{t-1})$ depends on certain assumptions that we shall assume to be valid. $\operatorname{cov}(Y_{t-1}, u_t) = 0$ because Y_{t-1} is determined before u_t is generated. Hence b_2 is a consistent estimator of β_2.

Limiting distributions

Next, we turn to the assertion that b_2 is asymptotically normally distributed. Here we have a problem that needs to be addressed. As the sample size increases, the distribution becomes taller and narrower and finally degenerates to a spike, so how can we say that b_2 is asymptotically normally distributed?

We encountered this problem when determining the asymptotic properties of IV estimators in Chapter 8. To deal with it, we again use the technique involving the use of a central limit theorem discussed in Section R.15. As a first step, we multiply the estimator by $\sqrt{T}$. This is sufficient to prevent the variance from tending to zero as T increases. However, $\sqrt{T}b_2$ does not have a limiting distribution, either, because b_2 tends to β_2 and $\sqrt{T}\beta_2$ increases without limit with T. So, instead, we consider $\sqrt{T}(b_2 - \beta_2)$. For the autoregressive model (11.60), it can be shown that the conditions for the application of a central limit theorem are satisfied, provided that $|\beta_2| < 1$, and that the limiting distribution is normal with zero mean and variance $(1 - \beta_2^2)$:

$$\sqrt{T}(b_2 - \beta_2) \xrightarrow{d} N(0, 1 - \beta_2^2). \qquad (11.64)$$

(The symbol $\xrightarrow{d}$ means 'has the limiting distribution'.)

This asymptotic result is all that we have in analytical terms. We cannot say anything analytically for finite samples.

However, given the limiting distribution, we can start working back tentatively to finite samples and make some plausible assertions. We can say that for large T the relationship may hold approximately. If this is the case, dividing the statistic by $\sqrt{T}$, we can then say that, as an approximation,

$$(b_2 - \beta_2) \sim N\left(0, \frac{1-\beta_2^2}{T}\right) \qquad \textbf{(11.65)}$$

for sufficiently large samples. (The symbol ~ means 'is distributed as'.) Hence, we can say that, as an approximation,

$$b_2 \sim N\left(\beta_2, \frac{1-\beta_2^2}{T}\right) \qquad \textbf{(11.66)}$$

for sufficiently large samples.

Of course, there remains the question of what might be considered to be a 'sufficiently large' sample. To answer this question, we turn to simulation.

Simulation reveals that the answer depends on the value of β_2 itself. We will start by putting $\beta_2 = 0.6$. Figure 11.4 shows the distributions of $\sqrt{T}(b_2 - 0.6)$ for $T = 25$, 50, 100, and 200. For the simulation, the disturbance term was drawn randomly from a normal distribution with zero mean and unit variance. According to the theory, the distribution of $\sqrt{T}(b_2 - 0.6)$ ought to converge to a normal distribution with mean zero and variance $(1 - 0.6^2) = 0.64$. This limiting normal distribution is shown as the dashed curve in the figure.

Although the overall shape of $\sqrt{T}(b_2 - 0.6)$ is not far from normal, even for T as small as 25, there are serious discrepancies in the tails, and it is the shape of the tails that matters for inference. Even for $T = 200$, the left tail is far too fat and the right tail far too thin. This implies that we should not expect (11.66) to be an accurate guide to the distribution of b_2.

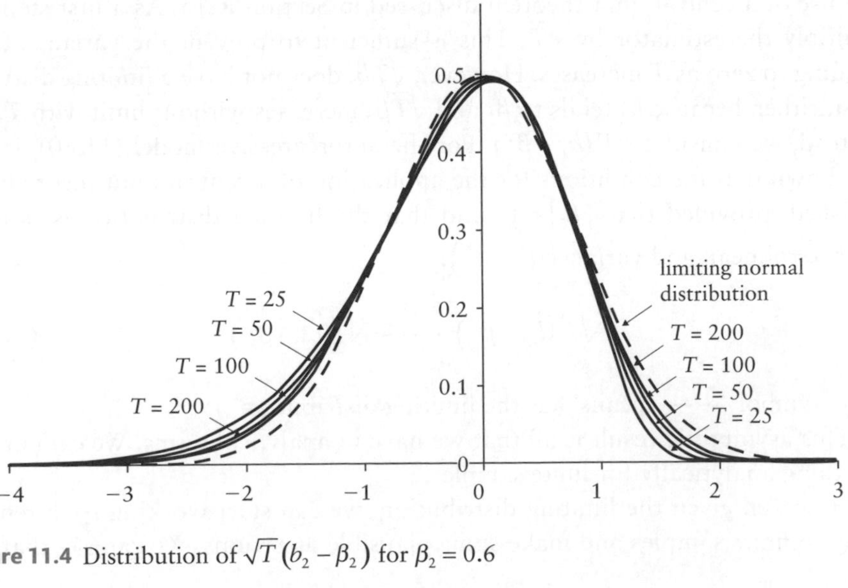

Figure 11.4 Distribution of $\sqrt{T}(b_2 - \beta_2)$ for $\beta_2 = 0.6$

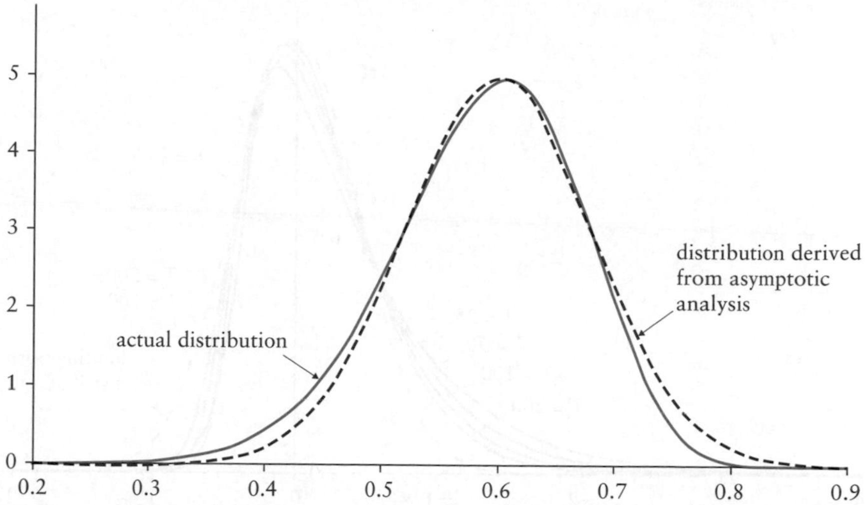

Figure 11.5 Actual and theoretical distributions of the OLS estimator of β_2 when $\beta_2 = 0.6$ and $T = 100$

This is confirmed by Figure 11.5. The figure compares the actual distribution of b_2 for $T = 100$, obtained by simulation, with the theoretical distribution given by (11.66) (still with $\beta_2 = 0.6$). Since $\sqrt{T}\left(b_2 - \beta_2\right)$ is just a linearly scaled function of b_2, the relationship between the actual distribution of b_2 and its theoretical distribution is parallel to that between $\sqrt{T}\left(b_2 - \beta_2\right)$ for $T = 100$ and its limiting normal distribution (11.64).

The finite-sample bias is the stronger, the closer that β_2 is to 1. Figure 11.6 shows the distribution of $\sqrt{T}\left(b_2 - \beta_2\right)$ when $\beta_2 = 0.9$. In this case, it is clear that, even for $T = 200$, the distribution is far from normal. The left tail contracts towards the limiting distribution as the sample size increases, as it did for $\beta_2 = 0.6$, but more slowly. The right tail actually shifts in the wrong direction as the sample size increases from $T = 25$ to $T = 50$. However, it then starts moving back in the direction of the limiting distribution, but there is still a large discrepancy even for $T = 200$.

t tests in an autoregressive model

Figures 11.4–11.6 show that, for finite samples, the tails of the distributions of $\sqrt{T}\left(b_2 - \beta_2\right)$ and b_2 differ markedly from their approximate theoretical distributions, even for $T = 200$, and this can be expected to cause problems for inference. This is indeed the case. We know that inference is asymptotically valid in a model with a lagged dependent variable. However, as always, we have to ask how large the sample should be in practice. We need to consider the effect on Type I error when the null hypothesis is true, and the effect on Type II error when the null hypothesis is false.

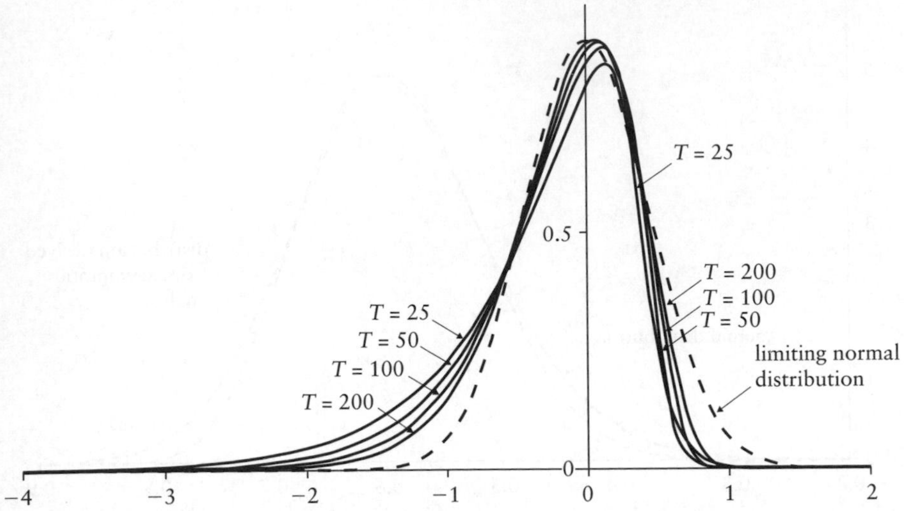

Figure 11.6 Distribution of $\sqrt{T}\,(b_2 - \beta_2)$ for $\beta_2 = 0.9$

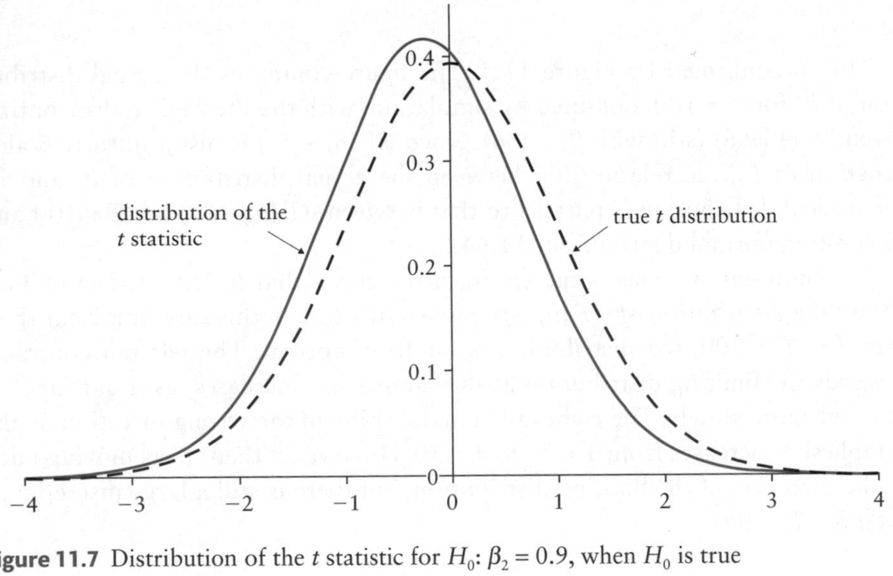

Figure 11.7 Distribution of the t statistic for H_0: $\beta_2 = 0.9$, when H_0 is true

We will start with the effect on Type I error and we again will illustrate the issue with the simple autoregressive model. Figure 11.7 shows the distribution of the t statistic for H_0: $\beta_2 = \beta_2^0$ when H_0 is true, $\beta_2^0 = 0.6$, and T = 100. The distribution is skewed, reflecting the fact that the distribution of b_2 is skewed. Further complexity is attributable to the fact that the standard error is also valid only asymptotically.

According to the tables, for a 5 percent two-sided test, with $T = 100$, the critical values of t are ±1.98. However, in reality the lower 2.5 percent tail of the distribution starts at −2.03 and the upper one at 1.89. This means that, if one uses the critical values from the table, the risk of a Type I error when the null hypothesis is true is greater than 2.5 percent when b_2 is negative and less than 2.5 percent when it is positive. As might be anticipated, the distortions are even worse for $\beta_2 = 0.9$. The true left 2.5 percent tail starts at −2.12 and the upper one starts at 1.75.

The potential effect on Type II error is often of greater practical importance, for normally our null hypothesis is that $\beta_2 = 0$ and if the process is truly autoregressive, the null hypothesis is false. Fortunately, for this null hypothesis, the t test is unlikely to mislead us seriously. If the true value of β_2 is low, the distorting effect of the failure of Assumption C.7 part (2) can be expected to be minor and our conclusions valid, even for finite samples. If the true value of β_2 is large, H_0 is likely to be rejected anyway, even though the t statistic does not have its conventional distribution and the nominal critical values of t are incorrect.

These remarks apply to the pure autoregressive model (11.61). In practice, the model will include other explanatory variables, with unpredictable consequences. The most that one can say is that, if there is a lagged dependent variable in the model, one should expect point estimates, standard errors, and t statistics to be subject to distortion and therefore one should treat them with caution, especially when the sample is small and when there is evidence that β_2 is large.

EXERCISE

11.17 It has been asserted that the distortions caused by the violation of Assumption C.7 part (2) when fitting

$$Y_t = \beta_2 Y_{t-1} + u_t$$

diminish with the size of β_2. Suppose that $\beta_2 = 0$ and you fit this relationship, not knowing that $\beta_2 = 0$. What can be said about (a) the asymptotic properties of b_2, (b) its finite-sample properties? What difference would it make if the true and fitted models included an intercept, again supposing $\beta_2 = 0$?

11.6 Simultaneous equations models

Simultaneous equations estimation is as much a feature of models using time series data as it is of those using cross-sectional data. Perhaps even more so. This is especially true of macroeconomic research, which almost exclusively uses time series data. Ever since its origins in the analysis of business cycles in the 1930s, there has been recognition that the only way to understand variations in economic growth, from boom to recession and back, has been to view the economy as a system of interactive relationships.

Most of the issues are similar to those that arise when using cross-sectional data. One needs to make a distinction between endogenous and exogenous variables, and between structural and reduced form equations, and find valid instruments, when necessary, for the endogenous variables. The main difference is the potential use of lagged endogenous variables as instruments.

We will use a simple macroeconomic model for a closed economy to illustrate the discussion. Private sector consumption, C_t, is determined by income, Y_t. Private sector investment, I_t, is determined by the rate of interest, r_t. Income is defined to be the sum of consumption, investment, and government expenditure, G_t. u_t and v_t are disturbance terms assumed to have zero mean and constant variance. Realistically, since both may be affected by economic sentiment, we should not assume that they are independent.

$$C_t = \beta_1 + \beta_2 Y_t + u_t \tag{11.67}$$

$$I_t = \alpha_1 + \alpha_2 r_t + v_t \tag{11.68}$$

$$Y_t = C_t + I_t + G_t. \tag{11.69}$$

As the model stands, we have three endogenous variables, C_t, I_t, and Y_t, and two exogenous variables, r_t and G_t. The consumption function is overidentified and we would use TSLS. The investment function has no endogenous variables on the right side and so we would use OLS. The third equation is an identity and does not need to be fitted. So far, so good. However, even in the simplest macroeconomic models, it is usually recognized that the rate of interest should not be treated as exogenous. We extend the model to the IS–LM model of conventional introductory macroeconomics by adding a relationship for the demand for money, M_t^d, relating it to income (the transactions demand for cash) and the interest rate (the speculative demand):

$$M_t^d = \gamma_1 + \gamma_2 Y_t + \gamma_3 r_t + w_t. \tag{11.70}$$

We assume that the money market clears with the demand for money equal to the supply, M_t^s, which initially we will assume to be exogenous:

$$M_t^d = M_t^s. \tag{11.71}$$

We now have five endogenous variables (the previous three, plus r_t and M_t^d) and two exogenous variables, G_t and M_t^s. On the face of it, the consumption and investment functions are both overidentified and the demand for money function exactly identified. However, we have hardly started with the development of the model. Government expenditure will be influenced by budgetary policy that takes account of government revenues from taxation. Tax revenues will be influenced by the level of income. The money supply will respond to various pressures, and so on. Ultimately, it has to be acknowledged that *all* important macroeconomic variables are likely to be endogenous and consequently that none is able to act as a valid instrument.

The solution is to take advantage of a feature of time series models that is absent in cross-sectional ones: the inclusion of lagged variables as explanatory variables. Suppose, as seems realistic, the static consumption function is replaced by the ADL(1,0) model

$$C_t = \beta_1 + \beta_2 Y_t + \beta_3 C_{t-1} + u_t. \tag{11.72}$$

C_{t-1} has already been fixed by time t and is described as a predetermined variable. Subject to an important condition, predetermined variables can be treated as exogenous variables at time t and can therefore be used as instruments. Hence, in the investment equation, C_{t-1} could be used as an instrument for r_t. To serve as an instrument, it must be correlated with r_t, but this is assured by the fact that it is a determinant of C_t, and thus Y_t, and so with r_t via the demand for money relationship.

To give another example, many models include the level of the capital stock, K_{t-1}, as a determinant of current investment (usually negatively: the greater the previous stock, the smaller the immediate need for investment, controlling for other factors). So the investment function becomes

$$I_t = \alpha_1 + \alpha_2 r_t + \alpha_3 K_{t-1} + v_t. \tag{11.73}$$

Then, since K_{t-1} is a determinant of I_t, and I_t is a component of Y_t, K_{t-1} can serve as an instrument for Y_t in the consumption function.

On the whole, it is reasonable to expect relationships to be dynamic, rather than static, and that lagged variables will feature among the regressors. Suddenly, a model that lacked valid instruments has become full of them.

It was mentioned above that there is an important condition attached to the use of predetermined variables as instruments. This concerns the properties of the disturbance terms in the model. We will discuss the point in the context of the use of C_{t-1} as an instrument for r_t in the investment equation. For C_{t-1} to be a valid instrument, it must be distributed independently of the disturbance term v_t. We acknowledge that C_{t-1} will be influenced by v_{t-1}. (Considering the interactions between the relationships at time $t-1$, v_{t-1} influences I_{t-1} by definition and hence Y_{t-1} because I_{t-1} is a component of it. Thus v_{t-1} also influences C_{t-1}, by virtue of the consumption function.) Now, the fact that C_{t-1} depends on v_{t-1} does not, in itself, matter. The requirement is that C_{t-1} should be distributed independently of v_t. So, provided that v_t and v_{t-1} are distributed independently of each other, C_{t-1} remains a valid instrument. But suppose that there is time persistence in the values of the disturbance term and v_t is correlated with v_{t-1}. Then C_{t-1} will not be distributed independently of v_t and will not be a valid instrument. We will return to the issue of time persistence in the disturbance term when we discuss autocorrelation (serial correlation) in Chapter 12.

EXERCISE

11.18* A researcher is fitting the following supply and demand model for a certain commodity, using a sample of time series observations:

$$Q_{dt} = \beta_1 + \beta_2 P_t + u_{dt}$$

$$Q_{st} = \alpha_1 + \alpha_2 P_t + u_{st},$$

where Q_{dt} is the amount demanded at time t, Q_{st} is the amount supplied, P_t is the market clearing price, and u_{dt} and u_{st} are disturbance terms that are not necessarily independent of each other. It may be assumed that the market clears and so $Q_{dt} = Q_{st}$. What can be said about the identification of (a) the demand equation, (b) the supply equation?

What difference would it make if supply at time t was determined instead by price at time $t-1$:

$$Q_{st} = \alpha_1 + \alpha_2 P_{t-1} + u_{st}.$$

What difference would it make if it could be assumed that u_{dt} is distributed independently of u_{st}?

11.19 Consider the following simple macroeconomic model:

$$C_t = \beta_1 + \beta_2 Y_t + u_{Ct}$$

$$I_t = \alpha_1 + \alpha_2 \left(Y_t - Y_{t-1}\right) + u_{It}$$

$$Y_t = C_t + I_t,$$

where C_t, I_t and Y_t are aggregate consumption, investment and income and u_{Ct} and u_{It} are disturbance terms. The first relationship is a conventional consumption function. The second relates investment to the change of output from the previous year (this is known as an 'accelerator' model.) The third is an income identity. What can be said about the identification of the relationships in the model?

11.7 Alternative dynamic representations of time series processes

Economy-wide macroeconomic models have always been imposing affairs. The first for the United States, Tinbergen (1939), constructed at a time when basic macroeconomic theory was still in its infancy, had 48 equations. This was nothing by comparison with the monumental structures developed subsequently by the Federal Reserve Bank, some universities, and other institutions, with impressive architecture and detail, painstaking refinement of the data, and the use of sophisticated econometric techniques in their construction. By the early 1950s there was a widespread conviction that, at long last, economic science was about to equip policymakers with the apparatus needed for making a decisive contribution to the rational planning of economic policy. In particular, there was the promise that it would henceforward be possible to avert catastrophes such as the Great Depression of the 1930s that had brought so much unnecessary hardship to so many.

However, when the time came to evaluate the predictive success of these magnificent constructions, there was an unpleasant surprise. The predictions were not obviously superior to those that could be obtained with simpler, even theory-free, methods. In one influential study, Cooper (1972) compared the predictions of six leading quarterly forecasting models of the time with those of a naïve autoregressive model. For a range of macroeconomic time series, he fitted the theory-free autoregressive process

$$Y_t = \theta_0 + \theta_1 Y_{t-1} + \theta_2 Y_{t-2} + \cdots + \theta_p Y_{t-p} + u_t \qquad \textbf{(11.74)}$$

with up to eight lags and showed that its predictive performance was just as good, if not better, than those of the leading major macroeconomic models of the day.

Acknowledgment of the fragility of the existing strategy for making macroeconomic predictions led to a number of developments, two of which will be outlined here in general terms. Some further technical detail will be added in Chapters 12 and 13.

Time series analysis

One reaction was an increase in interest in time series analysis. This is the name given to analysis based on univariate models (one variable model) where the current value of a variable is represented as being determined mainly, sometimes exclusively, by lagged values of itself and stochastic terms, with no theoretical content. (11.74) is a simple example. It had become evident that a successful macroeconomic model would have to capture the dynamics of the relevant variables as well as the behavioral relationships linking them. Time series analysts took this to an extreme, contending that it was sufficient, and best, to focus solely on the dynamics, dispensing with theory altogether.

This view was encouraged by the growing sophistication of time series methods. Time series forecasts already had a long history. From crude beginnings in 'no-change' models, where the predicted value of a series at time $t+1$ was just its value Y_t at time t, and 'same change' models, where the difference from time t to time $t+1$ was assumed to be equal to the difference between time $t-1$ and time t, the discipline had moved on to consider forecasts based on more elaborate procedures for smoothing and extrapolation. One model that appeared to be appropriate in some contexts was the 'exponentially weighted (meaning, geometrically declining) moving average' process

$$Y_t = \lambda Y_{t-1} + \lambda(1-\lambda)Y_{t-2} + \lambda(1-\lambda)^2 Y_{t-3} + \cdots + \varepsilon_t. \qquad \textbf{(11.75)}$$

Note the use of ε_t, rather than the usual u_t, for denoting the disturbance term. From this point onwards we will increasingly encounter disturbance terms that have dynamic structures and it is convenient to have special notation for the basic building block, ε_t, which is defined to be an IID random variable with zero mean. ε_t is often described as an innovation or, alternatively, white noise. Provided that $|\lambda| < 1$, and hence $|1-\lambda| < 1$, (11.75) is capable of a very simple alternative representation. Lagging it by one time period, and multiplying through by $(1-\lambda)$, one has

$$(1-\lambda)Y_{t-1} = \lambda(1-\lambda)Y_{t-2} + \lambda(1-\lambda)^2 Y_{t-3} + \lambda(1-\lambda)^3 Y_{t-4} + \cdots + (1-\lambda)\varepsilon_{t-1}. \quad \textbf{(11.76)}$$

Subtracting this from (11.75), one obtains

$$Y_t = Y_{t-1} + \varepsilon_t - (1-\lambda)\varepsilon_{t-1}. \quad \textbf{(11.77)}$$

The next step is to recognize that this process is a simple special case of the general **autoregressive moving-average process**

$$Y_t = \theta_0 + \theta_1 Y_{t-1} + \theta_2 Y_{t-2} + \cdots + \theta_p Y_{t-p} + \phi_1 \varepsilon_t + \phi_2 \varepsilon_{t-1} + \cdots + \phi_{q+1}\varepsilon_{t-q}. \quad \textbf{(11.78)}$$

'Autoregressive' in this context refers to the fact that Y_t depends on lagged values of itself. 'Moving-average' refers to the fact that the compound disturbance term is a linear combination of current and recent values of the innovations. For short, (11.78) is described as an **ARMA**(p, q) process, p and q referring to the maximum lags of Y and ε.

The critical difference between (11.78) and (11.74) is the inclusion of dynamics in the disturbance term as well as in the variable itself. This allows great flexibility in the representation of a time series, typically with low values of p and q.

As it stands, (11.78) represents a purely descriptive univariate model that is subject to no external factors other than the stochastic process. It can readily be extended to model the effect of external interventions, for example, in the form

$$Y_t = \theta_0 + \theta_1 Y_{t-1} + \beta X_t + \varepsilon_t, \quad \textbf{(11.79)}$$

where X_t is known as a **forcing process**. X may be completely exogenous, or it might be an intervention intended to exert control on Y. Typically, its characterization is mechanistic with known properties. We now have some overlap with conventional econometric models, but this is as far as the time series analyst is prepared to go.

ARMA models may be traced back to 1927 and contributions by Slutsky and Yule (Diebold, 2001), but it was not until they were thoroughly analyzed and developed in the landmark study of Box and Jenkins (1970) that they became prominent in the literature. Box and Jenkins proposed methods for determining p and q and for estimating the θ and ϕ parameters, and they investigated the implications for control. In recognition of their work, the ARMA approach to time series forecasting is often described as the Box–Jenkins method.

Many of the examples in Box and Jenkins (1970) involve aspects of chemical processes. This might be expected, given that Box had spent his early career working as a statistician for a major chemical engineering company. So when Box and Jenkins claimed that their methodology could be useful for forecasting any kind of time series process, their assertion encountered resistance. The stochastic component in chemical processes could be expected to be relatively uncomplicated. That their methodology would also be useful for forecasting economics time series was not self-evident.

Nevertheless, there quickly emerged a substantial time series literature that has left practitioners divided into two opposing camps. Time series analysts assert that, by focusing on dynamics, they produce forecasts at least as good as those of the conventional econometricians, notwithstanding the absence of theory, and that they typically do it with a minimal data burden, since they require data only on the time series being forecasted and not on all the variables that constitute a conventional econometric model.

Despite their very different approach, time series analysts have had a major impact on the methodology of conventional econometricians using time series data. From the start, their focus on representing processes as difference equations led time series analysts to classify processes as stable, explosive, and borderline. As we shall see in Chapter 13, the importance of these distinctions is now recognized by everyone using time series data.

Vector autoregressions

Another response to the predictive failure of conventional multivariate models has been the development of the vector autoregresssion (VAR) approach, dating from the seminal study of Sims (1980). Sims argued that the construction of conventional models had typically proceeded on an intuitive, ad hoc basis. As a consequence, such models incorporated implausible assumptions concerning exogeneity and imposed restrictions of doubtful validity. According to his line of thinking, it would be better to start with the assumption that *all* variables are endogenous. A structural equation for any variable would thus include, as regressors, the current values of all other variables in the system, its own lagged values, and the lagged values of all other variables. To avoid the problem of simultaneous equations bias, one would solve out the current values of the other variables, and would then be left with a reduced form equation in which the current value of the dependent variable would be expressed in terms of the lagged values of itself and the other variables only. This representation is known as the VAR.

As an illustration, suppose that you have a system of just two variables, Y and X, with structural equations

$$Y_t = \beta_1 + \beta_2 Y_{t-1} + \beta_3 X_t + \beta_4 X_{t-1} + u_t \qquad (11.80)$$

$$X_t = \alpha_1 + \alpha_2 X_{t-1} + \alpha_3 Y_t + \alpha_4 Y_{t-1} + v_t. \qquad (11.81)$$

The VAR would then be

$$Y_t = \frac{1}{1-\alpha_3\beta_3}\left(\beta_1 + \alpha_1\beta_3 + [\beta_2 + \alpha_4\beta_3]Y_{t-1} + [\beta_4 + \alpha_2\beta_3]X_{t-1} + u_t + \beta_3 v_t\right) \tag{11.82}$$

$$X_t = \frac{1}{1-\alpha_3\beta_3}\left(\alpha_1 + \alpha_3\beta_1 + [\alpha_2 + \alpha_3\beta_4]X_{t-1} + [\alpha_4 + \alpha_3\beta_2]Y_{t-1} + \alpha_3 u_t + v_t\right) \tag{11.83}$$

or

$$Y_t = \beta_1^* + \beta_2^* Y_{t-1} + \beta_3^* X_{t-1} + u_t^* \tag{11.84}$$

$$X_t = \alpha_1^* + \alpha_2^* X_{t-1} + \alpha_3^* Y_{t-1} + v_t^*, \tag{11.85}$$

where $\beta_1^* = \dfrac{\beta_1 + \alpha_1\beta_3}{1-\alpha_3\beta_3}$, etc.

There are a number of obvious issues:

1. The fact that one has to decide which variables should appear in the VAR means that some subjective judgment is inescapable.
2. There is a need to find some method for determining the appropriate number of lags.
3. There will be an inevitable problem of multicollinearity in estimating the parameters.
4. In general, the model will be underidentified. The VAR equations are, effectively, reduced form equations and it will not be possible to obtain estimates of the structural equations that might be hypothesized to underlie the VAR.
5. One has to be careful about the characterization of the disturbance terms. This will be discussed further in Chapter 12.

With all of these problems, one may wonder why there is so much interest in VARs. However, if the motivation for constructing the VAR is to obtain better forecasts than those provided by conventional models, then the issues of multicollinearity and identification are not relevant. Multicollinearity does not adversely affect the precision of forecasts, for essentially the same reason that it does not adversely affect a test of the joint explanatory power of the affected variables. As for identification, forecasts may be made directly from the VAR equations using the estimates of the β^* and α^* coefficients. There is no need to recover the underlying structural parameters.

Further, if the disturbance terms in the original equations are innovations, and provided that all lagged variables appear in every equation, one may efficiently estimate the VAR equation by equation, using nothing more complicated than OLS.

In a general VAR, the lagged values of every variable in principle affect every variable in the model and there is no discernible structure. However, empirically, it may turn out that some coefficients may not be significantly different from zero, and the imposition of zero restrictions allows some structure to emerge. Granger causality is one such structure. One variable is said to Granger-cause another if its lagged values influence the other variable, controlling for the lagged values of that variable, but the reverse is not the case. In equations (11.84) and (11.85), X is said to Granger-cause Y if α_3^* is not significantly different from zero, while β_3^* is. In that model, there was only one lagged value of either variable, and so a t test would suffice. In models with a greater number of lags, one should use an F test of the joint explanatory power of the lagged values.

The literature on VARs has become very extensive and complex. In the same way that a univariate process may, under certain conditions, be represented as an ARMA process, then, generalizing to vectors, it may be possible to represent a VAR in VARMA (vector autoregressive moving average) form. Similarly, the notion of an error-correction model has been generalized to VECM (vector error correction model) form. A discussion of VARMA and VECM models, like, indeed VARs themselves, requires the use of linear algebra and is therefore beyond the scope of this text.

Diebold (2001) provides a comprehensive general primer on forecasting, covering conventional regression models, time series analysis, and the use of VARs. For macroeconomic forecasting, there is no dominant technique. If there is any consensus, it is that any model needs to be supplemented by out-of-model information for producing forecasts, particularly for predicting turning points. Thus, macroeconomic forecasting remains as much of an art as a science, a conclusion that would surely disappoint the pioneering model builders of half a century ago. Diebold (1998) provides a slickly written account of its evolution after the contributions of Sims.

Key terms

- adaptive expectations model
- ADL(p, q) model
- AR(1) process
- autoregressive distributed lag model
- autoregressive moving-average process
- data generation process (DGP)
- dependence
- grid search
- habit persistence model
- observational equivalence
- parsimonious lag structure
- partial adjustment model
- persistence
- predetermined variable
- short-run effect
- time series analysis
- univariate model
- vector autoregression (VAR)

- innovation
- lag structure
- lagged dependent variable
- white noise
- long-run effect

EXERCISES

11.20 Suppose that X_t in equation (11.79) is a dummy variable that is equal to 0 for $t < t^*$ and 1 for $t \geq t^*$. Show that the impact on Y_{t^*+s} is an increase of $\beta\left(1+\theta_1+\ldots+\theta_1^s\right)$, and hence that the long-run effect is an increase of $\beta/1-\theta_1$.

12. Autocorrelation

12.1 Definition and consequences of autocorrelation

We come now to Assumption C.6, that the value taken by the disturbance term in any observation be determined independently of its values in all the other observations, and hence that $\mathrm{cov}(u_t, u_{t'}) = 0$, for $t' \neq t$. When the condition is not satisfied, the disturbance term is said to be subject to autocorrelation, or serial correlation. The terms are interchangeable.

Autocorrelation normally occurs only in regression analysis using time series data. The disturbance term in a regression equation picks up the influence of those variables affecting the dependent variable that have not been included in the regression equation. If the value of u in any observation is to be independent of its value in the previous one, the value of any variable hidden in u must be uncorrelated with its value at the time of the previous observation.

Persistence of the effects of excluded variables is probably the most frequent cause of positive autocorrelation, the most common type in economic analysis. In Figure 12.1, Y depends on X and a number of minor variables not included explicitly in the specification. The disturbance term in the model is generated by the combined effects of these excluded variables. In the first observation, the excluded variables have a net positive effect and the disturbance term is positive. If the excluded variables change slowly, their positive effect will persist and the disturbance term will remain positive. Eventually the balance will change and the net effect of the excluded variables becomes negative. Now the persistence effect works the other way and the disturbance term remains negative for a few observations. The duration and amplitude of each positive and negative sequence are essentially random, but overall there will be a tendency for positive values of the disturbance term to be followed by positive ones and for negative values to be followed by negative ones.

One important point to note is that autocorrelation is on the whole more likely to be a problem, the shorter the interval between observations. Obviously, the longer the interval, the less likely are the effects of the excluded variables to persist from one observation to the next.

In principle, one may also encounter negative autocorrelation. This occurs when the correlation between successive values of the disturbance term is

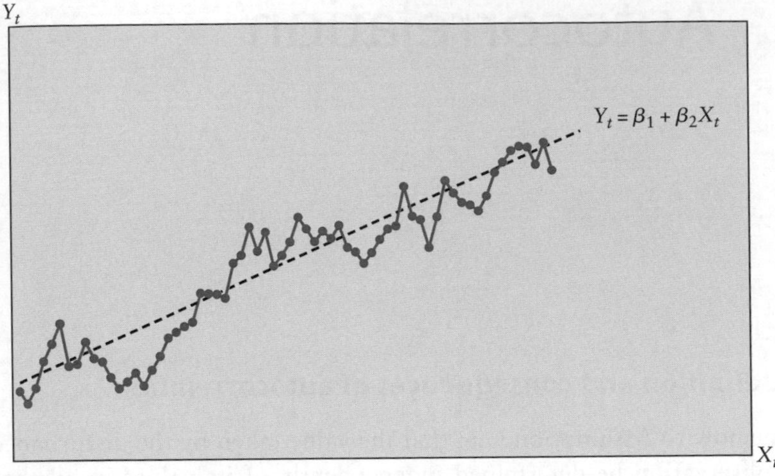

Figure 12.1 Positive autocorrelation

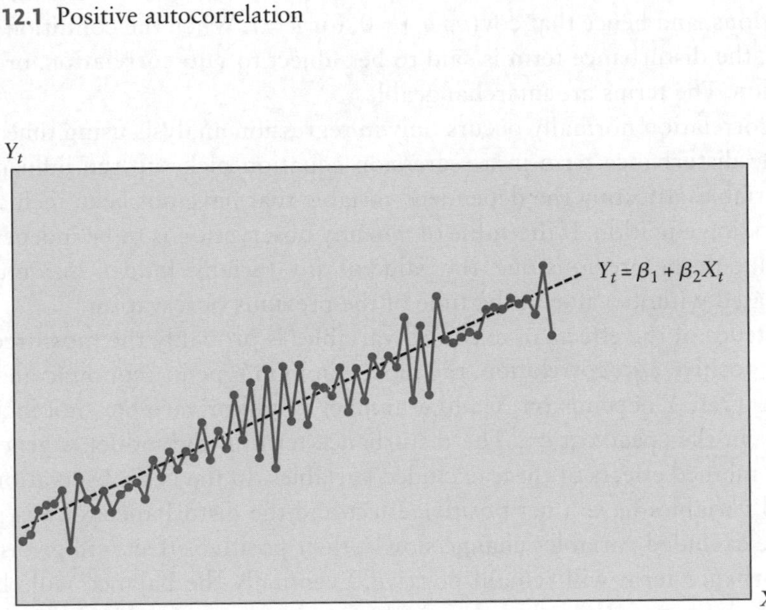

Figure 12.2 Negative autocorrelation

negative. A positive value in one observation is more likely to be followed by a negative value than a positive value in the next, and vice versa, the scatter diagram looking like Figure 12.2. A line joining successive observations to one another would cross the line relating Y to X with greater frequency than one would expect if the values of the disturbance term were independent of each other. Economic examples of negative autocorrelation are relatively uncommon, but sometimes it is induced by manipulations used to transform the original specification of a model into a form suitable for regression analysis.

We will mostly be concerned with first-order autoregressive autocorrelation, often denoted AR(1), where the disturbance term u in the model

$$Y_t = \beta_1 + \beta_2 X_t + u_t \tag{12.1}$$

is generated by the process

$$u_t = \rho u_{t-1} + \varepsilon_t, \tag{12.2}$$

where ε_t is an IID innovation with mean zero. By definition, the value of ε_t in any observation is independent of its value in all the other observations. This type of autocorrelation is described as autoregressive because u_t is being determined by lagged values of itself plus the fresh element of randomness ε_t, sometimes described as an innovation. It is described as first order because u_t depends only on u_{t-1} and the innovation. A process of the type

$$u_t = \rho_1 u_{t-1} + \rho_2 u_{t-2} + \rho_3 u_{t-3} + \rho_4 u_{t-4} + \rho_5 u_{t-5} + \varepsilon_t \tag{12.3}$$

would be described as fifth-order autoregressive autocorrelation, denoted AR(5). The main alternative to autoregressive autocorrelation is moving average autocorrelation, where u_t is determined as a weighted sum of current and previous values of ε_t. For example, the process

$$u_t = \lambda_0 \varepsilon_t + \lambda_1 \varepsilon_{t-1} + \lambda_2 \varepsilon_{t-2} + \lambda_3 \varepsilon_{t-3} \tag{12.4}$$

would be described as MA(3).

We will focus on AR(1) autocorrelation because it appears to be the most common type, at least as an approximation. It is described as positive or negative according to the sign of ρ in (12.2). Figures 12.1 and 12.2 illustrate AR(1) autocorrelation for $\rho = 0.6$ and $\rho = -0.6$, respectively. Note that if $\rho = 0$, there is no autocorrelation after all.

Consequences of autocorrelation

The consequences of autocorrelation for OLS are somewhat similar to those of heteroscedasticity. In general, the regression coefficients remain unbiased, but OLS is inefficient because one can find an alternative regression technique that yields estimators with smaller variances. The other main consequence, which should not be mixed up with the first, is that in the presence of autocorrelation the standard errors are estimated wrongly, often being biased downwards. Finally, although in general autocorrelation does not cause OLS estimates to be biased, there is an important special case where it does.

Unbiasedness is easily demonstrated, provided that Assumption C.7 is satisfied. In the case of the simple regression model

$$Y_t = \beta_1 + \beta_2 X_t + u_t, \tag{12.5}$$

we have seen that the OLS estimator of the slope coefficient can be decomposed as

$$b_2 = \beta_2 + \sum_{t=1}^{T} a_t u_t, \tag{12.6}$$

where

$$a_t = \frac{X_t - \bar{X}}{\sum_{s=1}^{T} (X_s - \bar{X})^2}. \tag{12.7}$$

Now, if Assumption C.7 is satisfied, a_t and u_t are distributed independently and we can write

$$E(b_2) = \beta_2 + E\left(\sum_{t=1}^{T} a_t u_t\right) = \beta_2 + \sum_{t=1}^{T} E(a_t u_t) = \beta_2 + \sum_{t=1}^{T} E(a_t) E(u_t). \tag{12.8}$$

At no point have we made any assumption concerning whether u_t is or is not subject to autocorrelation. All that we now require is $E(u_t) = 0$ and this is easily demonstrated. For example, in the AR(1) case, lagging (12.2) one time period, we have

$$u_{t-1} = \rho u_{t-2} + \varepsilon_{t-1}. \tag{12.9}$$

Substituting for u_{t-1} in (12.2), (12.2) becomes

$$u_t = \rho^2 u_{t-2} + \rho \varepsilon_{t-1} + \varepsilon_t . \tag{12.10}$$

Continuing to lag and substitute, we have

$$u_t = \varepsilon_t + \rho \varepsilon_{t-1} + \rho^2 \varepsilon_{t-2} + \cdots \tag{12.11}$$

Since, by definition, the expected value of each innovation is zero, the expected value of u_t is zero. For higher-order AR autocorrelation, the demonstration is essentially similar. For moving average autocorrelation, the result is immediate.

For multiple regression analysis, the demonstration is the same, except that a_t is replaced by a_t^*, where a_t^* depends on all of the observations on all of the explanatory variables in the model.

We will not pursue analytically the other consequences of autocorrelation. Suffice to mention that the proof of the Gauss–Markov theorem, which guarantees the efficiency of the OLS estimators, does require no autocorrelation, as do the expressions for the standard errors.

Autocorrelation with a lagged dependent variable

If the model specification includes a lagged dependent variable, OLS estimators are biased and inconsistent if the disturbance term is subject to autocorrelation. This will be demonstrated for the AR(1) case. Suppose that, for period t, the relationship is

$$Y_t = \beta_1 + \beta_2 X_t + \beta_3 Y_{t-1} + u_t. \tag{12.12}$$

Then, for period $t - 1$, it is given by

$$Y_{t-1} = \beta_1 + \beta_2 X_{t-1} + \beta_3 Y_{t-2} + u_{t-1}. \tag{12.13}$$

Thus Y_{t-1} depends on u_{t-1}. If there is AR(1) autocorrelation and

$$u_t = \rho u_{t-1} + \varepsilon_t, \tag{12.14}$$

then u_t also depends on u_{t-1}. Hence in (12.12) we then have a violation of part (1) of Assumption C.7. One of the explanatory variables, Y_{t-1}, is partly determined by u_{t-1}, which is also a component of the disturbance term. As a consequence, OLS will yield inconsistent estimates.

EXERCISES

12.1 Consider the model

$$Y_t = \beta_1 + \beta_2 X_t + \beta_3 Y_{t-1} + u_t$$
$$u_t = \rho u_{t-p} + \varepsilon_t,$$

where $p > 1$. What may be said about the properties of the OLS estimators of the parameters of the equation for Y_t?

12.2 Consider the model

$$Y_t = \beta_2 Y_{t-1} + u_t$$
$$u_t = \rho u_{t-1} + \varepsilon_t.$$

Show that plim b_2^{OLS} is given by

$$\text{plim } b_2^{\text{OLS}} = \frac{\beta_2 + \rho}{1 + \beta_2 \rho}.$$

12.2 Detection of autocorrelation

We will initially confine the discussion of the detection of autocorrelation to its most common form, the AR(1) process, and the simple regression model. If the disturbance term follows the AR(1) process, it is reasonable to hypothesize that, as an approximation, the residuals will conform to a similar process:

$$e_t = \rho e_{t-1} + \text{error}. \qquad \textbf{(12.15)}$$

After all, provided that the conditions for the consistency of the OLS estimators are satisfied, as the sample size becomes large, the regression parameters will approach their true values, the location of the regression line will converge on the true relationship, and the residuals will coincide with the values of the disturbance term. Hence, a regression of e_t on e_{t-1} is sufficient, at least in large samples. Of course, there is the issue that, in this regression, e_{t-1} is a lagged dependent variable, but that does not matter in large samples. This is illustrated with the simulation shown in Figure 12.3. The true model is

$$Y_t = 10 + 2.0t + u_t, \qquad \textbf{(12.16)}$$

with u_t being generated as an AR(1) process with $\rho = 0.7$. The values of the parameters in (12.16) make no difference to the distributions of the estimator of ρ in Figure 12.3. As can be seen, when (12.15) is fitted, the distribution of the estimator is left skewed and heavily biased downwards for $T = 25$. The mean of the distribution is 0.47. However, as the sample size increases, the downwards bias diminishes and it is clear that it is converging on 0.7 as the sample becomes large. Inference in finite samples will be approximate, given the autoregressive nature of (12.15).

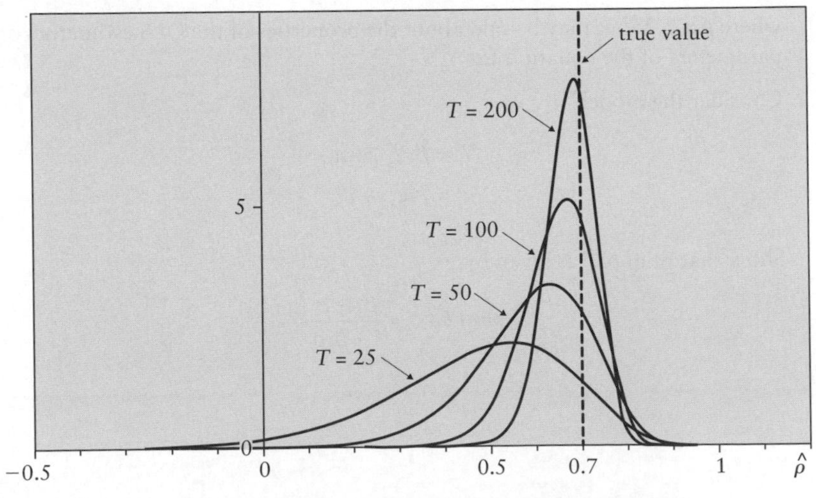

Figure 12.3 Distribution of the estimator of ρ, $T = 25$, 50, 100, and 200

The Breusch–Godfrey test

The simple estimator of the autocorrelation coefficient depends on Assumption C.7 part (2) being satisfied when (12.16) is fitted. Generally, one might expect this not to be the case. If the model contains a lagged dependent variable as a regressor, or violates Assumption C.7 part (2) in any other way, the estimates of the parameters will be inconsistent if the disturbance term is subject to autocorrelation. As a repercussion, (12.15) will produce an inconsistent estimate of ρ. The solution is to include all of the explanatory variables in the original model in the residuals autoregression. If the original model is

$$Y_t = \beta_1 + \sum_{j=2}^{k} \beta_j X_{jt} + u_t, \qquad \textbf{(12.17)}$$

where, say, one of the X variables is Y_{t-1}, then the residuals regression would be

$$e_t = \gamma_1 + \sum_{j=2}^{k} \gamma_j X_{jt} + \rho e_{t-1}. \qquad \textbf{(12.18)}$$

The idea is that, by including the variables, one is controlling for the effects of any endogeneity on the residuals. The underlying theory is complex and relates to maximum likelihood estimation, as does the test statistic. The original version of the test was proposed by Durbin (1970). In its present form, it is now known as the Breusch–Godfrey test. Various asymptotically equivalent tests have been proposed. The most popular involves the computation of the lagrange multiplier statistic nR^2 when (12.18) is fitted, n being the actual number of observations in the regression. Asymptotically, this is distributed as a chi-squared statistic with one degree of freedom. A simple t test on the coefficient of e_{t-1} has also been proposed, again with asymptotic validity.

The procedure can be extended to test for higher-order autocorrelation. If AR(q) autocorrelation is suspected, the residuals regression becomes

$$e_t = \gamma_1 + \sum_{j=2}^{k} \gamma_j X_{jt} + \sum_{s=1}^{q} \rho_s e_{t-s}. \qquad \textbf{(12.19)}$$

For the lagrange multiplier version of the test, the test statistic remains nR^2 (with n smaller than before, the inclusion of the additional lagged residuals leading to a further loss of initial observations). Under the null hypothesis of no autocorrelation, it has a chi-squared distribution with q degrees of freedom. The t test version becomes an F test comparing RSS for (12.19) with RSS for the same specification without the residual terms. Again, the test is valid only asymptotically. The lagrange multiplier version of the test has been shown to be asymptotically valid for the case of MA(q) moving average autocorrelation.

The Durbin–Watson test

The first major test to be developed and popularized for the detection of autocorrelation was the **Durbin–Watson test** for AR(1) autocorrelation (Durbin and Watson, 1950) based on the **Durbin–Watson *d* statistic** calculated from the residuals using the expression

$$d = \frac{\sum_{t=2}^{T}(e_t - e_{t-1})^2}{\sum_{t=1}^{T} e_t^2}. \tag{12.20}$$

It can be shown (see Appendix 12.1) that in large samples

$$d \rightarrow 2 - 2\rho. \tag{12.21}$$

Thus, if there is no autocorrelation present, $\rho = 0$ and d should be close to 2. If there is positive autocorrelation, d should be less than 2. If there is negative autocorrelation, it should be greater than 2. The Durbin–Watson test assumes that ρ lies in the interval $-1 < \rho < 1$ and hence that d lies between 4 and 0.

The null hypothesis for the test is that $\rho = 0$. Of course, even if H_0 is true, d will not be exactly equal to 2, except by freak chance. However, a value of d much lower than 2 leaves you with two choices. One is to assume that H_0 is true and that the low value of d has arisen as a matter of chance. The other is that the disturbance term is subject to positive autocorrelation. As usual, the choice is made by establishing a critical value d_{crit} below which d would not sink, say, more than 5 percent of the time. If d were below d_{crit}, you would then reject H_0 at the 5 percent significance level.

The critical value of d at any significance level depends, as might be expected, on the number of explanatory variables in the regression equation and the number of observations in the sample. A complication arises from the fact that the critical value also depends on the particular values taken by the explanatory variables. Thus, it is not possible to construct a table giving the exact critical values for all possible samples, as one can with the t test and the F test. However, it is possible to calculate upper and lower *limits* for the critical value of d. Those for positive autocorrelation are usually denoted d_U and d_L. Figure 12.4

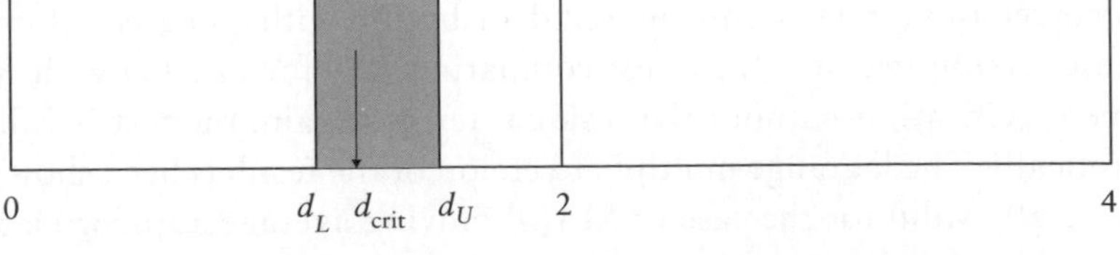

Figure 12.4 Durbin–Watson test for autocorrelation, showing the zone of indeterminacy in the case of suspected positive autocorrelation

represents the situation schematically, with the arrow indicating the critical level of d, which will be denoted d_{crit}.

There are three possible outcomes for the test:

1. d is less than d_L. In this case, it must be lower than d_{crit}, so you would reject the null hypothesis and conclude that positive autocorrelation is present.
2. d is greater than d_U. In this case, d must be greater than d_{crit}, so you would fail to reject the null hypothesis.
3. d lies between d_L and d_U. In this case, d might be greater or less than d_{crit}. The outcome is indeterminate.

Table A.5 at the end of this text gives d_L and d_U cross-classified by number of explanatory variables and number of observations, for the 5 percent and 1 percent significance levels, for the case of positive AR(1) autocorrelation. The zone of indecision between d_L and d_U decreases as the sample size increases.

Testing for negative autocorrelation follows a similar pattern, with the zone containing the critical value symmetrically located to the right of 2. Since negative autocorrelation is relatively uncommon, you are expected to calculate the limits of the zone yourself from the figures for positive autocorrelation for the corresponding number of explanatory variables and number of observations. This is easy enough to do. As is illustrated in Figure 12.5, $4 - d_U$ gives the lower limit, below which you fail to reject the null hypothesis of no autocorrelation, and $4 - d_L$ gives the upper one, above which you conclude that there is evidence of negative autocorrelation.

The Durbin-Watson test is valid only when all the explanatory variables are deterministic. This is in practice a serious limitation since usually interactions and dynamics in a system of equations cause Assumption C.7 part (2) to be violated. In particular, if the lagged dependent variable is used as a regressor, the statistic is biased towards 2 and therefore will tend to under-reject the null hypothesis. It is also restricted to testing for AR(1) autocorrelation. Despite these shortcomings, it remains a popular test and some major applications produce the d statistic automatically as part of the standard regression output. It does have the appeal of being computable directly from the regression output

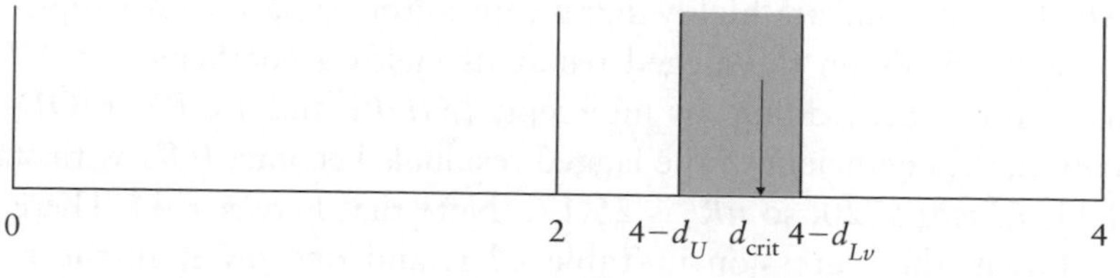

Figure 12.5 Durbin–Watson test for autocorrelation, showing the zone of indeterminacy in the case of suspected negative autocorrelation

and of being appropriate for finite samples, subject to the zone of indeterminacy and the deterministic regressor requirement.

Durbin's *h* test

Durbin (1970) proposed two tests for the case where the use of the lagged dependent variable as a regressor made the original Durbin–Watson test inapplicable. One was the precursor to the Breusch–Godrey test. The other was the Durbin *h* test, appropriate for the detection of AR(1) autocorrelation. The Durbin *h* statistic is defined as

$$h = \hat{\rho}\sqrt{\frac{n}{1 - ns^2_{b_{Y(-1)}}}}, \tag{12.22}$$

where $\hat{\rho}$ is an estimate of ρ in the AR(1) process, $s^2_{b_{Y(-1)}}$ is an estimate of the variance of the coefficient of the lagged dependent variable, and n is the number of observations in the regression. There are various ways in which one might estimate ρ but, since this test is valid only for large samples, it does not matter which is used. The most convenient is to take advantage of the large-sample relationship between d and ρ:

$$d \to 2 - 2\rho. \tag{12.23}$$

From d, an estimate of ρ is obtained as $(1 - ½d)$. The estimate of the variance of the coefficient of the lagged dependent variable is obtained by squaring its standard error. Thus h can be calculated from the usual regression results. In large samples, under the null hypothesis of no autocorrelation, h is distributed as a normal variable with zero mean and unit variance.

An occasional problem with this test is that the h statistic cannot be computed if $ns^2_{b_{Y(-1)}}$ is greater than 1, which can happen if the sample size is not very large. An even worse problem occurs when $ns^2_{b_{Y(-1)}}$ is near to, but less than, 1. In such a situation, the h statistic could be enormous, without there being any problem of autocorrelation.

Examples

The output shown in Table 12.1 gives the result of a logarithmic regression of expenditure on food on disposable personal income and the relative price of food. All the tests indicate highly significant autocorrelation. A simple regression of the residuals on the lagged residuals yields a coefficient of 0.79 with standard error 0.11. Adding an intercept, *LGDPI* and *LGPRFOOD* to the specification, the coefficient of the lagged residuals becomes 0.81 with standard error 0.11. R^2 is 0.5720, so nR^2 is 25.17. (Note that here $n = 44$. There are 45 observations in the regression in Table 12.1, and one fewer in the residuals regression.) The critical value of chi-squared with one degree of freedom at the 0.1 percent level is 10.83. The Durbin–Watson statistic is 0.48. d_L is 1.24 for a 1

Table 12.1

Dependent Variable: LGFOOD
Method: Least Squares
Sample: 1959 2003
Included observations: 45

Variable	Coefficient	Std. Error	t-Statistic	Prob.
C	2.236158	0.388193	5.760428	0.0000
LGDPI	0.500184	0.008793	56.88557	0.0000
LGPRFOOD	-0.074681	0.072864	-1.024941	0.3113

R-squared	0.992009	Mean dependent var	6.021331
Adjusted R-squared	0.991628	S.D. dependent var	0.222787
S.E. of regression	0.020384	Akaike info criter	-4.883747
Sum squared resid	0.017452	Schwarz criterion	-4.763303
Log likelihood	112.8843	Hannan-Quinn crite	-4.838846
F-statistic	2606.860	Durbin-Watson stat	0.478540
Prob(F-statistic)	0.000000		

Table 12.2

Dependent Variable: LGFOOD
Method: Least Squares
Sample (adjusted): 1960 2003
Included observations: 44 after adjustments

Variable	Coefficient	Std. Error	t-Statistic	Prob.
C	0.985780	0.336094	2.933054	0.0055
LGDPI	0.126657	0.056496	2.241872	0.0306
LGPRFOOD	-0.088073	0.051897	-1.697061	0.0975
LGFOOD(-1)	0.732923	0.110178	6.652153	0.0000

R-squared	0.995879	Mean dependent var	6.030691
Adjusted R-squared	0.995570	S.D. dependent var	0.216227
S.E. of regression	0.014392	Akaike info criter	-5.557847
Sum squared resid	0.008285	Schwarz criterion	-5.395648
Log likelihood	126.2726	Hannan-Quinn crite	-5.497696
F-statistic	3222.264	Durbin-Watson stat	1.112437
Prob(F-statistic)	0.000000		

percent significance test (2 explanatory variables, 45 observations). Adding the residual lagged two periods to the residuals regression makes very little difference to the results.

Table 12.2 gives the result of a parallel logarithmic regression with the addition of lagged expenditure on food as an explanatory variable. Again, there is strong evidence that the specification is subject to autocorrelation. A simple regression of the residuals on the lagged residuals yields a coefficient of 0.43 with standard error 0.14. With an intercept, *LGDPI*, *LGPRFOOD*, and *LGFOOD(–1)* added to the specification, the coefficient of the lagged residuals becomes 0.60 with standard error 0.17. R^2 is 0.2469, so nR^2 is 10.62, not quite significant at the 1 percent level. (Note that here $n = 43$.) The Durbin–Watson statistic is 1.11. From this one obtains an estimate of ρ as $1 - \frac{1}{2}d = 0.445$. The standard error of the coefficient of the lagged dependent variable is 0.1102. Hence the h statistic is

$$h = \hat{\rho}\sqrt{\frac{n}{1 - ns^2_{b_{Y(-1)}}}} = 0.445\sqrt{\frac{44}{1 - 44(0.1102)^2}} = 4.33. \quad (12.24)$$

Under the null hypothesis of no autocorrelation, the h statistic has a standardized normal distribution, so this value is above the critical value at the 0.1 percent level, 3.29. As might be expected, adding the residual lagged two periods to the residuals regression makes very little difference to the results.

EXERCISES

12.3 Perform the Breusch–Godfrey and Durbin–Watson tests for autocorrelation for the logarithmic demand function that you fitted in Exercise 11.4. Is there evidence of autocorrelation? If so, what are the implications for the statistical tests you performed?

12.4 If your regression application allows you to graph or print the residuals from a regression, do this in the case of your logarithmic demand function. Does an inspection of the residuals corroborate the presence (or absence) of autocorrelation found in Exercise 12.3?

12.3 Fitting a model subject to AR(1) autocorrelation

For treating autocorrelation, we will consider only the AR(1) case. This is sufficient for illustrating the most important issues. The AR(1) case has received the most attention in the literature because it appears to be the most common form of autocorrelation, persistence in the constituents of the disturbance term giving rise to it in many situations, and there is generally insufficient evidence to make it worthwhile considering more complicated models. If the observations are taken quarterly or monthly, however, other models may be more suitable, but we will not investigate them here.

AR(1) autocorrelation can be eliminated by a simple manipulation of the model. Suppose that the model is

$$Y_t = \beta_1 + \beta_2 X_t + u_t, \quad (12.25)$$

with u_t generated by the process

$$u_t = \rho u_{t-1} + \varepsilon_t. \tag{12.26}$$

If we lag equation (12.25) by one time period and multiply by ρ, we have

$$\rho Y_{t-1} = \beta_1 \rho + \beta_2 \rho X_{t-1} + \rho u_{t-1}. \tag{12.27}$$

Subtract (12.27) from (12.25):

$$Y_t - \rho Y_{t-1} = \beta_1(1-\rho) + \beta_2 X_t - \beta_2 \rho X_{t-1} + u_t - \rho u_{t-1}. \tag{12.28}$$

Hence,

$$Y_t = \beta_1(1-\rho) + \rho Y_{t-1} + \beta_2 X_t - \beta_2 \rho X_{t-1} + \varepsilon_t. \tag{12.29}$$

The model is now free from autocorrelation because the disturbance term has been reduced to the innovation ε_t. In the case of the more general multiple regression model

$$Y_t = \beta_1 + \beta_2 X_{2t} + \cdots + \beta_k X_{kt} + u_t, \tag{12.30}$$

with u_t following an AR(1) process, we follow the same procedure. We lag the equation and multiply it by ρ:

$$\rho Y_{t-1} = \beta_1 \rho + \beta_2 \rho X_{2,t-1} + \cdots + \beta_k \rho X_{k,t-1} + \rho u_{t-1}. \tag{12.31}$$

Subtracting (12.31) from (12.30) and rearranging, we again derive a model free from autocorrelation:

$$\begin{aligned} Y_t = {} & \beta_1(1-\rho) + \rho Y_{t-1} + \beta_2 X_{2t} - \beta_2 \rho X_{2,t-1} + \cdots \\ & + \beta_k X_{kt} - \beta_k \rho X_{k,t-1} + \varepsilon_t. \end{aligned} \tag{12.32}$$

Issues

There are a number of issues relating to the fitting of specifications such as (12.32).

1. The model incorporates the nonlinear restriction that the coefficient of the lagged value of each X variable is equal to minus the product of the coefficients of its current value and Y_{t-1}. This means that if OLS were used to fit it, there would be no guarantee that the coefficients would conform to the theoretical restrictions in finite samples. Thus, one has to use some nonlinear estimation procedure instead. The most common are nonlinear least squares, on the lines discussed in Chapter 4, and maximum likelihood estimation. Neither of these purports to yield unbiased estimates and inference is valid only asymptotically.
2. The restrictions should be tested. If they are not rejected, this will encourage us to believe that the model is an adequate representation of the data. If they are rejected, of course, the model is inadequate and needs to be improved. We will discuss the common factor test later in this section.

3. The model includes the lagged dependent variable as a regressor and so part (2) of Assumption C.7 is violated. The consequences are the same as for the first issue.
4. The inclusion of the lagged variables as regressors may give rise to an element of multicollinearity, although this may be mitigated if the estimation technique imposes the restrictions.
5. The lagged variables are not defined for the first observation in the sample, so the first observation is lost.

The last issue can be countered by the **Prais–Winsten correction**, in which the untransformed first observation is included in the sample when estimating the parameters:

$$Y_1 = \beta_1 + \beta_2 X_1 + u_1. \tag{12.33}$$

The disturbance term u_1 will be distributed independently of the disturbance terms in the other observations, $\varepsilon_2, \ldots, \varepsilon_T$, since they are generated randomly after the first period. However, the inclusion of the first observation gives rise to a problem of heteroscedasticity, since (12.26) implies that

$$\sigma_u^2 = \frac{1}{1-\rho^2}\sigma_\varepsilon^2, \tag{12.34}$$

where σ_u^2 and σ_ε^2 are the variances of u and ε. The heteroscedasticity may be eliminated by weighting the first observation by $\sqrt{1-\rho^2}$. The proofs of (12.34) and this assertion are left as an exercise.

As a consequence of issues (1), (3), and (4), it is not always clear that fitting (12.32) will yield results that are preferable to the original OLS specification subject to autocorrelation, especially if the autocorrelation is weak. An early Monte Carlo simulation (Park and Mitchell, 1980) suggested that, using the mean square error as the criterion, the distributions of the OLS point estimates were not seriously inferior to those obtained by Prais–Winsten or similar techniques, even for ρ as high as 0.8, if the data were strongly trended. However, inference was adversely affected since OLS tended to underestimate standard errors. If the data were not trended, the advantage of using other techniques was more obvious.

Inference

As in the case of heteroscedasticity, robust standard errors are available for use with OLS, the **Newey–West standard errors** being the most popular. As in the case of heteroscedasticity, the standard errors are valid only asymptotically.

Example

Tables 12.3 and 12.4 show the results of a logarithmic regression of housing services on disposable personal income and the relative price of housing

Table 12.3

```
Dependent Variable: LGHOUS
Method: Least Squares
Sample (adjusted): 1960 2003
Included observations: 44 after adjusting endpoints
Convergence achieved after 12 iterations
LGHOUS=C(1)*(1-C(2))+C(2)*LGHOUS(-1)+C(3)*LGDPI-C(2)*C(3)
      *LGDPI(-1)+C(4)*LGPRHOUS-C(2)*C(4)*LGPRHOUS(-1)
```

	Coefficient	Std. Error	t-Statistic	Prob.
C(1)	0.154815	0.354990	0.436111	0.6651
C(2)	0.719102	0.115689	6.215838	0.0000
C(3)	1.011295	0.021830	46.32636	0.0000
C(4)	-0.478070	0.091594	-5.219434	0.0000

R-squared	0.999205	Mean dependent var	6.379059
Adjusted R-squared	0.999145	S.D. dependent var	0.421861
S.E. of regression	0.012333	Akaike info criter	-5.866567
Sum squared resid	0.006084	Schwarz criterion	-5.704368
Log likelihood	133.0645	Durbin-Watson stat	1.901082

Table 12.4

```
Dependent Variable: LGHOUS
Method: Least Squares
Sample (adjusted): 1960 2003
Included observations: 44 after adjusting endpoints
Convergence achieved after 9 iterations
```

Variable	Coefficient	Std. Error	t-Statistic	Prob.
C	0.154815	0.354989	0.436111	0.6651
LGDPI	1.011295	0.021830	46.32642	0.0000
LGPRHOUS	-0.478070	0.091594	-5.219437	0.0000
AR(1)	0.719102	0.115689	6.215836	0.0000

R-squared	0.999205	Mean dependent var	6.379059
Adjusted R-squared	0.999145	S.D. dependent var	0.421861
S.E. of regression	0.012333	Akaike info criter	-5.866567
Sum squared resid	0.006084	Schwarz criterion	-5.704368
Log likelihood	133.0645	F-statistic	16757.24
Durbin-Watson stat	1.901081	Prob(F-statistic)	0.00000
Inverted AR Roots	.72		

services, using the nonlinear specification represented by equation (12.32). The model is

$$\begin{aligned} LGHOUS_t = {} & \beta_1(1-\rho) + \rho LGHOUS_{t-1} + \beta_2 LGDPI_t - \beta_2\rho LGDPI_{t-1} \\ & + \beta_3 LGPRHOUS_t - \beta_3\rho LGPRHOUS_{t-1} + \varepsilon_t. \end{aligned} \quad \textbf{(12.35)}$$

In Table 12.3, the regression model has been fitted using the nonlinear estimation facility that is a feature of EViews. This involves specifying the relationship in equation form, with C(1), C(2),... being the constants. Here C(1), C(2), C(3), and C(4) refer to β_1, ρ, β_2, and β_3, respectively. The fitted equation is therefore

$$\begin{aligned}\widehat{LGHOUS} &= C(1)[1 - C(2)] + C(2)LGHOUS(-1)\\ &\quad + C(3)LGDPI - C(2)C(3)LGDPI(-1)\\ &\quad + C(4)LGPRHOUS - C(2)C(4)LGPRHOUS(-1). \qquad \textbf{(12.36)}\end{aligned}$$

The estimate of ρ is high, 0.72, suggesting that there was severe autocorrelation in the original specification. The estimates of the income and price elasticities are similar to those in the OLS regression. This is what we would expect. Autocorrelation does not cause OLS estimates to be biased, but the AR(1) estimates will in principle be more efficient and therefore should tend to be more accurate.

We have noted that most regression applications designed for time series analysis include the Durbin–Watson statistic as a standard component of the output. In the same way, they usually have a built-in option for fitting models where the disturbance term has an AR(1) specification, making it in fact unnecessary to use a nonlinear equation such as (12.36) to spell out the structure of the model. In the case of EViews, adding AR(1) to the list of regressors converts the specification from OLS to that appropriate for AR(1) autocorrelation. This short-cut is welcome because it is often time-consuming to specify the model in equation form and easy to make mistakes.

The output for the logarithmic demand function for housing using the AR(1) short-cut is shown in Table 12.4. You can see that the regression results are identical to those for the explicit nonlinear specification. Note that the coefficient of AR(1) is the estimate of ρ, the coefficient of the lagged dependent variable, and corresponds to C(2) in the previous regression.

The coefficients of the lagged explanatory variables are not reported. If for some reason you need them, you could calculate them easily yourself, as minus the product of the coefficient of Y_{t-1} and the coefficients of the corresponding current explanatory variables. The fact that the lagged variables, other than Y_{t-1}, do not appear explicitly in the regression output does not mean that they have not been included.

Early regression applications tended to use the Cochrane–Orcutt iterative procedure described in Box 12.1. It effectively enables the nonlinear AR(1) model to be fitted using linear regression analysis, a major benefit when computers were still in their infancy and nonlinear estimation was so time-consuming that it was avoided if possible. Now that nonlinear regression is a standard feature of major regression applications, the Cochrane–Orcutt iterative procedure is mainly of historical interest and most applications designed for time series analysis offer alternative methods.

BOX 12.1 The Cochrane-Orcutt iterative procedure for eliminating AR(1) autocorrelation

The starting point for the Cochrane–Orcutt iterative procedure is equation (12.28), which may be rewritten

$$\tilde{Y}_t = \beta_1' + \beta_2 \tilde{X}_t + \varepsilon_t,$$

where $\tilde{Y}_t = Y_t - \rho Y_{t-1}$, $\tilde{X}_t = X_t - \rho X_{t-1}$, and $\beta_1' = \beta_1(1-\rho)$. If the value of ρ were known, $\tilde{Y}_t$ and $\tilde{X}_t$ could be constructed from the data on Y and X, and a simple regression of $\tilde{Y}_t$ on $\tilde{X}_t$ could be performed. The coefficient of $\tilde{X}_t$ would be a direct estimate of β_2, and the intercept could be used to derive an estimate of β_1. Of course, ρ is not known and has to be estimated, along with the other parameters of the model. The Cochrane–Orcutt iterative procedure does this by assuming that if the disturbance term follows an AR(1) process, the residuals will do so as well (approximately), and hence a regression of e_t on e_{t-1} will yield an estimate of ρ. The procedure involves the following steps:

1. Y is regressed on X with the original, untransformed data.
2. The residuals are calculated.
3. e_t is regressed on e_{t-1} to obtain an estimate of ρ.
4. $\tilde{Y}_t$ and $\tilde{X}_t$ are calculated using this estimate of ρ and the equation at the top of the box is fitted. The coefficient of $\tilde{X}_t$ provides a revised estimate of β_2 and the estimate of β_1' yields a revised estimate of β_1.
5. The residuals are recalculated and the process returns to step 3.

The process alternates between revising the estimates of β_1 and β_2, and revising the estimate of ρ, until convergence is obtained, that is, until the estimates at the end of the latest cycle are the same as the estimates at the end of the previous one, to a pre-specified number of decimal places.

The common factor test

We have seen that, in a simple regression of Y_t on X_t, AR(1) autocorrelation in the disturbance term may be eliminated by respecifying the model as

$$Y_t = \beta_1(1-\rho) + \rho Y_{t-1} + \beta_2 X_t - \beta_2 \rho X_{t-1} + \varepsilon_t. \quad \textbf{(12.37)}$$

This is a restricted version of the more general ADL(1,1) model (autoregressive distributed lag, the first argument referring to the maximum lag in the Y variable and the second to the maximum lag in the X variable(s))

$$Y_t = \lambda_1 + \lambda_2 Y_{t-1} + \lambda_3 X_t + \lambda_4 X_{t-1} + \varepsilon_t, \quad \textbf{(12.38)}$$

with the restriction

$$\lambda_4 = -\lambda_2 \lambda_3. \quad \textbf{(12.39)}$$

The presence of this implicit restriction provides us with an opportunity to perform a test of the validity of the model specification known as the common factor test. The theory behind the test procedure will not be presented here (for a summary, see Hendry and Mizon, 1978), but the usual F test of a restriction is not appropriate because the restriction is nonlinear. Instead we calculate the statistic

$$n \log(RSS_R / RSS_U), \tag{12.40}$$

where RSS_R and RSS_U are the residual sums of squares from the restricted model (12.37) and the unrestricted model (12.38), and the logarithm is, as always, to base e. n, the number of observations in the regression, will be one less than the number of observations in the sample because the first observation is lost when (12.37) and (12.38) are fitted. Strictly speaking, this is a large-sample test. If the original model has only one explanatory variable, as in this case, the test statistic has a chi-squared distribution with one degree of freedom under the null hypothesis that the restriction is valid.

If we had started with the more general model

$$Y_t = \beta_1 + \beta_2 X_{2t} + \cdots + \beta_k X_{kt} + u_t, \tag{12.41}$$

the restricted model would have been

$$Y_t = \beta_1(1 - \rho) + \rho Y_{t-1} + \beta_2 X_{2t} - \beta_2 \rho X_{2,t-1} + \cdots + \beta_k X_{kt} - \beta_k \rho X_{k,t-1} + \varepsilon_t. \tag{12.42}$$

There are now $k - 1$ restrictions because the model imposes the restriction that the coefficient of the lagged value of each explanatory variable is equal to minus the coefficient of its current value multiplied by the coefficient of the lagged dependent variable Y_{t-1}. Under the null hypothesis that the restrictions are valid, the test statistic has a chi-squared distribution with $k - 1$ degrees of freedom.

If the null hypothesis is not rejected, we conclude that the AR(1) model is an adequate specification of the data. If it is rejected, we have to work with the unrestricted ADL(1,1) model

$$Y_t = \lambda_1 + \lambda_2 Y_{t-1} + \lambda_3 X_{2t} + \lambda_4 X_{2,t-1} + \cdots + \lambda_{2k-1} X_{kt} + \lambda_{2k} X_{k,t-1} + \varepsilon_t, \tag{12.43}$$

including the lagged value of Y and the lagged values of all the explanatory variables as regressors. The problem of multicollinearity will often be encountered when fitting the unrestricted model, especially if there are several explanatory variables. Sometimes it can be alleviated by dropping those variables that do not have significant coefficients, but precisely because multicollinearity causes t statistics to be low, there is a risk that you will end up dropping variables that do genuinely belong in the model.

There is an interpretational implication of the test. The coefficient of Y_{t-1} may be interpreted as an estimate of ρ if the null hypothesis is not rejected. If it is rejected, the whole of the AR(1) story is abandoned and the coefficient of Y_{t-1} in the unrestricted version does not have any special interpretation.

Example

The output for the AR(1) regression for housing services has been shown in Table 12.4. The residual sum of squares was 0.006084. The unrestricted version of the model yields the output shown in Table 12.5.

Before we perform the common factor test, we should check that the unrestricted model is free from autocorrelation. Otherwise neither it nor the AR(1) model would be satisfactory specifications. R^2 for the residuals regression is 0.0077 and so nR^2 is 0.33, not remotely significant. Durbin's h statistic is given by

$$h = 0.1182 \times \sqrt{\frac{44}{1 - 44 \times (0.0585)^2}} = 0.85. \tag{12.44}$$

This is below 1.96 and so, for this test also, we do not reject the null hypothesis of no autocorrelation.

Next we will check whether the coefficients appear to satisfy the restrictions implicit in the AR(1) model. Minus the product of the lagged dependent variable and the income elasticity is $-0.7259 \times 0.2755 = -0.20$. The coefficient of lagged income is numerically much lower than this. Minus the product of the lagged dependent variable and the price elasticity is $-0.7259 \times -0.2291 = 0.17$, which is a little higher than the coefficient of lagged price. Hence, the restriction for the price side of the model appears to be nearly satisfied, but that for the income side does not.

The common factor test confirms this preliminary observation. The residual sum of squares has fallen to 0.001456. The test statistic is 44 log(0.006084/0.001456) = 62.92. The critical value of chi-squared at the 0.1 percent level with two degrees of freedom is 13.82, so we reject the restrictions

Table 12.5

Dependent Variable: LGHOUS
Method: Least Squares
Sample (adjusted): 1960 2003
Included observations: 44 after adjusting endpoints

Variable	Coefficient	Std. Error	t-Statistic	Prob.
C(1)	0.041458	0.065137	0.636465	0.5283
LGDPI	0.275527	0.067914	4.056970	0.0002
LGPRHOUS	-0.229086	0.075499	-3.034269	0.0043
LGHOUS (-1)	0.725893	0.058485	12.41159	0.0000
LGDPI (-1)	-0.010625	0.086737	-0.122502	0.9031
LGPRHOUS (-1)	0.126270	0.084296	1.497928	0.1424

R-squared	0.999810	Mean dependent var	6.379059
Adjusted R-squared	0.999785	S.D. dependent var	0.421861
S.E. of regression	0.006189	Akaike info criter	-7.205830
Sum squared resid	0.001456	Schwarz criterion	-6.962531
Log likelihood	164.5282	F-statistic	39944.40
Durbin-Watson stat	1.763676	Prob(F-statistic)	0.000000

implicit in the AR(1) model and conclude that we should use the unrestricted ADL(1,1) model instead.

We note that the lagged income and price variables in the unrestricted model do not have significant coefficients, so we consider dropping them. If we are going to drop both of them, we have to satisfy ourselves that their joint explanatory power is not significant. *RSS* for the regression omitting them is 0.001566. The *F* statistic for the null hypothesis that both their coefficients are zero is

$$F(2,38) = \frac{(0.001566 - 0.001456)/2}{0.001456/38} = 1.44. \qquad \textbf{(12.45)}$$

BOX 12.2 Could two wrongs make a right? AR(1) and MA(1) autocorrelation in an adaptive expectations model

In Section 11.4 it was shown that the adaptive expectations model,

$$Y_t = \beta_1 + \beta_2 X^e_{t+1} + u_t \qquad \textbf{(5)}$$

$$X^e_{t+1} - X^e_t = \lambda(X_t - X^e_t) \qquad \textbf{(6)}$$

could be transformed into an ADL(1,0) model of observable variables:

$$Y_t = \beta_1\lambda + (1-\lambda)Y_{t-1} + \beta_2\lambda X_t + u_t - (1-\lambda)u_{t-1}.$$

As a consequence of the transformation, the disturbance term is subject to moving average autocorrelation. Given the presence of the lagged dependent variable in the model, OLS would yield inconsistent estimates if used to fit it. Y_{t-1} and the MA(1) disturbance term would have the component u_{t-1} in common.

However, this conclusion is based on the assumption that u_t is IID. Suppose instead that it is subject to AR(1) autocorrelation:

$$u_t = \rho u_{t-1} + \varepsilon_t.$$

Then

$$u_t - (1-\lambda)u_{t-1} = \rho u_{t-1} + \varepsilon_t - (1-\lambda)\,u_{t-1} = \varepsilon_t - (1-\lambda-\rho)\,u_{t-1}.$$

Now it is reasonable to suppose that both λ and ρ will lie between 0 and 1, and hence it is possible that their sum might be close to 1. If this is the case, the disturbance term in the fitted model will be approximately equal to ε_t, and the MA(1) and AR(1) autocorrelation will have approximately neutralized each other.

Thus, if fitting an adaptive expectations model, it makes sense to regress the transformed model first, despite the apparent presence of MA(1) autocorrelation. One then tests for autocorrelation. If none is found, well and good. If there is evidence of autocorrelation, one should then fit the nonlinear model

$$Y_t = \beta_1 + \beta_2\lambda X_t + \beta_2\lambda(1-\lambda)X_{t-1} + \beta_2\lambda(1-\lambda)^2 X_{t-2} + \dots + u_t,$$

which remains free from autocorrelation if u_t is IID. (See equations (11.40)–(11.46) for a derivation of this model within the context of the Friedman permanent income hypothesis.)

The critical value of $F(2,38)$ at the 5 percent level is 3.24. Hence, we conclude that we can drop the variables and we arrive at the partial adjustment model specification already considered above. As we saw, the h statistic is 0.66, and we conclude that this may be a satisfactory specification.

EXERCISES

12.5 Perform a logarithmic regression of expenditure on your commodity on income and relative price, first using OLS and then using the option for AR(1) regression. Compare the coefficients and standard errors of the two regressions and comment.

12.6* Prove that σ_u^2 is related to σ_ε^2 as shown in (12.34), and show that weighting the first observation by $\sqrt{1-\rho^2}$ eliminates the heteroscedasticity.

12.7 A researcher has annual data on aggregate consumer expenditure on financial intermediaries, F_t, aggregate disposable personal income, X_t, and the relative price index for consumer expenditure on financial intermediaries, P_t, for the United States for the period 1959–2003 and fits the following logarithmic regressions (standard errors in parentheses; method of estimation as indicated, d = Durbin–Watson d statistic, BG = Breusch–Godfrey test statistic for AR(1) or MA(1) autocorrelation = nR^2 from first-order residuals regression):

	1: OLS	2: AR(1)	3: OLS	4: OLS
X	1.56	1.51	0.04	0.42
	(0.04)	(0.08)	(0.60)	(0.17)
P	−0.26	0.07	0.03	−0.10
	(0.21)	(0.21)	(0.20)	(0.15)
$F(-1)$	–	–	0.70	0.73
			(0.11)	(0.11)
$X(-1)$	–	–	0.43	–
			(0.61)	
$P(-1)$	–	–	−0.22	–
			(0.20)	
constant	−7.40	−8.53	−1.68	−1.80
	(0.77)	(1.04)	(1.02)	(1.01)
$\hat{\rho}$	–	0.70	–	–
		(0.11)		
R^2	0.984	0.991	0.993	0.992
RSS	0.317	0.164	0.138	0.144
d	0.65	1.87	1.68	1.78
BG	20.42	–	2.43	0.83

Explain the relationship between the second and third specifications, perform a common factor test, and discuss the adequacy of each specification.

12.8 Perform a logarithmic regression of expenditure on your category of consumer expenditure on income and price using an AR(1) estimation technique. Perform a second regression with the same variables but adding the lagged variables as regressors and using OLS. With Breusch–Godfrey and Durbin h tests, check that the second specification is not subject to autocorrelation.

Explain why the first regression is a restricted version of the second, stating the restrictions, and check whether the restrictions appear to be satisfied by the estimates of the coefficients of the second regression. Perform a common factor test. If the AR(1) model is rejected, and there are terms with insignificant coefficients in the second regression, investigate the consequences of dropping them.

12.9* The table gives the results of three logarithmic regressions using the Cobb–Douglas data for Y_t, K_t, and L_t, index number series for real output, real capital input, and real labor input, respectively, for the manufacturing sector of the United States for the period 1899–1922, reproduced in Exercise 11.6 (method of estimation as indicated; standard errors in parentheses; d = Durbin–Watson d statistic; BG = Breusch–Godfrey test statistic for first-order autocorrelation):

	1: OLS	2: AR(1)	3: OLS
log K	0.23 (0.06)	0.22 (0.07)	0.18 (0.56)
log L	0.81 (0.15)	0.86 (0.16)	1.03 (0.15)
log $Y(-1)$	–	–	0.40 (0.21)
log $K(-1)$	–	–	0.17 (0.51)
log $L(-1)$	–	–	–1.01 (0.25)
constant	–0.18 (0.43)	–0.35 (0.51)	1.04 (0.41)
$\hat{\rho}$	–	0.19 (0.25)	–
R^2	0.96	0.96	0.98
RSS	0.0710	0.0697	0.0259
d	1.52	1.54	1.46
BG	0.35	–	3.17

The first regression is that performed by Cobb and Douglas. The second fits the same specification, allowing for AR(1) autocorrelation. The third specification uses OLS with lagged variables. Evaluate the three regression specifications.

12.10* Derive the final equation in Box 12.2 from the first two equations in the box. What assumptions need to be made when fitting the model?

12.11 Consider the model

$$Y_t = \beta_1 + \beta_2 t + u_t, \quad (1)$$

where $t = 1,\ldots, T$ is a time trend, and the disturbance term u_t is subject to an AR(1) process $u_t = \rho u_{t-1} + \varepsilon_t$ where ε_t is IID with zero mean and finite variance and $|\rho| < 1$.

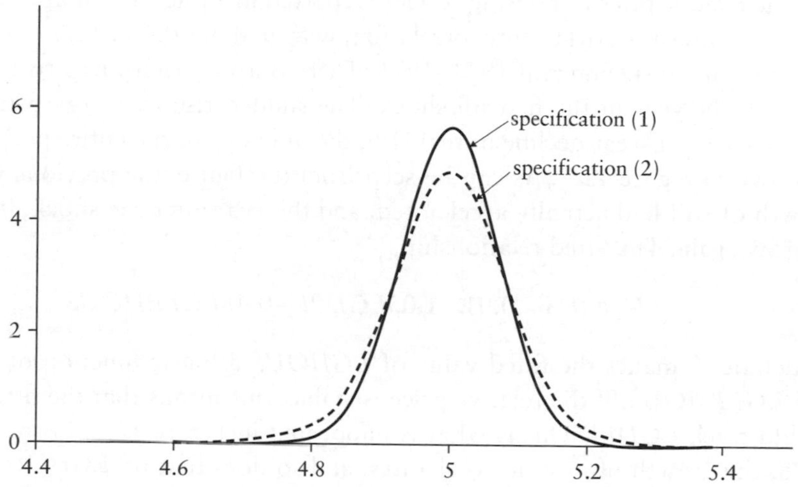

Derive a representation of the time series process for Y_t that is free from autocorrelation. This will be called specification (2). Explain whether specification (2) may be fitted using OLS. Explain the potential advantages and disadvantages of fitting specification (2) instead of specification (1). Assume that fitting specification (2) using OLS yields consistent estimates of the parameters. Show how one might obtain an estimate of β_2 from the regression results and demonstrate that it is consistent.

The figure compares the distributions of the estimates of β_2 obtained using specification (1) and those using the method determined via specification (2), using a simulation with the true values chosen as follows: $\beta_1 = 10$, $\beta_2 = 5$, and $\rho = 0.9$. Comment on the relationship between the distributions in the light of your answers to earlier parts of this exercise. The sample size was 50.

12.4 Apparent autocorrelation

Tests for autocorrelation often pick up patterns in the residuals that have got nothing to do with the type of autocorrelation for which they were designed. Sometimes the pattern may be caused by some other type of autocorrelation, but often the pattern is attributable to misspecification and has got nothing to do with the process generating the disturbance term. In such a case we would describe it as apparent autocorrelation. The most prominent cause of apparent autocorrelation is misspecification in the form of the omission of an important variable from the regression specification. Its omission effectively means that it becomes part of the disturbance term, and if it has a persistent effect from one time period to the nest, this will be revealed by the residuals.

Consider Figure 12.6. This shows the residuals from the static logarithmic regression of expenditure on housing services on disposable personal income and the relative price of housing services reported in Table 11.2. It appears to be a classic pattern of AR(1) autocorrelation, with ρ about 0.6 or 0.7.

Now look at the interval 1971–1975. There is a very sharp negative residual in 1973, the year of the first oil shock. The sudden rise in energy prices gave rise to a year-on-year decline in real DPI, the only one in the entire period. This is shown in Figure 12.7. As can be seen from the figure, the previous year the growth of DPI had actually accelerated, and the year after the shock, it started to grow again. The fitted relationship,

$$\widehat{LGHOUS} = 0.01 + 1.03LGDPI - 0.48LGPRHOUS \qquad \textbf{(12.46)}$$

by definition makes the fitted value of $LGHOUS$ a linear function of $LGDPI$ and $LGPRHOUS$. If the relative price is stable, this means that the fitted value should track $LGDPI$. This is what is happening in Figure 12.7. From 1972 to 1973, the growth of income accelerates, and so does that of $\widehat{LGHOUS}$. From 1973 to 1974, $LGDPI$ falls. $\widehat{LGHOUS}$ does not fall, but only because the relative price fell sharply in this period. From 1974 to 1975, $LGDPI$ resumes its previous rate of growth, and $\widehat{LGHOUS}$ matches it.

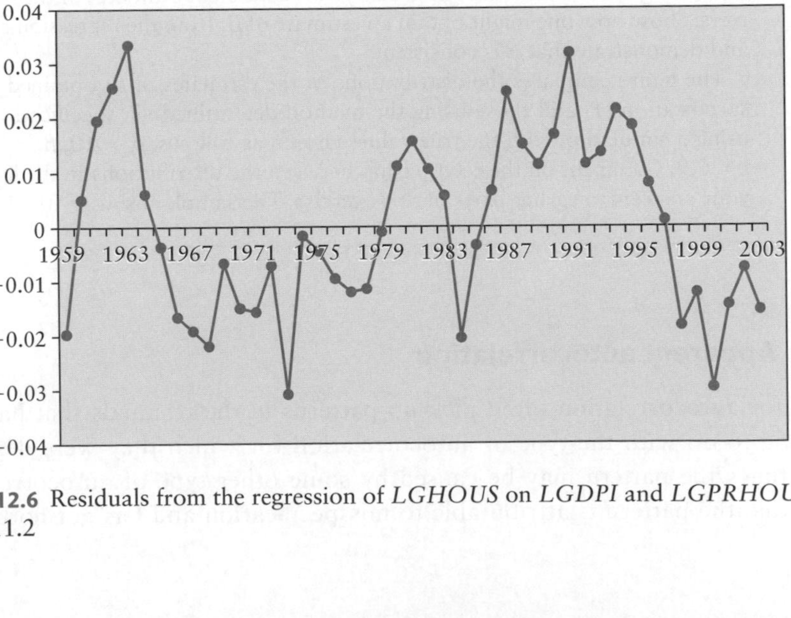

Figure 12.6 Residuals from the regression of *LGHOUS* on *LGDPI* and *LGPRHOUS* in Table 11.2

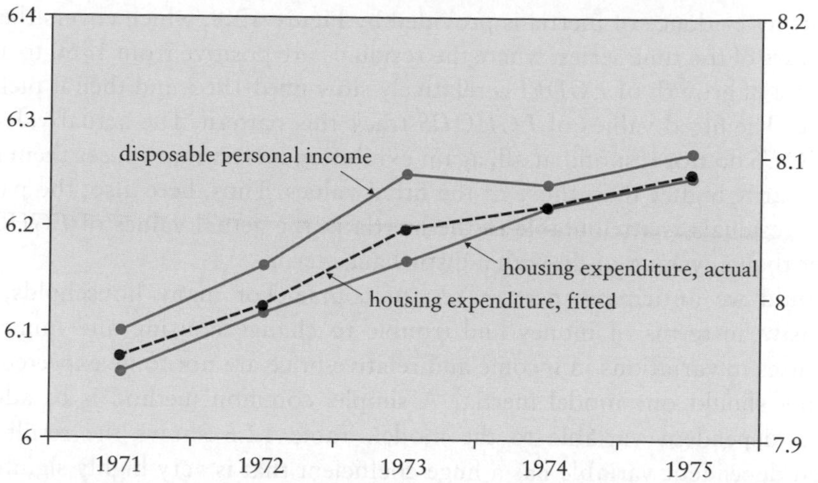

Figure 12.7 Logarithms of DPI (right scale) and actual and fitted expenditure on housing (left scale), 1971–1975

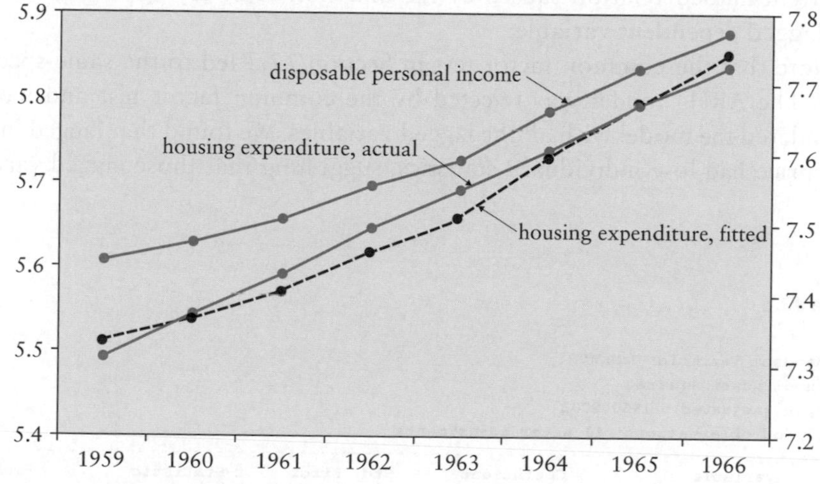

Figure 12.8 Logarithms of DPI (right scale) and actual and fitted expenditure on housing (left scale), 1959–1966

In the meantime, what is happening to the actual value, *LGHOUS*? Nothing. It maintains its existing trend with virtually no variation, and no response to the changes in the rate of growth of either income or price.

So what accounts for the sudden large negative residual in Figure 12.6? Not the disturbance term. There is hardly any evidence of a disturbance term, so stable is the rate of growth of *LGHOUS*. It is the fitted value, tracking the variations in *LGDPI*, that is responsible for the residual. The failure of the actual value of *LGHOUS* to respond to short-term variations in price is evidence of momentum and inertia.

Further evidence of inertia is provided by Figure 12.8, which covers the first few years of the time series, where the residuals are positive from 1960 to 1964. The rate of growth of *LGDPI* is relatively slow until 1963 and then it picks up a little. The fitted values of *LGHOUS* track this pattern. The actual values of *LGHOUS* do not respond at all, again exhibiting inertia that causes them to be temporarily higher than those of the fitted values. Thus, here also, the pattern in the residuals is attributable to the inertia in the actual values of *LGHOUS*, rather than anything to do with a disturbance term.

Would we anticipate inertia? Yes, of course. For many households, it is expensive in terms of money and trouble to change housing and immediate responses to variations in income and relative price are not to be expected.

How should one model inertia? A simple, common method is to add the lagged dependent variable to the model. Table 12.6 shows the result. The lagged dependent variable has a huge coefficient that is very highly significant. The Breusch–Godfrey test statistic for first-order autocorrelation is 0.20, not remotely significant. The Durbin h statistic is 0.66, also not remotely significant. We conclude that the autocorrelation found in the static model was in reality apparent autocorrelation caused by the omission of a very important variable, the lagged dependent variable.

Note that the common factor test in Section 12.3 led to the same specification. The AR(1) model was rejected by the common factor test and we then considered the model with all the lagged variables. We found that lagged income and price had low individual t statistics, suggesting that those lagged variables

Table 12.6

Dependent Variable: LGHOUS
Method: Least Squares
Sample (adjusted): 1960 2003
Included observations: 44 after adjustments

Variable	Coefficient	Std. Error	t-Statistic	Prob.
C	0.073957	0.062915	1.175499	0.2467
LGDPI	0.282935	0.046912	6.031246	0.0000
LGPRFOOD	-0.116949	0.027383	-4.270880	0.0001
LGHOUS(-1)	0.707242	0.044405	15.92699	0.0000

R-squared	0.999795	Mean dependent var	6.379059
Adjusted R-squared	0.999780	S.D. dependent var	0.421861
S.E. of regression	0.006257	Akaike info criter	-7.223711
Sum squared resid	0.001566	Schwarz criterion	-7.061512
Log likelihood	162.9216	Hannan-Quinn crite	-7.163560
F-statistic	65141.75	Durbin-Watson stat	1.810958
Prob(F-statistic)	0.000000		

were redundant. The F test showed that they did not have significant joint explanatory power and confirmed that they could be removed, leaving us with the specification in Table 12.6.

Although this example of apparent autocorrelation arose from the omission of the lagged dependent variable, it could arise from the omission of any important variable from the regression specification. It could also arise from functional misspecification. In particular, if the true relationship is a convex curve, as in Exercise 12.12, and a straight line regression is fitted, one will obtain a sequence of positive residuals in the first part of the sample, a sequence of negative residuals in the middle, and a sequence of positive residuals in the last part. Similarly, if the true relationship is a concave curve, one would obtain negative residuals followed by positive ones and then positive ones again. In both cases, tests for autocorrelation would pick up the pattern and signal autocorrelation. Of course, this apparent autocorrelation disappears if one fits an appropriate nonlinear specification.

EXERCISES

12.12* Using the 50 observations on two variables Y and X shown in the diagram, an investigator runs the following five regressions (estimation method as indicated; standard errors in parentheses; all variables as logarithms in the logarithmic regressions; d = Durbin–Watson d statistic; BG = Breusch–Godfrey test statistic):

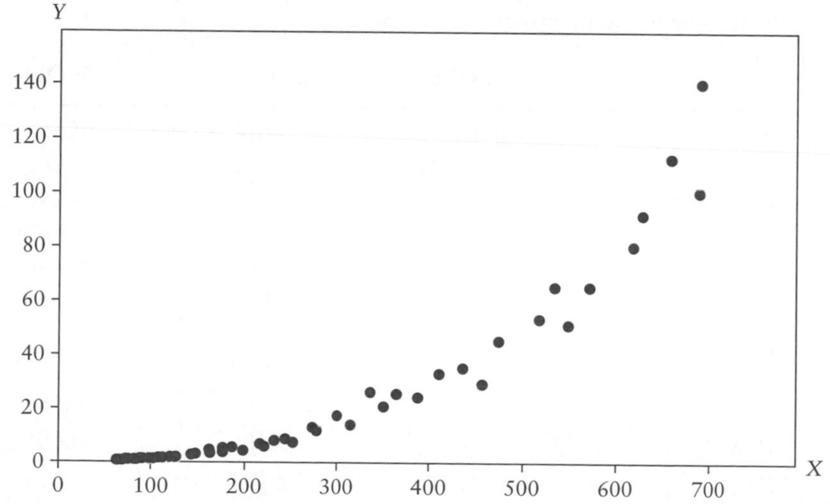

	1	2	3	4	5
	linear		*logarithmic*		
	OLS	AR(1)	OLS	AR(1)	OLS
X	0.16 (0.01)	0.03 (0.05)	2.39 (0.03)	2.39 (0.03)	1.35 (0.70)
Y(–1)	–	–	–	–	–0.11 (0.15)
X(–1)	–	–	–	–	1.30 (0.75)
$\hat{\rho}$	–	1.16 (0.06)	–	–0.14 (0.15)	–
constant	–21.88 (3.17)	–2.52 (8.03)	–11.00 (0.15)	–10.99 (0.14)	–12.15 (1.67)
R^2	0.858	0.974	0.993	0.993	0.993
RSS	7663	1366	1.011	0.993	0.946
d	0.26	2.75	2.17	1.86	21.95
BG	39.54	–	0.85	–	1.03

Discuss each of the five regressions, explaining which is your preferred specification.

12.13* Using the data on food in the Demand Functions data set, the following regressions were run, each with the logarithm of food as the dependent variable: (1) an OLS regression on a time trend *T* defined to be 1 in 1959, 2 in 1960, etc.; (2) an AR(1) regression using the same specification; and (3) an OLS regression on *T* and the logarithm of food lagged one time period, with the results shown in the table (standard errors in parentheses):

	1: OLS	2: AR(1)	3: OLS
T	0.017 (0.0004)	0.016 (0.002)	0.002 (0.001)
LGFOOD(–1)	–	–	0.880 (0.069)
constant	5.636 (0.010)	5.666 (0.054)	0.696 (0.388)
$\hat{\rho}$	–	0.880 (0.069)	–
R^2	0.978	0.995	0.995
RSS	0.049	0.009	0.009
d	0.210	1.193	1.193
BG	35.15	–	8.74

Discuss why each regression specification appears to be unsatisfactory. Explain why it was not possible to perform a common factor test.

12.5 Model specification: specific-to-general versus general-to-specific

Let us review our findings with regard to the demand function for housing services. We started off with a static model and found that it had an unacceptably low Durbin–Watson statistic. Under the hypothesis that the relationship was subject to AR(1) autocorrelation, we ran the AR(1) specification. We then tested the restrictions implicit in this specification, and found that we had to reject the AR(1) specification, preferring the unrestricted ADL(1,1) model. Finally we found that we could drop off the lagged income and price variables, ending up with a specification that could be based on a partial adjustment model. This seemed to be a satisfactory specification, particularly given the nature of the type of expenditure, for we do expect there to be substantial inertia in the response of expenditure on housing services to changes in income and relative price. We conclude that the reason for the low Durbin–Watson statistic in the original static model was not AR(1) autocorrelation but the omission of an important regressor (the lagged dependent variable).

The research strategy that has implicitly been adopted can be summarized as follows:

1. On the basis of economic theory, experience, and intuition formulate a provisional ad hoc model.
2. Locate suitable data and fit the model.
3. Perform diagnostic checks.
4. If any of the checks reveal inadequacies, revise the specification of the model with the aim of eliminating them.
5. When the specification appears satisfactory, congratulate oneself on having completed the task.

The danger with this strategy is that the reason that the final version of the model appears satisfactory is that you have massaged its specification to fit your particular data set, not that it really corresponds to the true model. The econometric literature is full of two types of indirect evidence that this happens frequently, particularly with models employing time series data, and particularly with those modelling macroeconomic relationships. It often happens that researchers investigating the same phenomenon with access to the same sources of data construct internally consistent but mutually incompatible models, and it often happens that models that survive sample period diagnostic checks exhibit miserable predictive performance. The literature on models of the determinants of aggregate investment is especially notorious in both respects. Further evidence, if any were needed, has been provided by experiments showing that it is not hard to set up nonsense models that survive the conventional checks (Peach and Webb, 1983). As a consequence, there is growing recognition of the fact that the tests eliminate only those models with the grossest misspecifications, and the survival of a model is no guarantee of its validity.

This is true even of the tests of predictive performance, where the models are subjected to an evaluation of their ability to fit fresh data. There are two problems with such tests. First, their power is often rather low. Second, there is the question of what the investigator does if a test is failed. Understandably, it is unusual for an investigator to quit, acknowledging defeat. The natural course of action is to continue tinkering with the model until the predictive performance test is passed, but of course the test then has no more integrity than the usual sample period diagnostic checks.

This unsatisfactory state of affairs has generated interest in two interrelated topics: the possibility of eliminating some of the competing models by confronting them with each other, and the possibility of establishing a more systematic research strategy that might eliminate bad model-building in the first place.

Comparison of alternative models

The comparison of alternative models can involve much technical complexity and the present discussion will be limited to a very brief and partial outline of some of the issues involved. We will begin by making a distinction between nested and non-nested models. A model is said to be nested inside another if it can be obtained from it by imposing a number of restrictions. Two models are said to be non-nested if neither can be represented as a restricted version of the other. The restrictions may relate to any aspect of the specification of the model, but the present discussion will be limited to restrictions on the parameters of the explanatory variables in a single equation model. It will be illustrated with reference to the demand function for housing services, with the logarithm of expenditure written Y and the logarithms of the income and relative price variables written X_2 and X_3.

Three alternative dynamic specifications have been considered: the ADL(1,1) model including current and lagged values of all the variables and no parameter restrictions, which will be denoted A; the model that hypothesized that the disturbance term was subject to an AR(1) process (B); and the model with only one lagged variable, the lagged dependent variable (C). For good measure we will add the original static model (D).

$$\text{(A)} \quad Y_t = \lambda_1 + \lambda_2 Y_{t-1} + \lambda_3 X_{2t} + \lambda_4 X_{2,t-1} + \lambda_5 X_{3t} + \lambda_6 X_{3,t-1} + \varepsilon_t, \tag{12.47}$$

$$\begin{aligned}\text{(B)} \quad Y_t = {} & \lambda_1(1-\lambda_2) + \lambda_2 Y_{t-1} + \lambda_3 X_{2t} - \lambda_2\lambda_3 X_{2,t-1} \\ & + \lambda_5 X_{3t} - \lambda_2\lambda_5 X_{3,t-1} + \varepsilon_t,\end{aligned} \tag{12.48}$$

$$\text{(C)} \quad Y_t = \lambda_1 + \lambda_2 Y_{t-1} + \lambda_3 X_{2t} + \lambda_5 X_{3t} + \varepsilon_t, \tag{12.49}$$

$$\text{(D)} \quad Y_t = \lambda_1 + \lambda_3 X_{2t} + \lambda_5 X_{3t} + \varepsilon_t, \tag{12.50}$$

The ADL(1,1) model is the most general specification and the others are nested within it. For B to be a legitimate simplification, the common factor test should not lead to a rejection of the restrictions. For C to be a legitimate

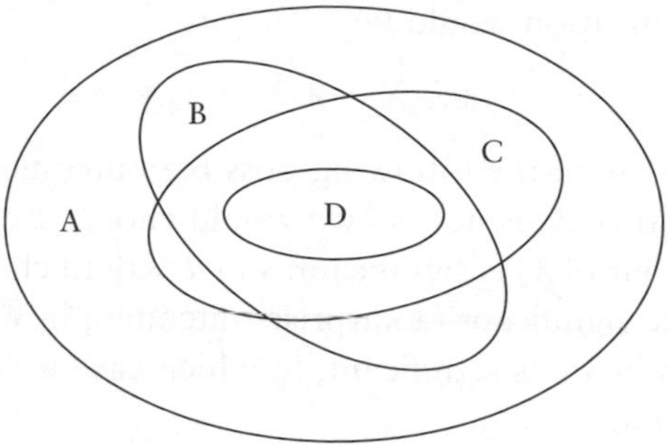

Figure 12.9 Nesting structure for specifications A, B, C, and D

simplification, H_0: $\lambda_4 = \lambda_6 = 0$ should not be rejected. For D to be a legitimate simplification, H_0: $\lambda_2 = \lambda_4 = \lambda_6 = 0$ should not be rejected. The nesting structure is represented by Figure 12.9.

In the case of the demand function for housing, if we compare B with A, we find that the common factor restrictions implicit in B are rejected and so it is struck off our list of acceptable specifications. If we compare C with A, we find that it is a valid alternative because the estimated coefficients of lagged income and price variables are not significantly different from zero, either individually (via t tests on their coefficients) or jointly (via an F test of their joint explanatory power). Finally, D must be rejected because the restriction that the coefficient of Y_{t-1} is zero is rejected by a simple t test. (In the whole of this discussion, we have assumed that the test procedures are not substantially affected by the use of a lagged dependent variable as an explanatory variable. This is strictly true only if the sample is large.)

The example illustrates the potential both for success and for failure within a nested structure: success in that two of the four specifications are eliminated and failure in that some indeterminacy remains. Is there any reason for preferring A to C or vice versa? Some would argue that C should be preferred because it is more parsimonious in terms of parameters, requiring only four instead of six. It also has the advantage of lending itself to the intuitively appealing interpretation involving short-run and long-run dynamics discussed in Chapter 11. However, the efficiency/potential bias trade-off between including and excluding variables with insignificant coefficients discussed in Chapter 6 makes the answer unclear.

What should you do if the rival specifications are not nested? One possible procedure is to create a union specification embracing the two rivals as restricted versions and to see if any progress can be made by testing each against the union. For example, suppose that the rival specifications are

(E) $$Y = \lambda_1 + \lambda_2 X_2 + \lambda_3 X_3 + \varepsilon_t, \tag{12.51}$$

(F) $$Y = \lambda_1 + \lambda_2 X_2 + \lambda_4 X_4 + \varepsilon_t. \tag{12.52}$$

Then the union specification would be

$$\text{(G)} \qquad Y = \lambda_1 + \lambda_2 X_2 + \lambda_3 X_3 + \lambda_4 X_4 + \varepsilon_t. \qquad \textbf{(12.53)}$$

We would then fit G, with the following possible outcomes: the estimate of λ_3 is significant, but that of λ_4 is not, so we would choose E; the estimate of λ_3 is not significant, but that of λ_4 is significant, so we would choose F; the estimates of both λ_3 and λ_4 are significant (a surprise outcome), in which case we would choose G; neither estimate is significant, in which case we could test G against the simple specification

$$\text{(H)} \qquad Y = \lambda_1 + \lambda_2 X_2 + \varepsilon_t, \qquad \textbf{(12.54)}$$

and we might prefer the latter if an *F* test does not lead to the rejection of the null hypothesis H_0: $\lambda_3 = \lambda_4 = 0$. Otherwise we would be unable to discriminate between the three specifications.

There are various potential problems with this approach. First, the tests use G as the basis for the null hypotheses, and it may not be intuitively appealing. If E and F are constructed on different principles, their union may be so implausible that it could be eliminated on the basis of economic theory. The framework for the tests is then undermined. Second, the last possibility, indeterminacy, is likely to be the outcome if X_3 and X_4 are highly correlated. For a more extended discussion of the issues, and further references, see Kmenta (1986), pp. 595–598.

The general-to-specific approach to model specification

We have seen that, if we start with a simple model and elaborate it in response to diagnostic checks, there is a risk that we will end up with a false model that satisfies us because, by successive adjustments, we have made it appear to fit the sample period data, 'appear to fit' because the diagnostic tests are likely to be invalid if the model specification is incorrect. Would it not be better, as some writers urge, to adopt the opposite approach. Instead of attempting to develop a specific initial model into a more general one, using what has been described as the specific-to-general approach to model specification, should we not instead start with a fully general model and reduce it to a more focused one by successively imposing restrictions (after testing their validity)?

Of course the general-to-specific approach is preferable, at least in principle. The problem is that, in its pure form, it is often impracticable. If the sample size is limited, and the initial specification contains a large number of potential explanatory variables, multicollinearity may cause most or even all of them to have insignificant coefficients. This is especially likely to be a problem in time series models. In an extreme case, the number of variables may exceed the number of observations, and the model could not be fitted at all. Where the model may be fitted, the lack of significance of many of the coefficients may appear to give the investigator considerable freedom to choose which variables to drop. However, the final version of the model may be highly sensitive to this initial arbitrary decision. A variable that has an insignificant coefficient initially and is dropped might have had a significant coefficient in a cut-down version of the model, had it been retained. The conscientious application of the general-to-specific principle, if applied systematically, might require the exploration of an unmanageable number of possible model-reduction paths. Even if the number were small enough to be explored, the investigator may well be left with a large number of rival models, none of which is dominated by the others.

Therefore, some degree of compromise is normally essential, and of course there are no rules for this, any more than there are for the initial conception of a model in the first place. A weaker but more operational version of the approach is to guard against formulating an initial specification that imposes restrictions that might be rejected. However, it is probably fair to say that the ability to do this is one measure of the experience of an investigator, in which case the approach amounts to little more than an exhortation to be experienced. For a nontechnical discussion of the approach, replete with entertainingly caustic remarks about the shortcomings of specific-to-general model-building and an illustrative example by a leading advocate of the general-to-specific approach, see Hendry (1979).

Key terms

- apparent autocorrelation
- autocorrelation
- autoregressive autocorrelation
- Breusch–Godfrey test
- Cochrane–Orcutt iterative procedure
- common factor test
- Durbin *h* statistic
- Durbin *h* test
- Durbin–Watson *d* statistic
- Durbin–Watson test
- first-order autoregressive autocorrelation AR(1)
- general-to-specific approach
- moving average autocorrelation
- negative autocorrelation
- Newey–West standard errors
- positive autocorrelation
- Prais–Winsten correction
- serial correlation
- specific-to-general approach

EXERCISES

12.14 A researcher is considering the following alternative regression models:

$$Y_t = \beta_1 + \beta_2 Y_{t-1} + \beta_3 X_t + \beta_4 X_{t-1} + u_t \qquad (1)$$

$$\Delta Y_t = \gamma_1 + \gamma_2 \Delta X_t + v_t \qquad (2)$$

$$Y_t = \delta_1 + \delta_2 X_t + w_t \qquad (3)$$

where $\Delta Y_t = Y_t - Y_{t-1}$, $\Delta X_t = X_t - X_{t-1}$, and u_t, v_t, and w_t are disturbance terms.

(a) Show that models (2) and (3) are restricted versions of model (1), stating the restrictions.

(b) Explain the implications for the disturbance terms in (1) and (2) if (3) is the correct specification and w_t satisfies the regression model assumptions. What problems, if any, would be encountered if ordinary least squares were used to fit (1) and (2)?

12.15 Explain how your answer to Exercise 12.14 illustrates some of the methodological issues discussed in this section.

APPENDIX 12.1 DEMONSTRATION THAT THE DURBIN–WATSON STATISTIC APPROXIMATES 2–2ρ IN LARGE SAMPLES

$$d = \frac{\sum_{t=2}^{T}(e_t - e_{t-1})^2}{\sum_{t=1}^{T} e_t^2} = \frac{\sum_{t=2}^{T}\left(e_t^2 - 2e_t e_{t-1} + e_{t-1}^2\right)}{\sum_{t=1}^{T} e_t^2}$$

$$= \frac{\sum_{t=2}^{T} e_t^2}{\sum_{t=1}^{T} e_t^2} + \frac{\sum_{t=2}^{T} e_{t-1}^2}{\sum_{t=1}^{T} e_t^2} - 2\frac{\sum_{t=2}^{T} e_t e_{t-1}}{\sum_{t=1}^{T} e_t^2} \rightarrow 2 - 2\frac{\sum_{t=2}^{T} e_t e_{t-1}}{\sum_{t=1}^{T} e_t^2}$$

as the sample size becomes large because both $\frac{\sum_{t=2}^{T} e_t^2}{\sum_{t=1}^{T} e_t^2}$ and $\frac{\sum_{t=2}^{T} e_{t-1}^2}{\sum_{t=1}^{T} e_t^2}$ tend to 1. Since $\frac{\sum_{t=2}^{T} e_t e_{t-1}}{\sum_{t=1}^{T} e_t^2}$ is an estimator of ρ, d tends to $2 - 2\rho$.

13. Introduction to Nonstationary Time Series

This chapter offers a brief and limited exposition of some of the concepts and issues that arise when regression analysis is applied to nonstationary time series. The treatment has been guided by the need to avoid complexity that would be inappropriate in an introductory econometrics course. For this reason, there is no mention of some important mathematical tools, such as lag operators, and the discussion barely scratches at the surface of those topics that are included. Rather than attempting to provide tools for immediate use, the overriding objective has been to convince a reader intending to work with time series data that there is a need for further study at a higher level, and that further study would be worthwhile.

The first task, obviously, is to explain what is meant by stationarity and nonstationarity. We will then turn to statistical inference, addressing the following questions relating to the estimators of coefficients in regressions using both stationary and nonstationary time series:

1. Under what conditions will the estimators be consistent?
2. If consistent, under what conditions will they be normally distributed, at least in large samples?
3. If the estimators are consistent and normally distributed, can we perform standard t and F tests?

13.1 Stationarity and nonstationarity

Stationary time series

We will start by defining a stationary time series process. We will begin with a very simple example, the AR(1) process

$$X_t = \beta_2 X_{t-1} + \varepsilon_t, \tag{13.1}$$

where $|\beta_2| < 1$ and ε_t is IID—independently and identically distributed—with zero mean and finite variance.

As noted in Chapter 11, we make a distinction between the potential values $\{X_1, \ldots, X_T\}$, before the sample is generated, and a realization of actual values $\{x_1, \ldots, x_T\}$. Statisticians write the potential values in upper case, and the actual values of a particular realization in lower case, as we have done here, to emphasize the distinction. Figure 13.1 shows an example of a realization starting with $X_0 = 0$, with $\beta_2 = 0.8$ and the innovation ε_t being drawn randomly for each time period from a normal distribution with zero mean and unit variance.

Because history cannot repeat itself, we will only ever see one realization of a time series process. Nevertheless, it is meaningful to ask whether we can determine the potential distribution of X at time t, given information at some earlier period, for example, time 0. As usual, there are two approaches to answering this question: mathematical analysis and simulation. We shall do both for the time series process represented by (13.1), starting with a simulation.

Figure 13.2 shows 50 realizations of the process. For the first few periods, the distribution of the realizations at time t is affected by the fact that they have a common starting point of 0. However, the initial effect soon becomes unimportant and the distribution becomes stable from one period to the next. Figure 13.3 presents a histogram of the values of X_{20}. Apart from the first few time points, histograms for other time points would look similar. If the number of realizations were increased, each histogram would converge to the normal distribution shown in Figure 13.3.

The AR(1) process (13.1) is said to be stationary, the adjective referring, not to X_t itself, but to the potential distribution of its realizations, ignoring transitory initial effects. X_t itself changes from period to period, but the potential distribution of its realizations at any given time point does not. The potential distribution at time t is described as the **ensemble distribution** at time t, to emphasize the fact that we are talking about the distribution of a cross-section of realizations, not the ordinary distribution of a random variable.

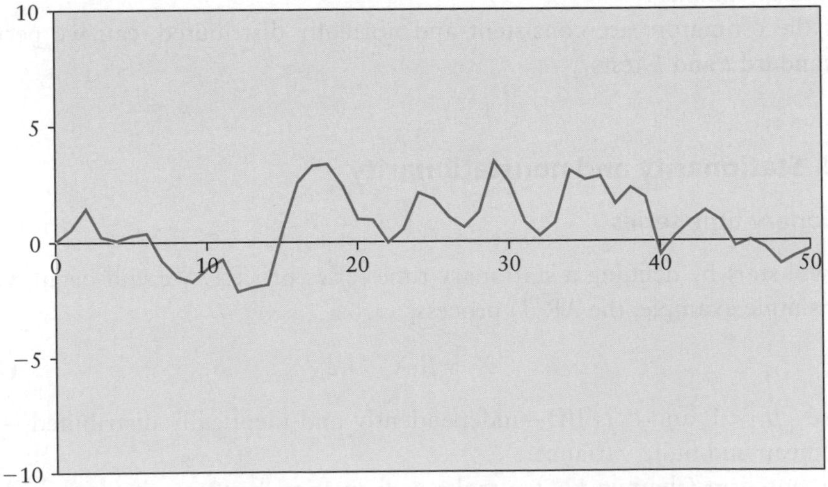

Figure 13.1 A realization of the AR(1) process (13.1)

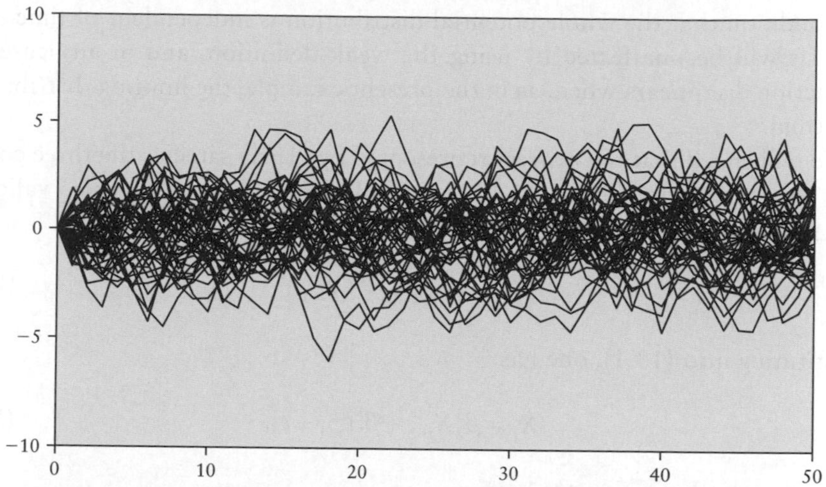

Figure 13.2 50 realizations of the AR(1) process (13.1)

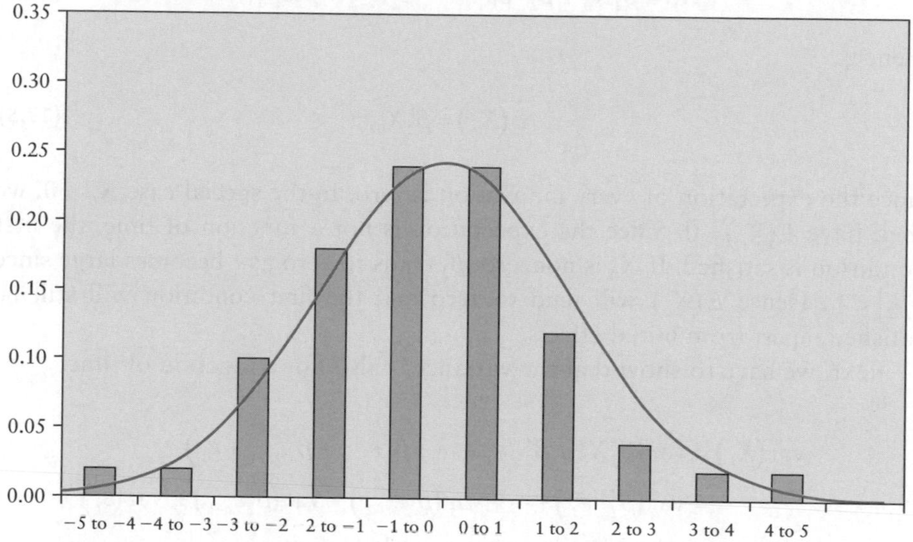

Figure 13.3 Ensemble distribution of AR(1) process after 20 periods, and limiting ensemble distribution

In general, a time series process is said to be stationary if its ensemble distribution satisfies three conditions:

1. The mean of the distribution is independent of time.
2. The variance of the distribution is independent of time.
3. The covariance between its values at any two time points depends only on the distance between those points, and not on time.

This definition of stationarity is known as weak stationarity or covariance stationarity. For the definition of strong stationarity, (1) and (2) are replaced by the condition that the whole potential distribution is independent of time. Our analysis will be unaffected by using the weak definition, and in any case the distinction disappears when, as in the present example, the limiting distribution is normal.

We will check that the process represented by (13.1) satisfies the three conditions for stationarity. First, if (13.1) is valid for time period t, it is also valid for time period $t-1$:

$$X_{t-1} = \beta_2 X_{t-2} + \varepsilon_{t-1}. \tag{13.2}$$

Substituting into (13.1), one has

$$X_t = \beta_2^2 X_{t-2} + \beta_2 \varepsilon_{t-1} + \varepsilon_t. \tag{13.3}$$

Lagging and substituting $t-1$ times,

$$X_t = \beta_2^t X_0 + \beta_2^{t-1}\varepsilon_1 + \cdots + \beta_2^2 \varepsilon_{t-2} + \beta_2 \varepsilon_{t-1} + \varepsilon_t . \tag{13.4}$$

Hence,

$$E(X_t) = \beta_2^t X_0, \tag{13.5}$$

since the expectation of every innovation is zero. In the special case $X_0 = 0$, we then have $E(X_t) = 0$. Since the expectation is not a function of time, the first condition is satisfied. If X_0 is nonzero, β_2^t tends to zero as t becomes large since $|\beta_2| < 1$. Hence $E(X_t)$ will tend to zero and the first condition will still be satisfied, apart from initial effects.

Next, we have to show that the variance is also not a function of time.

$$\begin{aligned}
\text{var}(X_t) &= \text{var}\left(\beta_2^t X_0 + \beta_2^{t-1}\varepsilon_1 + \cdots + \beta_2^2 \varepsilon_{t-2} + \beta_2 \varepsilon_{t-1} + \varepsilon_t\right) \\
&= \text{var}\left(\beta_2^{t-1}\varepsilon_1\right) + \cdots + \text{var}\left(\beta_2^2 \varepsilon_{t-2}\right) + \text{var}\left(\beta_2 \varepsilon_{t-1}\right) + \text{var}\left(\varepsilon_t\right) \\
&= \beta_2^{2(t-1)}\sigma_\varepsilon^2 + \cdots + \beta_2^4 \sigma_\varepsilon^2 + \beta_2^2 \sigma_\varepsilon^2 + \sigma_\varepsilon^2 \\
&= \left(\beta_2^{2(t-1)} + \cdots + \beta_2^4 + \beta_2^2 + 1\right)\sigma_\varepsilon^2 \\
&= \left(\frac{1-\beta_2^{2t}}{1-\beta_2^2}\right)\sigma_\varepsilon^2 .
\end{aligned} \tag{13.6}$$

(*Notes*: There are no covariances in the second line because the innovations are assumed to be generated independently. In the third line, the constants are squared when taken out of the variance expressions. The step from the fourth to the last line involves the standard summation of a geometric progression.)

Given that $|\beta_2|<1$, β_2^{2t} tends to zero as t becomes large. Thus, ignoring transitory initial effects,

$$\operatorname{var}(X_t)\to\sigma_\varepsilon^2\left(\frac{1}{1-\beta_2^2}\right) \tag{13.7}$$

and is independent of time. This is the variance of the ensemble distribution shown in Figures 13.2 and 13.3.

It remains for us to demonstrate that the covariance between X_t and X_{t+s} is independent of time. From (13.1) we have

$$X_{t+s}=\beta_2X_{t+s-1}+\varepsilon_{t+s}. \tag{13.8}$$

Lagging and substituting s times, this implies

$$X_{t+s}=\beta_2^sX_t+\beta_2^{s-1}\varepsilon_{t+1}+\cdots+\beta_2^2\varepsilon_{t+s-2}+\beta_2\varepsilon_{t+s-1}+\varepsilon_{t+s}. \tag{13.9}$$

Then

$$\begin{aligned}\operatorname{cov}(X_t,X_{t+s})&=\operatorname{cov}(X_t,\beta_2^sX_t)\\&\quad+\operatorname{cov}\left(X_t,\left[\beta_2^{s-1}\varepsilon_{t+1}+\cdots+\beta_2^2\varepsilon_{t+s-2}+\beta_2\varepsilon_{t+s-1}+\varepsilon_{t+s}\right]\right).\end{aligned} \tag{13.10}$$

The second term on the right side is zero because X_t is independent of the innovations after time t. The first term can be written $\beta_2^s\operatorname{var}(X_t)$. As we have just seen, $\operatorname{var}(X_t)$ is independent of t, apart from a transitory initial effect. Hence, the third condition for stationarity is also satisfied.

Variation

Suppose next that the process includes an intercept β_1:

$$X_t=\beta_1+\beta_2X_{t-1}+\varepsilon_t. \tag{13.11}$$

How does this affect its properties? Is it still stationary? Lagging and substituting t times, (13.4) becomes

$$\begin{aligned}X_t&=\beta_2^tX_0+\beta_1\left(\beta_2^{t-1}+\ldots+\beta_2^2+\beta_2\right)+\beta_2^{t-1}\varepsilon_1+\ldots+\beta_2^2\varepsilon_{t-2}+\beta_2\varepsilon_{t-1}+\varepsilon_t\\&=\beta_2^tX_0+\beta_1\frac{1-\beta_2^t}{1-\beta_2}+\beta_2^{t-1}\varepsilon_1+\ldots+\beta_2^2\varepsilon_{t-2}+\beta_2\varepsilon_{t-1}+\varepsilon_t,\end{aligned} \tag{13.12}$$

Taking expectations,

$$E(X_t)=\frac{\beta_1}{1-\beta_2}, \tag{13.13}$$

provided that t is large enough for the term $\beta_2^tX_0$ to be so small that it can be neglected. Thus the expectation is now nonzero, but it remains independent of time.

The variance is unaffected by the addition of a constant in the expression for X_t:

$$\begin{aligned}\operatorname{var}(X_t) &= \operatorname{var}\left(\beta_1 \frac{1-\beta_2^t}{1-\beta_2} + \beta_2^{t-1}\varepsilon_1 + \cdots + \beta_2^2\varepsilon_{t-2} + \beta_2\varepsilon_{t-1} + \varepsilon_t\right) \\ &= \operatorname{var}\left(\beta_2^{t-1}\varepsilon_1 + \cdots + \beta_2^2\varepsilon_{t-2} + \beta_2\varepsilon_{t-1} + \varepsilon_t\right) \\ &= \left(\frac{1-\beta_2^{2t}}{1-\beta_2^2}\right)\sigma_\varepsilon^2 \rightarrow \frac{\sigma_\varepsilon^2}{1-\beta_2^2}.\end{aligned} \tag{13.14}$$

The last line draws on (13.6). Thus the variance remains independent of time, apart from initial effects.

Finally, we need to consider the covariance of X_t and X_{t+s}. Lagging and substituting s times, the relationship between X_t and X_{t+s} becomes

$$X_{t+s} = \beta_1\left(\beta_2^{s-1} + \ldots + \beta_2^2 + \beta_2\right) + \beta_2^s X_t + \beta_2^{s-1}\varepsilon_{t+1} + \ldots + \beta_2^2 X_{t+s-2} + \beta_2\varepsilon_{t+s-1} + \varepsilon_{t+s}. \tag{13.15}$$

The covariance of X_t and X_{t+s} is not affected by the inclusion of the term $\beta_1\left(\beta_2^{s-1} + \ldots + \beta_2^2 + \beta_2\right)$ because it is a constant. Hence, the covariance is equal to $\beta_2^s \operatorname{var}(X_t)$, as before, and remains independent of t.

Pure stationary process with no initial effects

We have seen that the process (13.11) has a limiting ensemble distribution with mean $\beta_1/(1-\beta_2)$ and variance $\sigma_\varepsilon^2/(1-\beta_2^2)$. However, the process exhibits transient time-dependent initial effects associated with the starting point X_0. We can get rid of the transient effects by determining X_0 as a random draw from the ensemble distribution

$$X_0 = \frac{\beta_1}{1-\beta_2} + \sqrt{\frac{1}{\left(1-\beta_2^2\right)}}\varepsilon_0, \tag{13.16}$$

where ε_0 is a random draw from the distribution of ε at time zero. (In Exercise 13.2 you can check that X_0 has the ensemble mean and variance.) If we determine X_0 in this way, the expectation and variance of the process both become strictly independent of time.

(13.12) becomes

$$\begin{aligned}X_t &= \beta_2^t\left(\frac{\beta_1}{1-\beta_2} + \sqrt{\frac{1}{\left(1-\beta_2^2\right)}}\varepsilon_0\right) + \beta_1\frac{1-\beta_2^t}{1-\beta_2} + \beta_2^{t-1}\varepsilon_1 + \ldots + \beta_2^2\varepsilon_{t-2} + \beta_2\varepsilon_{t-1} + \varepsilon_t \\ &= \frac{\beta_1}{1-\beta_2} + \beta_2^t\sqrt{\frac{1}{\left(1-\beta_2^2\right)}}\varepsilon_0 + \beta_2^{t-1}\varepsilon_1 + \ldots + \beta_2^2\varepsilon_{t-2} + \beta_2\varepsilon_{t-1} + \varepsilon_t,\end{aligned} \tag{13.17}$$

and so the expectation is now strictly independent of time. (13.14) becomes

$$\begin{aligned}\operatorname{var}(X_t) &= \operatorname{var}\left(\frac{\beta_1}{1-\beta_2} + \beta_2^t\sqrt{\frac{1}{(1-\beta_2^2)}}\varepsilon_0 + \beta_2^{t-1}\varepsilon_1 + \cdots + \beta_2\varepsilon_{t-1} + \varepsilon_t\right) \\ &= \operatorname{var}\left(\beta_2^t\sqrt{\frac{1}{(1-\beta_2^2)}}\varepsilon_0 + \beta_2^{t-1}\varepsilon_1 + \cdots + \beta_2\varepsilon_{t-1} + \varepsilon_t\right) \\ &= \frac{\beta_2^{2t}}{(1-\beta_2^2)}\sigma_\varepsilon^2 + \left(\frac{1-\beta_2^{2t}}{1-\beta_2^2}\right)\sigma_\varepsilon^2 = \frac{\sigma_\varepsilon^2}{1-\beta_2^2}. \end{aligned} \tag{13.18}$$

and so the variance is also strictly independent of time.

Figure 13.4 shows 50 realizations with X_0 treated in this way. This is the counterpart of Figure 13.2, with $\beta_2 = 0.8$ as in that figure. As can be seen, the initial effects have disappeared. The other difference in the figures results from the inclusion of a nonzero intercept. In Figure 13.2, $\beta_1 = 0$. In Figure 13.4, $\beta_1 =$ 1.0 and the mean of the ensemble distribution is $\beta_1/(1-\beta_2) = 1.0/(1-0.8) = 5$.

As will be seen in Section 13.4, evaluation of the power of tests for nonstationarity can be sensitive to the assumption regarding X_0, and typically the most appropriate way of characterizing a stationary process is to avoid transient initial effects by treating X_0 as a random draw from the ensemble distribution.

Nonstationary time series

A process that violates any of the three conditions for stationarity is described as being nonstationary. We will take as our first example a variation on the

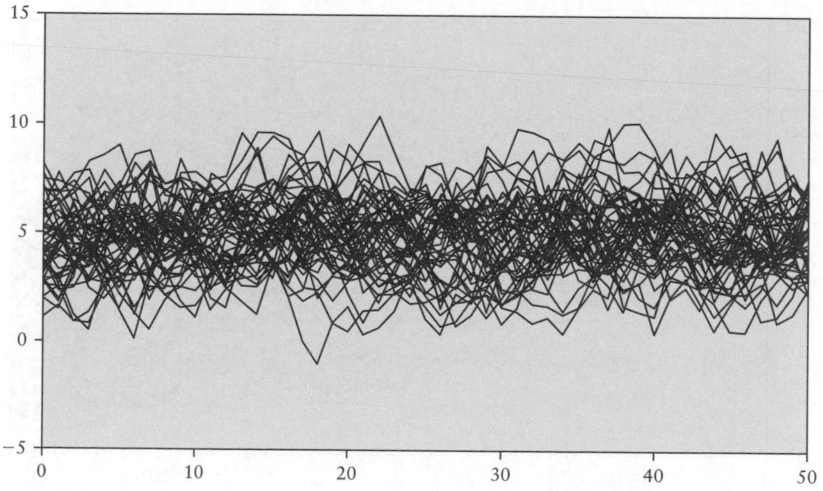

Figure 13.4 Stationary process with $\beta_1 = 1.0, \beta_2 = 0.8$, and initial value stochastic

stationary process (13.1). Suppose $\beta_2 = 1$. Then

$$X_t = X_{t-1} + \varepsilon_t. \quad \textbf{(13.19)}$$

In words, the value of X in one time period is equal to its value in the previous time period, plus a random adjustment. This is known as a random walk. Figure 13.5 shows an example realization of a random walk for the case where ε_t has a normal distribution with zero mean and unit variance.

Figure 13.6 shows the results of a simulation with 50 realizations. It is obvious that the ensemble distribution is not stationary. The distribution changes as t increases, becoming increasingly spread out. We will confirm this mathematically.

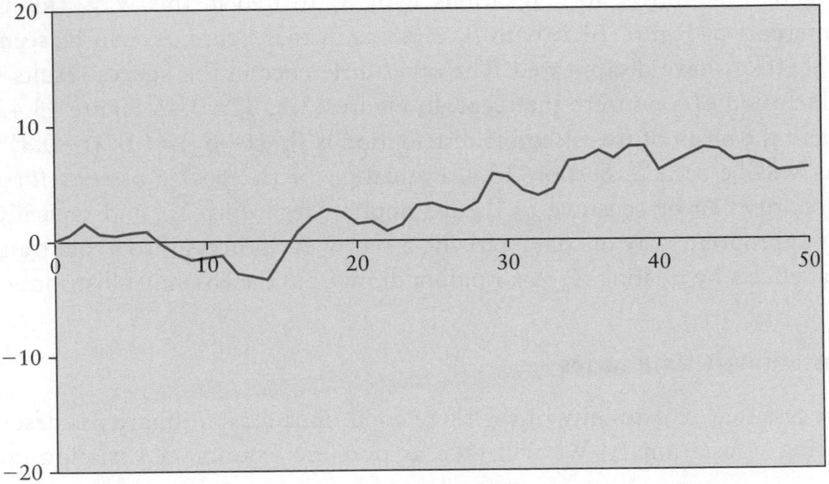

Figure 13.5 Random walk

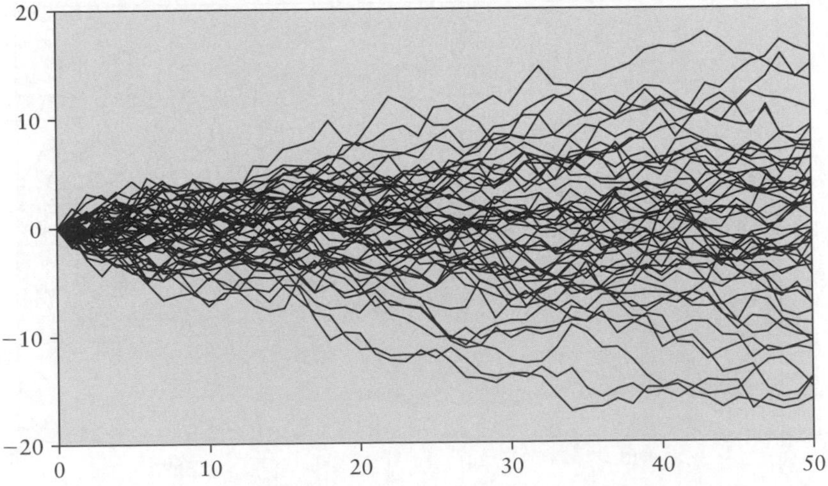

Figure 13.6 50 realizations of a random walk

The first condition for stationarity is not violated by a random walk. If (13.19) is true for t, it is also true for $t-1$:

$$X_{t-1} = X_{t-2} + \varepsilon_{t-1}. \tag{13.20}$$

Substituting into (13.19),

$$X_t = X_{t-2} + \varepsilon_{t-1} + \varepsilon_t. \tag{13.21}$$

Lagging and substituting t times,

$$X_t = X_0 + \varepsilon_1 + \cdots + \varepsilon_{t-2} + \varepsilon_{t-1} + \varepsilon_t. \tag{13.22}$$

Hence, given that $X_0 = 0$, $E(X_t) = 0$ as before. This can be confirmed by looking at Figure 13.6. The distribution at any time point t is distributed symmetrically about zero and so the mean remains at zero.

However, the second condition, that the variance should not change with time, is violated.

$$\begin{aligned}\operatorname{var}(X_t) &= \operatorname{var}(X_0 + \varepsilon_1 + \cdots + \varepsilon_{t-2} + \varepsilon_{t-1} + \varepsilon_t)\\ &= \operatorname{var}(\varepsilon_1) + \cdots + \operatorname{var}(\varepsilon_{t-2}) + \operatorname{var}(\varepsilon_{t-1}) + \operatorname{var}(\varepsilon_t)\\ &= \sigma_\varepsilon^2 + \cdots + \sigma_\varepsilon^2 + \sigma_\varepsilon^2 + \sigma_\varepsilon^2\\ &= t\sigma_\varepsilon^2.\end{aligned} \tag{13.23}$$

The variance is proportional to t, and this accounts for the spreading out of the distribution in Figure 13.6. We have thus confirmed graphically and mathematically that the ensemble distribution of (13.19) changes over time and therefore, by definition, that it is not stationary.

Variation

Suppose we add an intercept to the process, as in (13.24):

$$X_t = \beta_1 + X_{t-1} + \varepsilon_t. \tag{13.24}$$

What difference would this make? If (13.24) is true for time period t, it is true for $t-1$:

$$X_{t-1} = \beta_1 + X_{t-2} + \varepsilon_{t-1}. \tag{13.25}$$

Substituting into (13.24), we have

$$X_t = 2\beta_1 + X_{t-2} + \varepsilon_{t-1} + \varepsilon_t. \tag{13.26}$$

Lagging and substituting t times, this becomes

$$X_t = X_0 + t\beta_1 + \varepsilon_1 + \cdots + \varepsilon_{t-2} + \varepsilon_{t-1} + \varepsilon_t. \tag{13.27}$$

As a consequence,

$$E(X_t) = t\beta_1 \tag{13.28}$$

and the mean of the process becomes a function of time, violating the first condition for stationarity.

This process is known as a random walk with drift, the drift referring to the systematic change in the expectation from one time period to the next. Figure 13.7 shows 50 realizations of such a process. It can be seen that the ensemble distribution changes in two ways with time. The mean changes. In this case, it is drifting upwards because β_1 has been taken to be positive. If β_1 were negative, it would be drifting downwards. And, as in the first example, the distribution spreads out around the mean.

Deterministic trend

Random walks are not the only type of nonstationary process. Another common example of a nonstationary time series is one possessing a time trend:

$$X_t = \beta_1 + \beta_2 t + \varepsilon_t . \tag{13.29}$$

This type of trend is described as a deterministic trend, to differentiate it from the trend found in a model of a random walk with drift. Since

$$E(X_t) = \beta_1 + \beta_2 t + E(\varepsilon_t) = \beta_1 + \beta_2 t, \tag{13.30}$$

the expected value of X_t is not independent of t and so X_t is nonstationary. Figure 13.8 shows 50 realizations of a variation,

$$X_t = \beta_1 + \beta_2 t + u_t, \tag{13.31}$$

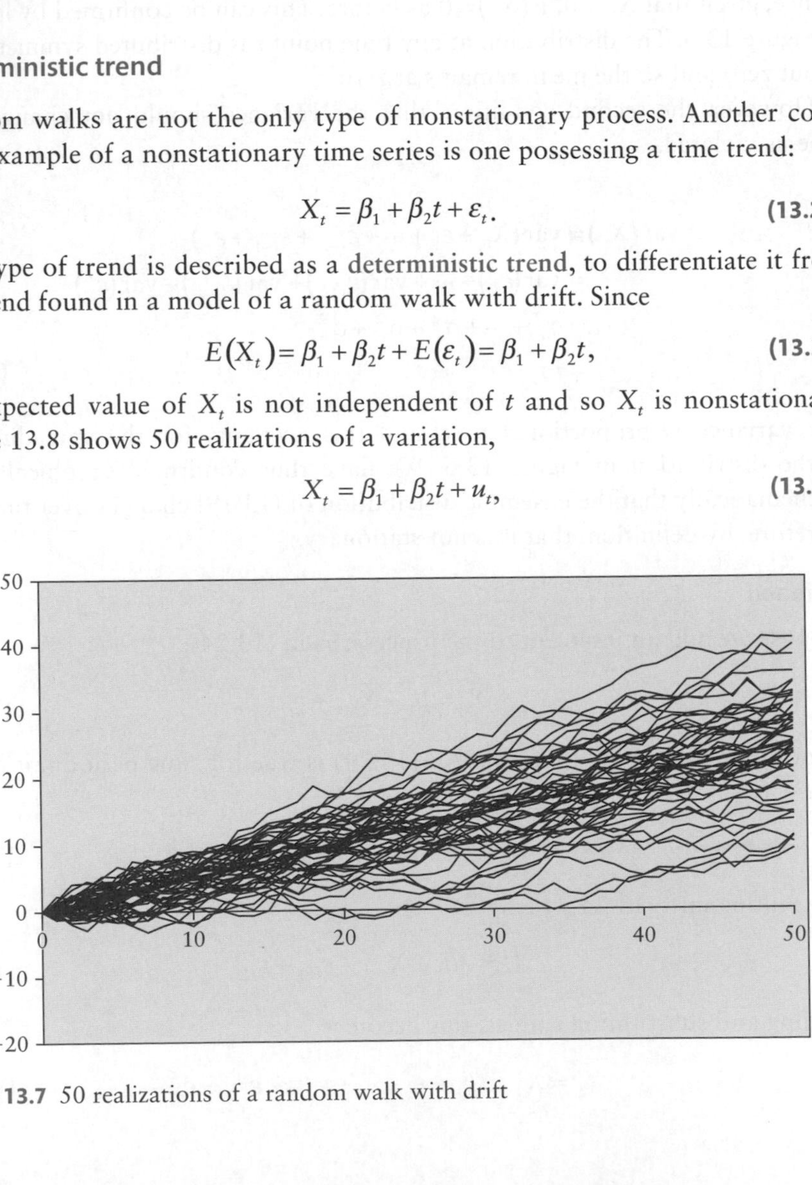

Figure 13.7 50 realizations of a random walk with drift

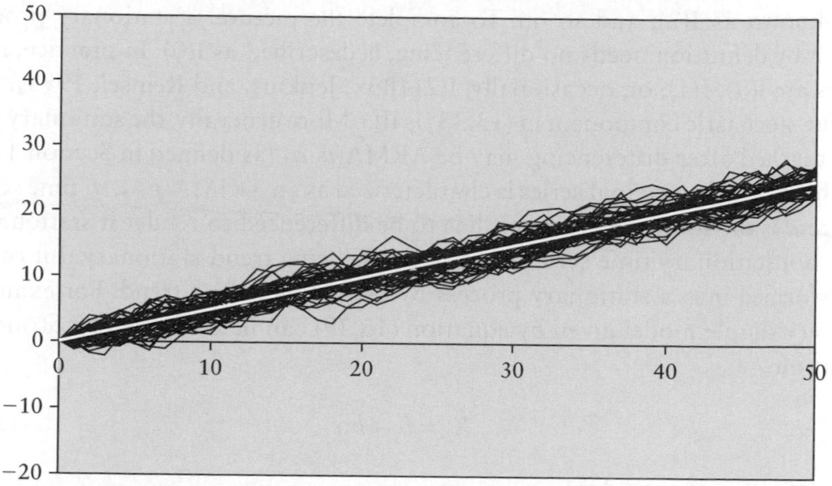

Figure 13.8 50 realizations of a deterministic trend with an AR(1) stationary process

where u_t is the stationary process

$$u_t = 0.8u_{t-1} + \varepsilon_t \tag{13.32}$$

displayed in Figures 13.1 and 13.2. The underlying trend line is shown in white.

The key difference between a deterministic trend and a random walk with drift is that in the former, the series must keep coming back to a fixed trend line. In any given observation, X_t will be displaced from the trend line by an amount u_t, but, provided that this is stationary, it must otherwise adhere to the trend line. By contrast, in a random walk with drift, the displacement from the underlying trend line at time t is the random walk $\sum \varepsilon_t$. Since the displacement is a random walk, there is no reason why X_t should ever return to its trend line.

Difference-stationarity and trend-stationarity

In the discussion that follows, a distinction will be made between difference-stationarity and trend-stationarity. If a nonstationary process can be transformed into a stationary process by differencing, it is said to be difference-stationary. A random walk, with or without drift, is an example. If X_t is a random walk with drift, as in equation (13.24),

$$\Delta X_t = X_t - X_{t-1} = \beta_1 + \varepsilon_t. \tag{13.33}$$

This is a stationary process with population mean β_1 and variance σ_ε^2, both independent of time. If a nonstationary time series can be transformed into a stationary process by differencing once, as in this case, it is described as integrated of order 1, or I(1). If a time series can be made stationary by differencing twice, it is known as I(2), and so on. To complete the picture, a stationary process, which by definition needs no differencing, is described as I(0). In practice, most series are I(0), I(1), or, occasionally, I(2) (Box, Jenkins, and Reinsel, 1994).

The stochastic component in (13.33) is IID. More generally, the stationary process reached after differencing may be ARMA(p, q) (as defined in Section 11.7), in which case the original series is characterized as an ARIMA(p, d, q) time series, where d is the number of times it has to be differenced to render it stationary.

A nonstationary time series is described as being trend-stationary if it can be transformed into a stationary process by extracting a time trend. For example, the very simple model given by equation (13.29) can be detrended by fitting the equation

$$\hat{X}_t = b_1 + b_2 t \tag{13.34}$$

and defining a new variable

$$\tilde{X}_t = X_t - \hat{X}_t = X_t - b_1 - b_2 t. \tag{13.35}$$

The new, detrended, variable is of course just the residuals from the regression of X on t.

The distinction between difference-stationarity and trend-stationarity is important for the analysis of time series. At one time it was conventional to assume that macroeconomic time series could be decomposed into trend and cyclical components, the former being determined by real factors, such as the growth of GDP, and the latter being determined by transitory factors, such as monetary policy. Typically, the cyclical component was analyzed using detrended versions of the variables in the model. However, as Nelson and Plosser (1982) point out, this approach is inappropriate if the process is difference-stationary. Although detrending may remove any drift, it does not affect the increasing variance of the series, and so the detrended component remains nonstationary. Further, because it ignores the contribution of real shocks to economic fluctuations, the approach causes the role of transitory factors in the cycle to be overestimated.

EXERCISES

13.1* Demonstrate that the MA(1) process

$$X_t = \varepsilon_t + \alpha_2 \varepsilon_{t-1}$$

is stationary. Does the result generalize to higher-order MA processes?

13.2* A stationary AR(1) process

$$X_t = \beta_1 + \beta_2 X_{t-1} + \varepsilon_t,$$

with $|\beta_2| < 1$, has initial value X_0, where X_0 is defined as

$$X_0 = \frac{\beta_1}{1-\beta_2} + \sqrt{\frac{1}{(1-\beta_2^2)}}\varepsilon_0$$

Demonstrate that X_0 is a random draw from the ensemble distribution for X.

13.2 Spurious regressions

To motivate the discussion that will consume the rest of this chapter, we now turn to the problem of spurious regressions. There are actually two literatures on spurious regressions. The first, which dates back to the beginning of econometrics as a formal discipline, concerns regressions involving variables with deterministic trends. The other involves regressions with random walks.

Spurious regressions with variables possessing deterministic trends

Suppose you have two unrelated variables Y_t and X_t, both generated by deterministic trends:

$$Y_t = \beta_1 + \beta_2 t + u_t \tag{13.36}$$

$$X_t = \alpha_1 + \alpha_2 t + v_t. \tag{13.37}$$

What happens if Y_t is regressed on X_t? The answer is obvious. The common dependence on t will cause the variables to be correlated, and hence a regression of one on the other will yield 'significant' coefficients, provided that the sample is large enough.

This problem was recognized very early in the history of econometrics. A popular response was to detrend the variables before performing the regression. Y_t and X_t would separately be regressed on time and the residuals saved, say as e_{Yt} and e_{Xt}. e_{Yt} and e_{Xt} would retain all the variation in Y_t and X_t other than that attributable to the time trend. If there were a genuine relationship between Y_t and X_t, it would be revealed in a regression of e_{Yt} on e_{Xt}. Eventually it was pointed out (Frisch and Waugh, 1933) that one did not actually need to go to the trouble of detrending Y_t and X_t before performing the regression. Exactly the same results would be obtained by including a time trend in a multiple regression of (unadjusted) Y_t on (unadjusted) X_t. (This was the origin of the Frisch–Waugh–Lovell theorem discussed in Section 3.2. Lovell (1963) generalized the result.)

The inclusion of a time trend in a regression of Y_t on X_t makes it relatively difficult to obtain significant results. Since it possesses a trend, the series for X_t will be correlated with t, and hence the problem of multicollinearity inevitably arises to some extent. However, performing the regression with the detrended versions of Y_t and X_t does not lead to any better results because they must be exactly the same.

Spurious regressions with variables that are random walks

The problem of spurious regressions caused by deterministic trends is easy to understand and easy to treat. Much more dramatic, and ultimately important, were the findings of a celebrated simulation undertaken by Granger and Newbold (1974). They found that, if they generated two independent random walks and regressed one on the other, the slope coefficient was likely to have a significant t statistic, despite the fact that the series were unrelated. They generated 100 pairs of random walks, with sample size 50 time periods. In 77, the slope coefficient was significant at the 5 percent level. This means that there were 77 instances of Type I error in the 100 regressions. With a 5 percent significance test, there ought to have been about 5. The incidence of Type I error when performing a 1 percent significance test was not much lower.

The study made an immediate impact because there was a growing consensus that many economic time series are plausibly characterized as being random walks, possibly with drift. Drift would of course aggravate the problem of spurious association. The findings of Granger and Newbold are all the more remarkable because their series were pure random walks.

We will undertake a similar simulation here. Our model will be

$$Y_t = \beta_1 + \beta_2 X_t + u_t \tag{13.38}$$

and we will regress Y_t on X_t where Y_t and X_t are generated as independent random walks. For comparison, we will also regress Y_t on X_t where Y_t and X_t are generated as independent white noise processes. In both cases, since Y_t and X_t are unrelated, the true value of β_2 is zero. In both cases, we generate 10 million samples for four sample sizes: 25, 50, 100, and 200.

Figures 13.9 and 13.10 show the distributions of b_2 and its t statistic for the regression where Y_t and X_t were white noise processes drawn independently

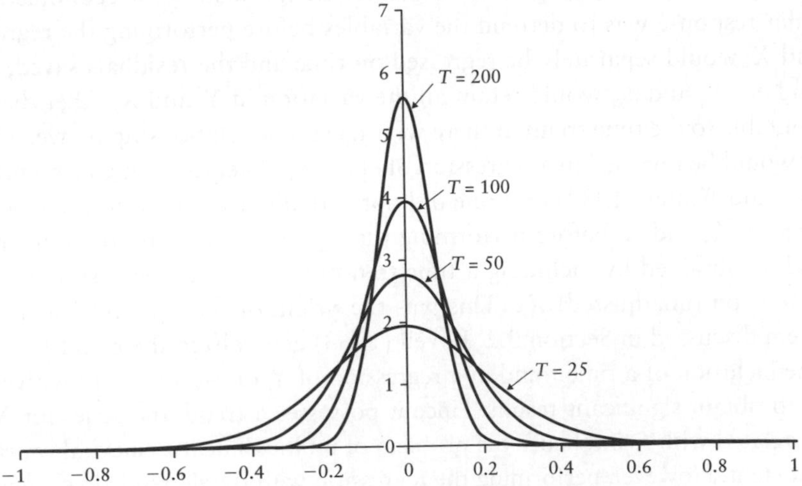

Figure 13.9 Distribution of b_2, white noise regressions

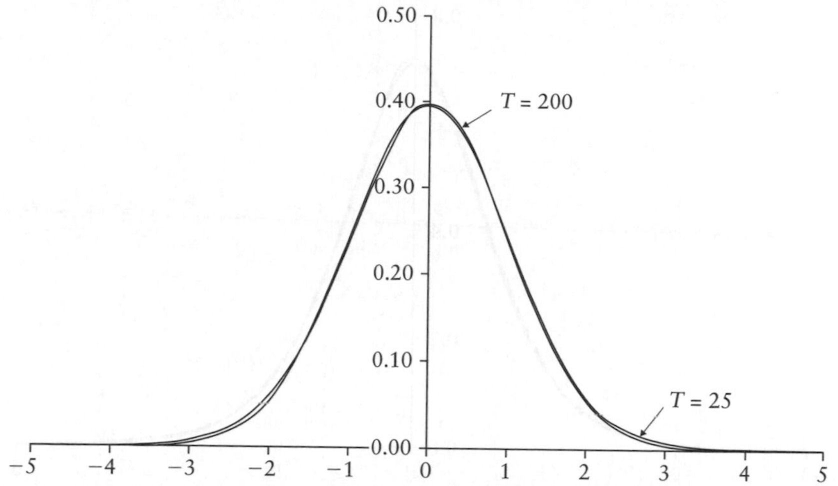

Figure 13.10 Distribution of t statistic for b_2, white noise regressions

from a normal distribution with zero mean and unit variance. The results of these regressions are intended to serve as a benchmark illustration of standard theory.

According to standard theory, the distribution of b_2 should have mean zero and standard deviation inversely proportional to $\sqrt{T}$, where T is the sample size. The height of the distribution should therefore be proportional to $\sqrt{T}$ since the total area must remain constant at unity. Thus, one would expect the distribution for 100 to be twice as tall as that for 25, and that for 200 to be twice as tall as that for 50. This is easy to check visually. Figure 13.9 confirms the theory.

Standard theory tells us that the distribution of the t statistic should have mean zero irrespective of the sample size and that it should converge to a normal distribution with zero mean and unit variance as the sample size becomes large. Figure 13.10 confirms this. It shows only the distributions for $T = 25$ and $T = 200$. Those for $T = 50$ and $T = 100$ are not shown because they are virtually coincidental with the other two. The distribution for $T = 200$ is the one with the very slightly higher mode and the thinner tails. It has converged on the normal distribution. The distribution for $T = 25$ is very similar. The body of the distribution has also almost converged on the normal distribution. It is only in the tails, which are marginally fatter than those for a normal distribution, that the distribution has not fully converged.

Figures 13.11, 13.12, and 13.13 provide similar information for the random walk regressions. Figures 13.11(a) and (b) demonstrate a truly remarkable result. If you regress one random walk on another, the slope coefficient does not tend to zero, no matter how large is the sample size. It tends to a limiting distribution. This is a complete break from what we have seen so far. It is the first time that we have come across an estimator that is inconsistent because its

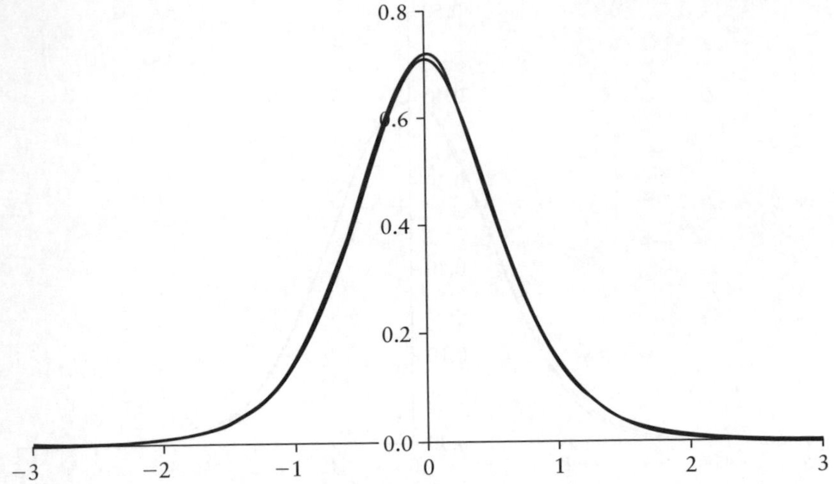

Figure 13.11(a) Distribution of b_2, random walk regressions, $T = 25, 50, 100$, and 200

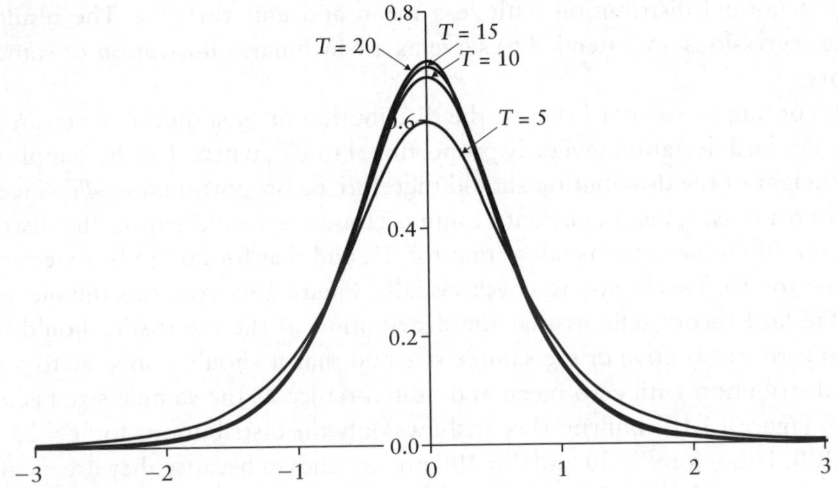

Figure 13.11(b) Distribution of b_2, random walk regressions, $T = 5, 10, 15$, and 20

distribution fails to collapse to a spike. The two requirements of a consistent estimator are:

1. Its distribution should collapse to a spike.
2. The spike should be at the true value of the parameter being estimated.

In previous encounters with inconsistent estimators, for example, OLS estimators in the presence of measurement error or simultaneity, the distributions did collapse to a spike, but the spike was at the wrong place. In this case, there is no

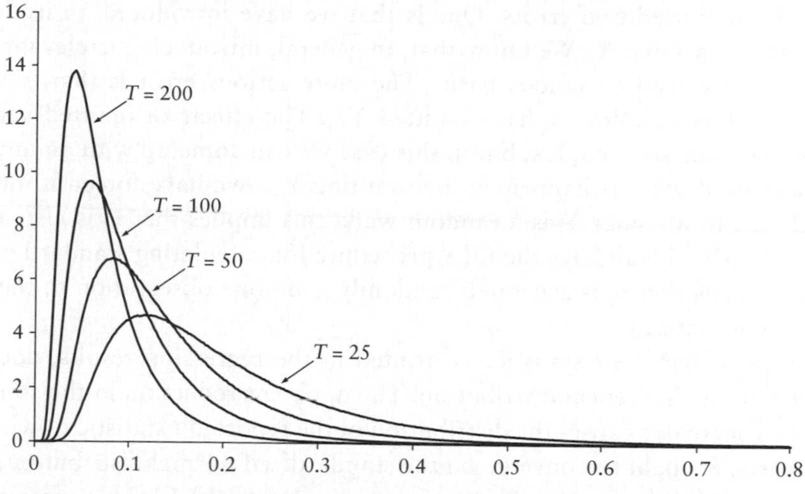

Figure 13.12 Distribution of standard error of b_2, random walk regressions

bias, so if the distribution had collapsed, the estimator would have been consistent. But it refuses to collapse. Phillips (1986) presents the mathematical theory for the failure to collapse. Since it involves advanced mathematics (stochastic calculus), a treatment will not be attempted here. We will be content with the simulation results.

Figure 13.11(a) shows the distributions of b_2 for $T = 25$, 50, 100, and 200. They are virtually identical. For a sample size of 25, the distribution has already virtually reached its limiting distribution. To see the process of convergence, one must look at even smaller sample sizes. This is done in Figure 13.11(b), where $T = 5$, 10, 15, and 20. The variance of the distribution falls when one increases the sample size from 5 to 10, and it falls further when one increases the sample size to 15. There is hardly any further change when one increases the sample size to 20 because the distribution is already close to its limit.

Figure 13.12 gives the distributions of the standard errors, *as printed out in the regression results*, for T equal to 25, 50, 100, and 200. These distributions ought to be almost identical, given that the standard error provides an estimate of the standard deviation, and Figure 13.11(a) has shown that the standard deviations for these sample sizes are almost the same. However, Figure 13.12 suggests that the standard deviation decreases with the sample size, in the usual way. This is incorrect, and the reason for the aberration is that the model is misspecified. Since Y_t is a random walk, the true process is

$$Y_t = Y_{t-1} + \varepsilon_{Yt}, \qquad \textbf{(13.39)}$$

where ε_{Yt} is a white noise process. When we fit

$$Y_t = \beta_1 + \beta_2 X_t + u_t, \qquad \textbf{(13.40)}$$

we have committed two errors. One is that we have introduced an irrelevant explanatory variable X_t. We know that, in general, introducing irrelevant variables does not lead to serious harm. The more serious error is that, since Y_t is generated as (13.39), we have omitted Y_{t-1}. The effects of omitted variable misspecification are complex, but in this case we can come up with an intuitive explanation of what is happening. By omitting Y_{t-1}, we have forced it into the disturbance term. Since Y_t is a random walk, this implies that u_t is also a random walk. This invalidates the OLS procedure for calculating standard errors, which assumes that u_t is generated randomly from one observation to the next (no autocorrelation).

It follows that the t statistic, as printed in the regression results, does not conform to its theoretical distribution. The apparent reduction in the standard error as T increases causes the distribution of the reported t statistic to widen as T increases. It ought to converge on the standardized normal distribution, as in Figure 13.10, but instead it widens, as shown in Figure 13.13. This accounts for the very high incidence of Type I errors found by Granger and Newbold.

Before drawing the implications of these findings, we will consider one further example. Suppose that, instead of being random walks, Y_t and X_t are (independent) AR(1) processes with coefficient 0.95:

$$Y_t = 0.95Y_{t-1} + \varepsilon_{Yt} \tag{13.41}$$

$$X_t = 0.95X_{t-1} + \varepsilon_{Xt}, \tag{13.42}$$

ε_{Yt} and ε_{Xt} being independent white noise processes. What happens if one regresses Y_t on X_t? Figure 13.14 shows the distribution of b_2 for sample sizes 25, 50, 100, and 200. The distribution does contract as the sample size increases, and if we

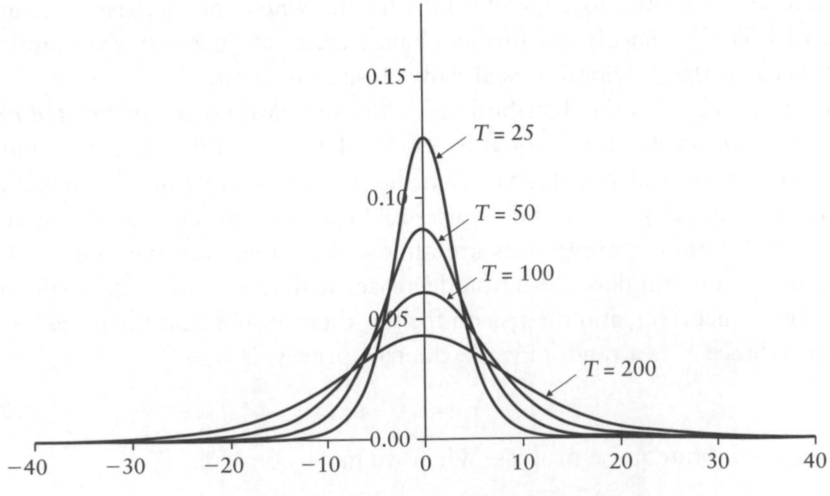

Figure 13.13 Distribution of t statistic for b_2, random walk regressions

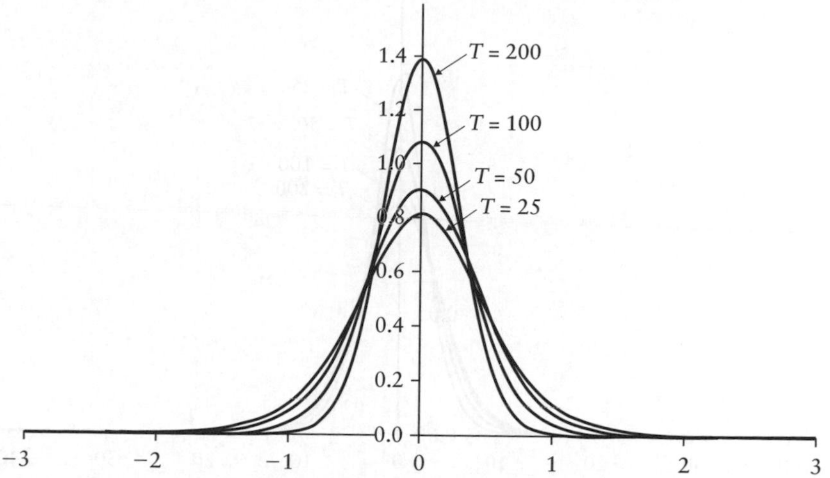

Figure 13.14 Distribution of b_2, AR(1) regressions with $\rho = 0.95$

continued to increase the sample size, it will progressively contract to a spike at zero. So, in contrast to the regressions with random walks, b_2 is a consistent estimator. But the rate of reduction of the standard deviation (and hence the increase in height) of the distribution is less than the $\sqrt{T}$ that we would expect from standard theory and that we found in Figure 13.9 with the white noise regressions. This is especially noticeable for small sample sizes.

As with the random walk case, the standard errors are computed incorrectly and the t statistics are not valid. The reasons are parallel to those in the case of the random walks. When we fit

$$Y_t = \beta_1 + \beta_2 X_t + u_t \tag{13.43}$$

instead of

$$Y_t = \beta_1 + \beta_2 Y_{t-1} + u_t, \tag{13.44}$$

we have included the redundant variable X_t, which does not matter, and have omitted Y_{t-1}, which does. Again, Y_{t-1} is forced into u_t and so u_t is an autocorrelated process with $\rho = 0.95$. Figure 13.15 gives the t distribution for the different sample sizes. It is nonstandard, although not as distorted as that for the random walks.

Of course, the autocorrelation should be revealed by a formal test. This is the case. For this purpose, it is sufficient to use the d statistic for the Durbin–Watson test, despite its imperfections. Figure 13.16 shows the distribution of this statistic for the four sample sizes. Even with T as small as 25, it indicates autocorrelation significant at the 1 percent level in most of the 10 million samples. For larger samples, it indicates significant autocorrelation almost all of the time.

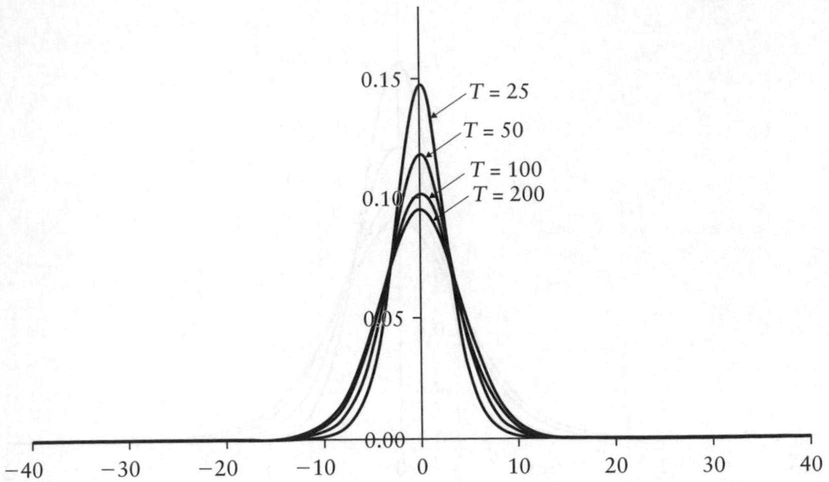

Figure 13.15 Distribution of t statistic for b_2, AR(1) regressions with $\rho = 0.95$

Once aware of the problem, we know how to treat it. We eliminate the autocorrelation by fitting the model

$$Y_t = \beta_1(1-\rho) + \rho Y_{t-1} + \beta_2 X_t - \beta_2 \rho X_{t-1} + \varepsilon_t. \quad \textbf{(13.45)}$$

If we do this, we will find that the coefficients of X_t and X_{t-1} are both zero and that the coefficient of Y_{t-1} is 0.95, subject of course to sampling error and the finite-sample bias caused by the presence of the lagged dependent variable in the specification. The fitted model then reveals the truth, that Y_t depends only on Y_{t-1} with coefficient 0.95, and that it does not depend on X_t at all.

Could we not treat the random walk case, where, under the null hypothesis, the disturbance term itself is a random walk, as an extreme case of autocorrelation with $\rho = 1$? In some ways, we can. As with the $\rho = 0.95$ case, the Durbin–Watson statistic almost invariably indicates severe positive autocorrelation. The distributions of the Durbin–Watson statistic for the various sample sizes are similar to those in Figure 13.16, shifted even further to the left. What happens if we fit (13.45) for this case? The results are much the same as for the case $\rho = 0.95$. We will discover that $\rho = 1$, that $\beta_2 = 0$, and the relationship simplifies to the definition of the random walk that is the true relationship for Y_t. This is not quite the full story because, as we will see in the next section, there are further surprises when we come to test the (true) null hypothesis that the coefficient of Y_{t-1} is equal to 1. However, it is a reasonable first approximation.

The AR(1) regressions demonstrate that the problem of excess Type I errors arising from nonstandard t distributions found by Granger and Newbold did not depend on the nonstationarity of their processes. It occurs with any AR(1) process, being more evident, the more closely the slope coefficient approximates unity.

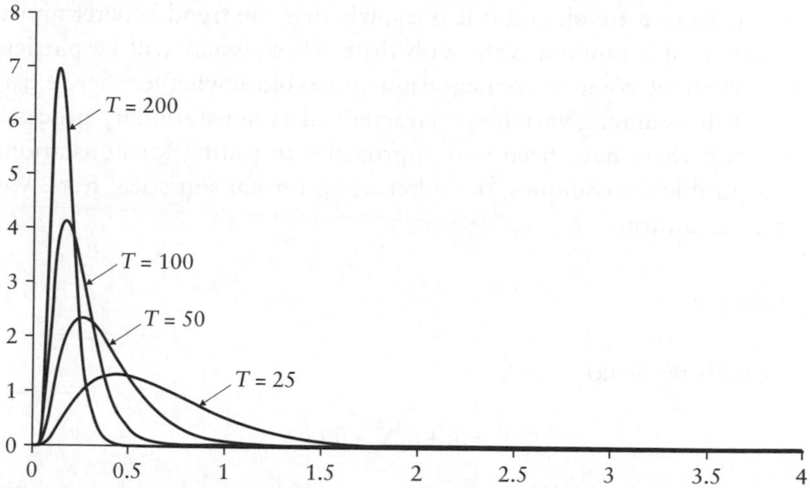

Figure 13.16 Distribution of Durbin–Watson statistic, AR(1) regressions with $\rho = 0.95$

The lesson to be learnt from the Granger–Newbold simulations is the one that motivated their article and was articulated by them at the time. This was that there is a substantial risk of apparently obtaining significant results, where no relationship exists, if you ignore evidence of autocorrelation, as was once quite common in applied work. The fact that Granger and Newbold used nonstationary processes, in the form of random walks, to make their point is not important. They could have made it just as well by using independent stationary AR(1) processes. But the effect is the more dramatic, the greater the value of ρ, and most obvious when one goes to the extreme value of 1, the random walk.

Although the objective of the Granger–Newbold simulations was to highlight the dangers of ignoring evidence of autocorrelation in time series models, their experiments also contributed to a growing awareness that standard theory did not necessarily apply to the properties of regression estimators, and associated statistical inference, for regressions using nonstationary time series data.

These concerns were reinforced by the fact that the use of nonstationary variables in model-building was very common. Macroeconomic analysis, in particular, routinely used variables such as aggregate income and aggregate consumption that invariably possessed time trends when measured in levels and were unquestionably nonstationary, the only issue being whether they were better characterized as random walks with drift (as argued by Nelson and Plosser, 1982) or as subject to deterministic trends. This stimulated a literature, now enormous and still growing, concerning the determination of the conditions under which such regressions with nonstationary time series could yield consistent estimates with valid statistical inference.

The first step was to develop a means for identifying whether a time series is, or is not, nonstationary in the first place, and if it is nonstationary, whether or not it possesses a trend, and if it does, whether the trend is deterministic or is the outcome of a random walk with drift. These issues will be particularly important when we come to cointegration and explore whether there exist genuine relationships among variables characterized as nonstationary processes.

Historically, there have been two approaches to testing for nonstationarity, one using graphical techniques, the other using formal statistical tests. We will consider each in turn.

EXERCISE

13.3 Consider the model

$$Y_t = \beta_1 + \beta_2 X_t + \beta_3 t + u_t$$

and suppose that X_t has a strong time trend. As a consequence, the estimation of β_2 will be subject to multicollinearity and the standard error relatively large. Suppose that one detrends the data for Y and X and instead regresses the model

$$e_{Yt} = \beta_2 e_{Xt} + u_t.$$

This is a simple regression and so the problem of multicollinearity does not arise. Nevertheless, by virtue of the Frisch–Waugh–Lovell theorem, the estimate of β_2 and its standard error will be exactly the same. Explain intuitively why the standard error has not decreased, despite the elimination of the problem of multicollinearity.

13.3 Graphical techniques for detecting nonstationarity

Section 11.7 outlines the time series analysis approach to representing a time series as a univariate ARMA(p, q) process

$$Y_t = \theta_0 + \theta_1 Y_{t-1} + \theta_2 Y_{t-2} + \ldots + \theta_p Y_{t-p} + \phi_1 \varepsilon_t + \phi_2 \varepsilon_{t-1} + \ldots + \phi_{q+1} \varepsilon_{t-q} \qquad \textbf{(13.46)}$$

for appropriate choice of p and q. Much earlier than conventional econometricians, time series analysts recognized the importance of nonstationarity and the need for eliminating it by differencing, generalizing the ARMA(p, q) model to the ARIMA(p, d, q) model where d was the number of times the series had to be differenced to render it stationary. The key tool for determining d, and subsequently p and q, was the correlogram. The autocorrelation function of a series X_t gives the theoretical correlation between the value of a series at time t and its value at time $t + k$, for values of k from 1 to (typically) about 20, being defined as the series

$$\rho_k = \frac{E((X_t - \mu_X)(X_{t+k} - \mu_X))}{\sqrt{E((X_t - \mu_X)^2)E((X_{t+k} - \mu_X)^2)}} \quad \text{for } k = 1, \ldots \qquad \textbf{(13.47)}$$

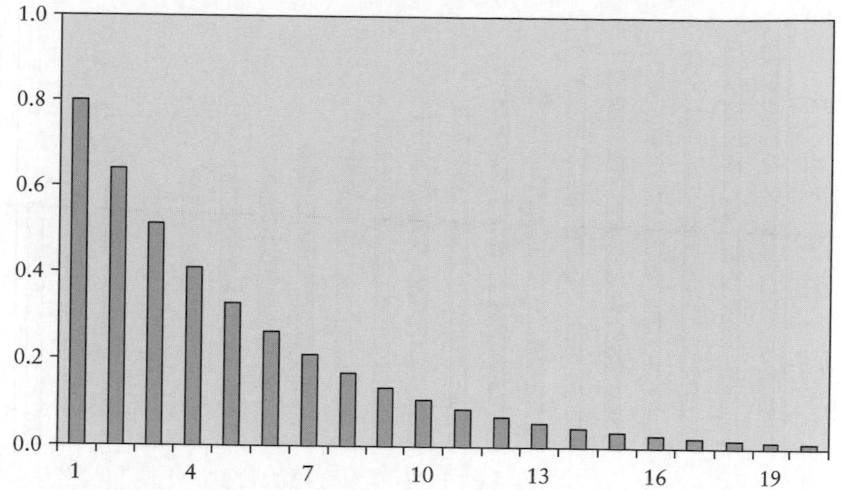

Figure 13.17 Correlogram of an AR(1) process with $\beta_2 = 0.8$

The correlogram is its graphical representation.

For example, the autocorrelation function for an AR(1) process $X_t = \beta_2 X_{t-1} + \varepsilon_t$ is

$$\rho_k = \beta_2^k, \tag{13.48}$$

the coefficients decreasing exponentially with the lag provided that $\beta_2 < 1$ and the process is stationary. The corresponding correlogram is shown in Figure 13.17 for β_2 equal to 0.8.

Higher-order stationary AR(p) processes may exhibit a more complex mixture of damped sine waves and damped exponentials, but they retain the feature that the weights eventually decline to zero.

By contrast, an MA(q) process has nonzero weights for only the first q lags and zero weights thereafter. In particular, the first autocorrelation coefficient for the MA(1) process

$$X_t = \varepsilon_t + \alpha_2 \varepsilon_{t-1} \tag{13.49}$$

is given by

$$\rho_1 = \frac{\alpha_2}{1 + \alpha_2^2} \tag{13.50}$$

and all subsequent autocorrelation coefficients are zero. The proof is left as an exercise.

In the case of nonstationary processes, the theoretical autocorrelation coefficients are not defined but one may be able to obtain an expression for $E(r_k)$, the expected value of the sample autocorrelation coefficients, and for long time series, these coefficients decline slowly. For example, in the case of a random walk,

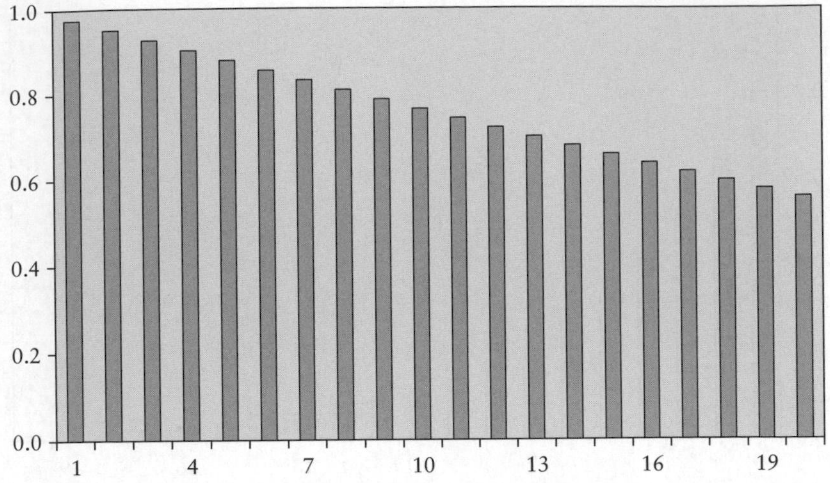

Figure 13.18 Correlogram (expected values of r_k) for a random walk, $n = 200$

the correlogram for a series with 200 observations is as shown in Figure 13.18 (Wichern, 1973).

Time series analysts exploit this fact in a two-stage procedure for identifying the orders of a series believed to be of the ARIMA(p, d, q) type. In the first stage, if the correlogram exhibits slowly declining coefficients, the series is differenced d times until the series exhibits a stationary pattern. Usually one differencing is sufficient, and at most two.

The second stage is to inspect the correlogram of the differenced series and its partial correlogram, a related tool, to determine appropriate values for p and q. This is not an exact science. It requires judgment, a reading of the tea-leaves, and different analysts can come up with different values. However, when that happens, alternative models are likely to imply similar forecasts, and that is what matters. Time series analysis is a pragmatic approach to forecasting. As Box, a leading exponent, once said, 'All models are wrong, but some are useful' (Box and Draper, 1987). In any case, the complexity of the task is limited by the fact that in practice most series are adequately represented by a process with the sum of p and q no greater than 2 (Box, Jenkins, and Reinsel, 1994).

There are, however, two problems with using correlograms to identify nonstationarity. One is that a correlogram such as that in Figure 13.18 could result from a stationary AR(1) process with a high value of β_2. The other is that the coefficients of a nonstationary process may decline quite rapidly if the series is not long. This is illustrated in Figure 13.19, which shows the expected values of r_k for a random walk when the series has only 50 observations.

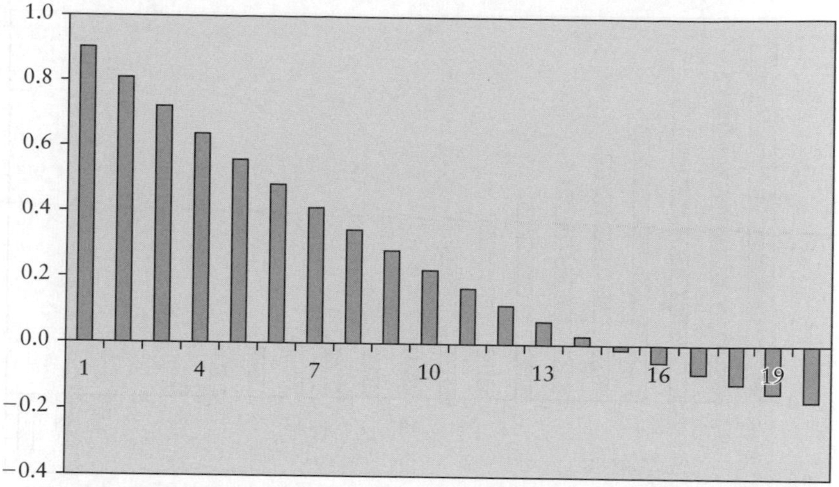

Figure 13.19 Correlogram (expected values of r_k) of a random walk, $n = 50$

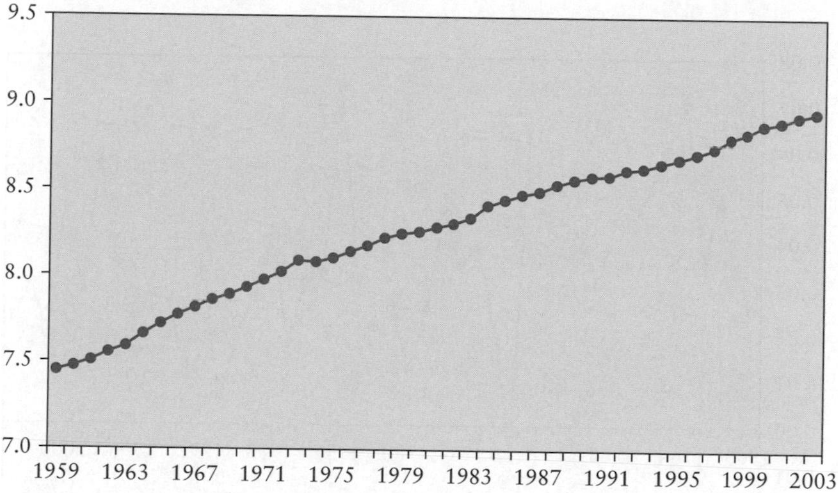

Figure 13.20 Logarithm of *DPI*, 1959–2003

Example

Figure 13.20 presents the data for the logarithm of *DPI* for 1959–2003 and Figure 13.21 presents the sample correlogram. At first sight, the falling autocorrelation coefficients suggest a stationary AR(1) process with a high value of β_2. Although the theoretical correlogram for such a process, shown in Figure 13.17, looks a little different in that the coefficients decline exponentially to zero without becoming negative, a sample correlogram would have negative values similar to those in Figure 13.21. However, the correlogram in Figure 13.21 is also very similar to that for the finite nonstationary process shown in Figure 13.19.

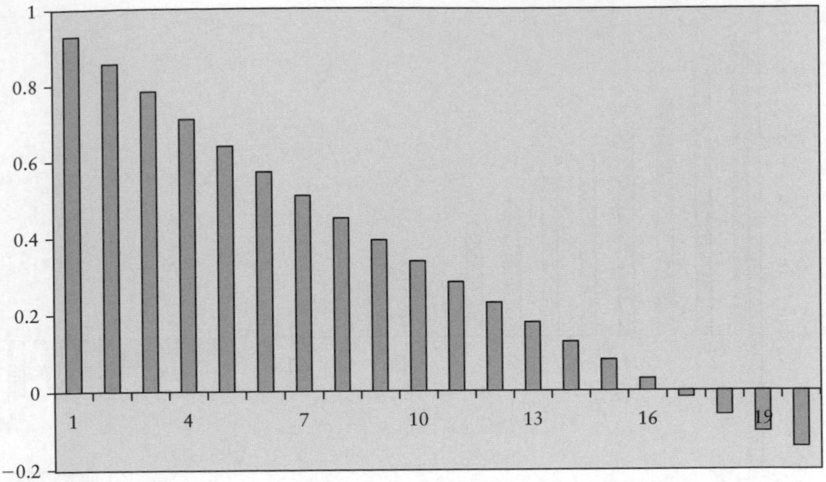

Figure 13.21 Sample correlogram of the logarithm of *DPI*

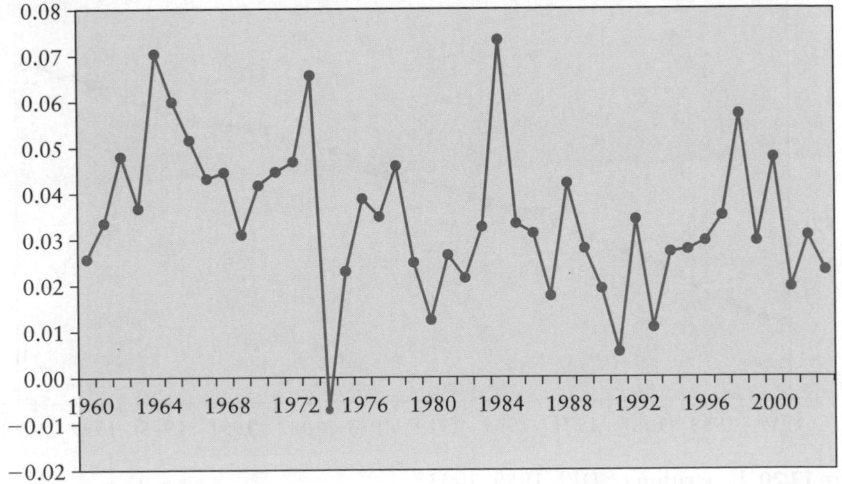

Figure 13.22 Differenced logarithm of *DPI*

Figure 13.22 shows the differenced series, which appears to be stationary around a mean annual growth rate of between 2 and 3 percent. Possibly there might be a downward trend, and equally possibly there might be a discontinuity in the series at 1972, with a step down in the mean growth rate after the first oil shock, but these hypotheses will not be investigated here. Figure 13.23 shows the corresponding correlogram, whose low, erratic autocorrelation coefficients provide support for the hypothesis that the differenced series is stationary.

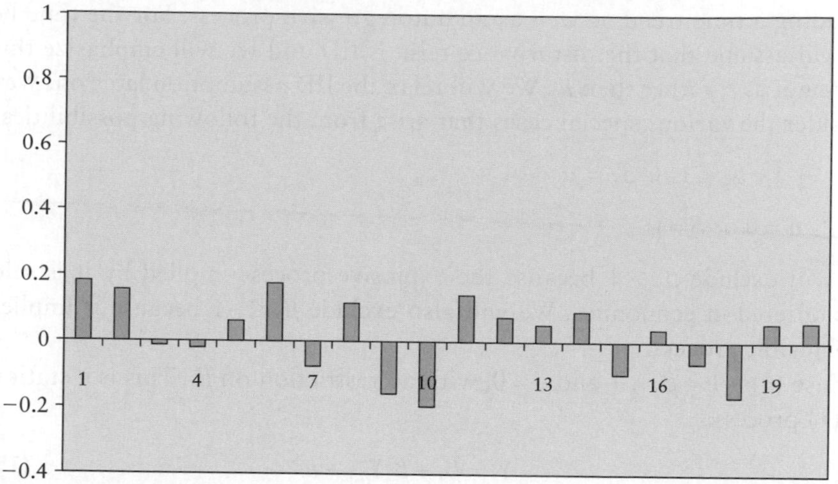

Figure 13.23 Sample correlogram of the differenced logarithm of *DPI*

EXERCISES

13.4 Prove that the autocorrelation function for an MA(1) process is given by (13.50) for the first autocorrelation, and 0 for higher ones.

13.5 Derive the autocorrelation function for an MA(2) process.

13.4 Tests of nonstationarity

The graphical approach appears to have served the time series analysts satisfactorily, but on the whole econometricians prefer more formal methods and tests for nonstationarity are no exception. They are often described as tests for unit roots, for reasons related to the theory of difference equations that need not concern us here.

Before embarking on tests of nonstationarity, it is prudent to recognize that we should not have unrealistic expectations concerning what can be achieved. To illustrate the discussion, suppose that we believe a process can be represented by

$$Y_t = \beta_2 Y_{t-1} + \varepsilon_t. \quad \textbf{(13.51)}$$

If $\beta_2 = 1$, the process is nonstationary. If $\beta_2 = 0.99$, it is stationary. Can we really expect to be able to discriminate between these two possibilities? Obviously not. We are seldom able to make such fine distinctions in econometrics. We have to live with the fact that we are unlikely ever to be able to discriminate between nonstationarity and highly autocorrelated stationarity.

We will start with the first-order autoregressive model

$$Y_t = \beta_1 + \beta_2 Y_{t-1} + \delta t + \varepsilon_t \quad \textbf{(13.52)}$$

including a time trend as well as an autoregressive process. For the time being we will assume that the disturbance term is IID and we will emphasize this by writing it as ε_t rather than u_t. We will relax the IID assumption later on. We will consider the various special cases that arise from the following possibilities:

- $-1 < \beta_2 < 1$ or $\beta_2 = 1$;
- $\delta = 0$ or $\delta \neq 0$.

We will exclude $\beta_2 > 1$ because the explosive process implied by it is seldom encountered in economics. We will also exclude $\beta_2 \leq -1$ because it implies an implausible process.

Case (a): $-1 < \beta_2 < 1$ and $\delta = 0$, with no restriction on β_1. This is a stationary AR(1) process:

$$Y_t = \beta_1 + \beta_2 Y_{t-1} + \varepsilon_t. \tag{13.53}$$

Case (b): $\beta_1 = 0, \beta_2 = 1$, and $\delta = 0$. The process is a random walk:

$$Y_t = Y_{t-1} + \varepsilon_t. \tag{13.54}$$

Case (c): $\beta_1 \neq 0, \beta_2 = 1$, and $\delta = 0$. The process is a random walk with drift:

$$Y_t = \beta_1 + Y_{t-1} + \varepsilon_t. \tag{13.55}$$

Case (d): $-1 < \beta_2 < 1$ and $\delta \neq 0$. This is a stationary autoregressive process around a deterministic trend:

$$Y_t = \beta_1 + \beta_2 Y_{t-1} + \delta t + \varepsilon_t. \tag{13.56}$$

Case (e): $\beta_2 = 1$ and $\delta \neq 0$. The model is doubly nonstationary, being a random walk (with drift if $\beta_1 \neq 0$) around a deterministic time trend.

Case (e) can be excluded because it is implausible. It implies

$$\begin{aligned} Y_t &= \beta_1 + Y_{t-1} + \delta t + \varepsilon_t \\ &= \beta_1 + \left(\beta_1 + Y_{t-2} + \delta(t-1) + \varepsilon_{t-1}\right) + \delta t + \varepsilon_t \\ &= 2\beta_1 + 2\delta t - \delta + Y_{t-2} + \varepsilon_{t-1} + \varepsilon_t \end{aligned} \tag{13.57}$$

after lagging and substituting once. Lagging and substituting t times, we can express Y_t in terms of the initial Y_0, the innovations, and a convex quadratic expression for t:

$$Y_t = t\beta_1 + \frac{t(t+1)}{2}\delta + Y_0 + \sum_{s=1}^{t} \varepsilon_s. \tag{13.58}$$

It is not reasonable to suppose that any (ordinary) time series process can be characterized as a convex quadratic function of time.

Our objective is to determine which of cases (a)–(d) provides the best representation of a given process. Two approaches have been advocated.

One is to start with the most general model, (13.52), and then conduct a series of tests that might lead to a simplification to one of cases (a)–(d) (see, for example, Holden and Perman, 2007). This has the intellectual appeal of implementing the general-to-specific approach. However, as will be seen, the tests involved often have low power, and this can give rise to ambiguity that cannot be resolved.

The other approach (see, for example, Hamilton, 1994) is pragmatic. One starts by plotting the data and assessing whether there is evidence of a trend. If there is not, then one limits the investigation to cases (a) and (b). If there is, one considers cases (c) and (d). This is the approach that will be adopted here.

Untrended process

If there is no evidence of a trend, we can drop the time trend and are therefore left with the two alternatives of a stationary process and a random walk:

$$Y_t = \beta_1 + \beta_2 Y_{t-1} + \varepsilon_t \tag{13.59}$$

$$Y_t = Y_{t-1} + \varepsilon_t . \tag{13.60}$$

Note that there is an asymmetry in the specification under the two possibilities. If the process is a random walk, there must be no intercept. Otherwise the process would be a random walk with drift and therefore trended. If the process is stationary, the intercept may, and in general, will, be nonzero. For this reason, in the discussion below, it should be assumed that the fitted model includes an intercept, as in (13.59), and that we are interested in testing the restrictions $\beta_2 = 1$ and $\beta_1 = 0$.

In Section 11.5 we investigated the properties of the OLS estimator of β_2 in the autoregressive process

$$Y_t = \beta_2 Y_{t-1} + \varepsilon_t . \tag{13.61}$$

We were not able to say anything analytically about the finite-sample properties of the estimator, but we saw that it is consistent and that

$$\sqrt{T}\,(b_2 - \beta_2) \xrightarrow{d} N\left(0,\ 1 - \beta_2^2\right). \tag{13.62}$$

From this, we could assert that, as an approximation, for sufficiently large samples

$$b_2 \sim N\left(\beta_2,\ \frac{1 - \beta_2^2}{T}\right) \tag{13.63}$$

and we investigated the closeness of the approximation using simulation methods. Including an intercept does not affect these conclusions qualitatively. What happens if $\beta_2 = 1$, as in (13.60)? If we try to apply (13.62) when $\beta_2 = 1$, we immediately get into trouble. It implies that the limiting distribution of the scaled estimator has zero variance.

This is actually correct. To understand what is happening, we will look at the distribution of the estimated values of β_2, when $\beta_2 = 1$, for $T = 25, 50, 100$, and 200. Figure 13.24 shows the distribution of b_2 for the different sample sizes when we fit (13.59). As expected, the OLS estimator is biased for finite samples but consistent. The distribution collapses to a spike as the sample size increases, and the spike is at the true value $\beta_2 = 1$.

This is as anticipated since we know that OLS is a consistent estimator for all AR(1) processes (Rubin, 1950). What is surprising is the rate at which the distribution contracts. In all applications so far, the variance of the OLS estimator has been inversely proportional to the size of the sample. Hence the standard deviation is inversely proportional to $\sqrt{T}$, and since the area is constant at 1, the height of the distribution is proportional to $\sqrt{T}$. Figure 13.9 provides a typical example. However, in Figure 13.24 it can be seen that the height is proportional to T. The height doubles from $T = 25$ to $T = 50$, it doubles again from $T = 50$ to $T = 100$, and it doubles once more from $T = 100$ to $T = 200$. This means that the variance of the distribution of b_2 is inversely proportional to T^2, not T. Multiplying by $\sqrt{T}$ is not enough to prevent the distribution contracting. Figure 13.25 illustrates this.

Because the distribution is contracting to the true value faster than the standard rate, the estimator is described as **superconsistent**. When $\beta_2 = 1$, to obtain a limiting distribution relevant to the OLS estimator, we must consider $T(b_2 - 1)$, not $\sqrt{T}(b_2 - 1)$. Figure 13.26 shows that this statistic does have a limiting distribution, and reaches it quite quickly, since the distribution for $T = 25$ is almost the same as that for $T = 200$. (The distributions for $T = 50$ and $T = 100$ have been omitted, for clarity.)

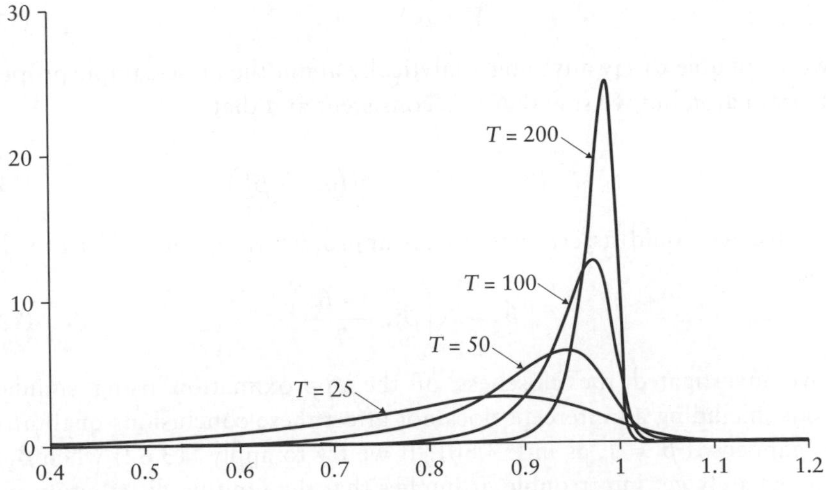

Figure 13.24 Distribution of slope coefficient, true model a random walk

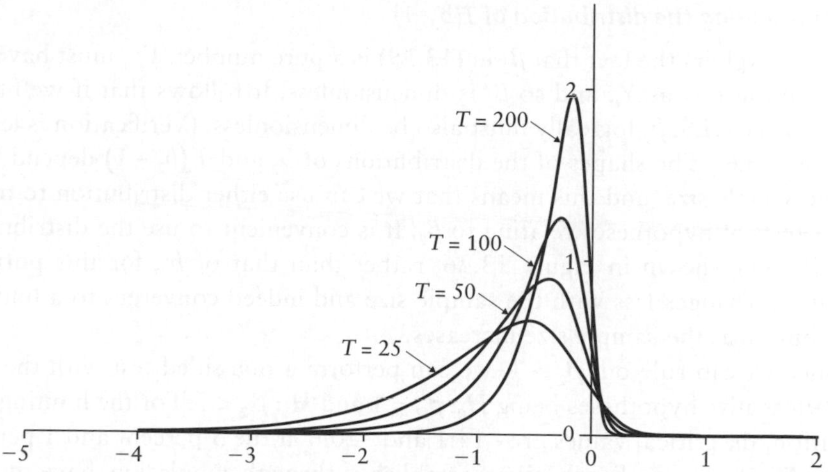

Figure 13.25 Distribution of $\sqrt{T}\,(b_2 - 1)$, true model a random walk

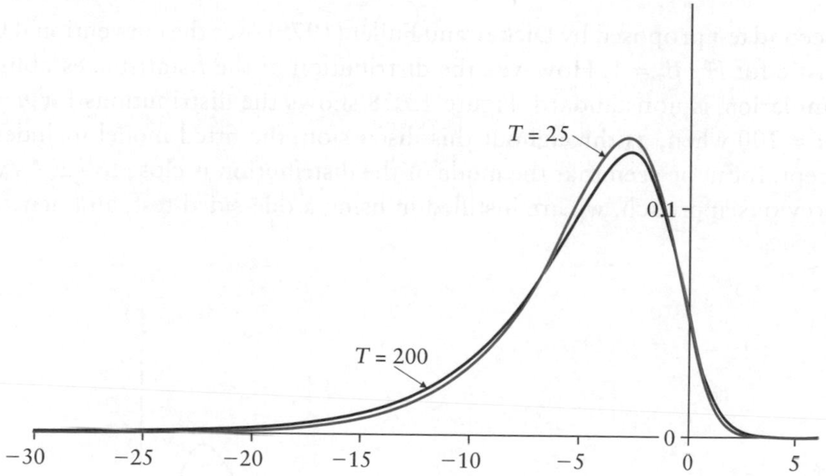

Figure 13.26 Distribution of $T\,(b_2 - 1)$, true model a random walk

However, we now have a further surprise. The distribution is not normal. This means that, if we work back from the limiting distribution to distributions in finite samples, as in (13.62) and (13.63), we cannot claim that the estimator is approximately normal, even in large samples.

In their original articles (1979 and 1981), Dickey and Fuller proposed three tests for nonstationarity in an autoregressive process: a direct test using the distribution of b_2, a t test, and an F test. We will consider each in turn.

Direct test using the distribution of T(b₂–1)

This test exploits the fact that β_2 in (13.59) is a pure number. Y_{t-1} must have the same dimensions as Y_t, and so β_2 is dimensionless. It follows that if we fit the model using OLS, b_2 logically must also be dimensionless. (Verification is left as Exercise 13.6.) The shapes of the distributions of b_2 and $T(b_2-1)$ depend only on the sample size, and this means that we can use either distribution to make direct tests of hypotheses relating to β_2. It is convenient to use the distribution of $T(b_2-1)$, shown in Figure 13.26, rather than that of b_2, for this purpose because it changes less with the sample size and indeed converges to a limiting distribution as the sample size increases.

Since we can rule out $\beta_2 > 1$, we can perform a one-sided test with the null and alternative hypotheses being H_0: $\beta_2 = 1$ and H_1: $\beta_2 < 1$. For the limiting distribution, the critical values are –14.1 and –20.6 at the 5 percent and 1 percent levels. Finite-sample distributions, established through simulation, have thinner left tails and so the critical values are smaller. Figure 13.27 shows the rejection regions for one-sided 5 percent (limit –12.1) and 1 percent (limit –16.6) tests for $T = 25$. Table A.6 gives the critical values of $T(b_2-1)$ for finite samples.

t test

The second test proposed by Dickey and Fuller (1979) uses the conventional OLS t statistic for H_0: $\beta_2 = 1$. However, the distribution of the t statistic, established by simulation, is nonstandard. Figure 13.28 shows the distributions for $n = 25$ and $n = 200$ when, as throughout this discussion, the fitted model includes an intercept. It can be seen that the mode of the distribution is close to –2. As with the previous approach, we are justified in using a one-sided test, and hence the

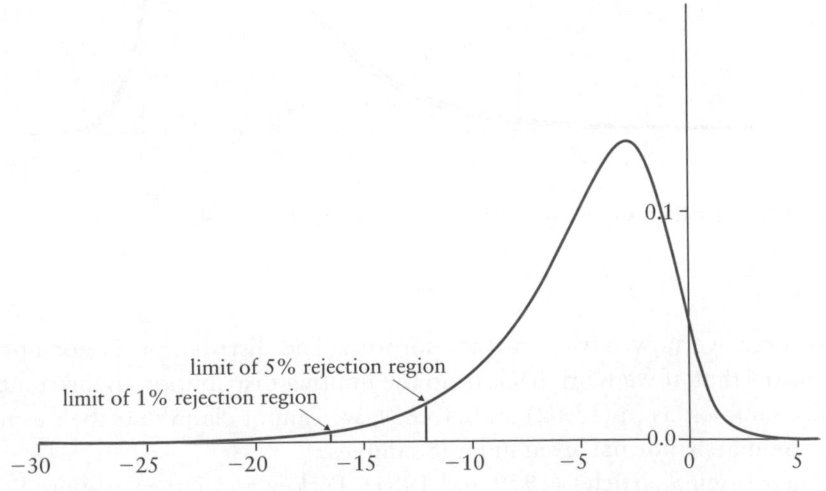

Figure 13.27 Rejection regions of the distribution of $T(b_2-1)$, true model a random walk, $T = 25$

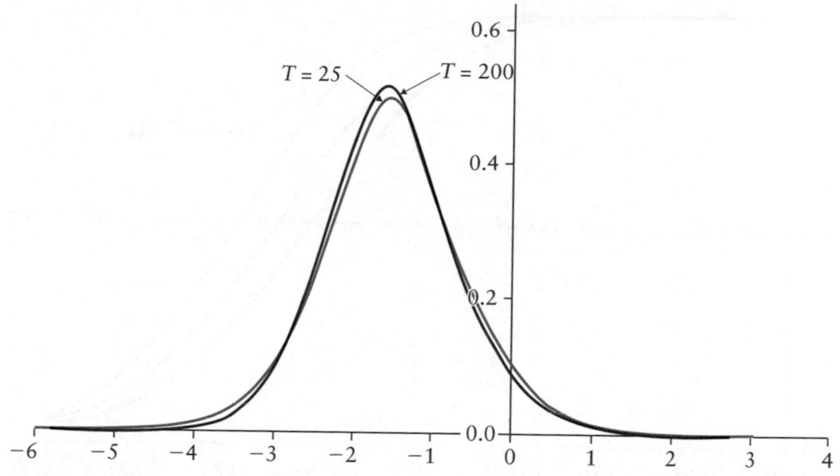

Figure 13.28 Distribution of t statistic for H_0: $\beta_2 = 1$, true model a random walk

critical value for any given significance level will be much more negative than the conventional critical value. For example, the critical value at the 5 percent level for $T = 25$ is −2.99. The conventional critical value for a one-sided test with 23 degrees of freedom is 1.71. Table A.6 gives critical values, established by simulation, for different sample sizes.

F test

The third Dickey–Fuller test exploits the fact that, under H_0, the model is a restricted version of that under H_1 with two restrictions: $\beta_2 = 1$ and, also, $\beta_1 = 0$. The first two tests do not make use of this second restriction. To test the joint restrictions, it is sufficient to construct the OLS F statistic in the usual way. However, as might be anticipated, it does not have a standard distribution. Table A.6 provides critical values.

Power of the tests

We now have three ways of testing H_0 against H_1 and there is no guarantee that they will lead to the same conclusion. There are two obvious questions that we should ask. How good are these tests, and which is the best? To answer these questions, we need to be more specific about what we mean by 'good' and 'best'. For any given significance level, we would like a test to have the least risk of a Type II error, that is, of failing to reject the null hypothesis when it is false. The power of a test is defined to be probability of rejecting the null hypothesis when it is false, so we want our tests to have high power, and the best test will be that with the highest power. We fit the model

$$Y_t = \beta_1 + \beta_2 Y_{t-1} + \varepsilon_t \qquad \textbf{(13.64)}$$

for $|\beta_2| < 1$ and test H_0: $\beta_2 = 1$.

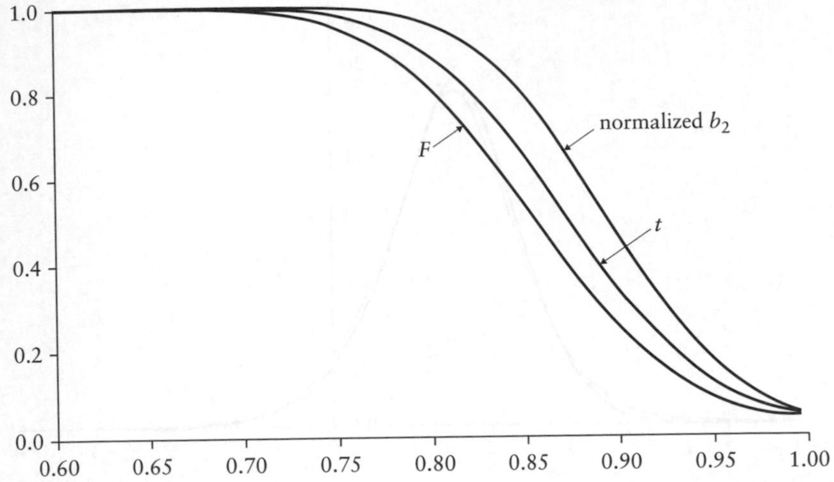

Figure 13.29 Comparison of the power of unit root tests as a function of β_2

Figure 13.29, which illustrates a variation on a simulation in Dickey and Fuller (1981), shows the power of the three tests as a function of β_2, using a 5 percent significance level for each of them. The figure seems to answer our questions. The power of the test based on $T(b_2 - 1)$ is greatest for all values of $\beta_2 < 1$. The t test is next, and the F test least powerful. The tests all have high power when $\beta_2 < 0.8$. For values above 0.8, the power rapidly diminishes and becomes low. For $\beta_2 = 0.9$, for example, even the test based on $T(b_2 - 1)$ will fail to reject the null hypothesis 50 percent of the time. This demonstrates the difficulty of discriminating between nonstationary processes and stationary processes that are highly autoregressive.

The inferiority of the F test in this comparison may come as a surprise, given that it is making more use of the data than the other two. However, there is a simple reason for this. The other two tests are one-sided and this increases their power, holding the significance level constant.

When deriving power functions such as those in Figure 13.29, one has to make potentially important assumptions relating to the characterization of the initial value of the series, Y_0, and the value of β_1. In the present case, it has been assumed that Y_0 should be drawn randomly from the ensemble distribution and be generated by (13.16). This eliminates initial effects and is appropriate if the process has a substantial history prior to the sample period. When Y_0 is determined in this way, the power functions are not affected by the value of β_1.

A common alternative assumption is to assign the value of 0 to Y_0. This might be appropriate if the process started at the beginning of the sample period. There is an extensive literature on power functions associated with tests of nonstationarity, not just the three developed by Dickey and Fuller, but also the many others that have been proposed. If there is a consensus, it is that the random draw initial condition is typically more realistic than setting $Y_0 = 0$, but that the appropriate use of power functions depends on the researcher's understanding of the context.

Trended process

If an inspection of the graph of a process reveals evidence of a trend, we need to consider whether the process is better characterized as a random walk with drift

$$Y_t = \beta_1 + Y_{t-1} + \varepsilon_t \quad \text{with } \beta_1 \neq 0 \tag{13.65}$$

or a deterministic trend

$$Y_t = \beta_1 + \beta_2 Y_{t-1} + \delta t + \varepsilon_t \quad \text{with } |\beta_2| < 1. \tag{13.66}$$

To do this, we generate Y_t using (13.65) and fit (13.66) with no assumption about the parameters. We can then test H_0: $\beta_2 = 1$ using as our test statistic either $T(b_2 - 1)$ or the t statistic for b_2, as before. The inclusion of the time trend in the specification causes the critical values under the null hypothesis to be different from those in the untrended case. They are determined by simulation methods, as before. We can also perform an F test. We have argued that a process cannot combine a random walk with drift and a time trend, so we can test the composite hypothesis H_0: $\beta_2 = 1$, $\delta = 0$. Critical values for the three tests are given in Table A.7 at the end of the text.

If the null hypothesis is false, and Y_t is therefore a stationary autoregressive process about a deterministic trend, the OLS estimators of the parameters are $\sqrt{T}$ consistent, and the conventional test statistics asymptotically valid.

Two special cases should be mentioned, if only as econometric curiosities. In general, if a plot of the process exhibits a trend, we will not know whether it is caused by a deterministic trend or a random walk with drift, and we have to allow for both by fitting (13.66) with no restriction on the parameters. But if, for some reason, we know that the process is either a deterministic trend or, alternatively, a random walk with drift, and if we fit the model appropriately, there is a spectacular improvement in the properties of the OLS estimator of the slope coefficient.

Special case where the process is known to be a deterministic trend

In the special case where $\beta_2 = 0$ and the process is just a simple deterministic trend, we encounter a surprising result. If it is known that there is no autoregressive component, and the regression model is correctly specified with t as the only explanatory variable, the OLS estimator of δ is **hyperconsistent**, its variance being inversely proportional to T^3. This is illustrated for the case $\delta = 0.2$ in the left chart in Figure 13.30. Since the standard deviation of the distribution is inversely proportional to $T^{3/2}$, the height is proportional to $T^{3/2}$, and so it more than doubles when the sample size is doubled. If Y_{t-1} is mistakenly included in the regression model, the loss of efficiency is dramatic. The estimator of δ reverts to being only $\sqrt{T}$ consistent. Further, it is subject to finite-sample bias. This is illustrated in the right chart in Figure 13.30.

In this special case, if the regression model is correctly specified, and the disturbance term is normally distributed, OLS t and F tests are valid for finite

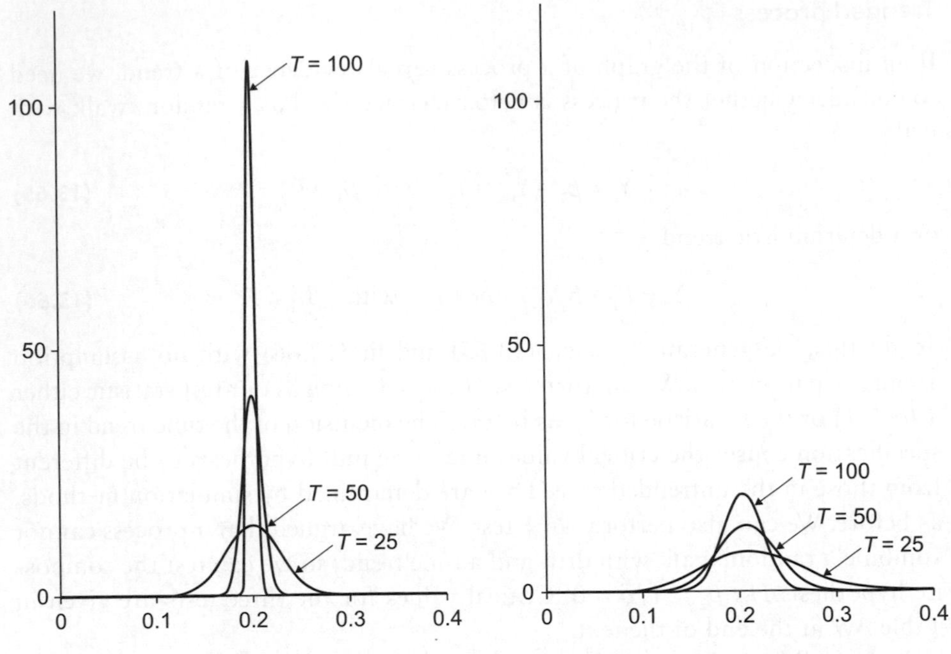

Figure 13.30 Distribution of estimator of δ, simple trend, Y_{t-1} excluded (left), included (right)

samples, despite the hyperconsistency of the estimator of δ. If the disturbance term is not normal, but has constant variance and finite fourth moment, the t and F tests are asymptotically valid.

Special case where the process is known to be a random walk with drift

Similarly, in the special case where the process is known to be a random walk with drift, so that $\beta_2 = 1$ and $\delta = 0$, and the model is correctly specified with Y_{t-1} as the only explanatory variable, the OLS estimator of β_2 is hyperconsistent. The t and F tests are asymptotically valid, but not valid for finite samples because the process is autoregressive.

Augmented Dickey–Fuller tests

So far we have considered only the first-order autoregressive process

$$Y_t = \beta_1 + \beta_2 Y_{t-1} + \varepsilon_t. \quad \textbf{(13.67)}$$

We need to generalize the discussion to higher-order processes. We will start with the second-order process

$$Y_t = \beta_1 + \beta_2 Y_{t-1} + \beta_3 Y_{t-2} + \varepsilon_t. \quad \textbf{(13.68)}$$

To be stationary, the parameters now need to satisfy several conditions. The most important in practice is $|\beta_2 + \beta_3| < 1$. To test this, it is convenient to reparameterize the model. Subtract Y_{t-1} from both sides, add and subtract $\beta_3 Y_{t-1}$ on the right side, and group terms together:

$$\begin{aligned} Y_t - Y_{t-1} &= \beta_1 + \beta_2 Y_{t-1} - Y_{t-1} + \beta_3 Y_{t-1} - \beta_3 Y_{t-1} + \beta_3 Y_{t-2} + \varepsilon_t \\ &= \beta_1 + (\beta_2 + \beta_3 - 1)Y_{t-1} - \beta_3 (Y_{t-1} - Y_{t-2}) + \varepsilon_t . \end{aligned} \quad \textbf{(13.69)}$$

Thus, the model becomes

$$\begin{aligned} \Delta Y_t &= \beta_1 + (\beta_2 + \beta_3 - 1)Y_{t-1} + \beta_3 \Delta Y_{t-1} + \varepsilon_t \\ &= \beta_1 + (\beta_2^* - 1)Y_{t-1} + \beta_3^* \Delta Y_{t-1} + \varepsilon_t . \end{aligned} \quad \textbf{(13.70)}$$

where $\beta_2^* = \beta_2 + \beta_3$, $\beta_3^* = -\beta_3$, and $\Delta Y_{t-1} = Y_{t-1} - Y_{t-2}$. Under the null hypothesis H_0: $\beta_2^* = 1$, the process is nonstationary. One may usually perform a one-sided test with alternative hypothesis H_1: $\beta_2^* < 1$ since $\beta_2^* > 1$ implies an explosive process. Under the null hypothesis, the estimator of β_2^* is superconsistent and the test statistics $T(b_2^* - 1)$, t, and F have the same distributions, and therefore critical values, as before. If a deterministic time trend is suspected, it may be included and the critical values are those for the first-order specification with a time trend.

Generalizing to the specification

$$Y_t = \beta_1 + \beta_2 Y_{t-1} + \cdots + \beta_{p+1} Y_{t-p} + \varepsilon_t , \quad \textbf{(13.71)}$$

a condition for stationarity is $\left|\beta_2 + \cdots + \beta_{p+1}\right| < 1$ and it is convenient to reparameterize the model as

$$\Delta Y_t = \beta_1 + (\beta_2^* - 1)Y_{t-1} + \beta_3^* \Delta Y_{t-1} + \cdots + \beta_{p+1}^* \Delta Y_{t-p} + \varepsilon_t , \quad \textbf{(13.72)}$$

where $\beta_2^* = \beta_2 + \cdots + \beta_{p+1}$ and $\beta_3^*, \ldots, \beta_{p+1}^*$ are appropriate linear combinations of $\beta_3, \ldots, \beta_{p+1}$. Under the null hypothesis of non-explosive nonstationarity, the test statistics $T(b_2^* - 1)$, t, and F asymptotically have the same distributions and critical values as before. In practice, the t test is particularly popular and is generally known as the **augmented Dickey–Fuller (ADF) test**.

There remains the issue of the determination of p. Two main approaches have been proposed and both start by assuming that one can hypothesize some maximum value $p^{\max}$. In the F test approach, (13.72) is fitted with $p = p^{\max}$ and a t test is performed on the coefficient of $\Delta Y_{t-p^{\max}}$. If this is not significant, this term may be dropped. Next, an F test is performed on the joint explanatory power of $\Delta Y_{t-p^{\max}}$ and $\Delta Y_{t-p^{\max}-1}$. If this is not significant, both terms may be dropped. The process continues, including further lagged differences in the F test until the null hypothesis of no joint explanatory power is rejected. The last lagged difference included in the test becomes the term with the maximum lag. Higher-order lags may be dropped because the previous F test was not significant. Provided that the disturbance term is IID, the normalized coefficient of Y_{t-1} and its t statistic will have the same (non-standard) distributions as for the Dickey–Fuller test.

The other method is to use an information criterion such as the Bayes Information Criterion (BIC), also known as the Schwarz Information Criterion (SIC). This requires the computation of the statistic

$$BIC = \log\left(\frac{RSS}{T}\right) + \frac{k\log T}{T} = \log\left(\frac{RSS}{T}\right) + \frac{(p+2)\log T}{T} \qquad (13.73)$$

and choosing p so as to minimize the expression. The first term falls as p increases, but the second term increases, and the trade-off is such that asymptotically the criterion will select the true value of p. A common alternative is the Akaike Information Criterion (AIC)

$$AIC = \log\left(\frac{RSS}{T}\right) + \frac{2k}{T}. \qquad (13.74)$$

This imposes a smaller penalty on overparameterization and will therefore tend to select a larger value of p, but simulation studies suggest that it may produce better results in practice.

Whether one uses the F test approach or information criteria, it is necessary to check that the residuals are not subject to autocorrelation, for example, using a Breusch–Godfrey lagrange multiplier test. Autocorrelation would provide evidence that there remain dynamics in the model not accounted for by the specification and that the model does not include enough lags.

Other tests

The 1979 and 1981 Dickey–Fuller papers were truly seminal in that they have given rise to a very extensive research literature devoted to the improvement of testing for nonstationarity and of the representation of nonstationary processes. The low power of the Dickey–Fuller tests was acknowledged in the original papers and much effort has been directed to the problem of distinguishing between nonstationary processes and highly autoregressive stationary processes.

Remarkably, the original Dickey–Fuller tests, particularly the t test in augmented form, are still widely used, perhaps even dominant. Other tests with superior asymptotic properties have been proposed, but some underperform in finite samples, as far as this can be established by simulation. The augmented Dickey–Fuller t test has retained its popularity on account of robustness and, perhaps, theoretical simplicity. However, a refinement, the ADF–GLS (generalized least squares) test due to Elliott, Rothenberg, and Stock (1996) appears to be gaining in popularity and is implemented in major regression applications. Simulations indicate that its power to discriminate between a nonstationary process and a stationary autoregressive process is uniformly closer to the theoretical limit than the standard tests, irrespective of the degree of autocorrelation.

Example

The EViews output in Table 13.1 shows the result of performing an ADF test on the logarithm of *DPI* with the number of lags determined by the BIC (SIC). The coefficient of $LGDPI_{t-1}$ is −0.09, close to zero. The t statistic, reproduced at the top of the output where it is designated the ADF test statistic, is −1.78. Under the null hypothesis of nonstationarity, the critical value of t at the 5 percent level, also given at the top of the output, is −3.52, and hence the null hypothesis of nonstationarity is not rejected. Notice that the critical value is much larger than 1.69, the conventional critical value for a one-sided test at the 5 percent level for a sample of this size.

Table 13.1

```
Augmented Dickey-Fuller Unit Root Test on LGDPI
Null Hypothesis: LGDPI has a unit root
Exogenous: Constant, Linear Trend
Lag Length: 0 (Automatic based on SIC, MAXLAG=9)
--------------------------------------------------------------------------------
                                                    t-Statistic    Prob.*
--------------------------------------------------------------------------------
Augmented Dickey-Fuller test statistic               -1.784362     0.6953
Test critical values1% level                         -4.180911
                    5% level                         -3.515523
                    10% level                        -3.188259
--------------------------------------------------------------------------------
*MacKinnon (1996) one-sided p-values.

Augmented Dickey-Fuller Test Equation
Dependent Variable: D(LGDPI)
Method: Least Squares
Sample (adjusted): 1960 2003
Included observations: 44 after adjustments
--------------------------------------------------------------------------------
Variable           Coefficient    Std. Error       t-Statistic        Prob.*
--------------------------------------------------------------------------------
LGDPI(-1)           -0.090691      0.050826         -1.784362         0.0818
C                    0.723299      0.381112          1.897865         0.0648
@TREND(1959)         0.002622      0.001705          1.537390         0.1319
--------------------------------------------------------------------------------
R-squared            0.164989           Mean dependent var         0.034225
Adjusted R-squared   0.124257           S.D. dependent var         0.016388
S.E. of regression   0.015336           Akaike info criter        -5.451443
Sum squared resid    0.009643           Schwarz criterion         -5.329794
Log likelihood       122.9317           Hannan-Quinn crite        -5.406330
F-statistic          4.050580           Durbin-Watson stat         1.776237
Prob(F-statistic)    0.024814
--------------------------------------------------------------------------------
```

Table 13.2 gives the EViews output for an ADF test on the differenced series. The coefficient of $\Delta LGDPI_{t-1}$ is -0.82, well below zero, and the t statistic is -5.31, allowing the null hypothesis of nonstationarity to be rejected at the 1 percent level (critical value -3.59). The tests therefore suggest that the logarithm of DPI is generated as an I(1) process. ADF–GLS tests produce very similar results for both levels and first differences.

Further complications

If a process obviously possesses a trend, it should be possible to discriminate between the null hypothesis of a unit root and the alternative hypothesis of a deterministic trend, despite the low power of the tests that have been proposed, if one has enough observations. However, the standard tests assume that, under the alternative hypothesis, the deterministic trend is truly fixed, apart from a stationary random process around it. The picture becomes blurred if one allows

Table 13.2

```
Augmented Dickey-Fuller Unit Root Test on D(LGDPI)

Null Hypothesis: D(LGDPI) has a unit root
Exogenous: Constant
Lag Length: 0 (Automatic based on SIC, MAXLAG=9)
-----------------------------------------------------------------------
                                              t-Statistic    Prob.*
-----------------------------------------------------------------------
Augmented Dickey-Fuller test statistic         -5.311020     0.0001
Test critical values1% level                   -3.592462
                    5% level                   -2.931404
                    10% level                  -2.603944
-----------------------------------------------------------------------
*MacKinnon (1996) one-sided p-values.

Augmented Dickey-Fuller Test Equation
Dependent Variable: D(LGDPI,2)
Method: Least Squares
Sample (adjusted): 1961 2003
Included observations: 43 after adjustments
-----------------------------------------------------------------------
Variable          Coefficient     Std. Error     t-Statistic     Prob.*
-----------------------------------------------------------------------
D(LGDPI(-1))      -0.817536       0.153932       -5.311020       0.0000
C                  0.028136       0.005872        4.791700       0.0000
-----------------------------------------------------------------------
R-squared           0.407574     Mean dependent var    -6.15E-05
Adjusted R-squared  0.393124     S.D. dependent var     0.021111
S.E. of regression  0.016446     Akaike info criter    -5.332042
Sum squared resid   0.011090     Schwarz criterion     -5.250126
Log likelihood      116.6389     Hannan-Quinn crite    -5.301834
F-statistic         28.20694     Durbin-Watson stat     2.035001
Prob(F-statistic)   0.000004
-----------------------------------------------------------------------
```

for the possibility that the deterministic trend may be periodically subject to shocks, for then the process begins to look a little like a random walk with drift and the difficulty of rejecting a unit root is increased.

For example, in their influential study, Nelson and Plosser (1982) concluded that the logarithm of GDP, along with several other important macroeconomic variables, was subject to a unit root. However, others have shown that the data are also consistent with a representation of the process as a deterministic trend subject to breaks such as those that could reasonably be associated with major events such as the Great Depression and the Second World War.

Another layer of complexity is added if the assumption of a constant variance of the disturbance term is relaxed. If this is relaxed, it becomes harder still to discriminate between the competing hypotheses. In the case of GDP, increased volatility appears to be associated with the same major events that may have been responsible for breaks. These issues remain an active research area in the literature and make an understanding of the context all the more necessary for the selection of an appropriate representation of a process.

EXERCISES

13.6 Suppose that Y_t is a process generated by

$$Y_t = \beta_1 + \beta_2 Y_{t-1} + \varepsilon_t.$$

Demonstrate that the OLS estimator of β_2 is dimensionless.

13.7* Suppose that Y_t is generated by the autoregressive process

$$Y_t = \beta_1 + \beta_2 Y_{t-1} + u_t,$$

where u_t is generated by an AR(1) process. Demonstrate that the appropriate specification for the ADF test is that given by (13.70).

13.8 Perform augmented Dickey–Fuller tests for difference-stationarity on the logarithms of expenditure on your commodity and the relative price series. Calculate the first differences and test for difference-stationarity.

13.9 Suppose that Y_t is determined by the process

$$Y_t = Y_{t-1} + \varepsilon_t + \lambda \varepsilon_{t-1},$$

where ε_t is IID. Show that the process for Y_t is nonstationary unless λ takes a certain value.

13.10* We have seen that the OLS estimator of δ in the model

$$Y_t = \beta_1 + \delta t + \varepsilon_t$$

is hyperconsistent. Show also that it is unbiased in finite samples, despite the fact that Y_t is nonstationary.

13.5 Cointegration

In general, a linear combination of two or more time series will be nonstationary if one or more of them is nonstationary, and the degree of integration of the combination will be equal to that of the most highly integrated individual series. Hence, for example, a linear combination of an I(1) series and an I(0) series will be I(1), that of two I(1) series will also be I(1), and that of an I(1) series and an I(2) series will be I(2).

However, if there is a long-run relationship between the time series, the outcome may be different. Consider, for example, Friedman's Permanent Income Hypothesis and the consumption function

$$C_t^P = \beta_2 Y_t^P v_t, \tag{13.75}$$

where C_t^P and Y_t^P are permanent consumption and income, respectively, and v_t is a multiplicative disturbance term. In logarithms, the relationship becomes

$$\log C_t^P = \log \beta_2 + \log Y_t^P + u_t, \tag{13.76}$$

where u_t is the logarithm of v_t. If the theory is correct, in the long run, ignoring short-run dynamics and the differences between the permanent and actual measures of the variables, consumption and income will grow at the same rate and the mean of the difference between their logarithms will be $\log \beta_2$. Figure 13.31 shows plots of the logarithms of aggregate disposable personal income, *DPI*, and aggregate personal consumer expenditure, *PCE* (left scale), and their difference (right scale) for the United States for the period 1959–2003. It can be seen that the gap between the two has been fairly stable, increasing a little in the first part of the period and declining a little thereafter. Thus, although the series for

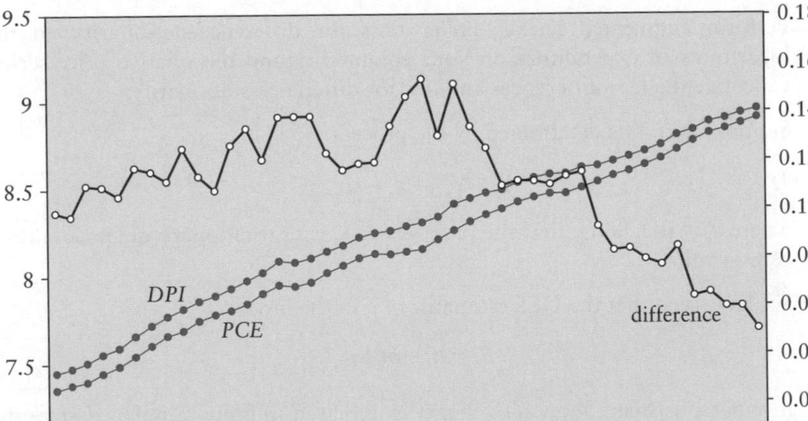

Figure 13.31 Logarithms of *DPI* and *PCE* (left scale) and difference (right scale)

DPI and *PCE* are nonstationary, they appear to be wandering together. For this to be possible, u_t must be a stationary process, for if it were not, the two series could drift apart indefinitely, violating the theoretical relationship.

When two or more nonstationary time series are linked in such a way, they are said to be cointegrated. In this example, the slope coefficient of $\log Y^P$ in (13.76) is theoretically equal to 1, making it possible to inspect the divergence graphically in Figure 13.31. More generally, if there exists a relationship

$$Y_t = \beta_1 + \beta_2 X_{2t} + \cdots + \beta_k X_{kt} + u \qquad \textbf{(13.77)}$$

between a set of variables $Y_t, X_{2t}, \ldots, X_{kt}$, the disturbance term u_t can be thought of as measuring the deviation between the components of the model:

$$u_t = Y_t - \beta_1 - \beta_2 X_{2t} - \cdots - \beta_k X_{t}. \qquad \textbf{(13.78)}$$

In the short run the divergence between the components will fluctuate, but if the model is genuinely correct there will be a limit to the divergence. Hence, although the time series are nonstationary, u_t will be stationary.

If there are more than two variables in the model, it is possible that there may be multiple cointegrating relationships, the maximum number in theory being equal to $k - 1$.

To test for cointegration, it is necessary to evaluate whether the disturbance term is a stationary process. In the case of the example of consumer expenditure and income, it is sufficient to perform a standard ADF unit root test on the difference between the two series. The results are shown in Table 13.3, with the difference between the logarithms being denoted *Z*. The ADF test statistic is –1.63, which is less than –3.52, the critical value at the 5 percent level under the null hypothesis of nonstationarity. This is a surprising result, for other studies have found the logarithms of consumer expenditure and income to be cointegrated (for example, Engle and Granger, 1987). Part of the problem is the low power of the test against an alternative hypothesis of u_t being a stationary process with high autocorrelation. The coefficient of the lagged residual is –0.13, suggesting that the process is approximately AR(1) with autocorrelation 0.87, but the standard error is too large for the null hypothesis of nonstationarity to be rejected. It is likely that persistence in the way that consumers behave is responsible for this. As consumers become more savings conscious, as they seem to have done from 1959 to about 1984, the gap between the logarithms widens. As they become less savings conscious, as seems to have been the case since 1984, it narrows. However, these changes evidently have long cycles, and so even over a period as long as 45 years it is difficult to discriminate between the hypothesis that the gap is a random walk and the alternative that it is stationary, with strong autocorrelation. However, a sufficiently long time series would show that the gap is stationary, for it is not possible for it to decrease indefinitely.

In the more general case of a model such as (13.77), where the cointegrating relationship has to be estimated, the test is an indirect one because it must be

Table 13.3

Augmented Dickey-Fuller Unit Root Test on Z

Null Hypothesis: Z has a unit root
Exogenous: Constant, Linear Trend
Lag Length: 0 (Automatic based on SIC, MAXLAG=9)

		t-Statistic	Prob.*
Augmented Dickey-Fuller test statistic		-1.630141	0.7646
Test critical values	1% level	-4.180911	
	5% level	-3.515523	
	10% level	-3.188259	

*MacKinnon (1996) one-sided p-values.

Augmented Dickey-Fuller Test Equation
Dependent Variable: D(Z)
Method: Least Squares
Sample (adjusted): 1960 2003
Included observations: 44 after adjustments

Variable	Coefficient	Std. Error	t-Statistic	Prob.*
Z(-1)	-0.125404	0.076928	-1.630141	0.1107
C	0.548443	0.334069	1.641706	0.1083
@TREND(1959)	-0.000340	0.000143	-2.370707	0.0225

R-squared	0.125214	Mean dependent var	-0.001099
Adjusted R-squared	0.082542	S.D. dependent var	0.010878
S.E. of regression	0.010420	Akaike info criter	-6.224498
Sum squared resid	0.004451	Schwarz criterion	-6.102848
Log likelihood	139.9389	Hannan-Quinn crite	-6.179384
F-statistic	2.934303	Durbin-Watson stat	2.402963
Prob(F-statistic)	0.064415		

performed on the residuals from the regression, rather than on the disturbance term. In view of the fact that the least squares coefficients are chosen so as to minimize the sum of the squares of the residuals, and that the mean of the residuals is automatically zero, the time series for the residuals will tend to appear more stationary than the underlying series for the disturbance term. To allow for this, the critical values for the test statistic are even higher than those for the standard test for nonstationarity of a time series. Asymptotic critical values for the case where the cointegrating relationship involves two variables are shown in Table 13.4. The test assumes that a constant has been included in the cointegrating relationship, and the critical values depend on whether a trend has been included as well.

Table 13.4 Asymptotic critical values of the Dickey–Fuller statistic for a cointegrating relationship with two variables

	5 percent	1 percent
Constant, no trend	−3.34	−3.90
Constant and trend	−3.78	−4.32

Source: Davidson and MacKinnon (1993).

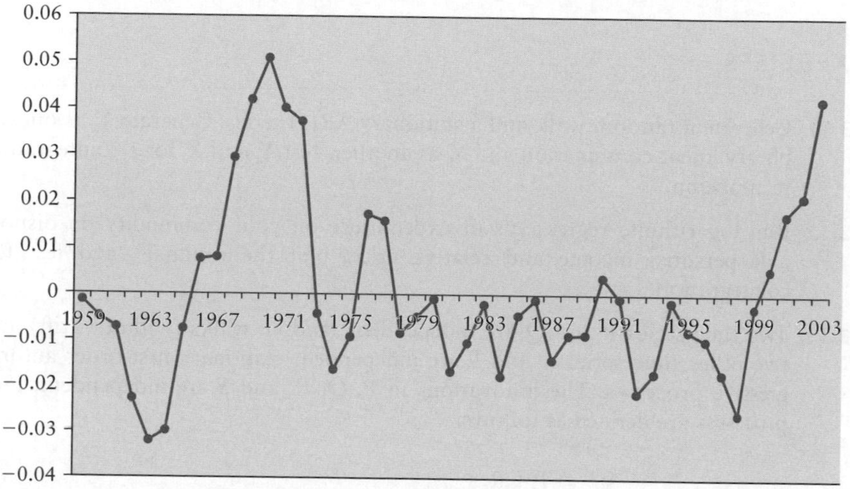

Figure 13.32 Residuals from a logarithmic regression of food on income and relative price

In the case of a cointegrating relationship, least squares estimators can be shown to be superconsistent (Stock, 1987). An important consequence is that OLS may be used to fit a cointegrating relationship, even if it belongs to a system of simultaneous relationships, for any simultaneous equations bias tends to zero asymptotically.

Example

A logarithmic regression of expenditure on food on *DPI* and the relative price of food was performed using the Demand Functions data set, the fitted equation being

$$\widehat{LGFOOD} = \underset{(0.39)}{2.24} + \underset{(0.01)}{0.50}\, LGDPI - \underset{(0.07)}{0.07}\, LGPRFOOD \quad R^2 = 0.992. \qquad \textbf{(13.79)}$$

The residuals are shown in Figure 13.32. The pattern is mixed and it is not possible to say whether it looks stationary or nonstationary. The Engle–Granger statistic is −1.93, not significant even at the 5 percent level. The failure to reject the null hypothesis of nonstationarity suggests that the variables are not cointegrated. Nevertheless, the coefficient of the lagged residuals is −0.21, suggesting an AR(1) process with ρ equal to about 0.8. Thus, once again, the failure of the test to reject the null hypothesis of nonstationarity may merely reflect its low power against the alternative hypothesis that the disturbance term is a highly autocorrelated stationary process. Consequently, it is possible that the variables are in fact cointegrated.

EXERCISES

13.11 Generate a random walk and a stationary AR(1) series. Generate Y_t as one arbitrary linear combination and X_t as another. Test Y_t and X_t for a cointegrating relationship.

13.12 Run logarithmic regressions of expenditure on your commodity on disposable personal income and relative price, plot the residuals, and test for cointegration.

13.13 Two time series P and Q are independent random walks (without drift) and two other time series R and S are independent stationary first-order autoregressive processes. The innovations in P, Q, R, and S are independent. Five processes are defined as follows:

$$\begin{aligned} V &= P + R \\ W &= P - R \\ X &= P + Q \\ Y &= P - Q \\ Z &= R + S. \end{aligned}$$

Taking the five processes V, W, X, Y, and Z pairwise, explain whether or not they are cointegrated. [*Note*: There are 10 pairs to consider.]

13.6 Fitting models with nonstationary time series

The poor predictive power of early macroeconomic models, despite excellent sample period fits, gave rise to two main reactions. One was a resurgence of interest in the use of univariate time series for forecasting purposes, described in Section 11.7. The other, of greater appeal to economists who did not wish to give up multivariate analysis, was to search for ways of constructing models that avoided the fitting of spurious relationships. We will briefly consider three of them: detrending the variables in a relationship, differencing the variables in a relationship, and constructing error correction models.

Detrending

As noted in Section 13.2, for models where the variables possess deterministic trends, the fitting of spurious relationships can be avoided by detrending the variables before use. This was a common procedure in early econometric analysis with time series data. Alternatively, and equivalently, one may include a time trend as a regressor in the model. By virtue of the Frisch–Waugh–Lovell theorem, the coefficients obtained with such a specification are exactly the same as those obtained with a regression using detrended versions of the variables. (The standard errors will be marginally different. The specification with the time trend will calculate them correctly, while the specification with the detrended variables will fail to take account of the fact that detrending consumes one degree of freedom.)

However, there are potential problems with this approach. Most importantly, if the variables are difference-stationary rather than trend-stationary—and Nelson and Plosser (1982) have shown that for many macroeconomic variables there is evidence that this is the case—the detrending procedure is inappropriate and likely to give rise to misleading results. In particular, if a random walk X_t is regressed on a time trend as in

$$X_t = \beta_1 + \beta_2 t + \varepsilon_t, \tag{13.80}$$

the null hypothesis H_0: $\beta_2 = 0$ is likely to be rejected more often than it should, given the significance level (Durlauf and Phillips, 1988). Although the least squares estimator of β_2 is consistent, and thus will tend to zero in large samples, its standard error is biased downwards. As a consequence, in finite samples deterministic trends will appear to be detected, even when not present.

Further, if a series is difference-stationary, the procedure does not make it stationary. In the case of a random walk, extracting a non-existent trend in the mean of the series can do nothing to alter the trend in its variance. As a consequence, the series remains nonstationary. In the case of a random walk with drift, the procedure can remove the drift, but again it does not remove the trend in the variance. In either case, the problem of spurious regressions is not resolved, and for this reason detrending is now not usually considered to be an appropriate procedure.

Differencing

In early time series studies, if the disturbance term in a model

$$Y_t = \beta_1 + \beta_2 X_t + u_t \tag{13.81}$$

was believed to be subject to severe positive AR(1) autocorrelation

$$u_t = \rho u_{t-1} + \varepsilon_t, \tag{13.82}$$

a common rough-and-ready remedy was to regress the model in differences rather than levels:

$$\begin{aligned}\Delta Y_t &= \beta_2 \Delta X_t + \Delta u_t \\ &= \beta_2 \Delta X_t + (\rho - 1)u_{t-1} + \varepsilon_t\end{aligned} \quad \textbf{(13.83)}$$

Of course differencing overcompensated for the autocorrelation, but if ρ was near 1, the resulting weak negative autocorrelation was held to be relatively innocuous. Unknown to practitioners of the time, the procedure is also an effective antidote to spurious regressions, and was advocated as such by Granger and Newbold (1974). If both Y_t and X_t are unrelated I(1) processes, they are stationary in the differenced model and the absence of any relationship will be revealed.

A major shortcoming of differencing is that it precludes the investigation of a long-run relationship. In equilibrium $\Delta Y = \Delta X = 0$, and if one substitutes these values into (13.83) one obtains, not an equilibrium relationship, but an equation in which both sides are zero.

Error correction models

We have seen that a long-run relationship between two or more variables is given by a cointegrating relationship, if it exists. On its own, a cointegrating relationship sheds no light on short-run dynamics, but its very existence indicates that there must be some short-term forces that are responsible for keeping the relationship intact, and thus that it should be possible to construct a more comprehensive model that combines short-run and long-run dynamics. A standard means of accomplishing this is to make use of an error correction model of the kind discussed in Section 11.4. It will be seen that it is particularly appropriate in the context of models involving nonstationary processes.

It will be convenient to rehearse the theory. Suppose that the relationship between two I(1) variables Y_t and X_t is characterized by the ADL(1,1) model

$$Y_t = \beta_1 + \beta_2 Y_{t-1} + \beta_3 X_t + \beta_4 X_{t-1} + \varepsilon_t. \quad \textbf{(13.84)}$$

In equilibrium,

$$\bar{Y} = \beta_1 + \beta_2 \bar{Y} + \beta_3 \bar{X} + \beta_4 \bar{X}. \quad \textbf{(13.85)}$$

Hence,

$$\bar{Y} = \frac{\beta_1}{1 - \beta_2} + \frac{\beta_3 + \beta_4}{1 - \beta_2} \bar{X} \quad \textbf{(13.86)}$$

and

$$Y_t = \frac{\beta_1}{1 - \beta_2} + \frac{\beta_3 + \beta_4}{1 - \beta_2} X_t \quad \textbf{(13.87)}$$

is the cointegrating relationship.

The ADL(1,1) relationship (13.84) may be rewritten to incorporate this relationship by subtracting Y_{t-1} from both sides, subtracting $\beta_3 X_{t-1}$ from the right side and adding it back again, and rearranging:

$$\begin{aligned} Y_t - Y_{t-1} &= \beta_1 + (\beta_2 - 1)Y_{t-1} + \beta_3 X_t + \beta_4 X_{t-1} + \varepsilon_t \\ &= \beta_1 + (\beta_2 - 1)Y_{t-1} + \beta_3 X_t - \beta_3 X_{t-1} + \beta_3 X_{t-1} + \beta_4 X_{t-1} + \varepsilon_t \\ &= (\beta_2 - 1)\left(Y_{t-1} - \frac{\beta_1}{1-\beta_2} - \frac{\beta_3 + \beta_4}{1-\beta_2} X_{t-1} \right) + \beta_3 (X_t - X_{t-1}) + \varepsilon_t . \end{aligned} \qquad \textbf{(13.88)}$$

Hence, we obtain the error correction model

$$\Delta Y_t = (\beta_2 - 1)\left(Y_{t-1} - \frac{\beta_1}{1-\beta_2} - \frac{\beta_3 + \beta_4}{1-\beta_2} X_{t-1} \right) + \beta_3 \Delta X_t + \varepsilon_t . \qquad \textbf{(13.89)}$$

The model states that the change in Y in any period will be governed by the change in X and the discrepancy between Y_{t-1} and the value predicted by the cointegrating relationship. The latter term is denoted the error correction mechanism, the effect of the term being to reduce the discrepancy between Y_t and its cointegrating level and its size being proportional to the discrepancy.

The feature that makes the error correction model particularly attractive when working with nonstationary time series is the fact that all of the terms ΔY_t, ΔX_t, and $\left(Y_{t-1} - \beta_1/(1-\beta_2) - (\beta_3 + \beta_4)X_{t-1}/(1-\beta_2)\right)$ in (13.89) are I(0), the latter by virtue of being just the lagged disturbance term in the cointegrating relationship. Hence, the model may be fitted using least squares in the standard way.

Of course, the β parameters are not known and the cointegrating term is unobservable. One way of overcoming this problem, known as the Engle–Granger two-step procedure, is to use the values of the parameters estimated in the cointegrating regression to compute the cointegrating term. Engle and Granger (1987) demonstrate that asymptotically the estimators of the coefficients of (13.89) will have the same properties as if the true values had been used. As a consequence, the lagged residuals from the cointegrating regression can be used for the cointegrating term.

Example

The EViews output in Table 13.5 shows the results of fitting an error correction model for the demand function for food using the Engle–Granger two-step procedure, on the assumption that (13.79) is a cointegrating relationship. The coefficient of the error correction term, *ZFOOD*(−1), the lagged residuals, indicates that about 15 percent of the disequilibrium divergence tends to be eliminated in one year.

Table 13.5

Dependent Variable: DLGFOOD

Method: Least Squares

Sample(adjusted): 1960 2003

Included observations: 44 after adjusting endpoints

Variable	Coefficient	Std. Error	t-Statistic	Prob.*
ZFOOD(-1)	-0.148063	0.105268	-1.406533	0.1671
DLGDPI	0.493715	0.050948	9.690642	0.0000
DPFOOD	-0.353901	0.115387	-3.067086	0.0038

R-squared	0.343031	Mean dependent var	0.018243
Adjusted R-squared	0.310984	S.D. dependent var	0.015405
S.E. of regression	0.012787	Akaike info criter	-5.815054
Sum squared resid	0.006704	Schwarz criterion	-5.693405
Log likelihood	130.9312	Durbin-Watson stat	1.526946

EXERCISES

13.14 Fit an error correction model for your commodity, assuming that a cointegrating relationship has been found in Exercise 13.12.

13.15 A researcher has time series data for aggregate consumption, C, and aggregate disposable personal income, Y, for a certain country. She establishes that the logarithms of both series are I(1) (integrated of order one) and she correctly hypothesizes that the long-run relationship between them may be represented as

$$C = \lambda Y v, \tag{1}$$

where λ is a constant and v is a multiplicative disturbance term. It may be assumed that $\log v$ is normally distributed with zero mean and constant variance.

The researcher believes that log C and log Y are cointegrated. How should she demonstrate this?

The relationship implies that the long-run growth rate of consumption is equal to that of income. Explain whether it is correct to describe the growth rates as being cointegrated.

The researcher is also interested in the short-run dynamics of the relationship and correctly hypothesizes that they may be represented by the relationship

$$\log C_t = \beta_1 + \beta_2 \log C_{t-1} + \beta_3 \log Y_t + \beta_4 \log Y_{t-1} + \varepsilon_t, \tag{2}$$

where ε_t is identically and independently distributed and drawn from a normal distribution with zero mean. State the restriction that has to be satisfied by the parameters if the short-run relationship (2) is to be compatible with the long-run relationship (1).

Show how the restricted version of (2) may be reparameterized as an error correction model. Explain why fitting the error correction model, rather than (2) directly, avoids a potentially important problem.

Key terms

- ARIMA(p, d, q) time series
- ARMA(p, q) time series
- augmented Dickey–Fuller (ADF) test
- cointegrated time series
- correlogram
- deterministic trend
- difference stationarity
- error correction model
- integrated time series
- nonstationarity
- random walk
- random walk with drift
- stationarity
- trend stationarity
- unit root

14. Introduction to Panel Data Models

14.1 Introduction

If the same units of observation in a cross-sectional sample are surveyed two or more times, the resulting observations are described as forming a **panel** or **longitudinal data set**. The National Longitudinal Survey of Youth that has provided data for many of the examples and exercises in this text is such a data set. The NLSY started with a baseline survey in 1979 and the same individuals have been reinterviewed many times, annually until 1994 and biennially since then. However, the units of observation of a panel data set need not be individuals. They may be households, or enterprises, or geographical areas, or indeed any set of entities that retain their identities over time.

Because panel data have both cross-sectional and time series dimensions, the application of regression analysis to fit econometric models is more complex than that for simple cross-sectional data sets. Nevertheless, panel data sets are increasingly being used in applied work and the aim of this chapter is to provide a brief introduction. For comprehensive treatments see Hsiao (2003), Baltagi (2005), and Wooldridge (2002).

There are several reasons for the increasing interest in panel data sets. An important one is that their use may offer a solution to the problem of omitted variable bias caused by unobserved heterogeneity, a common problem in the fitting of models with cross-sectional data sets. This will be discussed in the next section.

A second reason is that it may be possible to exploit panel data sets to reveal dynamics that are difficult to detect with cross-sectional data. For example, if one has cross-sectional data on a number of adults, it will be found that some are employed, some are unemployed, and the rest are economically inactive. For policy purposes, one would like to distinguish between frictional unemployment and long-term unemployment. Frictional unemployment is inevitable in a changing economy, but long-term unemployment can indicate a social problem that needs to be addressed. To design an effective policy to counter long-term unemployment, one needs to know the characteristics of those affected or at risk. In principle, the necessary information might be captured with a cross-sectional survey using retrospective questions about past employment status, but in practice the scope for this is often very limited. The further back in the past one goes, the worse are the problems of a lack of records and fallible memories, and the greater becomes the problem of measurement error. Panel studies avoid this problem in that the need for recall is limited to the time interval since the previous interview, typically no more than a year.

A third attraction of panel data sets is that they often have very large numbers of observations. If there are n units of observation and if the survey is undertaken in T time periods, there are potentially nT observations consisting of time series of length T on n parallel units. In the case of the NLSY, there were just over 6,000 individuals in the core sample. The survey has been conducted 21 times as of 2010, generating well over 100,000 observations. Further, because it is expensive to establish and maintain them, such panel data sets tend to be expertly designed and rich in content.

A panel is described as **balanced** if there is an observation for every unit of observation for every time period, and as **unbalanced** if some observations are missing. The discussion that follows applies equally to both types. However, if one is using an unbalanced panel, one needs to take note of the possibility that the causes of missing observations may be endogenous to the model. Equally, if a balanced panel has been created artificially by eliminating all units of observation with missing observations, the resulting data set may not be representative of its population.

Example of the use of a panel data set to investigate dynamics

In many studies of the determinants of earnings, it has been found that married men earn significantly more than single men. One explanation is that marriage entails financial responsibilities—in particular, the rearing of children—that may encourage men to work harder or seek better-paying jobs. Another is that certain unobserved qualities that are valued by employers are also valued by potential spouses and hence are conducive to getting married, and that the dummy variable for being married is acting as a proxy for these qualities. Other explanations have been proposed, but we will restrict attention to these two. With cross-sectional data it is difficult to discriminate between them. However, with panel data one can find out whether there is an uplift at the time of marriage or soon after, as would be predicted by the increased productivity hypothesis, or whether married men tend to earn more even before marriage, as would be predicted by the unobserved heterogeneity hypothesis.

In 1988 there were 1,538 NLSY males working 30 or more hours a week, not also in school, with no missing data. The respondents were divided into three categories: the 904 who were already married in 1988 (dummy variable $MARRIED = 1$); a further 212 who were single in 1988 but who married within the next four years (dummy variable $SOONMARR = 1$); and the remaining 422 who were single in 1988 and still single four years later (the omitted category). Divorced respondents were excluded from the sample. The following earnings function was fitted (standard errors in parentheses):

$$\widehat{LGEARN} = \underset{(0.028)}{0.163}\, MARRIED + \underset{(0.037)}{0.096}\, SOONMARR + \text{constant} + \text{controls} \qquad R^2 = 0.27. \tag{14.1}$$

The controls included years of schooling, *ASVABC* score, years of tenure with the current employer and its square, years of work experience and its square, age and its square, and dummy variables for ethnicity, region of residence, and living in an urban area.

The regression indicates that those who were married in 1988 earned 16.3 percent more than the reference category (strictly speaking, 17.7 percent, if the proportional increase is calculated properly as $e^{0.163} - 1$) and that the effect is highly significant. However, it is the coefficient of *SOONMARR* that is of greater interest here. Under the null hypothesis that the marital effect is dynamic and marriage encourages men to earn more, the coefficient of *SOONMARR* should be zero. The men in this category were still single as of 1988. The t statistic of the coefficient is 2.60 and so the coefficient is significantly different from zero at the 1 percent level, leading us to reject the null hypothesis at that level.

However, if the alternative hypothesis is true, the coefficient of *SOONMARR* should be equal to that of *MARRIED*, but it is lower. To test whether it is significantly lower, the easiest method is to change the reference category to those who were married by 1988 and to introduce a new dummy variable *SINGLE* that is equal to 1 if the respondent was single in 1988 and still single four years later. The omitted category is now those who were already married by 1988. The fitted regression is (standard errors in parentheses)

$$\widehat{LGEARN} = \underset{(0.028)}{-0.163}\, SINGLE - \underset{(0.034)}{0.066}\, SOONMARR + \text{constant} + \text{controls} \qquad R^2 = 0.27. \tag{14.2}$$

The coefficient of *SOONMARR* now estimates the difference between the coefficients of those married by 1988 and those married within the next four years, and if the second hypothesis is true, it should be equal to zero. The t statistic is -1.93, so we (just) do not reject the second hypothesis at the 5 percent level. The evidence seems to provide greater support for the second hypothesis, but it is possible that neither hypothesis is correct on its own and the truth might reside in some compromise.

In the foregoing example, we used data only from the 1988 and 1992 rounds of the NLSY. In most applications using panel data it is normal to exploit the data from all the rounds, if only to maximize the number of observations in the sample. A standard specification is

$$Y_{it} = \beta_1 + \sum_{j=2}^{k} \beta_j X_{jit} + \sum_{p=1}^{s} \gamma_p Z_{pi} + \delta t + \varepsilon_{it}, \tag{14.3}$$

where Y is the dependent variable, the X_j are observed explanatory variables, and the Z_p are unobserved explanatory variables. The index i refers to the unit of observation, t refers to the time period, and j and p are used to differentiate between different observed and unobserved explanatory variables. ε_{it} is a disturbance term assumed to satisfy the usual regression model conditions. A trend term t has been introduced to allow for a shift of the intercept over time. If the implicit assumption of a constant rate of change seems too strong, the trend can be replaced by a set of dummy variables, one for each time period except the reference period.

The X_j variables are usually the variables of interest, while the Z_p variables are responsible for unobserved heterogeneity and as such constitute a nuisance component of the model. The following discussion will be confined to the (quite common) special case where it is reasonable to assume that the unobserved heterogeneity is unchanging and accordingly the Z_p variables do not need a time subscript. Because the Z_p variables are unobserved, there is no means of obtaining information about the $\sum \gamma_p Z_{pi}$ component of the model and it is convenient to rewrite (14.3) as

$$Y_{it} = \beta_1 + \sum_{j=2}^{k} \beta_j X_{jit} + \alpha_i + \delta t + \varepsilon_{it}, \tag{14.4}$$

where

$$\alpha_i = \sum_{p=1}^{s} \gamma_p Z_{pi}. \tag{14.5}$$

α_i, known as the **unobserved effect**, represents the joint impact of the Z_{pi} on Y_i. Henceforward it will be convenient to refer to the unit of observation as an individual, and to the α_i as the individual-specific unobserved effect, but it should be borne in mind that the individual in question may actually be a household or an enterprise, etc. If α_i is correlated with any of the X_j variables, the regression estimates from a regression of Y on the X_j variables will be subject to omitted variable bias. Even if the unobserved effect is not correlated with any of the explanatory variables, its presence will in general cause OLS to yield inefficient estimates and invalid standard errors. We will now consider ways of overcoming these problems.

First, however, note that if the X_j controls are so comprehensive that they capture all the relevant characteristics of the individual, there will be no relevant unobserved characteristics. In that case, the α_i term may be dropped and a pooled OLS regression may be used to fit the model, treating all the observations for all of the time periods as a single sample.

14.2 Fixed effects regressions

The two main approaches to the fitting of models using panel data are known as **fixed effects regressions**, discussed in this section, and **random effects regressions**, discussed in the next. Three versions of the fixed effects approach will be described. In the first two, the model is manipulated in such a way that the unobserved effect is eliminated.

Within-groups fixed effects

In the first version, the mean values of the variables in the observations on a given individual are calculated and subtracted from the data for that individual. In view of (14.4), one may write

$$\bar{Y}_i = \beta_1 + \sum_{j=2}^{k} \beta_j \bar{X}_{ij} + \delta\bar{t} + \alpha_i + \bar{\varepsilon}_{it}. \tag{14.6}$$

Subtracting this from (14.4), one obtains

$$Y_{it} - \bar{Y}_i = \sum_{j=2}^{k} \beta_j \left(X_{ijt} - \bar{X}_{ij}\right) + \delta(t - \bar{t}) + \varepsilon_{it} - \bar{\varepsilon}_i \tag{14.7}$$

and the unobserved effect disappears. This is known as the **within-groups regression** model. For the group of observations relating to a given individual, it is explaining the variations of the dependent variable about its mean in terms of the variations of the explanatory variables about their means. The possibility of tackling unobserved heterogeneity bias in this way is a major attraction of panel data for researchers.

However, there are some prices to pay. First, the intercept β_1 and any X variable that remains constant for each individual will drop out of the model. The elimination of the intercept may not matter, but the loss of the unchanging explanatory variables may be frustrating. Suppose, for example, that one is fitting an earnings function to data for a sample of individuals who have completed their schooling, and that the schooling variable for individual i in period t is S_{it}. If the education of the individual is complete by the time of the first time period, S_{it} will be the same for all t for that individual and $S_{it} = \bar{S}_i$ for all t. Hence $(S_{it} - \bar{S}_i)$ is zero for all time periods. If all individuals have completed their schooling by the first time period, $(S_{it} - \bar{S}_i)$ will be zero for all i and t. One cannot include a variable whose values are all zero in a regression model. Thus, if the object of the exercise were to obtain an estimate of the returns to schooling untainted by unobserved heterogeneity bias, one ends up with no estimate at all.

A second problem is the potential impact of the disturbance term. We saw in Chapter 3 that the precision of OLS estimates depends on the mean square deviations of the explanatory variables being large in comparison with the variance of the disturbance term. The analysis was in the context of the simple regression model, but it generalizes to multiple regression. The variation in $(X_j - \bar{X}_j)$ may well be much smaller than the variation in X_j. If this is the case, the impact of the disturbance term may be relatively large, giving rise to imprecise estimates. The situation is aggravated in the case of measurement error, since this will lead to bias, and the bias is the greater, the smaller the variation in the explanatory variable in comparison with the variance of the measurement error.

A third problem is that we lose a substantial number of degrees of freedom in the model when we manipulate the model to eliminate the unobserved effect: we lose one degree of freedom for every individual in the sample. If the panel is balanced, with nT observations in all, it may seem that there would be $nT - k$ degrees of freedom. However, in manipulating the model, the number of degrees of freedom is reduced by n, for reasons that will be explained later in this section. Hence, the true number of degrees of freedom will be $n(T - 1) - k$. If T is small, the impact can be large. (Regression applications with a fixed effects regression facility will automatically make the adjustment to the degrees of freedom when implementing the within-groups method.)

First differences fixed effects

In a second version of the fixed effects approach, the first differences regression model, the unobserved effect is eliminated by subtracting the observation for the previous time period from the observation for the current time period, for all time periods. For individual i in time period t, the model may be written

$$Y_{it} = \beta_1 + \sum_{j=2}^{k} \beta_j X_{ijt} + \delta t + \alpha_i + \varepsilon_{it}. \tag{14.8}$$

For the previous time period, the relationship is

$$Y_{it-1} = \beta_1 + \sum_{j=2}^{k} \beta_j X_{ijt-1} + \delta(t-1) + \alpha_i + \varepsilon_{it-1}. \tag{14.9}$$

Subtracting (14.9) from (14.8), one obtains

$$\Delta Y_{it} = \sum_{j=2}^{k} \beta_j \Delta X_{ijt} + \delta + \varepsilon_{it} - \varepsilon_{it-1} \tag{14.10}$$

and again the unobserved heterogeneity has disappeared. However, the other problems remain. In particular, the intercept and any X variable that remains fixed for each individual will disappear from the model and n degrees of freedom are lost because the first observation for each individual is not defined. In addition, this type of differencing gives rise to autocorrelation if ε_{it} satisfies the regression model conditions. The error term in (14.10) for time period t is $(\varepsilon_{it} - \varepsilon_{it-1})$. That for the previous observation is $(\varepsilon_{it-1} - \varepsilon_{it-2})$. Thus the two error terms both have a component ε_{it-1} with opposite signs and negative moving average autocorrelation has been induced. However, if ε_{it} is subject to autocorrelation:

$$\varepsilon_{it} = \rho\varepsilon_{it-1} + v_{it}, \tag{14.11}$$

where v_{it} is a well-behaved innovation, the moving average disturbance term is equal to $v_{it} - (1 - \rho)\varepsilon_{it-1}$. If the autocorrelation is severe, the $(1 - \rho)\varepsilon_{it-1}$ component could be small and so the first differences estimator could be preferable to the within-groups estimator.

Least squares dummy variable fixed effects

In the third version of the fixed effects approach, known as the least squares dummy variable (LSDV) regression model, the unobserved effect is brought explicitly into the model. If we define a set of dummy variables A_i, where A_i is equal to 1 in the case of an observation relating to individual i and 0 otherwise, the model can be rewritten

$$Y_{it} = \sum_{j=2}^{k} \beta_j X_{ijt} + \delta t + \sum_{i=1}^{n} \alpha_i A_i + \varepsilon_{it}. \tag{14.12}$$

Formally, the unobserved effect is now being treated as the coefficient of the individual-specific dummy variable, the $\alpha_i A_i$ term representing a fixed effect on the dependent variable Y_i for individual i (this accounts for the name given to the fixed effects approach). Having re-specified the model in this way, it can be fitted using OLS.

Note that if we include a dummy variable for every individual in the sample as well as an intercept we will fall into the dummy variable trap described in Section 5.2. To avoid this, we could define one individual to be the reference category, so that β_1 is its intercept, and then treat the α_i as the shifts in the intercept for the other individuals. However, the choice of reference category is often arbitrary and accordingly the interpretation of the α_i in such a specification not particularly illuminating. Alternatively, we can drop the β_1 intercept and define dummy variables for all of the individuals, as has been done in (14.12). The α_i now become the intercepts for each of the individuals. Note that, in common with the first two versions of the fixed effects approach, the LSDV method requires panel data. With cross-sectional data, one would be defining a dummy variable for every observation, exhausting the degrees of freedom. The dummy variables on their own would give a perfect but meaningless fit.

If there are a large number of individuals, using the LSDV method directly is not a practical proposition, given the need for a large number of dummy variables. However, it can be shown mathematically that the method is identical to the within-groups method. The only apparent difference is in the number of degrees of freedom. It is easy to see from (14.12) that there are $nT - k - n$ degrees of freedom if the panel is balanced. In the within-groups approach, it seemed at first that there were $nT - k$. However, n degrees of freedom are consumed in the manipulation that eliminates the α_i.

Given that it is equivalent to the within-groups approach, the LSDV method is subject to the same problems. In particular, we are unable to estimate coefficients for the X variables that are fixed for each individual. Suppose that X_{ij} is equal to c_i for all the observations for individual i. Then

$$X_j = \sum_{i=1}^{n} c_i A_i . \tag{14.13}$$

To see this, suppose that there are four individuals and three time periods, as in Table 14.1, and consider the observations for the first individual. X_j is equal to c_1 for each observation. A_1 is equal to 1. All the other A dummies are equal to 0. Hence, both sides of the equation are equal to c_1. Similarly, both sides of the equation are equal to c_2 for the observations for individual 2, and similarly for individuals 3 and 4.

Table 14.1 Individual-specific dummy variables and an unchanging X variable

Individual	*Time period*	A_1	A_2	A_3	A_4	X_j
1	1	1	0	0	0	c_1
1	2	1	0	0	0	c_1
1	3	1	0	0	0	c_1
2	1	0	1	0	0	c_2
2	2	0	1	0	0	c_2
2	3	0	1	0	0	c_2
3	1	0	0	1	0	c_3
3	2	0	0	1	0	c_3
3	3	0	0	1	0	c_3
4	1	0	0	0	1	c_4
4	2	0	0	0	1	c_4
4	3	0	0	0	1	c_4

Thus, there is an exact linear relationship linking X_j with the dummy variables and the model is subject to exact multicollinearity. Accordingly, X_j cannot be included in the regression specification.

Example

To illustrate the use of a fixed effects model, we return to the example in Section 14.1 and use all the available data from 1980 to 1996, 20,343 observations in all. Table 14.2 shows the extra hourly earnings of married men and of men who are single but married within the next four years. The controls (not shown) are the same as in Section 14.1. The first column gives the estimates obtained by simply pooling the observations and using OLS with robust standard errors. The second column gives the fixed effects estimates, using the within-groups method, with single men as the reference category. The third gives the fixed effects estimates with married men as the reference category. The fourth and fifth give the random effects estimates, discussed in the next section.

The OLS estimates are very similar to those in the wage equation for 1988 discussed in Section 14.1. The fixed effects estimates are considerably lower, suggesting that the OLS estimates were inflated by unobserved heterogeneity. Nevertheless, the pattern is the same. Soon-to-be-married men earn significantly more than single men who stay single. However, if we fit the specification corresponding to equation (14.2), shown in the third column, we find that soon-to-be-married men earn significantly less than married men. Hence, both hypotheses relating to the marriage premium appear to be partly true.

14.3 Random effects regressions

As we saw in the previous section, when the variables of interest are constant for each individual, a fixed effects regression is not an effective tool because

Table 14.2 Earnings premium for married and soon-to-be-married men, NLSY 1980–96

	OLS	*Fixed effects*		*Random effects*	
Married	0.184 (0.007)	0.106 (0.012)	—	0.134 (0.010)	—
Single, married within 4 years	0.096 (0.009)	0.045 (0.010)	−0.061 (0.008)	0.060 (0.009)	−0.075 (0.007)
Single, not married within 4 years	—	—	−0.106 (0.012)	—	−0.134 (0.010)
R^2	0.358	0.268	0.268	0.346	0.346
DWH test	—	—	—	205.8	205.8
n	20,343	20,343	20,343	20,343	20,343

such variables cannot be included. In this section, we will consider an alternative approach, known as a random effects regression that may, subject to two conditions, provide a solution to this problem.

The first condition is that it is possible to treat each of the unobserved Z_p variables as being drawn randomly from a given distribution. This may well be the case if the individual observations constitute a random sample from a given population as, for example, with the NLSY where the respondents were randomly drawn from the US population aged 14 to 21 in 1979. If this is the case, the α_i may be treated as random variables (hence the name of this approach) drawn from a given distribution and we may rewrite the model as

$$Y_{it} = \beta_1 + \sum_{j=2}^{k} \beta_j X_{jit} + \alpha_i + \delta t + \varepsilon_{it}$$

$$= \beta_1 + \sum_{j=2}^{k} \beta_j X_{jit} + \delta t + u_{it}, \qquad \textbf{(14.14)}$$

where

$$u_{it} = \alpha_i + \varepsilon_{it}, \qquad \textbf{(14.15)}$$

We have thus dealt with the unobserved effect by subsuming it into the disturbance term.

The second condition is that the Z_p variables are distributed independently of all of the X_j variables. If this is not the case, α, and hence u, will not be uncorrelated with the X_j variables and the random effects estimation will be biased and inconsistent. We would have to use fixed effects estimation instead, even if the first condition seems to be satisfied.

If the two conditions are satisfied, we may use (14.14) as our regression specification, but there is a complication. u_{it} will be subject to a special form of autocorrelation and we will have to use an estimation technique that takes account of it.

First, we will check the other regression model conditions relating to the disturbance term. Given our assumption that ε_{it} satisfies the usual regression model conditions, we can see that u_{it} satisfies the condition that its expectation be zero, since

$$E(u_{it}) = E(\alpha_i + \varepsilon_{it}) = E(\alpha_i) + E(\varepsilon_{it}) = 0 \quad \text{for all } i \text{ and } t. \qquad \textbf{(14.16)}$$

Here we are assuming without loss of generality that $E(\alpha_i) = 0$, any nonzero component being absorbed by the intercept, β_1. u_{it} will also satisfy the condition that it should have constant variance, since

$$\sigma^2_{u_{it}} = \sigma^2_{\alpha_i+\varepsilon_{it}} = \sigma^2_\alpha + \sigma^2_\varepsilon + 2\sigma_{\alpha\varepsilon} = \sigma^2_\alpha + \sigma^2_\varepsilon \quad \text{for all } i \text{ and } t. \qquad \textbf{(14.17)}$$

The $\sigma_{\alpha\varepsilon}$ term is zero on the assumption that α_i is distributed independently of ε_{it}. u_{it} will also satisfy the regression model condition that it be distributed independently of the values of X_j, since both α_i and ε_{it} are assumed to satisfy this condition.

However, there is a problem with the regression model condition that the value of u_{it} in any observation be generated independently of its value in all other observations. For all the observations relating to a given individual, α_i will have the same value, reflecting the unchanging unobserved characteristics of the individual. This is illustrated in Table 14.3 for the case where there are four individuals and three time periods.

Since the disturbance terms for individual i have a common component α_i, they are correlated. For individual i in period t, the disturbance term is $(\alpha_i + \varepsilon_{it})$. For the same individual in any other period t' it is $(\alpha_i + \varepsilon_{it'})$. The population covariance between them is

$$\sigma_{u_{it},u_{it'}} = \sigma_{(\alpha_i+\varepsilon_{it}),(\alpha_i+\varepsilon_{it'})} = \sigma_{\alpha_i,\alpha_i} + \sigma_{\alpha_i,\varepsilon_{it'}} + \sigma_{\varepsilon_{it},\alpha_i} + \sigma_{\varepsilon_{it},\varepsilon_{it'}} = \sigma_\alpha^2. \qquad (14.18)$$

For observations relating to different individuals, the problem does not arise because then the α components will be different and generated independently.

As in the case of autocorrelated disturbance terms in a time series model, OLS remains unbiased and consistent, but it is inefficient and the OLS standard errors are computed wrongly.

In the case of autocorrelated disturbance terms in a time series model, the solution was to transform the model so that the transformed disturbance term satisfied the regression model condition, and a similar procedure is adopted in

Table 14.3 Example of disturbance term values in a random effects model

Individual	*Time period*	u
1	1	$\alpha_1 + \varepsilon_{11}$
1	2	$\alpha_1 + \varepsilon_{12}$
1	3	$\alpha_1 + \varepsilon_{13}$
2	1	$\alpha_2 + \varepsilon_{21}$
2	2	$\alpha_2 + \varepsilon_{22}$
2	3	$\alpha_2 + \varepsilon_{23}$
3	1	$\alpha_3 + \varepsilon_{31}$
3	2	$\alpha_3 + \varepsilon_{32}$
3	3	$\alpha_3 + \varepsilon_{33}$
4	1	$\alpha_4 + \varepsilon_{41}$
4	2	$\alpha_4 + \varepsilon_{42}$
4	3	$\alpha_4 + \varepsilon_{43}$

the present case. However, while the transformation in the case of autocorrelation was very straightforward, in the present case it is more complex. Known as feasible generalized least squares, its description requires the use of linear algebra and is therefore beyond the scope of this text. It yields consistent estimates of the coefficients and therefore depends on n being sufficiently large. For small n its properties are unknown.

Assessing the appropriateness of fixed effects and random effects estimation

When should you use fixed effects estimation rather than random effects estimation, or vice versa? In principle, random effects estimation is more attractive because observed characteristics that remain constant for each individual are retained in the regression model. In fixed effects estimation, they have to be dropped. Also, with random effects estimation, we do not lose n degrees of freedom, as is the case with fixed effects.

However, if either of the preconditions for using random effects is violated, we should use fixed effects instead. One precondition is that the observations can be described as being drawn randomly from a given population. Judging whether this is satisfied is mostly a matter of understanding the nature of the data. In the case of the NLSY, this is a reasonable assumption because that data set was designed to be a random sample from the corresponding age group in the US population. By contrast, it would not be a reasonable assumption if the units of observation in the panel data set were countries and the sample consisted of those countries that are members of the Organization for Economic Cooperation and Development (OECD). These countries certainly cannot be considered to represent a random sample of the 200-odd sovereign states in the world.

The other precondition is that the unobserved effect be distributed independently of the X_j variables. How can we tell if this is the case? The standard procedure is yet another implementation of the **Durbin–Wu–Hausman test** used to help us choose between OLS and IV estimation in models where there is suspected measurement error (Section 8.5) or simultaneous equations endogeneity (Section 9.3). The null hypothesis is that the α_i are distributed independently of the X_j. If this is correct, both random effects and fixed effects are consistent, but fixed effects will be inefficient because, looking at it in its LSDV form, it involves estimating an unnecessary set of dummy variable coefficients. If the null hypothesis is false, the random effects estimates will be subject to unobserved heterogeneity bias and will therefore differ systematically from the fixed effects estimates.

As in its other applications, the DWH test determines whether the estimates of the coefficients, taken as a group, are significantly different in the two regressions. If any variables are dropped in the fixed effects regression, they are excluded from the test. Under the null hypothesis, the test statistic has a chi-squared distribution. In principle, this should have degrees of freedom equal to the number of slope coefficients being compared but, for technical reasons that require matrix algebra for an explanation, the actual number may be lower. A regression application that implements the test, such as Stata, should determine the actual number of degrees of freedom.

Example

The fixed effects estimates, using the within-groups approach, of the coefficients of married men and soon-to-be-married men in Table 14.2 are 0.106 and 0.045, respectively. The corresponding random effects estimates are considerably higher, 0.134 and 0.060, inviting the suspicion that they may be inflated by unobserved heterogeneity. The DWH test involves the comparison of 13 coefficients (those of *MARRIED*, *SOONMARR*, and 11 controls). Stata reports that there are in fact only 12 degrees of freedom. The test statistic is 205.8. With 12 degrees of freedom, the critical value of chi-squared at the 0.1 percent level is 32.9, so we definitely conclude that we should be using fixed effects estimation.

Our findings are the same as in the simpler example in Section 14.1. They confirm that married men earn more than single men. Part of the differential appears to be attributable to the characteristics of married men, since men who are soon-to-marry but still single also enjoy an earnings premium. However, part of the marriage premium appears to be attributable to the effect of marriage itself, since married men earn significantly more than those who are soon-to-marry but still single.

Random effects or OLS?

Suppose that the DWH test indicates that we can use random effects rather than fixed effects. We should then consider whether there are any unobserved effects at all. It is just possible that the model has been so well specified that the disturbance term

$$u_{it} = \alpha_i + \varepsilon_{it} \tag{14.19}$$

consists only of the purely random component ε_{it} and there is no individual-specific α_i term. In this situation, we should use pooled OLS, with two advantages. There is a gain in efficiency because we are not attempting to allow for non-existent within-groups autocorrelation, and, for inference, we will be able to take advantage of the finite-sample properties of OLS, instead of having to rely on the asymptotic properties of random effects.

Various tests have been developed to detect the presence of random effects. The most common, implemented in some regression applications, is the Breusch–Pagan lagrange multiplier test, the test statistic having a chi-squared distribution with one degree of freedom under the null hypothesis of no random effects. In

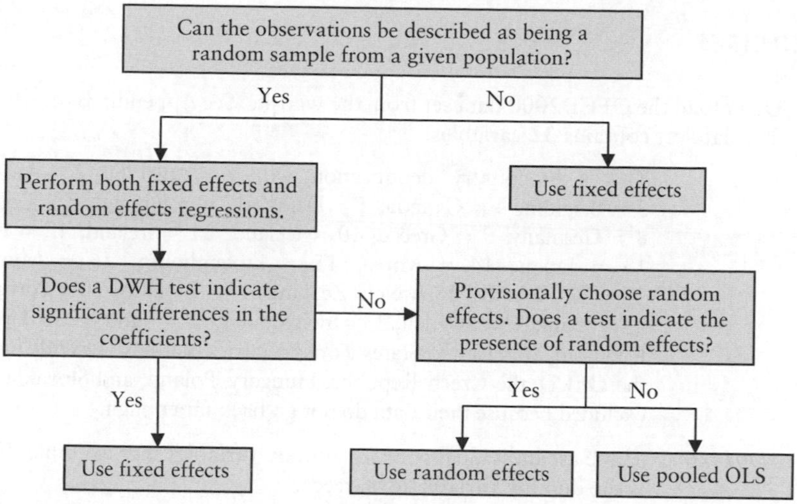

Figure 14.1 Choice of regression model for panel data

the case of the marriage effect example, the statistic is very high indeed, 20,007, but in this case it is meaningless because we have already discovered that we should not use random effects estimation.

Figure 14.1 summarizes the decision-making process for fitting a model with panel data.

A note on the random effects and fixed effects terminology

It is generally agreed that the random effects/fixed effects terminology can be misleading, but that it is too late to change it now. It is natural to think that random effects estimation should be used when the unobserved effect can be characterized as being drawn randomly from a given population and that fixed effects should be used when the unobserved effect is considered to be non-random. The second part of that statement is correct. However, the first part is correct only if the unobserved effect is distributed independently of the X_j variables. If it is not, fixed effects should be used instead to avoid the problem of unobserved heterogeneity bias.

Key terms

- balanced panel
- Durbin–Wu–Hausman test
- first differences regression
- fixed effects
- least squares dummy variable (LSDV) regression
- longitudinal data set
- panel data set
- pooled OLS regression
- random effects
- unbalanced panel
- unobserved effect
- within-groups regression

EXERCISES

14.1 Download the OECD2000 data set from the website. See Appendix B for details. The data set contains 32 variables:

ID	This is the country identification, with 1 = Australia, 2 = Austria, 3 = Belgium, 4 = Canada, 5 = Denmark, 6 = Finland, 7 = France, 8 = Germany, 9 = Greece, 10 = Iceland, 11 = Ireland, 12 = Italy, 13 = Japan, 14 = Korea, 15 = Luxembourg, 16 = Mexico, 17 = Netherlands, 18 = New Zealand, 19 = Norway, 20 = Portugal, 21 = Spain, 22 = Sweden, 23 = Switzerland, 24 = Turkey, 25 = United Kingdom, 26 = United States. Four countries that have recently joined the OECD, the Czech Republic, Hungary, Poland, and Slovakia, are excluded because their data do not go back far enough.
ID01–26	These are individual country dummy variables. For example, *ID09* is the dummy variable for Greece.
E	Average annual percentage rate of growth of employment for country i during time period t.
G	Average annual percentage rate of growth of GDP for country i during time period t.
TIME	There are three time periods, denoted 1, 2, and 3. They refer to average annual data for 1971–80, 1981–90, and 1991–2000.
TIME2	Dummy variable defined to be equal to 1 when *TIME* = 2, 0 otherwise.
TIME3	Dummy variable defined to be equal to 1 when *TIME* = 3, 0 otherwise.

Perform a pooled OLS regression of *E* on *G*. Regress *E* on *G*, *TIME2*, and *TIME3*. Perform appropriate statistical tests and give an interpretation of the regression results.

14.2 Using the OECD2000 data set, perform a (within-groups) fixed effects regression of *E* on *G*, *TIME2*, and *TIME3*. Perform appropriate statistical tests, give an interpretation of the regression coefficients, and comment on R^2.

14.3 Perform the corresponding LSDV regression, using OLS to regress *E* on *G*, *TIME2*, *TIME3*, and the country dummy variables (a) dropping the intercept, and (b) dropping one of the dummy variables. Perform appropriate statistical tests and give an interpretation of the coefficients in each case. Explain why either the intercept or one of the dummy variables must be dropped.

14.4 Perform a test for fixed effects in the OECD2000 regression by evaluating the explanatory power of the country dummy variables as a group.

14.5 Download the NLSY2000 data set from the website. See Appendix B for details. This contains the variables found in the *EAEF* data sets for the years 1980–94, 1996, 1998, and 2000 (there were no surveys in 1995, 1997, or 1999). Assuming that a random effects model is appropriate, investigate the apparent impact of unobserved heterogeneity on estimates of the coefficient of schooling by fitting the same earnings function, first using pooled OLS, then using random effects.

14.6 The *UNION* variable in the NLSY2000 data set is defined to be equal to 1 if the respondent was a member of a union in the year in question and 0 otherwise. Assuming that a random effects model is appropriate, add *UNION* to the earnings function specification and fit it using pooled OLS and random effects.

14.7 Using the NLSY2000 data set, perform a fixed effects regression of the earnings function specification used in Exercise 14.5 and compare the estimated coefficients with those obtained using OLS and random effects. Perform a Durbin–Wu–Hausman test to discriminate between random effects and fixed effects.

14.8 Using the NLSY2000 data set, perform a fixed effects regression of the earnings function specification used in Exercise 14.6 and compare the estimated coefficients with those obtained using OLS and random effects. Perform a Durbin–Wu–Hausman test to discriminate between random effects and fixed effects.

14.9 The NLSY2000 data set contains the following data for a sample of 2,427 males and 2,392 females for the years 1980–2000: weight in pounds, years of schooling, age, marital status in the form of a dummy variable *MARRIED*, defined to be 1 if the respondent was married, 0 if single, and height in inches. Hypothesizing that weight is influenced by schooling, age, marital status, and height, the following regressions were performed for males and females separately:

(1) an ordinary least squares regression pooling the observations;

(2) a within-groups fixed effects regression;

(3) a random effects regression.

The results of these regressions are shown in the table. Standard errors are given in parentheses.

	Males			*Females*		
	OLS	*FE*	*RE*	*OLS*	*FE*	*RE*
Years of schooling	−0.98 (0.09)	−0.02 (0.23)	−0.45 (0.16)	−1.95 (0.12)	−0.60 (0.27)	−1.25 (0.18)
Age	1.61 (0.04)	1.64 (0.02)	1.65 (0.02)	2.03 (0.05)	1.66 (0.03)	1.72 (0.03)
Married	3.70 (0.48)	2.92 (0.33)	3.00 (0.32)	−8.27 (0.59)	3.08 (0.46)	1.98 (0.44)
Height	5.07 (0.08)	dropped	4.95 (0.18)	3.48 (0.10)	dropped	3.38 (0.21)
constant	−209.52 (5.39)	dropped	−209.81 (12.88)	−105.90 (6.62)	dropped	−107.61 (13.43)
R^2	0.27	—	—	0.17	—	—
n	17,299	17,299	17,299	13,160	13,160	13,160
DWH $\chi^2(3)$			7.22			92.94

Explain why height is excluded from the FE regression.

Evaluate, for males and females separately, whether the fixed effects or random effects model should be preferred.

For males and females separately, compare the estimates of the coefficients in the OLS and FE models and attempt to explain the differences.

Explain in principle how one might test whether individual-specific fixed effects jointly have significant explanatory power, if the number of individuals is small. Explain why the test is not practical in this case.

14.10 The within-groups version of the fixed effects regression model involves subtracting the group mean relationship

$$\overline{Y}_i = \beta_1 + \sum_{j=2}^{k} (\beta_j \overline{X}_{ij}) + \delta\overline{t} + \alpha_i + \overline{\varepsilon}_{it}$$

from the original specification in order to eliminate the individual-specific effect α_i. Regressions using the group mean relationship are described as between effects regressions. Explain why the between effects model is in general inappropriate for estimating the parameters of a model using panel data. (Consider the two cases where the α_i are correlated and uncorrelated with the X_j controls.)

APPENDIX A: Statistical tables

Table A.1 Cumulative standardized normal distribution

A(z) is the integral of the standardized normal distribution from ∞ to *z* (in other words, the area under the curve to the left of *z*). It gives the probability of a normal random variable not being more than z standard deviations above its mean. Values of *z* of particular importance:

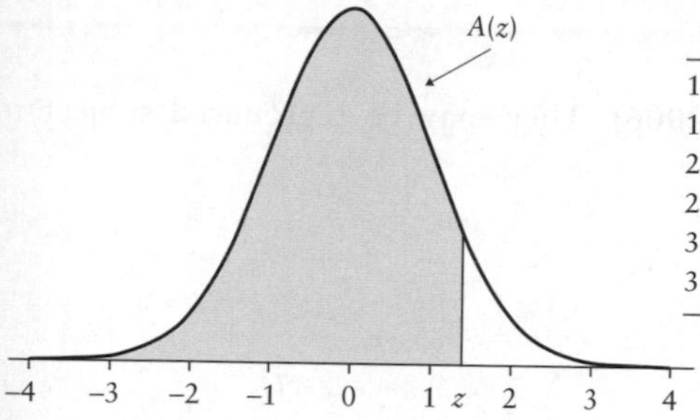

z	*A(z)*	
1.645	0.9500	Lower limit of right 5% tail
1.960	0.9750	Lower limit of right 2.5% tail
2.326	0.9900	Lower limit of right 1% tail
2.576	0.9950	Lower limit of right 0.5% tail
3.090	0.9990	Lower limit of right 0.1% tail
3.291	0.9995	Lower limit of right 0.05% tail

z	0.00	0.01	0.02	0.03	0.04	0.05	0.06	0.07	0.08	0.09
0.0	0.5000	0.5040	0.5080	0.5120	0.5160	0.5199	0.5239	0.5279	0.5319	0.5359
0.1	0.5398	0.5438	0.5478	0.5517	0.5557	0.5596	0.5636	0.5675	0.5714	0.5753
0.2	0.5793	0.5832	0.5871	0.5910	0.5948	0.5987	0.6026	0.6064	0.6103	0.6141
0.3	0.6179	0.6217	0.6255	0.6293	0.6331	0.6368	0.6406	0.6443	0.6480	0.6517
0.4	0.6554	0.6591	0.6628	0.6664	0.6700	0.6736	0.6772	0.6808	0.6844	0.6879
0.5	0.6915	0.6950	0.6985	0.7019	0.7054	0.7088	0.7123	0.7157	0.7190	0.7224
0.6	0.7257	0.7291	0.7324	0.7357	0.7389	0.7422	0.7454	0.7486	0.7517	0.7549
0.7	0.7580	0.7611	0.7642	0.7673	0.7704	0.7734	0.7764	0.7794	0.7823	0.7852
0.8	0.7881	0.7910	0.7939	0.7967	0.7995	0.8023	0.8051	0.8078	0.8106	0.8133
0.9	0.8159	0.8186	0.8212	0.8238	0.8264	0.8289	0.8315	0.8340	0.8365	0.8389
1.0	0.8413	0.8438	0.8461	0.8485	0.8508	0.8531	0.8554	0.8577	0.8599	0.8621
1.1	0.8643	0.8665	0.8686	0.8708	0.8729	0.8749	0.8770	0.8790	0.8810	0.8830
1.2	0.8849	0.8869	0.8888	0.8907	0.8925	0.8944	0.8962	0.8980	0.8997	0.9015
1.3	0.9032	0.9049	0.9066	0.9082	0.9099	0.9115	0.9131	0.9147	0.9162	0.9177
1.4	0.9192	0.9207	0.9222	0.9236	0.9251	0.9265	0.9279	0.9292	0.9306	0.9319
1.5	0.9332	0.9345	0.9357	0.9370	0.9382	0.9394	0.9406	0.9418	0.9429	0.9441
1.6	0.9452	0.9463	0.9474	0.9484	0.9495	0.9505	0.9515	0.9525	0.9535	0.9545
1.7	0.9554	0.9564	0.9573	0.9582	0.9591	0.9599	0.9608	0.9616	0.9625	0.9633
1.8	0.9641	0.9649	0.9656	0.9664	0.9671	0.9678	0.9686	0.9693	0.9699	0.9706
1.9	0.9713	0.9719	0.9726	0.9732	0.9738	0.9744	0.9750	0.9756	0.9761	0.9767

Table A.1 *(Continued)*

z	0.00	0.01	0.02	0.03	0.04	0.05	0.06	0.07	0.08	0.09
2.0	0.9772	0.9778	0.9783	0.9788	0.9793	0.9798	0.9803	0.9808	0.9812	0.9817
2.1	0.9821	0.9826	0.9830	0.9834	0.9838	0.9842	0.9846	0.9850	0.9854	0.9857
2.2	0.9861	0.9864	0.9868	0.9871	0.9875	0.9878	0.9881	0.9884	0.9887	0.9890
2.3	0.9893	0.9896	0.9898	0.9901	0.9904	0.9906	0.9909	0.9911	0.9913	0.9916
2.4	0.9918	0.9920	0.9922	0.9925	0.9927	0.9929	0.9931	0.9932	0.9934	0.9936
2.5	0.9938	0.9940	0.9941	0.9943	0.9945	0.9946	0.9948	0.9949	0.9951	0.9952
2.6	0.9953	0.9955	0.9956	0.9957	0.9959	0.9960	0.9961	0.9962	0.9963	0.9964
2.7	0.9965	0.9966	0.9967	0.9968	0.9969	0.9970	0.9971	0.9972	0.9973	0.9974
2.8	0.9974	0.9975	0.9976	0.9977	0.9977	0.9978	0.9979	0.9979	0.9980	0.9981
2.9	0.9981	0.9982	0.9982	0.9983	0.9984	0.9984	0.9985	0.9985	0.9986	0.9986
3.0	0.9987	0.9987	0.9987	0.9988	0.9988	0.9989	0.9989	0.9989	0.9990	0.9990
3.1	0.9990	0.9991	0.9991	0.9991	0.9992	0.9992	0.9992	0.9992	0.9993	0.9993
3.2	0.9993	0.9993	0.9994	0.9994	0.9994	0.9994	0.9994	0.9995	0.9995	0.9995
3.3	0.9995	0.9995	0.9995	0.9996	0.9996	0.9996	0.9996	0.9996	0.9996	0.9997
3.4	0.9997	0.9997	0.9997	0.9997	0.9997	0.9997	0.9997	0.9997	0.9997	0.9998
3.5	0.9998	0.9998	0.9998	0.9998	0.9998	0.9998	0.9998	0.9998	0.9998	0.9998
3.6	0.9998	0.9998	0.9999							

Table A.2 *t* distribution: critical values of *t*

		Significance level					
Degrees of freedom	*Two-tailed test:*	10%	5%	2%	1%	0.2%	0.1%
	One-tailed test:	5%	2.5%	1%	0.5%	0.1%	0.05%
1		6.314	12.706	31.821	63.657	318.309	636.619
2		2.920	4.303	6.965	9.925	22.327	31.599
3		2.353	3.182	4.541	5.841	10.215	12.924
4		2.132	2.776	3.747	4.604	7.173	8.610
5		2.015	2.571	3.365	4.032	5.893	6.869
6		1.943	2.447	3.143	3.707	5.208	5.959
7		1.894	2.365	2.998	3.499	4.785	5.408
8		1.860	2.306	2.896	3.355	4.501	5.041
9		1.833	2.262	2.821	3.250	4.297	4.781
10		1.812	2.228	2.764	3.169	4.144	4.587
11		1.796	2.201	2.718	3.106	4.025	4.437
12		1.782	2.179	2.681	3.055	3.930	4.318
13		1.771	2.160	2.650	3.012	3.852	4.221
14		1.761	2.145	2.624	2.977	3.787	4.140
15		1.753	2.131	2.602	2.947	3.733	4.073
16		1.746	2.120	2.583	2.921	3.686	4.015
17		1.740	2.110	2.567	2.898	3.646	3.965
18		1.734	2.101	2.552	2.878	3.610	3.922
19		1.729	2.093	2.539	2.861	3.579	3.883
20		1.725	2.086	2.528	2.845	3.552	3.850

Table A.2 (*Continued*)

Degrees of freedom	*Two-tailed test:* / *One-tailed test:*	*Significance level*					
	Two-tailed test:	10%	5%	2%	1%	0.2%	0.1%
	One-tailed test:	5%	2.5%	1%	0.5%	0.1%	0.05%
21		1.721	2.080	2.518	2.831	3.527	3.819
22		1.717	2.074	2.508	2.819	3.505	3.792
23		1.714	2.069	2.500	2.807	3.485	3.768
24		1.711	2.064	2.492	2.797	3.467	3.745
25		1.708	2.060	2.485	2.787	3.450	3.725
26		1.706	2.056	2.479	2.779	3.435	3.707
27		1.703	2.052	2.473	2.771	3.421	3.690
28		1.701	2.048	2.467	2.763	3.408	3.674
29		1.699	2.045	2.462	2.756	3.396	3.659
30		1.697	2.042	2.457	2.750	3.385	3.646
32		1.694	2.037	2.449	2.738	3.365	3.622
34		1.691	2.032	2.441	2.728	3.348	3.601
36		1.688	2.028	2.434	2.719	3.333	3.582
38		1.686	2.024	2.429	2.712	3.319	3.566
40		1.684	2.021	2.423	2.704	3.307	3.551
42		1.682	2.018	2.418	2.698	3.296	3.538
44		1.680	2.015	2.414	2.692	3.286	3.526
46		1.679	2.013	2.410	2.687	3.277	3.515
48		1.677	2.011	2.407	2.682	3.269	3.505
50		1.676	2.009	2.403	2.678	3.261	3.496
60		1.671	2.000	2.390	2.660	3.232	3.460
70		1.667	1.994	2.381	2.648	3.211	3.435
80		1.664	1.990	2.374	2.639	3.195	3.416
90		1.662	1.987	2.368	2.632	3.183	3.402
100		1.660	1.984	2.364	2.626	3.174	3.390
120		1.658	1.980	2.358	2.617	3.160	3.373
150		1.655	1.976	2.351	2.609	3.145	3.357
200		1.653	1.972	2.345	2.601	3.131	3.340
300		1.650	1.968	2.339	2.592	3.118	3.323
400		1.649	1.966	2.336	2.588	3.111	3.315
500		1.648	1.965	2.334	2.586	3.107	3.310
600		1.647	1.964	2.333	2.584	3.104	3.307
∞		1.645	1.960	2.326	2.576	3.090	3.291

Table A.3 *F* distribution: critical values of *F* (5% significance level)

v_1 / v_2	1	2	3	4	5	6	7	8	9
1	161.45	199.50	215.71	224.58	230.16	233.99	236.77	238.88	240.54
2	18.51	19.00	19.16	19.25	19.30	19.33	19.35	19.37	19.38
3	10.13	9.55	9.28	9.12	9.01	8.94	8.89	8.85	8.81
4	7.71	6.94	6.59	6.39	6.26	6.16	6.09	6.04	6.00
5	6.61	5.79	5.41	5.19	5.05	4.95	4.88	4.82	4.77
6	5.99	5.14	4.76	4.53	4.39	4.28	4.21	4.15	4.10
7	5.59	4.74	4.35	4.12	3.97	3.87	3.79	3.73	3.68
8	5.32	4.46	4.07	3.84	3.69	3.58	3.50	3.44	3.39
9	5.12	4.26	3.86	3.63	3.48	3.37	3.29	3.23	3.18
10	4.96	4.10	3.71	3.48	3.33	3.22	3.14	3.07	3.02
11	4.84	3.98	3.59	3.36	3.20	3.09	3.01	2.95	2.90
12	4.75	3.89	3.49	3.26	3.11	3.00	2.91	2.85	2.80
13	4.67	3.81	3.41	3.18	3.03	2.92	2.83	2.77	2.71
14	4.60	3.74	3.34	3.11	2.96	2.85	2.76	2.70	2.65
15	4.54	3.68	3.29	3.06	2.90	2.79	2.71	2.64	2.59
16	4.49	3.63	3.24	3.01	2.85	2.74	2.66	2.59	2.54
17	4.45	3.59	3.20	2.96	2.81	2.70	2.61	2.55	2.49
18	4.41	3.55	3.16	2.93	2.77	2.66	2.58	2.51	2.46
19	4.38	3.52	3.13	2.90	2.74	2.63	2.54	2.48	2.42
20	4.35	3.49	3.10	2.87	2.71	2.60	2.51	2.45	2.39
21	4.32	3.47	3.07	2.84	2.68	2.57	2.49	2.42	2.37
22	4.30	3.44	3.05	2.82	2.66	2.55	2.46	2.40	2.34
23	4.28	3.42	3.03	2.80	2.64	2.53	2.44	2.37	2.32
24	4.26	3.40	3.01	2.78	2.62	2.51	2.42	2.36	2.30
25	4.24	3.39	2.99	2.76	2.60	2.49	2.40	2.34	2.28
26	4.22	3.37	2.98	2.74	2.59	2.47	2.39	2.32	2.27
27	4.21	3.35	2.96	2.73	2.57	2.46	2.37	2.31	2.25
28	4.20	3.34	2.95	2.71	2.56	2.45	2.36	2.29	2.24
29	4.18	3.33	2.93	2.70	2.55	2.43	2.35	2.28	2.22
30	4.17	3.32	2.92	2.69	2.53	2.42	2.33	2.27	2.21
35	4.12	3.27	2.87	2.64	2.49	2.37	2.29	2.22	2.16
40	4.08	3.23	2.84	2.61	2.45	2.34	2.25	2.18	2.12
50	4.03	3.18	2.79	2.56	2.40	2.29	2.20	2.13	2.07
60	4.00	3.15	2.76	2.53	2.37	2.25	2.17	2.10	2.04
70	3.98	3.13	2.74	2.50	2.35	2.23	2.14	2.07	2.02
80	3.96	3.11	2.72	2.49	2.33	2.21	2.13	2.06	2.00
90	3.95	3.10	2.71	2.47	2.32	2.20	2.11	2.04	1.99
100	3.94	3.09	2.70	2.46	2.31	2.19	2.10	2.03	1.97
120	3.92	3.07	2.68	2.45	2.29	2.18	2.09	2.02	1.96
150	3.90	3.06	2.66	2.43	2.27	2.16	2.07	2.00	1.94
200	3.89	3.04	2.65	2.42	2.26	2.14	2.06	1.98	1.93
250	3.88	3.03	2.64	2.41	2.25	2.13	2.05	1.98	1.92
300	3.87	3.03	2.63	2.40	2.24	2.13	2.04	1.97	1.91
400	3.86	3.02	2.63	2.39	2.24	2.12	2.03	1.96	1.90
500	3.86	3.01	2.62	2.39	2.23	2.12	2.03	1.96	1.90
600	3.86	3.01	2.62	2.39	2.23	2.11	2.02	1.95	1.90
750	3.85	3.01	2.62	2.38	2.23	2.11	2.02	1.95	1.89
1000	3.85	3.00	2.61	2.38	2.22	2.11	2.02	1.95	1.89

Table A.3 (*Continued*)

v_1 / v_2	10	12	14	16	18	20	25	30	35
1	241.88	243.91	245.36	246.46	247.32	248.01	249.26	250.10	250.69
2	19.40	19.41	19.42	19.43	19.44	19.45	19.46	19.46	19.47
3	8.79	8.74	8.71	8.69	8.67	8.66	8.63	8.62	8.60
4	5.96	5.91	5.87	5.84	5.82	5.80	5.77	5.75	5.73
5	4.74	4.68	4.64	4.60	4.58	4.56	4.52	4.50	4.48
6	4.06	4.00	3.96	3.92	3.90	3.87	3.83	3.81	3.79
7	3.64	3.57	3.53	3.49	3.47	3.44	3.40	3.38	3.36
8	3.35	3.28	3.24	3.20	3.17	3.15	3.11	3.08	3.06
9	3.14	3.07	3.03	2.99	2.96	2.94	2.89	2.86	2.84
10	2.98	2.91	2.86	2.83	2.80	2.77	2.73	2.70	2.68
11	2.85	2.79	2.74	2.70	2.67	2.65	2.60	2.57	2.55
12	2.75	2.69	2.64	2.60	2.57	2.54	2.50	2.47	2.44
13	2.67	2.60	2.55	2.51	2.48	2.46	2.41	2.38	2.36
14	2.60	2.53	2.48	2.44	2.41	2.39	2.34	2.31	2.28
15	2.54	2.48	2.42	2.38	2.35	2.33	2.28	2.25	2.22
16	2.49	2.42	2.37	2.33	2.30	2.28	2.23	2.19	2.17
17	2.45	2.38	2.33	2.29	2.26	2.23	2.18	2.15	2.12
18	2.41	2.34	2.29	2.25	2.22	2.19	2.14	2.11	2.08
19	2.38	2.31	2.26	2.21	2.18	2.16	2.11	2.07	2.05
20	2.35	2.28	2.22	2.18	2.15	2.12	2.07	2.04	2.01
21	2.32	2.25	2.20	2.16	2.12	2.10	2.05	2.01	1.98
22	2.30	2.23	2.17	2.13	2.10	2.07	2.02	1.98	1.96
23	2.27	2.20	2.15	2.11	2.08	2.05	2.00	1.96	1.93
24	2.25	2.18	2.13	2.09	2.05	2.03	1.97	1.94	1.91
25	2.24	2.16	2.11	2.07	2.04	2.01	1.96	1.92	1.89
26	2.22	2.15	2.09	2.05	2.02	1.99	1.94	1.90	1.87
27	2.20	2.13	2.08	2.04	2.00	1.97	1.92	1.88	1.86
28	2.19	2.12	2.06	2.02	1.99	1.96	1.91	1.87	1.84
29	2.18	2.10	2.05	2.01	1.97	1.94	1.89	1.85	1.83
30	2.16	2.09	2.04	1.99	1.96	1.93	1.88	1.84	1.81
35	2.11	2.04	1.99	1.94	1.91	1.88	1.82	1.79	1.76
40	2.08	2.00	1.95	1.90	1.87	1.84	1.78	1.74	1.72
50	2.03	1.95	1.89	1.85	1.81	1.78	1.73	1.69	1.66
60	1.99	1.92	1.86	1.82	1.78	1.75	1.69	1.65	1.62
70	1.97	1.89	1.84	1.79	1.75	1.72	1.66	1.62	1.59
80	1.95	1.88	1.82	1.77	1.73	1.70	1.64	1.60	1.57
90	1.94	1.86	1.80	1.76	1.72	1.69	1.63	1.59	1.55
100	1.93	1.85	1.79	1.75	1.71	1.68	1.62	1.57	1.54
120	1.91	1.83	1.78	1.73	1.69	1.66	1.60	1.55	1.52
150	1.89	1.82	1.76	1.71	1.67	1.64	1.58	1.54	1.50
200	1.88	1.80	1.74	1.69	1.66	1.62	1.56	1.52	1.48
250	1.87	1.79	1.73	1.68	1.65	1.61	1.55	1.50	1.47
300	1.86	1.78	1.72	1.68	1.64	1.61	1.54	1.50	1.46
400	1.85	1.78	1.72	1.67	1.63	1.60	1.53	1.49	1.45
500	1.85	1.77	1.71	1.66	1.62	1.59	1.53	1.48	1.45
600	1.85	1.77	1.71	1.66	1.62	1.59	1.52	1.48	1.44
750	1.84	1.77	1.70	1.66	1.62	1.58	1.52	1.47	1.44
1000	1.84	1.76	1.70	1.65	1.61	1.58	1.47	1.47	1.43

Table A.3 (*Continued*)

v_1 / v_2	40	50	60	75	100	150	200
1	251.14	251.77	252.20	252.62	253.04	253.46	253.68
2	19.47	19.48	19.48	19.48	19.49	19.49	19.49
3	8.59	8.58	8.57	8.56	8.55	8.54	8.54
4	5.72	5.70	5.69	5.68	5.66	5.65	5.65
5	4.46	4.44	4.43	4.42	4.41	4.39	4.39
6	3.77	3.75	3.74	3.73	3.71	3.70	3.69
7	3.34	3.32	3.30	3.29	3.27	3.26	3.25
8	3.04	3.02	3.01	2.99	2.97	2.96	2.95
9	2.83	2.80	2.79	2.77	2.76	2.74	2.73
10	2.66	2.64	2.62	2.60	2.59	2.57	2.56
11	2.53	2.51	2.49	2.47	2.46	2.44	2.43
12	2.43	2.40	2.38	2.37	2.35	2.33	2.32
13	2.34	2.31	2.30	2.28	2.26	2.24	2.23
14	2.27	2.24	2.22	2.21	2.19	2.17	2.16
15	2.20	2.18	2.16	2.14	2.12	2.10	2.10
16	2.15	2.12	2.11	2.09	2.07	2.05	2.04
17	2.10	2.08	2.06	2.04	2.02	2.00	1.99
18	2.06	2.04	2.02	2.00	1.98	1.96	1.95
19	2.03	2.00	1.98	1.96	1.94	1.92	1.91
20	1.99	1.97	1.95	1.93	1.91	1.89	1.88
21	1.96	1.94	1.92	1.90	1.88	1.86	1.84
22	1.94	1.91	1.89	1.87	1.85	1.83	1.82
23	1.91	1.88	1.86	1.84	1.82	1.80	1.79
24	1.89	1.86	1.84	1.82	1.80	1.78	1.77
25	1.87	1.84	1.82	1.80	1.78	1.76	1.75
26	1.85	1.82	1.80	1.78	1.76	1.74	1.73
27	1.84	1.81	1.79	1.76	1.74	1.72	1.71
28	1.82	1.79	1.77	1.75	1.73	1.70	1.69
29	1.81	1.77	1.75	1.73	1.71	1.69	1.67
30	1.79	1.76	1.74	1.72	1.70	1.67	1.66
35	1.74	1.70	1.68	1.66	1.63	1.61	1.60
40	1.69	1.66	1.64	1.61	1.59	1.56	1.55
50	1.63	1.60	1.58	1.55	1.52	1.50	1.48
60	1.59	1.56	1.53	1.51	1.48	1.45	1.44
70	1.57	1.53	1.50	1.48	1.45	1.42	1.40
80	1.54	1.51	1.48	1.45	1.43	1.39	1.38
90	1.53	1.49	1.46	1.44	1.41	1.38	1.36
100	1.52	1.48	1.45	1.42	1.39	1.36	1.34
120	1.50	1.46	1.43	1.40	1.37	1.33	1.32
150	1.48	1.44	1.41	1.38	1.34	1.31	1.29
200	1.46	1.41	1.39	1.35	1.32	1.28	1.26
250	1.44	1.40	1.37	1.34	1.31	1.27	1.25
300	1.43	1.39	1.36	1.33	1.30	1.26	1.23
400	1.42	1.38	1.35	1.32	1.28	1.24	1.22
500	1.42	1.38	1.35	1.31	1.28	1.23	1.21
600	1.41	1.37	1.34	1.31	1.27	1.23	1.20
750	1.41	1.37	1.34	1.30	1.26	1.22	1.20
1000	1.41	1.36	1.33	1.30	1.26	1.22	1.19

Table A.3 F distribution: critical values of F (1% significance level)

v_1 / v_2	1	2	3	4	5	6	7	8
1	4052.18	4999.50	5403.35	5624.58	5763.65	5858.99	5928.36	5981.07
2	98.50	99.00	99.17	99.25	99.30	99.33	99.36	99.37
3	34.12	30.82	29.46	28.71	28.24	27.91	27.67	27.49
4	21.20	18.00	16.69	15.98	15.52	15.21	14.98	14.80
5	16.26	13.27	12.06	11.39	10.97	10.67	10.46	10.29
6	13.75	10.92	9.78	9.15	8.75	8.47	8.26	8.10
7	12.25	9.55	8.45	7.85	7.46	7.19	6.99	6.84
8	11.26	8.65	7.59	7.01	6.63	6.37	6.18	6.03
9	10.56	8.02	6.99	6.42	6.06	5.80	5.61	5.47
10	10.04	7.56	6.55	5.99	5.64	5.39	5.20	5.06
11	9.65	7.21	6.22	5.67	5.32	5.07	4.89	4.74
12	9.33	6.93	5.95	5.41	5.06	4.82	4.64	4.50
13	9.07	6.70	5.74	5.21	4.86	4.62	4.44	4.30
14	8.86	6.51	5.56	5.04	4.69	4.46	4.28	4.14
15	8.68	6.36	5.42	4.89	4.56	4.32	4.14	4.00
16	8.53	6.23	5.29	4.77	4.44	4.20	4.03	3.89
17	8.40	6.11	5.18	4.67	4.34	4.10	3.93	3.79
18	8.29	6.01	5.09	4.58	4.25	4.01	3.84	3.71
19	8.18	5.93	5.01	4.50	4.17	3.94	3.77	3.63
20	8.10	5.85	4.94	4.43	4.10	3.87	3.70	3.56
21	8.02	5.78	4.87	4.37	4.04	3.81	3.64	3.51
22	7.95	5.72	4.82	4.31	3.99	3.76	3.59	3.45
23	7.88	5.66	4.76	4.26	3.94	3.71	3.54	3.41
24	7.82	5.61	4.72	4.22	3.90	3.67	3.50	3.36
25	7.77	5.57	4.68	4.18	3.85	3.63	3.46	3.32
26	7.72	5.53	4.64	4.14	3.82	3.59	3.42	3.29
27	7.68	5.49	4.60	4.11	3.78	3.56	3.39	3.26
28	7.64	5.45	4.57	4.07	3.75	3.53	3.36	3.23
29	7.60	5.42	4.54	4.04	3.73	3.50	3.33	3.20
30	7.56	5.39	4.51	4.02	3.70	3.47	3.30	3.17
35	7.42	5.27	4.40	3.91	3.59	3.37	3.20	3.07
40	7.31	5.18	4.31	3.83	3.51	3.29	3.12	2.99
50	7.17	5.06	4.20	3.72	3.41	3.19	3.02	2.89
60	7.08	4.98	4.13	3.65	3.34	3.12	2.95	2.82
70	7.01	4.92	4.07	3.60	3.29	3.07	2.91	2.78
80	6.96	4.88	4.04	3.56	3.26	3.04	2.87	2.74
90	6.93	4.85	4.01	3.53	3.23	3.01	2.84	2.72
100	6.90	4.82	3.98	3.51	3.21	2.99	2.82	2.69
120	6.85	4.79	3.95	3.48	3.17	2.96	2.79	2.66
150	6.81	4.75	3.91	3.45	3.14	2.92	2.76	2.63
200	6.76	4.71	3.88	3.41	3.11	2.89	2.73	2.60
250	6.74	4.69	3.86	3.40	3.09	2.87	2.71	2.58
300	6.72	4.68	3.85	3.38	3.08	2.86	2.70	2.57
400	6.70	4.66	3.83	3.37	3.06	2.85	2.68	2.56
500	6.69	4.65	3.82	3.36	3.05	2.84	2.68	2.55
600	6.68	4.64	3.81	3.35	3.05	2.83	2.67	2.54
750	6.67	4.63	3.81	3.34	3.04	2.83	2.66	2.53
1000	6.66	4.63	3.80	3.34	3.04	2.82	2.66	2.53

Table A.3 (*Continued*)

v_1 / v_2	9	10	12	14	16	18	20	25
1	6022.47	6055.85	6106.32	6142.67	6170.10	6191.53	6208.73	6239.83
2	99.39	99.40	99.42	99.43	99.44	99.44	99.45	99.46
3	27.35	27.23	27.05	26.92	26.83	26.75	26.69	26.58
4	14.66	14.55	14.37	14.25	14.15	14.08	14.02	13.91
5	10.16	10.05	9.89	9.77	9.68	9.61	9.55	9.45
6	7.98	7.87	7.72	7.60	7.52	7.45	7.40	7.30
7	6.72	6.62	6.47	6.36	6.28	6.21	6.16	6.06
8	5.91	5.81	5.67	5.56	5.48	5.41	5.36	5.26
9	5.35	5.26	5.11	5.01	4.92	4.86	4.81	4.71
10	4.94	4.85	4.71	4.60	4.52	4.46	4.41	4.31
11	4.63	4.54	4.40	4.29	4.21	4.15	4.10	4.01
12	4.39	4.30	4.16	4.05	3.97	3.91	3.86	3.76
13	4.19	4.10	3.96	3.86	3.78	3.72	3.66	3.57
14	4.03	3.94	3.80	3.70	3.62	3.56	3.51	3.41
15	3.89	3.80	3.67	3.56	3.49	3.42	3.37	3.28
16	3.78	3.69	3.55	3.45	3.37	3.31	3.26	3.16
17	3.68	3.59	3.46	3.35	3.27	3.21	3.16	3.07
18	3.60	3.51	3.37	3.27	3.19	3.13	3.08	2.98
19	3.52	3.43	3.30	3.19	3.12	3.05	3.00	2.91
20	3.46	3.37	3.23	3.13	3.05	2.99	2.94	2.84
21	3.40	3.31	3.17	3.07	2.99	2.93	2.88	2.79
22	3.35	3.26	3.12	3.02	2.94	2.88	2.83	2.73
23	3.30	3.21	3.07	2.97	2.89	2.83	2.78	2.69
24	3.26	3.17	3.03	2.93	2.85	2.79	2.74	2.64
25	3.22	3.13	2.99	2.89	2.81	2.75	2.70	2.60
26	3.18	3.09	2.96	2.86	2.78	2.72	2.66	2.57
27	3.15	3.06	2.93	2.82	2.75	2.68	2.63	2.54
28	3.12	3.03	2.90	2.79	2.72	2.65	2.60	2.51
29	3.09	3.00	2.87	2.77	2.69	2.63	2.57	2.48
30	3.07	2.98	2.84	2.74	2.66	2.60	2.55	2.45
35	2.96	2.88	2.74	2.64	2.56	2.50	2.44	2.35
40	2.89	2.80	2.66	2.56	2.48	2.42	2.37	2.27
50	2.78	2.70	2.56	2.46	2.38	2.32	2.27	2.17
60	2.72	2.63	2.50	2.39	2.31	2.25	2.20	2.10
70	2.67	2.59	2.45	2.35	2.27	2.20	2.15	2.05
80	2.64	2.55	2.42	2.31	2.23	2.17	2.12	2.01
90	2.61	2.52	2.39	2.29	2.21	2.14	2.09	1.99
100	2.59	2.50	2.37	2.27	2.19	2.12	2.07	1.97
120	2.56	2.47	2.34	2.23	2.15	2.09	2.03	1.93
150	2.53	2.44	2.31	2.20	2.12	2.06	2.00	1.90
200	2.50	2.41	2.27	2.17	2.09	2.03	1.97	1.87
250	2.48	2.39	2.26	2.15	2.07	2.01	1.95	1.85
300	2.47	2.38	2.24	2.14	2.06	1.99	1.94	1.84
400	2.45	2.37	2.23	2.13	2.05	1.98	1.92	1.82
500	2.44	2.36	2.22	2.12	2.04	1.97	1.92	1.81
600	2.44	2.35	2.21	2.11	2.03	1.96	1.91	1.80
750	2.43	2.34	2.21	2.11	2.02	1.96	1.90	1.80
1000	2.43	2.34	2.20	2.10	2.02	1.95	1.90	1.79

Table A.3 (*Continued*)

v_1 / v_2	30	35	40	50	60	75	100	150	200
1	6260.65	6275.57	6286.78	6302.52	6313.03	6323.56	6334.11	6344.68	6349.97
2	99.47	99.47	99.47	99.48	99.48	99.49	99.49	99.49	99.49
3	26.50	26.45	26.41	26.35	26.32	26.28	26.24	26.20	26.18
4	13.84	13.79	13.75	13.69	13.65	13.61	13.58	13.54	13.52
5	9.38	9.33	9.29	9.24	9.20	9.17	9.13	9.09	9.08
6	7.23	7.18	7.14	7.09	7.06	7.02	6.99	6.95	6.93
7	5.99	5.94	5.91	5.86	5.82	5.79	5.75	5.72	5.70
8	5.20	5.15	5.12	5.07	5.03	5.00	4.96	4.93	4.91
9	4.65	4.60	4.57	4.52	4.48	4.45	4.41	4.38	4.36
10	4.25	4.20	4.17	4.12	4.08	4.05	4.01	3.98	3.96
11	3.94	3.89	3.86	3.81	3.78	3.74	3.71	3.67	3.66
12	3.70	3.65	3.62	3.57	3.54	3.50	3.47	3.43	3.41
13	3.51	3.46	3.43	3.38	3.34	3.31	3.27	3.24	3.22
14	3.35	3.30	3.27	3.22	3.18	3.15	3.11	3.08	3.06
15	3.21	3.17	3.13	3.08	3.05	3.01	2.98	2.94	2.92
16	3.10	3.05	3.02	2.97	2.93	2.90	2.86	2.83	2.81
17	3.00	2.96	2.92	2.87	2.83	2.80	2.76	2.73	2.71
18	2.92	2.87	2.84	2.78	2.75	2.71	2.68	2.64	2.62
19	2.84	2.80	2.76	2.71	2.67	2.64	2.60	2.57	2.55
20	2.78	2.73	2.69	2.64	2.61	2.57	2.54	2.50	2.48
21	2.72	2.67	2.64	2.58	2.55	2.51	2.48	2.44	2.42
22	2.67	2.62	2.58	2.53	2.50	2.46	2.42	2.38	2.36
23	2.62	2.57	2.54	2.48	2.45	2.41	2.37	2.34	2.32
24	2.58	2.53	2.49	2.44	2.40	2.37	2.33	2.29	2.27
25	2.54	2.49	2.45	2.40	2.36	2.33	2.29	2.25	2.23
26	2.50	2.45	2.42	2.36	2.33	2.29	2.25	2.21	2.19
27	2.47	2.42	2.38	2.33	2.29	2.26	2.22	2.18	2.16
28	2.44	2.39	2.35	2.30	2.26	2.23	2.19	2.15	2.13
29	2.41	2.36	2.33	2.27	2.23	2.20	2.16	2.12	2.10
30	2.39	2.34	2.30	2.25	2.21	2.17	2.13	2.09	2.07
35	2.28	2.23	2.19	2.14	2.10	2.06	2.02	1.98	1.96
40	2.20	2.15	2.11	2.06	2.02	1.98	1.94	1.90	1.87
50	2.10	2.05	2.01	1.95	1.91	1.87	1.82	1.78	1.76
60	2.03	1.98	1.94	1.88	1.84	1.79	1.75	1.70	1.68
70	1.98	1.93	1.89	1.83	1.78	1.74	1.70	1.65	1.62
80	1.94	1.89	1.85	1.79	1.75	1.70	1.65	1.61	1.58
90	1.92	1.86	1.82	1.76	1.72	1.67	1.62	1.57	1.55
100	1.89	1.84	1.80	1.74	1.69	1.65	1.60	1.55	1.52
120	1.86	1.81	1.76	1.70	1.66	1.61	1.56	1.51	1.48
150	1.83	1.77	1.73	1.66	1.62	1.57	1.52	1.46	1.43
200	1.79	1.74	1.69	1.63	1.58	1.53	1.48	1.42	1.39
250	1.77	1.72	1.67	1.61	1.56	1.51	1.46	1.40	1.36
300	1.76	1.70	1.66	1.59	1.55	1.50	1.44	1.38	1.35
400	1.75	1.69	1.64	1.58	1.53	1.48	1.42	1.36	1.32
500	1.74	1.68	1.63	1.57	1.52	1.47	1.41	1.34	1.31
600	1.73	1.67	1.63	1.56	1.51	1.46	1.40	1.34	1.30
750	1.72	1.66	1.62	1.55	1.50	1.45	1.39	1.33	1.29
1000	1.72	1.66	1.61	1.54	1.50	1.44	1.38	1.32	1.28

Table A.3 *F* distribution: critical values of *F* (0.1% significance level)

v_1 / v_2	1	2	3	4	5	6	7	8
1	4.05e05	5.00e05	5.40e05	5.62e05	5.76e05	5.86e05	5.93e05	5.98e05
2	998.50	999.00	999.17	999.25	999.30	999.33	999.36	999.37
3	167.03	148.50	141.11	137.10	134.58	132.85	131.58	130.62
4	74.14	61.25	56.18	53.44	51.71	50.53	49.66	49.00
5	47.18	37.12	33.20	31.09	29.75	28.83	28.16	27.65
6	35.51	27.00	23.70	21.92	20.80	20.03	19.46	19.03
7	29.25	21.69	18.77	17.20	16.21	15.52	15.02	14.63
8	25.41	18.49	15.83	14.39	13.48	12.86	12.40	12.05
9	22.86	16.39	13.90	12.56	11.71	11.13	10.70	10.37
10	21.04	14.91	12.55	11.28	10.48	9.93	9.52	9.20
11	19.69	13.81	11.56	10.35	9.58	9.05	8.66	8.35
12	18.64	12.97	10.80	9.63	8.89	8.38	8.00	7.71
13	17.82	12.31	10.21	9.07	8.35	7.86	7.49	7.21
14	17.14	11.78	9.73	8.62	7.92	7.44	7.08	6.80
15	16.59	11.34	9.34	8.25	7.57	7.09	6.74	6.47
16	16.12	10.97	9.01	7.94	7.27	6.80	6.46	6.19
17	15.72	10.66	8.73	7.68	7.02	6.56	6.22	5.96
18	15.38	10.39	8.49	7.46	6.81	6.35	6.02	5.76
19	15.08	10.16	8.28	7.27	6.62	6.18	5.85	5.59
20	14.82	9.95	8.10	7.10	6.46	6.02	5.69	5.44
21	14.59	9.77	7.94	6.95	6.32	5.88	5.56	5.31
22	14.38	9.61	7.80	6.81	6.19	5.76	5.44	5.19
23	14.20	9.47	7.67	6.70	6.08	5.65	5.33	5.09
24	14.03	9.34	7.55	6.59	5.98	5.55	5.23	4.99
25	13.88	9.22	7.45	6.49	5.89	5.46	5.15	4.91
26	13.74	9.12	7.36	6.41	5.80	5.38	5.07	4.83
27	13.61	9.02	7.27	6.33	5.73	5.31	5.00	4.76
28	13.50	8.93	7.19	6.25	5.66	5.24	4.93	4.69
29	13.39	8.85	7.12	6.19	5.59	5.18	4.87	4.64
30	13.29	8.77	7.05	6.12	5.53	5.12	4.82	4.58
35	12.90	8.47	6.79	5.88	5.30	4.89	4.59	4.36
40	12.61	8.25	6.59	5.70	5.13	4.73	4.44	4.21
50	12.22	7.96	6.34	5.46	4.90	4.51	4.22	4.00
60	11.97	7.77	6.17	5.31	4.76	4.37	4.09	3.86
70	11.80	7.64	6.06	5.20	4.66	4.28	3.99	3.77
80	11.67	7.54	5.97	5.12	4.58	4.20	3.92	3.70
90	11.57	7.47	5.91	5.06	4.53	4.15	3.87	3.65
100	11.50	7.41	5.86	5.02	4.48	4.11	3.83	3.61
120	11.38	7.32	5.78	4.95	4.42	4.04	3.77	3.55
150	11.27	7.24	5.71	4.88	4.35	3.98	3.71	3.49
200	11.15	7.15	5.63	4.81	4.29	3.92	3.65	3.43
250	11.09	7.10	5.59	4.77	4.25	3.88	3.61	3.40
300	11.04	7.07	5.56	4.75	4.22	3.86	3.59	3.38
400	10.99	7.03	5.53	4.71	4.19	3.83	3.56	3.35
500	10.96	7.00	5.51	4.69	4.18	3.81	3.54	3.33
600	10.94	6.99	5.49	4.68	4.16	3.80	3.53	3.32
750	10.91	6.97	5.48	4.67	4.15	3.79	3.52	3.31
1000	10.89	6.96	5.46	4.65	4.14	3.78	3.51	3.30

Table A.3 (*Continued*)

v_1	9	10	12	14	16	18	20	25	30
v_2									
1	6.02e05	6.06e05	6.11e05	6.14e05	6.17e05	6.19e05	6.21e05	6.24e05	6.26e05
2	999.39	999.40	999.42	999.43	999.44	999.44	999.45	999.46	999.47
3	129.86	129.25	128.32	127.64	127.14	126.74	126.42	125.84	125.45
4	48.47	48.05	47.41	46.95	46.60	46.32	46.10	45.70	45.43
5	27.24	26.92	26.42	26.06	25.78	25.57	25.39	25.08	24.87
6	18.69	18.41	17.99	17.68	17.45	17.27	17.12	16.85	16.67
7	14.33	14.08	13.71	13.43	13.23	13.06	12.93	12.69	12.53
8	11.77	11.54	11.19	10.94	10.75	10.60	10.48	10.26	10.11
9	10.11	9.89	9.57	9.33	9.15	9.01	8.90	8.69	8.55
10	8.96	8.75	8.45	8.22	8.05	7.91	7.80	7.60	7.47
11	8.12	7.92	7.63	7.41	7.24	7.11	7.01	6.81	6.68
12	7.48	7.29	7.00	6.79	6.63	6.51	6.40	6.22	6.09
13	6.98	6.80	6.52	6.31	6.16	6.03	5.93	5.75	5.63
14	6.58	6.40	6.13	5.93	5.78	5.66	5.56	5.38	5.25
15	6.26	6.08	5.81	5.62	5.46	5.35	5.25	5.07	4.95
16	5.98	5.81	5.55	5.35	5.20	5.09	4.99	4.82	4.70
17	5.75	5.58	5.32	5.13	4.99	4.87	4.78	4.60	4.48
18	5.56	5.39	5.13	4.94	4.80	4.68	4.59	4.42	4.30
19	5.39	5.22	4.97	4.78	4.64	4.52	4.43	4.26	4.14
20	5.24	5.08	4.82	4.64	4.49	4.38	4.29	4.12	4.00
21	5.11	4.95	4.70	4.51	4.37	4.26	4.17	4.00	3.88
22	4.99	4.83	4.58	4.40	4.26	4.15	4.06	3.89	3.78
23	4.89	4.73	4.48	4.30	4.16	4.05	3.96	3.79	3.68
24	4.80	4.64	4.39	4.21	4.07	3.96	3.87	3.71	3.59
25	4.71	4.56	4.31	4.13	3.99	3.88	3.79	3.63	3.52
26	4.64	4.48	4.24	4.06	3.92	3.81	3.72	3.56	3.44
27	4.57	4.41	4.17	3.99	3.86	3.75	3.66	3.49	3.38
28	4.50	4.35	4.11	3.93	3.80	3.69	3.60	3.43	3.32
29	4.45	4.29	4.05	3.88	3.74	3.63	3.54	3.38	3.27
30	4.39	4.24	4.00	3.82	3.69	3.58	3.49	3.33	3.22
35	4.18	4.03	3.79	3.62	3.48	3.38	3.29	3.13	3.02
40	4.02	3.87	3.64	3.47	3.34	3.23	3.14	2.98	2.87
50	3.82	3.67	3.44	3.27	3.41	3.04	2.95	2.79	2.68
60	3.69	3.54	3.32	3.15	3.02	2.91	2.83	2.67	2.55
70	3.60	3.45	3.23	3.06	2.93	2.83	2.74	2.58	2.47
80	3.53	3.39	3.16	3.00	2.87	2.76	2.68	2.52	2.41
90	3.48	3.34	3.11	2.95	2.82	2.71	2.63	2.47	2.36
100	3.44	3.30	3.07	2.91	2.78	2.68	2.59	2.43	2.32
120	3.38	3.24	3.02	2.85	2.72	2.62	2.53	2.37	2.26
150	3.32	3.18	2.96	2.80	2.67	2.56	2.48	2.32	2.21
200	3.26	3.12	2.90	2.74	2.61	2.51	2.42	2.26	2.15
250	3.23	3.09	2.87	2.71	2.58	2.48	2.39	2.23	2.12
300	3.21	3.07	2.85	2.69	2.56	2.46	2.37	2.21	2.10
400	3.18	3.04	2.82	2.66	2.53	2.43	2.34	2.18	2.07
500	3.16	3.02	2.81	2.64	2.52	2.41	2.33	2.17	2.05
600	3.15	3.01	2.80	2.63	2.51	2.40	2.32	2.16	2.04
750	3.14	3.00	2.78	2.62	2.49	2.39	2.31	2.15	2.03
1000	3.13	2.99	2.77	2.61	2.48	2.38	2.30	2.12	2.02

Table A.3 (*Continued*)

v_1 / v_2	35	40	50	60	75	100	150	200
1	6.28e05	6.29e05	6.30e05	6.31e05	6.32e05	6.33e05	6.35e05	6.35e05
2	999.47	999.47	999.48	999.48	999.49	999.49	999.49	999.49
3	125.17	124.96	124.66	124.47	124.27	124.07	123.87	123.77
4	45.23	45.09	44.88	44.75	44.61	44.47	44.33	44.26
5	24.72	24.60	24.44	24.33	24.22	24.12	24.01	23.95
6	16.54	16.44	16.31	16.21	16.12	16.03	15.93	15.89
7	12.41	12.33	12.20	12.12	12.04	11.95	11.87	11.82
8	10.00	9.92	9.80	9.73	9.65	9.57	9.49	9.45
9	8.46	8.37	8.26	8.19	8.11	8.04	7.96	7.93
10	7.37	7.30	7.19	7.12	7.05	6.98	6.91	6.87
11	6.59	6.52	6.42	6.35	6.28	6.21	6.14	6.10
12	6.00	5.93	5.83	5.76	5.70	5.63	5.56	5.52
13	5.54	5.47	5.37	5.30	5.24	5.17	5.10	5.07
14	5.17	5.10	5.00	4.94	4.87	4.81	4.74	4.71
15	4.86	4.80	4.70	4.64	4.57	4.51	4.44	4.41
16	4.61	4.54	4.45	4.39	4.32	4.26	4.19	4.16
17	4.40	4.33	4.24	4.18	4.11	4.05	3.98	3.95
18	4.22	4.15	4.06	4.00	3.93	3.87	3.80	3.77
19	4.06	3.99	3.90	3.84	3.78	3.71	3.65	3.61
20	3.92	3.86	3.77	3.70	3.64	3.58	3.51	3.48
21	3.80	3.74	3.64	3.58	3.52	3.46	3.39	3.36
22	3.70	3.63	3.54	3.48	3.41	3.35	3.28	3.25
23	3.60	3.53	3.44	3.38	3.32	3.25	3.19	3.16
24	3.51	3.45	3.36	3.29	3.23	3.17	3.10	3.07
25	3.43	3.37	3.28	3.22	3.15	3.09	3.03	2.99
26	3.36	3.30	3.21	3.15	3.08	3.02	2.95	2.92
27	3.30	3.23	3.14	3.08	3.02	2.96	2.89	2.86
28	3.24	3.18	3.09	3.02	2.96	2.90	2.83	2.80
29	3.18	3.12	3.03	2.97	2.91	2.84	2.78	2.74
30	3.13	3.07	2.98	2.92	2.86	2.79	2.73	2.69
35	2.93	2.87	2.78	2.72	2.66	2.59	2.52	2.49
40	2.79	2.73	2.64	2.57	2.51	2.44	2.38	2.34
50	2.60	2.53	2.44	2.38	2.31	2.25	2.18	2.14
60	2.47	2.41	2.32	2.25	2.19	2.12	2.05	2.01
70	2.39	2.32	2.23	2.16	2.10	2.03	1.95	1.92
80	2.32	2.26	2.16	2.10	2.03	1.96	1.89	1.85
90	2.27	2.21	2.11	2.05	1.98	1.91	1.83	1.79
100	2.24	2.17	2.08	2.01	1.94	1.87	1.79	1.75
120	2.18	2.11	2.02	1.95	1.88	1.81	1.73	1.68
150	2.12	2.06	1.96	1.89	1.82	1.74	1.66	1.62
200	2.07	2.00	1.90	1.83	1.76	1.68	1.60	1.55
250	2.03	1.97	1.87	1.80	1.72	1.65	1.56	1.51
300	2.01	1.94	1.85	1.78	1.70	1.62	1.53	1.48
400	1.98	1.92	1.82	1.75	1.67	1.59	1.50	1.45
500	1.97	1.90	1.80	1.73	1.65	1.57	1.48	1.43
600	1.96	1.89	1.79	1.72	1.64	1.56	1.46	1.41
750	1.95	1.88	1.78	1.71	1.63	1.55	1.45	1.40
1000	1.94	1.87	1.77	1.69	1.62	1.53	1.44	1.38

Table A.4 χ^2 (chi-squared) distribution: critical values of χ^2

	Significance level		
Degrees of freedom	5%	1%	0.1%
1	3.841	6.635	10.828
2	5.991	9.210	13.816
3	7.815	11.345	16.266
4	9.488	13.277	18.467
5	11.070	15.086	20.515
6	12.592	16.812	22.458
7	14.067	18.475	24.322
8	15.507	20.090	26.124
9	16.919	21.666	27.877
10	18.307	23.209	29.588
12	21.026	26.217	32.909
15	24.996	30.578	37.697
20	31.410	37.566	45.315
30	43.773	50.892	59.703

Table A.5 Durbin–Watson d statistic: d_L and d_U, 5% significance level

n	$k = 2$		$k = 3$		$k = 4$		$k = 5$		$k = 6$	
	d_L	d_U	d_L	d_U	d_L	d_U	d_L	d_U	d_L	d_U
15	1.08	1.36	0.95	1.54	0.82	1.75	0.69	1.97	0.56	2.21
16	1.10	1.37	0.98	1.54	0.86	1.73	0.74	1.93	0.62	2.15
17	1.13	1.38	1.02	1.54	0.90	1.71	0.78	1.90	0.67	2.10
18	1.16	1.39	1.05	1.53	0.93	1.69	0.82	1.87	0.71	2.06
19	1.18	1.40	1.08	1.53	0.97	1.68	0.86	1.85	0.75	2.02
20	1.20	1.41	1.10	1.54	1.00	1.68	0.90	1.83	0.79	1.99
21	1.22	1.42	1.13	1.54	1.03	1.67	0.93	1.81	0.83	1.96
22	1.24	1.43	1.15	1.54	1.05	1.66	0.96	1.80	0.86	1.94
23	1.26	1.44	1.17	1.54	1.08	1.66	0.99	1.79	0.90	1.92
24	1.27	1.45	1.19	1.55	1.10	1.66	1.01	1.78	0.93	1.90
25	1.29	1.45	1.21	1.55	1.12	1.66	1.04	1.77	0.95	1.89
26	1.30	1.46	1.22	1.55	1.14	1.65	1.06	1.76	0.98	1.88
27	1.32	1.47	1.24	1.56	1.16	1.65	1.08	1.76	1.01	1.86
28	1.33	1.48	1.26	1.56	1.18	1.65	1.10	1.75	1.03	1.85
29	1.34	1.48	1.27	1.56	1.20	1.65	1.12	1.74	1.05	1.84
30	1.35	1.49	1.28	1.57	1.21	1.65	1.14	1.74	1.07	1.83
31	1.36	1.50	1.30	1.57	1.23	1.65	1.16	1.74	1.09	1.83
32	1.37	1.50	1.31	1.57	1.24	1.65	1.18	1.73	1.11	1.82
33	1.38	1.51	1.32	1.58	1.26	1.65	1.19	1.73	1.13	1.81
34	1.39	1.51	1.33	1.58	1.27	1.65	1.21	1.73	1.15	1.81
35	1.40	1.52	1.34	1.58	1.28	1.65	1.22	1.73	1.16	1.80
36	1.41	1.52	1.35	1.59	1.29	1.65	1.24	1.73	1.18	1.80
37	1.42	1.53	1.36	1.59	1.31	1.66	1.25	1.72	1.19	1.80
38	1.43	1.54	1.37	1.59	1.32	1.66	1.26	1.72	1.21	1.79
39	1.43	1.54	1.38	1.60	1.33	1.66	1.27	1.72	1.22	1.79
40	1.44	1.54	1.39	1.60	1.34	1.66	1.29	1.72	1.23	1.79
45	1.48	1.57	1.43	1.62	1.38	1.67	1.34	1.72	1.29	1.78
50	1.50	1.59	1.46	1.63	1.42	1.67	1.38	1.72	1.34	1.77
55	1.53	1.60	1.49	1.64	1.45	1.68	1.41	1.72	1.38	1.77
60	1.55	1.62	1.51	1.65	1.48	1.69	1.44	1.73	1.41	1.77
65	1.57	1.63	1.54	1.66	1.50	1.70	1.47	1.73	1.44	1.77
70	1.58	1.64	1.55	1.67	1.52	1.70	1.49	1.74	1.46	1.77
75	1.60	1.65	1.57	1.68	1.54	1.71	1.51	1.74	1.49	1.77
80	1.61	1.66	1.59	1.69	1.56	1.72	1.53	1.74	1.51	1.77
85	1.62	1.67	1.60	1.70	1.57	1.72	1.55	1.75	1.52	1.77
90	1.63	1.68	1.61	1.70	1.59	1.73	1.57	1.75	1.54	1.78
95	1.64	1.69	1.62	1.71	1.60	1.73	1.58	1.75	1.56	1.78
100	1.65	1.69	1.63	1.72	1.61	1.74	1.59	1.76	1.57	1.78

n = number of observations; k = number of parameters.

Reprinted from Durbin and Watson (1951) with the kind permission of the Biometrika Trustees

Table A.5 Durbin–Watson d statistic: d_L and d_U, 1% significance level

n	$k = 2$		$k = 3$		$k = 4$		$k = 5$		$k = 6$	
	d_L	d_U	d_L	d_U	d_L	d_U	d_L	d_U	d_L	d_U
15	0.81	1.07	0.70	1.25	0.59	1.46	0.49	1.70	0.39	1.96
16	0.84	1.09	0.74	1.25	0.63	1.44	0.53	1.66	0.44	1.90
17	0.87	1.10	0.77	1.25	0.67	1.43	0.57	1.63	0.48	1.85
18	0.90	1.12	0.80	1.26	0.71	1.42	0.61	1.60	0.52	1.80
19	0.93	1.13	0.83	1.26	0.74	1.41	0.65	1.58	0.56	1.77
20	0.95	1.15	0.86	1.27	0.77	1.41	0.68	1.57	0.60	1.74
21	0.97	1.16	0.89	1.27	0.80	1.41	0.72	1.55	0.63	1.71
22	1.00	1.17	0.91	1.28	0.83	1.40	0.75	1.54	0.66	1.69
23	1.02	1.19	0.94	1.29	0.86	1.40	0.77	1.53	0.70	1.67
24	1.04	1.20	0.96	1.30	0.88	1.41	0.80	1.53	0.72	1.66
25	1.05	1.21	0.98	1.30	0.90	1.41	0.83	1.52	0.75	1.65
26	1.07	1.22	1.00	1.31	0.93	1.41	0.85	1.52	0.78	1.64
27	1.09	1.23	1.02	1.32	0.95	1.41	0.88	1.51	0.81	1.63
28	1.10	1.24	1.04	1.32	0.97	1.41	0.90	1.51	0.83	1.62
29	1.12	1.25	1.05	1.33	0.99	1.42	0.92	1.51	0.85	1.61
30	1.13	1.26	1.07	1.34	1.01	1.42	0.94	1.51	0.88	1.61
31	1.15	1.27	1.08	1.34	1.02	1.42	0.96	1.51	0.90	1.60
32	1.16	1.28	1.10	1.35	1.04	1.43	0.98	1.51	0.92	1.60
33	1.17	1.29	1.11	1.36	1.05	1.43	1.00	1.51	0.94	1.59
34	1.18	1.30	1.13	1.36	1.07	1.43	1.01	1.51	0.95	1.59
35	1.19	1.31	1.14	1.37	1.08	1.44	1.03	1.51	0.97	1.59
36	1.21	1.32	1.15	1.38	1.10	1.44	1.04	1.51	0.99	1.59
37	1.22	1.32	1.16	1.38	1.11	1.45	1.06	1.51	1.00	1.59
38	1.23	1.33	1.18	1.39	1.12	1.45	1.07	1.52	1.02	1.58
39	1.24	1.34	1.19	1.39	1.14	1.45	1.09	1.52	1.03	1.58
40	1.25	1.34	1.20	1.40	1.15	1.46	1.10	1.52	1.05	1.58
45	1.29	1.38	1.24	1.42	1.20	1.48	1.16	1.53	1.11	1.58
50	1.32	1.40	1.28	1.45	1.24	1.49	1.20	1.54	1.16	1.59
55	1.26	1.43	1.32	1.47	1.28	1.51	1.25	1.55	1.21	1.59
60	1.38	1.45	1.35	1.48	1.32	1.52	1.28	1.56	1.25	1.60
65	1.41	1.47	1.38	1.50	1.35	1.53	1.31	1.57	1.28	1.61
70	1.43	1.49	1.40	1.52	1.37	1.55	1.34	1.58	1.31	1.61
75	1.45	1.50	1.42	1.53	1.39	1.56	1.37	1.59	1.34	1.62
80	1.47	1.52	1.44	1.54	1.42	1.57	1.39	1.60	1.36	1.62
85	1.48	1.53	1.46	1.55	1.43	1.58	1.41	1.60	1.39	1.63
90	1.50	1.54	1.47	1.56	1.45	1.59	1.43	1.61	1.41	1.64
95	1.51	1.55	1.49	1.57	1.47	1.60	1.45	1.62	1.42	1.64
100	1.52	1.56	1.50	1.58	1.48	1.60	1.46	1.63	1.44	1.65

n = number of observations; k = number of parameters.

Reprinted from Durbin and Watson (1951) with the kind permission of the Biometrika Trustees

Table A.6 Critical values for Dickey–Fuller unit root tests for models with no time trend

	$T(b_2-1)$		t		F	
observation	5%	1%	5%	1%	5%	1%
10	−9.86	−12.75	−11.27	−12.75	6.529	11.680
11	−10.14	−13.22	−11.57	−13.22	6.278	10.886
12	−10.39	−13.64	−11.89	−13.64	6.072	10.290
13	−10.61	−14.01	−12.17	−14.01	5.919	9.843
14	−10.81	−14.34	−12.43	−14.34	5.793	9.481
15	−10.98	−14.65	−12.65	−14.65	5.688	9.188
16	−11.13	−14.93	−12.86	−14.93	5.600	8.947
17	−11.28	−15.19	−13.05	−15.19	5.524	8.742
18	−11.40	−15.43	−13.22	−15.43	5.463	8.572
19	−11.52	−15.64	−13.38	−15.64	5.407	8.425
20	−11.63	−15.83	−13.53	−15.83	5.356	8.281
21	−11.73	−16.01	−13.66	−16.01	5.310	8.172
22	−11.83	−16.18	−13.79	−16.18	5.272	8.073
23	−11.91	−16.34	−13.90	−16.34	5.239	7.981
24	−11.99	−16.48	−14.00	−16.48	5.205	7.901
25	−12.06	−16.62	−14.11	−16.62	5.176	7.819
26	−12.13	−16.76	−14.20	−16.76	5.153	7.767
27	−12.20	−16.88	−14.29	−16.88	5.131	7.710
28	−12.26	−17.00	−14.37	−17.00	5.109	7.646
29	−12.31	−17.10	−14.45	−17.10	5.086	7.586
30	−12.36	−17.19	−14.51	−17.19	5.067	7.544
35	−12.58	−17.64	−14.83	−17.64	4.989	7.352
40	−12.76	−17.96	−15.05	−17.96	4.935	7.212
45	−12.89	−18.23	−15.23	−18.23	4.889	7.110
50	−13.00	−18.43	−15.39	−18.43	4.859	7.038
60	−13.18	−18.79	−15.63	−18.79	4.809	6.922
70	−13.30	−19.04	−15.81	−19.04	4.775	6.842
80	−13.40	−19.22	−15.94	−19.22	4.752	6.778
90	−13.46	−19.35	−16.03	−19.35	4.730	6.729
100	−13.54	−19.47	−16.13	−19.47	4.716	6.693
120	−13.63	−19.67	−16.24	−19.67	4.692	6.636
150	−13.72	−19.85	−16.38	−19.85	4.670	6.585
200	−13.80	−20.02	−16.50	−20.02	4.645	6.529
250	−13.86	−20.14	−16.59	−20.14	4.634	6.500
300	−13.91	−20.24	−16.64	−20.24	4.626	6.484
400	−13.95	−20.31	−16.71	−20.31	4.615	6.450
500	−13.97	−20.37	−16.73	−20.37	4.607	6.440
1000	−14.04	−20.51	−16.84	−20.51	4.595	6.413

Note: The true model is a random walk. The fitted model includes an intercept but no time trend. The number of observations is the number in the regression, not the sample. In the original Dickey–Fuller tables, the number refers to the number in the sample. Even allowing for this difference, there are minor unexplained differences.

Table A.7 Critical values for Dickey–Fuller unit root tests for models with a time trend

	$T(b_2-1)$		t		F	
observations	5%	1%	5%	1%	5%	1%
10	−13.24	−15.70	−4.000	−5.343	9.636	17.183
11	−13.73	−16.39	−3.926	−5.150	9.139	15.662
12	−14.18	−17.03	−3.869	−5.010	8.779	14.591
13	−14.58	−17.61	−3.826	−4.892	8.496	13.773
14	−14.94	−18.15	−3.789	−4.803	8.276	13.170
15	−15.27	−18.65	−3.758	−4.732	8.089	12.674
16	−15.57	−19.09	−3.731	−4.667	7.936	12.265
17	−15.84	−19.52	−3.711	−4.617	7.811	11.948
18	−16.09	−19.91	−3.690	−4.576	7.695	11.664
19	−16.32	−20.26	−3.672	−4.531	7.601	11.403
20	−16.53	−20.60	−3.658	−4.498	7.520	11.197
21	−16.73	−20.91	−3.644	−4.467	7.443	11.018
22	−16.90	−21.20	−3.633	−4.440	7.376	10.853
23	−17.07	−21.47	−3.621	−4.416	7.319	10.716
24	−17.24	−21.73	−3.612	−4.394	7.267	10.581
25	−17.38	−21.97	−3.602	−4.376	7.217	10.469
26	−17.52	−22.19	−3.594	−4.355	7.175	10.356
27	−17.65	−22.41	−3.588	−4.340	7.138	10.271
28	−17.78	−22.61	−3.582	−4.325	7.102	10.194
29	−17.88	−22.79	−3.574	−4.310	7.066	10.104
30	−17.99	−22.97	−3.568	−4.297	7.038	10.029
35	−18.46	−23.73	−3.544	−4.244	6.911	10.732
40	−18.82	−24.34	−3.526	−4.204	6.820	9.525
45	−19.10	−24.83	−3.512	−4.176	6.751	9.377
50	−19.34	−25.22	−3.502	−4.152	6.699	9.244
60	−19.72	−25.86	−3.487	−4.119	6.625	9.077
70	−19.97	−26.31	−3.475	−4.095	6.564	8.954
80	−20.18	−26.68	−3.467	−4.078	6.527	8.868
90	−20.33	−26.94	−3.460	−4.063	6.493	8.787
100	−20.46	−27.15	−3.455	−4.051	6.469	8.735
120	−20.67	−27.50	−3.447	−4.036	6.432	8.661
150	−20.86	−27.86	−3.439	−4.021	6.395	8.580
200	−21.06	−28.21	−3.432	−4.005	6.359	8.496
250	−21.19	−28.43	−3.428	−3.995	6.340	8.455
300	−21.28	−28.59	−3.425	−3.990	6.327	8.426
400	−21.39	−28.79	−3.422	−3.982	6.310	8.390
500	−21.44	−28.90	−3.419	−3.977	6.296	8.363
1000	−21.57	−29.12	−3.414	−3.967	6.277	8.319

Note: The true model is a random walk with drift. The fitted model includes an intercept and a time trend. The number of observations is the number in the regression, not the sample. In the original Dickey–Fuller tables, the number refers to the number in the sample. Even allowing for this difference, there are minor unexplained differences.

APPENDIX B: Data Sets

Nine data sets, downloadable from the OUP website http://www.oup.com, are intended to provide an opportunity for practical work.

By far the most important are the *Educational Attainment and Earnings Functions* (*EAEF*) and the *Demand Functions* (*DF*) data sets. They are used in an extensive series of exercises that are intended to provide continuity in practical work throughout the text. The repeated use of the same data sets is intended to have two benefits. One is to provide a sense of development. For both data sets, you will start with a very simple specification that will become more sophisticated as you work through the text and your understanding of the material grows. The other is to keep to a minimum the expenditure of time and energy that is required to become familiar with new data sets.

EAEF is a cross-sectional data set that provides exercises for most topics covered in Chapters 1–10 and *DF* is a time series data set with exercises for most topics in Chapters 11–13. These data sets are also used to provide many of the examples in the text.

The other seven data sets are more specialized in nature and are intended for use on specific topics.

All the data sets are provided in Stata, EViews and ASCII formats. To download a data set, click on its name and follow the instructions in the dialogue box. A Stata format data set should be ready for use. At the present time, an EViews data set will need renaming. For example, the Demand Functions data set will download with filename demand_wf1.bin. It should have extension wf1, not bin, so rename it as demand.wf1. To do this, go to My Computer, browse until you find the downloaded file, click on File and then Rename. You will now be able to delete the .bin extension and replace _wf1 with .wf1. EViews will now recognize it.

You should include a constant in all of the regressions, unless there is an instruction to the contrary. Most regression applications automatically assume that a constant should be included, unless specifically indicated otherwise. However some, including EViews, require you to specify a constant if you wish to include one.

Educational Attainment and Earnings Functions (*EAEF*)

In view of its relevance for social policy, it is not surprising that analysis of the closely related topics of the determinants of educational attainment and the determinants of earnings has long been a major application of econometrics. Particularly sensitive issues are those relating to differences in educational attainment and earnings attributable to ethnicity, sex, and genetic endowment, to interactions in the effects of these factors, and to changes through time. The data sets described here will allow you to explore some of these issues using a subset of a major US data base, the National Longitudinal Survey of Youth 1979– (NLSY79).

NLSY79 is a panel survey with repeated interviews of a nationally representative sample of young males and females aged 14 to 21 in 1979. From 1979 to 1994 the interviews took place annually. Since 1994 they have been conducted at two-year intervals. The core sample originally consisted of 3,003 males and 3,108 females. In addition, there are special supplementary samples (some now discontinued) of ethnic minorities, those in poverty, and those serving in the armed forces. Extensive background information was obtained in the base-year survey in 1979 and since then information has been updated each year on education, training, employment, marital status, fertility, health, child care, and assets and income. In addition, special sections have been added from time to time on other topics—for example, drug use. The surveys have been extremely detailed and the quality of the execution of the survey is very high. As a consequence, NLSY79 is regarded as one of the most important data bases available to social scientists working with US data.

This cross-section data set is supplied in the form of 22 parallel subsets each consisting of 540 observations, 270 drawn randomly from the male respondents in the source data set and the same number drawn randomly from the female respondents. The first 20 data sets are intended for use by members of a workshop. At the beginning of the course, the workshop instructor should assign a different data set to each member of the workshop. If you are working on your own, choose any one of the 20. Data Set 21 is used in examples in the text. You can use it to replicate the examples if you so wish. Data Set 22 is intended for use by instructors.

Each subset contains the same variables and they provide an opportunity for a small group to work through the exercises together with some variation in the results. As the name suggests, most of the exercises involve the fitting of educational attainment functions and earnings functions, starting with simple regression analysis and developing more complex models as new topics are encountered in the cross-sectional part of the text, Chapters 1–10.

Each subset contains data for each respondent on the following variables (C indicates a continuous variable, D a dummy variable):

Personal variables

FEMALE	D	Sex of respondent (0 if male, 1 if female)
MALE	D	Sex of respondent (1 if male, 0 if female)
Ethnicity:		
ETHBLACK	D	Black
ETHHISP	D	Hispanic
ETHWHITE	D	Non-black, non-hispanic
AGE	C	Age in 2002
S	C	Years of schooling (highest grade completed as of 2002)
Highest educational qualification:		
EDUCPROF	D	Professional degree
EDUCPHD	D	Doctorate
EDUCMAST	D	Master's degree
EDUCBA	D	Bachelor's degree
EDUCAA	D	Associate's (two-year college) degree
EDUCHSD	D	High school diploma or equivalent
EDUCDO	D	High school drop-out

Marital status		
SINGLE	D	Single, never married
MARRIED	D	Married, spouse present
DIVORCED	D	Divorced or separated
Scaled score on a component of the ASVAB battery		
ASVAB02	C	Arithmetic reasoning
ASVAB03	C	Word knowledge
ASVAB04	C	Paragraph comprehension
ASVAB05	C	Numerical operations (speed test)
ASVAB06	C	Coding speed (speed test)
ASVABC	C	Composite of *ASVAB02* (with double weight), *ASVAB03*, and *ASVAB04*
Faith:		
FAITHN	D	None
FAITHC	D	Catholic
FAITHJ	D	Jewish
FAITHP	D	Protestant
FAITHO	D	Other
HEIGHT	C	Height, in inches, in 1985
WEIGHT85	C	Weight, in pounds, in 1985
WEIGHT02	C	Weight, in pounds, in 2002

Family background variables

SM	C	Years of schooling of respondent's mother
SF	C	Years of schooling of respondent's father
SIBLINGS	C	Number of siblings
Living at age 14:		
L14TOWN	D	in a town or city
L14COUN	D	in the country, not on a farm
L14FARM	D	on a farm
LIBRARY	D	Member of family possessed a library card when respondent was 14
POV78	D	Family living in poverty in 1978

Work-related variables

EARNINGS	C	Current hourly earnings in $ reported at the 2002 interview
HOURS	C	Usual number of hours worked per week, 2002 interview
TENURE	C	Tenure (years) with current employer at the 2002 interview
EXP	C	Total out-of-school work experience (years) as of the 2002 interview.
COLLBARG	D	Pay set by collective bargaining, 2002
Category of employment		
CATGOV	D	Government
CATPRI	D	Private sector
CATSE	D	Self-employment
URBAN	D	Living in an urban area at 2002 interview

Living in 2002 in:

REGNC	D	North central census region
REGNE	D	North eastern
REGS	D	Southern
REGW	D	Western

Not all of the variables are used in the exercises suggested in the next section. You should feel free to experiment by trying alternative regression specifications with the extra variables.

Demand Functions (*DF*)

The data set is a subset of the National Income and Product Accounts published on a regular basis by the US Bureau of the Census. The data are aggregate (for the whole of the United States) annual observations for the period 1959–2003 on income, 20 categories of consumer expenditure, and price index series for these categories. The intention is that the exercises should provide material for practical work for a small group of students working in parallel, each student working with a different category of expenditure.

The income and expenditure variables are all measured in $ billion at 2000 constant prices. The price index series are all based with 2000=100. The variables are as follows:

Income and population

DPI	Aggregate disposable personal income
TPE	Aggregate personal expenditure
POP	Population, measured in thousands

Expenditure on nondurables

CLOT	Clothing and shoes
FLOW	Flowers, seeds, and potted plants
FOOD	Food purchased for off-premise consumption (this category should not be assigned for practical work because it is used for examples in the text)
GASO	Gasoline and oil
MAGS	Magazines, newspapers, and sheet music
TOB	Tobacco products
TOYS	Nondurable toys and sport supplies

Expenditure on services

ADM	Admissions to specified spectator amusements
BUSI	Personal business
DENT	Dentists
DOC	Physicians
GAS	Gas
HOUS	Housing (this category should not be assigned for practical work because it is used for examples in the text)

LEGL	Legal services
MASS	Local transportation: mass transit systems
REL	Religious and welfare activities
TELE	Telephone and telegraph

Expenditure on durables

BOOK	Books and maps
FURN	Furniture
OPHT	Ophthalmic products

The nominal price index series for the categories of expenditure have the name of the category prefixed by *P*: *PFOOD, PHOUS*, etc. The data set includes the nominal price index for total personal expenditure, *PTPE*. In the regressions, economic theory (and common sense) suggests that one should use real price indices rather than nominal ones in regression analysis, where a real price index is defined relative to general inflation as measured by *PTPE*. For example, the real (or relative) price index for food, *PRELFOOD*, is defined as

$$PRELFOOD = 100*(PFOOD/PTPE).$$

The data set also includes a trend variable *TIME* that is defined to be 1 for 1959, 2 for 1960, and so on.

You should choose, or be assigned by your instructor, one of the categories of expenditure listed above. In the exercises below you will develop a regression specification for this category, starting with a simple regression model and gradually improving it. If you are working with just one category of expenditure, it may be helpful to simplify the data set by deleting the expenditure and price variables relating to the other categories.

Consumer Expenditure Survey (*CES*)

This cross-sectional data set contains annual household expenditure on 21 categories of expenditure for 869 households in 1995. The suite of exercises provided for it is similar to that for *EAEF*, the data set being intended for extra practice for students out-of-class. Answers to all the exercises are provided in the *Study Guide*.

The data set has been derived from the Quarterly Interview Survey of the Consumer Expenditure Survey undertaken by the US Department of Labor, Bureau of Labor Statistics. The survey has a nationally representative sample of about 5,000 households, each household being interviewed five times, the first time to gather basic data about the household, and the other four times at quarterly intervals to gather data on expenditures. The households in the present data set entered the quarterly survey at the beginning of 1995 and the data give the total expenditure by category over the 1995 calendar year. The variables are as follows:

Household characteristics

SIZE	Number of persons in the household
SIZEAM	Number of adult males (males older than 15) in the household
SIZEAF	Number of adult females (females older than 15) in the household

SIZEJM	Number of junior males (males aged 2 through 15) in the household
SIZEJF	Number of junior females (females aged 2 through 15) in the household
SIZEIN	Number of children aged less than 2 in the household
REFAGE	Age of the reference person in the household (the individual who owns or rents the dwelling)
REFEDUC	Education of the reference person, coded as 0 Never went to school 1 Elementary school only (1–8 years) 2 Some high school, but did not graduate 3 High school graduate, no college 4 Some college, but did not graduate 5 College graduate 6 Graduate school
REFRACE	Ethnicity of the reference person, coded as 1 White 2 Black 3 American Indian, Aleut, Eskimo 4 Asian or Pacific Islander 5 Other
HHTENURE	Household tenure, coded as 1 Owned with mortgage 2 Owned without mortgage 3 Owned, mortgage not reported 4 Rented 5 Occupied without payment of cash rent 6 Student housing

Expenditure variables

EXP	Total household expenditure, including some items not listed as variables below
FDHO	Food and nonalcoholic beverages consumed at home
FDAW	Food and nonalcoholic beverages consumed away from home, excluding meals as pay in kind
HOUS	Housing, excluding expenditure on utilities, household operations, and household equipment. In the case of owned dwellings it comprises mortgage interest, property taxes, and the cost of maintenance, repairs, and insurance. In the case of rented dwellings, it consists of rent, including rent as pay in kind. *HOUS* also includes the recurrent costs of vacation houses, expenditure on lodging away from home, and the cost of school housing. Note that this category of expenditure does *not* include purchases of dwellings
TELE	Telephone services
DOM	Domestic services, such as condo housekeeping and management, gardening, and babysitting and child day care

TEXT	Household textiles such as bathroom, bedroom, kitchen and dining room linens, curtains and cushions
FURN	Furniture
MAPP	Major household appliances, such as dishwashers, refrigerators, clothes washers, stoves and ovens, air conditioners, floor cleaning machines and sewing machines
SAPP	Small appliances and miscellaneous housewares
CLOT	Clothing
FOOT	Footwear
GASO	Gasoline and motor oil
TRIP	Public transportation on out-of-town trips
LOCT	Local public transportation
HEAL	Health care, comprising health insurance, medical services, prescription drugs, and medical supplies
ENT	Entertainment, comprising fees and admissions, televisions, radios, and sound equipment, pets, toys, and playground equipment, and other related equipment and services
FEES	Membership fees of recreational and health clubs, fees for participant sports, admission fees for movies, theatre, concerts, opera, and sporting events, and fees for recreational instruction
TOYS	Toys, games, hobbies, playground equipment, and pets, including veterinarian expenses
READ	Reading matter, such as newspapers, magazines, and books
EDUC	Education, such as tuition fees, school books, supplies and equipment for elementary school, high school, and college, and other types of school
TOB	Tobacco products and supplies such as cigarettes, cigars, and pipe tobacco

All the expenditure variables are measured in current dollars. If you are working with just one category of expenditure, it may be helpful to simplify the data set by deleting the expenditure variables relating to the other categories.

OECD employment and GDP growth rates (*OECD*)

This data set is provided for Exercise 4.5, an investigation into alternative nonlinear functional forms. An answer is provided in the *Study Guide*. The data set contains the average annual growth rate of various macroeconomic aggregates for the period 1988–1997 for 26 OECD countries. It has been compiled from various issues of OECD *Economic Outlook* over the period 1990–2000. Missing values have been coded –9999, except in the Stata data set, where the missing value code has been used. The variables are

WAGES	Average annual rate of growth of nominal wages
PRICES	Average annual rate of growth of prices
GDP	Average annual rate of growth of real GDP
EMPLOY	Average annual rate of growth of employment
MONEY1	Average annual rate of growth of money and quasi-money

MONEY2	Average annual rate of growth of money and quasi-money, alternative data compiled from individual country tables in the IMF *International Financial Statistics Yearbook 2000*
UNEMPLOY	Average rate of unemployment

In regressions involving *EMPLOY*, the observation for Mexico should be excluded because the figure has been distorted by special circumstances. With the NAFTA agreement, US firms started moving their manufacturing plants to low-wage Mexico, recruiting workers, many of whom had previously been employed in the informal sector. The official employment statistics, collected by social security, measure only employment in the formal sector and therefore grossly overestimate the net increase in employment. In 1997 alone, employment increased by 13.3 percent according to the official figures, clearly nonsensical. Over the whole period, the average employment growth rate was greater than the average GDP growth rate, also nonsensical.

School Costs (*SC*)

This cross-sectional data set provides data on annual recurrent expenditure, numbers of students, type of curriculum, and other characteristics for 74 schools in Shanghai. The intention is to provide an opportunity for using dummy variables, investigating how type of curriculum affects the cost function.

The data set is an extract taken by the author with permission from a series of annual surveys of 105 Shanghai secondary schools undertaken by Fujian University staff during the period 1981–1985 with the support of the World Bank. The data in this data set relate to 1985. It was a time of rapid expansion of secondary education, both in terms of the number of schools and in the enrollments of some. To guard against the possibility that enrollments and budgets might be in disequilibrium, the 24 schools with enrollments that had increased (or decreased) by more than one-third over the previous year were excluded from the sample. Likewise seven schools with incomplete data were excluded, leaving 74 in the sample. The data on capital expenditure were very volatile and not susceptible to meaningful analysis. The recurrent cost data comprised staff costs, non-staff administrative expenditure, non-staff instructional expenditure, expenditure on books and expenditure on utilities. Maintenance expenditure was excluded because, like capital expenditure, it was very volatile and seemingly determined more by the availability of a budget rather than actual year-to-year need.

The variables are variables (C indicates a continuous variable, D a dummy variable):

COST	C	Annual recurrent cost, in yuan (worth about US$0.25 at the time)
N	C	Number of students enrolled
OCC	D	Occupational school (1 if technical or skilled worker's school, 0 if general or vocational school)
REGULAR	D	Regular school (1 if general or vocational school, 0 if technical or skilled worker's school)
TECH	D	Technical school (1 if technical school, 0 otherwise)
WORKER	D	Skilled workers' school (1 if skilled workers' school, 0 otherwise)
VOC	D	Vocational school (1 if vocational school, 0 otherwise)
GEN	D	General school (1 if general school, 0 otherwise)
RES	D	Residential school (1 if residential school, 0 otherwise)

Labor Force Participation (*LFP*)

This cross-section data set consists of data on labor force participation and background characteristics for 2,726 individuals in the US National Longitudinal Survey of Youth data set for 1994. See the *EAEF* entry above for a description of this survey. C indicates a continuous variable, D a dummy variable, T a coded variable.

Personal variables

AGE	C	Age in 1994
S	C	Years of schooling (highest grade completed as of 1994)
MALE	D	Sex of respondent (1 if male, 0 if female)
Ethnicity		
ETHBLACK	D	Black
ETHHISP	D	Hispanic
Scaled score on a component of the ASVAB battery		
ASVAB2	C	Arithmetic reasoning
ASVAB3	C	Word knowledge
ASVAB4	C	Paragraph comprehension
ASVABC	C	Composite of *ASVAB2* (with double weight), *ASVAB3*, and *ASVAB4*
CHILDREN	C	Number of children in the household
YOUNGEST	C	Age of youngest child
CHILDL06	C	Presence of a child aged < 6 in the household
CHILDL16	C	Presence of a child aged < 16, but no child aged < 6, in the household
MARISTAT	T	Marital status, coded as: 1 never married; 2 married, spouse present; 3 other
MARRIED	D	Married (*MARISTAT* = 2)

Work-related variables

EARNINGS	C	Current hourly earnings in $ reported at 1994 interview
WORKING	D	Working (has recorded earnings)
EMPSTAT	T	Employment status, coded as: 1 employed; 2 unemployed; 3 out of the labor force

Educational Expenditure (*EDUC*)

This data set contains cross-section data on aggregate expenditure on education, GDP, and population for a sample of 38 countries in 1997. It is provided for Exercises 7.6 and 7.9, an investigation into heteroscedasticity and measures to alleviate it. It contains three variables:

EDUC	Public recurrent expenditure on education (US$ million)
GDP	Gross domestic product (US$ million)
POP	Population (million)

NLSY panel data set (*NLSY2000*)

The data are drawn from the NLSY79 data set (see *EAEF* above) and relate to the years 1980–1994, 1996, 1998, and 2000. Note that there are many missing data. Obviously, if a respondent was not interviewed in a given year, all data for that year are missing. In addition, many data are missing for specific reasons.

The data are restricted to males whose marital status is either single or married, who are not in school, for whom *ASVAB* scores are available, who worked at least 30 hours per week, and whose reported hourly rate of pay was at least \$2.50 and not more than \$250.

The variables listed below were recorded for each respondent for each of the years 1980–1994, 1996, 1998, and 2000. Hence, there are potentially 18 observations for each respondent. However, owing to non-interviews or exclusions, the actual number is lower for many respondents and the panel is of the unbalanced type.

The variables *ID* and *TIME* should be used to identify the structure of the panel data set.

Time identifier

TIME	C	Defined as year – 1980. Values are 1–14, 16, 18, and 20

Personal variables

ID	C	Respondent identification number
AGE	C	age
AGESQ	C	square of *AGE*
S	C	years of schooling (highest grade completed)
		ethnicity:
ETHBLACK	D	black
ETHHISP	D	hispanic
HEIGHT85	C	height in inches in 1985
WEIGHT	C	weight in pounds
		score on a component of the *ASVAB* battery (scaled with mean 50, standard deviation 10)
ASVAB2	C	arithmetic reasoning
ASVAB3	C	word knowledge
ASVAB4	C	paragraph comprehension
ASVABC	C	composite of *ASVAB2* (with double weight), *ASVAB3*, and *ASVAB4*
SM	C	mother's years of schooling
SF	C	father's years of schooling
SIBLINGS	C	number of siblings
CHILDREN	C	number of children in the household
YOUNGEST	C	age of youngest child
MARRIED	D	married in the interview year
SINGLE	D	single in the interview year
SINGBOTH	D	single in the interview year and four years later
SOONMARR	D	single in the interview years but married four years later
URBAN	D	living in an urban area
		region of residence (census classification)
REGNE	D	north-east
REGNC	D	north-central
REGW	D	west
REGS	D	south

Work-related variables

EARNINGS	C	current hourly earnings in 1996 constant dollars
HOURS	C	hours worked per week
TENURE	C	years worked with present employer
TENURESQ	C	square of *TENURE*
EXP	C	total years of work experience
EXPSQ	C	square of *EXP*
		sector of employment
CLASSPRI	D	private sector employee
CLASSPUB	D	public sector
CLASSSE	D	self-employed
UNION	D	member of a union (question asked 1988–2000 only)
UNCOLB	D	wages set by collective bargaining

C indicates a continuous variable, D a dummy variable.

OECD2000

This data set is fully described in Exercise 14.1.

Bibliography

Amemiya, Takeshi (1981). Qualitative response models: a survey. *Journal of Economic Literature* 19(4): 1483–1536

Amemiya, Takeshi (1984). Tobit models: a survey. *Journal of Econometrics* 24(1): 3–61

Baltagi, Badi H. (2005). *Econometric Analysis of Panel Data* (third edition), Chichester, England: John Wiley

Box, George E.P., and David R. Cox (1964). An analysis of transformations. *Journal of the Royal Statistical Society Series B* 26(2): 211–243

Box, George E.P., and Norman R. Draper (1987). *Empirical Model-Building and Response Surfaces.* New York: Wiley

Box, George E.P., and Gwilym M. Jenkins (1970). *Time Series Analysis: Forecasting and Control.* San Francisco: Holden Day

Box, George E.P., Gwilym M. Jenkins, and Gregory C. Reinsel (1994). *Time Series Analysis: Forecasting and Control* (third edition). Englewood Cliffs, NJ: Prentice-Hall

Brown, T.M. (1952). Habit persistence and lags in consumer behaviour. *Econometrica* 20(3): 355–371

Card, David (1995). Using geographic variation in college proximity to estimate the return to schooling. In Louis N. Christofides, E. Kenneth Grant and Robert Swidinsky (editors), *Aspects of Labour Market Behaviour: Essays in Honour of John Vanderkamp.* Toronto: University of Toronto Press

Chow, Gregory C. (1960). Tests of equality between sets of coefficients in two linear regressions. *Econometrica* 28(3): 591–605

Cobb, Charles W., and Paul H. Douglas (1928). A theory of production. *American Economic Review* 18(1, Supplement): 139–165

Cooper, Ronald L. (1972). The predictive performance of quarterly econometric models of the United States. In Bert G. Hickman (editor), *Econometric Models of Cyclical Behavior.* New York: Columbia University Press

Court, Andrew T. (1939). Hedonic price indexes with automotive examples, in *The Dynamics of Automobile Demand*, Papers presented at a joint meeting of the American Statistical Association and the Econometric Society in Detroit, December 1938: General Motors Corporation

Davidson, James E.H. (2000). *Econometric Theory.* Oxford: Blackwell

Davidson, Russell, and James G. MacKinnon (1993). *Estimation and Inference in Econometrics.* New York: Oxford University Press

Dickey, David A., and Wayne A. Fuller (1979). Distribution of the estimators for autoregressive time series with a unit root. *Journal of the American Statistical Association* 74(366): 427–431

Dickey, David A., and Wayne A. Fuller (1981). Likelihood ratio statistics for autoregressive time series with a unit root. *Econometrica* 49(4): 1057–1072

Diebold, Francis X. (1998). The past, present, and future of macroeconomic forecasting. *Journal of Economic Perspectives* 12(2): 175–192

Diebold, Francis X. (2001). *Elements of Forecasting* (second edition), Cincinnati, Ohio: South-Western

Durbin, James (1954). Errors in variables. *Review of the International Statistical Institute* 22(1): 23–32

Durbin, James (1970). Testing for serial correlation in least-squares regression when some of the regressors are lagged dependent variables. *Econometrica* 38(3): 410–421

Durbin, James, and G.S. Watson (1950). Testing for serial correlation in least-squares regression I. *Biometrika* 37(3–4): 409–428

Durlauf, Steven N., and Peter C.B. Phillips (1988). Trends versus random walks in time series analysis. *Econometrica* 56(6): 1333–1354

Elliott, Graham, Thomas J. Rothenberg, and James H. Stock (1996). Efficient tests for an autoregressive unit root. *Econometrica* 64(4): 813–836

Engle, Robert F., and Clive W.J. Granger (1987). Co-integration and error correction representation, estimation, and testing. *Econometrica* 50(2): 251–276

Fowler, Floyd J. (2009). *Survey Research Methods* (fourth edition). Thousand Oaks, CA: Sage Publications

Friedman, Milton (1957). *A Theory of the Consumption Function*. Princeton, NJ: Princeton University Press

Frisch, Ragnar, and Frederick V. Waugh (1933). Partial time regressions as compared with individual trends. *Econometrica* 1(4): 387–401

Goldfeld, Stephen M., and Richard E. Quandt (1965). Some tests for homoscedasticity. *Journal of the American Statistical Association* 60(310): 539–547

Granger, Clive W.J., and Paul Newbold (1974). Spurious regressions in econometrics. *Journal of Econometrics* 2(2): 111–120

Gronau, Reuben (1974). Wage comparisons—a selectivity bias. *Journal of Political Economy* 82(6): 1119–1155

Hamilton, James D. (1994). *Time Series Analysis*. Princeton, NJ: Princeton University Press

Hausman, Jerry A. (1978). Specification tests in econometrics. *Econometrica* 46(6): 1251–1271

Heckman, James (1976). The common structure of statistical models of truncation, sample selection, and limited dependent variables and a simple estimator for such models. *Annals of Economic and Social Measurement* 5(4): 475–492

Hendry, David F. (1979). Predictive failure and econometric modelling in macroeconomics: the transactions demand for money. In Paul Ormerod (editor), *Modelling the Economy*. London: Heinemann

Hendry, David F., and Grayham E. Mizon (1978). Serial correlation as a convenient simplification, not a nuisance. *Economic Journal* 88(351): 549–563

Holden, Darryl, and Roger Perman (2007). Unit roots and cointegration for the economist. In B. Bhaskara Rao (editor), *Cointegration for the Applied Economist* (second edition). Basingstoke, UK: Palgrave Macmillan

Hsiao, Cheng (2003). *Analysis of Panel Data* (second edition). Cambridge: Cambridge University Press

Kmenta, Jan (1986). *Elements of Econometrics* (second edition). New York: Macmillan

Kuh, Edwin, and John R. Meyer (1957). How extraneous are extraneous estimates? *Review of Economics and Statistics* 39(4): 380–393

Lintner, John (1956). Distribution of incomes of corporations among dividends, retained earnings and taxes. *American Economic Review* 46(2): 97–113

Liviatan, Nissan (1963). Tests of the Permanent-Income Hypothesis based on a reinterview savings survey. In Carl Christ (editor), *Measurement in Economics.* Stanford, CA: Stanford University Press

Lovell, Michael C. (1963). Seasonal adjustment of economic time series. *Journal of the American Statistical Association* 58: 993–1010

MacKinnon, James G., and Halbert White (1985). Some heteroskedasticity-consistent covariance matrix estimators with improved finite sample properties. *Journal of Econometrics* 29(3): 305–325

Moser, Claus and Graham Kalton (1985). *Survey Methods in Social Investigation* (second edition). Aldershot: Gower

Nelson, Charles R., and Charles I. Plosser (1982). Trends and random walks in macroeconomic time series: some evidence and implications. *Journal of Monetary Economics* 10(2): 139–162

Nerlove, Marc (1963). Returns to scale in electricity supply. In Carl Christ (editor), *Measurement in Economics.* Stanford, CA: Stanford University Press

Park, Rolla E., and Bridget M. Mitchell (1980). Estimating the autocorrelated error model with trended data. *Journal of Econometrics* 13(2): 185–201

Peach, James T., and James L. Webb (1983). Randomly specified macroeconomic models: some implications for model selection. *Journal of Economic Issues* 17(3): 697–720

Phillips, Peter C.B. (1986). Understanding spurious regressions in econometrics. *Journal of Econometrics* 33(3): 311–340

Rubin, Herman (1950). Consistency of maximum-likelihood estimates in the explosive case. In T.C. Koopmans (editor), *Statistical Inference in Dynamic Economic Models*, New York: John Wiley

Sims, Christopher A. (1980). Macroeconomics and reality. *American Economic Review* 48(1): 1–48

Stock, James H. (1987). Asymptotic properties of least squares estimators of cointegrating vectors. *Econometrica* 55(5): 1035–1056

Tinbergen, Jan. (1939). *Statistical Testing of Business Cycle Theories. 2, Business Cycles in the United States of America, 1919–1932*, Geneva: League of Nations

Tobin, James (1958). Estimation of relationships for limited dependent variables. *Econometrica* 26(1): 24–36

Waugh, Frederick V. (1929). *Quality as a Determinant of Vegetable Prices*, New York: Columbia University Press

Wichern, Dean W. (1973). The behaviour of the sample autocorrelation function for an integrated moving average process. *Biometrika* 60(2): 235–239

White, Halbert (1980). A heteroskedasticity-consistent covariance matrix estimator and a direct test for heteroskedasticity. *Econometrica* 48(4): 817–838

Wooldridge, Jeffrey M. (2002). *Econometric Analysis of Cross Section and Panel Data*, Cambridge, MA: MIT Press

Wu, De-Min (1973). Alternative tests of independence between stochastic regressors and disturbances. *Econometrica* 41(4): 733–750

Author Index

Amemiya, Takeshi 357, 363, 373

Baltagi, Badi H. 514
Box, George E.P. 205, 424, 425, 474, 486
Brown, T.M. 405

Card, David 345
Chow, Gregory C. 245
Cobb, Charles W. 397
Cooper, Ronald L. 423
Court, Andrew T. 186
Cox, David R. 205

Davidson, James E.H. 110
Davidson, Russell 505
Dickey, David A. 493, 494, 496
Diebold, Francis X. 424, 427
Douglas, Paul H. 397
Draper, Norman R. 486
Durbin, James 326, 435, 436, 438
Durlauf, Steven N. 509

Elliott, Graham 500
Engle, Robert F. 505, 511

Fowler, Floyd J. 172
Friedman, Milton 311, 312
Frisch, Ragnar 156, 475
Fuller, Wayne A. 493, 494, 496

Goldfeld, Stephen M. 285
Granger, Clive W.J. 476, 505, 510, 511
Greene, William 3
Gronau, Reuben 375, 376

Hamilton, James D. 496
Hausman, Jerry A. 326
Heckman, James 376, 378
Hendry, David F. 446, 461
Holden, Darryl 491
Hsiao, Cheng 514

Jenkins, Gwilym M. 424, 425, 474, 486

Kalton, Graham 172
Kmenta, Jan 460
Kuh, Edwin 174

Lintner, John 410
Liviatan, Nissan 323
Lovell, Michael C. 156, 475

MacKinnon, James G. 295, 507
Meyer, John R. 174
Mitchell, Bridget M. 442
Mizon, Grayham E. 446
Moser, Claus 172

Nelson, Charles R. 474, 483, 503, 509
Nerlove, Marc 277
Newbold, Paul 476, 510

Park, Rolla E. 442
Peach, James T. 457
Perman, Roger 491
Phillips, Peter C.B. 479, 509
Plosser, Charles I. 474, 483, 503, 509

Quandt, Richard E. 285

Reinsel, Gregory C. 474, 486
Rothenberg, Thomas J. 500
Rubin, Herman 492

Sims, Christopher A. 425
Stock, James H. 500, 507

Tinbergen, Jan 422
Tobin, James 373

Watson, G.S. 436
Waugh, Frederick V. 156, 191, 475
Webb, James L. 457
White, Halbert 286, 294, 295
Wichern, Dean W. 486
Wooldridge, Jeffrey M. 514
Wu, De-Min 326

Subject Index

Acceptance region 40, 42–6
definition 40
Adaptive expectations 406–9
ADF test. *See* Nonstationarity, detection
Adjusted R^2 183–4
ADL. *See* Autoregressive distributed lag models
Akaike Information Criterion (AIC) 500
AR. *See* Autoregressive process
ARIMA. *See* Autoregressive integrated moving average process
ARMA. *See* Time series processes
Asymptotic properties of estimators
asymptotic normality
of IV estimators 318–22
of OLS estimators 305–6
central limit theorems
Lindeberg–Levy 74, 114, 124, 125
Lindeberg–Feller 114, 124
consistency 66–73
definition 68
hyperconsistency 497–8
of IV estimators 316–17
of OLS estimators 304–5
superconsistency 492, 499, 507
convergence in distribution 74–8
probability limit (plim) 67–72
rules for 70–1
simulations 72–73
Augmented Dickey–Fuller test. *See* Nonstationarity, detection
Autocorrelation (autocorrelated disturbance term)
apparent, attributable to model misspecification 451–5
functional misspecification 455
omission of important variable 452–5
autoregressive (AR) autocorrelation
first order AR(1) 431
higher order 431
causes of 429–430
consequences for OLS estimators 431–3
common factor test 445–448
definition 429–31
fitting a model subject to AR(1) autocorrelation 440–5
Cochrane–Orcutt iterative procedure 444, 445
Prais–Winsten correction 442
innovation 431, 441
lagged dependent variable and autocorrelation 433
moving average autocorrelation 431
negative autocorrelation 429
Newey–West standard errors 442
positive autocorrelation 429
length of observation interval 429
tests for 434–440
Breusch–Godfrey test 435
Durbin *h* test 438
Durbin–Watson *d* test 436–8
Autocorrelation function. *See* Time series processes
Autoregressive distributed lag (ADL) models 401–10
ADL(1,0) model 401–9
adaptive expectations 406–9
dynamics 402–4
partial adjustment 404–5
ADL(1,1) model 408–9
definition of ADL model 401
error correction model 405–6
properties of regression coefficient estimators 411–19
asymptotic normality of regression coefficients 415–19
consistency 414–15
finite-sample bias 413
inference 417–419
limiting distributions 415–419
t tests 417–19
Autoregressive integrated moving average (ARIMA) process 474, 484, 486
See also Time series processes
Autoregressive moving average (ARMA) process 424
See also Time series processes

Autoregressive (AR) process
  correlogram 485
  disturbance term subject to AR. *See* Autocorrelation
  stationarity conditions 498, 499

Balanced panel. *See* Panel data
Bayes Information Criterion (BIC) 500
Bias
  definition of 27
  possible trade-off with variance 30–2
    loss function 31
    mean square error criterion 31–2
BIC. *See* Bayes Information Criterion
  Binary choice models. *See* Linear probability model; Logit analysis; Probit analysis; Sample selection model; Tobit model
Breusch–Pagan lagrange multiplier test. 526–7
Brown's habit persistence model 405

Censored regression model. *See* Tobit model
Central limit theorem
  Lindeberg–Levy 74, 76, 114, 124, 125
  Lindeberg-Feller 114, 124
Chi-squared distribution, critical values. *See* Table A.4
Chow test 245–8
Cochrane–Orcutt iterative procedure 445
Coefficient of determination. *See* R^2
Cointegrated time series, Cointegration
  See Nonstationary time series processes
Common factor test 445–8
Confidence interval 51–56
  regression coefficients 142–143, 164
  predictions189
Consistency. *See* Asymptotic properties of estimators
Consumer Expenditure Survey data set 552–4
Consumption function
  Brown's habit-persistence model 405
  Friedman's Permanent Income Hypothesis
    critique of OLS estimation 311–12
    fitted using adaptive expectations model 407–9
    permanent income and consumption, definitions 311
    transitory income and consumption, definitions 311
Continuous random variables. *See* Random variables
Corrected R^2 183–4
Correlation coefficient
  population 22
  sample 34
Correlogram 465
Cov. *See* Covariance
Covariance
  definition 17
  estimator 34, 79–81
  rules 19–20
Cross-sectional data 110

Data
  Cross-sectional 110
  Panel 110
  Time series 110, 391–2
Data generation process (DGP) 304, 391–2
  realization 392
Data sets for exercises. *See* Appendix B
Demand functions data set 393, 551–552
De-meaning of regressors 214–16
Dependent variable in regression model 83
  two decompositions of 92–4
Deterministic trend 472–473, 475, 497–8
Detrending 475, 509
DGP. *See* Data generation process
Difference-stationarity 473–4
Dickey–Fuller test. *See* Nonstationarity, detection
Discrete random variables. *See* Random variables
Distributed lags. *See* Autoregressive distributed lag models
Disturbance term
  autocorrelated. *See* Autocorrelation
  estimation of variance
  innovation 424
    in context of autocorrelation 431
  noise 85
  origin of 83–5
  standard error of regression equation (s_u)
  white noise 424, 476–7, 481
  See also Regression model assumptions
Double structure of a random variable. *See* Random variable, double structure
Dummy variables
  benefits from use of 226
  Chow test 245–8
    relationship with *F* test for full set of dummy variables 247–8
  definition of 226
  dummy variable trap 235–7
  F test of the joint explanatory power of a set of dummy variables 233–4
  intercept dummy variable 226–7
  interpretation of coefficient, logarithmic dependent variable 229
  multiple categories of 230–7
    change of reference category 234–5
    choice of reference category 230–1, 234
    omitted category 231
    reference category 230

multiple sets of 237–9
slope dummy variable 240–4
definition 241
t tests of dummy variable coefficients 227–8
Durbin *h* test 438
Durbin–Watson *d* test 436–8
table of d_U and d_L. *See* Table A.5
Durbin–Wu–Hausman (DWH) test
in context of measurement errors 326–8
in context of simultaneous equations estimation 346–9
in context of fixed and random effects 525–6

EAEF. *See* Educational attainment and earnings functions
Educational attainment and earnings functions (*EAEF*) data sets 548–51
Educational expenditure data set (*EDUC*) 556
Efficiency 28–32
comparative concept 30
definition 28
mean square error criterion 31–2
Elasticity
definition 196
estimation 197
income, price elasticities 395
interpretation of elasticity 196–7
Endogenous variable. *See* Simultaneous equations estimation
Engel curve 197–200
Ensemble distribution 464–73
Error correction models 406, 510–12
Errors in variables. *See* Measurement errors
ESS. *See* Explained sum of squares
Estimator
consistency 66–73
definition of 24
difference between estimate and estimator 24
efficiency 28–9
of population mean 24
of regression coefficients. *See* Regression coefficients
unbiasedness 27
See also Indirect least squares; Instrumental variables; Maximum likelihood; Ordinary least squares; Two-stage least squares
Exact identification. *See* Simultaneous equations estimation
Exogenous variable. *See* Simultaneous equations estimation
Expectation. *See* Expected value
Expected value
of continuous random variable 18
of discrete random variable 8–9
of function of continuous random variable 18–19
of function of discrete random variable 9–10
rules 10–11
Explained sum of squares (*ESS*) 105
Explanatory variable 83. *See also* Regressor
Extraneous information used to mitigate multicollinearity

F distribution, critical values. *See* Table A.3
F statistic. *See F* tests
F tests
of goodness of fit of regression equation
multiple regression 177–9, 275
simple regression 145–7
of homoscedasticity (Goldfeld–Quandt test) 285–6
of joint explanatory power of group of explanatory variables 180–2
of set of dummy variables 233–4
of validity of combining two samples to fit regression (Chow test) 245–8
of validity of linear restriction 270, 274–5
First differences regression. *See* Panel data
Fitted model 86. *See also* Regression model
Fitted value 86
Fixed effects regression 518–22. *See also* Panel data
Friedman's Permanent Income Hypothesis. *See* Consumption function
Frisch–Waugh–Lovell theorem 156–8, 206
graphing relationship between two variables in multiple regression model 156–8
Functional misspecification. *See* Model misspecification
Gauss–Markov theorem 132–3, 149–50, 161, 303

Goldfeld–Quandt test 285–6
Goodness of fit, *F* test of 145–7, 177–9, 275. See also R^2
Granger causality 427
Granger–Newbold spurious regressions
gretl regression software 4

Habit persistence model. *See* Consumption function
Hausman test. *See* Durbin–Wu–Hausman test
Heckman two-step procedure. *See* Sample selection model
Hedonic pricing 185–9
Heteroscedasticity
apparent heteroscedasticity caused by functional misspecification 292–3
causes of 283–5

Heteroscedasticity (*cont.*)
consequences for OLS estimators 282–3, 295–7
definition of 281
heteroscedasticity-consistent standard errors 294–5, 297
measures to mitigate 288–92
tests for
Goldfeld–Quandt 285–6
White 286–7
weighted least squares (WLS) regression 289, 295–7
Homoscedasticity, definition 280–1
Hyperconsistency 497–8
Hypothesis
alternative, definition 37
null, definition 37
testing 36–46

Ideal proxy. *See* Proxy variables
Identification. *See* Simultaneous equations estimation
ILS. *See* Indirect least squares
Imperfect proxy variable. *See* Proxy variables
Inconsistency, definition 69
Independence of two random variables 19
Independent variable 83. *See also* Regressor
Indirect least squares (ILS) 348–9
equivalence with IV under exact identification 349
Innovation 424. *See also* Disturbance term
Instrument. *See* Instrumental variables
Instrumental variables (IV) 316–328
comparison with OLS
Durbin–Wu–Hausman test 326–8
simulation 318–20
consistency of IV estimator 317
definition of 316
multiple instruments 325–6
population variance of IV estimator
asymptotic 317–20
finite sample, simulation 320–3
requirements for use 318
use to fit Permanent Income Hypothesis model 323
use in simultaneous equations estimation 338–41
Integrated time series 473–4
Interactive regressors 213–16. *See also* Dummy variable, slope dummy variable
Inverse of Mills' ratio 376. *See also* Sample selection model
Irrelevant variables. *See* Model misspecification
IV. *See* Instrumental variables

Labor force participation (*LFP*) data set 556
Lag structure 398
parsimonious 401
Lagged dependent variable. *See* Autoregressive distributed lag models
Lagged variable, definition of 398–9
Least squares criterion
linear regression 85–87, 153–5
nonlinear regression 218–22
See also Regression analysis, ordinary least squares
Least squares dummy variable (LSDV) regression 520–2
LFP. *See* Labor force participation data set
Likelihood function 380. *See also* Maximum likelihood estimation
Likelihood ratio statistic, test 386–7
Lindeberg–Levy central limit theorem 74, 76, 114, 124, 125
Lindeberg-Feller central limit theorem 114, 124
Linear probability model 354–7
problems with, 355–6
Linear restriction. *See* Restriction
Linearity of regression model
in parameters 192
in variables 192
Linearization of nonlinear regression model 192–207
disturbance term assumptions 202–5
logarithmic model 196–200
semilogarithmic model 200–2
variable redefinition 192–5
Log-likelihood function 381. *See also* Maximum likelihood estimation
Logarithmic model 196–200
comparison with linear model 205–7, 388–90
Logarithmic transformations 196–207
rules for 198
Logit analysis, logit model 359–63
goodness of fit 362–3
marginal effects 360–2
Loglinear model 197
Longitudinal data set. *See* Panel data
Loss function 31–32
LSDV regression. *See* Least squares dummy variable regression

MA. *See* Moving average process
Maximum likelihood estimation (MLE) 378–87
asymptotic efficiency 379
goodness of fit 386
likelihood function 380
likelihood ratio test 386–7
log-likelihood function 381
maximum likelihood principle 380
simple regression model 385

Mean of a random variable
population 9
maximum likelihood estimator of 378–85
generalized unbiased estimator
sample
distribution 24–6
estimator of population mean
efficient 28–30
unbiased 27–8
variance of 25–6
Mean square error 31–2
Measurement errors 306–12
in dependent variable 309–10
in explanatory variable 306–9
imperfect proxy variables 310–11
proof of inconsistency of OLS estimators 306–8
See also Durbin–Wu–Hausman test; Friedman's Permanent Income Hypothesis
Mills' ratio 376. *See also* Sample selection model
MLE. *See* Maximum likelihood estimation
Model A, B, C. *See* Regression model
Model misspecification
functional form
potential cause of apparent autocorrelation 455
potential cause of apparent heteroscedasticity 292–3
irrelevant variables 250–1, 260–3
consequences of 250–1, 260–1
omitted variables 250–8
consequences of 250–4
derivation of bias 253
direction of bias 253, 256
effect on R^2 256–8
invalidation of statistical tests 254
potential cause of apparent autocorrelation 451–5
Model specification 457–61
comparison of alternative models 458–60
general-to-specific approach 460–1
nested and non-nested models 458
specific-to-general approach 460
See also Model misspecification
Monte Carlo experiment 121
See also Simulation experiment
Moving average (MA) process 424
correlogram 485
disturbance term subject to MA. *See* Autocorrelation
Multicollinearity 165–76
caused by correlated explanatory variables 165–6
caused by approximate linear relationship among explanatory variables 168
consequences 166
definition of 165–6
different impact on *F* tests and *t* tests 179
effect on prediction error 189–90
exact multicollinearity 166–8
dummy variable trap 235–7
measures to mitigate 169–76
combination of explanatory variables 172, 175
exclusion of explanatory variables 172–3
inclusion of additional explanatory variables 171–2
increase in sample size 170–1
increase in mean square deviation of explanatory variables 172
reduction in correlation of explanatory variables 172
use of extraneous information 173–4
use of theoretical restriction 174–6
Multiple regression analysis 151–5. *See also* Regression analysis, two explanatory variables

National Longitudinal Survey of Youth 2000 (*NLSY2000*) panel data set 556–8
See also Educational Attainment and Earnings Functions data set
Nested models. *See* Model specification
Newey–West standard error 442
NLSY2000. *See* National Longitudinal Survey of Youth 2000 panel data set
Noise. *See* Disturbance term
Nonlinear regression
fitted using grid search 409
fitted using iterative procedure 218–22
fitted using nonlinear specification 220–2
linearized by logarithmic transformation 196–207
linearized by redefining variables 192–5
use of
higher-order polynomials 211–13
interactive terms 213–16
quadratic variables 209–11
Nonlinear restriction. *See* Restriction
Nonsense regressions 457. *See also* Spurious regressions
Nonstationarity, detection
graphical techniques 485–9
autocorrelation function 484
correlogram 485–9
unit root tests
ADF–GLS test 500–501
Augmented Dickey Fuller (ADF) tests 498–500
Dickey–Fuller *t* test 494–5
Dickey–Fuller $T(b_2–1)$ test 494

Nonstationarity, detection (*cont.*)
Dickey–Fuller *F* test 495
for trended processes 497–8
for untrended processes 491–6
power of unit root tests 495–6, 500–501
Nonstationary time series processes 469–474, 504–12
cointegration 504–9
definition 504–5
simultaneous equations bias, asymptotic attenuation 507
superconsistency of OLS 507
tests for 505–7
conditions for stationarity 465, 469–74
deterministic trend 472–473
difference-stationarity 473–4
ensemble distribution 470–3
fitting models with nonstationary processes 508–512
detrending 509
differencing 509–10
error correction models 510–12
integrated processes 473–4
random walk 470–1
random walk with drift 471–2
tests for nonstationarity
trend-stationarity 473–4
See also Nonstationarity, detection; Spurious regressions
Nonstochastic regressors. *See* Regressor
Normal distribution 32–5
Normal distribution table. *See* Table A.1
Normal equations
multiple regression model 154, 155
simple regression model 91

OECD2000 data set 555
OLS. *See* Regression analysis, ordinary least squares
Omitted category. *See* Dummy variables
Omitted variables. *See* Model misspecification
One-sided test. *See t* tests; Tests, one-sided
Order condition for identification 344–5. *See also* Simultaneous equations estimation
Ordinary least squares (OLS). *See* Regression analysis, ordinary least squares
Outlier 278–9
Overidentification 342–4. *See also* Simultaneous equations estimation

p values 139–40. *See also t* tests
Panel data
appropriateness of OLS, fixed effects, random effects regressions 525–7
Breusch–Pagan Lagrange multiplier test 526–7
Durbin–Wu–Hausman test 525–6
balanced panel 515
definition 110, 514
fixed effects regressions 518–22
first differences 519–20
least squares dummy variable (LSDV) 520–2
within-groups 518–19
pooled OLS regression 518, 526
random effects regression 522–5
unbalanced panel 515
unobserved effect 517
Parameter of regression model 83
linearity in parameters 192
Partial adjustment model 404–5
Brown's habit persistence model 405
Permanent income hypothesis. *See* Consumption function
Plim. *See* Probability limit
Polynomial regression specification 211–13
Pooled OLS regression. *See* Panel data
Population covariance. *See* Covariance
Population mean. *See* Mean of a random variable
Population variance of a random variable. *See* Variance of a random variable
Population variance of sample mean. *See* Mean of a random variable
Power of a test 42–6
definition 42
See also Tests, one-sided; Nonstationarity, detection
Prediction 185–90
confidence interval 189
error 188
impact of multicollinearity 189–90
population variance 188–90
unbiasedness 188
Probability density function of random variable 14–17
Probability limit 66–73
definition of 67
rules 70–1
Probit analysis, probit model 365–7
marginal effects 365–7
Proxy variables 263–7
benefits from using 264
consequences of use of 264–5
ideal proxy 264–5
imperfect 265
unintentional 266–7

Quadratic regression specification 209–11
Qualitative response models. *See* Linear probability model; Logit analysis; Probit analysis; Sample selection model; Tobit model

Qualitative explanatory variables. *See* Dummy variables

R^2 104–8, 176–7
  adjusted (corrected) 183–4
  alternative interpretation 107–8
  coefficient of determination 105
  definition 105
  effect of omitted variable on 256–8
  F test of goodness of fit 146–7, 275
Ramsey's RESET test 216–7
Random effects regression 522–5. *See also* Panel data
Random variables
  continuous 6, 14–17
  discrete 6–13
  double structure 23, 25–27
  expected value 8, 18
  fixed and random components 12–13
  independence of two random variables 19
  standard deviation 11
  variance 11–12, 18–19
Random walk 470–1
  with drift 471–2
  Granger–Newbold spurious regressions 475–84
Realization 23, 392, 463–4. *See also* Data generation process
Reduced form equation 332. *See also* Simultaneous equations estimation
Redundant variable. *See* Model misspecification
Reference category. *See* Dummy variables
Regression analysis, ordinary least squares (OLS)
  simple regression analysis 83–5
  least squares criterion 87–92
  multiple regression analysis 151–5
  normal equations 91
  See also Disturbance term; Nonlinear regression analysis; R^2; Regression model assumptions; Residual
Regression coefficients, IV. *See* Instrumental variables
Regression coefficients, OLS
  as random variables 114–18
  asymptotic properties, Model B
    asymptotic normality 305–6
    consistency 304–5
    reason for interest 304
  confidence intervals 142–3, 164
  effects of changes in units of variables 92–99, 101, 122
  hypothesis testing 134–9
    alternative hypothesis
    null hypothesis
  inconsistency caused by
    measurement error in explanatory variable 306–9
    simultaneous equations bias 333–5
  interpretation
    linear 95–7
    logarithmic 196–200
    multiple regression model 156–8
    semilogarithmic 200–1
    simple regression model 95–7
  one explanatory variable
    analytical decomposition 114–18
    consistency 304–5
    derivation of expressions 90–2
    Monte Carlo experiment 121–5
    population variance 125–9
    standard errors 129–31
    unbiasedness 118, 302–3
  two explanatory variables
    analytical decomposition 160
    derivation of expressions 153–5
    population variance 161–4
    standard errors 162–4
    unbiasedness 160–1
  See also t tests
Regression model
  assumptions
    Model A 111–14, 159–60
    Model B 300–2
    Model C 391–3
  fitted 86
  types 110–11
Regressor (explanatory variable, independent variable) 83
  nonstochastic 110–11
  stochastic 300
reparameterizaton of model specification
  estimation of long-run effects in dynamic model 400–1
  standard error of linear combination of parameters 270–3
  t test of linear restriction 273–4
RESET test 216–7
Residual
  definition of 87
  use in improving model specification 278–9
  OLS regressions with intercept
    zero correlation with explanatory variables 103–4
  zero sample mean 103
Residual sum of squares (*RSS*) 90
Restriction
  benefits from exploitation 175, 268–9
  definition
    linear restriction 174, 269
    nonlinear restriction 269

Restriction (*cont.*)
tests
common factor test of nonlinear restriction 445–8
likelihood ratio test 386–7
F test of linear restriction 270
F test multiple linear restrictions 274–5
t test of linear restriction 273–4
use in mitigation of problem of multicollinearity 174–6, 268–9
zero restrictions 275
RSS. *See* Residual sum of squares

Sample selection model 374–8
Heckman two-step estimation procedure 376
Sample mean. *See* Mean of a random variable
Sample selection bias. *See* Sample selection model
School costs data set 555–6
Schwarz Information Criterion (SIC) 500
Semilogarithmic model 200–2
Serial correlation. *See* Autocorrelation
Significance level (size) of test, definition 40
Simple regression analysis 83–5. *See also* Regression analysis, one explanatory variable
Simulation experiment 72–3. *See also* Monte Carlo experiment
Simultaneous equations bias. *See* Simultaneous equations estimation
Simultaneous equations estimation
Durbin–Wu–Hausman test 346–50
endogenous variables 332
exogenous variables 332
identification
exact identification 342
order condition 344–5
overidentification 342–4
underidentification 341–2
indirect least squares 348–9
instrumental variables estimation 338–41
reduced form equation 332
simulation comparison with OLS 339–41
simultaneous equations bias 331, 333–7
structural equation 332
two-stage least squares 343–4
unobserved heterogeneity 345–6
Size of a test 40
Slope dummy variables. *See* Dummy variables
Specification error. *See* Model misspecification
Spurious regressions
deterministic trends, caused by 475
Granger–Newbold random walks 476–84
Standard deviation of a random variable 11
Standard error
regression coefficient. *See* Regression coefficients, OLS
regression equation (s_u) 130
sample mean 48
Static time-series models 393–6
Stationarity. *See* Stationary time series process
Stationary time series process 463–9
conditions for stationarity 465
definition of stationarity 464–6
difference-stationarity 473–4
ensemble distribution 464–9
trend stationarity 473–4
Stochastic regressor. *See* Regressor
Structural equation 332. *See also* Simultaneous equations estimation
Superconsistency 492, 499, 507

t distribution 48–9
table, critical values. *See* Table A.2
t statistic 48
t tests 47–51
degrees of freedom
estimation of sample mean 48
multiple regression analysis 164
simple regression analysis 135
equivalence of *t* test of slope coefficient and *F* test, simple regression 147–8
interpreted as marginal *F* test, multiple regression 182–3
one-sided tests
regression coefficients 140–2
sample mean 63–9
See also Tests, one-sided
p values 139–40
power 42–6
regression coefficients 134–9
reporting results 138–9
of linear restriction 273–4
equivalence to *F* test 279
significance level
definition 40
trade-off with power 44–6
Type I error 38, 40, 42–6
Type II error 38, 42–6
See also Regression coefficients; Tests, one-sided
Tests, one-sided 56–66
anomalous results 64–5
benefits from 59–60, 62–4
justification 65
logic underlying 57
power, compared with two-sided test 59–63
See also *t* tests
Time series analysis 423–425
autoregressive moving average (ARMA) models 424

Box–Jenkins method 424
forcing process 424
See also Nonstationarity, detection; Time series processes
Time series data 110, 391–392
Time series processes
alternative dynamic representations 422–7
vector autoregressive (VAR) 425–426
vector autoregressive moving average (VARMA) 427
vector error correction models (VECM) 427
autocorrelation function 467
autoregressive integrated moving average (ARIMA) 474, 484, 486
autoregressive moving average (ARMA) 424
correlogram 465
ensemble distribution 464–73
nonstationary 469–74
stationary 463–9
univariate 423
See also Nonstationary time series processes; Stationary time series processes; Time series analysis
Time series regression models
dynamics 398–401
estimation of long-run effects 400–1
simultaneous equations models 419–421
Granger causality 427
predetermined variable as instrument 421
static 393–396
See also Autoregressive distributed lag models; Time series analysis; Time series processes
Tobit analysis, tobit model 368–73
Total sum of squares (*TSS*) 105
Trend-stationarity 473–4
TSLS. *See* Two-stage least squares
TSS. *See* Total sum of squares
Two-stage least squares (TSLS) 343–4. *See also* Simultaneous equations estimation
Type I, Type II errors 38, 40, 42–6

Unbalanced panel. *See* Panel data
Unbiased estimator, unbiasedness
definition 27
of regression coefficients 118, 160–1, 302–3
of sample mean 27–8
possible trade-off with variance 30–2
Underidentification 341–2. *See also* Simultaneous equations estimation
Unit root tests. *See* Nonstationarity, detection
Unobserved effect. *See* Panel data
Unobserved heterogeneity 345–6

Var. *See* Variance of a random variable
VAR. *See* Vector autoregression
Variable misspecification. *See* Model misspecification
Variance of a random variable
continuous random variable 18–19
discrete random variable 11–12, 18
estimator 33, 79–81
maximum likelihood estimator 383–5
rules 21–2
Vector autoregression (VAR) 425–7
Granger causality 427
Vector autoregressive moving average (VARMA) process 427
Vector error correction model (VECM) 427

Weighted least squares (WLS) regression 289, 295–7
White heteroscedasticity-consistent standard errors 294–5
White noise 424, 476–7, 481. *See also* Disturbance term
White test for heteroscedasticity 286–7
Within-groups regression. *See* Panel data